1 MONTH OF
FREE
READING

at

www.ForgottenBooks.com

By purchasing this book you are eligible for one month membership to ForgottenBooks.com, giving you unlimited access to our entire collection of over 1,000,000 titles via our web site and mobile apps.

To claim your free month visit:
www.forgottenbooks.com/free977386

ISBN 978-0-260-85863-4
PIBN 10977386

For support please visit www.forgottenbooks.com

REPORT OF THE COMMITTEE

ON

Water Powers, Forestry, and Drainage

OF THE

Wisconsin Legislature

1910

MADISON, WIS.
DEMOCRAT PRINTING COMPANY, STATE PRINTER
1911

CONTENTS.

o his Excellency the Governor, and to the Honorable Legislature of Wisconsin:—

In compliance with the joint resolutions of the 1909 session f the legislature, appointing several committees to investigate ertain specified subjects, and recommend legislation relative hereto, this committee was assigned the subjects of Water Powrs. Forestry and Drainage, and the undersigned, members of uch committee, beg to submit this report, and the several bills d exhibits thereto attached.

Respectfully submitted this 30th day of December, A. D. 1910.

H. P. BIRD,
> Senator.

WILLIAM M. BRAY,
GEO. P. HAMBRECHT,
F. W. KUBASTA,
J. E. THOMAS,
> Assemblymen.

REPORT

OF

THE SPECIAL LEGISLATIVE COMMITTEE

APPOINTED TO INVESTIGATE

Water Powers, Forestry and Drainage

The special legislative committees created by the Wisconsin Legislature of 1909, for the purpose of investigating the subjects of Water Powers, Forestry and Drainage in the state, and to recommend such legislation relative thereto as it deemed advisable, beg leave to submit the following

REPORT.

The committee was created by joint resolutions Nos. 8-21 and 52, and consisted of the following members:

Senators Bird, Husting and Krumrey.

Assemblymen Bray, Hambrecht, Kubusta and Thomas.

The committee organized by choosing Senator H. P. Bird, chairman, and Assemblyman Geo. P. Hambrecht, secretary. The chairman, secretary and Assemblyman J. E. Thomas were chosen as a sub-committee to audit the expense accounts of the members. Later, owing to the illness of Senator Bird, Assemblyman Bray was chosen a member of the auditing committee, to act for Senator Bird, during the absence of the latter.

The committee accepted the invitation of the State Conservation Commission to attend the meeting of such commission on July 14, 1909, to learn what measures relating to matters referred to this committee and not brought before the legislature were under consideration.

From August 16th to the 27th, the Committee made a trip along the lower Fox River from Oshkosh to Kaukauna. Then to Shawano, and on to Neopit where lumbering is in progress under government regulation on the Menominee Indian reservation. Then to the interstate water power in process of development on the Menominee river about twenty miles above Marinette. Then along the Wisconsin river from Grand Rapids to Grandfather Falls fourteen miles above Merrill, stopping at intermediate points where water power has been developed, and at some points where the power has not been improved.

From October 18th, to the 29th, the Committee made a trip to Eagle River and vicinity, and up through a part of the Eagle chain of lakes, to observe the system of reservoirs now being constructed for the purpose of making a more uniform flow in the Wisconsin river. Then across to the Chippewa river drainage, and down branches of that stream. Continuing westward, via Ashland and Superior, the Committee visited Cass Lake, Minnesota, to observe the timber cutting on the Oneida Indian reservation under government supervision— this being the nearest point where slash burning and reforesting is in actual progress. On the return from Cass Lake, the Committee traveled forty-five miles up the Chippewa River, from Eau Claire, to observe the water powers on that stream.

The object of these trips was to familiarize the Committee, to some extent at least, with the physical conditions pertaining to water powers, both developed and undeveloped; also to observe the cut over lands in the north part of the state and the adaptation of the soil and other conditions relative to reforesting—also to see the reservoirs now being constructed on the head waters of the Wisconsin river.

At advantageous places along the route the Committee stopped for hearings, and invited everyone who was interested in the subjects under consideration to give testimony and information. So far as practicable, previous notice was given of these hearings so as to secure full attendance. During the first trip, hearings were held as follows:

1st at Log Cabin Inn, Neenah, Aug. 17th, 1909, about 30 present.

2nd at Kaukauna Town Hall, Aug. 18, 1909, about 100 present.

3rd at Shawano, Aug. 20, 1909, about 20 present.
4th at Wausau, Aug. 25, 1909, about 50 present.
5th at Wausau, Aug. 26, 1909, about 50 present.
On the second trip:
6th at Hackley, Oct. 19, 1909, about 20 present.
7th at Eagle River Dam, Oct. 20, 1909, about 40 present.
8th at Rhinelander, Oct. 21, 1909, about 35 present.
9th at Cass Lake, Minn., Oct. 24, 1909, about 30 present.
10th at Eau Claire, Oct. 27, 1909, about 100 present (3 sessions).

Also hearings in the club room of the Hotel Pfister, Milwaukee, as follows: December 2nd, 3rd, 4th, 7th, 8th, 9th, 13th, and 14th, 1909, attendance from twenty to one hundred at each hearing.

Hearings were also had at Madison, Wis., October 24th, 25th and 26th, 1910, and on December 8th, 9th and 10th, 1910, and later in the same month. In this connection your Committee would state that a two days' session was held at St. Paul, December 6th and 7th, 1910, with the Lake States Forest Fire Conference, at which Conference there were present prominent lumbermen, railroadmen, and members of the Forestry Department and state officials of the three states of Michigan, Wisconsin and Minnesota.

In addition to these formal meetings, individual members of the committee met for informal discussions and research work connected with the questions submitted to the committee. In this research work the committee employed Attorney M. C. Riley, of Milwaukee, who devoted a great deal of time to the questions submitted to him, and who rendered valuable services to the committee and members thereof, in gathering data for the use of the committee.

Mr. Henry D. Goodwin of Milwaukee rendered most efficient stenographic services to the Committee in taking down and transcribing the official proceedings of the Committee.

Many of the persons who appeared before the Committee during the trips to the northern part of the state were financially interested in water powers, several were lumbermen, some owners of summer resorts and the others were citizens generally interested in the proceedings of the Committee. At Cass Lake, Minnesota, those who have charge of the government timber, as well as several lumbermen who are engaged in cutting logs, testified. At Milwaukee. four University professors and the President of that institution, the State Forester, farmers and many others residing in different parts of the state rendered valuable aid to the Committee by the information given.

The testimony obtained by the Committee at these hearings is filed as a part of this report. A typewritten transcript of this testimony, (the official proceedings of the Committee), is filed with the Wisconsin Legislative Reference Library at Madison.

It was the purpose of the Committee in holding these hearings to learn, as far as possible, the sentiment of all classes of citizens in the parts of the state that would be most affected by changes in the laws relating to Water Powers, Forestry and Drainage. In this the Committee thinks it has been quite successful.

The Committee had heard statements and arguments covering, when reduced to typewritten form, over 3,000 closely printed pages.

Guided by the observations made and the testimony offered the Committee respectfully submits the following statement of *facts and recommendations:*

FACTS.

WATER POWERS.

It may be stated generally that there seems to be great and unanimous interest in and desire for further development of water powers in order to build up cities and furnish employment for the people.

Some objection has been made to the effect that dams and reservoirs destroy the natural beauty of the country, but the fact is, as the Committee finds it, that all things considered, the natural beauty of the country is greatly enhanced by these improvements.

Mr. M. C. Riley compiled for your Committee a series of tables, marked exhibits 1 to 6, inclusive, and made a part of this report, analyzing all of the dam charters granted by the legislature from the organization of the territory of Wisconsin to date. This analysis, arranged chronologically, gives the citation of the law granting the charter, the name of the grantee, the location of the dam, the duration and the purpose of the grant, the provisions for the safe-guarding of navigation, miscellaneous purposes included in the grant, whether or not the power of eminent domain was granted, whether or not fishways were provided for and whether or not a reserve clause to amend, alter or repeal the charter was made a part thereof. From the legislature 665 permits to construct dams. 244 permits were granted to improve navigation and to facilitate log driving, or both; 227 for hydraulic purposes; 52 to improve navigation and for hydraulic purposes; 79 to facilitate log driving and for hydraulic purposes, and 63 for other purposes, viz.: to feed canals, for pisciculture, to create ponds, to flow cranberry marshes, for the "public good," for general municipal purposes, and include 44 grants in which no purpose is specified, the context of the grants being indefinite.

These tables show further that out of the 665 permits granted 326 contained the power of eminent domain; 325 contained a reserve clause to alter, amend or repeal the grant, 31 were granted for a limited period, and 121 provided for fishways. The following table (page 2772 of the official proceedings), compiled from Professor Leonard S. Smith's report for the Federal Conservation Commission, shows the number and kind of plants operated by water power in Wisconsin, May, 1908:

TABLE.

NUMBER AND KIND OF PLANTS RUN BY WATER POWER MAY, 1908.—COMPILED FROM PROF. LEONARD S. SMITH'S REPORT PREPARED FOR FEDERAL CON-SERVATION COMMISSION.

Paper mills, pulp and fiber..........	43	Manufacturing hosiery	1
Flour, grain and feed...............	218	Manufacturing nails	1
Saw mills and planing mills..........	45	Manufacturing bee hives..........	1
Electric light and power..............	43	Manufacturing boxes (wood)......	1
Woolen mills, manufacturing yarn and carding........................	22	Manufacturing brushes	1
Manufacturing brick..................	1	Manufacturing sash and doors....	1
Manufacturing bridges...............	1	Manufacturing cutlery	1
Compressed air.....................	2	Manufacturing scales	1
Mill elevators.......................	2	Manufacturing cotton goods......	1
Manufacturing boots and shoes......	1	Creameries	1
Tannery	1	Floating logs	10
Machine shops......................	15	Manufacturing linen goods.......	2
Manufacturing wooden ware..........	1	Water works	4
Manufacturing furniture.............	2	Idle	5
Manufacturing hubs and spokes......	1	Not known	10
		Total	439

No person has appeared before this committee or given testimony criticising the improvement of any water power that has been developed in the state of Wisconsin, either as to the damage done to other property thereby, or as to injustice done to citizens by those who have made such improvements.

No person has appeared before this committee or has given testimony criticising the construction of any dam that has been built in this state, or has contended that the same was, by reason of faulty construction, a menace to any other property upon the stream, and no person has appeared and presented claim of any injury done to any person or thing by reason of such improvements.

The evidence presented to this committee shows that most of the water powers developed in Wisconsin have been financed by capital from within the state. Upon investigation your committee found no tendency toward a uniting of powers so as to form a water power trust or monopoly.

All the testimony and facts brought to the attention of this committee shows that every water power that has been improved in Wisconsin has, by virtue of such improvement, immediately become a great and useful feature in the development of industry at the location of such improved power, or in the vicinity thereof, and that in many places such improvement of a water power has been the determining factor, not only in locating a thriving and prosperous industry, but in promoting the general prosperity of a large region, and in greatly aiding the development of our state. This is especially true in the timber region of Wisconsin. The improvement of these powers has directly resulted in furnishing a large and profitable market to new settlers engaged in clearing timbered land for agricultural uses. Were it not for this industrial development, much of the timber cut from these agricultural lands would be waste products that would have to be destroyed on the premises and at a considerable cost.

The testimony discloses a demand from every community where water powers are located, and where testimony was taken, for every encouragement possible for the full development of all undeveloped water power, in order to stimulate the commercial activity of the community.

In all cases where any hydraulic power in Wisconsin is leased or sold to the public it is subject to the public utility laws of Wisconsin, and is under the direct supervision and regulation of the Wisconsin Railroad Commission the same as any other public utility product.

Wisconsin has no mountains, and the evidence presented to this committee shows that there is no erosion affecting in any manner the flow of any of the rivers in this state.

The testimony discloses that nearly all manufacturing plants operated by water power in this state have installed auxiliary steam plants to supplement the water power created either to add to the total power used or to compensate for the regular fluctuations in water levels.

On the *Lower Fox* river, between Lake Winnebago and Green Bay, most of the water power is developed, but not all. The Federal grants, in the interest of navigation, to large corporations which,in some cases have been conflicting, have influenced the development, with the result that at this time the General Government maintains the dams (with minor exceptions) and controls the amount of water required for navigation, the users of water power being permitted to use the surplus only. These grants are all under Federal control.

In connection with the water power development on the Fox river, Mr. L. M. Mann, Assistant Engineer for the Federal Government at Oshkosh, Wis., submitted to your Committee 5 tables marked "Exhibit 7" and attached to this report, as follows, to-wit:

Tables Furnished by the U. S. Engineer's Office, Oshkosh, Wis., to the Legislative Committee on Water Powers, Forestry and Drainage.

1. Water Powers on Lower Fox River, Wisconsin.
2. Fox and Wisconsin Improvement, Wisconsin.
3. Statement concerning Water Power at Existing Government Dams, Fox River, Wis.—Sheet 1.
4. Statement concerning Water Power at Existing Government Dams, Fox River, Wis.—Sheet 2.
5. Statement concerning Water Power at Existing Private Dams, Fox River, Wis.—Sheet 3.

On the *Wisconsin River* much progress has been made in developing water power, and in nearly all cases without litigation or misunderstandings between the operators themselves or the riparian owners. There still remains much undeveloped power on this river.

On the *Chippewa River* power is developed at Eau Claire and at Chippewa Falls only. Several large powers are still entirely undeveloped.

On the *Flambeau* but a small part of the possible power is developed. The rapid fall in that river makes large development possible.

Four powers on the *Menominee River*, an interstate stream,

are developed above Marinette, viz.: at upper and lower Quin nesee, at Niagara, and at a point locally known as Gran Rapids, near Marinette. Several powers are developed at Mari nette. Much remains unimproved.

On the *Peshtigo River* one power was developed years ag at Peshtigo Village, and another is now in progress at High Falls. This river has many rapids, and much more power can be developed.

The *Rock River*, on which much power is now being used, was not visited—nor were the many other rivers in the state, on some of which a part of the power is already developed and on others, none at all.

For the amount of developed and undeveloped water power in the state, see the following table:

The following table gives the most important facts regarding the principal water power rivers of Wisconsin.

River System	Drainage Area.	Total Fall.	Already Developed.	Easily Developed	Now Developed.	Now un-developed.
	Sq. Mi.	Feet.	Feet.	Feet.	H. P.	H. P.
Wisconsin	12,280	1,044	308	430	67,2 0	396,500
Fox	6,400	170	150	13	38,250	11,500
Wolf	3,650	800		400	2,580	34,000
Menominee	4,000	550	130	307	12,6 0	72,5 0
Peshtigo	1,123	1,040	50	880	2,100	33,80)
Oconto	934	245	60	725	2,885	21,000
Black	2,270	570	95	400	2,20)	16,500
Chippewa	9,573	730	300	700	20,000	156,00)
St. Croix	7,576	522	50	200	18,6 0	45,80)
Rock	3,500	132	67	14	7,700	1,000
Milwaukee	840	437	122	100	3,300	4,300
Flambeau	11,883	575	60	37)	5,:00	45,00)
Omitting Flambeau river					1·3,105	
Including Dore Flambeau						827.9 0

L. S. Smith, University of Wisconsin.
Wisconsin Engineer, June 1909, page 285

This report is kindly furnished to the Committee by Prof. Leonard S. Smith of the State University. It will be seen from this table that in June 1909, 183,105 horse power was developed, and that 827,900 horse power remained undeveloped—a total horse power in the state of 1,011,005.

The committee is not unmindful of the fact that conditions existing in the state make it extremely difficult to develop considerable of this water power in the immediate future, chiefly for the reason that there is no market for the power. The Committee also feels that every encouragement ought to be given water power companies to develop this power as early as possible in order to save on the wood and coal supply.

Prof. Smith also states that the figures set forth in this table, owing to the fact that the survey of many of our rivers is incomplete, and to the further fact that the measurement of water is not always made by the same methods, are only approximately correct.

The estimates of Prof. Smith are based upon. *theoretical* horse power, taking into consideration the total fall of the streams in the state and the volume of water. It is a difficult matter to get correct data for the whole state on *practical* horse power, which takes into consideration not only the two elements above, but as well the possibility, from a practical standpoint, to convert the theoretical horse power into practical commercial use. Mr. A. A. Babcock, Jr., of Wausau, has kindly furnished your committee with the following table, showing the development and possibility of development on the Wisconsin River from Conover to Prairie du Sac. Mr. Babcock's table shows both the theoretical and practical horse power on this particular river, together with drainage area and other data:

WATER POWERS ON THE WISCONSIN RIVER

Location.	Fall in Feet.			Drainage area in square miles.	Flow in feet per second based on 7-10 cu. ft. per second per square mile of drainage area.	Horse Power.		
	Theoretical.	Practical.	Developed.			Hydraulic based on theoretical head.	Actual on wheel shaft, based on practical head, wheel efficiency 85 per cent. practical.	Based on wheel shaft, based on wheel head, 85 per cent.
Conover	*8	.....	.....	150	103	95	....	....
Otter Rapids	19	13	12	475	333	720	419	887
Rainbow Rapids	8	8	.....	700	490	400	340	....
Rhinelander	32	32	31¾	810	567	2,660	1,750	1,722
Hat Rapids	21½	20	19½	1,070	749	1,830	1,445	1,427
Nigger Island(Whirlpool Rapids)	*44	*(40)	.....	1,123	786	3,930	....	....
Kings (Pine Creek Rapids)	19½	19	*(19)	1,193	835	1,850	1,530	....
Tomahawk	16½	15	15	1,913	1,339	2,360	1,940	1,940
Grandmother	21	20	.....	1,950	1,865	3,260	2,640	....
Grandfather (Upper)	33½	30	29½	2,160	1,512	5,760	4,890	4,817
Grandfather (Lower)	60½	60	.....	2,160	1,512	10,380	8,750	....
Bill Cross	26½	25	.....	2,200	1,540	4,570	3,680	....
Merrill (Upper)	25	20	.....	2,380	1,666	4,730	3,220	....
Merrill (Lower)	15	14½	14½	2,600	1,820	3,110	2,550	2,550
Trapp Rapids	20½	20	.....	2,780	1,946	5,580	4,590	....
Brokaw	16	15¾	15¾	2,893	2,068	3,680	3,080	3,080
Wausau	25	25	20	2,920	2,044	5,810	4,940	3,952
Rothchilds	20	20	20	3,840	2,688	6,110	5,190	5,190
Mosinee	28	28	16	3,930	2,751	8,750	7,440	4,250
Battle Island	*20	*(20)	.....	4,360	3,052	6,940	....	....
Stevens Point (Upper)	12	12	7	4,740	3,318	4,530	3,850	2,247
Stevens Point (Lower)	19	17	17	4,760	3,332	7,190	5,470	5,4'0
Plover	10	8	7½	4,970	3,479	3,060	2,690	2,522
Biron	13	13½	12½	5,170	3,619	5,340	4,360	4,3 0
Grand Rapids	30	29	29	5,220	3,654	12,460	10,250	10,2'0
South Centralia	13	11	11	5,230	3,661	5,410	3,870	3,870
Port Edwards	18	17	17	5,240	3,668	7,500	6,020	6,020
Nekoosa	19	18¾	18¾	5,410	3,787	8,180	6,830	6,830
Old Barnum	*10	*(10)	.....	5,700	2,900	4,540	....	....
Necedah	*10	*(10)	.....	6,000	4,200	4,780	....	....
Kilbourn	17	17	17	7,610	5,327	10,300	10,800	10,300
Prairie du Sac	15	*(15)	.....	8,700	6,000	10,390	....	....
Total	664½	622½	349¾	.....	....	166,655	111,514	60,704

*Estimated.

Totals for Comparison:
Theoretical fall ....376.50 feet
Practical fall ....355.50 feet, 94½%
Developed fall ....330 75 feet, 80¾%
Theoretical horse power................................105,060.00
Practical horse power................................86,784.00   86¼%
Developed horse power................................60,684.00   80¼%
Total fall in river................................664.50 feet
Total practical fall in river................................622.50 feet 93½%
Total developed fall in river................................349.75 feet 52¾%

In connection with this table, Mr. Babcock states:

"You will note that several of the locations are marked with a star, and by this we wish to call your attention to the fact that we are not thoroughly posted on the heads at these places, and so have simply estimated same.

Under the head of Fall in Feet, the column headed theoretical means the total fall in the river from the head to the foot of the rapids, while that under the head of practical, means approximately the head that could be utilized economically, and that under the head of developed, is the head which is being used at the present time. The next column explains itself and is the number of square miles in the drainage area above each of the various locations given. The next column gives the flow in cubic feet of water per second that would be supplied from the drainage area above each of the several locations on the basis of 7/10 of a cubic foot of water per second per square mile of drainage area. I want to say here, that the minimum flow that can be expected on the Wisconsin river is about 3/10 of a cubic foot per second per square mile of drainage area, while the freshet flow has gone up to over $2\frac{1}{2}$ cubic feet per second per square mile. The average flow for the whole year, for normal year, would be about 75/100 cubic feet per second per square mile. Inasmuch as there is quite a little time that the flow is below the average, it has not been considered economical to keep a plant with too much machinery. This is liable to stand idle some portion of the time, so the conservative equipment would be one that would utilize a flow of about 7/10 of a cubic foot per second per square mile of drainage area. Therefore, it is for this reason that we have used 7/10 cubic feet for the making of this comparison.

You can readily understand that these figures would be increased proportionately were you to call the average 8/10, 9/10 or one cubic foot, but, personally, we do not think this would give the proper conception of horse power on the Wisconsin river, or in fact any other river of similar character. You understand that these figures do not take into consideration anything but the natural run-off. Such service as is rendered by reservoir system in regulating the flow in the Wisconsin river would increase the minimum flow and decrease the freshet flow and exert its influence towards raising the average

flow, but for the purpose of comparison, which you will probably desire to make, believe it is much better to give you figures
based on natural conditions.

Under the last heading of horsepower the first column is
designated as ''hydraulic'' and means the amount of theoretical
horsepower that 7/10 cubic foot flow would give if the whole
theoretical head could be utilized. (If you should desire to
reduce this to actual horsepower you can take 85 per cent of
these figures given.) The next column headed "Actual" represents the amount of actual horsepower that would be available on the water wheel shaft during the 7/10 cubic foot flow,
under what we have termed the practical head and the efficiency of the water wheels is figured at 85 per cent. The last
column headed "developed" is the amount of actual horsepower that would be delivered on the water wheel shaft by this
7/10 cubic foot flow under the developed head. The efficiency
of the water wheels being figured at 85 per cent.

In giving you the totals for comparison at the bottom of the
table we want to speak of one of the locations not touched by
Mr. Jones.

First: Otter Rapids: You will note that there is a theoretical fall of 19′ at this place. There is no question but what
the greater part of this 19′ could be utilized, but the expense
would be enormous for raising the water from the 13′, or practical head, to 19′ flow. As Evarts', Folzes, The Hemlock and
many other resorts, together with a number of private cottages
on the lower Eagle Chain, which of course, would have to be
condemned and purchased, and it is practically out of the question to consider such an increase in the head at this place.

The first three totals that are given you for comparison are
computed from the developed powers only. The totals for
horsepower take into consideration the same developed power,
while the last three totals take in the total fall in the river.''

The importance of the wise development of water power in
this state, to the end that all classes of citizens may receive the
greatest possible benefit therefrom, at the present time as well
as in future years, is deeply impressed upon this Committee,
nor scarcely can it be overestimated. The industrial development of the state is largely dependent upon the wise use of
this water power.

The Committee is pleased to note that in nearly every case where water power has been developed, flourishing villages and cities have grown up as a result, thus adding largely to the population and immensely increasing the taxable property of the state. It should be noted also that water power is especially adapted to the manufacture of paper which is one of the causes leading to the great advancement of this industry, and which has caused the invesment of such large amounts of capital in this state. The paper manufacturer very opportunely followed, in many cases, the passing of the lumber industry, thus affording continued employment to the labor that otherwise would have been compelled to leave the state, and furnished use for property that otherwise would have been of very little value.

Ten of the leading paper industries of the Wisconsin river furnished Mr. A. A. Babcock, Jr., from their books, data from which he compiled the following financial statement:

Average total monthly pay roll, exclusive of salaries......................	$110,280 00
Annually	$1,323,360 00
Number of hands employed, 2,166—representing 10,830 individuals on the basis of families of five persons.	
Amount of taxes paid...	$100,839 00
Amount of total taxes of communities wherein industries are located...	$403,840 00
Proportion of total taxes paid by this industry in the valley, 25 per cent. and ranges in various localities from 1 1-5 per cent, to 95 per cent.	
Total capital invested..	$11,325,000 00
Pulp wood used annually, cords...	217,160
Value of same...	$1,843,800 00
Annual tonnage of incoming freight, including pulp wood, tons............	647,100
Estimated value of same..	$3,495,900 00
Estimated freight charges on same.......................................	675,375 00
Annual tonnage of outgoing freight, tons.................................	201,250
Estimated value of same...	$7,042,500 00
Estimated freight charges on same.......................................	$584,450 00

This statement does not include the unfinished paper mill at the **Marathon Paper Mills Company** at Rothschilds, five miles below Wausau. Your Committee is informed that the amount invested in this plant is about $2,000,000.00. Neither does this statement include the money invested in public utilities operated by water power, nor many other industries that are dependent on water power for their operation.

Your Committee prepared a list of fifty questions pertaining to the industrial development of water powers, and, through its committee clerk, Mr. Oscar Lind, sent copies of these questions to owners and users of developed water powers throughout the state. Answers, more or less complete, were received from various parts of the state and tabulated by Mr. Lind. The questions submitted are as follows:

1. State name of corporation.
2. Date of organization.
3. When was franchise secured from the legislature?
4. If franchise was purchased, state from whom and sum paid therefor.
5. What is the present location of corporation?
6. From what river is power derived?
7. Give list of officers and directors with office held by each.
8. What is the capital stock of the corporation?
9. What is the nature of its business?
10. Is the corporation owner or lessee of water power? If lessee, state name of lessor.
11. If lessee, state when power was first leased and the amount paid per annum per horsepower.
12. State dimensions of dam, and of what material it is built.
13. What is the amount of the fall?
14. State average daily flow in hydraulic feet per second at both high water and low water periods.
15. What is the average amount of unused power at both high water and low water periods on your level?
16. State approximately the undeveloped horsepower on the stream where plant is located.
17. State amount of developed and undeveloped horsepower owned by corporation.
18. What is the total horsepower of water power used per annum?

19. If steam power is used in connection with water power, what is the total amount of steam power used per annum?

20. What is the specific purpose to which the water power is devoted?

21. What is the total amount of manufactured product per annum? If reporting on more than one plant, state each separately.

22. What is the value of the output of the corporation per annum?

23. If power is leased to others, what is the gross and net income derived therefrom per annum, and what is the total per horsepower charged for water and for steam separately?

24. Does the corporation sell power, and if so, what quantity per annum and to whom?

25. If power is sold to public utilities, state the amount per annum charged for water and steam separately.

26. If power is sold to municipal corporations, state the amount per horsepower charged per annum for water and steam separately.

27. If power is sold to private individuals, state the amount per horsepower per annum charged for water and steam separately.

28. For what purposes is power sold?

29. State amount of expenses charged up for power per annum. a. Steam. b. Water power.

30. What is the monthly payroll of the corporation?

31. If steam power is used in connection with water power, state the cost of coal at point of location of plant.

32. In connection with the operation of the plant, what expenditure is made per horsepower reduced? a. steam? b. Water power?

33. Do you own flowage rights, and if so, state their nature and how they were secured, whether by purchase or otherwise.

34. What is the cost of erection and equipment of dam and water power including flowage rights?

35. What is the cost of maintenance of plant?

36. State difference in cost of manufacture as between water power and steam power.

37. To what extent, if any, does plant afford a market for forest products which would otherwise be unmarketable?

38. Where does the raw material used in plant come from?

39. What amount is set aside annually on account of depreciation of the property?

40. Is reservoir a practical necessity? If so, state reasons.

41. To what extent, if at all, has the reservoir system been developed on stream?

42. If the reservoir system is already partially or fully developed, state the percentage of increased efficiency resulting therefrom.

43. Enumerate transportation facilities of corporation.

44. Give estimate of the enhancement in the value of property in the vicinity of the plant in dollars and in percentage, due to the development of the water power.

45. What is the assessed value of the property owned by the corporation?

46. Give actual value of same.

47. If water power franchise is assessed separately, state amount of assessment.

48. What proportion of the taxes of the village, town or city in which plant is located is paid by corporation?

49. If the water power is bonded, state amount of bonded indebtedness.

50. Is there any agreement between your company and any other water power company, either as owner or lessee, to regulate or control the water power in your vicinity or within this state, either as to valuation or horsepower or otherwise? If so, state the nature of this agreement.

The list of answers received, tabulated as aforesaid, is marked "Exhibit 8" made a part of this report, and filed with the Wisconsin Legislative Reference Library, at Madison.

2

RECOMMENDATIONS.

WATER POWERS.

Cheap and available power is the basis and prequisite of extensive and diversified development. The principal sources of this power are coal and water. Wisconsin has no coal, but she ranks foremost among the states east of the Rocky Mountains in water power. Power from water is much cheaper than power from coal. While water power is cheaper, its use, until recent years was confined to the immediate localities where it was developed; but with the great improvements in methods for transforming such power into electric energy and in storing and transmitting the same over long distances, water is destined to become the chief source of power in industrial development. Wisconsin's water power is remarkably well distributed so that it can be carried by electrical transmission to many places remote from the source of power, when the demand for such power exists. Our state has realized this great public benefit, and is foremost among the states in recognizing the public utility of such transmission and sale of power, by placing it under the complete control of the Wisconsin Railroad Commission, insuring to the users of this power adequate service at reasonable rates, permitting the promoters and investors of such development a reasonable return only, on the capital invested, thus preventing for all time, the possibility of extortion by owners of such power, by reason of monopoly or otherwise.

Your entire committee heartily commends the Wisconsin Public Utility law in this respect, not only to the regulation of the more commonly known public utilities, but in its special application to the sale of power to the public.

Your committee is unanimous in recommending that permits and franchises to erect dams in navigable waters, be granted by the Wisconsin Railroad Commission, with proper and reasonable safeguards for the public rights.

Not more than a fourth part of the total water power in the state is fully developed, and a considerable part of that developed is now being used by private manufacturing plants. The prosperity and industrial welfare of the state is vitally concerned in a wise and efficient development of the water powers, and to that end all such development should be encouraged by all proper and reasonable means.

The right and scope of public control over water powers, when used as a public utility, is clear and adequate.

Your Committee is unanimous in believing, and recommends that, in the interest of the public welfare, all *franchises* granted to create power should be indeterminate, the same as in the case of other public utilities. This insures to the public, lower rates and faster development of our resources, and at the same time the public, through a system of reasonable regulation by the Wisconsin Railroad Commission, is safeguarded against extortion by those who sell power.

In this connection, and in order to stimulate enterprise by those who sell power, your Committee would urge upon the attention of the legislature, the application, so far as practicable, of the law of "sliding scale of returns" to water power companies selling power, *after* rates have become fixed by the Railroad Commission. For a more detailed analysis of this system of "sliding scale of returns," Mr. Hambrecht of this Committee submits his brief on "The Sliding Scale of Returns to Public Utilities," marked "Exhibit 9," and made a part of this report.

Mr. Hambrecht further submits to the Committee a series of 15 briefs, prepared by him, with the assistance of Mr. M. C. Riley, employed by the Committee. These briefs are more specifically referred to later in the report. The following is a list of subjects briefed, to-wit:

1. Definition of navigable streams.   (a) Wisconsin, (b) Federal.

2. Distinction between floatable streams and streams which are navigable in the broader sense of that word.

3. The relation of the United States, State and of the individual to the navigable waters of the state of Wisconsin.

4. Constitutional provisions relating to navigable waters.

5. Does the ordinance of 1787 make navigable rivers in Wisconsin public for all purposes. Effect of this ordinance on water powers in Wisconsin.

6. Does the "Right of Navigation" mean the right of passage over navigable rivers for purposes of commerce and profit, only, or does it include as well the right of passage over such rivers for pleasure and recreation?

7. The doctrine of riparian rights.

8. In what way did the arid states in the perfection of their irrigation and mining laws evade the doctrine of riparian rights?

9. The law governing the great ponds of Massachusetts.

10. To what extent has Congress or the State Legislature power to authorize the interference with or obstructions of navigable streams?

11. The nature of a franchise. Does a franchise differ from a permit?

12. Has the Legislature power to destroy the navigation of a navigable stream in the interest of drainage of submerged or swamp lands?

13. Legislative control over private and quasi public corporations.

14. Power of the Legislature to alter, amend or repeal corporate charters where the power is expressly reserved. Effect on acquired property under charter.

15. The nature of a public utility.

16. The sliding scale of returns to public utilities.

17. Government regulation of industry and the price of commodities.

18. Taxation of manufacturing, mercantile, transportation, and transmission corporations in the United States.

There has been some division of opinion in your Committee as to the precise nature of the public rights in the navigable streams, as distinguished from the riparian rights of the property owner along the shore. Also as to the conditions that should be imposed upon the grantees of authority to erect and maintain dams to develop power.

Messrs. Bray and Thomas express their views, as to the rights of the state in navigable waters and the conditions that should accompany **grants authorizing** the construction of dams in such waters, **in a bill marked** ''Exhibit A'' and made a part of this report.

General Summary of "Exhibit A."

The **Railroad Commission** of Wisconsin, after making certain findings, **is empowered** by this bill to grant authority to erect dams in **navigable waters** for the purpose of improving the navigation thereof and for developing hydraulic power. All such **grants, the bill provides,** shall be made to corporations only and for an **indeterminate** period; shall be accompanied by the power of eminent domain. when necessary, and are franchises The **right is reserved** to the state, whenever it has constitutional power, and to any municipality to purchase any water power plant authorized by the bill, the compensation to be paid therefor and the terms of the sale to be determined by the railroad commission. **Existing** grants, authorizing the maintenance of dams in **navigable waters,** are amended so that all will terminate in twenty-five **years,** and the manner in which the grantees of the permits or franchises so amended shall come in under the provisions **of the bill** is provided for. The bill reserves to the legislature the right to charge the grantees of any franchise a franchise rental. but provides that no such rental shall be charged or collected until twenty-five years hence. and provides further that in no case shall such franchise rental reduce the net income of such grantee to less than a reasonable return on investment. The Railroad Commission is given broad powers over the development and distribution of power by the grantees of these franchises. Upon a showing of public convenience and necessity. and of possibility, such commission may order additional development of hydraulic power. and upon similar showing may order that all hydraulic power, not reasonably necessary for the use of the grantee. be transformed into electric power and that such electric power be transmitted for sale to the public. The bill in many respects follows very closely the Wisconsin public utility law. Several sections framed to prevent the formation of a water power trust or monopoly are included in the bill. For more detailed information see ''Exhibit A.''

Messrs. Hambrecht. Bird and Kubasta would recommend that the state grant franchises or permits, as the case may be, for the development of water powers, not upon the theory of *improvement of navigation*, (unless such improvement is *in fact* contemplated), but rather on the theory that the development of water power, in and of itself, is the main purpose of the grant. In other words, the state, *in order to impose conditions*, should not attempt, under the guise of *improving navigation*, to do *indirectly* that which it could not do directly, when, as the fact often is, navigation is *impeded* by the development of hydraulic power. With this in mind, the Railroad Commission should make a distinction in the nature of the grant to develop water power, between power to be used by a riparian for his own *private business* and power to be generated and sold to the *public*. In the latter case the power company becomes a public utility. In the former case a private concern. The *use* to which one puts his property, rather than the property itself, is the determining factor as to whether or not a particular business is a public utility. Public *service* is the underlying principle for all public utilities. For a detailed analysis of this question Mr. Hambrecht submits his brief on "The Nature of a Public Utility," marked "Exhibit 10," and made a part of this report.

When a riparian, or any one else, about to develop a water power, asks for and receives the power of eminent domain from the state, it *must* be for a *public purpose* and should then be under the control of the Wisconsin Railroad Commission, as to rates charged, service rendered, and in all other respects, as other public utilities. It is otherwise when no right of eminent domain is granted, and the water power is used by the riparian for his own *private business*. In the former case, the grant from the state would be in the nature of a *franchise*. In the latter case it would be a bare *permit*. For a more detailed analysis of the distinction between a *franchise* and a *permit*, Mr. Hambrecht submits his brief on "The Nature of a Franchise. Does it Differ from a Permit?", marked "Exhibit 11" and made a part of this report.

Messrs. Hambrecht, Bird and Kubasta would further distinguish and classify the streams in the state, in so far as public rights are concerned, into three classes:

1. *Navigable Streams* in the broad sense of the word. Such streams to include those in which commerce is carried on, *up*

and *down* stream, by barges and boats. The Fox river, now under federal control, affords us an example of such stream in this state.

2. *Floatable Streams,* or those which can be used only to float the products of the soil *down stream.* Logging streams and the like furnish examples of this class.

3. *Non-navigable Streams,* or those not navigable for any purpose.

In class (1) the riparian right of the shore owner is, in all cases, subordinate to that of the public. This principle should be recognized by the state, through the Railroad Commission, in granting dam franchises or permits, and should, whenever possible, make the improvement of *navigation,* the paramount object in granting dam franchises. All such navigation improvement companies should, in all respect, be under the strict supervision and control of the Railroad Commission.

In class (2) the rights of the riparian owner and of the public are both to be enjoyed with due regard to the existence and preservation of the other. Neither is *paramount* to the other, but the respective rights of the riparian owner and of the public are to be enjoyed concurrently. Each must be enjoyed reasonably, and without any unnecessary interference with the enjoyment of the other, and without negligence. On such streams the Railroad Commission should grant *franchises* or *permits,* as the case may be, upon proper showing, if they are satisfied that the proposed development will not materially interfere with such down stream navigation as the particular stream in question affords.

In class (3) the rights of the public do not attach, and legislative permission is not necessary to construct a dam in such streams.

For a more detailed analysis of the distinction between class (1) and class (2) Mr. Hambrecht submits his brief on "The Distinction between Floatable Streams and Streams which Are Navigable in the Broader Sense of that Word," marked "Exhibit 12" and made a part of this report.

The right of a riparian owner to use water flowing over his land, for the development of hydraulic power, is a property right incident to the realty of the riparian owner. This riparian property right is limited and modified, as above stated, though not extinguished, by the public right of navigation and other community rights in navigable streams. The state, through its railroad commission, should recognize the riparian rights of applicants for grants to erect dams and at the same time should protect and preserve all the community rights of the public in navigable streams of the state when such grants are made.

For a more detailed analysis of the nature of the *public* rights and of the *riparian* rights in navigable streams in this state, Mr. Hambrecht submits a series of briefs, prepared by him for his report, marked as exhibits and made a part hereof, as follows, to-wit:

Exhibit 13: "Definition of Navigable Streams: (a) in Wisconsin, (b) Federal."

Exhibit 14: "The Relation of the United States, State and of the Individual to the Navigable Waters of the State of Wisconsin."

Exhibit 15: "Constitutional Provisions Relating to Navigable Waters."

Exhibit 16: "Does the Ordinance of 1787 Make Navigable Rivers in Wisconsin Public for All Purposes? Effect on Water Powers."

Exhibit 17: "Does the *Right of Navigation* mean the right of passage over navigable Rivers for purposes of Commerce and profit only, or does it include as well the right of passage over such Rivers for Pleasure and Recreation?".

Exhibit 18: "The Doctrine of Riparian Rights."

Exhibit 19: "In what way did the Arid States, in the Perfection of their Irrigation and Mining Laws, Evade the Doctrine of Riparian Rights?"

Exhibit 20: "The Law Governing the Great Ponds of Massachusetts."

Exhibit 21: "To what extent has Congress or the State Legislature Power to Authorize the Interference with or Obstruction of Navigation in Navigable Streams?"

Exhibit 22: "Has the Legislature Power to Destroy the Navigation of a Navigable Stream in the Interest of Drainage or Swamp Lands?"

Exhibit 23: "Extent of Legislative Control over Private and Quasi-public Corporations."

Exhibit 24: "Power of the Legislature to Alter, Amend or Repeal Corporate Charters where the Power is Expressly Reserved. Effect of acquired property under such charter."

Exhibit 25: ''Government Regulation of Industry and the Price of Commodities.''

These briefs state the law as found, upon research, and it is hoped that the analysis of the questions treated will prove to be of assistance to those interested in the general proposition of the Conservation of our Natural Resources, as applied to Water Powers in this State.

Taxation of Water Powers.

The property of water power companies, like all other property, should be assessed at its full market value and taxed accordingly. When water power is developed and operated by a private corporation, the whole property of such corporation, including its water power, should be assessed and taxed like the property of other similar corporations. When water power is being used as a public utility, the property of the operating company, including the water power, should be assessed, for the purpose of taxation, the same as the property of other similar public service companies.

Messrs. Hambrecht, Kubasta, Bird and Thomas would therefore recommend that, after the entire properties of these companies have been fully taxed, on the basis of their full market value, no additional taxes, in the nature of a franchise rental, should be imposed by the state.

In the interest of the public welfare, and in order to prevent over-capitalization, through an unearned increment, no element of value should ever be given to any permit, license or franchise granting authority to erect and maintain a dam in navigable waters for the development of hydraulic power or for other purposes.

The question of an adequate system of taxation for corporations, private and quasi-public, has not yet received detailed attention in many states owing to the newness of many phases of our industrial development. For an analysis of the systems of taxation of corporations, in vogue in 30 representative states, with certain recommendations based thereon, Mr. Hambrecht submits his brief on ''Taxation of Corporations—Manufacturing, Mercantile, Transportation and Transmission and their Shareholders and Bondholders,'' marked ''Exhibit 26'' and made a part of this report.

RESERVOIRS.

The Committee found that the Wisconsin Valley Improvement Company had made good progress in constructing reservoirs on the headwaters of the Wisconsin river, and that the work was still progressing. This work is done under the authority and strict supervision of the state, but the expense is borne by the water power owners and the actual cost of maintenance is divided pro rata, based on the amount of horsepower that each one has developed.

The following map, prepared by Mr. C. B. Stewart, engineer for the Wisconsin State Board of Forestry, shows the extent and location of the Wisconsin Valley Improvement Company's reservoirs at the headwaters of the Wisconsin river.

Map showing reservoirs operated by Wisconsin Valley Improvement Company, September, 1910:

The following table, submitted by the Wisconsin Valley Improvement Company, shows the distribution of tolls for storage of water on the Wisconsin and Tomahawk Rivers for a period of six (6) months, ending June 30, 1909, subject to the approval of the Railroad Commission of Wisconsin.

The committee heartily favors the extension of the reservoir plan, similar to the plan now developed on the Wisconsin River, wherever it can be done, and recommends that the bills applying to the Wolf and Chippewa rivers, referred to this committee, become laws.

The natural conditions in that part of the state are very favorable for storing water, the country being generally level, and containing very many—perhaps a thousand—lakes. At one point a dam fifteen feet in height causes a water storage fully fifteen miles in length spreading over about fifty square miles, including many of the lakes, thus forming an immense reservoir. When it is remembered that one square mile of water,

Plate I.

	Reservoir			Location of Dam			Areas in square miles		Capacity of storage million cu. ft.	
	Name	Location								
1	Vieux des sert	42	11	17	42	11	8 ½	26	780	780
2	Twin	41-42	11	19	41	11	5 ½	25	330	380
3	Long on Deerskin	41-42	12	7	41	12	4 ⅜	23	370	400
4	" " Eagle	37-40	11-12	5	39	11	6 ¾	109	376	750
5	Lower 9 mile	39-40	11	4	39	11	2 ½	10	325	325
6	Upper 9	40	11-12	36	40	11	½	3	38	38
7	Seven mile	39	11-12	11	39	11	1	5	135	135
8	Minocqua	38-40	6-7	10	39	6	9 ½	79	330	840
9	Little Deerskin	40-41	10-11	33	41	11	½	8	28	28
10	Sugar Camp	38-39	8-10	17	39	9	3 ⅛	50	500	500
11	Big St Germain	40-41	7-8	30	40	8	2 ½	64	210	210
12	Little St Germain	40	8-9	35	40	8	1 ⅛	20	95	95
13	Buckatahpon	41	9	24	41	9	1 ¼	10	110	110
14	Pickerel	39-40	7-8	18	39	8	½	11	30	50
15	Squirrel Lake	39	5	30	39	5	2	17	120	138
16	North Pelican	36-39	9-11	4	36	10	2 ¼	89	0	135
17	South Pelican	35	10-11	11	35	10	3 ½	18	0	280
18	Rice Lake	36-37	7	8	36	7	½	12	40	40
19	Hancock Lake	36	7	15	36	7	⅜	6	30	30
	Totals						58 ⅜	578	3839	5241

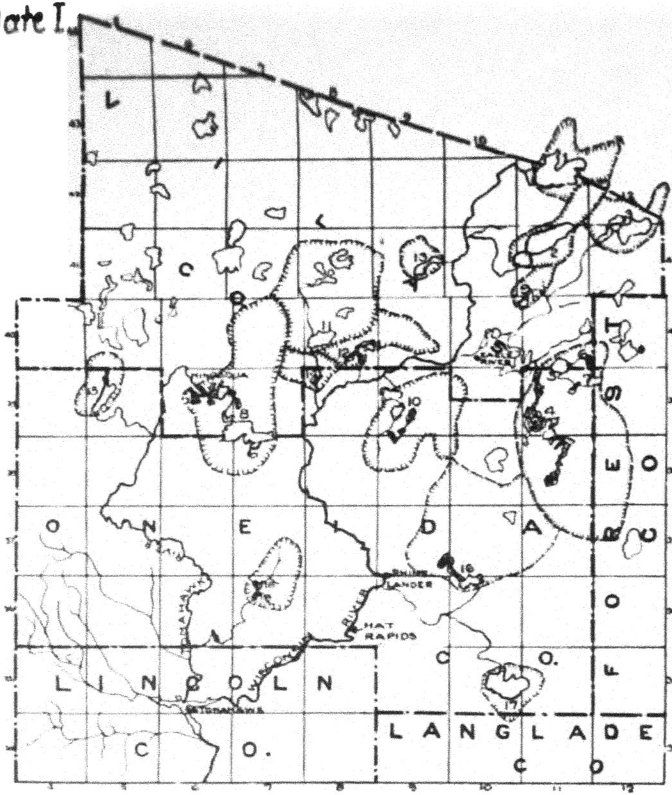

MAP
SHOWING
RESERVOIRS
OPERATED BY
WISCONSIN VALLEY IMPROVEMENT CO.

SEPT.-1910

☐ Represents drainage area.

COMPILED FROM DATA OF WIS. VAL. IMP. CO.

Power St	Remarks
Prairie Rapids	ᴇᵛELOPED
Tomahawk	₄, but wasting water at all times.
Tomahawk Rapids	" " " " "
Otter Rapids	ANDER Paper Co. Rhinelander, Wis
Rhinelander	ANDER Power Co. Rhinelander, Wis.
Hat Rapids	DEVELOPED
Nigger Island	"
Kings	HAWK Paper & Pulp Co. Tomahawk, Wis.
Tomahawk	
Grandmother	EVELOPED.
Upper Grandfa	FATHER Falls Co. Merrill, Wis.
Lower "	EVELOPED.
Bill Cross	"
Merrill (Upper	"
" (Lowe	UER Pulp & Mfg. Co. Merrill, Wis.
Trap Rapids	EVELOPED.
Brokaw	AU Paper Mills Co. Brokaw, Wis.
Wausau	₄, but wasting water at all times.
Rothchilds	EVELOPED.
Mosinee	"
Battle Islan	"
Stevens Point	₄, but wasting water at all times.
Stevens "	SIN River Paper & Pulp Co. Stevens Point, Wis.
"	R Paper Co. Plover, Wis.
Plover	Rapids Paper & Pulp Co. Grand Rapids, Wis.
Biron	LIDATED Water Power & Pulp Co Grand Rapids, Wis.
Grand Rapid	LIA Pulp & Water Power Co. Grand Rapids, Wis.
South Centr	
Port Edwar	SA–Edwards Paper Co. Port Edwards, Wis.
Nekoosa	EVELOPED.
Kilbourn	

12 inches deep, contains nearly 28 million cubic feet, and that the reservoir referred to is but one of several to be constructed, some idea of the vast storage possibilities will be realized. The impounding of so large an amount of water during time of excess will have an important effect in the prevention of destructive floods, not alone in the rivers of our state, but to some extent in the Mississippi river. This impounded water drawn off when the stage of water in the river is low, will supplement the natural flowage and will be of very great benefit to all water power users along the river. Reservoir systems, when fully developed on the head waters of the Wisconsin and other rivers, will be an important factor in increasing the amount of water power of the state.

The height to which the water may be raised in the lakes included in the storage districts, and the level to which it may be lowered is, under authority of the legislature, determined by the State Board of Forestry, and is indicated by permanent grade posts or bench marks. Some of these grade posts are already in place and the remainder will soon be established. The surface of the lakes is much more uniform in height under this plan than in former years under natural conditions. This renders the banks very favorable for summer cottages, a considerable number of which have already been erected on these lakes. Pleasure seekers are much gratified at the increase of water in the small streams, locally called "thoroughfares," connecting the lakes. When the reservoir system is completed there will be many long stretches across lakes and connecting thoroughfares over which small boats and launches, such as hunters and tourists use, can pass uninterruptedly. One such stretch of fifty miles is now available on the headwaters of the Wisconsin River.

This reservoir system will, to a considerable extent, make the water power in the river below a *controllable* power. This is a matter of vital importance to all industries using such power.

The courage and enterprise of the men who initiated the reservoir system and who are carrying it forward so successfully deserve high commendation and encouragement by the state. In the judgment of the committee this method of *increasing* and *controlling* water power is of vast importance; the benefits will be perpetual and of greater extent than is now generally understood. So far as the committee has learned the development of a state reservoir system by private citizeus at their own expense, but under the supervision and control of the state, has never before been undertaken—but the result in Wisconsin thus far is very satisfactory. and there is nothing to indicate that it will not be permanently so.

Your committee therefore recommends for favorable consideration by the legislature such bills as come before it providing for storage reservoirs similar to that now established at the headwaters of the Wisconsin River by the Wisconsin Valley Improvement Company under its charter granted by the Wisconsin Legislature of 1907, being Chapter 335 of the Laws of 1907. .

Mr. C. B. Stewart. on request of the State Board of Forestry, made a recent survey of the conditions of the reservoir system on the Wisconsin River, as operated by the Wisconsin Valley Improvement Company, and by request of Mr. Stewart and the State Board of Forestry, his findings are marked ''Exhibit 27,'' and are made a part of this report.

FORESTRY.

The forest primeval, stately, unscarred and perfect, is not now found, nor has it ever existed in this state save in small areas. Wind and fire have ever been the enemies of the forest, striving for its destruction;—while nature, silently and patiently is ever working for its restoration and improvement. Add to these destructive elements the work of man, and the result is the condition now existing in the Northern part of our state. The pine is practically gone, the supply of hemlock and hardwood is greatly reduced. Forest fires have followed timber cutting, with the result that many thousand of acres of land are now a barren waste covered with blackened stumps, worthless shrubs, wild grass and woods. On some areas where fires have not been severe, or have never passed over, new forest growth is springing up that will become of commercial value in the future. In some of the earlier cuttings, certain varieties of timber were left as being of no value at that time, but which are now valuable. The vegetable mold which nature had been accumulating for many years to fertilize the soil has been burned away, leaving the soil unproductive and uninviting to one pioneer farmer. There are also many thousands of acres in the northern part of the state which are not adapted to farming, and can be utilized for forestry or water storage only. Under present conditions all of these are assessed at a very low price, and justly so, with the result that the state derives very small revenue in taxes therefrom.

That the prosperity of the entire state is in a large measure dependent upon the restoration of the forests in the northern part needs no argument, but brief mention may be made that from this section alone can our future lumber supply, upon which the retaining and continuing of many of our factories depend, be secured within our state. The stock for paper mills.

poles for telegraph and telephone lines and fence posts, as well as timber for general building and miscellaneous use, are also dependent upon forest restoration. The forest also gives a covering to the head waters of the main rivers and retards the rapid run-off of snow and ice in spring time and prolongs the flow into the dry season. The prevention of forest fires will also add to the agricultural value of certain large areas, thus increasing the population and property value of the state.

It was with these purposes in view that Forestry legislation was initiated. The first measures introduced years ago by Ex-Senator Burroughs, now deceased, were followed by others until the session of 1905 when a general forestry law, (Chapter 264, laws of 1905) was passed. Under this law forestry work is now being conducted.

There has been considerable conflict of expert opinion on the relation of forests to stream flow, and therefore your committee cannot do better than to refer to two government publications, treating on this subject, and to incorporate in this report, as exhibits, two prepared opinions by experts, setting out the matters in dispute. The two Government Reports referred to are:

(1) "A Report on the Influence of Forest on Climate and on Floods," by Professor Willis L. Moore, Chief of the United States Weather Bureau. House of Representatives Report, United States Committee on Agriculture, 1910.

(2) Relation of Deforestation to Precipitation and Run-off in Wisconsin," by Mr. William C. Devereaux, Local Forecaster, Milwaukee, Wisconsin, dated, June 3, 1910; printed by order of the Chief of Bureau in Monthly Weather Review, 1910, 38: 720–723. Reprinted in pamphlet form.

The two expert opinions prepared for your committee are:

(1) "The Intimate Relation of Forest Cover to Stream Flow," by Mr. E. M. Griffith, State Forester, Madison, Wisconsin, (1910). This article is marked "Exhibit 28" and made a part of this report.

(2) "Statement of Professor D. W. Mead, of Madison, Wisconsin, to the committee on Water Powers, Forestry and Drainage of the Wisconsin Legislature. Revised 1910," marked "Exhibit 29", and made a part of this report. Professor Mead's article deals with other matters referred to this committee in a comprehensive and thorough manner, and his entire article is included in the exhibit, for helpful information furnished.

Under the present forestry law all state land north of Town 33, (corresponding with the north line of Oconto and Taylor counties), was withdrawn from sale, except such portions as should be found upon examination to be better adapted for agriculture, the intention being to retain such lands for the purpose of reforesting the same. The general government has since granted to the state 20,000 acres to be added to this state forest reserve. Parts of these lands consisted of small isolated pieces, which the forestry board was authorized to sell or to exchange for other lands, so as to make the state forest reserve compact and therefore more easily protected from forest fires.

These holdings are now largely in Oneida and Vilas counties, with small tracts in Forest, Iron and Price Counties, the total state holding being nearly 300,000 acres. These lands are largely within the wonderful lake region on the head waters of the many branch streams that unite farther down and form the Wisconsin, Chippewa and Wolf Rivers. The lands of private owners, however, are scattered amongst the state holdings, and these should be purchased in order to enlarge the forest reserve and to render fire protection more effectual which is possible only when the land is in a compact body.

Because of the importance of growing timber in our own state, (which will become an important source of revenue to the state before many years), in order that the prevention of forest fires may be made possible, that our wonderful lake region may be made more beautiful and attractive to tourists by forest covered banks, and in order to conserve the waters at the head waters of our principal rivers, and because of the fact that some parts of the land in the vicinity of the state forest reserve is not adapted to agriculture, your committee is of the opinion that the purchase of land to enlarge the state forest reserve should be continued until approximately two million acres have been secured. Much of this land can now be secured at a very low price. A considerable amount was bought by the Forestry board in 1909 at $2.50 per acre. This opportunity to buy at low price will not long continue—perhaps has already passed, and greater advance in price in the near future is believed to be certain. Land upon which merchantable timber is growing will naturally cost more, and is worth more.

Your committee was impressed with the fact that fire is the

great destroyer of the forest, and the preventive to new growth
of timber. Under favorable conditions a forest fire sweeps over
a section of country with the swiftness of the wind, and licks
its fiery tongue about the seedlings and saplings by the millions, and about the larger trees as well, leaving blackness and
desolation in its wake. The *prevention* of forest fires is an *absolute condition* to foresting.

The present method of preventing these fires is by town fire
wardens. This system has resulted in much good but is inefficient, especially during certain seasons of the year, and during times of drought. The expense of these wardens, after report and approval by the State Forester, is paid by the towns.
A change from town to county wardens will add to the convenience of controlling these officials and will increase their efficiency. Your committee recommends for passage a bill marked
"Exhibit B", and made a part of this report. This bill, in
addition to increasing the salary of the state forester and enlarging his powers provides for a change from the *town* to the
county fire warden system and provides for an increased appropriation for forestry purposes.

But this is not enough. Some method to prevent the *starting* of forest fires is necessary, for once under full headway it
is beyond human power, in most cases, to stop such a fire. It
may be controlled in some degree by back firing or by other
methods, and sometimes may be stopped by previously established fire lines, but safety lies in prevention alone. A system
of patrols has been instituted in some of the Western states, and
with satisfactory results. The federal government adopted this
plan years ago. No better method has yet been devised, and in
the opinion of the Committee this plan should be at once
adopted in this state; this patrol to consist of experienced men,
well organized and disciplined, a few of whom should be on
duty during all the summer months, and the remainder subject to call as needed. The main purpose of such patrol would
be to prevent the starting of forest fires.

Should the conservation bill, marked "Exhibit F" and referred to later, become a law, then and in that event so much of
the provisions of "Exhibit B" as are in conflict therewith
should be changed.

The Lake States Forest Fire Conference held at St. Paul,
Minnesota, December 6th and 7th, 1910, after mature delibera-

tion concerning their recommendations for the prevention of forest fires, adopted the following resolutions:

"This Conference after mature deliberation adopted resolutions affecting the question of preventing forest fires, of which the following is a copy, to-wit:

Your Resolutions Committee beg to submit the following results of its deliberations:

Resolved, that we recommend to the legislatures of our States:

1st. That the forest fire protection of each State and such other branches of State work as may be deemed best to combine with it, be placed under the control of a nonpartisan Commission empowered, as fully as possible under the constitutions of the different states, to carry on the work and under civil service rules. Such commission should represent all the interests involved as far as possible, and we recommend that such commission place the work in charge of a chief forester who should be a professional graduate forester and that the commission employ such trained foresters and other assistants as may be necessary; define their duties and fix their salaries; said employes to be engaged under such civil service regulations as the Commission may prescribe.

2nd. *Resolved*, That it is the sense of this Conference that the present Forest Fire Warden Service of Michigan, Wisconsin and Minnesota is totally inadequate to meet the existing fire hazard to both life and property, and that forest protection service, to become efficient must be greatly extended. To this end we recommend an adequate forest patrol system, maintained by the state, organized and operated by the commission referred to.

3rd. *We Further Recommend*, That the commission be authorized to co-operate with the national government, the several adjoining states, and such associations and organizations as the commission may find necessary to best protect the timber resources of the state.

4th. *Resolved*, That this Conference is opposed to a general slash burning law, as experience has proven it unsatisfactory, impracticable and dangerous. We recommend, however, that the commission should be given authority to order the disposal of dangerous slashings sufficient to establish a safe fire line around standing timber or other valuable property.

5th. *Resolved*, That this Conference advocates legislation providing strict regulation of the burning of brush and debris in clearing land during the dry season, such burning to be under the direction of state fire patrolmen, under such regulations as the commission may prescribe.

6th. *We Further Recommend*, That the burning of all debris on the rights of way of the various railroads be under the control and direction of the state forest patrol. Further, that under special conditions as directed by the state patrol the railway companies maintain a patrol, properly equipped following their trains, also that all railroad and logging locomotives and traction engines must be equipped with the most practical spark arresting devices (subject to inspection and approval of the commission.)

7th. WHEREAS, The building of fire lines around exposed property including settlements, villages and towns, has proven a most effective means for the control and extinguishment of fires.

We Recommend, That one of the principal duties of the patrolmen working under the direction of the commission, should be to establish such fire lines where necessary for protection of property.

8th. *We Recommend*, As the most effective measures for preventing and fighting serious fires, adequate means of transportation and communication, to include trails, telephone lines and lookout stations, and that the efforts of the commission should be exerted toward the construction and establishment of the same as rapidly as consistent.

9th. The appalling sacrifice of life and the continued great loss of state and private property resulting from fires in our forested area, are a disgrace to our civilization and a most serious drain upon our natural resources, and we believe that the expenditure of such amount as may be necessary to prevent these losses is fully justified.

We Therefore Recommend, That the appropriations by the state legislature to maintain forest protection should be sufficient to provide for a forest patrolman for each forty thousand acres requiring protection as well as for the ex-

penses necessary to successfully carry out all of the measures, suggested by these resólutions.

10th. *We recommend,* in addition to the patrol system, an
auxiliary county fire fighting force to be appointed by and
under the direction of the commission, to be paid by the
state and charged back to the counties. Such expenses to
be ultimately borne by the counties or towns, in which the
fires occur.

Further Be It Resolved, That as it is shown by statistics
that there are a large number of fires set each season
through the carelessness of the general public, including
campers, fishermen, hunters and others, *We Recommend,*
That a campaign of education be energetically carried on
through every possible channel to the end that this hazard
be reduced through a better understanding of forest conditions by all the people.

Resolved Further, That the sincere thanks of all the delegates and attendants here be extended to the officials of
the state of Minnesota, and the city of St. Paul, who have
contributed so largely to the success of this Conference, to
the Manufacturers and Jobbers' Association of St. Paul for
the courtesies shown, to the management of the St. Paul
hotel for the facilities so freely extended, and to the press
for its treatment of the proceedings of this Lake States
Forest Fire Conference.''

Your committee after a full hearing discussing the various
objects referred to is in hearty accord with these resolutions and
we believe that legislation enacted along the lines therein indi-
ated would be of advantage to this state. It was the purpose
of this Conference to secure so far as practicable, uniform legis-
ation to prevent forest fires in the three lake states of Michigan,
Wisconsin and Minnesota.

Your committee also recommends that the penalty for setting
forest fires and for failure to extinguish camp and other fires
that endanger the forests, be made more severe, and a bill, made
a part of this report and marked ''Exhibit C,'' is recommended
for passage.

In order to purchase the land for enlarging the state forest
reserve, and to provide for the expense of preventing forest
fires, principally by the patrol system, your committee has pre-

pared a bill levying a tax of two-tenths of a mill on the property of the state, and submits such bill to the favorable consideration of the legislature. This bill is marked "Exhibit D" and is made a part of this report.

Mr. Thomas would recommend that the proceeds derived from the two-tenths mill tax shall not be used for patrolling private holdings.

In further explanation of the need of this fund for forestry purposes, Mr. E. M. Griffith, state forester, submits the following statement.

"This bill, Digest of Substitute Amendment No. 2 S., for No. 502, S., which is before your committee, is amended so as to provide for a state tax of two-tenths of one mill for a period of twenty years. The bill as introduced by the committee on forestry in the session of 1909 provided for a tax of one-tenth of a mill for a period of ten years.

In 1905, through the enactment of Chapter 264, the state took the first step towards a broad and comprehensive policy to gradually acquire adequate forest reserves at the headwaters of the most important rivers of the state. This law withdrew from sale and set aside for forest reserve purposes all state lands north of Town 33, and the most effective provision of the bill was that the state board of forestry might dispose of the agricultural and scattered lands, not suitable for forestry, the proceeds of such sales to constitute a "forest reserve fund" to be available for the purchase of lands to be added to the forest reserves.

The state lands north of town 33, which remained unsold in 1905, were so badly scattered that they could not be systematically managed as forest reserves, or adequately protected from fire and timber trespass. The state forester, therefore, after examining the lands and consulting with the higher officers of the U. S. forest service, recommended to the state board of forestry that the main forest reserve to be located in the wonderful lake region, lying at the headquarters of the Wisconsin and Chippewa rivers in Oneida and Vilas counties, and that the agricultural and scattering lands in other counties should be appraised and sold, at public sale, at such times as the lands and timber could be disposed of to the best advantage. In 1905 the state lands in Oneida and Vilas counties comprised 50,346 acres, and up to January 1st, 1910, the state board of forestry have purchased 58,218 acres in these two counties, so that the present acreage is 108,564 acres. In addition to these lands there are some 35,656 acres in Forest county, 29,174 in Iron county, and 27,634 acres in Price County, most of which will be retained within the permanent reserves, so that the foundation of our future forest reserves is now 201,028 acres. There remain some 71,364 acres of agricultural and scattered lands to be disposed of in other counties and they will be offered for sale as general business conditions warrant.

The sale of these remaining lands, however, will not begin to provide sufficient funds to purchase the lands which it is absolutely necessary to procure in order to block up the reserves and thus make forestry management possible. As previously stated, the lake region in Oneida and Vilas counties, at the headwaters of the Wisconsin and Chippewa rivers, is very unusual in the number, extent and beauty of the lakes. Those lakes also have a very important economic value, for if the forest growth upon their watersheds is protected, and some of the lakes also used as reservoirs, the flow of the rivers rising in this region can be made remarkably uniform, and thereby the value of these rivers both in the development of power and for any possible future needs of navigation, will be assured to the people of the state for all time.

But this lake region, which is such a valuable asset to the state, cannot be protected until the necessary lands are acquired and placed under forestry management. The cut over lands which are adjacent to, and mixed in among, the state's holdings, owned largely by non-residents and uncared for, are a serious and constant menace to the forest reserves, as they are the source from which start many of the destructive forest fires. The truest economy on the part of the state will be to acquire these lands as soon as possible, so that the young growth which is coming up may be protected and denuded lands reforested.

The state board of forestry has secured the 58,218 acres, already purchased in this region, at the very low average price of $2.50 per acre, but timbered lands which should be secured to protect the shores of the rivers and lakes, and which will prove to be most profitable investments, cannot of course be purchased at such a low figure. The state board of forestry has, during the past five years, examined the acres which should be purchased and it has been found that the state should own and control at least 2,000,000 acres in forest reserves. It is the intention to appoint forest rangers who will live in the reserves, act as fire patrols to prevent the setting or spread of forest fires, build fire lines, roads and trials, plant acres which have been denuded, and scale the mature timber which is cut from reserve lands by the purchasers.

As stated, the lands necessary to block up the reserves should be purchased as soon as possible and an executive organizaticn perfected so that the reserves shall be brought into cendition to yield an increasing revenue to the state. I therefore recommend as an urgent necessity the passage of bill No. 502 S. so amended as to provide a state tax of two-tenths of one mill for each dollar of the assessed valuation of the taxable property in the state, to be collected annually for a period of twenty years, the tax when levied and collected to constitue "a forestry investment fund," to be used for the purchase, improvement and protection of forest reserve lands. Such a tax, of two-tenths of one mill, will make it possible for the state board of forestry to at once enter into land contracts to secure the lands which are needed and to pay for them as the money becomes available.

This may appear to be a large sum to devote to forestry work, but it should be remembered that the purchase of forest reserve lands will be a most excellent investment for the state for the following reasons:

1. The young timber on the reserves will be protected and denuded acres planted so that in future years the state will receive a direct and increasing revenue from the sale of mature timber which can be cut and removed from time to time, and at the same time improve the character of the forest.

2. Indirectly the state will receive even a greater revenue by retaining industries within the state which will become more and more dependent upon the forest reserves for raw material as the forests are cut off of private lands.

3. In the same way the state will gain an indirect revenue from the preservation and improvement of the water powers, which will be assured by extensive forests at the headwaters.

4. Preserving the forests in the beautiful lake regions of northern Wisconsin will both protect and greatly enhance its present attractiveness as a resort region for not only the citizens of this state, but the entire Mississippi Valley as well. The value of such a resort region is not generally understood, even from the dollar view-point, but the report of the Bureau of Labor of New Hampshire for 1905 shows that the resort business yielded in that year over $10,000,000, and the report of the forest, fish and game commission of New York for the same year states that it was over $7,000,000.

If we protect our lakes, rivers and forests in northern Wisconsin they will attract summer visitors from all over the country, and not only will the settlers have an near and ready market for all they can raise, but a large amount of money will be paid to hotels, boarding houses, resorts, guides, etc.

A small section of the reserves should also be set apart for consumptives, where they can live a healthy life in the bracing air of Northern Wisconsin, and those who are in need of financial assistance be given enough light work, such as planting, to at least pay for their keep. In time it will also be desirable to set apart a portion of the reserves as a bird and game preserve.

As will be noted from the following statement both New York and Pennsylvania through generous annual appropriations are rapidly acquiring splendid forest reserves, which they appreciate are investments that will constantly increase in value.

New York.

Forest Reserve Lands.

Purchased, 1907 ....   46,156 acres
Area, 1908.. .... 1,548,450 acres
Purchased, 1908 ....   63,367 acres
                                    _____
Area, 1909 .... 1,611,817 acres
Purchased, 1909 ....   43,943 acres
                                    _____
    Total .... 1,655,760 acres
Appropriation, 1908, for purchase lands $603, 516.

Pennsylvania.

Forest Reserve Lands.

Area 1904 ....549,563 acres
                                    _____
Area 1906 ....701,297 acres
Contracted for in 1906................100,000 acres
                                    _____
    Total ....801,297 acres
Appropriation for 1907 and 1908...........$600,000 00

Bill No. 502, S., as amended provides for the employment of a forest fire patrol. The severe forest fires during this month (May, 1910) in many of the northern counties, which have done an enormous amount of damage, have again emphasized the urgent necessity of a patrol system, which backed by the necessary laws will largely prevent the starting of forest fires. Such a patrol system must be very elastic, as only a few men will be required at certain seasons, but the force must be rapidly enlarged during a dangerously dry season. Of course it will only be necessary to employ patrols from about April 1st to December 1st, but it is planned to employ camp foremen who have been tested by the lumber companies. The state would employ these men as forest fire patrols from say April 1st to December 1st, and the lumber companies the remainder of the year. Thus the state without employing the men throughout the year would secure a permanent force which is of course very essential to good work. In some heavily timbered counties from four to five patrols would be needed, in others one would usually be sufficient. The county fire wardens should be under them and the patrols should pick competent men in each county whom they could employ as deputy patrols in times of necessity. It is estimated that the patrol system for 32 northern counties would cost in ordinary seasons from $75,000 to $100,000. The cost of the system would be paid from the proceeds of the two-tenths of a mill tax, and it is strongly recommended that the state board of forestry should not be limited as to the percentage of the mill tax which it may expend for the patrol system, as it must be very elastic to meet changing conditions of danger. Wisconsin must stop the fearful annual loss of forest resources by forest fires."

SLASH BURNING.

The committee observed with interest that the Hackley-Phelps-Bonnell Company at Hackley, in Vilas County, was utilizing the waste in hardwood timber cuttings for the manufacture of charcoal, wood alcohol and acetate of lime. An expensive plant is required to do this distilling economically, yet from such facts as were submitted to the committee, a fair margin of profit seemed to be practically certain. A plant of this sort should be run in connection with a lumber manufacturing plant, in order that the refuse from the lumber might furnish fuel for the distilling. Apparently the margin in this distilling would warrant the shipping of hardwood waste, under ordinary freight conditions, for a hundred miles or so, and still leave some margin of gain to the shipper and to the distiller.

Since small hardwood limbs, down to about an inch in diameter, are included in this stock for distilling, your committee expresses the hope that the solution of the disposition of hardwood slash will be solved by this process.

Your Committee does not, at this time, recommend any general "slash burning" law for this state. This is based on physical conditions in Wisconsin and on the reported failure of the operation of the general "slash burning" law of Minnesota, where conditions appear to be much more favorable for the working of such a law than in this state. Your Committee was impressed with the failure of the general "slash burning" law of Minnesota after a full discussion of the subject by foresters, and others in attendance at the Lake States Forest Fire Conference held at St Paul, Minnesota, December 6th and 7th, 1910. In place of such general slash burning law your committee has seen fit to adopt the resolutions prepared by the above conference, already referred to.

DRAINAGE.

The committee is advised by authority believed to be re-
ble, that approximately three million acres of land in the
te, which is now too wet for cultivation, can be drained.
part of this land would become high grade agricultural
nd if properly drained, while other parts are not suitable
r agriculture, and can be used for water storage or for
rowing certain kinds of forest trees only.

All of the swamp and overflowed land is now assessed at
om one dollar to eight or ten dollars per acre, while in some
ases, the adjoining high land is assessed from fifty to one hun-
red dollars. In some part of the state, especially the southern
nd central, this wet land would be of the same value as the
higher land, if well drained. This has been proved by actual
experiments.

Statistics collected from drainage actually done in the state
up to this time show that the average cost is from six to
seven dollars an acre, and the average increase in value of such
drained land is about forty dollars per acre.

During the earlier years of our state's existence, and extending as far back as territorial days, dams were erected on many
steams for local purposes, largely to run mills to grind the grain
of the early settlers. A considerable number of these dams are
still standing, and in some cases, after twenty years of existence, public rights, that cannot be disturbed by later demands,
have vested. Some of these dams are now of no practical use,
while the impounded water overflows thousands of acres of land
hat would otherwise be high grade agricultural land, and
re in demand for such use. The state should grant authority
o secure relief in such cases, upon fair conditions. In other
ases the overflow caused by such dams is of small area, the
nd has come to be considered as a permanent lake; residences,
ghways and other improvements have been made to conform

to the present water level, thus promoting the beauty as well as the utility of the location. Such conditions should not be disturbed.

In other localities, especially in certain places in the northern part of the state, the wet and overflowed lands would be of no more value, at least for many years, if drained than under present conditions. Some of these wet lands can be utilized for cranberry culture; some for growing certain varities of timber; while other parts of these low lands can profitably be drained for agricultural purposes. Several drainage districts are already established, with the prospects of highly satisfactory results.

It is evident to the committee that no uniform rule for the physical work of drainage can be adopted, but that the local conditions must govern in each case. After the advantages and disadvantages have been carefully considered by competent and impartial authority, the course of procedure as to drainage should be determined.

It has been brought to the attention of your committee that the present drainage laws, which have many times been changed and amended, make the proceedings too expensive for residents of a proposed drainage district, to determine whether or not a drainage proposal will be favorably considered, also to initiate proceedings in case it is so considered.

In view of the foregoing conditions, it has been determined that the welfare and material advantage of the State will be promoted by having all of the present laws relating to drainage rewritten, making them as plain and brief as practicable. This your committee, with the assistance of Mr. Thomas M. Kearney of Racine and of Mr. B. M. Vaughan, of Grand Rapids, has done. Your committee submits a bill, proposing an amendment, revision and codification of our present drainage laws. This bill is marked "Exhibit E" and is made a part of this report.

Your committee wishes to express their appreciation to Messrs. Kearney and Vaughan for valuable assistance rendered in this matter.

A CONSERVATION COMMISSION.

our committee heartily favors and recommends a whole-
e conservation of the natural resources of the state. These
tural resources such as lands, forests, waterways and fish
d game are very closely allied, and in order to bring about
e best results along the lines of conservation, your committee
commends that a Conservation Commission, composed of three
mpetent commissioners, be created, and that such Commission
given plenary jurisdiction and broad powers over matters
rtaining to natural resources and their conservation.

It is the opinion of your Committee that the Conservation
ommission at this time should be given power and jurisdic-
on over all matters pertaining to forestry, to the fish and
ame of the state, to waterways, except water power develop-
ent which the committee recommends be placed under the
pervision and jurisdiction of the Railroad Commission of
isconsin, and, in certain cases, to drainage of swamp or sub-
erged lands.

This Conservation Commission should be composed of a
forester, a commissioner conservant with matters relating to
fish and game, and an hydraulic engineer. The Commission
should have supervision over all matters now under the control and supervision of the State Board of Forestry and of
the State Game Warden and over such other matters pertaining
to natural resources as is deemed expedient.

The creation of such a Commission should merge the departments of the State Board of Forestry and the State Game
Warden. By merging these two departments much by way
of duplication can be avoided. Instead of the State employing
corps of game wardens and a corps of fire wardens, rangers,
tc., the Commission can employ one corps of men with au-
hority to enforce both forestry and fish and game laws. In
is way the expense of the enforcement of these laws can be

reduced to such an extent that the creation of the Conservation Commission will throw no extra financial burden upon the State. The efficiency of any conservation movement will be promoted by the creation of a commission as recommended.

Your committee respectfully submits a bill for the creation of a Conservation Commission, and recommends its enactment into law. This bill is marked "Exhibit F" and is made a part of this report.

Senator Bird recommends, Assemblymen Hambrecht, Thomas and Kubusta concurring, that in addition to the powers already given to the proposed Conservation Commission, their duties shall also include the duties now belonging to the State Land Office.

"EXHIBIT A."

A Bill.

o amend section 1596 of the statutes relating to the erection
of dams, bridges or other obstructions in or over any
navigable river or stream, and to create sections 1596—1 to
1596—50 of the statutes relating to the granting of franchises for the improvement of navigation and for the development of hydraulic power.

he people of the state of Wisconsin, represented in senate and assembly, do enact as follows:

SECTION 1. Section 1596 of the statutes is amended to read:
Section 1596. All rivers and streams which have been
meandered and returned as navigable by the surveyors employed by the government of the United States *and all rivers*
nd streams navigable in fact for any purpose, are hereby declared navigable (so far as the same have been meandered)
the extent that no dam, bridge or other obstruction shall be
e in or over the same without the permission of the legislature; but this section shall not be construed to impair the
wers granted by law to towns, countries or cities, to construct such bridges over such rivers and streams. The consent of
is state is hereby given to the acquisition by the United
tates of all lands and appurtenances in this state which have
n or may be acquired by the United States for the purpose of
cting thereon dams, abutments, locks, lock-keepers' dwell-
. chutes or other structures necessary or desirable in improving the navigation of the rivers or other waters within
d on the borders of this state, and the United States may
old, use and occupy such lands and other property and

exercise exclusive jurisdiction and control over the same, subject to the right of this state to have civil and criminal process issued out of any of its courts executed within and upon said lands.

Section 2. There are added to the statutes fifty (50 new sections to read:

SECTION 2. There are added to the statutes fifty (50) new used in this act shall mean the railroad commission of Wisconsin.

2. The term "navigable waters" as used in this act shall mean all streams, rivers, lakes and connecting waters in the state of Wisconsin navigable in fact for any purpose.

(3) The term "franchise" as used in this act shall mean a grant of legislative authority to a corporation organized as herein prescribed to improve the navigation of navigable waters and to develop hydraulic power.

(4) The term "applicants" as used in this act shall mean any number of persons, not less than three (3), who propose to organize as a corporation under sections 1777 to 1777c, both inclusive of the statutes of 1898 and acts amendatory thereof, and who apply to the railroad commission for a franchise as defined in this act.

(5) The term 'improvement" or "improvements" as used in this act shall mean all improvements made or all improvements proposed to be made under authority of any franchise granted pursuant to this act for the improvement of navigation and the development of hydraulic power.

Section 1596—2. Every franchise granted pursuant to the provisions of this act shall be granted for the purpose of improving the navigation of navigable waters and for the development of hydraulic power.

Section 1596—3. Every grant of legislative authority under the provisions of this act to improve the navigation of navigable waters and to develop hydraulic power is hereby declared to be a franchise.

Section 1596—4. Every franchise granted pursuant to the provisions of this act is accepted, taken and held subject to the terms, conditions, and provisions of such franchise and of this act, and is so accepted, taken and held in consideration of the powers, privileges and prerogatives conferred by said franchise.

Section 1596—5. Every franchise granted under this act shall be granted only to corporations oroganized pursuant to sections 1777 to 1777e, both inclusive of the statutes of 1898 and acts amendatory thereof.

Section 1596—6. Any number of persons, not less than three (3), desiring to secure a franchise under this act shall propose to form a corporation pursuant to Sections 1777 to 1777e, both inclusive of the statutes of 1898 and acts amendatory thereof, and shall file with the railroad commission a verified application which shall set forth and include the following:

(1) The name and location of the waters sought to be improved.

(2) The nature, the scope and the manner of making said proposed improvements.

(3) Whether or not the applicants are riparian owners of lands abutting upon said proposed improvement, and, if so, the extent by metes and bounds of such riparian ownership. If the applicants are not riparian owners abutting said proposed improvement or do not own all the riparian lands affected or likely to be affected by said improvement, they shall state the names of the owners of such riparian land not owned or controlled by said applicants.

(4) A general description of any dam or works proposed to be erected and a general statement as to the construction of the same.

(5) The approximate amount of hydraulic power that will be developed in connection with such improvement, and the use or uses to which it is proposed to put said power.

(6) The location of any existing dam or works in the vicinity of said improvement, and the extent, if any, to which the dam or works will be affected thereby.

(7) A map on the scale of not less than four inches to the mile, showing the lands that may be affected by the erection and maintenance of any proposed dam or works or by any flowage that may be caused thereby, and approximately the outline of such flowage.

(8) Such additional and other information as shall be prescribed by the railroad commission.

Section 1596—7. Upon receipt of the verified application pro-

vided for in section 1596—6, the railroad commission shall, as
soon thereafter as may be possible, advertise, once each week
for four consecutive weeks, in at least one newspaper published
in each county in which such improvement is proposed to be
made, the fact that such application for a franchise has been
received. The railroad commission shall in such advertisement,
invite other applications for a franchise to improve the navigation of such waters and to develop hydraulic power at the
proposed location, or at other points in such vicinity on the
waters designated, and shall set a date thirty (30) days after
the date of the last publication within which such applications
shall be received, and shall also in such advertisement fix a
time and place for a public hearing.

2. At the time and place fixed for such hearing the railroad
commission shall carefully consider all applications and the
qualifications of the different applicants and shall hear all arguments for and against the proposed improvements and for
and against the different applicants. Such hearing may be
continued from time to time.

Section 1596—8. 1. As soon as practicable after said hearing
the railroad commission shall make such examination and investigation of the location, nature and scope of the proposed
improvements as it shall deem necessary. Upon the conclusion
of said hearing and investigation the railroad commission shall
find which of the proposed improvements is the most efficient
and advantageous for the public and which of the applicants
is best qualified to make the same. The railroad commission
may, however, reject any or all applications received.

2. In making such findings the railroad commission shall
take into consideration the scope, location, manner of making
and permanency of the proposed improvements, the extent to
which such power can be put, the navigable character of the
waters to be improved; which, if any, of the applicants are
riparian owners abutting said improvement, the relative financial ability of the applicants to complete and maintain properly such improvement, the uses to which the respective
applicants propose to put any hydraulic power resulting from
the improvement, and any and all other relevant and material
facts and shall give to each its proper weight.

Section 1596—9. If the riparian owner or owners of the
land upon which any dam or works necessary for such pro-

posed improvement is to be wholly or partly erected and maintained apply for such franchise and agree and specify to make and maintain such improvement upon terms and conditions equally as efficient and advantageous for the public as those specified by other applicants, then the railroad commission shall give such riparian owner or owners preference over all other applicants in the granting of such franchise.

Section 1596—10. The improvement found as aforesaid to be the most efficient and advantageous for the public is hereby authorized to be made, subject to the provisions of this act, by the applicants found as aforesaid by the railroad commission to be the best qualified to make the same, and a franchise for said purpose is hereby granted to such applicants. The railroad commission shall certify its findings provided for in sections 1596—8 and 1596—9 to the secretary of the state who shall thereupon issue to the designated applicants a certificate under the seal of the state evidencing the authority hereby conferred.

Section 1696—11. The applicants whose proposed improvement has been found by the railroad commission to be the most efficient and advantageous for the public and to whom a certificate has been issued, shall, before commencing any work ' on said improvement, prepare and submit to the said railroad commission detailed plans and specifications for all dams and works to be erected in connection with such authorized improvement and map showing such topographical and hydrographic data as may be necessary for a satisfactory understanding of the same.

2. Such plans and specifications and map shall be subject to the approval of the railroad commission. After such approval no deviation whatsoever therefrom, either before or after the completion of the improvement, shall be made without obtaining the written approval of the said commission.

Section 1596—12. Every franchise granted under the provisions of this act shall continue in force for an indeterminate period, subject to all the terms, conditions and provisions of this act, and subject to the provisions that the state of Wisconsin, whenever it may have the constitional power, or any municipality may purchase, the property of such corporation at any time as provided herein, paying therefor just compensation

to be determined by the railroad commission and according to
the terms and condition fixed by said commission. Any such
municipality is authorized to purchase such property at the
value and according to the terms and conditions as herein
provided.

Section 1596—13. The compensation for any such property
purchased from any such corporation by the state or by any
municipality shall be determined by the railroad commission, and in making such purchase and determining such compensation the procedure for acquiring the property of a public utlity by a municipality outlined in sections 1797m—80
to 1797m—86, both inclusive of the statutes, shall govern and
be followed.

Section 1596—14. Every grantee, its successors or assigns,
of any franchise granted pursuant to the provisions of this
act, in consideration of the rights, privileges and prerogatives
conferred by such franchise and by this act, shall, if the legislature so provides, pay annually into the state treasury a
franchise rental. The precise amount of such franchise rental
shall be fixed in a manner to be provided by law. .

2. However, no such franchise rental shall be levied against,
collected from or paid by any such grantee, its successors or assigns, until twenty-five (25) years after the passage and publication of this act; and, in no case shal lthe collection or payment of such franchise rental reduce the net income of any such
guarantee in all dams, works, property and rights necessary
for the improvement of navigation and the development of hydraulic power authorized by such franchise.

Section 1596—15. Any franchise granted pursuant to the provision of this act shall be null and void unless the improvement
thereby authorized be completed within three (3) years from
the time when such franchise becomes effective and in force.
The railroad commission may, however, upon good and sufficient cause being shown, grant a reasonable extension o rexten-
sions of the time for the completion of the improvement.

Section 1596—16. When such improvement is completed
it shall be maintained continously, and its maintenance and
operation shall not be discontinued or cease for any length of
time exceeding three (3) years. The railroad commission may
however, upon good and sufficient cause being shown, extend

such period or discontinuance or suspension for a reasonable additional time.

Section 1596—17. Every corporation developing hydraulic power under a franchise granted pursuant to the provision of this act is authorized and required to lease or dispose of said power to the public without discrimination and at a reasonable rate. However, said corporation may retain and use as much of said power as shall be reasonably necesary for its own purpose.

Section 1596—18. If any dam or works used in connection therewith, maintained under a franchise granted pursuant to the provisions of this act, shall be owned, leased, trusteed, possesed or controlled by any device permanently, temporarily, directly, indirectly, tactily or in any maner whatsoever so that the same form part of, or in any way effect any combination or shall in any wise controlled by and combination in the form or an unlawful trust, or form the subject of any contract or conspiracy to limit the output of any hydraulic power or electric energy derived therefrom or in restraint of trade in the generation, sale or distribution of hydraulic power of electric energy derived therefrom, the franchise granted authorizing the erection and maintenance of said dam and the improvement of navigation and the development of hydraulic power by the guarantee thereof, it successors or assigns, shal be forfeited to the state of Wisconsin by proceedings instituted by the attorney general in the courts for that purpose.

Section 1596—19. All dams and works authorized by any franchise granted under this act shall be erected and maintained under the following conditions:

(1) When required by the railroad commission, every such dam or works shall be provided with suitable slides and chutes for the passage of logs and timber products, and such slides and chutes shall at all times be kept in good repair.

(2) If the water sin or across which any such dam or works is erected and maintained, are navigable for purposes of commerce or for pleasure boats and crafts, every such dam or works, shall, when required by the railroad commission, be equipped and maintained with a lock, boat hoist, marine railway or other efficient device of a size and construction to be approved by the railroad commission. Such lock, boat hoist, marine railway, or other efficient device when constructed shall

at all times be maintained in good repair and working order.

(3) When required by the railroad commission every such dam or works shall be provided with a good and sufficient fishway and said fishway when constructed shall at all times be kept in good repair and open for the free and easy descent and ascent of fish.

When required by the railroad commission every such dam or works shall be quipped and maintained with spillways or flood gates capable of permitting the passage through or over the same of any or all floods during freshets and during all seasons of the year.

(5) Subject to the approval of the railway commission, there shall be erected and maintained by the owner thereof, two permanent monuments at every such dam or works marking the height to which the head of water may be maintained in accordance with the franchise.

Section 1596—20. In case it shall be necessary for any corporation to take or flow any lands or property for the purpose of any improvement authorized by any franchise granted under this act, said corporation shall be subjected to all the provisions, remedies and liabilities, and shall be entitled to all the benefits, privileges, remedies and provisions of chapter 146 of the statutes, which are applicable and not inconsistent with this act. but nothing contained in the section shall be taken to preclude said corporation from acquiring title to or the right to use any and all such lands or property by purchase, lease, license, or by any usual method or means of acquisition of title by act of parties.

Section 1596—21. Also for the purpose of acquiring the necesary lands or easements or privileges in lands, so that the complete improvement under this act and any franchise granted hereunder may be successfully carried out, such corporation ma yenjoy the right granted to and conferred uoon corporations by sections 1777 to 1777e, both inclusive of the statutes and laws amendatory thereof, and may also enjoy the rights granted to and conferred upon corporations by sections 1850 to 1857, both inclusive of the statutes and laws amendatory thereof.

Section 1596—22. All franchises, licenses or permits heretofore granted conferring upon any person, firm or corporation the right to erect or maintain any dam or other works in or across and navigable waters of this state for any purpose whatsoever are hereby amended so that the same and each of them shall terminate twenty-five (25) years after the passage and publication of this act.

Section 1596—23. Any person, firm or corporation maintaining a dam or works pursuant to any franchise, license or permit amended by section 1596—22 desiring to obtain a franchise under this act, may, at any time prior to termination of the franchise so amended, file with the railroad commission and with the secretary of state a written instrument, duly executed, agreeing to surrender such franchise, liscense or permit upon receiving in lieu thereof a franchise granted pursuant to the povisions of this act, and shall at the same time file, in the manner provided in section 1596—6, a written application for a franchise to maintain such dam or works in accordance with the provisions of this act.

Section 1596—24. Within a reasonable time after the receipts of the agreement and application provided for in section 1596--23 the railraod commission shall make an examination and investigation of such dam or works, and if the railroad commission shall find and certify to the secretary of state that such dam or works is properly constructed and advantageously located for the most efficient improvement of the navigation of such waters and the development of hydraulic power, then such applicants are hereby authorized to maintain such dam or works for such purposes, and a franchise subject to all the terms. provisions and conditions of this act is hereby granted to such applicants. The secretary of the state shall issue to the said applicants a certificate under the seal of the state evidencing the authority hereby conferred.

Section 1596—25. If the railroad commission upon the examination and investigation provided for in section 1596—24 finds that such dam or works is not properly constructed and advantageously located for the most efficient improvement of the navigation of such waters and the development of hydraulic power, then the railroad commission shall find what form of construction and what location is most advantageous for such purposes. The railroad commission shall furnish the applicants with a copy of such findings, and if the applicants file a written instrument with the railroad commission and with the secretary of state agreeing toalter the construction or to change the location of the dam or works examined and investigated so as to conform with the findings of the railroad commision, then a franchise subject to all the terms and conditions of this act is hereby granted to such applicants. The secretary of state shall issue to the said applicants a certificate under the seal of the state evidencing the authority hereby conferred.

Section 1596—26. A franchise granted to any applicants pursuant to section 1596—24 or 1596—25 shall become effecive and be in force upon compliance by the grantees thereof with the provisions of section 1596—30 of this act. Such franchise shall be granted and accepted in lieu of and shall render null and void and of no effect any franchise, license or permit heretofore granted to such applicants, or any or either of them, authorizing the erection and maintenance of a dam or owrks for any purpose whatsoever at the location specified in said franchise granted pursuant to said section 1596—24 or 1596—25.

Section 1596—27. 1. If any person, firm or corporation maintaining any dam or works in or across any navigable waters of this state under any franchise, license or permit heretofore granted, fails to make application for a franchise as provided in section 1596—23, the right to maintain such dam or works for the improvement of navigation and the development of hydraulic power shall be subject to be applied for. The railroad commission may advertise as provided in Section 1596—6 for applications for a franchise to maintain such dam or works for such purposes.

2. If any franchise granted under this act be forfieted or otherwise terminated before the expiration thereof, the right to continue the improvement of navigation and the development of hydraulic power authorized by such franchise shall be subject to be applied for, and the railroad commission may advertise as provided in Section 1596—6 for applications therefor.

Section 1596—28. The railroad commission shall receive all applications made as a result of the advertisements provided for in section 1596—26, hold hearings and as soon as practicable thereafter shall, in the manner hereinbefore prescribed, find which improvement is the most efficient and advantageous for the public and which applicants are best qualified to maintain the same. The improvement thus found to be the most efficient and advantageous for the public is hereby authorized to be maintained by the applicants thus designated and a franchise

therefor is hereby granted to said applicants subject to all
the terms, conditions and provisions of this act. The railroad
commision shall certify its findings to the secretary of state
who shal lthereupon issue to the designated applicants under
the seal of the state, a certificate evidencing the authority
hereby conferred.

Section 1596—29. 1. At the termination of any franchise,
license or permit granting authority to erect and maintain
any dam or works in or across any navigable waters of this
state by expiration, forfeiture or otherwise, all dams and works
of improvement or any part thereof, erected and maintained
under such franchise, license or permit may be taken by the
grantee of a franchise to maintain such dam or works for the
improvement of navigation and the development of hydaulic
power, and the same, subject to the approval of the railroad
commission, may be used for such purposes.

2. Said grantee is further authorized and empowered to acquire and hold title to all lands and flowage rights, dams,
weirs, tunnels, races, flumes, sluices, pits, and other structures
or others in connection with or appertaining to said improvement for the maintenance thereof or for the utilization of hydraulic power created thereby.

3. If the parties are unable to agree upon the value of the
dam or works rescribed and to be taken, the grantee of the
franchise to maintain such dam or works for the improvement
of navigation and the development of hydraulic power is authorized and empowered to acquire the same by and through
condemnation proceedings under the power of eminent domain,
as provided in sections 1596—20 and 1596—21 of this act.

Section 1596—30. 1. Any franchise granted pursuant to
the provisions of this act shall become effective and be in force
upon the incorporation under the provisions of sections 1777
:.. 1777e. both inclusive, of the statutes and acts amendatory
thereof. of the applicants to whom such franchise is granted,
and upon the filing with the secretary of state by such applicants so incorporated of a written acceptance of such franchise.

2. Such written acceptance shall be filed within ninety (90)
days after notice from the railroad commission to such appli-
ants that a franchise has been granted to them. In case of
failure to file such acceptance within the time herein prescribed.
the franchise granted to such applicants shall be null and void.

Section 1596—31. Any corporation operating under a franchise granted pursuant to this act, shall be subject to all the duties and liabilities imposed by the statutes and laws of this state upon river improvement companies organized under the general law, and shall be entitled to all such reasonable tolls by reason of facilities or improvement furnished in aid of navigation, and shall be entitled to all rights and remedies in relation thereto as are given to river improvement companies by the statutes and laws of this state; but the tolls to be charged and collected shall at all times be subject to regulation and restriction by the railroad commission of Wisconsin in the same manner as railroad rates may be regulated by said commission.

Section 1596—32. During the continuance of any franchise granted pursuant to the provisions of this act, the grantee thereof, its successors or assigns, shall keep and maintain all dams, weirs, tunnels, races, flumes, sluices, pits, fishways, locks, boat hoists, and other structures and works necessary for the improvement of navigation and for the proper maintenance of any dam or works in accordance with such franchise in good repair and condition, and shall not wilfully or otherwise injure or destroy the same or any part thereof, or remove the same or any part thereof unless such removal be first approved in writing by the railroad commission.

Section 1596—33. 1. The railroad commission shall have supervision over the sale and distribution of and may regulate and fix a reasonable rate to be charged for any and all power resulting from any improvement authorized under any franchise granted pursuant to the provisions of this act. In the exercise of such supervision and regulation and fixing of rates, said railroad commission shall have all the rights, powers and privileges conferred upon such commission by sections 1797m—1 to 1797m—108, both inclusive, of the statutes.

2. Any corporation offering for sale any power resulting by reason of any improvement authorized under this act shall be subject to all the provisions of sections 1797m—1 to 1797m—108, both inclusive, of the statutes, and shall enjoy all privileges and rights conferred upon public utilities by said sections of the statutes.

Section 1596—34. Upon complaint made against any corporation operating under a franchise granted under this act, by any mercantile, agricultural, or manufacturing society or by any body politics or municipal organization, or by any twenty-five (25) persons, firms, corporations or associations, that the supply of hydraulic power of such corporation is inadequate or cannot be obtained because of the failure or refusal of such corporation to develop a reasonable amount or all of the hydraulic power capable of development in connection with any improvement authorized by such franchise, or because such corporation fails or refuses to transform and transmit for sale to the public a reasonable amount of the hydraulic power created in connection with any such improvement, the railroad commission shall proceed, with or without notice, to make such investigation as it may deem necessary or convenient. But no order affecting such service shall be entered by the railroad commission without a formal hearing.

Section 1596—35. The railroad commission shall, prior to such formal hearing, notify the corporation complained of that a complaint has been made, and ten (10) days after such notice has been given the railroad commission may proceed to set a time and place for a hearing and an investigation as hereinbefore provided.

Section 1596—36. The railroad commission shall give the corporation complained of and the complainant ten (10) days' notice of the time and place, when and where such hearing and investigation will be held and such matters considered and determined. Both the corporation and complainant shall be entitled to be heard and shall have process to enforce the attendance of witnesses.

Section 1596—37. 1. If upon such investigation it shall be found that for the reason or reasons set out in the complaint the supply of hydraulic power of any corporation is inadequate or cannot be obtained, and if a showing be made at such hearing that public convenience and necessity require it, the railroad commission shall have to order such corporation to develop and dispose of to the public all or any additional part of the hydraulic power capable of development in connection with any improvement authorized by the franchise granted to such corporation and not used or necessary for its purposes, and may also, upon such showing, order that all or any part of such developed hydraulic power not used or necessary for the purposes of such grantee, be transformed into electrical power and that the same be transmitted for sale to the public.

2. However, in no case shall any such corporation be ordered or required to develop additional power or to transform and transmit any such power except upon a showing that a reasonable return on the additional investment necessary for such additional development or for such transformation and transmission shall accrue to such corporation.

Section 1596—89. If upon such investigation the allegations of the complaint shall be found to be true, the expenses incurred by the railroad commission in making such investigation may be assessed by the said commission against the corporation complained of.

Section 1596—39. Whenever the railroad commission shall believe that public convenience and necessity require the development of all the hydraulic power capable of development in connection with any improvement authorized by any franchise granted under this act, or the transformation of any or all of such hydraulic power into electrical power and the transmission of the same for sale to the public, said commission may on its own motion summarily investigate the same, with or without notice.

Section 1596—40. If, after making such summary investigation, the railroad commission becomes satisfied that sufficient grounds exist to warrant a formal hearing being ordered as to the matters so summarily investigated, such commission shall furnish the corporation interested a statement notifying such corporation of the matters under investigation. Ten (10) days after such notice has been given the railroad commission may proceed to set a time and place for a hearing and investigation as hereinbefore provided.

Section 1596—41. Notice of the time and place for such hearing shall be given to the corporation and to such other interested persons as the railroad commission shall deem necessary, as provided in section 1596—35, and thereafter procedure shall be had and conducted in reference to the matter investigated in like manner as though complaint had been filed with the railroad commission, relative to the matter investigated, and the same order or orders may be made in reference thereto as if such investigation had been made on complaint.

Section 1596-42. For the purpose of carrying into effect sections 1596—34 to 1596—41, both inclusive of this act, the railroad commission shall have all the rights, powers and privileges conferred upon said commission by section 1797m—43 to 1797m—73, both inclusive of the statutes, and shall be governed in its procedure by said sections of the statutes; and for such purpose every corporation operating under a franchise granted pursuant to this act shall be subject to all the provisions of said section 1797m43 to 1797—73, both inclusive of the statutes, and shall enjoy all the rights and privileges conferred by said sections of the statutes upon public utilities against which complaint has been made as for inadequacy of service.

Section 596—43. The improvement of the navigation of all navigable waters of this state, and the construction and maintenance of all dams and works constructed and maintained in connection with the development of hydraulic power, shall be under the supervision of the railroad commission. Such railroad commission or any member thereof or any person appointed by said railroad commission for such purpose shall, during the construction thereof and at all other times, have free access to any and all parts of the premises, structures, and works necessary and constructed and maintained in connection with such improvement.

Section 1596—44. 1. Every corporation operating under a franchise granted pursuant to the provisions of this act shall furnish to the railroad commission all information required by it to carry into effect the provisions of this act, and shall make specific answers to all questions submitted by the railroad commission, and shall make any and all reports required by said commission..

2. Every such corporation receiving from the railroad commission any blanks with directions to fill the same, shall cause the same to be properly filled out so as to answer fully and correctly each question therein propounded, and said answers shall be verified under oath by the president, secretary, superintendent or general manager of such corporation and returned to the railroad commission at its office within the period fixed by said commission.

Section 1956—45. The railroad commission or any member of such commission or any person or persons employed by such commission for that purpose, shall, upon demand, have the right to inspect the books, accounts, papers, records and memoranda of any corporation operating under a franchise granted pursuant to this act, and to examine under oath, any officer, agent or employe of such corporation in relation to its business and affairs.

Section 1596—46. 1. The railroad commission and each member of such commission for the purposes mentioned in this act, shall have power to administer oaths, certify to official acts, issue subpoenas, compel the attendance of witnesses and the production of books, accounts, papers, documents and testimony.

2. In case of the disobedience on the part of any person or persons to comply with any order of the railroad commission or any commissioner or any subpoena, or, upon the refusal of any witnesses to testify to any matter regarding which he may lawfully be interrogated before the railroad commission, it shall be the duty of the circuit court of any county or the judge thereof, on applictaion of a member of the railroad commission, to compel obedience by attachment proceedings for contempt as in the case of disobedience of the requirements of a subpoena issued from such court or a refusal to testify therein.

Section 1596—37. 1. Each witness who shall appear before the railroad commission by its order, shall receive for his attendance the fees and mileage now provided for witnesses in civil cases in courts of record, which shall be audited and paid by the state in the same manner as other expenses are audited and paid, upon the presentation of proper vouchers sworn to by such witness and approved by the chairman of the railroad commission.

2. No witness subpoenaed at the instance of parties other than the railroad commission shall be entitled to compensation from the state for attendance or travel unless the railroad commission shall certify that his testimony was material to the matter investigated.

Section 1596—48. The provisions of this act shall not apply to corporations hereofore organized in whole or in part to establish, maintain or operate a system of water reservoirs for the purpose of regulating the flow of the waters of any river in the state.

Section 1596—49. No assignment, sale or transfer of any franchise granted under the provisions of this act shall be made to any corporation unless the railroad commission shall first find in the manner hereinbefore prescribed that such corporation is qualified to maintain the improvement authorized by such franchise in an efficient and advantageous manner for the public. Whenever there shall be any such transfer or assignment, the same shall be in writing and a certified copy thereof shall, within ten (10) days after the execution thereof, be filed with the secretary of state and with the railroad commission of Wisconsin.

Section 1596—50. If any corporation operating under any franchise granted pursuant to the provisions of this act fails substantially to comply with any of the provisions of this act, or its franchise, or of law, or if any such corporation fails to comply with any ruling, finding, stipulation, or determination of the railroad commission, the franchise of such corporation shall be forfeited. The railroad commission shall notify the attorney general of any such failure, and upon proper suit being brought by the attorney general, such franchise shall be forfeited and all rights thereunder shall terminate and cease.

SECTION 3. This act shall take effect and be in force from and after its passage and publication.

"EXHIBIT B."

A BILL.

To repeal section. 1494-44a, relating to the duties of the state board of forestry, and to amend sections 1494-42, 1494-43, 1449-46, 1494-47, 1494-48, 1494-49, 1494-50, 1494-55, 1494-60 and 1494-62 of the statutes relative to the state forester, his assistants and to forestry and to the appropriation therefor.

The people of the State of Wisconsin, represented in senate and assembly, do enact as follows:

SECTION 1. Section 1494-44a of the statute is repealed.

SECTION 2. Sections 1494-42, 1494-43, 1494-46, 1494-47, 1494-48, 1494-49, 1494-50, 1494-55, 1494-59, 1494-60, 1494-62, 4405a and 4406 of the statutes are amended to read:

Section 1494--42. 13. There shall be a state forester who shall be a technically trained forester, appointed by the state board of forestry, and whether any candidate for this position is a techniaclly trained forester shall be detemined by certificates from the secretary of the United Stats department of agriculture.

He shall receive a salary of ~~twenty five hundred~~ *four thousand* dollars per year, and the actual and necessary traveling and field expenses, incurred in the conduct of his official business, be empowered to appoint a clerk whose salary shall not exceed ~~eight~~ *fifteen* hundred dollars per annum; be supplied with suitable offices in the capitol building, be entitled from the superintendent of public property to such stationery, postage and other office supplies and equipment as may be necessary, be authorized to purchase all necessary field supplies, equipment and instruments, be furnished by the state all necessary printed forms and notices and the publications hereinafter provided, and shall act as secretary of the state board of forestry.

3. He shall, under the supervision of the state board of forestry, execute all matters pertaining to forestry within the jurisdiction of the state, direct the management of the state forest reserve, *depute one of his assistants to act during his absence or disability,* collect data relative to forest destruction and conditions, take such action as is authorized by law to prevent and

extinguish forest fires and to prevent forest trespass; cooperate in forestry as provided under ~~section 5 of this act~~ 1494-45 *of the statutes;* and advance as he may deem wise by the issuing of publications and by lectures, the cause of forestry within the state; ~~and may, upon invitation of the board of regents of the University of Wisconsin, supervise such courses in forestry as may hereafter be provided for at said university.~~ He shall prepare ~~annually~~ *biennially* a report to the state board of forestry on the progress and condition of state forest work, and recommend therein plans for improving the state system of forest protection, management, replacement and taxation. The state board of forestry shall report ~~annually~~ *biennially* a summary of such facts to the governor.

Section ~~1494~~ 43. *1.* The sale of all lands belonging to the state north of town 33 shall cease upon the passage of this act, and such lands *and all lands reverting to the state* north of town 33 *and all state lands within the Menominee. Stockbridge and Munsie Indian reservations* shall constitute the state forest reserve; provided, that those state lands within said forest reserve which after examination by the state forester are found by him to be more suitable for other purposes than for the purpose of the state forest reserve, because of their character, condition, extent or situation, ~~may~~ *shall* be sold by the commissioners of the public lands, upon the recommendation of the state forester and with the approval of the state board of forestry.

2. The state forester shall, under the supervision of the state board of forestry, direct the management of the state forest reserve to, which end he may employ the necessary assistance, and may upon said reserve institute conservative lumbering, make and maintain forest nurseries, plantations and fire lines and execute other silvicultural and protective measures necessary to the highest permanent usefulness of said reserve to the state. *He may build roads, erect township and section corners and other permanent monuments, construct and maintain telephone lines and service, camps and rangers' cabins and a field office: he shall have authority to purchase all necessary field supplied and equipment, and field office supplies, and to provide such means of transportation within the reserve as are necessary to the efficiency of the field force and for the conveyance of field supplies, and he shall have authority to do all*

*things necessary for the accomplishment of the purpose of
the forest reserve.* In such conservative lumbering the state
forester is authoried, under the supervision of the state board of
forestry, to remove or cause to be removed *and sell,* when and
in such manner as he may deem advisable, wood, timber or
other products from said reserve. ~~Such wood, timber or other
products shall be sold to the highest bidder under contracts
executed and signed by the state forester, on behalf of the
state, subject to the approval of the state board of forestry.~~

Section 1494–46. There shall be an assistant state forester,
who shall be a technically trained forester, appointed by the state
forester with the approval of the state board of forestry. He
shall receive a salary of ~~fifteen~~ *not to exceed twenty-five* hundred dollars per year, and the actual and necessary traveling
and field expenses, incurred in the conduct of his official business. He shall perform such duties as may be assigned to him
by the state forester, and shall represent the latter in case of
disability or absence.

Section 1494–47. The state forester shall also be state fire
warden, and the assistant state forester shall be assistant state
fire warden. The state forester shall appoint ~~one or more town~~
as many county fire wardens *as he deems necessary* ~~for these
organized towns in which he deems it necessary, or for such
portions of organized towns as he may define,~~ and he may
remove any fire warden from office. He shall give the necessary instructions to said fire wardens and supervise the execution of their work. *He may provide each fire warden with an
official badge.*

Section 1494–48. *1.* Each ~~town~~ *county* fire warden, before
entering upon his duties, shall take an oath of office and file
the same with the state forester. All ~~town~~ fire wardens shall
take prompt and effective measures against the spread and illegal setting of forest, marsh or swamp fires within their own
and adjoining ~~towns~~ *counties* and have the power of sheriffs to
arrest without warrant for violations of the provisions of ~~this
act.~~ *Sections 1494-11 to 1194-62, inclusive, and of sections
4405a and 4406 of the statutes.* They shall have authority to
call upon any able bodied citizen, in territory in which they act,
to assist in extinguishing forest, marsh or swamp fires in such
manner as they may direct. *They shall have authority to serve
notice upon town officers to remove or destroy any rubbish,*

such as logs, stumps, brush, tree tops or branches, found in the highway in any town of this state, which, in the opinion of the state fire warden, is liable to become a contributing cause of forest fire or the spread thereof; and if such rubbish is not removed or destroyed within thirty days of the date upon which such notice is served, then the county fire wardens are authorized to remove or destroy such rubbish. The ~~town~~ *county* fire wardens shall first submit to the state forester itemized accounts for their own services and the services of their assistants, and no accounts shall be paid ~~out of the treasury of the town in which such services have been rendered~~ without the written approval of the state forester.

2. The ~~town~~ *county* fire wardens and those assisting them shall receive ~~such compensation~~ for their services in carrying out the provisions of this section ~~as the town board shall allow~~, *not less than fifteen cents nor more than* twenty-five cents per hour for the time actually employed; provided that the total of such accounts *in any county in any one year* shall not exceed *three* hundred dollars for each ~~thirty-six sections in any one year in any one town~~ *township contained in said county, except in case of emergency, when the above amount may be exceeded upon vote of the county board of supervisors. The bills of the county fire wardens when approved by the state forester or the acting state forester, shall be paid by the state treasurer, and the amounts so paid shall be collected by the state treasurer from the respective counties.* The state forester is authorized to approve for payment not to exceed fifty per centum of the clear proceeds of any fine collected in an action brought for a violation of any of the provisions of sections ~~17 or 18 of this act~~ *1494-57 or 1494-58 of the statutes*, or sections 4405a or 4406, statutes of 1898, relating to setting, failure to put out or care of fires, where the evidence to secure a conviction is furnished by a ~~town~~ *county* fire warden or any other person, *the same to be paid by the county treasurer out of the fine so collected and credit to be taken therefor in his settlement with the state treasurer.*

Section 1494-49. Any ~~town~~ *county* fire warden who shall refuse *or neglect* to carry out the provisions of ~~the preceding sections~~ *1494-48 or 1494-50 of the statutes* or any able bodied citizen who shall refuse to render assistance as provided by ~~said section~~ *1494-48 of the statutes*, shall be punished by a fine of not less than ten nor more than fifty dollars, or by imprisonment in the county jail for not less than ten days or more than thirty days, or by both such fine and imprisonment.

Section 1494–50. Each ~~town~~ county fire warden shall post or cause to be posted conspicuously in those parts of this ~~town~~ *county* where fires are likely to occur, all notices furnished him for that purpose by the state forester, and he shall receive therefor compensation at the rate provided in section ~~8 of this act~~ *1491–18 of the statutes. Fire wardens shall also be compensated in the same manner for the time actually employed in warning settlers, calling out citizens, making arrests, and carry out any measures for the prevention of forest fires.*

Section 1494–55. Whenever an arrest shall have been made for any violation of any provision of ~~this act~~ *section 1494–41s to 1494–64 inclusive or of section 4405a or 4406 of the statutes,* or whenever any information of such violation shall have been lodged with him, it shall be the duty of the district attorney of the county in which the criminal act was committed to prosecute the offender or offenders. If any district attorney shall fail to comply with the provisions of this section, he shall be guilty of a misdemeanor and upon conviction shall be fined not less than $100 nor more than $1,000, or be imprisoned not less than thirty days nor more than one year, or both in the discretion of the court. The penalties of this section shall apply to any magistrate, with proper authority, who refuses or neglects without cause to issue a warrant for the arrest and prosecution of any person or persons when complaint, under oath, of violation of any terms ~~of this act~~ *of sections 1494–41 to 1494–64 inclusive or of section 4405a or 1106 of the statutes* has been lodged with him.

Section 1494–59. Every person who, unlawfully cuts, or injures any kind of wood or timber standing, lying or growing upon the lands of another, or of the state, or of the United States, or upon any public highway, or unlawfully and wilfully injures or destroys or carries away any of the products of such wood or timber lands is guilty of a misdemeanor, and upon conviction, shall be fined not less than $25 nor more than $1,000 or be imprisoned not less than fifteen days nor more than three years, or by both such fine and imprisonment.

Section 1494–60. In addition to the penalties provided in section ~~19~~ *1494–59 of the statutes* for *negligent or* wilful trespass on forest lands, the state, the county or the private owners upon whose lands the *negligent or* wilful trespass was committed, may recover in a civil action ~~double~~ *triple* the amount of damages suffered *and any reasonable expense necessarily incurred in determining the extent of the trespass.*

~~This section shall not apply to the cutting of wood or timber from uncultivated woodland for the repair of a public highway or bridge upon or adjacent to the land.~~

Section 1494–62.   There is hereby appropriated out of any funds in the state treasury not otherwise appropriated an annual appropriation of ~~nine thousand eight hundred~~ *thirty-five thousand* dollars to pay the annual salaries provided by the terms of ~~this act~~ *sections 1494–41 to 1494–64 inclusive of the statutes,* and for carrying out the provisions of ~~this act~~ *such sections of the statutes.* If all of said sum be not expended in any one year the balance not so expended may be used for the purpose aforesaid in any subsequent year.

SECTION 3.   This act shall take effect and be in force from and after its passage and publication.

EXHIBIT C.

A BILL

To amend sections 4405a and 4406 of the statutes, relating to protection of forests from fires and providing a penalty for failure to extingush fires.

The people of the state of Wisconsin, represented in Senate and Assembly, do enact as follows:

SECTION 1. Sections 4405a and 4406 of the statutes are amended to read:

Section 4405a. ~~Whenever the fire warden of any town becomes convinced that a dangerously dry time exists in its vicinity and that it is imprudent to set fires on any land he shall post or cause to be posted a notice in three public places in such town forbidding the setting of such fires therein, and after the posting of such notices no person shall set any fire upon any land in said town, except for warming the person or cooking food, until written permission has been received from one of the fire wardens of said town.~~ *No fires shall be set except for warming the person or for cooking food, from the first day of April to the first day of November, without the written permission of a county fire warden; upon any land within the territory now contained in the following counties: Adams, Ashland, Barron, Bayfield, Burnett, Chippewa, Clark, Douglas, Dodge, Dunn, Eau Claire, Florence, Forest, Iron, Jackson, Juneau, Langlade, Lincoln, Marathon; Marinette, Monroe, Oconto, Oneida, Polk, Portage, Price, Rusk, Sawyer, Shawano, Taylor, Vilas, Washburn, Waupaca and Wood.* All persons who start camp fires shall exercise all reasonable precautions to prevent damage therefrom and shall entirely extinguish the same before leaving them. Every person violating any provision of this section shall be punished by a fine of not *less than $25* nor more than ~~$50~~ *$100* or by imprisonment in the county jail not more than six months for each offense.

Section 4406. Any person who shall build a fire on any lands in this state not his own or under his control, except as hereinafter provided, shall, before leaving the same, totally extinguish it, and upon failure to do so shall be punished by a fine *of* not ~~exceeding~~ *less than twenty-five dollars nor more than one* hundred dollars or by imprisonment in the county jail not exceeding one month, or by both such fine and imprisonment. Any person who shall willfully or negligently set fire to or assist another to set fire on any land, whereby such land is injured or endangered, or shall willfully or negligently suffer any fire upon his land to escape beyond the limits thereof, to the injury of the land of another, shall be punished as hereinbefore provided and *shall in addition* be liable *in civil action* to the person injured for all damage that may be caused by the fire, *and to the county for all expense incurred by it in fighting such fire.*

SECTION 2.   This act shall take effect and be in force from and after its passage and publication.

EXHIBIT D.

A Bill.

To create section 1072—1 of the statutes, providing for an annual tax for a period of ten years, the proceeds of which to be used as therein provided in promoting forestry in this state.

The people of the state of Wisconsin, represented in Senate and assembly, do enact as follows:

SECTION 1. There is added to the statutes a new section to read:

Section 1072—1. 1. There shall be levied and collected annually for a period of twenty years, beginning with the year 1911, a state tax of two-tenths of one mill for each dollar of the assessed valuation of the taxable property in the state, as ascertained and fixed by the tax commission of Wisconsin for appointment of the state tax to the several counties, which amount when levied and collected shall constitute the forestry investment fund, and any and all interest received from the said investment fund, shall be added to and become a part of said fund. All moneys in such fund are appropriated and shall be used to purchase forest reserve lands and for the increase, improvement and protection of the state forest reserve, for the employment of a forest fire patrol to protect the timber and wild lands of the state, and for such other purpose as the state board of forestry shall deem to the best advantage in the promotion of forestry in this state. Any part of the tax so levied and collected not used in any year for such purpose shall be available and may be used for such purpose in any subsequent year.

2. The state forester under the supervision of the state board of forestry is authorized to enter into contracts to purchase lands as additions to the forest reserve and to make payments on such lands from the forestry investment fund as moneys become available.

Section a. This act shall take effect and be in force from and after its passage and publication.

"EXHIBIT E."

A Bill.

o repeal sections 1379—11 to 1379—28, inclusive, sections 1379—22L, 1379—22m, 1379—22n, section 1379—24m, sections 1379—29 to 1379—31, inclusive, sections 1379—30a, 1379—30b, 1379—30c, 1379—30d, 1379—30e, sections 1379—31a, 1379—31b, 1379—31c, 1379—31e, 1379—31f, 1379—31g, 1379—31h, 1379—31i, 1379—31j, 1379—31k, 1379—31L, 1379—31m, 1379—31n, 1379—31o, 1379—31p, 1379—31q, 1379—31r, 1379—31s, 1379—31t, 1379—31u, 1379—31cm, 1379—31gm, section 1379—32, and sections 1379—32a and 1379—32b of the statutes relating to the drainage of lands, and to create sections 1379—11 to 1379—28, inclusive, sections 1379—31b, 1379—31c, 1379—31d, 1379—31e, 1379—31f, 1379—31g, 1379—31h, 1379—31i, 1379—31j, 1379—31k, 1379—31L, 1379—31m, 1379—31n, 1379—31o, 1379—31p, 1379—31q, 1379—31r, 1379—31s, 1379—31t, 1379—31u, section 1379—32, and section 1379—32a of the statutes constituting an amendment, revision and codification of the draining laws.

The people of the state of Wisconsin, represented in senate and assembly, do enact as follows:

SECTION 1.   Sections 1379—11 to 1379—28, inclusive, sections 1379—22L, 1379—22m, 1379—22n, section 1379—24m, sections 1379—29 to 1379—31, inclusive, sections 1379—30a, 1379—30b, 1379—30c, 1379—30d, 1379—30e, sections 1379—31a, 1379—31b, 1379—31c, 1379—31d, 1379—31c, 1379—31f, 1379—31g, 1379—31h, 1379—31i, 1379—31j, 1379—31k, 1379—31L, 1379—31m, 1379—31n, 1379—31o, 1379—31p, 1379—31q, 1379—31r, 1379—31s, 1379—31t, 1379—31u, 1379—31cm, 1379—31gm, section 1379—32 and sections 1379—32a and 1379—32b of the statutes, except for the purpose of completing the organization of any drainage district now in process of organization, are repealed.

SECTION 2. There are added to the statutes forty-four new sections to read:

Section 1379—11. 1. Whenever a majority of the owners of lands within any district of land, who shall represent one-third in area of the land within said district to be reclaimed and benefited or whenever the owners of more than one-half of the lands within such districts desire to construct one or more drains, ditches, levees or other works, across the lands of others for the promotion of the public health or welfare and the drainage of such lands, or desire to maintain and keep in repair any such drain, ditch or levee heretofore constructed under any law of this state, such owners may file in the Circuit Court of any county in which the lands or any part of them shall lie, a petition setting forth:

(1) The proposed name of said drainage district;

(2) The necessity for the proposed work, describing the necessity;

(3) A general or a detail description of the proposed starting points, routes and termini of the proposed drains, ditches, and levees;

(4) A general or a detail description of the lands proposed to be included in said district;

(5) The names of the owners of all lands in said district, then known;

(6) If the purpose of said petitioners is the enlargement, repair and maintenance of a ditch, drain, levee or other work heretofore constructed under any law of this state, said petition shall give general description of the same, with such particulars as may be deemed important;

(7) Said petition shall pray for the organization of a drainage district by the name and with the boundaries proposed and for the appointment of commissioners for the execution of such proposed work, according to the provisions of this and the following sections.

2. No petition having as many signers as are required by this section shall be declared void, but the court may at any time prior to the appointment of commissioners permit the petition to be amended in form and substance to conform to the facts, if the facts justify the organization of drainage district. Several similar petitions for the organization of the same district may be circulated and when filed shall together be regarded as one

petition having as many signers as there are separate signers to
the several petitions filed who own lands within said proposed
drainage district. All petitions for the organization of said district filed prior to the hearing on said petition shall be considered by the court the same as if filed with the first petitions
placed on file, and the signatures thereon contained shall be
counted in determining whether sufficient land owners have
signed said petition.

3. Said territory need not be contiguous, provided that it be
so situated that the public health or welfare will be promoted
by such drainage of each part thereof and the benefits of the
proposed work in each part will exceed the damages from and
cost of said proposed work in each part; and provided, that the
court shall be satisfied that said proposed work can be more
cheaply done if in a single district than otherwise.

4. If any minor or incompetent persons have any interest in
any lands included with the drainage district proposed to be organized under this act, the general guardian of such minor or
incompetent person may, for and on behalf of such minor or
incompentent person, join in the petition for the organization
and establishment of such district.

5. All lands and interest in lands in said proposed district
owned by such minor or incompetent person, whose guardian
signed said petition under the authority herein granted, shall
be counted in determining whether sufficient land owners have
signed said petition, the same as if such minors or incompetent
persons had been adults and competent.

Section 1379—12. 1. On such petition being filed, the court
or judge thereof shall make an order fixing a time and place of
hearing and ordering notice. Thereupon the clerk of said court
for the county in which the proceedings are instituted shall
cause twenty (20) days' notice of the filing of such petition to
be given by posting notice thereof in at least five (5) public
places within the boundaries of the district proposed in the petition; by serving or causing to be served a copy of such notice
on each owner of land within said proposed district in any
county in which any lands in said proposed district are situated,
either personally or by leaving a copy thereof at his usual place
of abode with a person of suitable age and discretion, to whom
its contents shall be explained, and by publishing a copy thereof
at least once a week for three successive weeks in some news-

paper published in each county from which any part of the district is proposed to be taken. If there be no newspaper in any such county, such notice may be published in a newspaper published in an adjoining county. However, if any such owner of land is absent from said county and no person of suitable age and discretion is at his usual place of abode, upon proof by proper oath of such facts, publication of such notice shall be sufficient service upon said land owner.

2. Such notice shall specify in what court said petition is filed, shall give a general description of the proposed work, a general description of all of the lands included within the boundaries of said proposed district, the name proposed for said drainage district, and shall state the time and place by the court fixed in said order, when and where the petitioners will ask a hearing on said petition.

3. If any of the owners of land in said district are non-residents of the county or counties in which the proposed district lies, the petition shall be accompanied by an affidavit giving the names and post office addresses of such non-residents, if such are known, and if unknown, shall state that upon diligent inquiry their names or post office addresses (whichever may be the fact) cannot be ascertained. The clerk of the court shall mail a copy of the notice aforesaid to each of said non-resident owners whose post office address is known, within ten (10) days after the first publication of the same.

4. The certificate of the clerk of the court, or other public officer, or the affidavit of any other person who knows the facts, attached to a copy of said notice, shall be sufficient evidence of the posting, serving, mailing or publication thereof.

5. Personal service of said notice on (or service by leaving at the last usual place of abode of) all owners of lands or easements or interests in lands within said district shall give the court complete jurisdiction without posting, publication or mailing of said notice.

6. It shall not be necessary to make service upon persons owning and holding mortgages or liens upon any of the lands within the boundaries of said proposed district.

7. The posting, publication, serving and mailing of said notices of hearing shall give the court jurisdiction of the persons and lands within said boundaries and the subject matter of said proceeding, for all of the purposes of this act.

Section 1379—13. 1. If it shall be found at or before the hearing on a petition for the organization of a drainage district that one or more owners of land in said district have not been duly served with notice of hearing on said petition, the court or presiding judge shall not thereby lose jurisdiction. The court or presiding judge in such case shall adjourn the hearing, make an order directing the serving of said notice upon said land owner and fixing the time and manner of service of such notice, which notice shall notify him to appear at such adjourned time and place and be heard on said petition.

2. Said notice shall be served personally or by leaving at the last usual place of abode of said unserved owners, not less than eight (8) days before said adjourned hearing.

3. Upon the adjourned day, the same proceedings, adjournments, trial, findings and orders may be had as in case of complete service of notice in the first instance. In case of failure to mail said notice as herein required, the court or judge may order the same mailed later and shall adjourn said hearing so that said notice shall be mailed at least ten (10) days before said adjourned hearing. In case of failure to publish or post notice as in this act required, the court or judge may adjourn said hearing for sufficient time to permit due posting and publication of said notice and shall order said notice posted or published as provided in section 1379—12. In case of adjournment to permit notice to be given, the notice served, published or posted shall state the fact of such adjournment and the time and place of such hearing, pursuant to said adjournment.

Section 1379—14. 1. On the day fixed for hearing on such petition, all parties owning lands or any interest or easement in land within said proposed district, or who would be affected thereby, may appear and contest the sufficiency of the petition; the sufficiency of the signers of the petition; the sufficiency of the notice; the constitutionality of the law; or the jurisdiction of the court, specifying their objections to such jurisdiction; and the petitioners and contestants may on the trial offer any competent evidence in regard thereto.

2. All notices of contest shall be in writing and shall clearly specify the grounds of contest and shall be verified by the oath of the contestant and shall be filed with the clerk of the court in which said proceeding is pending, at least (5) days before the time set for hearing, and a copy thereof shall be served upon

the attorney for the petitioners at least five (5) days before
said time set for hearing.

3. The court shall hear and determine whether or not the
petition contains the signature of a majority of the owners of
lands within the said proposed district and who represent one-
third in area of the lands proposed to be affected by said work
or the signatures of the owners of more than one-half of such
lands, and shall determine all questions of law arising on said
contest. The circuit court in which said petition shall be filed
or the judge thereof may adjourn the hearing on said petition
from time to time for the want of sufficient notice, or to give or
prepare for trial, or for other good cause.

4. The affidavit of any three or more of the signers of said
petition, stating that they have examined it and are acquainted
with the locality of said district and that said petition is signed
by a sufficient number of owners of lands in said district to
satisfy the provisions of this act, shall be taken by the court
or judge as prima facie evidence of the facts therein stated.

5. All deeds made for the purpose of establishing or defeat-
ing the prayer of said petition, and not made in good faith and
for a valuable consideration, shall be held to be a fraud and the
holders of such deeds shall not be considered as the owners of
the land described therein.

6. If the court or presiding judge thereof, after hearing any
and all competent evidence that may be offered for and against
said petition, shall find that the same has not been signed as
herein required, the said petition shall be dismissed at the cost
of the petitioners and judgment shall be entered against said
petitioners for the amount of said costs.

7. But if it shall appear that the petition has been so signed,
the court or judge shall so find and order any necessary amendments thereto, and shall appoint three suitable, competent persons as commissioners and fix their preliminary bond. If the
proposed district is situated in two or more counties, not more
than two of said commissioners shall reside in any one of said
counties. Ownership of land within the district shall not dis-
qualify a person from acting as a commissioner.

8. After such petition for the organization of a drainage
district shall have been filed in court, no person shall be per
mitted to withdraw his signature from said petition, excepting

only with the consent in writing of a majority of the signers of said petition. .

Section 1379—15. 1. Before entering upon their duties such commissioners shall take and subscribe an oath to support the Constitution of the United States and the Constitution of the state of Wisconsin, to faithfully and impartially discharge their duties as such commissioners, and to render a true account of their doings to the court by which they were appointed whenever required by law or the order of the court, and shall execute a bond running to the clerk of the said court and his successors in office as obligees, to be filed with said clerk for the benefit of the parties interested, in an account to be fixed by the court or presiding judge, and with sureties to be approved by the court or presiding judge, conditioned for the faithful discharge of their duties as such commissioners, and the faithful accounting for and application of all moneys which shall come into their hands as such commissioners. A majority shall constitute a quorum, and a concurrence of a majority in any matter within their duties shall be sufficient to its determination.

2. The commissioners first appointed shall hold their office until the first Tuesday in July next succeeding the time of the completion of the work proposed in the petition, but not to exceed the first Tuesday in the fifth succeeding July following the date of the order organizing such district, and until their respective successors are appointed and qualified. The commissioners appointed to succeed the first board, excepting those appointed to fill vacancies, shall hold their respective offices as follows: one for one year, one for two years, and one for three years, and until their successors are appointed and qualified, and the commissioners thereafter appointed shall hold their respective offices for the term of three years each and until their successors are appointed and qualified.

3. Appointments to fill expired terms in the office of Drainage Commissioner shall be made by the presiding judge of the circuit court of the county having jurisdiction of the drainage district, at the court house therein, on the first Tuesday of July in each succeeding year, or as soon thereafter as possible.

4. Vacancies in the board may be filled by such judge at any time, and the commissioner appointed to fill a vacancy shall serve for the residue of the unexpired term and until his successor is appointed and qualified. The removal of any com-

missioner from the county or counties in which lands of such
district are situated shall render his office vacant.

5. The commissioners shall keep an accurate record of all
moneys collected on account of the work under their charge,
and of all payments made by them, and shall take vouchers for
such payments, and shall keep full, accurate and true minutes
of their proceedings. They shall receive for their services three
dollars and fifty cents ($3.50) per day, and their actual reason-
able expenses. They shall at all times be under the control and
direction of the court or presiding judge, and shall obey its or
his directions. For failure so to do they shall forfeit their compensation and be dealt with summarily as for contempt.

6. Suits may also be brought upon their bonds in the name
of the clerk of the court, and the amount recovered shall be
applied to the construction of the work or to the injured party
as justice may require.

7. If the petition provided for in section 1379—11 contains
a detailed description of the proposed work, and a detailed description of the extent of the proposed district, and is accompanied by exhibits showing profiles and maps and the estimated
cost and benefits of the proposed work, and prays that the commissioners appointed be ordered by the court to omit the preliminary report in section 1379—16 provided and to proceed
directly with the preparation of the report in section 1379—18
of this act provided, and if the court is satisfied by the evidence
at hand that the benefits of said proposed work will exceed the
cost thereof, including all damages and expenses, and that the
work proposed in the petition will not in any manner enter
upon any navigable water of the state, and that the omission
of such preliminary report is justifiable, said court shall so
order.

Section 1379—16. 1. Within ten days after said commissioners shall be appointed and qualified they shall meet and organize by electing one of their number secretary, and as soon as
may be thereafter, except as hereinbefore provided, they shall
personally examine the lands in said district and make a preliminary report to the court, which report shall state:

(1) Whether said proposed work is necessary or would be of
utility in carrying out the purpose of the petition.

(2) Whether the proposed work would promote the public
health.

(3) Whether the proposed work would promote the public welfare.

(4) Whether the total benefits from said proposed work will exceed the cost thereof together with the damages resulting therefrom, and in arriving at this they shall include the benefits and damages resulting therefrom both within and without said proposed district, and they shall estimate and assess separately the amount of benefits which will result to each government or smaller subdivision of lands of each separate land owner within said district, which estimate and assessment shall be known as the assessment of benefits.

(5) Whether in doing the work proposed, or work which they may propose, it will be necessary to enter upon and do work in any navigable stream or other navigable waters of the state, the character thereof and whether the proposed work will in any wise permanently obstruct or interfere with the general navigability thereof.

2. Said commissioners shall in said report fix and report to the court the boundaries of said proposed drainage district according to the lines of government subdivisions or fractions thereof. Said boundaries shall not be so changed from those in the petition described as to deprive the court of jurisdiction by reason of not having on the petition the required number of signers owning land within said changed boundaries.

3. If said proposed work as in the petition described is not best suited to carry out the purpose of the petition the commissioners shall consider and base their report upon the plan best suited to carry out those purposes, and shall report to the court the one by them considered.

4. Any person or corporation owning land within the district proposed by the original petition or adjoining thereto, or within or adjoining the district as changed or enlarged by the first report of the commissioners, may at any time file in court a request to be joined as a petitioner, and the court may by order permit such person or corporation to be joined as petitioner with like force and effect as if he had signed the original petition, and thereafter such owner so brought in shall be counted as an original petitioner for all purposes. The original and any other petition filed herein may be signed by the owner in person or by an agent or attorney authorized in writing to sign such

6

owner's name, which written authority shall be filed with the petition.

Section 1379—17. 1. Upon the filing of the preliminary report, the court or the presiding judge thereof shall, by order, fix a time and place when and where the same shall be heard at some general or special term of said court, not less than thirty days nor more than sixty days from the filing of said report. Notice of the time and place of hearing upon said preliminary report shall be given to all interested persons by publishing a brief notice of the filing of said report in one newspaper published in each county in which any land in said proposed drainage district shall be situated, or if no newspaper is published in said county, in one newspaper in an adjoining county, once in each week for three successive weeks prior to the day appointed for hearing thereof. Said notice shall describe all lands by said report included in said district which were not included therein by the petition and state that such lands are to be included in said district, and shall describe all lands excluded from said district which were by the petition included therein, and shall state that said lands are to be excluded from said district.

2. When lands are added to the proposed district by the commissioners, the owners thereof shall be served with said notice as provided for service of notice of hearing on the petition.

3. Upon the day fixed for hearing upon said report, said court may adjourn said hearing for good cause or may proceed to hear, try and determine all issues arising upon said report.

4. Any interested party may appear and remonstrate against said report or any material part thereof. All remonstrances shall be in writing, be verified on oath, be filed at least five days before the day for hearing, and shall set forth the facts upon which they are based.

5. All issues arising upon said preliminary report shall be tried by the court without a jury.

6. If the court shall find in favor of the remonstrants, or if said report be that the proposed work will not promote the public health and will not promote the public welfare, or that the benefits from said proposed work will not exceed the damages and cost of construction, and no remonstrance against said report is filed, the petition shall be dismissed and the costs taxed against the petitioner, and judgment entered therefor as in Sec-

tion 1379—21 hereinafter provided; but if the preliminary report be that the benefits of said proposed work or works by the commissioners proposed will exceed the damages and costs of construction, and that the public health will be promoted thereby, or that the public welfare will be promoted thereby, and no remonstrance thereto is filed; or if on the trial of the issues made on said report, the court finds that the benefits will exceed the damages and the cost of construction, and that the public health or the public welfare will be promoted by said proposed work, the court shall make and file such findings in writing and make an order confirming said report or directing the amendment of the report to conform to the findings of said court, and when so amended, the court shall by order confirm the same and direct said commissioners to proceed with said work with all convenient speed.

7. Said findings and order shall be final and conclusive unless appealed from to the supreme court within thirty days after the filing thereof.

8. If it shall appear from said report or upon the hearing upon said report that it will be necessary to enter upon any navigable waters of the state or remove any mill dams or obstructions from navigable streams, or clean out, widen, deepen and straighten any navigable stream, the said drainage commissioners shall within thirty days after the filing of the order confirming the preliminary report file with the Conservation Commission of the state of Wisconsin a certified copy of the petition and all other papers and orders filed with the circuit court in said proceeding, together with an application setting forth that the public health and the public welfare demands that certain mill dams or other obstructions shall be removed from a navigable stream or that it is necessary to enter upon any navigable stream for the purpose of straightening, cleaning out, deepening and widening the same, and that said proposed work will not permanently obstruct or impede the general navigability of such navigable waters, which application shall be duly verified and shall be accompanied with detail plans, profiles and specifications of the work proposed in and upon such navigable waters.

9. Upon receiving an application under the provisions of this act, the Conservation Commission shall forthwith set a time and place for the hearing of such application, which time shall not

be less than three weeks nor more than eight weeks from the date of filing application, and the place shall be at the court house at the county seat of the county in which said proceeding is pending, or at some other place if the Commission shall deem the latter more convenient.

· 10· The Conservation Commission shall thereupon give to the drainage commissioners a notice of the time and place of said hearing, which notice shall be published by the drainage commissioners at least once each week for two successive weeks preceding such hearing, in one newspaper in each county in which any part of said proposed district is located, and satisfactory proof of publication of the notice of hearing on such applicaton shall be filed by the applcants with said Conservation Commission. Said drainage commissioners shall also serve a copy of said notice of hearing upon the secretary of state of the State of Wisconsin and also upon the attorney general of the State of Wisconsin, at least ten days prior to such hearing, and satisfactory proof of such service shall be filed by the drainage commissioners with said Conservation Commission.

11. At such hearing or any adjournment thereof, the Conservation Commission shall carefully consider such application and shall hear such drainage commissioners by counsel or agents, in support thereof, and any person, corporation or municipality, in person or by counsel or agents, in opposition thereto, and upon demand of the drainage commissoiners or any person or corporation or municipality appearing in opposition, take evidence and testimony orally or by deposition in support of the application or in opposition thereto.

12. Said Conservation Commission shall have power to subpoena witnesses and to compel the production of books, documents and papers, to adminster oaths and to punish for disobedience of any order of the Commission or any commissioner or of a subpoena or for refusal of a witness to be sworn or to testify.

13. If it should develop upon such hearing that the plans, profiles and specifications proposed and submitted by the drainage commissioners are not best adapted for the work proposed on such navigable waters, then said Conservation Commission may modify, amend or make new plans and specifications and approve such plans, profiles and specifications as in their judgment are best adapted for such work.

14. Upon the conclusion of the hearings on said application as above provided, said Conservation Commission shall carefully consider all the evidence submitted, and if the said Conservation Commission, or a majority of them, shall find that the work proposed is necessary and will promote the public welfare will promote the public welfare and will not permanently obstruct or impede the general navigability of any such navigable waters, the said Conservation Commission shall forthwith grant and issue a certificate that the work proposed is necessary and will promote the public health or will promote the public welfare and will not permanently obstruct or impede the general navigabiity of any such navigable waters, which said certificate shall be filed in the office of the secretary of state, and a copy thereof, certified by the secretary of state, shall be filed in the office of the clerk of the Circuit Court in which said drainage proceedings is pending and in the matter of said proceeding.

15. The said Conservation Commission shall also approve the plans, specifications and profiles for the work proposed upon and in such navigable waters, or such amended and modified plans, specifications and profiles which they may adopt, and shall file the same in the office of the secretary of state and shall file with the clerk of the court in which said proceeding is pending and in the matter of said proceeding, a duly certified copy of said plans, specifications and profiles.

16. Such certificate and the plans approved shall constitute conclusive authority to such drainage commissioners and to do any acts necessary in and about the surveying, laying out, constructing, repairing, altering, enlarging, cleaning, deepening, widening, protecting and maintaining any ditch, drain, levee or other work upon the navigable rivers, streams or other navigable waters, both within and beyond the limits of the drainage district: the procuring, purchasing, or condemning, under proceedings similar to the proceedings had under the award of damages hereunder, of riparian rights, rights of flowage, dams and water powers in such navigable streams, channels, and waters, both within and beyond the limits of the drainage district.

17. If upon the conclusion of said hearing on said application, said Conservation Commission, or a majority of them, shall find and determine that the work proposed in said navigable

streams and waters is not necessary and will not promote the public health or will not promote the public welfare, and will permanently obstruct and impede the general navigability of such navigable waters, then said Conservation Commission shall refuse to grant said certificate and refuse to approve said plans and specifications and shall make an order refusing to grant the same.and shall file said order in the office of the secretary of state, and a copy thereof, certified by the secretary of state, shall be filed in the office of the clerk of the circuit court of the county in which such drainage proceeding is pending, and upon the filing of such certified copy of said order, if it shall be made to appear to the court that the objects of the petition cannot be accomplished without entering upon such navigable waters, then the court shall make and enter an order dismissing the petition and all proceedings had thereon, and costs shall be taxed against the petitioners and judgment entered therefor as in section 1379—21 hereinafter provided.

18. If said Conservation Commission shall grant and issue to the drainage commissioners a certificate that the work proposed is necessary and will promote the public health or will promote the puplic welfare and will not permanently obstruct or impede the general navigability of such navigable waters, then and upon the filing of such certified copy of said certificate in the office of the clerk of said circuit court in which said drainage proceedings is pending, said drainage district shall be and is hereby declared to be organized as a drainage district by the name mentioned in said petition, or such other name as the court shall fix, with the boundaries fixed by the order confirming the report of such commissioners, to be a body corporate by said name fixed in said order, with the right to sue and be sued, to use and adopt a seal and to have perpetual succession ; and all proceedings in said matter shall be stayed until after said Conservation Commission shall have rendered its decision.

19. The commissioners appointed as aforesaid, and their successors in office, shall, from the entry of said order of confirmation and the filing of such certificate of the Conservation Commission, constitute the corporate authority of said drainage district, and shall exercise all functions conferred on them by law, and do all things and perform all acts necessary to the construction and preservation of the proposed work.

20. All proceedings herein required prior to the entry of such

order of confirmation of record shall be deemed to be, and are hereby declared to be, necessary to the formation of said body corporate, and any defect therein falling within the purview of any curative provision herein contained may be cured thereunder.

Section 1379—18. 1. As soon as may be after the confirmation of said preliminary report, or within such time as the court may direct, said commissioners shall proceed to have all necessary levels taken and surveys made, and lay out said proposed work, make a map thereof and plans and profiles and other specifications therefor, and report in writing to the court:

(1) Whether the starting point, routes and termini of the proposed work and the proposed location thereof as in the petition contained are in all respects proper and feasible, and if not, shall report such as are most proper and feasible.

(2) What lands within the district as by them reported will be injured by the proposed work, if any, and if so, therein award to each tract, lot, easement or interest by whomsoever held, the amount of damages which they shall determine to be caused to the same by the proposed work.

(3) They shall also determine and report to the court the total cost of the proposed work, which cost shall include all incidental expenses of organizing such district, the damages to lands both within and without the district, together with attorneys' fees for the petitioners, which cost will hereinafter be referred to as cost of construction.   ,

2. If the cost of construction of any particular part of the work so proposed to be done should be assessed upon any particular tract or tracts, lot or lots of land, easement or easements, or upon any corporation or corporations, the commissioners shall so specify, and in their report they shall fix and determine the sums which should be assessed against said tracts, lots and corporations, and assess said sum against said lots, tracts, easement and corporations.

3. And if any corporation would in the judgment of said commissioners derive special benefits from the whole or any part of such proposed work, the commissioners shall so report and assess those benefits, and assess against the same its proportionate share of the cost of said proposed work.

4. The word "corporation," wherever in this act contained,

shall be construed to include private corporations of all kinds; towns; cities; villages; drainage districts and counties.

5. They shall apportion and assess the part of this cost of construction not assessed as above against the several benefited tracts, lots and easements in said drainage district in propor-tion to the benefits which they have assessed against the same in their preliminary report, by setting down opposite each lot, tract or easement the sum which they assess against the same for construction. The assessments which together make up the cost of construction as above defined, are herein referred to as assessments for construction.

6. The commissioners shall further report to the court the probable cost of keeping said proposed work in repair after it is completed.

7. In case the purpose of the petition is repairing, enlarging or maintaining a drain, ditch, levee or other work heretofore constructed under any law of this state, it shall be the duty of the commissioners to examine such drain, ditch, levee or other work and the lands intended to be reclaimed or benefited thereby, and to report to the court: (a) Whether in their opin-ion such levee, drain or ditch with proper enlargement or repair can be made sufficient to protect permanently said lands from overflow, or to drain the same; (b) the probable annual expense of keeping the same in repair; (c) what lands will be benefited thereby, giving accurate description by government or smaller subdivisions, the names of the owners, when known, and the cost of all necessary work with all incidental expenses, and an assess-ment of such cost on each tract, lot or easement, which assess-ment shall be apportioned on the actual benefits to be had, and if any particular part of such cost should be assessed upon any particular tract, lot or easement, they shall so specify; and if any corporation derive a public or special benefit from such work, they shall so determine and report, and assess such cor-poration its equitable proportion of such cost; (d) whether the aggregate amount of such cost will exceed the benefits resulting to the lands and interests assessed; (e) whether the proposed district will embrace all of the lands that may be benefited by the enlargement, repair or maintenance of such levee, drain or ditch, and if not, what additional lands will be so affected.

8. They shall include in their said report maps, plans and other specifications, and file the same with their report.

9. The commissioners shall not be confined to the point of commencement, routes or termini of the ditches or drains, or the number, extent or size of the same, or the location, plan or extent of any ditch, levee or other work as proposed by the petitioners, but shall locate, design, lay out and plan the same in such manner as to them shall seem best to promote public health and welfare and to drain or protect the lands of the parties interested with the least damage and greatest benefit to all lands affected thereby; and any plan proposed by the commissioners may, on the application of any person interested, in the way hereinbefore provided for, or on the application of the commissioners, be altered by the court by written order in such manner as shall appear to the court to be just.

Section 1379—19. 1. Upon the filing of said report the court shall make out and enter an order fixing the time and place when and where all persons interested may appear and remonstrate against the confirmation thereof, and the court shall cause notice of the time and place of such hearing to be given to all parties interested, by publication thereof, which notice shall be signed by the clerk of said court and shall state that the final report of the commissioners has been filed with the clerk of said court, which report contains the aware of damages and the assessment for construction against the several tracts, parcels, easements and corporations owning lands within said district and that the same can be seen and examined by any interested party at the office of said clerk of said court, and shall also state the time and place when all parties may be heard upon said report.

2. Said notice shall be published for at least three successive weeks prior to the date set for hearing in one newspaper published in each county in which said lands or any part thereof within said district shall be located (and if no newspaper is published in said county, in some newspaper published in an adjoining county), and by serving a copy of said notice on the attorneys for all persons or corporations who have appeared in said proceeding.

Section 1379—20. 1. Any owner of lands or of any easement or interest therein within said district, or any person or corporation affected by the proposed work, may appear on the day set for hearing of said report and remonstrate against the whole or any part of the proposed work. Such remonstrances shall be verified by affidavit and shall state the objections of the affiant whether they go to the jurisdiction of the commissioners or of the court, or whether they rest on any other fact such

2. As that some lands or corporations are assessed too high or too low or improperly,

3. Or that lands are assessed which ought not to be assessed,

4. Or that lands or corporations should be assessed which are not assessed,

5. Or that damages allowed to any parcel easement, lot or to any corporation are excessive,

6. Or that the plan for said proposed work should be changed. specifying the change,

. 7. Or that any person or corporation to whom damages are allowed may remonstrate because the damages allowed are inadequate.

8. Such remonstrances shall be filed with the clerk of the circuit court in which said proceeding is pending at least five days before the time set for hearing upon said report, and a copy thereof shall be served upon the attorneys for the commissioners at least five days before said time of hearing.

9. The circuit court of said county, or the presiding judge thereof, may affix a time at any term of court, or appoint a special term for hearing remonstrances, and on demand of any person or corporation assessed for or awarded damages may frame issues in said matter, empanel a jury and take its verdict upon the trial of such issues.   (1) Whether the amount of damages awarded by the commissioners to any remonstrant is excessive or inadequate, and (b) whether the assessment for construction to any remonstrant demanding the review by a jury is too high or too low; and the jury may award such damages and assess for construction in their verdict as they may consider proper.   All other issues arising on any remonstrance, excepting those for construction and damages, where a demand is made for jury trial, shall be tried by the court.

10. If the court finds that the report requires modifications, the same may by order of the court be referred back to the commissioners to be modified in accordance with said order of the court, and said commissioners shall immediately modify the same and file such modified and amended report with the court.

11. In any case between the commissioners and any remon-

strant, the court may award and apportion the costs. Costs awarded against the commissioners shall not go against them personally, but shall be paid out of the funds realized from the assessments for construction.

12. If there be no remonstrance, or if the finding be in favor of the validity of the proceeding, or after the report shall have been modified to conform to the findings, the court shall confirm the report and the order of confirmation shall be final and conclusive and the proposed work shall be established and authorized and the proposed assessments approved and confirmed, unless within thirty days an appeal be taken to the supreme court. Said order of confirmation shall also fix the commissioners' bond.

13. Said order of confirmation may at the same time or at any subsequent term of said court be revised, modified or changed, on petition of the commissioners after the publication of such notice as the court, or a judge thereof, may require, to parties adversely interested.

14. At any time after the filing of such report, and prior to making the order confirming said report, the court may permit the commissioners to present and file a supplemental report, or amend their report, as to any matter which, pursuant to the provisions hereof, shall or might be included in the original report presented by them, and after the publication of reasonable notice to all parties interested in such manner as the court shall direct, the court may upon the hearing in said matter make such order as the case may require.

Section 1379—21. 1. In case the petition or proceedings are dismissed as provided in this act, judgment shall be entered against the petitioners and in favor of the commissioners for the costs, expenses and liabilities incurred in said proceeding and for the benefit of those who have rendered services or advanced money in the prosecution of such proceeding, or have recovered costs on successful contests therein and who have loaned money for the purpose of prosecuting the proceeding and work under this act.

2. Before any such judgment is entered said commissioners shall file with the clerk of the circuit court in which said proceedings were instituted, an itemized statement of such costs, expenses and indebtedness, duly verified, upon which an order shall issue requiring said petitioners to show cause before said

court at a time and place named, why judgment should not be
entered against said petitions for the amount of said costs and
expenses. Notice of the hearing of such order to show cause
shall be given to said petitions by publication of the same in
one newspaper published in the county where the proceedings
are pending, at least three successive weeks prior to the date
set for hearing. Said notice need not contain an itemized
statement of said account.

3. The petitioners shall among themselves contribute in the
payment of said judgment in proportion to the benefits their
lands within the boundaries of the proposed district at the time
of filing said petition would have sustained in case the work
proposed had been completed, and contribution shall be based
upon the estimate of benefits contained in the preliminary
report of said commissioners as confirmed.

Section 1379—22. 1. At the time of the confirmation of such
report, it shall be competent for the court to order the assessment for construction of new work to be paid in not more than
fifteen (15) instalments of such amounts and at such times as
will be convenient for the accomplishment of the proposed
work, or for the payment of the principal and interest of such
notes or bonds of said district as the court shall grant authority
to issue for the construction of the new work. The court may
also by such order fix the date on which the first instalment
of the assessments for construction shall become due, which
shall be January 1st, not more than five (5) years after the
date of the order, and each of said instalments shall draw interest from the date of said order, said interest to be paid annually.

2. Unless otherwise provided by said order, such assessments
shall be payable at once, and from the time of the entry of said
order the assessments for construction of new work and additional assessments and interest thereon shall be a first lien upon
the lands assessed until paid, and shall take precedence over
the lien of all other liens and mortgages, even though such
other liens and mortgages were acquired and held prior to the
time of the filing of the petition under this act, excepting only
liens for general or special taxes.

3. And the owner of land or any corporation assessed for
construction may, at any time before the commissioners have
entered into a contract to borrow money upon the notes or

bonds of said drainage district based upon said assessment, pay into court the amount of the assessment against his land, or any tract thereof, or against such corporation, together with the interest thereon at the rate of six per cent from the time of the entry of said order up to the date of said payment. Said payment shall relieve said lands from the lien of said assessment, and said person or corporation from all liability thereon.

4. Whenever the commissioners shall desire to borrow money upon the notes or bonds to be paid during a series of years and after a period exceeding three (3) years, they shall by public advertisement first invite proposals to furnish the money desired at the most favorable rate of interest, or if bonds or notes shall be issued at six per centum, proposals to take the same at the best premium, and until such advertisement is made without success, they shall not privately negotiate such notes or bonds as aforesaid.

5. On or before the fifteenth day of January and July in each year from the time of their appointment until their final discharge, the commissioners shall make and file with the clerk of the circuit court in which said proceeding was instituted an itemized account of their reports and expenditures during the half year ending with the last day of the preceding month, in which shall be set down the balance on hand at the date of their prior report, the dates, sources and amount of receipts, the dates. purposes for and amounts of expenditures, all as actually having occurred, and the balance then on hand, and the vouchers of said expenditures shall be filed with such account. Such account shall be verified by the oath of one or more of the commissioners, and, together with the vouchers, be carefully preserved by the clerk as part of the papers in the proceeding.

6. At any time within thirty (30) days after the filing of such account, any land owner within said district may file exceptions thereto, specifying the items objected to and the grounds of objection, and give notice in writing to the commissioners thereof: Thereupon the exceptions shall stand for trial before the court and judgment shall be rendered for or against the district, with right of appeal as in other cases. Costs may be adjudged to the commissioners against the party filing exceptions if they are not sustained, and in the discretion of the court, if but partly sustained. If the items excepted to be

wholly disallowed, and in all other cases when the commissioners shall exceed their authority, the taxable costs of proceedings shall be adjudged against the commissioners, and not against the district.

Section 1379—23.   1.   Assessments for keeping any drain, ditch, levee or other work in repair under these provisions, shall become due and payable on the first Tuesday of September annually.   Commissioners having charge of any completed drain, ditch or levee or other work shall, between the fifteenth day of May and the first day of June in each year, file with the clerk of the court having jurisdiction of such drainage district, a report in which they shall specify in detail the labor necessary for the preservation and protection of the work under their control, the places where repairs are specially needed, the estimated cost of such repairs and the sum to be assessed against each tract, lot, easement or corporation to pay for the same.

2. No notice of the filing of such report shall be necessary. All such assessments for repairs shall be apportioned on each tract of land within said drainage district in the same proportion as the assessments of benefits for the construction of the work which were confirmed by the court.   Such annual report shall be heard by the court on the last Tuesday of June of each year or as soon thereafter as may be convenient, and the presiding judge shall examine said report, hear all objections to the same, fix and determine the amount of such assessments and cause such adjudication to be entered of record in said court and a certified copy to be delivered to said commissioners.

3. The amount to be collected under the order of said court for the preservation and maintenance of said work as aforesaid, together with all other assessments theretofore levied, shall, not in the aggregate exceed the total amount of the assessments for benefits as levied in the preliminary report of the commissioners as confirmed by the court.

4. The commissioners of each drainage district, when they make the report provided for with reference to the repairs of said ditches, shall include therein their estimates of the incidental expenses of caring for said district for the ensuing year and shall assess the same with their assessments for repairs.

Section 1379—24. 1. In all cases, after assessments for construction or repairs are confirmed by the court, the commissioners shall, within twenty (20) days after such confirmation, give notice of the entry of the order of confirmation and of the time and place where the assessments may be paid, by mailing to each owner of land within said district, at his last known post office address, a notice, which notice shall contain a statement of the amount assessed against his land and the time and place of payment, and no other notice of the making of said order shall be necessary to set the thirty (30) days for appeal running.

2. If assessments against lands are not paid when due, they shall certify the same to the clerk of the town, city or village in which the delinquent lands are situated, as due and unpaid for such work. and such clerk shall enter the same in the tax roll of such town, city or village, next thereafter to be made. against the lands benefited, but in a separate column thereof, and the same shall be collected in the same manner in which state. county and town taxes are collected, except only that the personal property of natural persons and private corporations and all lands other than those against which the assessments shall have been made shall not be liable to seizure and sale therefor.

3. Any town treasurer, village treasurer or city treasurer who shall collect drainage assessments pursuant to this act, shall, on or before the last Tuesday of March in each year, transmit the drainage moneys so collected by him to the commissioners of the drainage district entitled thereto.

4. Any town treasurer, village treasurer or city treasurer who shall fail to transmit to the proper drainage commissioners the drainage moneys belonging to their district. within the time hereinbefore limited, shall forfeit one hundred dollars ($100) to said drainage district which forfeitures and the cost of collecting the same may be collected before any justice of the peace of the county where said treasurer resides, in any suit in which the drainage district to which said drainage money belongs shall be the plaintiff and said treasurer defendant. Said treasurer and the sureties on his bond shall be liable for such drainage money collected by him and not transmitted to the proper drainage commissioners.

Section 1379—25. 1. Such assessments as are not paid to the commissioners or to the town. city, or village treasurer shall be returned by the town, city or village treasurer to the county

treasurer in the same manner and at the same time as delin
quent taxes, but separately therefrom. The county treasurer
shall advertise the same in his list of lands to be sold for unpaid taxes and, unless paid to him prior to the tax sale, he
shall sell said lands for the taxes and drainage assessments
against the same, treating said drainage assssments the same
as unpaid taxes but keeping them separate from the taxes on his
record. When he issues certificates of sale of land for taxes
and drainage assessments, he shall issue a separate certificate
for the amount of drainage assessments on said land. No extra
advertising for sale fee shall be added to the certificate of sale
for drainage assessments when the land was at the same time sold
for taxes as well as for drainage assessments. In case the
tax on any land shall be paid and the drainage assessments not
paid said county treasurer shall proceed to sell said land for
drainage assessment or assessments in the same manner in
which he would proceed if the taxes thereon were unpaid. The
tax certicfiate and the drainage assessment certificate on the
same land may be assigned separately or together, but at the
public sale they shall be offered and sold together.

2. The county treasurer of any county of the state in which
the whole or any part of a drainage district is situated shall, in
the books of account of said county keep a separate account
with each such drainage district. In each account he shall
credit the proper drainage district which (a) all sums received
by the county in payment of drainage assessments of that district; (b) all sums received by the county as principal on sale
of drainage assessment certificates at the tax sale (except such
certificates as shall be sold to the county) ; (c) all sums receievd
by the county for principal and interest on sale or assessment
of drainage assessment certificates after the county has bid in
such certificates; (d) the face and accrued interest on all drainage assessment certificates up to the date of the drainage assessment deed, in case the county has taken deed to itself on any
drainage assessment certificates; (e) any and all other sums
received by said county on account of such drainage district.

3. In such accounts said county treasurer shall charge to each
district on its separate account all sums paid to the commissioner
of said district.

4. The county treasurer of any county in which the whole
or any part of a drainage district is situated shall, on demand

of the commissioners of any such drainage district, pay to said commissioners the balance of moneys held by the county for such drainage district, and shall take and file in his office receipts of such commissioners for such payments.

5. After the expiration of three years from the issuing of said drainage assessment certificate, a deed shall issue upon any certificate of sale for unpaid drainage assessments, in the same manner and upon the same notice or affidavit of non-occupancy now required for the issuance of tax deeds, which deeds shall be in form substantially the same as tax deeds, provided that no such drainage assessment deed shall cut off or adversely affect any drainage assessment or installment of any assessment falling due after the assessment or installment upon which such deed is issued or, shall cut off or adversely affect any additional assessment or assessments for repairs that may hereafter be made or fall due. No tax deed shall cut off any drainage assessment, nor shall any drainage assessment cut off any tax deed.

6. The rules of law applying to the collection of taxes and sale of land for taxes and tax deeds shall, unless in conflict with this act, apply to the collection of and sale of lands for drainage assessment except that said drainage assessment certificates shall draw ten (10) per centum of interest annually. When commissioners shall fail to certify to the town, city or village clerk of the proper town, city or village any one or more drainage assessments for construction or repair, or additional assessment against any land in said district, at the proper time, they may certify the same to the town, city or village clerk at any time thereafter within the same or any subsequent year.

Section 1379—26. Immediately after the entry of any order confirming any assessment for construction or additional assessment, or any assessment for repairs and maintenance of the work, the clerk of the court shall make out and certify to the register of deeds in each county where assessed lands are situated, a true copy of the list of the lands in said county assessed and the sum assessed against such tract or parcel thereof or easement therein, and said register shall thereupon enter such order of record and the same shall be notice of the lien of said assessment to all persons. The lien of said assessments shall be dated from the filing of said certified list with the register of deeds. The register of deeds shall record such certificate and list with him filed and shall receive the usual fees therefor.

Section 1397—27. If assessments for the construction of new work be payable installments, each installment shall draw interest at the rate of six (6) per cent per annum from the date of the order fixing and affirming the assessments until paid, interest payable annually; and in case said interest is not paid when due, its collection shall be enforced in the same manner as are assessments for construction.

Scetion 1379—28. When duly qualified and after having obtained the certificate of public necessity, in case the work proposed requires the entry upon and doing of work in navigable streams and waters, the drainage commissioners shall have power to do any and all necessary acts in and about the surveying, laying out, constructing, repairing, altering, enlarging, cleaning, protecting and maintaining of any ditch, drain, levee or other work for which they may have been appointed, including the constructing of all necessary bridges, crossings, embankments, protections, dams and lateral drains; the cleaning out and straightening of navigable and non-navigable channels and streams; and the removal of obstructions therefrom, both within and beyond the limits of the drainage district; the procuring, purchasing or condemning, under proceedings similar to proceedings had under the award of damages hereunder, or riparian rights, rights of flowage, dams and water powers in streams and channels. both navigable and non-navigable, and both within and beyond the limits, of the drainage districts; and for such purposes may use any moneys in their hands arising from the assessments made. as in this act provided.

Section 1379—28a. The commissioners, their agents, servants and employees. shall at all times, after the appointment of the commissioners have the right to go upon any and all lands within said drainage district and upon the lands along any drain. ditch, levee or embankment in the district, to inspect, deepen, widen and repair the same whenever necessary, not doing unnecessary damage. and shall not be liable for trespass therefor.

Section 1379—29. 1. Said commissioners shall have the right to lay out and construct all necessary drains, ditches and levees across any railway right of way or yards in their district, and any railway company whose right of way or yards, crosses the line of any proposed drain, ditch or levee, shall open its right of way or yards and permit such drain, ditch or levee to cross the same as soon as such drain, ditch or levee is constructed to such right of way or yards. The terms "railway company" as used in this act shall include steam, electric, interurban and street railways.

2. Every drainage district shall be liable to the railway company whose right of way or yard of tracks any of its drains, ditches or levees cross for the reasonable cost of the culverts and bridges made necessary by said ditch, drain or levee crossing said right of way, yards or tracks, but not of more expensive character than average other culverts or bridges being constructed on said division of railway crossing streams or ditches of approximately the same width and depth and within one hundred miles of said drainage district ditches.

3. Upon receiving fifteen days' notice in writing, any railway company across whose right of way any such drain, ditch or levee is laid out, shall open its right of way or yards to permit said commissioners and their contractors, agents or employes to construct said drain, ditch or levee across said right of way and yards, and shall permit the passage of dredges and other machinery used in the construction of said work through said right of way.

4. For every day that such railway company fails, after the end of said fifteen days, to open their said right of way or yards as hereinbefore required, it shall forfeit twenty-five dollars to said drainage district, to be collected in an action as other forfeitures are collected or set off against any damages that may have been awarded to said company. If said railway company fails to open its right of way or yard along the line of said drain. ditch or levee, the commissioners may, at any time after the expiration of said fifteen days, open such right of way or yards along the lines of said drains, ditches and levees, and construct the same, provided, however, that said drainage district, its agents and employes, shall in all cases, so prosecute the work through such railway right of way and yards as not to delay traffic upon said railway for a longer time than is absolutely necessary to construct the work upon said right of way and yards.

Section 1379—30. If in the first assessment for construction the commissioners shall have reported to the court a smaller sum than is needed to complete the work of construction, or if in any year an additional sum is necessary to pay the interest or lawful indebtedness of said drainage district, further additional assessments of the lands and corporations benefited, proportioned on the last assessment of benefits which has been approved by the court, shall be made by the commissioners of the said drainage district under the order of the court or presiding judge thereof, provided, however, that said assessment and the first assessment for construction shall not exceed the total amount of the benefits which will be received by the lands within said drainage district, as estimated in the preliminary report of the commissioners, which said additional assessment shall be made without notice, and may be made payable in installments as specified in section 1379—22 hereof, and shall be treated and collected in the same manner as the original assessments for construction confirmed by the court in said drainage proceedings.

2. The commissioners of said drainage district shall have the same power to borrow money or issue notes or bonds based upon such further and additional assessment herein provided for that is given to them by section 1379—31b of this act.

Section 1379—31. 1. Omission to assess benefits or to assess for construction or to make additional assessment or to make asesments for repairs or to award damages to any one or more tracts of land or assessments in the drainage district, or to assess benefits, or to assess for construction or to assess for repairs or to make additional assessments against any corporation which shall have been assessed, shall neither affect the jurisdiction of the court to confirm the report nor render the benefits assessed or the assessments for construction or additional assessment or assessments for repairs against other lands or assessments against any corporation voidable, but the commissioners of said drainage district shall thereafter, as soon as they discover the omission or as soon as notified thereof, either agree with the omitted parties upon the proper assessments and awards of damage, or assess such benefits or make such assessments for construction and make such additional assessments against the omitted lands and corporations and award such damages as shall be just, and report the facts together with such assessments and awards, to the court.

2. The court shall thereupon, by order, fix a time and place of hearing on such report and therein specify what notice shall be given to the owner or owners of said lands or said corpora-

tion, and the time and manner of serving the same. The owner of said lands or assessments therein, or such owner or corporations affected, may file a verified written remonstrance against the confirmation thereof because said assessment is too high or the award of damages too low, which remonstrance shall set forth the facts on which remonstrance relies as provided in Section 1379—20 of this act.

3. Said remonstrance shall be filed with the clerk of the court at least five (5) days before the time set for hearing and a copy thereof shall be served upon the attorney for the commissioners at least five (5) days before said time of hearing. The issues arising upon such report and remonstrance shall be made up and tried as provided in Section 1379—20 hereof. If said failure to assess benefits, assess for construction, make additional assessments or assess for repairs, or award damages, is brought to the court's attention prior to the confirmation of the report in which the failure occurs, the court shall adjourn the hearing thereon until the omitted lands and corporations are assessed and the owners of such lands and corporations are served with the notice which the court may order served.

4. This action shall be retroactive and shall apply to failures to assess benefits, failures to assess for construction, failures to assess for repair, failure to make additions, assessments and failures to award damages occurring in any drainage district.

Section 1379—81b. 1. The commissioners may borrow money not exceeding the amount of assessments for construction, additional assessments and assessments for repairs unpaid at the time of borrowing, for the construction or repair of any work which they shall be authorized to construct or repair or for the payment of any indebtedness they may have lawfully incurred, and may secure the same by notes, or bonds, bearing interest at the rate not to exceed six per cent per annum and not running beyond one year after the last installment of the assessment on the account of which the money borrowed shall fall due, which notes or bonds shall not be held to make the commissioners personally liable, but shall constitute a lien upon the assessments for the repayment of the principal and interest of such notes and bonds.

2. And the court may, on the petition of the commissioners authorize them to refund any lawful indebtedness of the district by taking up and cancelling all of its outstanding notes

and bonds as fast as they become due or before if the holders thereof will surrender the same, and issue in lieu thereof new notes or bonds of such district, payable in such longer time as the court shall deem proper, not to exceed in the aggregate the amount of all notes and bonds of the district then outstanding and the unpaid accrued interest thereon, and bearing interest not to exceed six per cent per annum.

3. And the court may, on the petition of the commissioners, order that the collection of any installment of assessments be postponed to such time as the court may deem proper and reasonable.

4. The court may, upon the petition of the commissioners, at any time after the organization of the drainage district, and before the confirmation of the report levying the assessments for cost of construction, enter an order authorizing said commissioners to borrow money upon the note or notes of said drainage district, for the purpose of surveying and laying out the necessary work and for the purpose of carrying on the proceedings, the said note or notes not to run for more than one year and to bear interest at a rate of not exceeding six per cent per annum.

Section 1379—31o. In all cases where the work to be done at any time under the direction of the commissioners shall in their opinion cost to exceed five hundred dollars ($500), the same shall be let to the lowest responsible bidder, and the commissioners shall advertise for sealed bids by notice published in some newspaper published in the county in which the petition is filed, and may advertise in one or more newspapers published elsewhere. fI there be no newspapers published in the county in which the petition is filed, they shall advertise in some newspapers published in an adjoining county, which said notice shall particularly set forth the time and place when and where the bids advertised for will be opened, the kind of work to be let and the terms of payment. Said commissioners may continue the letting from time to time, if in their judgment the same shall be necessary, and shall reserve the right to reject any and all bids, and they shall not during their term of office be interested directly or indirectly in any contract for the construction of any drain, ditch, levee or other work in said drainage district, or in the sale of materials therefor, or in the wages of, or supplies of men or teams employed on any such work in said district.

Section 1379—31d. The net damages allowed to the owners of lands shall be paid or tendered before the commissioners, shall be authorized to enter upon the lands, for damage to which the award is made for the construction of any drains, ditches or levees proposed thereon. If the owner is unknown, or there shall be a contest in regard to the ownership of the lands, or the owner will not receive payment or there exists a mortgage or lien against the same, or the commissioners cannot for any other reason safely pay him, they may deposit the said damage with the clerk of the court for the benefit of the owner or parties interested, to be paid or distributed as the court shall direct, and such payment shall have the same effect as the tender to and acceptance of the damages awarded by the true owner of the land.   This section shall not, however. prevent said commissioners, their agents, servants or employes, going upon said lands to do any and all work found necessary prior to making their assessments of benefits and award of damages and the trial of their report thereof.

Section 1379—31e. 1. When any person or persons owning lands within the district, which have been assessed for cost of construction of any ditch or drain, shall present to the commissioners of any organized drainage district an affidavit satisfying such commissioners, that he, or they, own real estate of such character (describing the same) within said drainage district. and that the same has been assessed for construction and needs drainage and is shut off from access to any drain of said district; (or that, by reason of the slope of the land it is impractical for him or them to drain said real estate to any such drain) without crossing the lands of other owners, and that he. or they, cannot purchase from the owner or owners of the lands, lying between his or their lands and such drain, to which his or their land must be drained, a right of way for a private drain thereto, over or along or through the lands or such other owners along a practicable route, or that said right of way cannot be purchased except at an exhorbitant price, stating the lowest price for which the same can be purchased, and asking that a drain be laid out from affiant's lands to such drain, the said commissioners shall fix a time and place of hearing upon said application, and within thirty days after the filing of said affidavits, shall give notice of the time and place of meeting therefor, by posting notice thereof in three public places in said draining district at least ten days before the time fixed for hearing theron, and by serving said notice at least five days before such hearing on the occupants of all lands through or along which such drain may pass, and upon the owners of said lands, if such owners reside within the district.

2. Such notice shall be served personally or by leaving a copy thereof at the usual place of abode of each occupant, and each owner of said lands residing in said district, across, through or along which lands it is proposed to lay out such drain.

3. At the time and place fixed by said notice said commissioners shall meet, and if the facts set out in said application are true and they decide that a drain is necessary, they shall by order lay out said drain as a public drain, and shall assess the benefits which said drain will be to the lands across or along which the same shall be laid, and other lands in the district benefited thereby, and determine and award the damages to said several tracts by reason of the construction of said drain and assess the cost of said drain to the benefited lands.

4. Said assessments, determination and award shall be in writing, and shall specify the benefits or damages which they determine that said drain will cause to said several tracts of lands, and each assessment therein, across or along which the same shall be laid out. Said order, assessment and determination they shall file and record in their office.

5. Said applicants shall cause notice of said assessment and determination to be served upon each occupant of assessed land and lands across or along which said drain shal be laid, and upon each owner who resides in said district, in the same manner as the previous notice is herein required to be served, within ten days after the making of said order laying out the said drain

6. The order laying out said drain shall describe the same by describing the line along which the same shall be laid, and give the slope of sides of the same, grades, depths and width

8. Written proof of the service of said several notices shall

7. Said orders shall be final unless appealed from to the circuit court having jurisdiction of the district, within thirty days after the serving of said last notice.

8. Written proof of the service of said several notices shall be filed in the office of the clerk of said court.

9. A copy of said order shall be filed in the office of the clerk of the court within thirty days after the said order is made.

10. Said commissioners shall determine the cost of the said drain; which cost shall include the damages awarded to the propertes through or along which said drain shall be laid, together with cost of constructing the same, and all preliminary costs necessary to the laying out of the same, together with the filing fees of the register of deeds.

11. Within eight months after the time for appeal from the order laying out said drain is past, the owner or owners filing said affidavit shall deposit with said commissioners the cost of such drain as by them determined, whereupon said commissioners shall construct said drain, and the same shall become a public drain and part of the system of drains of said drainage district.

12. In case the assessment of benefits against the lands or any easement or interest therein, across or along which said drain s laid, shall exceed the damages thereto and no appeal is taken from the said determination of said commissioners (or on appeal benefits are confirmed) and said cost of said drains is deposited with said commissioners as herein required, said commissioners shall assess against the land and easements benefited the cost of said drain in proportion to the benefits assessed and shall file with the register of deeds of said county a certified statement of their order laying out said drain of such assessments for the cost of said drain, and the land against which the same are assessed, setting down to each tract the sum assessed against the same, and the register of deeds shall record the same, and thereupon said assessments for the cost of said drain, shall become liens upon said several parcels, tracts and easements of said lands against which they are assessed.

13. Unless said assessments for construction for the cost of said drain are paid to said commissioners within one year from the making of said order, they shall certify the same to the clerk of said town, the same as an original assessment, to be collected as are other assessments against said lands, by placing the same upon the tax roll of said town.

14. When collected and paid to said commissions, said com-

missioners shall pay the same to the party or parties who paid for the construction of said drain, his or their heirs, personal representatives or assigns, in the proportion in which said party or parties originally paid the same.

15. In case two or more persons file said affidavit asking for a drain to be used by them in common, the cost of said drain shall be apportioned to said owners in proportion to the assessment of benefits then in force against their lands benefited thereby.

16. When practicable, said drains herein provided for shall be laid out and constructed on the side of the public highways.

Section 1379—31f. 1. Whenever owners of land contiguous to any drainage districts formed under these provisions may desire to be admitted to the benefits of said district, they shall file in the office of the clerk of the court having jurisdiction of such district, a petition signed by more than one half of the adult owners of lands in said territory, which said signers shall represent more than one-third of the lands in said proposed extension or addition, or signed by the owners of more than one-half of the lands in said new territory, together with a description of the lands which they desire admitted to said district, and the names of the owners so far as the same are known or can be ascertained, with a plat showing the original district and proposed new territory.

2. Upon the filing of such petition, the court or judge thereof shall by order fix a time and place of hearing thereon before the court at some general or special term or before the presiding judge thereof, and direct that notice of the time and place of such hearing be served upon all of the owners of such lands as are sought to be admitted to the benefits of said district, in the same manner that notice is required to be served on land owners by section two of this act.

3. At the time and place fixed for a hearing on said petition, any interested party may appear and contest the prayer of the petition, (1) because insufficient in form or substance; (2) because it has not the required number of signers. The same proofs or ownership may be accepted as provided in section four hereof.

4. If the court or judge shall find said petition insufficient in form or substance, the same may be amended. If the court shall

find that the petition, including all copies thereof filed prior
to hearing thereon, has not the required number of signers, the
petition shall be dismissed and judgment for costs entered
against the petitioners. But if the court or judge finds the
petition is in substance sufficient, or if it is amended so that it
is in substance sufficient, and also finds that it has sufficient
number of signers, the court or judge shall make such findings
in writing and refer the petition to the commissioners of the district to which it is sought to admit the new territory. Said
hearing may be adjourned to obtain other signers, serve notice
on unserved land owners, or for other good cause.

5. Said commissioners shall, as soon as possible after said petition is referred to them, examine said lands and make report on
them to the court:

(1) Whether the public health will be promoted by the proposed work.

(2) Whether the public wilfare will be promoted by the proposed work: and

(3) Whether the benefits will exceed the damages and cost of
construction of the proposed work.

6. Said commissioners shall as soon as possible, file said report with the court. Similar notice shall be given thereon, similar proceedings and hearings had thereon and similar findings
made thereon as on the preliminary report provided for in sections six and seven hereof. If the court shall find that the public
health or welfare will be promoted by the proposed work and
that the benefits will exceed the damages and cost of construction, the court shall make written findings of those facts and order that said lands, or so much thereof as the court shall direct,
be admitted to the benefits of the original drainage district, and
it shall thereafter be a part of the original drainage district, and
the lands therein shall thereafter be chargeable with assessments
for the preservation, repair and maintenance of the works in
said district in the same manner as are the lands in the original
district.

7. After the confirmation of said preliminary report, said commissioners shall proceed substantially as provided in section
eight thereof. In fixing the first assessment for construction
on such new terrtiory, the commissioners shall, in addition to the
cost of whatever work must necessarily be done therein, to place
such lands on the same footing as to drainage facilities as that

enjoyed by the lands in the original district, assess thereon such further sum as will make the amount to be paid on account of each acre of said lands in said new territory equal to the amount paid for the original drainage work of the same kind on account of each acre of the original drainage district similarly situated. If no land in said district is similarly situated, they shall assess thereon such further sum as shall be equitable, which shall be apportioned upon the benefits to such lands in all cases. The additional amount so received shall be held by the commissioners for the benefit of the entire drainage district.

8. Upon filing the report assessing benefits, assessing for construction and awarding damages in the matter of such addition, the same notice shall be served and proceedings had as in case of the report in an original district assessing benefits, assessing for construction and awarding damages.

9. The several orders confirming said reports shall be final and conclusive unless appealed from to the supreme court within thirty days after the rendering and entry thereof.

10. The provisions of this section shall, apply to proceedings now pending for the addition of new territory to any drainage district, unless the court order such proceedings or proceed under Section 1379—38 of the statutes of 1898 until completed.

Section 1379—31g. 1. Whenever any lands outside of a drainage district are receiving the benefits of the drains of said district, by direct or indirect, natural or artificial connection therewith, the commissioners of said district may report such facts to the court and ask that said lands, describing them, be brought into said district and assessed for the benefits by them received from the drains, ditches or levees of said district.

2. Upon the filing of said report, the court shall order the owners of such lands to be notified of the filing of said report and the contents thereof, and shall require such owners to show cause at a time and place therein fixed, not less than twenty days thereafter, why their said lands should not be brought into said district and assessed for said benefits.

3. At the time and place fixed for hearing said report, any of said land owners may appear and remonstrate against the confirmation of said report. All remonstrances shall be in writing, verified and shall set forth the facts on which they are based. All issues arising on said report shall be tried by the court without a jury.

4. If the court shall find that said lands or any of them are receiving the benefits of any such drain, ditch or levee, the court shall so find in writing and shall order said lands to be annexed to and made a part of said district, and benefits to be assessed against the same by the commissioners of said district.

5. Said order shall be final and conclusive unless appealed from to the supreme court within thirty days from the date of entry thereof.

6. Said commissioners shall, after the time for appeal is past, assess against each parcel, tract and easement of and in said annexed lands, reasonable and just benefits, and shall assess against said lands for construction and repairs such sum as shall be just. If lands similarly situated shall be assessed a like sum of benefits and damages as said lands in the said district to which they are sought to be annexed, and a sum for construction of said work which shall be equal to all sums assessed for the complete construction of the drainage system in the district to which they are sought to be annexed against lands having the same assessment of benefits in said district.

7. The commissioners shall file their said report and assessments in court. The court shall by order require said owners to show cause at a time and place therein fixed, not less than twenty days after the services of said order, why said report and assessments should not be confirmed. And on the hearing of said order to show cause, if a jury trial is demanded, the court shall frame issues on benefits and damages and empanel a jury or adjourn the hearing thereon until some term of court when a jury is in attendance and take the verdict of a jury on such issues. All other issues arising on said report shall be tried by the court. The court shall order all necessary amendments of said report and make written findings of fact, and when said report is amended shall by order confirm the same.

Section 1379—31h. 1. In all proceedings in this act provided for, the court shall appoint some reputable attorney as guardian ad litem to represent all infants and incompetent persons interested in said proposed work. In case the interests of such infants or incompetents shall appear to the court to be adverse to each other, the court shall appoint as many different attorneys to be guardian ad litem as the circumstances of the case may require.

2. The attorneys so appointed shall appear for and represent

their wards in all matters connected with said proceedings and shall be paid such sum as the court may fix out of the moneys in the hands of the commissioners.

3. In case of failure to serve notice upon an infant or incompetent, or assess his or her lands or award them damages in the first instance, said infant or incompetent may be brought into the court under the various curative sections of this act, a guardian ad litem appointed and the same proceedings had as in case of a competent person.

4. In case of failure to appoint a guardian ad litem for any interested infant or incompetent person in the first instance upon that fact becoming known to the court either before or after the hearing the court may order the infant or incompetent served with proper notice, a guardian ad litem appointed, and proceed as if a guardian ad litem has been appointed in the first instance, and if judgment be already rendered, may order the infant or incompetent and his guardian ad litem to show cause why the lands of said infant or incompetent should not be bound by all orders, findings, and judgments theretofore made in said matter.

Section 1379—31i. The lands embraced in any such drainage district shall be liable for any and all damages that result to lands lying outside of its boundaries because of the work done in said district. The word "damages" in this section shall be construed to mean such damages and only such damages as could be recovered against natural persons for life injury, resulting from life work. Such damages may be agreed upon between the commissioners and the damaged party subject to the approval of the court, or may be recovered in any action at law.

Section 1379—31j. The boundaries of such drainage district shall in no manner conflict with any other drainage district above it or below it, and if through the construction of any proposed ditch, drain or levee increased cost shall be entailed upon a lower district in providing means to carry off the water or remove the sediment flowing from the higher district, the lands in the higher district shall be liable for such increased cost. The amount of such increased cost may be agreed upon between the commissioners of said districts subject to the approval of the court, or may be recovered in an action at law between said districts.

Section 1379—31k. 1. In case any tract of land in a drainage district assessed for benefits as a single tract is divided in ownership, the commissioners of said drainage district shall apportion the sum to be collected in any year thereafter for construction, additional assessments or repair against said tract, in such manner as shall be just and equitable between the several divisions of the divided tract.

2. In case of easements granted in any tract of land, when such easement shall bear any portion of said assessment for construction, repair or additional assessment, the commissioners shall each year apportion the amount of said assessment to be collected that year justly between the owner of the dominant and servient estates.

Section 1379—31L. Any commissioner may resign to the court having jurisdiction over his district, and said court may accept his resignation and appoint his successor, who shall serve out the unexpired term of the resigned commissioner and until his successor is appointed and qualified. The court shall by appointment fill all vacancies in said commission, however, occurring.

Section 1379—31m. 1. The court shall at all times have supervision of said commissioners, and may at any time require them to make a report on any matter or matters connected with their duties as commissioners, and after due hearing may remove from office any or all of said commissioners for neglect of duty or malfeasance in office or for other good cause. The court or presiding judge may at any time require the commissioners to give new bonds to the clerk of the court and may fix the amount thereof, and said bonds shall be submitted to the court or the presiding judge thereof for approval.

2. The court shall at all times have supervision over all matter pertaining to drainage districts and may make such orders with respect to all matters pertaining to the carrying on of the work of said district or shall be for the best interest of said district, and for that purpose may, at any time, permit or require, as the circumstances may demand, the bringing in of new parties upon such terms as shall be just, with like force and effect as if they were original parties to said proceedings; and the rules of equity practice shall apply to all proceedings had under this act, and the court shall have the equitable supervision over all matters pertaining to drainage district

proceedings, with like force and effect as if said proceeding were a case of equity.

3. Any person owning land contiguous to the boundaries of any drainage district may at any time make application to the court to have said land included in said drainage district, and the court may, after due notice of said application, make an order adding said land to said district, with like force and effect as if the same had been included in the original petition or the preliminary report of the commissioners, and said lands shall be admitted in said drainage district upon the payment by the person owning the same to the funds ot said drainage district of such sum as the court may require, which sum shall be a lien upon said lands and shall be collected in the same manner as assessments for benefits.

Section 1379—31n. Where drainage districts are in process of organization under the statutes as they have heretofore existed, said organization shall be perfected under the laws as they heretofore existed, unless the court otherwise order, but after said organization is completed and corporate authorities acquired under said statutes, all further proceedings shall be had under this act where there is any section of this act to apply to such proceedings. All drainage districts heretofore organized under sections of law hereby reppealed, shall, after the passage hereof, be governed by this act; but nothing herein contained shall in any way render more difficult of collection any bonds or notes by said districts issued, or impair the obligation of any contract made in behalf of said district.

Section 1379—31o.—Whenever any assessment is made and confirmed against any city, village or town, the sum to be paid by said city, village or town shall be by the clerk of the court, at the request of the commissioners, certified to the clerk of said city, village or town, and by said clerk placed upon the next tax roll of said city, village or town among and as a part of the taxes to be collected that year, provided that whenever the sum assessed for construction or additional assessment against any city, village or town exceeds one per centum of the assessed value of the property in said city, village or town for the last previous assessment for taxation, as by its assessor and board of review fixed, the court shall, by order, direct that said assessment for construction against said city, village or town to be paid in installments. Said installments, except the last, shall each be one per cent of the assessed value of the city, village or town for the year of collection, but not less in any year than one per cent of the assessed value of said city, village or town for the year on which said first installment is computed, and each installment shall bear interest at the rate of six per cent per annum from the date of the entry of the order of confirmation, interest payable annually.

Section 1397—31p. Each and every sum assessed for construction, for additional assessment or for repairs against any land or against any corporation, as soon as such assessment is confirmed by the court, shall be and is declared to be a judgment of the circuit court in favor of said drainage district and against said land corporation, and unless some other method of collection is herein provided shall be collected in the same manner as any other money judgment is collected, provided that whenever said assessment is a lien upon land it shall only be collected out of said land on which it is a lien.

Section 1379—31q. The commissioners shall in the first instance construct all bridges and grades on highways that exist across their drains, ditches or levees prior to or at the time of the construction of their drains, ditches or levees. The town in which any drain, ditch or levee shall be crossed by any highway constructed afterward shall build all necesary bridges and grades. Said town shall maintain and repair all bridges and grades made necessary by any drain, ditch or levee dug or constructed by the commissioners of any drainage district to which this act shall apply.

Section 1379—31r. Commissioners of drainage districts are hereby declared to be public officers. The presumption shall be in favor of the regularity and validity of all their official acts. Whenever any report of the commissioners of any drainage district or any part of any such report is contested, remonstrated against or called in question, the burden of proof shall rest upon the contestant, remonstrant or questioner.

Section 1379—31s. 1. In case of failure to serve any notice of any proceeding or hearing in this act provided for, upon any person or corporation, such person or corporation may ap-

8

pear in court and waive such defect of service, or may waive
it by filing in court or delivering to the commissioners of the
drainage district to be filed in court a written waiver of such
defect, in which waiver said defect shall be described; which
waiver shall be signed by such party and witnessed and
acknowledged before a proper officer having power to make
acknowledgements of deeds.

2. In case of a city the mayor or clerk, by direction of the
city council, shall execute and acknowledge said waiver; in
case of a village the president and clerk, by direction of the
village trustees shall execute and acknowledge said waiver;
in case of town board a majority of the same shall execute
and acknowledge said waiver. When said waiver is filed in
court, it shall have the same effect as due service upon said
omitted party would have had in the first instance.

3. In case of omission to assess any corporation or land that
should be assessed for benefits, or construction, or repair, or
additional assessment, or to award damages, said omitted
party and the owner of omitted land may in writing agree
with the commissioner of said district what the assessment
should be against the land, or against said corporation, or what
said damages should be, and such agreement shall be acknowledged and witnesed as provided above for waivers, and be
filed in the court and recorded in the office of the register of
deeds of the county in which said lands lie.

4. The provisions of this section shall be retroactive and
apply to drainage districts heretofore organized, and those
now in process of organization as well as to districts organized
·under this act.

Section 1379—1t. 1. When any assessment for construction,
or additional assessment, or any installment thereof, or any
assessment for repairs shall have been fully paid, on demand
of any interested party and presentation of a receipt showing
that said assessment or installment has been paid, said commisioners shall, in writing, under seal of their said drainage district, satisfy the lien of said assessment. Said satisfaction
shall be witnessed and acknowledged so as to entitle it to
record and be recorded in the office of the register of deeds
of the county in which said lands or any of them lie.

2. Said commissioners shall keep in their office a complete
record of the assessed lands and the assessments against the

same and shall on said record mark "paid" any and all assessments and installments that are paid, whether to them or to the town treasurer or county treasurer.

Section 1379—31u. 1. Whenever the commisioners of any drainage district organized under the laws of the state, having at least eight miles of open ditches, drains or levees within its boundaries, file in the office of the clerk of the circuit court of the county having jurisdiction of such drainage district, a petition setting forth: (a) that it is necessary to make annual repairs to said ditches, drains or levees in order to properly maintain them; (b) that in order to make such repairs, certain machinery and appliances are necessary, specifying what machinery is best adapted; (c) that it will be more economical for the district to own the necessary machinery and appliances and to do the work itself than to have it done under contract; (d) and praying that the commissioners of such drainage district be authorized by order of the court to purchase, operate and maintain such machinery, dredges and other appliances which may be necessary to keep in repair the ditches, drains or levees within their drainage district, and to employ labor, and do all other things necessary to be done in order to satisfactorily operate said machinery and appliances, the court shall make and enter an order fixing the time and place of hearing upon said petition.

2. The clerk of said court shall give notice of the time and place of hearing upon said petition to all persons interested, by publishing a notice thereof, setting forth briefly the filing of said petition and the relief prayed for, together with the time and place of hearing thereon, for three successive weeks, in one newspaper published in each county in which any lands of said district are situated.

3. At the time of said hearing, all persons owning lands within the drainage district may appear and contest the allegation set forth in said petition, and the court shall hear all proofs offered, both for and against the same, and shall make and enter findings thereon.

4. If the court shall find that it will not be economical, or that it is not for the best interests of the district to own the necessary machinery and to do the work itself than it have it done under contract, then said petition shall be dismissed and the costs of the proceeding paid out of the general funds of the district.

5. If the court shall find that it will be more economical for the district to own the necessary machinery and to do the work itself than to have it done under contract, it shall enter an order authirizing and empowering the commission of the district to purchase, operate and maintain any machinery, dredges or other appliances which may be necessary to keep in repair the ditches, drains or levees within their drainage district, and to employ labor and to do all other things necessary to be done in order to satisfactorily operate said machinery and appliances.

6. If there is no money in the hands of the commissioners with which to pay for the machinery so authorized to be purchased, the commissioners shall levy an additional assessment in all the assessable lands in said district, based on the last assessment of benefits approved by the court, to pay for the cost of such machnery and other appliances, together with the cost of such machnery and other appliances, together with the cost of this proceeding, provided, however, that said assessment shall not exceed fifteen (15) per cent of the original assessment for the construction of the entire work within said district, and that it, together with all former assessments for construction and repairs, shall not exceed the estimate of benefits contained in the preliminary report as confirmed.

Section 1379—32. Whenever it shall become necessary for any corporation organized under the laws of the state for the purpose of constructing, maintaining and operating drains, ditches, canals or the like for the drainage and for reclaiming wet, submerged, overflowed and swamp lands, in order to promote the public health and welfare, to acquire any real estate for the purpose of constructing, maintaining or operating any canals, drains, ditches or the like, it may purchase the same with the approval of the court, or may acquire such real estate in the manner hereinafter provided.

Section 1379—32a. The provisions of Section 1379—11 to Section 1379—32a, inclusive, of this act shall be liberally construed to promote the public health or welfare by reclaiming wet or overflowed lands, building embankments or levees, and the preservation of any system of drainage heretofore constructed according to law.

Section 3. This act shall take effect and be in force from and after its passage and publication.

"EXHIBIT F."

A BILL.

To create sections 1498—21 to 1498—32, inclusive, of the statutes, create a conservation commission to direct and supervise the care and protection of forests, fish and game and drainage, and to render appropriations heretofore made of this act.

The people of the state of Wisconsin, represented in senate and assembly, do enact as follows:

SECTION 1. There are added to the statutes twelve new sections to read:

SECTION 1498—21. A conservation commission, consisting of three commissioners and which shall be known as the Conservation Commission of Wisconsin, is hereby created, and shall be composed as follows:

(1) One member of such commission shall be a technically trained forester. Whether any candidate for this position is a technically trained forester shall be determined by a certificate from the secretary of the United States department of agriculture. Such commissioner shall, under the supervision of the commission, have special charge of all matters pertaining to forestry within the jurisdiction of the commission.

(2) One member of the commission shall have a general and special knowledge of matters relating to fish and game, and shall, under the supervision of the commission, have special charge of all matters pertaining to the protection, hunting and taking of fish and game within the jurisdiction of the commission. The state commission of fisheries shall furnish the governor with the names of at least five men whom it considers fitted to perform the duties hereby imposed upon such commissioner, and from such list the appointment shall be made.

(3) One member of the commission shall be a competent hydraulic engineer and shall also have a general and special knowledge of waterways and drainage and shall, under the

supervision of the commission, have special charge of all matters pertaining to waterways, drainage and lakes within the jurisdiction of the commission. The board of directors of the Wisconsin society of engineers shall furnish the governor with the names of at least five men whom it considers fitted to perform the dutes hereby imposed upon such commisioner, and from such list the appointment shall be made.

SECTION 1498—22. Immediately after the passage of this act the governor shall, by and with the advice and consent of the senate, appoint such commissioners. The term of one such appointee shall terminate on the first Monday in February, 1913; the term of the second such appointee shall terminate the first Monday in February, 1915, and the term of the third such appointee shall terminate on the first Monday in February, 1917.

SECTION 1498—23. In January, 1913, and bienially thereafter, there shall be appointed, as provided in Section 1498—22, one commissioner for the term of six years from the first Monday in February of such year. Each commissioner so appointed shall hold his office until his successor is appointed and qualified. Any vacancy in the conservation commission of Wisconsion, due to the resignation, removal or death of any commissioner or due to any other cause, shall be filled by appointment by the governor for the unexpired term, subject to confirmation by the senate, but any such appointment shall be in full force until acted upon by the state.

SECTION 1498—24. No commissioner, nor the secretary of the commission, hereinafter provided for, while holding such position, shall hold any other office or position or profit or trust, or pursue any other business or vocation, or serve on or upon any committee of any political party, but shall devote his entire time to the duties of his office.

SECTION 1498—25. Before entering upon the duties of his office, each of said commissioners, and the secretary hereinafter provided for, shall take and subscribe the constitutional oath of office, and shall in addition thereto swear (or affirm) that he holds no other office of profit; nor any position under any political committee or party; which oath, or affirmation, shall be filed in the office of the secretary of state.

SECTION 1498—26. The governor may at any time remove any commissioner for inefficiency, neglect of duty, or malfeasance in office. Before such removal he shall give such commissioner a copy of the charges against him and shall fix a time when he can be heard in his own defense, which shall not be less than ten days thereafter, and said hearing shall be open to the public. If he shall be removed, the governor shall file in the office of the secretary of state a statement of all charges made against such commissioner and his finding thereon, with the record of the proceedings.

SECTION 1498—27. The commission shall keepp its office at the state capitol, and the superintendent of public property is directed to provide suitable rooms for that purpose, also the necessary office furniture, supplies, postage and stationery. The commission is authorized to purchase the necessary field supplies, equipment and instruments, to procure printed forms and notices, and to issue special publications pertaining to its work, the cost of which shall be audited and paid the same as other expenses of the state are audited and paid. The commission may hold session at other places than the capitol, whenever in its judgment, the interest of the state can best be served by so doing.

SECTION 1498—28. In case of the necessary absence of one of the commissioners, a majority of the commission shall constitute a quorum to transact business, and it shall:

(1) Elect one of its members chairman.

(2) Appoint a secretary who shall keep a full and correct account of all transactions and proceedings of the commission and shall perform such other duties as may be required by the commission.

(3) Appoint and employ the necessary clerks and stenographers to perform the clerical work of the office, and appoint and employ such foresters, experts and employes as may be necessary to carry out the provisions of Sections 1498—21 to 1498—32 of the statutes. The commission shall fix the compensation of such clerks, stenographers, foresters, wardens, experts and employes. The experts and temporary employes shall be exempt from the operation of chapter 363, laws of 1905, and amendatory acts.

SECTION 1498—29. Each of the three commissioners provided for in Section 1498—21 shall receive an annual salary of five thousand dollars. The secretary shall receive an annual salary not exceeding fifteen hundred dollars.

SECTION 1498—30. 1. All duties, liabilities. authority, powers and privileges heretofore or hereafter imposed or conferred by law upon the state board of forestry and its members, and upon the state fish and game warden, are hereby imposed and conferred upon the Wisconsin conservation commission and its members; and such conservation commission shall have such further supervision and control over all matters pertaining to waterways, water reservoir systems, lakes, and the drainage of submerged or swamp lands as may hereafter be provided by law and shall have such other superivison and control over and pertaining to other matters as may be conferred upon such commission.

2. All duties, liabilities, authority, powers, and privileges heretofore or hereafter imposed or conferred by law upon the special or additional deputy game wardens, upon the county game wardens, upon the state fire wardens, trespass agents. and upon the assistant state forester, are hereby imposed and conferred upon the foresters, wardens, agents and assistants provided for herein, upon each thereof all such duties, liabilities, authority, powers and privileges.

3. All laws relating to said state board of forestry and its members, to the state forester, to the waterways commission and its members, to the fish and game warden, to all deputy. special and county game wardens, to the state, county and town fire wardens, to trespass agents, and to the assistant state forester, shall apply to and be deemed to relate to the commission hereby created and the officers hereby provided for so far as the said laws are appplicable.

4. All funds, apppropriations and moneys heretofore or hereafter made available by law for carrying out the purposes set forth in the laws creating. regulating, providing for, and relating to such state board of forestry and its members, such state forester, such waterway commission and its members, and such state fish and game wardens, and in the laws creating, regulating, providing for and relating to all clerks, employes. assistants, deputies, wardens. special and additional deputy wardens, county wardens. fire wardens, county or town fire wardens, trespass agents and assistant foresters and all funds. appropriations and moneys under the control of any such state board of forestry and its members, such state forester, waterways commission and its members, and such state fish and game wardens and all clerks, employes, assistants. depu-

ties, wardens, special and additional deputy wardens, county wardens, fire wardens, town fire wardens, trespass agents, and assistant foresters, shall be available to and under the control of the conservation commission of Wisconsin.

5. The special funds designated as the hunting license fund and the forest reserve fund; the annual appropriation contained in section 1494—62 of the statutes as it now exists or may hereafter be amended, and the annual appropriation of six thousand five hundred dollars made by chapter 429 of the laws of 1907, to carry out the provisions of sections 1797m, 1797n, 1797o, 1797p, 1797q, 1797r, 1797s, 1797u, and 1797v, of the statutes, are hereby transferred to and placed under the control of the conservation commission of Wisconsin and made available to carry out the provisions of sections 1498—21 to 1498—32 of the statutes.

6. All laws relating to the collection, carrying, transfer, custody and disbursement of said funds, appropriations and moneys, or relating to any clerical or ministerial act involved in such collection, carrying, transfer, custody and disbursement thereof, shall apply to the collection, carrying, transfer, custody and disbursement of said funds when under the control of the conservation commission of Wisconsin.

7. Any amendment hereafter made relative to the duties, liabilities, authority, powers and privileges of or relative to funds, appropriations and moneys available to or under the control of any of the commissioners or officers named in this section, including the state land office, shall be deemed to relate to the duties, liabilities, authority, powers and privileges imposed and conferred upon the conservation commission of Wisconsin hereby created and the officers herein provided for, and to the funds, appropriations and moneys available to or under the control of such commission and officers herein created and provided for.

SECTION 1498—31. All acts and parts of acts conflicting with the provisions of this act are repealed in so far as they are inconsistent herewith.

SECTION 1498—32. This act is hereby declared to be a public act and for the accomplishment of public purposes and shall be favorably construed to the accomplishment of said purposes.

SECTION 2. This act shall take effect and be in force from and after its passage and publication.

EXHIBIT 1.

ANALYSIS OF THE FRANCHISES

FOR THE

CONSTRUCTION OF DAMS

BY THE

LEGISLATURE OF WISCONSIN.

TOWN, VILLAGE AND CITY GRANTEES.

By M. C. Riley, January, 1910.

ANALYSIS OF THE FRANCHISES FOR THE CONSTRUCTION OF DAMS BY THE LEGISLATURE.

Town, Village and City Grantees.

Citation.	Grantee.	Stream, Location, County.	Duration of grant.	Purposes.
'46,p. 140	Madison, village of.	Catfish. At outlet of Fourth lake.	No limit.	Improvement navigation and hydraulic.
'75,353 '76,231	Eau Claire, city of.	Chippewa river. Within limits of said city. Eau Claire county.	No limit	For water power.
'87,447 '85,434	Milwaukee, city of.	Milwaukee river. Between Racine St. and Humboldt Ave. Milwaukee. Co.	No limit	Hydraulic and sanitary.
91.277	Kilbourn city....	Wisconsin river.	No limit	Water works other municipal purposes and improvement of navigation.
'91,284	Town of Newport, Columbia Co.	Wis. river. In town of Newport. Columbia Co.	No limit	Protect'ng highways & improvement of navigation.
'07· c. 35* '03· 59	City of EauClaire	Chippewa river Below mouth of Eau Claire. Eau Claire Co.	No limit	Improvement of navigation to improve sanitary conditions of city. for electric lighting. water works, etc.
'05· 11	Village of Spooner.	Yellow river. N W. qr of S. E qr. Sec. 31. T. 39 N.,R. 12 W. Washburn Co.	No limit	To operate system of water works & electric lights.
'05· 470	City o' Greenwood,	Black river. Sec. 34 T. 27. R. 2 W. Clark Co.	No limit	Lighting. heating, plumbing etc
'05, 483	Town of Eagle River.	Wisconsin river. Government lots 7 and 8, Sec. 36, T. 40 N.,R. 9 E. Town of Eagle River. Vilas Co.	No limit	Lighting. waterworks. etc.
'07, c. 590	City of Washburn.	Sioux river. N. hf of N. E. qr, Sec. 19, T. 49 N., R. 4 W. Bayfield Co.	No limit	General municipal purposes.
'07, 58	City of Ashland.	White river. W hf of N. E. qr Sec 34. T. 47 N., R. 4 W. Ashland Co.	No limit	General municipal purposes.

*Height of dam, eminent domain, leasing of power, etc.

ANALYSIS OF THE FRANCHISES FOR THE CONSTRUCTION OF DAMS BY THE
LEGISLATURE—Continued.

Town, Village and City Grantees.

Protection of navigation.	Miscellaneous purposes.	Eminent domain.	Reserve clause.	Fish-ways.
Provides for slides.	Right to lease power.	Not granted.....	No................	Yes,
Slides for logs, etc. Locks for boats.	Right to lease power for hydraulic purposes.	Not granted, ...	No................	No.
None............	None............	Granted..........	Yes..............	No.
None............	Proposition to be left to vote of people.	Granted as per mill dam act.	No................	No.
None............	None.............	Granted as per mill dam act.	No................	No.
Slides for logging. etc.	May lease excess power for period not to exceed 22 years.	Granted..........	Yes............	Yes.
None............	None............	Granted as per mill dam act.	Yes..............	Yes.
Slides for logging, etc.	Sec. 350, '05.grant to W. H. Dick to be constructed within 4 years.	Granted..........	Yes............ ..	Yes.
Slides for logging etc.	Sec. 350, '05.grant to W. H. Dick to be constructed within 4 years.	Granted..........	Yes..............	Yes.
Slides for logs. etc.	May let excess power for any lawful private purpose for not longer than 10 yrs.	Granted..........	Yes..............	Yes.
Slides for logs, etc.	May lease excess power for any lawful private purpose, for not more than 10 yrs.	Granted..........	Yes..............	Yes.

EXHIBIT 2.

ANALYSIS OF THE FRANCHISES

FOR THE

CONSTRUCTION OF DAMS

BY THE

LEGISLATURE OF WISCONSIN.

CORPORATE GRANTEES.

By M. C. Riley, January, 1910.

ANALYSIS OF THE FRANCHISES FOR THE CONSTRUCTION OF DAMS BY THE LEGISLATURE OF WISCONSIN, CORPORATE GRANTEES.

Citation.	Grantee.	Stream, Location, County.	Duration of grant.	Purposes.
(1)	Wm. Dickinson, et al.	Fox river. Rapids des Peres. Brown Co.	No limit.........	Hydraulic........
'38, 95	Rochester & Des Moines Hydraulic and Mfg. Com'y. (corp.)	Des Moines river near Rochester.	No limit.........	Hydraulic........
'39, 57	Milwaukee Mfg. & Hydraulic Co. (corp.)	Milwaukee frac. Sec. 21, T. 7 N., R. 22 E. Mil. Co.	No limit.........	Hydraulic........
'43, p. 68 '40, p. 7	W. H. Bruce, et al.	Manitowoc river. Manitowoc Co. Secs. 23, 25 and 26, T. 19, R. 23 E.	No limit.	Hydraulic........
'42, p. 26	Fox River Improvement Com'y (corp.)	Fox river. Depere to La Fontaine.	No limit.........	Improvement of navigation.
'43, p. 17	Prairieville Mfg. Co. (corp.)	Any stream in town of Prairieville. Milwaukee Co.	No limit.........	Hydraulic........
'45, p. 9 '46, p. 26	Wisconsin river navigation Com'y (corp.)	Wisconsin river. Below Little Bull Falls. S. E. qr S. 29, T. 27 N., R. 7 E.	No limit.........	Improving navigation.
'46, p. 201	Carrollton Mfg. Co. (corp.)	Any stream. Within Sec. 28, T. 15 N., R. 23 E. Sheboygan Co.	No limit.........	Hydraulic........
'50. 94* '54. 87 '55. 100	Ira Miltimoore.	Rock river. Sec. 21, 22, 27, 28, T. 2, R. 12 E. Rock Co.	No limit..... ..	Hydraulic........
'50. 257	Upper Wis. navigation improvement Co. (Corp.)	Wisconsin river. From point Boise to main fork of said river next above the Beaulieux rapids.	No limit.........	Improvement of navigation.
'52. 87	Appleton Water-power Co. (corp.)	On any land owned or leased by Co. No. particular stream or streams designated.	No limit.........	Hydraulic........

(1) Mich. Terr. Laws Vol. III, p. 1355, 1835, 14, '36 and 33, '38 incorporates Co. to complete work.
* Transferred to Afton manufacturing company (corp.)

ANALYSIS OF THE FRANCHISES FOR THE CONSTRUCTION OF DAMS BY THE LEGISLATURE OF WISCONSIN, CORPORATE GRANTEES—Continued.

Protection of navigation.	Miscellaneous provisions.	Eminent domain	Reserve clause	Power
Lock for boats. etc.	None............	Granted..........	Yes..............	No.
Dam not to extend across main channel of stream	None............	Not granted.....	Yes..............	No.
Slides for logs, etc., and lock for boats.	Property owners on opposite side of river may use power on that side upon payment to said Co. of one-half the cost of the dam and lock.	Granted..........	Yes..............	Yes.
Locks if river make navigable for boats and large above said dam— free. Slide for timber.	None............	Not granted.	Yes..............	No.
Locks for boats. etc.	None............	Granted..........	Yes..............	No.
None............	Mill dam act supplies.	Granted..........	Yes..............	No.
Locks when necessary. Slides for timber, etc.	Work to be commenced within 1 and completed within 2 years.	Not granted.....	Yes..............	No.
None............	None............	Not granted.....	Yes..............	No.
Slide for timber. Locks as soon as river made navigable for boats.	Right to sell or lease. Right to use power.	Not granted ...	Yes..............	Yes.
None............	Power of using or leasing the water power created by such improvements.	Not granted.....	No..............	No.
None............	None............	Not granted....	No............	No.

9

ANALYSIS OF THE FRANCHISES FOR THE CONSTRUCTION OF DAMS BY
THE LEGISLATURE OF WISCONSIN, CORPORATE GRANTEES—Continued.

Citation.	Grantee.	Stream, Location, County.	Duration of grant.	Purposes.
'52, 391	Waukesha Mfg. Co. (corp.)	On land owned or leased by Co. No particular stream or streams designated.	No limit.........	Hydraulic........
'53, 30* '54, 28 '54, 341 '66, 171* '68, 394* '76, 298 '78, 236	Wisconsin river improvement Co. (corp.)	Wis. river. From Stevens Point to point Bass. Portage Co.	No limit.........	Improvement of navigation.
'53, 81*	Hartfort Iron Co. (corp.)	On any land owned or leased by Co. No particular stream or streams designate.	No limit.........	Hydraulic.......
'54, 95*	Washington Iron Co. (Corp.)	On any land which may hereafter be loaned or leased by said Co.	No limit.........	Hydraulic...... ..
'54, 133*	Horicon Iron & Mfg. Co. (corp.)	On any land which may hereafter be owned by said company, also authorized to maintain dam already across Rock river. At village of Horicon. Dodge Co.	No limit.........	Hydraulic & improvement of navigation.
'54, 274*	Richland Mfg. Co. (corp.)	On any land owned or leased by Co. In Richland Co.	No limit.........	Hydraulic........
'54, 331*	Beaver Dam Mfg. Co. (corp.)	On land owned by Co. Authorized also to maintain upper dam across Beaver Dam creek. Village of Beaver Dam.	No limit.........	Hydraulic and Improvement of of navigation.
'55, 50*	Appleton water power Co. (corp.)	On any land owned or leased by Co. No streams designated.	No limit.........	Hydraulic........
'55, 330	Wisconsin river Hydraulic Co. (corp.)	Wis. Sec. 9, 10 and 15, T. 12 N., R. 6 E. Columbia and Sauk Co.	No limit.........	Hydraulic boomage, etc.
'56, 294 '68, 304 '89, 53	Pokoosa Lumbering Co. (corp.)	Wis. T. 21, R. 5 E. Portage Co.	No limit.........	Facilitate log driving.
'56, 405* '65, 286 '66, 509	Chippewa river Improvement Co. (corp.)	*All bayous and sloughs that make out of the Chippewa river.	No limit.	Improvement of navigation.

ANALYSIS OF THE FRANCHISES FOR THE CONSTRUCTION OF DAMS BY THE LEGISLATURE OF WISCONSIN, CORPORATE GRANTEES—Continued.

Protection of navigation.	Miscellaneous provisions.	Eminent domain.	Reserve clause.	Fishways.
None............	None............	Not granted.....	No............ ...	No.
None............	None............	Granted.........	Yes.............	No.
None............	None............	Not granted.....	No...............	No.
None............	None............	Not granted.....	No...............	No.
...ide for passage of rafts, etc.	May lease or sell surplus water power created.	Granted.........	No............ ...	Yes.......
None............	None....	Not granted.....	No...............	No.
...les for passage of timber.	May lease or sell for grist or saw mills, or for other mfg. purposes, any surplus water created by said dams.	Granted.........	No...............	Yes.
None............	None............	Not granted.....	No...............	No.
...les for logs locks for ...ts.	None............	Granted.........	No...............	No.
...les for logs.	None............	Not granted.....	No...............	No.
None............	County board authorized to aid and levy tax therefor.	Not granted.....	No...............	No.

ANALYSIS OF THE FRANCHISES FOR THE CONSTRUCTION OF DAMS BY
THE LEGISLATURE OF WISCONSIN, CORPORATE GRANTEES—Continued.

Citation.	Grantee.	Stream. Location. County.	Duration of grant.	Purposes.
'56, 481*	Apple River Dam Co. (corp.)	Apple river. Sec. 33, T. 33 N., R. 16 W. Polk Co.	12 yrs.	Facilitate log driving.
'57, 91*	St. Croix Mfg. & Imp. Co.	St. Croix river. (One or more dams) above head of steamboat navigation.	No limit.	Facilitate logging.
'57, 170* '80, 34* '68, 398* '69, 186* '71, 116* '73, 12 '73, 131 '74, 294 '81, 44 '82, 156	Yellow River Imp. Co. (corp.)	Yellow river. In Wood and Juneau Counties.	No limit.	Improvement of navigation and logging.
'57*	Suamico Lumbering Co. (corp.)	On any lands of said Company. No streams named.	No limit	Facilitate logging.
'57, 235* '62, 72	Chippewa Falls Lumbering Co. (corp.)	Chippewa river (on one or more dams) T. 28 N., R. 8 W. Chippewa Co.	No limit.	Imp. of nav. logging.
'57, 233*	Beloit Imp. Co. (corp.)	On land now or hereafter to be owned by Co. No stream named.	No limit.	Hydraulic. . . . . .
'57, 382	Shawano Mfg (corp).	At outlet of Shawana Lake and and at Red River where empting into Wolf river.	No limit.	Improvement of navigation.
'59, 133* '60, 59* '61, 26* '63, 146* '65, 139* '66, 320* '67, 122* '70, 93* '71, 242* '82, 13	Peshtigo Lumber and Mfg. Co. (corp).	Peshtigo river from mouth as far up as Co. is disposed to go.	No limit	Imp. of nav. and logging.
'59, 200*	Black River Imp. Co. (corp).	Black river above Shepherd & Valentine's mill.	20 years.	Imp. of nav. and logging.
'62, 35* '64, 157*	Eau Claire River L. D. Co. (corp).	Eau Claire river. no particular portion.	No limit	Imp. nav. an logging.
'64, 84* '66, 447* '80, 225 '82, 283	Black River Improvement Co. (corp)	Black river. Near its mouth. Clark, Trempeleau, Jackson and La Crosse Cos.	No limit.	Improve navigation & logging

ANALYSIS OF THE FRANCHISES FOR THE CONSTRUCTION OF DAMS BY THE LEGISLATURE OF WISCONSIN, CORPORATE GRANTEES—Continued.

Protection of navigation.	Miscellaneous provisions.	Eminent domain.	Reserve clause.	Fishways.
Flood gates for logs etc.	May collect toll.	Not granted.....	No......	No.
None.............	None.............	Not granted.....	No................	No.
None.............	Right to collect tolls.	Granted..........	No...............	No.
None	None.............	Not granted......	No......	No.
None....	None.............	Not granted......	No................	No.
None.............	None.	Not granted......	No................	No.
None.............	None.............	Granted..........	No................	No.
None.............	None.............	Granted......	No................	No.
...obstructed ...ration.	Charge toll......	Granted..........	No..........	No.
...le for logs.	None.............	Not granted......	No................	No.
None... ....,	None.	Granted..........	No................	No... .....

ANALYSIS OF THE FRANCHISES FOR THE CONSTRUCTION OF DAMS BY THE LEGISLATURE OF WISCONSIN, CORPORATE GRANTEES—Continued.

Citation.	·Grantee.	Stream, Location, County.	Duration of grant.	Purposes.
'64, 302* '68, 366* '77, 234†	Willow River Dam Co. (corp)	Willow river. T. 32, R. 15.	12 years..........	Facilitate logging.
'67, 26* '75, 147	Cedar Creek Hydraulic Co.	Cedar Creek. In Washington and Ozaukee Cos.	No limit..........	Hydraulic........
'67, 328* '73, 231	Eagle Rapids flooding, dam and boom Co. (corp)	Chippewa. Sec. 28, T. 29 N. R. 8 W. Eagle Rapids. Chippewa Co.	No limit....... .	Logging and Imp. of navigation.
'67, 145	Big Plover river log driving Co.	Big Plover river. General.	No limit..........	Improvement of navigation and logging.
'67, 334* '69, 413* '70, 186*	Lemonweir Improvement Co. (corp)	Lemonweir river. In Juneau, Monroe. and Jackson Cos.	No limit..........	Improvement of navigation.
'67, 408 '68, 260	Kinnickinnic. Slack water and Hydraulic Co. (corp)	Kinnickinnic. (From mouth to Village of River Falls). all in Pierce Co.	No limit..........	Improvement navigation.
'67, 454	Mechanics Union Mfg. Co. (corp)	Rock river. At Horicon. Dodge Co.	No limit..........	Hydraulic........
'67, 503* '68, 220* '75, 296 Repealed '82, 297	Wis. Mfg. Co. et al.	Little Wolf. S. E. ¼ of S. W. ¼ Sec. 8. T. 22 N. R. 14 E. Waupaca Co.	No limit..........	Logging and improvement of navigation.
'68, 430* '69, 108* '73, 259 '76, 45 '76, 366 '78, 206 '82, 134 continues 10 years Repealed	Apple River Log Driving Co,	Apple river and tributaries.	10 years..........	Log driving and improving of navigation.
'69, 76* '73, 207 '74, 106	Embarrass River Improvement Co. (corp)	Embarrass river. Above mouth of north fork. Sec. 8. T. 26, R. 14, Shawano Co. (Includes north fork of branch, middle fork of branch; south fork of branch.)	No limit..........	Improvement of navigation and log driving.

†Dam and rights transferred to C. Buckhardt 361, '69, 154 '82.

ANALYSIS OF THE FRANCHISES FOR THE CONSTRUCTION OF DAMS B THE LEGISLATURE OF WISCONSIN, CORPORATE GRANTEES—Continued.

Protection of navigation.	Miscellaneous purposes.	Eminent domain.	Reserve clause.	Fishways.
Keep gates of dams open for passage and sluicing of logs.	None............	Granted, subject to all provisions of mill dam act (ch. 56 R. S.)	No....	No.
None..............	None............	Granted	No..............	No.
Slide for logs, etc.	May collect toll.	Granted..........	No..............	No.
None............	May collect toll.	Not granted.	No..............	No.
None...........	May collect toll. state grants 12 secs. swamp land in above counties to company.	Granted..........	No............	No.
None.............	None............	Granted..........	No..............	No.
Slide for logs etc.	None...	Not granted except to state lands.	No..............	No.
Slide for logs, etc	May collect toll.	Not Granted.....	No...............	No.
None............	May collect toll	Not granted.....	No..............	No.
None............	May collect toll.	Not granted.....	No..............	No.

ANALYSIS OF THE FRANCHISES FOR THE CONSTRUCTION OF DAMS BY THE LEGISLATURE OF WISCONSIN, CORPORATE GRANTEES—Continued.

Citation.	Grantee	Stream, location, county.	Duration of grant.	Purposes.
'09, 86*	Union Lumbering Co. (corp)	Chippewa river and tributaries. Above steamboat navigation: Sec. 26, 33, 34, and 35 T. 29 N, R. 8 W. and secs. 2, 3, 4, 5, 6, 7, and 8, T. 28 N. R. 8 W. and secs. 11 and 12, T. 28, R. 9 W. Chippewa Co.	No limit..........	Hydraulic and log driving.
'69, 452* '70, 164* '71, 405* '76, 405 '77, 124 '78, 207 '85, 43 '85, 74 '83, 73 (Repealed Authority to dam Nimakogan river.) '87, 344 '89, 40	Nimakogan & Totagotic Dam Co.	Nimakogan river. T. 43 R. 6 W. Ashland Co. Totogatic river. Sec. 12, T. 42, R. 10 West Burnett Co. Eau Claire river. T. 44. R. 10 W. St. Croix river. Between mouth of Eau Claire and of Moose river. Yellow river. (4 dams) one at T. 40, R. 16 W. one at T. 39. R 14 W. one at T. 38, R. 13 W., one at T. 39. R. 12 W. Clam river. T. 39. R. 16 W. Nimakogan river. (2 dams) one at sec. 35, T. 41, R. 10, one at sec. 6, T. 41, R. 8.	15 years........ .	Improvement of navigation and log driving.
'70, 93*	Northeastern Improvement Co.	Peshtigo river. Between lower boundry of sec. 24, T. 32, R. 19 E. and upper boundary of sec. 10. T. 35 N., R. 17 E.	No limit.......	Improvement of navigation.
'70, 268*	Baraboo River Improvement Co.	Baraboo river. Between lower boundry of sec. 33, T. 12 N., R. 6 E.	No limit..........	Improvement of navigation.

ANALYSIS OF THE FRANCHISES FOR THE CONSTRUCTION OF DAMS BY THE LEGISLATURE OF WISCONSIN, CORPORATE GRANTEES—Continued.

Protection of navigation.	Miscellaneous purposes.	Eminent domain.	Reserve clause.	Fishways.
None............	None.............	Not granted.	No.................	No.
Must permit all ly driving to use dams.	May collect toll.	Granted...........	No................	No.
Passage at all times for boats, logs. etc.	May collect tolls, commence within 2 years, complete within 5 years.	Not granted.....	No................	No.
None.............	May close up sloughs and tributaries and may direct channel of river so as to connect with the Wisconsin at any point above city of Portage. May collect tolls for all boats. logs. etc. run through said improvement. Towns may subscribe. 1 year to commence. 10 years to complete.	Granted...........	No................	No.

ANALYSIS OF THE FRANCHISES FOR THE CONSTRUCTION OF DAMS BY
THE LEGISLATURE OF WISCONSIN, CORPORATE GRANTEES—Continued.

Citation.	Grantee.	Streams, Location, County.	Duration of grant.	Purposes.
'70, 480* '75, 226	Little Wolf river Improvement Co. (corp.)	Little Wolf river (7 dams, 4 flood dams and 3 may be flood or rolling dams) one at or near head of Cedar Rapids; one at or near Big Falls; one at or near Dells Rapids one at or near Reneer Rapids; three anywhere between Reneer Rapids and E. line sec. 1, T. 25, R. 10.	No limit..........	Improvement of navigation.
'71, 144*	Darlington Water Power Imp. Co.	Pecatonico river. Town of Darlington. La Fayette Co.	No limit..........	Hydraulic ....
'71, 241	Beloit water-power Co.	Black River (dam already erected). City of Beloit, Rock Co.	No limit........	Hydraulic .....
'71, 326	Huntington Mfg. Co. (corp.)	Apple River T. 31 N. R. 12 W. St. Croix Co.	No limit..........	Hydraulic ......
'71, 332*	Wagon landing dam and mill Co. (corp.)	Apple River T. 32 N., R. 17 W. Polk Co	No limit..........	Hydraulic ......
'71, 357*	Pine River Imp. Co. (corp.)	Pine River, from mouth where emptying into Wis. to mills in village of Richland Center. Richland Co.	No limit..........	Improvement of navigation.
'71, 467*	East Shioc Imp. Co.	East Shioc. E. ½ Secs. 7, 8 and 9. T. 25 N. R. 17 E.	No limit........	Imp. of nav. and log driving.
'71, 483*	White River Dam Log Driving & Boom Co. (corp.)	White River (dam or dams.) Towns 45, 46 and 47. Ranges 4, 6 and 7. Bayfield and Ashland Co.	20 yrs	Imp. of navigation and log driving.

ANALYSIS OF THE FRANCHISES FOR THE CONSTRUCTION OF DAMS B
THE LEGISLATURE OF WISCONSIN, CORPORATE GRANTEES—Continued.

Protection of Navigation.	Miscellaneous Purposes.	Eminent domain.	Reserve clause.	Fishways.
None............	May collect tolls for timber, etc. passing over dams.	Granted..........	No...............	No.
None............	None............	Not granted.....	No...............	No.
None............	None............	Granted as per mill dam act.	No...............	No
Slides for logs. etc.	None............	Not granted......	No...............	No.
Slides for logs. etc.	None............	Not granted....	No...............	No.
Locks............	Co. has exclusive right to carry property and persons on said river from mouth to Richland Center. Must establish and publish uniform tariff. All persons to have right to use river for navigation upon payment therefor.	Empowered to occupy and use banks (no provisions for payment to owners of banks).	No...............	No.
None............	May collect toll.	Not granted....	No...............	No.
Open channel at all times for rafts, logs, etc.	May collect toll Stockholder in Co. to have preference over others in the storage of their logs but are required to receive all logs or timber coming into White River and drive same.	Granted..........	No...............	No.

ANALYSIS OF THE FRANCHISES FOR THE CONSTRUCTION OF DAMS BY THE LEGISLATURE OF WISCONSIN, CORPORATE GRANTEES—Continued.

Citation.	Grantee.	Stream, location, county.	Duration of grant.	Purposes.
'71, 494*	Mill Creek Imp. Co. (corp.)	Mill Creek Wood & Portage Cos.	No limit	Facilitate log driving.
'71, 498*	Wausau Creek Imp. (corp.)	Outlet of Rush Lake. Town of Nepenskem, Winnebago, Co.	No limit	Hydraulic
'74, 288 '76, 375 '81, 163 '83, 95	Shaw, Daniel et al. (corp.)	Thorn Apple river branch of Chippewa.	No limit	Facilitate log driving.
.75, 169 '67, 257	Rounds, J. M. & Co. (corp.)	Little Wolf. N. W. ¼ of S. W. Sec. 15, T. 23 N. R. 13 W. Waupaca Co.	15 years	Facilitate log driving.
'75, 254	Holman Franklin, et al.	Rice Creek, (dam or dams) S. W. ¼ Sec. 21, T. 33 N. R. S. W. Chippewa Co.	No limit	Facilitate log and Imp. of navigation.
'75, 288	Greeley Elam, et al. (corp.)	Sand Creek. E. ¼ S. W. ¼ Sec. 5, T. 36 N. R 14 W., Barron Co.	15 years	Facilitate log driving.
'78, 113 act amended '76, 249	Trow, A. S. et al. (corp.)	Embarrass River,	No limit	Facilitate log driving.
'87, 29	Centralia Pulp & Water Power Co.	Wis. River Sec 24, T. 32 N. R. 5 E.	No limit	Hydraulic
'89, 77	Freeman & Fellows Lumbering Co. (corp.)	Four Mill creek, (dam and improve.) Burnett Co.	No limit	Facilitate log driving.
'93, 118 Amended act of '66, 424	Kilbourn Mfg Co. (corp.)	Wisconsin Secs. 3, 4, 9, and 10. T. 13 N. R. 6 E., Sauk and Columbia Cos.	No limit	Hydraulic
,93, 207	Meiklejohn & Co. (corp.)	Embarrass river. S. ¼ and N. W. ¼ frac. of N. E. ¼ Sec 5, T. 26 N. R. 13 E., Shawano Co.	No limit	Facilitate log driving.
'95, 98	Hickerson Roller Mill Co. (corp.)	Wood river N. W. ¼ of S. W. ¼ Sec. 14 T. 38 N., R. 19 W. Burnett Co.	15 yrs	Hydraulic and flooding.

ANALYSIS OF THE FRANCHISES FOR THE CONSTRUCTION OF DAMS BY THE LEGISLATURE OF WISCONSIN, CORPORATE GRANTEES—Continued.

Protection of navigation.	Miscellaneous purposes.	Eminent domain.	Reserve clause.	Fishways.
None............	May collect tolls.	Not granted....	No............	No.
None............	If dam does permanent injury to land on Rush Lake, it may be declared a nuisance in action brought in circuit court.	Granted.........	No............	No.
None............	May collect toll. Dam to be commenced within one and completed within two yrs.	Not granted....	No............	No'
Slides for logs, etc.	May collect toll.	Not granted...	No..........	No.
Slides for logs, etc.	May collect toll.	Not granted....	No............	No.
Slides for logs, etc.	May collect toll.	Not granted....	No............	No.
None............	May collect toll.	Not granted....	No............	No.
Slide for log.	None............	Not granted....	Yes............	No.
Slides for logs	May collect toll.	Granted.........	Yes............	No.
None............	None............	Not granted....	No............	No.
Slides for logs, etc.	May collect tolls; mill dam act applies.	Granted	Yes............	No.
Slide for logs.	Subject to mill dam act.	Granted as per mill dam act.	Yes	No.

ANALYSIS OF THE FRANCHISES FOR THE CONSTRUCTION OF DAMS BY THE LEGISLATURE OF WISCONSIN, CORPORATE GRANTEES—Continued.

Citation.	Grantee.	Stream, Location, County.	Duration of grant.	Purposes.
'96, 341	Butternut Waterpower Co. (corp.)	Butternut Creek.	No limit.........	Facilitate log driving.
'01. 300	Foster. Geo. E., Lumber Co. (corp.)	Pine river. Town of Pine River.Lincoln Co.	No limit........	Hydraulic......
'03, 24	St. Croix Falls, Wis. Imp. Co.	St. Croix River near village St. Croix Falls, Polk Co.	No limit...	Imp. of navigation and hydraulic.
'03, 26	Antigo Island Club.	Pelican River, outlet of Pelican Lake.	No limit	Imp. of navigation and protection of fish.
'03, 178	Cornell Land & Power Co.	Chippewa River, Sec. 18, T. 31 R. 6. W. Chippewa Co.	No limit........	Hydraulic......
'03, 180	Long Lake Imp. Co. (corp.)	Long Lake north shore. S. side gov't. lot 3, Sec. 18 T. 32 N. R. 8 W. Chippewa Co	No limit........	Imp. of navigation of Lake.
'03, 182	La Crosse and Black River R. R. Co. (corp.)	Black River lots 2 and 8. 1. T. 21. R. 4 W. Jackson Co.	Work to be commenced within 4 yrs.	Imp. of navigation and hydraulic. (Transmission of power.)
'03, 206	La Crosse and Northern Ry. Co. (corp.)	Black River lot 5, Sec. 1 or lot 7, Sec. 2, T. 18 N., R. 8. W. La Crosse Co.	No limit	Imp. of navigation and hydraulic. (Transmission of power.)
'05, 39	Stevens Point Power Co.	Big Plover River, N. E. ¼ Sec. 12, T. 24, N. R. ½. E. Portage Co.	No limit	Hydraulic......
'05, 408	Stolle Barnde Lbr. Co.	Big Some river; T. Sec. 4, T. 35 N. R. 4. E., Lincoln Co.	No limit	Imp. of navigation, logging and hydraulic.
'07, 329	Wausau Lbr. Co.	Big Rib river. Floating dams Sec. 30. T. 31 N. R. 4 E., Lincoln Co. Sec. 28, T. 32 N., R. 3 E. Taylor Co.	No limit	Facilitate log driving.
'07, 335 '09, 301 Private bridge.	Wis. Valley Imp. Co.	Tributaries of Wisconsin north of south line, T. 34 N.	No limit	Improve navigation of Wis. and Tomahawk rivers by system of reservoirs.

ANALYSIS OF THE FRANCHISES FOR THE CONSTRUCTION OF DAMS BY THE LEGISLATURE OF WISCONSIN, CORPORATE GRANTEES—Continued.

Protection of Navigation.	Miscellaneous Provisions.	Eminent domain.	Reserve clause.	Fishways.
Slides for logs, etc.	May collect toll.	Granted........	Yes.............	No.
Slides for logs, etc.	None............	Granted.........	Yes.............	Yes.
Slides for logs, etc.	May sell or lease power in whole or in part.	Granted.........	Yes.............	Yes.
None............	None............	Not granted....	Yes.............	Yes.
Slides for logs, etc.	None............	Granted.........	Yes.............	Yes.
None............	None............	Granted.........	Yes.............	Yes.
Slides etc. for logs.	None............	Granted.........	Yes.............	Yes.
Slides for logs etc.	Dam to be constructed within 6 yrs.	Granted.........	No.............	Yes.
None............	None............	Granted.........	Yes.............	No.
Slides for logs etc.	See C. 350, '05. grant to W. H. Dick to be constructed within 4 yrs.	Granted.........	Yes.............	Yes.
None............	None............	Not granted....	Yes.............	No.
Slides for logs, etc.	May collect toll, take over all dams, etc. exceptions stated.	Granted.........	Yes.............	Yes.

ANALYSIS OF THE FRANCHISES FOR THE CONSTRUCTION OF DAMS BY THE LEGISLATURE OF WISCONSIN, CORPORATE GRANTEES—Continued.

Citation.	Grantee.	Streams, Location, County.	Duration of grant.	Purposes.
'07, 405	Crivitz Pulp and Paper Co.	Peshtigo River, Sec. 24, T. 32 N., R. 19 E. Marinette Co.	No limit	Imp. of navigation and hydraulic.
'07, 549	Watertown Gas and El. Co. (successors of Calvin & Jas. Benton p. 37, '44.)	Rock River W. ½ Sec. 3, T. 8, R. 15. Jefferson Co.	No limit	Hydraulic ......
'07, 626	John Arpin Lbr. Co.	Chippewa, Sec. 10, T. 37, N. R. 7 W. Sawyer Co.	No limit	Imp. of navigation and hydraulic.
'07, 644	Beans Eddy Power Co.	Wisconsin Secs. 6, 7, and 8, T. 26 N., R. 7 E., Marathon Co.	No limit	Imp. of navigation and hydraulic.

ANALYSIS OF THE FRANCHISES FOR THE CONSTRUCTION OF DAMS BY
THE LEGISLATURE OF WISCONSIN, CORPORATE GRANTEES—Continued.

Protection of Navigation.	Miscellaneous Provisions.	Eminent domain	Reserv. 1. S. OWEN use	ays.
Slides for logs, etc.	See c. 350 '05. Construction to commence within 4 yrs.	Granted.........	Yes.............	Yes.
Slides for logs, etc.	See 350, '05· Approval of City of Watertown prerequisite.	Granted.........	Yes.............	Yes.
Slides for logs, etc.	See 350. '05. Work to be commenced within 2 yrs.	Granted.........	Yes..	Yes.
Slides for logs, etc.	Sec. 350, '05 (Reasonable. price question to be decided by jury in Circuit Court.) Instead of by arbitrators as in Sec. 7. Ch. 350, Laws of 1905.	Granted.........	Yes.....·........	Yes.

10

EXHIBIT 3.

ANALYSIS OF THE FRANCHISES

FOR THE

CONSTRUCTION OF DAMS

BY THE

LEGISLATURE OF WISCONSIN.

INDIVIDUAL GRANTEES.

By M. C. Riley, January, 1910.

ANALYSIS OF THE FRANCHISES FOR THE CONSTRUCTION OF DAMS BY THE
LEGISLATURE—Continued.

Individual Grantees.

Citation.	Grantee.	Stream, Location, County.	Duration of grant.	Purposes.
'38. 40 43. p. 68	Slaugter Wm. B. (Ind.)	Manitowoc river, Manitowoc Co., sec. 10, T.19 N. R. 23 E.	No limit	Hydraulic.
'39, 45	Charles F. H. et al	Rock River Johnson's Rapids. sec. 4, T 8, R. 15 E. Jefferson Co.	No limit	Hydraulic.
'39,49	Albert E. Ellis. et al.	Rock river sec. 6 or 7, T 11, R. 16 E. Dodge Co.	No limit	Hydraulic.
'41.68 '43,61 (locks required)	Samuel H.Farnsworth. (Ind.)	Menominee river. So. branch, Brown Co.,	No limit	Hydraulic.
'41.69	Wm. P. Owen. (Ind.)	Rock river Jefferson Co. sec. 19, T. 8, R 16.	No limit	Hydraulic.
'42. p. 8	Asa Clark.(Ind.)	Outlet of Pewaukee Lake S. W. ¼ sec. 9. T. 7 N. R 19 E, Waukesha Co.	No limit	Hydraulic.
'42. p. 84 '52,20 (All rights transferred to Jones & Arodt)	George Lurwick. (Ind.)	Oconto river Brown Co. lots 6 and 7, sec. 24. T. 28, R. 21 E.	No limit	Hydraulic.
'42, p. 83	James H. Rogers et al. (Ind.)	Milwaukee river. Milwaukee Co. Spring St. to Wisconsin St.	No limit	For passage over streams.
'42, p. 9 '47, p. 17	Kendall D. G. et al.	Rock river Jefferson Co. sec. 2 or 11, T. 6, R. 14 E.	No limit	Improvement of navigation; hydraulic.
'42, p. 11 '43, p. 68	Oliver C. Hubbard. (Ind.)	Manitowoc river, Manitowoc Co. Lots 4 and 7. sec. 23, T. 19 E, R. 23 E.	No limit	Hydraulic.
'42, p. 44	Lucius I. Barber and E.G. Darling. (Ind.)	Crawfish, Jefferson Co. sec. 11, T. 6 R. 14 E.	No limit	Improvement of navigation and hydraulic, locks to be constructed where dam is located.
'43, p. 21 '54, 150 (Repealed requirements for locks and slides)	Henry Thien.	Milwaukee river, Washington Co. N. W. Frac. ¼ sec. 23, T. 9 N. R. 21 E.	No limit	Hydraulic.

ANALYSIS OF THE FRANCHISES FOR THE CONSTRUCTION OF DAMS BY THE LEGISLATURE—Continued.

Individual Grantees.

Protection of Navigation.	Miscellaneous purposes.	Eminent domain.	Reserve clause.	Fishways.
Provides for locks free.	None...... ...	Granted..........	Reserves the right to amend or to further improve navigation.	No.
Locks when Rock river becomes navigable.	Grantees subject to all laws made for protection of fish and navigation.	Not granted	Yes...	Yes.
Locks for boats. etc.	None.........	Not granted......	Alter or amend at any time so as to facilitate navigation of said river.	Yes.
Provides for lock for boats when-ever river is made navigable there-for free.	None....·..........	Not granted......	Yes.............	Yes.
Provides for locks for boats when-ever river is made navigable there-for.	None.....	Not granted	Yes.............	Yes.
None	Provision of mill dam act applies.	Granted as per mill dam act.	No...............	No.
Slides for logs. etc.	Mill dam act ap-plies.	Granted as per mill dam act.	Yes....,........	No.
Must not hamper navigation	None.............	Not granted.....	Yes.............	No.
Provides for locks free and for a chute for tim-ber.	Mill dam act ap-plies.	Granted as per mill dam act.	Yes	Yes.
Provides for locks for boats whenever river is made navigable therefor	Mill dam act ap-plies.	Granted as per mill dam act.	Yes.............	No.
Mill dam act applies.	Inserted as per mill dam act.	Granted as per mill dam act.	Yes.	Yes.
Locks provided for slides for tim-ber, etc.	Mill dam act ap-plies.	Granted as per mill dam act.	Yes..	No.

ANALYSIS OF THE FRANCHISES FOR THE CONSTRUCTION OF DAMS BY THE
LEGISLATURE—Continued.

Individual Grantees.

Citation.	Grantee.	Stream, Location, Count.	Duration of grant.	Purposes.
'43, p. 22 '45, p. 95	Levi Godfrey, et al.	Fox River, town of Rochester, Racine Co. sec. 11 and 2 T. 3, R. 19.	No limit............	Hydraulic........
'43, p. 32	Silas Peck, et al.	Fox river, Racine Co. sec. 32, T. 3 N. R. 19 E.	No limit..........	Hydraulic........
'43, p. 34 '51, 333 '57, 116	Clamden and Luke Stoughton. (Ind.)	Rock river sec.21, T. 4, R. 12, Rock Co.	No limit..........	Hydraulic. Right to sell or lease right to use power
'43, p. 25 '46, p. 116 '48, p. 13 '55, 355	Wm. H. H. Bailey et al (Ind.)	Rock river. sec. 36, T. 3 N. R. 12 E. Rock Co.	No limit..	Hydraulic. Right to sell or lease. Right to use power.
'43, p. 35 '51, 333 '57, 116				
'43, p. 35 '51, 333. '57, 116	Anson W. et al. (Ind.)	Rock river, sec. 14 and 15, T. 3 N. R. 12 E. Rock Co.	No limit..........	Improvement of navigation and hydraulic.
'43, p. 26	Ira Hersey et al. (Ind.)	Rock river. sec. 35 or 26 T. 1 N. R. 12 E.	No limit..........	Hydraulic........
'44, p. 36	David Jones and Erastus Bailey.	Peshtigo river, sec. 19, T. 30 N. R. 33 E. Marinette Co.	No limit..........	Hydraulic........
'44, p. 38	John P. Arndt.	Oconto River. S. E. ¼ sec. 30, T. 28 N. R. 21 E. Oconto county.	No limit..........	Hydraulic........
'44, p. 71	James Campbell and Thomas Stewart.	Sugar river, Green county, sec. 28, T. 3 N. R. 9 E.	No limit..........	Hydraulic.........
'44, p. 37	James H. Rogers	Milwaukee river, Milwaukee Co. S. W. frac. ¼ sec. 4. T. 7 N, R. 22 E.	No limit..........	Hydraulic........
'44, P. 37 '07, 549	Calvin M. and Joseph Bonton.	Rock River. Jefferson Co. (Dam previously constructed). W. ¼ sec. 3. T. 8. R. 15.	No limit..........	none specified ...
'45, p. 99	John Hustis.	Rock river, Dodge county. E.¼ sec. 9, T. 10 N. R. 16 E.	No limit..........	Hydraulic........

ANALYSIS OF THE FRANCHISES FOR THE CONSTRUCTION OF DAMS BY THE
LEGISLATURE—Continued.

Individual Grantees.

Protection of Navigation.	Miscellaneous purposes.	Eminent domain.	Reserve clause.	Fishways.
None.............	Mill dam act applies.	Granted as per mill dam act.	Yes...............	Yes.
None.............	Mill dam act applies.	Granted as per mill dam act.	Yes...............	Yes.
Provides for lock for boats and slides for timber and fish.	Mill dam act applies.	Granted as per mill dam act.	Yes...............	Yes.
Locks for boats and slides for timber etc.	Mill dam act applies.	Granted as per mill dam act.	No...............	
Locks and slides for timber etc.	Mill dam act applies.	Granted as per mill dam act.	Yes...............	Yes.
Locks for boats and slides for timber. etc.	Mill dam act applies.	Granted as per mill dam act.	Yes...............	Yes.
Object to amendment whenever river above dam is improved so as to admit of the passage of boats. slide timber.	Mill dam act applies.	Granted as per mill dam act.	Yes...............	No.
Slide for timber. etc.	Mill dam act applies.	Granted as per mill dam act.	Yes...............	No.
None.............	Mill dam act applies.	Granted as per mill dam act.	Yes...............	No.
Slides for timber etc.. and locks when necessary.	Mill dam act applies.	Granted as per mill dam act.	Yes...............	No.
Locks for boats and slides for timber, etc.	Mill dam act applies.	Granted as per mill dam act.	Yes...............	Yes.
Locks when necessary and slides for timber. etc.	Mill dam act applies.	Granted as per mill dam act.	Yes...............	Yes.

ANALYSIS OF THE FRANCHISES FOR THE CONSTRUCTION OF DAMS BY THE LEGISLATURE—Continued.

Individual Grantees

Citation.	Grantee.	Stream, Location, County.	Duration of grant.	Purposes.
'45, p. 104	Joachim Green-hogen.	Milwaukee river. Milwaukee Co. secs. 19 or 20, T. 8 N. R. 22 E.	No limit.........	Hydraulic........
'45, p. 100	Horace R. Jerome.	Menominee river Whites Rapids.	No limit..........	Hydraulic........
'45, p. 100	I. Cary Hall.	Menominee river - Lot 4, sec. 1, T. 32 N. R. 22 E. Brown Co.	No limit.........	Hydraulic...... .
'46, p. 93 '55, 155	None named.	Milwaukee river. Washington county. E ½ of N. E. ¼ sec. 25 T. 11, R. 21.	No limit	Hydraulic........
'44, p. 113	Abraham Brawley.	Wis. River. Portage Co. Between secs. 31 and 32, T. 24 N. R. 8 E.	No limit..........	Hydraulic ....
'47. p. 16	Lyman E. Boomer, et al.	Rock river. Jefferson Co. Secs. 8 and 9, T. 3 N, R 15 E.	No limit..........	Hydraulic ....
'47, p. 44, '51, 88 (2 frac. all rights etc. to John Werner.)	Eliphalet S. Miner, et al.	Wis. river. Grand Rapids. N. W. ¼ sec. 6, T. 22 N, R. 6 E.	No limit.........	Improvement of navigation.
'47, p. 46	William Jones...	Sugar river. Green Co. S. E. ¼, sec. 15, T. 2 N. R. 9 E.	No limit..........	Hydraulic.......
'47, p. 103	Michael Bratt....	Mil. river. Washington Co. Sec. 34, T. 12 N. R. 21. E.	No limit..........	Hydraulic.......
'47, p. 103	Phineas M. Johnson.	Mil. river. Washington Co. N. E. ¼, sec. 24, T. 10 N, R. 21 E	No limit..........	Hydraulic.......
'47, p. 103	Benjamin H. Mooers.	Mil. river. Washington Co. Sec. 25 T. 10 F., R. 21 E.	No limit........	Hydraulic ....
'47, 104, Repealed p. 130, '48.	Harvey Jones et al. (Ind).	Fox river. Sec. 21, and lot 3, 4, 7, 8, 9 and 10 in sec. 22, T. 20 N. R. 17 E.	No limit..........	Hydraulic ....
'47, p. 121	Samuel H. Farnsworth (Ind.)	Wolf river. (150 miles from mouth) on or between secs. 24, 25, T. 27 N. R. 15 E. Shawano Co.	No limit	Hydraulic.......

ANALYSIS OF THE FRANCHISES FOR THE CONSTRUCTION OF DAMS BY THE LEGISLATURE—Continued.

Individual Grantees.

Protection of Navigation.	Miscellaneous purposes.	Eminent domain.	Reserve clause.	Fishways.
Locks for boats, and slides for timber. etc.	Mill dam act applies.	Granted as per mill dam act.	Yes............... Yes...............	No. No.
Locks when necessary and slides for timber. etc.	Mill dam act applies.	Granted as per mill dam act.	Yes...............	No.
Locks when necessary. Slides for timber. etc.	Mill dam act applies.	Granted as per mill dam act.	Yes...............	No.
Slides for timber. etc.	Mill dam act applies.	Granted as per mill dam act.	Yes...............	No.
Slides for boats and timbers.	Mill dam act applies.	Granted as per mill dam act.	Yes...............	No.
Locks when stream made navigable for boats, and slides for timber. etc.	Mill dam act applies.	Granted as per mill dam act.	Yes...............	Yes.
Chute in dam across main channel.	Right to charge toll for timber passing through other than main channel dam.	Not granted.....	Yes...............	Yes.
None.............	Mill dam act applies.	Granted as per mill dam act.	Yes,.............	No.
Slide for timber. etc.	None	Not granted.....	Yes...............	No.
Slide for timber. etc.	None	Not granted......	Yes...............	No.
Slide for timber. etc	None	Not granted......	Yes...............	No.
Locks	Mill dam act applies.	Granted as per mill dam act.	Yes...............	No.
Slides for craft. timber. etc.	Mill dam act applies.	Granted as per mill dam act.	No...............	No.

ANALYSIS OF THE FRANCHISES FOR THE CONSTRUCTION OF DAMS BY THE LEGISLATURE—Continued.

Individual Grantees.

Citation.	Grantee.	Stream. Location. County.	Duration of grant.	Purposes.
'47· p. 179	Samuel Ormsby.	Sheboygan river. Sheboygan Co. Sec. 28, T. 15, R. 23.	No limit.........	Hydraulic ....
48. p. 38	Elisha Morran...	Oconto river. Brown Co. Lots 2 and 3. sec. 26 and lots 2 and 4, sec. 35, T. 28 N. R. 20 E.	No limit.........	Hydraulic ....
'48· p. 43	Joseph Carley and Benjamin Brown (Ind).	Milwaukee river. Washington Co. Sec. 6, T. 11, R. 21.	No limit.........	Hydraulic ....
'48· p. 68	C. C. Washburne and Cyrus Woodman (Ind.)	Pecatonica river. Green Co. Secs. 20 and 21, T. 1 N. R. 6 E.	No limit.........	Hydraulic ....
'48· p. 126	Barton Sallsbury	Milwaukee river. Washington Co. Sec. 12, T. 11 N. R. 20 E.	No limit.........	Hydraulic ....
'48· 129	Curtis Reed......	North branch Fox river (outlet of Winnebago) fraction of sec. 22. T. 20 N. R. 17 F.	No limit...... ..	Hydraulic ....
'48· p. 13 '50· 214	Ira Millimore et al.	Rock river. Secs. 1 and 2 N, T. 2, R. 12 E.	No limit.........	Hydraulic ....
'48· p. 139	Cicero Comstock and Chas. H. Williams (Ind).	Milwaukee river. Milwaukee Co. Secs. 4 and 5, T. 7, R. 22 E.	No limit.........	Hydraulic ....
'48. p. 142	J. Sprague Pardee.	Fox river. Columbia Co. Sec. 3, T. 12 N. R. 10 F.	No limit.........	Hydraulic ....
'48. p. 132	Samuel Young..	Pecatonica river. La Fayette Co. Sec. 1, T. 1, R. 5.	No limit.........	Hydraulic ....
'48· p. 83T	Wm. A. Barston.	Fox river. Frac. sec. 17, T. 15 N. R. 10 E.	No limit.........	Hydraulic ....
'48. 106 '67· 188	Edward S. Hanchett et al.	Pecatonica river. Green Co. Secs. 31 and 32. T. 1, R. 6 E.	No limit.........	Hydraulic ....
'48 S. p. 145 Repealed '58, 317	S. Norman Pratt.	Crawfish in Jefferson Co. Sec. 4. T. 7 N. R. 14 F.	No limit.........	Hydraulic ....

ANALYSIS OF THE FRANCHISES FOR THE CONSTRUCTION OF DAMS BY THE
LEGISLATURE—Continued.

Individual Grantees.

H. S. OWEN.

Protection of navigation.	Miscellaneous purposes.	Eminent domain.	Reserve clause.	Fishways.
None..............	Mill dam act applies.	Granted as per mill dam act.	Yes..............	No.
Free passage for rafts, crafts or boats."	Mill dam act applies.	Granted as per mill dam act.	No..............	No.
Free passage for rafts, timber, etc.	None............	Not granted.....	Yes..............	No.
Free passage for all ascending water craft.	Mill dam act applies.	Granted as per mill dam act.	No..............	No.
Free passage for rafts, timber, etc.	Mill dam act applies.	Granted as per mill dam act.	Yes..............	No.
None..............	Mill dam act applies.	Granted as per mill dam act.	No..............	No.
Locks where stream made navigable, for boats, slides for timber.	Right to use or lease right to use power.	Not granted.....	Yes..............	Yes.
Free passage of rafts, timber, etc.	Mill dam act applies.	Granted as per mill dam act.	Yes..............	Yes.
slides for craft and timber.	Mill dam act applies.	Granted as per mill dam act.	No..............	No.
Free passage for rafts, water crafts	Mill dam act applies.	Granted	Yes..............	No.
Locks............	Mill dam act applies. Right to sell or lease right to use power.	Granted as per mill dam act.	No..............	No.
Free passage for rafts, water craft.	Mill dam act applies.	Granted as per mill dam act.	No..............	No.
slides for timber, etc., locks where river is made navigable for boats.	Mill dam act applies.	Granted..........	No..............	Yes.

ANALYSIS OF THE FRANCHISES FOR THE CONSTRUCTION OF DAMS BY THE
LEGISLATURE—Continued.

Individual Grantees

Citation.	Grantee.	Stream, Location, County.	Duration of grant.	Purposes.
'48T. p. 9	F. William Allerding.	Milwaukee river. Frac. lots 2 and 3. sec. 4, T. 7 N. R. 22 E. Milwaukee Co.	No limit.........	Hydraulic.......
'48T. p. 44	George C. Daniels.	Milwaukee river. Town of Grafton. Washington Co. Sec. 1, T. 10, R. 21.	No limit.........	Hydraulic.......
'49T. 40	Day, Oscar......	Milwaukee river. Washington Co. Frac. lot 5, being the N. E. frac. of S. E. 4. sec. 10, T. 11, R. 31 E.	No limit.........	Hydraulic.......
'49. 78	Cyrus Curtis....	Rock river. Near Ft. Atkinson. Jefferson Co. Sec. 4. T. 5, R 14.	No limit.........	Hydraulic.......
'49. 200	John M. Keep...	Pecatonica. La Fayette Co. Sec. 3, T. 2 N, R. 3 E.	No limit........	Hydraulic.......
'50. 118	Pliney Pearce.	Manitowoc river. Manitowoc Co., lots 2 and 8, sec. 14, T 19, R, 23 E.	No limit.........	Hydraulic.......
'50, 120	James Catlin...	Fox river. Racine Co. Near S. line of sec. 33, T. 3 N. R. 19 E.	No Limit	Hydraulic.......
'50, 189	Thomas C. Snow and Charles Waldo.	Grand river. Marquette Co. Sec. 13, T. 14, R. 11 and sec. 7, T. 14, R. 12 E.	No limit.........	None specified...
'50, 277	Joshua F. Cox.	Fox river Rapids at Depere. (To complete improvements.)	No limit....	Improvement of navigation.
'51, 36	Richard H. McGoon	Pecatonica. La Fayette Co. Sec 20, T. 3 N, R. 3 E.	No limit	None specified...

ANALYSIS OF THE FRANCHISES FOR THE CONSTRUCTION OF DAMS BY THE LEGISLATURE—Continued.

Individual Grantees.

Protection of navigation.	Miscellaneous purposes.	Eminent domain.	Reserve clause.	Fishways.
Free passage for timber, etc.	Mill dam act applies.	Granted as per mill dam act.	No...........	No.
Free passage for raft, timber, etc.	None...........	Not granted.....	Yes............	No.
None.............	None...........	Not granted.....	No..............	No.
Slide for timber, etc.	None...........	Not granted	No..............	Yes.
Free passage for rafts and water crafts.	Mill dam act ap	Granted	Yes.............	No.
Slide for timber, locks where river is made navigable for boats.	None...........	Not granted.....	Yes	Yes.
Must not obstruct navigation.	None...........	Not granted....	Yes............	No.
None.	None...........	Not granted.....	No..............	No
None.	In consideration for Cox's completing improvement without cost to state, state grants to him the free use of all the surplus water created by the dam for hydraulic purposes. Cox to keep dam and locks in repair and shall at all times pass and repass boats, rafts, etc., free of charge.	Not granted.....	No..............	No.
Locks where river is made navigable for boats.	None...........	Not granted.....	Yes	Yes

ANALYSIS OF THE FRANCHISES FOR THE CONSTRUCTION OF DAMS BY THE
LEGISLATURE—Continued.

Individual Grantees.

Citation.	Grantee.	Stream. Location. County.	Duration of grant.	Purposes.
'51, 81 '55, 88	George W. Foster.	Milwaukee river. Washington Co. Sec. 29, T. 12, R. 21 E.	No limit..	Hydraulic... ...
'51, 126	Alvin B. Carpenter.	Sugar river. Rock Co. Sec. 20, T. I. N. R. 10 E.	No limit..........	Hydraulic.....
'51, 129 '62, 32 '93.190	Merrick Murphy.	Oconto river. Lots 2 and 7, sec. 34, T. 28, R. 20.	No limit	Hydraulic.......
'51, 173	Napoleon B. Millard and A. D. Bonesteel. (Ind.)	Little Wolf river. 2½ miles above Grignan's mill.	No limit	Hydraulic.......
'51, 203	Ebeniger Dakin.	White river. Marquette Co. Sec. 17, T. 17. R.11.	No limit....	Hydraulic improvement of navigation..
'51, 206	Harrison C. Hobart, et al.	Outlet of Long Pond. Fond du Lac Co. Secs. 25 and 26, T. 14 N. R. 19 E.	No limit....	Hydraulic.......
'51, 208	Charles Klingholtz.	Manitowoc river. Manitowoc Co. Lots 1, 2 or 3. sec. 26 T. 19 N. R. 23 E.	No limit····	Hydraulic.... ..
'51, 248 '54, 151	Henry Thien	Milwaukee river. Milwaukee Co. Lots 1 and 4. sec. 20, T. 8. R. 22.	No limit	Hydraulic......
'51, 259 Repealed '57, J59	Samuel George..	Pecatonica river. La Fayette Co. N. W. qr. sec. 1, T. 2 N. R. 3 E.	No limit··········	Hydraulic.... ..
'51,383	Ann Garrison. ...	Baraboo river, Sec 27, T. 12, R. 7 E. Sauk Co.	No limit....·......	Hydraulic.......
'52,59	Charles and Richard Klingholtz.	Manitowoc. Manitowoc Co. N E. ¼ sec. 16, T. 19 N., R. 23 E.	No limit...... ...	Hydraulic.......
52,76	Joseph Davenport.	Fox river. Onehalf sec. 30, T. 1. N. R. 20 E.	No limit	Hydraulic ....
52,116	Edward D. Beardsley.	Manitowoc, onehalf Manitowoc Co., lots 2 and 6, sec. 10, T. 19 N, R. 23 E.	No limit	Hydraulic ....
52,275	Frederick Davis.	Menomonee. Shioc. One mile above its junction wit h Wolf.	No limit ....—...	None specified...

ANALYSIS OF THE FRANCHISES FOR THE CONSTRUCTION OF DAMS BY THE
LEGISLATURE—Continued.

Individual Grantees.

Protection of navigation.	Miscellaneous Purposes.	Eminent domain.	Reserve clause.	Fishways.
None	Shall not flow lands of others.	Not granted.....	No...............	No.
None....	None.............	Not granted.....	No...............	No.
Slides for rafts and boats.	None.............	Not granted.....	Yes	No.
Slides for rafts and boats.	None.............	Not granted.....	Yes	No.
None............	None.............	Not granted.. ...	No...............	No.
None......	None.............	Not granted.....	No...............	No.
None.............	Must not over-flow lands of others.	Not granted.....	No...............	No.
Slides for timber. locks where river is made navigable for boats.	None.............	Granted	Yes	No.
Slide for rafts and watercrafts.	None.............	Not granted.....	Yes	No.
Slide provided for rafts. Locks wherever river is made navigable for boats.	Right to sell or lease right to use power.	Not granted.....	Yes	No.
None.............	None.............	Not granted.....	No...............	No.
None......	None.............	Granted	No...............	No.
Slides for timber	None...:....	Not granted.....	Yes	No.
Slides for timber. etc.	None.............	Not granted.....	Yes	No.

ANALYSIS OF THE FRANCHISES FOR THE CONSTRUCTION OF DAMS BY THE LEGISLATURE—Continued.

Individual Grantees.

Citation.	Grantee.	Stream. Location. County.	Duration of grant.	Purposes.
'52.403	John M. Sewood.	Grand river. (N. W. qr. sec. 14. T. 14. R. 12.)	No limit	None specified...
'52.501	John B. Sewood..	Grand river. Sec. 7, T. 14. R. 13. Green Lake.	No limit	None specified...
'53, 23*	Peter Bender et al.	Milwaukee river. N. E. sec. 30 T. 8 N., R 22 E. Milwaukee Co.	No limit	Hydraulic.......
'53,141*	William Duntan.	Wisconsin river. N. E. qr of S. E. qr sec. 8, T. 23 N. R. 8 E..	No limit	None specified...
'53.152* '89.32	Luther Hanchett et al.	Wisconsin river. Frac. lot 8 to frac. lot 9 sec. 30. T. 22 N., R. 5 E.	No limit	Hydraulic......
'53,177	Monroe Palmer	La Crosse river. N. E. qr of N. E. qr Sec. 34. & S. E. qr of S. E. qr Sec. 27, T. 17 N., R. 6W. La Crosse Co.	No limit	Hydraulic.......
'53.208 *'05.491 '05,177	Jacob Spalding. (City of Black river Falls. J. J. McGilloway successor).	Black river. E. E. qr of S. E. qr Sec 15, T. 21 N., R. 4. W. Jackson Co.	No limit (t) be constructed in 4 yrs).	Hydraulic.......
'53,212	Richard McGoon.	Pekatonico. Sec 27. T. 3 N., R. 3, E. La Fayette Co.	No limit...... ...	Hydraulic.......
'53.221	Nathan H. Wood.	Baraboo. Town of Caledonia.	No limit.........	None specified..
'53.226	Asahel W. Benham.	Fox river. on Sec 30. T. 1 N., R. 20. E. Kenosha Co.	No limit	None specified ..
'53.247	George Neaves. et al.	Wisconsin. Grand Rapids. Portage Co. Opp. Sec. 18. T. 22. R. 6, E.	No limit.........	Hydraulic......
'53,258	George J. Wright et al.	Wolf. At La Motte. Shawano Co.	No limit.........	None specified...

* (As to height of dam and imposes conditions upon grantees).

ANALYSIS OF THE FRANCHISES FOR THE CONSTRUCTION OF DAMS BY THE LEGISLATURE—Continued.

Individual Grantees.

Protection of navigation.	Miscellaneous purposes.	Eminent domain.	Reserve clause.	Fishways.
None............	None............	Not granted.....	No...............	No.
None............	None............	Not granted.....	No...............	No.
Locks as soon as river becomes navigable.	None............	Granted.........	No...............	No.
If dam or boom shall interfere with or obstruct or prevent of rafts, boats, same shall be deemed public nuisance.	Ch. 62 of laws of 1849 applies ("An act to prevent obstructions of the same Wis. river", etc.) ("How dams shall be constructed," etc.)	Not granted.....	No...............	No.
Slides and locks.	Right to sell or lease right to use power.	Not granted.....	Yes	No.
Free passage for rafts. etc.	None............	Not granted.....	Yes	No.
Shall be so constructed as to admit free passage of rafts. etc.	Sec 305. '05 grant to W. H. Dick.	Not granted......	Yes.............	Yes.
None............	None............	Not granted......	Yes.............	No.
Slides for timber. Locks where river rendered navigable for rafts.	Not to interfere with any water privileges now improved on said stream.	Not granted......	No...............	No.
None............	None............	Not granted......	No...............	No.
Slides for boats and rafts.	None............	Not granted......	No...............	No.
Slides for rafts. boat & water mills.	None............	Not granted......	No...............	No.

11

ANALYSIS OF THE FRANCHISES FOR THE CONSTRUCTION OF DAMS BY THE
LEGISLATURE—Continued.

Individual Grantees.

Citation.	Grantee.	Stream, Location, County.	Duration of grant.	Purposes.
'53,270 Repeal '60, 69	John Marshall et al.	Wisconsin. On N. hf Sec. 15, T. 13 N., R. 6, E.	No limit	Hydraulic........
'53,342	Ernest Prieger.	Honey creek. Spring St. road, Sec. 28, T. 7. R. 21. Milwaukee Co.	No limit.........	None specified...
'53,376 '73,187 Repealed '74, 10	John W. Stewart.	Pecatonica. Secs. 3, 4, 9 or 10, T. 1 N., R. 5, E. La Fayette Co.	No limit.........	Hydraulic......
'53,408	Evan Edwards.	North Duck Creek, N. W. qr Sec. 6, T. 12, N. R. 12, E. Columbia Co.	No limit.........	None ....
'54, 9	Charles Quentin et al.	Milwaukee river Sec. 31, T. 10 N., R. 22, E. Ozaukee Co.	No limit.........	Hydraulic........
'54, 82	Chas. Shuter et al.	Wisconsin river. T. 29 N., R. 7, E. Marathon Co.	No limit.........	None specified...
'54, 96	Jonathon Leighton.	Sheboygan river Between lots 2, 3 & 5, in Sec. 31, T. 15 N., R. 23, E. Town and County of Sheboygan.	No limit.........	Hydraulic........
'54,111	Joseph Goss......	Sugar river. Sec. 26, T. 2 N., R. 9, E. Green Co.	No limit.........	Hydraulic........
'54,140	Austin McCracken.	Grand River. Sec. 8. T. 14, R. 13. Marquette Co.	No limit.........	Hydraulic........
'54,231	Monroe Palmer.	La Crosse river. N. E. qr Sec. 34, & N. E. qr of S. E. hf Sec. 27. T. 17 N., R. 6, W. La Crosse Co.	No limit.........	Hydraulic........
'54,250	John J. Jarvis...	Baraboo river. S. E. qr of S. E. qr Sec. 29, T. 12 N., R. 5. E. Sauk Co.	No limit.........	Hydraulic......
'54,275	Charles Klingholtz.	Manitowoc river. Lot 1, Sec. 26, T. 19 N., R. 23, E. Manitowoc Co.	No limit.........	Hydraulic.......
'54,249 '64,264 '67, 99 '68,112	Swedes Iron Company. (Corp.)	On any land which may be hereafter owned or leased by Co. No stream specified.	No limit.........	Hydraulic.......

ANALYSIS OF THE FRANCHISES FOR THE CONSTRUCTION OF DAMS BY THE LEGISLATURE—Continued.

Individual Grantees.

Protection of navigation.	Miscellaneous purposes.	Eminent domain.	Reserve clause.	
Locks and slides for timber, boats, etc.	None	Granted	Yes	No.
None	None	Not granted	No	No.
Slides for timber, etc. Locks where river made navigable.	Not to interfere with any now erected. May sell or lease the right to use power.	Not granted	No	Yes.
None specified	None	Granted	No	No.
None	None	Not granted	No	No.
Not to obstruct	None	Not granted	No	No.
Free passage for water crafts, timber, etc.	None	Not granted	No	No.
Slide for timber, etc.	Right to sell or lease the right to use power.	Granted	No	No.
None	None	Not granted	No	No.
None	None	Not granted	No	No.
Slide for rafts & timber.	None	Granted	No	No.
Free passage for descending timber.	Shall not flow land of others.	Not granted	No	No.
None	None	Not granted	No	No.

ANALYSIS OF THE FRANCHISES FOR THE CONSTRUCTION OF DAMS BY THE
LEGISLATURE—Continued.

Individual Grantees.

Citation.	Grantee.	Stream. Location. County.	Duration of grant.	Purposes.
'55, 88	George W. Foster.	Milwaukee river. Sec. 28, T. 12, R. 21, E.	No limit.........	Hydraulic.......
'55,142	Silas D. Whitlock.	Rubicon(stream) S. W. qr Sec. 25. T. 10, R. 17. Dodge Co	No limit	Hydraulic.......
'55,144	George Rossman et al.	Rubicon(stream) N. E. qr Sec. 21. T. 10, R. 18. E. Washington Co.	No limit.........	Hydraulic.......
'55,149	Henry F. Belitz et al.	Sheboygan river. S. E. qr Sec. 30. T. 17 N.. R. 22. E. Manitowoc Co.	No limit.........	Hydraulic.......
'55,186	Thomas W. Baker et al.	Manitowoc river. Sec. 10. T. 19 N., R. 23. E. Manitowoc Co.	No limit.........	Hydraulic......
'55,188 Repealed '79, 48	Ezra Wescott....	Peckatonica river. Sec. 1, or 2. T. 1 N.. R. 4. E. La Fayette Co.	No limit.........	Hydraulic.......
'55, 214	Jacob Ten Eyck.	Sugar river. Secs. 2 & 3. T. 1. R. 9. E. Green Co.	No limit.........	Hydraulic......
'55,228	John M. Crawford	Baraboo river, sec. 20, T. 12 N.. R. 9. E town of Calidonia.	No limit.........	none specified...
'55,251	John H. Knapp, et al.	Red Cedar river, lot 1. sec. 24. T. 26, R. 13. W. Dunn Co.	No limit.........	Hydraulic.......
'55,288	C. D. Gordan.....	Mullett river at outlet of Mullet Lake. hf Fond du Lac Co.	No limit.........	Hydraulic.......
'55,313	Thomas, J. L. V.	Bass Creek. sec. 14, T. 2. R. 11 E.	No limit.........	Hydraulic.......
'55,325	Caleb S. Ogden, et al.	St. Lawrence creek. sec. 22, T. 23. N.. R. 12 E. Waupaca Co	No limit.........	Hydraulic.......
'55,361	Joel Bishop.....	Baraboo river, N. W. qr. sec. 35. T. 14, R.. 2 E Adams county.	No limit............	Hydraulic.......

ANALYSIS OF THE FRANCHISES FOR THE CONSTRUCTION OF DAMS BY THE LEGISLATURE—Continued.

Individual grantees.

Protection of navigation.	Miscellaneous purposes.	Eminent domain.	Reserve clause.	Fishways.
None	None	Not granted	No,	No.
None	None	Granted	No	No.
None	None	Granted	No	No.
Free passage for timber and water rafts.	None	Not granted	No	No.
Free passage for descending rafts.	None	Not granted	Yes	No.
Lock for timber. Locks where public interest requires.	None	Granted	Yes	Yes.
Slide for rafts timber, etc.	None	Granted	No	Yes.
Slide for descending timber, rafts etc. Locks river rendered navigable.	None	Not granted	No	No.
Lock for boats, timber, etc.	None	Granted	No	Yes.
None	None	Granted	No	No.
None	May sell or lease right to use power	Granted	No	No.
None	None	Granted	No	No.
Slide for timber,	None	Granted	No	No.

ANALYSIS OF THE FRANCHISES FOR THE CONSTRUCTION OF DAMS BY THE
LEGISLATURE—Continued.

Individual Grantees.

Citation.	Grantee.	Stream, Location, County.	Duration of grant.	Purposes.
'55,385	Delos E. Durkee	Rubicon S. E. qr. sec. 35, T. 10, R.17 E. Dodge county.	No limit	Hydraulic
'56,58 '57,187	Joseph MacKay.	Baraboo river W. hf s c. 10. T. 12, R. 4 E. Sauk county.	No limit	Mill dam for the benefit and convenience of public and for the public good.
'56,80	William Carson, et al.	Clearwater river, S. W. qr. sec. 14, T. 27, R. 9 W. Chippewa Co.	No limit	Hydraulic
'56,136	Cyrus Woodmen	Kickapoo, T. 7 N., R. 4 W.	No limit	Hydraulic
'56,176	Milton M. Maughs.	Lemonweir river, S. hf of N. W. frac. qr sec. 7, T. 15 N, R. 4 E. Juneau Co.	No limit	For the benefit and convenience of the public and for the public good.
'56,305	George Smith	Little river, sec. 24, T. 28 N, R. 20E	No limit	None specified.
'56,308	Noah Daven	Bad Fish creek, N. E. qr sec. 1, T. 4 N., R. 10 E. Rock county.	No limit	Hydraulic
'56,353	Rufus Washburn	Milwaukee river S. hf sec. 34, T. 12 N. R. 21 E. Ozaukee Co.	No limit	Hydraulic
,56,376	Mortimer L. Sayles, et al.	White cre·k, S. W, qr. sec. 25, T. 6, R. 68 E. Waukesha Co.	No limit	Hydraulic
'56,397	Lloyd L. Lewis.	Flemming's crk. N. E. qr. sec. 24, T. 18 N. R. 7 W. LaCrosse Co.	No limit	Hydraulic
'56,511	George W. & John L. Brower.	No stream named, N. W. qr. sec. 35, T. 13 N. R. 13 E. Dodge Co.	No limit	Hydraulic

ANALYSIS OF THE FRANCHISES FOR THE CONSTRUCTION OF DAMS BY THE LEGISLATURE—Continued.

Individual Grantees.

Protection of navigation	Miscellaneous purposes.	Eminent domain.	Reserve clause.	Fishways.
None............	None............	Granted..........	No................	No.
None............	Commrs. to determine as to necessity and as to height, etc, of dam.	Granted..........	No................	No.
Slide for logs, etc.	None............	Granted..........	Yes................	No.
Slide for logs, etc.	None............	Granted..........	No................	No.
None............	Commrs. to determine as to necessity and as to height, etc. of dam.	Granted..........	No................	No.
None............	None............	Not granted......	No................	No.
None............	Right to sell or lease the right to use such wat r.	Granted..........		
None............	None............	Granted..........		
None............	None............	Granted,.........	No................	No.
None............	None............	Granted..........	No...........	No.
None............	Commrs. to determine as to necessity and as to eight. etc. of dam.	Granted..........	No................	No.

ANALYSIS OF THE FRANCHISES FOR THE CONSTRUCTION OF DAMS BY THE LEGISLATURE—Continued.

Individual Grantees.

Citation.	Grantee.	Stream, Location, County.	Duration of grant.	Purposes.
'57,99	Chas. L. Goomer et al.	Waupaca river. sec. 36, T. 22 N. R. 12 E. Waupaca C o.	No limit..........	Hydraulic......
'57,183	James and Robert Scott.	Fox river. sec. 14, T. 3 N. R. 19 E. Racine Co.	No limit..........	Hydraulic.......
'57,195	Henry Vol z......	Oconto river, lots 1 and 2, sec. 25, T. 28, R. 19. Oconto Co.	No limit.	None specified...
'57,237	Amoca Wilson...	Lemonwelr riv-er. sec. 7 and 8, T. 16 R. 3 E. Juneau Co.	No limit..........	Hydraulic.......
'57,318	E. W. Chapin.....	"Stream running through the place usually called Batavia, town of Scott, Sheboygan Co.	No liml	Hydraulic.......
'57,164	Rufus Andrews.	Oconto river, lot 3 of Sec. 23 an lot 4 of sec. 26, T. 28 R. 19. Oconto Co.	No limit.....	None sp cified...
'57,335	Newell Dustin...	Lemonwelr river E .hf of N. E. qr. sec. 16, T. 15 N. R. 4 E. Juneau Co.	No limit..........	None specified...
'57,360	Benj. F. Phillips.	Little Wolf river S. E. qr of sec. 8, T. 22 N. R. 14 E. Waur aca Co.	No limit	Improvement of navigation and lo. ging.
'57,167	Joseph MacKey.	Bara' oo river. W. hf, sec. 10, T. 12. R. 4 E. Sauk Co.	No limit..........	None specified...
'57.412	John C. Hall.....	No stream named. (W ¼ of N. W. ¼, sec. 4, T. 11 N. R. 14 E. Dodge Co.)	No limit	Hydraulic ......
'57,368	Wm. H. Gleason.	Flambeau river At falls, T. 35 N. R. 5 W.	No limit...... ...	None specified...
'58.278	James Hart	Patrick Creek, Secs. 26 & 35, T. 13 N. R. 16 E. town of Le Roy. Dodge Co.	No limit..........	Hydraulic ....

ANALYSIS OF THE FRANCHISES FOR THE CONSTRUCTION OF DAMS BY THE LEGISLATURE—Continued.

Individual Grantees.

Protection of navigation.	Miscellaneous purposes.	Eminent domain.	Reserve clause.	Fishways
Slide for timber. etc.	None	Granted	No	No.
None	None	Not granted	No	No.
Slide for logs. etc.	None	Granted	No	No.
Free passage for logs. rafts. etc.	None	Not granted	No	No.
None	None	Granted	No	No.
Slide for logs. etc.	None	Not granted	No	No.
None	None	Granted	No	No.
Slide for logs. etc. and channel to be kept unobstructed.	Phillips becomes successor to Robert Grignow who maintained dam at above point, by virtue of art. 9. treaty with Menomonee Indians, Oct. 18, 1848.	Not granted	No	No.
None	None	Granted	No	No.
None	Commrs. to determine as to necessity and as to height, etc. of dam.	Granted	No	No.
None	None	Not granted	No	No.
None	None	Not granted	No	No.

ANALYSIS OF THE FRANCHISES FOR THE CONSTRUCTION OF DAMS BY THE
LEGISLATURE—Continued.

Individual Grantees.

Citation.	Grantee.	Stream, Location, County.	Duration of grant.	Purposes.
'58, 254	Anson Bangs	Menomonee river. Sec 13, T. 2. R.22 E. Oconto Co.	No limit.........	Hydraulic ......
'59, 111	Isaac Ferris	Wisconsin river. Sec. 17. T. 23, R. 8 E. Portage Co.	No limit..........	Hydraulic ......
'60, 74	William Knowles	Peck a t o n i c a. Sec. 11, T. 1 N., R. 5 E. La Fayette Co.	No limit..........	Hydraulic.. ......
'61, 20	A. L. Flint.......	Makan River. Sec. 7, T. 16, R. 11 E. Marquette Co.	No limit..........	None specified...
'61, 36	John H. Knapp.	Red Cedar river. Lots 2 and 3, sec. 26, T. 28, R. 13 W. Dunn Co.	No limit..........	Hydraulic........
'61, 42	Burrage B. Downs.	Red Cedar river. Lots 2, 3, 5. 7 & 8 in sec. 34, T. 27. R, 13 W. Dunn Co.	No limit..........	Hydraulic........
'61, 52	Andrew Sheppard.	Black River. Lots 4 and 5, sec. 33, T. 21, R. 4 W. Jackson Co.	No limit..........	None specified..
'61, 59	J. R. Slauson, et al.	Scarboror river. Sec. 35, T. 24 R. 23. Kewaunee Co.	No limit.	None specified...
'61, 69	Henry W. Stillman.	Milwaukee river. S. ½ sec. 3, T. 11, R. 21 E. Ozaukee Co.	No limit.	Hydraulic ......
'63, 153	John Ehlers.....	Milwaukee river. S. W. ¼ Sec. 1, T. 8 N. R. 21 E. Milwaukee Co.	No limit.	Hydraulic ......
'63, 327	Alexander Morrill, et al.	Honey Creek. N. E. ¼ Sec. 17, T. 9 N., R. 6 E. Sauk Co.	No limit..........	Hydraulic ......
'63, 349	Isaac R. & D. A. Lawt n.	Kickapoo river. N. W. ¼ Sec. 6, T. 12 N., R. 2 W. Richland Co.	No limit	Hydraulic........
'64, 300	Adin Randall.....	Chippewa river. Sec. 30. T. 30 N., R. 7 W. Chippewa Co.	No limit	Hydraulic and logging.
'64, 325	John H. Knapp, et al.	Red Cedar river. At foot of Rice Lake, frac. lots 2 and 3, sec. 21, T. 35, R. 11 W. Dallas Co.	No limit	Hydraulic and logging.

ANALYSIS OF THE FRANCHISES FOR THE CONSTRUCTION OF DAMS BY THE
LEGISLATURE—Continued.

Individual Grantees.

Protection of navigation.	Miscellaneous purposes.	Eminent domain.	Reserve clause.	Fishways
Slide for logs.	None	Granted	No	No.
Slide for logs.	None	Not granted	No.	No.
Slide for logs.	Right to sell or lease the right to use water.	Granted	No	No.
None	None	Not granted	No	No.
Slide for logs.	None	Not granted	No	No.
Slide for logs.	None	Not granted	No	No.
Slide for logs.	None	Not granted	No	No.
None	None	Granted	No	No.
None	None	Not granted	No	No.
None	None	Granted	No	No.
None	None	Granted	No	No.
Slide for logs.	None	Not granted	No	No.
Slide for logs.	None	Not granted	No	No.
None	None	Not granted	No	No.

ANALYSIS OF THE FRANCHISES FOR THE CONSTRUCTION OF DAMS BY THE
LEGISLATURE—Continued.

Individual Grantees.

Citation.	Grantee.	Stream. Location. County.	Duration of grant.	Purposes.
'64,389	Satterlee Warden.	Pecatonica. Sec. 4. T. 1. R. 4 E. La Fayette Co.	No limit	Hydraulic.....
'65,319	Andred Tainter.	Chetack river. Lot 2. sec. 30. T 33, R. 10 W. Barron Co.	No limit	Hydraulic and logging.
'66.82 Repealed '67.426	Harvey T. Rumsey, et al.	Trempealeau river, from mouth, to west line of B. 5 in T. 22, Jackson Co.	No limit	Improvement of navigation.
'66,99	John H. Knapp, et al.	Red Cedar river. S. ¼ sec. 20. T. 29 N., R. 12 W. Dunn Co.	No limit..........	Hydraulic and logging.
'66,122 amend '72,115	Daniel A. Baldwin, et al.	Willow river. At its mouth. Hudson. St. Croix Co.	limit.........	Free log driving
'66.183 amend '72.44	Daniel & Charles Sylvester.	Crooked Creek & Sanders Creek. Secs. 26, 35 and 36. Town of Boscobel.	To be completed in 2 years.	Hydraulic and to be used for protection against fire and for such other purposes as Boscobel as trustees may determine upon.
'67,563	Henry Nachtway.	West Twin river. S. ¼ of S. W. ¼ Sec. 27. T. 21. R. 23. Manitowoc Co.	No limit..........	Hydraulic and logging.
'67.568	John C. French. et al.	Chippewa river. T. 30 N., R. 7 W. Chippewa Co.	No limit...... ...	None specified
'67.503 '68,220	John Heath......	Little Wolf. S. W. ¼ of S. E. ¼ sec. 8 T. 22 N., R. 14 E. Waupaca Co.	No limit..... ...	Logging and improvement of navigation.
'67.586 '81,188	James Meikeljohn.	Little Wolf. S. E. qr Sec. 34. T. 23 N.. R. 13 E. Waupaca Co.	No limit..........	Facilitate logging.
'67.587	J. P. More & Bro.	Little Wolf. N. E. qr of N. E. qr Sec. 1. T. 20 N.. R. 13 E. Waupaca Co.	No limit..........	Facilitate logging.
'68.376 amend '72.100	Geo. A. Gore.....	Apple river. Sec. 12, T. 32 N. R. 17 W.	15 years..........	Logging.... ..
'68,216	John Hasemann.	Big Rib river. N. E. qr of N. E. qr Sec. 26, T. 29 N. R. 5 E. Marathon Co.	No limit..........	Hydraulic... ..

ANALYSIS OF THE FRANCHISES FOR THE CONSTRUCTION OF DAMS BY THE LEGISLATURE—Continued.

Individual Grantees.

Protection of navigation.	Miscellaneous purposes.	Eminent domain.	Reserve clause.	Fishways.
...le for logs.	None............	Granted as per mill dam act.	No...............	No.
None	None............	Not granted......	No...............	No.
None............	Given exclusive right to navigation upon improved portion of, for 25 years.	Granted as per mill dam act.	No...............	No.
None	None............	Not granted.	No...............	No.
None	None............	Granted as per mill dam act.	No...............	No.
None............	None............	Granted..........	No...............	No.
None	None............	Not granted......	No...............	No.
...e for logs.	None............	Granted as per mill dam act.	No...............	No.
...e for logs.	May collect toll.	Not granted.	No...............	No.
...e for logs, etc	May collect toll.	Not granted....	No...............	No.
...e for logs, etc	May collect toll.	Not granted.....	No.....	No.
...e for logs, etc	May collect toll.	Granted as per mill dam act.	No...............	No.
...e for logs, etc	None	Not granted......	No...............	No.

ANALYSIS OF THE FRANCHISES FOR THE CONSTRUCTION OF DAMS BY THE
LEGISLATURE—Continued.

Individual Grantees.

Citation.	Grantee.	Stream. Location. County.	Duration of grant.	Purposes.
'68,265	James R. Buck-staff et al.	Little Wolf. Sec. 11, T. 23 N., R. 13 E.	No limit,	Flood dam for logging.
'68,461	James Bracklin et al.	Vermillion river. S. W. qr of S. W. qr Sec. 26. T. 34 N., R. 12 W. Dalles Co.	No limit,	Facilitate logging.
'68,489	John Fitzgerald et al.	Lyndon Creek. Town of Kildare. Juneau Co.	No limit,	Hydraulic........
'68,302	W. A. A. Perkins	Bogus Creek. T 23 N. R. 15. Pepin Co.	10 years..........	Pisciculture.....
'69,223	Gustavus Lawrence et al.	Streams connecting White Clay & Mud Lake & Mud Lake & Shawano Lake. Shawano Co.	No limit..........	To improve navigation -log driving.
'69,290	E. R. Murdock..	Embarrass river. Lot 3, Sec. 19. T. 26, R. 15 E. Shawano Co.	No limit..........	To improve navigation and log driving.
'69,361	Christian Buckhardt.	Willow river. At falls St.Joseph. St. Croix Co. Dam formerly owned by Willow River Dam Co.	No limit..........	Hydraulic.......
'69,400	Andrew Thompson et al.	Black Creek. Sec. 31. T. 24 N., R. 18 E. Outagamie Co.	No limit..........	Log driving......
'69,195	John S. Sherman	Trout Creek. Sec. 14, T. 27. R. 10 W. Eau Claire Co.	No limit..........	Pisciculture......
'69,411	L. S. Linsey.....	Oconto river. Lot 2 and 3. Sec. 5, T. 27, R. 18 E.	No limit..........	Hydraulic.......
'70,32	John Linder.....	Big Rib river. Sec. 6. T. 38 N., R. 8 E. City and Co. of Marathon.	No limit..........	Hydraulic.......
'70,48	Warden Satterlee	Pecatonica river. Secs. 1 & 2. T. 1 N. R. 4 E. LaFayette Co.	No limit..........	Hydraulic.......
'70,270	Nathan Parker et al	Little Wolf. S. E. qr of S. E. qr Sec. 24, T. 25 N., R. 11 E. Waupaca Co.	No limit..........	Facilitate log driving.

ANALYSIS OF THE FRANCHISES FOR THE CONSTRUCTION OF DAMS BY THE LEGISLATURE—Continued.

Individual Grantees.

Protection of navigation.	Miscellaneous purposes.	Eminent domain.	Reserve clause.	Fishways,
slide for logs, etc	May collect toll.	Granted	No...............	No.
slide for logs....	None.............	Not granted......	No...............	Na,
None.............	None.............	Not granted......	No............	No.
None.............	None.............	Not granted	No...............	No.
slide for logs, etc	May collect toll,	Not granted......	No...............	No.
slides for logs.	May collect toll.	Granted..........	No...............	No.
None.............	Subject to all provisions of mill dam act. (c. 56. R. S.)	Granted..........	No.,..............	No.
slide for logs, etc	May collect toll.	Granted..........	No...............	No.
None	Grantee to own all fish in pond created by dam.	Not granted......	No...............	No.
slide for logs, etc	None.............	Not granted.....	No...............	No.
slide for logs, etc	None.............	Not granted	No...............	No.
None.............	Mill dam act applies.	Granted as per mill dam act.	No...............	No.
slide for logs, etc	May collect toll.	Granted..........	No...............	No.

ANALYSIS OF THE FRANCHISES FOR THE CONSTRUCTION OF DAMS BY THE LEGISLATURE—Continued.

Individual Grantees.

Citation.	Grantee.	Stream, Location, County.	Duration of grant.	Purposes.
'70,421	Charles Sherman	Pecatonica river branch. N. E. qr Sec. 10, T. 4 N., R. 2 E. La Fayette Co.	No limit..........	None specified...
'70,463	B. H. Overton...	Red river. Sec. 2, T. 27 N., R.14 E. Shawano Co.	No limit..........	Facilitate log driving.
'71,239	Christian Burkhardt.	Willow river. 200 rods from Willow falls, town of St. Joseph. St. Croix Co.	No limit..........	Hydraulic ....
'71,85	Julius Sizer......	Milwaukee river Lot 3. Sec. 11, T 11, R. 21 E. Ozaukee Co.	No limit..........	Hydraulic ....
'72,38 '93,213	Reuben C. Lyon	Wisconsin river. Sec. 8. T. 22 N., R. 6 E. Wood Co.	No limit..........	None spe ified...
'72,110	J, B. Schanbly .	Milwaukee river. Sec. 34, T. 12 N., R. 21 E. Ozaukee Co.	No limit..........	Hydraulic ... ...
'72,117	Orange Walker et al.	Eau Claire Lake or river. Lot 4 Sec. 16, T. 44, R. 9 W.	15 years..........	Facilitate log driving.
'72,133	John Linder......	Big Rib river. E. hf of S. W. qr Sec. 5 T. 28 N., R 6 E Marathon Co	No limit..........	Hydraulic ......
'76,80	Jesse Pramer...	Turtle Creek. T 2. R. 14 E., Sec. 27. Rock Co.	No limit..........	Hydraulic.......
'72,112	Emil Munch et al	Bean Brook, MacKey branch S. E. qr of S. E.qr. Sec. 12, T. 39, R. 11 W. and N.W. qr of N. E. qr. Sec. 18. T. 39, R. 11 W. Burnett Co.	15 years..........	Facilitate log driving.
'73,134 '74,69	Frederick A. Dresser.	Chimpanzee Brook. Sec. 28,T. 41, R, 10 W. Burnett Co. Bean Brook.(1 or more) Sec. 6, T. 39, R. 10 W. Burnett Co Sec. 8, T. 39, R. 10 W. Burnett Co.	20 years..........	Facilitate log driving.
'73,135	Samuel B. Dresser, et al. (Ind.)	Osceola Creek. T. 33. R. 19 W. Sec. 27. Polk Co.	No limit..........	Hydraulic ....

ANALYSIS OF THE FRANCHISES FOR THE CONSTRUCTION OF DAMS BY THE
LEGISLATURE—Continued.

Individual Grantees.

Protection of navigation.	Miscellaneous purposes.	Eminent domain.	Reserve clause.	Fishways.
None.............	Mill dam act applies.	Granted as per mill dam act.	No........	No.
None.............	None.....	Not granted. ..	No................	No.
None.............	Mill dam act applies.	Granted...... ...	No................	No.
None.............	None.............	Granted as per mill dam act.	No................	No.
Not to impede running of lumber. etc.	None.............	Not granted.....	No.....	No.
None	None.............	Granted..........	No................	No.
slides for logs. etc.	May collect toll.	Granted..........	No................	No,
slide for logs	None.............	Granted..........	No................	No.
None.............	None.	Granted..........	No................	No.
slide for logs. etc	May collect toll. Gates to remain open during July, Aug. and Sept.	Not granted.....	No................	No.
slide for logs. etc	May collect toll.	Not granted. ...	No................	No.
None	None.............	Granted..........	No.......	No.

ANALYSIS OF THE FRANCHISES FOR THE CONSTRUCTION OF DAMS BY THE
LEGISLATURE—Continued.

Individual Grantees.

Citation.	Grantee.	Stream. Location, County.	Duration of grant.	Purposes.
'73,150 '77.258 '78.92 '78,191 '87,226	S. C. Ogden et al.	Little Wolf. N. E. qr. Sec. 34. T. 24, R. 13. E. Waupaca Co.	15 years..........	Facilitate log driving.
'73. 245	Alvin N. Bugbee et al.	Wood river. North fork of north branch, N. W. ½ of N. E. ½ sec. 33. T. 39 N. R. 18 W. Burnett Co.	No limit.........	To flow cranberry marsh.
'73, 252	Aaron M. Chase.	Totogatic river. T. 43. R. 8. also T 42, R. 12, Bayfield Co.	No limit.........	Facilitate log driving.
'73, 275	Louis E. Torinus	Moose river. Sec 35, T. 45 N. R. 13, W. Douglas Co.	15 yrs...........	Facilitate log driving.
'74, 118	B. F. Cooper, et al.	Wisconsin river Sec. 12, T. 31 N. R. 6 E. Marathon Co.	No limit.........	Facilitate log driving.
'74. 153 '76, 2 7	W. A. Talboy, et al.	Clam river. North fork S. F. ½. N. E. ½. sec. 5. T. 37. R. 14 W. Barron Co.	10 yrs...........	Facilitata log driving.
'74. 154 '76, 263	David E. Tewksbury.	Clam river (dam or dams) one at S. W. ½ sec. 1. T. 37. R. 14 W. Barron Co. and one at N. W. ½. N. E. ½ sec. 10. T. 37. R. 14 W. Barron Co.	10 yrs...........	Facilitate log driving.
'74. 176	John H. Redfield	Elk river. Secs. 15 and 22. T. 40 N. R. 1. E. Chippewa Co.	20 yrs...........	Log driving......
'74. 204	V. Brooks et al.	Little Sandy (trib. of Little Eau Claire) Marathon Co.	No limit.........	Log driving......
'74. 228	L. D. Brewster..	Fisher river. (branch of Chippewa) Chippewa Co.	No limit.........	Facilitate log driving.
'74, 230	John M. Robinson.	Wisconsin. Secs 6. 7 and 8. T. 23 N R. 8 E. Portage Co.	No limit.........	Facilitate log driving.
'74. 276	John Edwards...	Wisconsin. Secs. 2 and 3, T. 21 N R. 5 E. Wood Co.	No limit.........	Facilitate log driving.

ANALYSIS OF THE FRANCHISES FOR THE CONSTRUCTION OF DAMS BY THE
LEGISLATURE—Continued.

Individual Grantees.

Protection of navigation.	Miscellaneous purposes.	Eminent domain.	Reserve clause.	Fishways.
Slides for logs. etc.	May collect toll for use of dam.	Granted..........	No................	No.
None..	None	Granted as per mill dam act.	No................	No.
None	None.............	Not granted.....	No................	No.
Slides for logs. etc.	May collect toll for use of dams.	Granted as per mill dam act.	No................	No.
Slides for logs. etc.	None	Not granted.....	No	No.
Slides for logs. etc,	May collect toll..	Not granted.....	No................	No.
Slides and gates for logs, etc.	May collect toll..	Granted..........	No................	No,
None.............	May collect toll..	Granted..........	No................	No.
None.............	May collect toll..	Not granted.....	No................	No.
Slides and gates for logs, etc.	May collect toll..	Not granted.....	No................	No.
Navigation of river for logs, etc.. Not to be obstructed.	None........	Not granted....	No................	No.
Not to be obstructed, navigation of river for logs, etc.	To be constructed only on lands owned by grantee	Not granted.....	No.............	No.

ANALYSIS OF THE FRANCHISES FOR THE CONSTRUCTION OF DAMS BY THE LEGISLATURE—Continued.

Individual Grantees.

Citation.	Grantee.	Stream, Location, County.	Duration of grant.	Purposes
'74, 289	W. D. Mihills, et al.	Little Wolf. S. branch N. W. ¼ of S. W. ¼ sec. 34, T. 25 N. R. 11, Waupaca Co.	No limit.........	Facilitate log driving.
'74, 304	John H. Knapp, et al.	Moons Creek. Sec. 16. T. 33 N. R. 14 W. Barron Co.	No limit.........	None.............
'74, 306	Hiram Russell..	Wisconsin, town of Rome. Adams Co.	No limit.........	Not to obstruct navigation for logs, etc.
'74, 231	John H. Knapp.	Branch of Yellow river. Sec. 34. T. 36 N. R. 13 W. Barron Co.	No limit.........	None........ ....
'74, 264	John H. Knapp, et al.	Lighting creek. Sec. 24, T. 34 N. R. 14 W Barron Co.	No limit.........	None........ ....
'75, 45	Dan. F. Smith...	South fork Clam river, at Clam Falls. Polk Co.	No limit.........	Slide for logs, etc
'75, 70	Canute Anderson et al.	Wood river near town of Grantsburg, Burnett Co.	15 yrs...........	Slides for logs, etc.
'75, 91	Charles Herman.	Milwaukee river. Lot 6, sec 18. T. 8, R. 22 E. Milwaukee Co.	No limit.........	None.............
'75, 195	J. H. McCourt...	South fork Clam river. N. W. ¼ of E. ¼. sec. 36, T. 37 N. R. 16 W. Polk Co.	15 yrs...........	Facilitate log driving.
'75, 326 amend '76, 265	Roberts & Wheelan.	Black river. (dams) one at sec. 27, T. 31. R. 1 E. Taylor Co.. one at sec. 21. T. 31. R. 1 E. Taylor Co., (3) one at sec. 14 and 15. T. 32. R. 1 E. Taylor Co., (4) one at sec. 34. T. 32, R. 1 E. Taylor Co., (5) one at sec. 21. T. 31. R. 1 E. Taylor Co., (6) one at sec. 27. T. 31. R. 1 E. Taylor Co.	No limits........	Facilitate log driving. + improvement of navigation.
'75, 327	John E. Glover..	South fork Clam river. N. E. ¼ of S. E. ¼, sec. 8. T. 36 N. R. 15 W. Polk Co.	15 yrs...........	Facilitate log driving.

ANALYSIS OF THE FRANCHISES FOR THE CONSTRUCTION OF DAMS BY THE LEGISLATURE—Continued.

Individual Grantees.

Protection of navigation.	Miscellaneous purposes.	Eminent domain.	Reserve clause.	Fishways.
Slides for logs. etc.	May collect toll	Granted	No...............	No.
None	Hydraulic and facilitate log driving.	Not granted.....	No................	No.
None	Facilitate log driving.	Not granted.....	No...............	No.
Must be erected upon land owned by grantee.	Facilitate log driving.	Not granted.....	No................	No.
None	Hydraulic........	Not granted.....	No...............	No.
May collect toll..	Facilitate log driving.	Not granted	No...............	No.
May collect toll..	Facilitate log driving.	Not granted.....	No...............	No.
Mill dam act applies.	Hydraulic........	Granted as per mill dam act.	No...............	No.
Slides for logs. etc.	May collect toll..	Not granted.....	No...............	No.
None	None.............	Granted as per mill dam act.	No............	No.
Slides for logs. etc.	May collect toll..	Not granted.....	No...............	No.

ANALYSIS OF THE FRANCHISES FOR THE CONSTRUCTION OF DAMS BY THE
LEGISLATURE—Continued.

Individual Grantees.

Citation.	Grantee.	Stream, Location, County.	Duration of grant.	Purposes.
'76, 34	William H. Decker.	Trempealeau river. Frac. lots 7 and 3, sec. 17, T. 20 N. R. 10 W. Trempealeau and Buffalo Counties	No limit.........	Hydraulic "and others."
'76, 103	Dudley J. Spaulding.	North and south forks Popple river and across Brett creek, one at sec. 17, T. 27. R. 1 E. Clark Co. One at secs 25 and 26, T. 28, R. 1 E. Clark Co. One at sec. 36, T. 29, R. 2 W. Clark Co., and one at secs. 22 and 23, T. 29, R. 1 W.. Clark Co.	15 years..........	Facilitate log driving.
'76, 195	Geo. H. Brickner	Sheboygan river. N. E. ¼ sec. 32, T. 15 N, R. 23 E. Sheboygan Co.	No limit.........	Hydraulic "and other"
'76, 250	L. W. Bliss.......	Little Wolf Sec. 10, T. 24, R. 13 E. Waupaca Co.	15 years..........	Facilitate log driving.
'76, 252	John Arbuckle..	Barhan stream. N. E. ¼, sec. 30, T. 38 N., R. 4 W. Burnett Co.	15 years..........	Facilitate log driving.
'76, 285	Solomon Leach..	Wisconsin river. Portage.	No limit..........	Hydraulic ....
'76, 287 Repealed '81, 39	John P. Jaconson	No stream designated. sec. 26, T. 38. R. 18. Burnette Co.	No limit..........	None specified...
'77, 412*	Rust William A.	North branch Eau Claire river. Clark Co.	No limit..........	Facilitate log driving.
'77, 43	William A. Rust.	S. branch Eau Claire river. Clark Co.	No limit..........	Facilitate log driving.
'77, 23	Peter Wilkinson et al.	Leach creek. Sec. 13, T. 12 N., R. 7 E. Sauk Co.	No limit..........	Improve navigation and protect from back water in time of freshets.

*(Act amends 219, '76, which held out inducements to anyone who improved the north branch of Eau Claire river, in Clark Co.)

ANALYSIS OF THE FRANCHISES FOR THE CONSTRUCTION OF DAMS BY THE
LEGISLATURE—Continued.

Individual Grantees.

Protection of navigation.	Miscellaneous purposes.	Eminent domain.	Reserve clause.	Fishways.
None............	None............	Granted..........	No...............	No.
Slides for logs, etc.	May collect toll..	Not granted.....	No...............	No.
None............	None............	Granted..........	No...............	No.
Slides for logs, etc.	May collect toll.	Not granted.....	No...............	No.
Slides for logs, etc.	May collect toll.	Not granted.....	No...............	No.
110 ft. of unobstructed channel on each side of dam erected in middle of stream.	None............	Not granted.....	No...............	No.
Slide for logs, etc.	None............	Granted as per mill dam act.	No...............	No.
None............	May collect toll.	Not granted.....		
None............	May collect toll.	Not granted.....	No...............	No.
None............	Towns through which stream runs authorized to appropriate money to aid in erection of dam	Not granted.....	No...............	No.

ANALYSIS OF THE FRANCHISES FOR THE CONSTRUCTION OF DAMS BY THE
LEGISLATURE—Continued.

Individual Grantees.

Citation.	Grantee	Stream. Location. County.	Duration of grant.	Purposes.
'77, 236	James Hewitt....	Wedge's creek. Sec. 10, T. 24 N., R. 3 W. Clark Co.	15 years...... ...	Slide for logs, etc.
'77, 247	Albert E. Pound.	Yellow river.....	No limit..........	Facilitate log driving.
'77, 267	Chauncy Blakeslee.	Cunningham creek. Clark Co.	No limit..........	Facilitate log driving.
'78, 163	Charles L. Fellows.	Stoney creek and tributaries. Door and Kewaukee counties.	No limit.........	Facilitate log driving.
'78, 239	William Miller..	Mondeau creek.	No limit.........,	None specified. .
'78, 271	Albert Wendroff	Little Rib river. N. W. ¼, sec. 11. T. 29 N., R. 6 E. Marathon Co.	No limit..........	Hydraulic.......
'78, 272	Henry Hewitt, Jr. et al.	Flambeau river. S. Fork. Secs. 22 and 23, T. 40, R. 3 E. Price Co.	No limit..........	Improvement of navigation and log driving.
'78, 283	John Quaderer..	Quaderer's creek. S. E. ¼, sec. 28, T. 34 N., R. 12 W. Barron Co.	No limit...... ...	Hydraulic and boomage.
'78, 284	John Quaderer..	Yellow river. N. E.¼ N. W.¼ sec. 28, T. 34 N., R. 12 W. Barron Co.	No limit.........,	Hydraulic and boomage.
'78, 291 Repealed '82, 86	W. L. Sadler.....	Sucker branch. Sec. 26, T. 33, R. 17 W. Polk. Co,	No limit..........	Facilitate log driving.
'78, 281 Repealed '82, 260	John McDonald, et al.	Bruny river. (Branch of Chippewa). between N. line of sec. 23, T. 40 N., R. 4 W. and S. line of sec. 34, T. 39 N., R. 6 W. Chippewa Co.	No limit ....,	Facilitate log driving.

* (Act amends ch. 12, '73, which held act inducements no anyone who improved Yellow river.

ANALYSIS OF THE FRANCHISES FOR THE CONSTRUCTION OF DAMS BY THE LEGISLATURE—Continued.

Individual Grantees.

Protection of navigation.	Miscellaneous purposes.	Eminent domain.	Reserve clause.	Fishways.
May collect toll.	Not granted.....	Not granted.....	No...............	No.
None...........	May collect toll. Others have right to use dams upon payment therefor.	Not granted.....	Yes.............	No.
None...........	May collect toll.	Not granted.....	No...............	No.
None...........	May collect toll.	Not granted.....	No...............	No.
Slide for logs, etc.	May charge toll.	Not granted.....	No...............	No.
Slide for logs, etc.	None............	Granted..........	No...............	No.
None...........	May collect toll.	Not granted.....	No...............	No.
Slides for logs, etc.	Subject to mill dam act.	Granted..........	No...............	No.
Slides for logs, etc.	Subject to mill dam act.	Granted..........	No.....	No.
Slides for logs, etc.	May collect toll.	Not granted.....	No...............	No.
None...........	May collect toll.	Not granted.....	No...............	No.

ANALYSIS OF THE FRANCHISES FOR THE CONSTRUCTION OF DAMS BY THE
LEGISLATURE—Continued.

Individual Grantees.

Citation.	Grantee.	Stream, Location, county.	Duration of grant.	Purposes.
'78, 318 '79, 27	Frederick G. Stanley.	Court Orielle river. (Dam or dams). N. of N. line, T. 38. R. 8 W. Chippewa Co.	No limit..........	Facilitate log driving.
'78. 337	William A. Rust.	Eau Claire river. Sec. 5 or 8, T. 26. R. 6 W. Eau Claire Co.	No limit..........	Improvement of navigation and facilitate log driving.
'79, 13	B. F. and C. S. McMillian.	Little Eau Claire river. sec. 17, T. 26 N., R. 3 E. Marathon Co.	No limit..........	Facilitate log driving.
'79, 21	J. J. White.......	Big Eau Pliene river. S. E. ¼, sec. 34, T. 29, R. 2 E. Marathon Co.	No limit..........	Hydraulic and boomage.
'79. 81	William T. Price	Onelle creek. Clark Co.	No limit....:......	Facilitate log driving.
'79,53	Mark Douglas...	Solf Maple Creek. Chippewa Co.	No limit..........	Improvement of navigation & facilitate log driving.
'79,55	Daniel Shaw et al	Deer Tail river. (Tributary of Chippewa) T. 33 & 34, R. 6, W. Chippewa Co.	No limit..........	Facilitate log driving.
'79,71	Nicholas Abrahamson.	Wiegor river. (Tributary of Chippewa) Sec 9. 16 & 21, T. 37. N. R. 7, W. Chippewa Co.	No limit........	Facilitate log driving.
'79,90	Carl B. & Alfred E. Long.	Yellow river. Sec. 34. T. 23, N. R. 3, E. Wood Co.	No limit..........	None specified.
'79,96	The Knapp Stout & Co.	Bear Creek. Sec. 18, T. 36. N. R. 11. W. Barron Co.	No limit	Hydraulic & facilitate log driving.
'79,112	William Johnson	William river. Sec. 29, T. 32. N. R 15. W. Polk Co.	15 yrs	Facilitate log driving.
'79,127 '89,179 (Granted changed to James H. Reddan.)	Geo.H. Ray......	Canley Creek Clark Co.	No limit..........	Improve navigation.

ANALYSIS OF THE FRANCHISES FOR THE CONSTRUCTION OF DAMS BY THE LEGISLATURE—Continued.

Individual Grantees.

Protection of navigation.	Miscellaneous purposes.	Eminent domain.	Reserve clause.	Fishways.
Slide for logs, etc.	May collect toll.	Not granted.....	No..............	No.
May collect tolls Dams and other improvements to be impartially operated during driving season	None............	Not granted.....	No..............	
Slide for logs, etc.	None............	Not granted.....	No..............	No.
Slides for logs, etc.	Subject to mill dam act.	Granted..........	No..............	No.
None.............	May collect toll. Partiality not to be shown.	Not granted.....	No..............	No.
None............	May collect toll.	Not granted.....	No..............	No.
Slides for logs, etc.	May collect tolls.	Not granted.....	No..............	No.
Slides for logs, etc.	May collect toll.	Not granted.....	No..............	No.
Slides for logs, rafts, etc.	None	Not granted.....	No..............	No.
None............	None	Not granted	No..............	No.
Slides for logs, etc.	May collect tolls.	Not granted	No..............	No.
Dam & other improvements to be operated in a practical manner.	May collect tolls.	Not granted	No..............	No.

ANALYSIS OF THE FRANCHISES FOR THE CONSTRUCTION OF DAMS BY THE LEGISLATURE—Continued.

Individual Grantees.

Citation.	Grantee.	Stream, Location, County.	Duration of Grant.	Purposes.
'79,136 amend '82,78	The Knapp Stout Co.	Red Cedar river. Sec. 25. T. 37. N. R. 10. W. Burnett Co.	No limit.........	Hydraulic & facilitate log driving.
'79,137 '81,253 '82,95	The Knapp Stout & Co.	Yellow river. Sec. 34, T. 36 N., R. 13. M. Barron Co.	No limit.........	Hydraulic & facilitate log driving.
'79,143	A. J. Haywood and W. E. McCard.	Little Chief river. N. E. qr of, N. E. qr Sec. 26. T. 40. R. 7. W. Chippewa Co.	No limit.........	Facilitate log driving.
'79,144	William McKeath.	Pine Creek. Sec. 14, T. 37 N., R. 3. W. Chippewa Co.	No limit.........	Facilitate log driving.
'79,147 '80,208	William Johnson	Willow river. Sec. 13, T. 31 N., R. 16. W. St. Croix Co.	15 yrs.............	Facilitate log driving.
'79,154	The Knapp Stout & Co.	Ten Mile Creek. Sec. 30. or 31. T. 33. N. R. 9. W. Chippewa Co.	No limit.........	Hydraulic & facilitate log driving.
'79,155	The Knapp Stout Co.	Yellow river. Sec. 7. T. 35. N. R. 12, W. Barron Co.	No limit	Hydraulic & facilitate log driving.
'79,191 '81,253 '85,95	William Baker..	Yellow river. S. Fork. Sec. 24, T. 32. R. 2. W. Taylor Co.	No limit.........	Improve navigation and log driving.
'79,201	G. E. & E. G. More	Little Wolf river. S. W. qr of N. E. qr Sec. 1. T. 22 N., R. 13. E. Waupaca Co.	No limit.........	Facilitate log driving.
'79,213 repealed '85,235	Chas. D. Wescott et al.	Wolf river. N. E. qr Sec. 25, T. 27 N., R. 15. E. Shawano Co.	No limit.........	Hydraulic and boomage.
'79,229	Jerome B. Garland.	Manedau Creek. Taylor Co.	No limit.........	Facilitate log driving.
'79,232	John E. Glover.	Clam river. (S. Fork) Sec. 31, T. 37. R. 15, W. Polk Co.	15 yrs.............	Facilitate log driving.
'80,7	Thomas Gay et al	Kickapoo river. Lots 1 & 2. Sec. 28. T. 10 N. R 4. W. Crawford Co.	No limit.........	Hydraulic & facilitate log driving.
'80,25	Gustof J. Erickson et al.	Wood river. S W. qr Sec. 16, T 38 N., R. 18. W. Burnett Co.	15 yrs.............	Hydraulic & facilitate log driving.

ANALYSIS OF THE FRANCHISES FOR THE CONSTRUCTION OF DAMS BY THE
LEGISLATURE—Continued.

Individual Grantees.

Protection of navigation.	Miscellaneous Purposes.	Eminent Domain	Reserve clause.	Fishways.
slide for logs. etc	Logs. etc. to be passed free.	Not granted	No..............	No.
slides for logs. etc.	Logs to be passed free.	Not granted......	No..............	No.
Slide for logs, etc	May collect toll.	Not granted......	No...............	No.
None............	May collect toll.	Not granted......	No...............	No.
Slides for logs. etc.	May collect toll.	Not granted......	No...............	No
None....	None	Not granted......	No...............	No.
Not to interfere w.h prior rights.	None.............	Not granted......	No...............	No.
None.............	May collect toll.	Not granted......	Yes	No.
slides to be maintained.	May collect toll.	Not granted......	No	No.
Slides to be maintained for logs, etc	Subject to mill dam act.	Granted as per mill dam act.	No...	No.
None.............	May collect toll.	Not granted......	No...............	No.
slides for logs. etc.	May collect toll.	Not granted......	No.........	No.
slide for logs, etc	None	Not granted......	No...............	No.
slide for logs, etc to pass free.	None	Not granted	No...............	No.

ANALYSIS OF THE FRANCHISES FOR THE CONSTRUCTION OF DAMS BY THE
LEGISLATURE—Continued.

Individual Grantees.

Citation.	Grantee.	Stream, Location, County.	Duration of grant.	Purposes.
'80,26	Stees, Frederick R.	Vermillion. Sec. 22, T. 35 N., R. 13, W. Barron Co.	No limit..........	Hydraulic........
'80,32	Knapp Stout & Co	Turtle Creek. Sec. 11, T. 33 N., R. 14, W. Barron Co.	No limit..........	Hydraulic & facilitate log driving.
'80,33	Knapp Stout Co.	Turtle Creek. Sec. 27, T. 34 N., R. 14, W. Barron Co.	No limit..........	Hydraulic & facilitate log driving.
'80,40	Knapp Stout Co.	Hemlock Creek. Sec. 36, T. 36 N., R. 10, W. Barron Co.	No limit..........	Hydraulic & facilitate log driving.
		Hemlock Creek. Sec. 29, T. 36 N., R. 9. W. Chippewa Co.	No limit..........	Hydraulic & facilitate log driving.
'80,49	F. S. Breed	Embarrass river. N. south branch. N. hf of S. W. qr, Sec. 10, T. 26 N., R. 12 E. Shawano Co.	No limit..... ...	Hydraulic and boomage.
'80,63	James McCrossen	Spirit river. S.E. qr of S. W. qr, Sec. 9, T. 34, R. 4 E. Lincoln Co.	No limit...:......	Facilitate log driving.
'80,75	Knapp, Stout & Co.	Hay river. Sec. 32, T. 34 N., R. 13 W. Barren Co.	No limit..........	Hydraulic & facilitate log driving.
'80,76	Knapp, Stout & Co.	Red Cedar river. Sec. 13, T. 28 N., R. 13 W. Dunn Co.	No limit..........	Hydraulic & facilitate log driving.
'80,77	A. E. Sawyer et al.	Black river. Sec. 30, T. 31. R. 1 W. Taylor Co.	No limit..........	Facilitate log driving.
'80,84	Charles W. Hanson.	Christmas Creek. N. hf of N. E. qr, Sec. 14, T. 31, R. 5 W. Chippewa Co.	No limit..........	Facilitate log driving.
'80,92	Knapp, Stout & Co.	Hemlock creek. Sec. 30, T.36 N., R. 6 W. Chippewa Co.	No limit..........	Hydraulic & facilitate log driving.
'80,97	Gustavus Werlich.	Big Rib river. S. W. qr of S. E. qr, Sec. 13, and N. W. qr of N.E. qr, Sec. 24, T. 30 N., R. 4 E. Marathon Co.	No limit..........	Hydraulic and boomage.
'80,102	K. A. Ostegreen.	Spirit river. N. W. qr, Sec. 10, T. 34, R. 4 E. Lincoln Co.	No limit.,.........	Hydraulic. ......

ANALYSIS OF THE FRANCHISES FOR THE CONSTRUCTION OF DAMS BY THE LEGISLATURE—Continued.

Individual Grantees.

Protection of navigation.	Miscellaneous purposes.	Eminent domain.	Reserve clause.	Fishways.
Slide for logs, etc to pass free.	Mill Dam act applies.	Granted (c, 146, R. S.)	No., ...	No.
Slide for logs, etc to pass free.	None	Not granted......	No...............	No.
Slide for logs, etc to pass free.	None.	Not granted.	No..., ...	No.
Slide for logs, etc to pass free.	None	Not granted	No...............	No.
Slide for logs, etc to pass free.	None	Not granted	No...............	No.
Slide for logs etc. To pass free.	None	Not granted......	No...............	No.
Slide for logs, etc	May collect toll..	Not granted......	No...............	No.
Slide for logs etc. To pass free.	None....	Not granted.....	No...............	No.
Slide for logs etc. To pass free.	None	Not granted.....	No...............	No.
Flood gates for logs etc.	May collect toll.	Not granted.....	No...............	No.
Slide for logs etc.	May collect toll.	Not granted.....	No...............	No.
Slide for logs etc.	None.............	Not granted.....	No...............	No.
Slides and gates for logs, etc.	None.......	Not granted.....	No...............	No.
Free passage for logs, etc.	Mill dam act applies.	Granted..........	No...............	No

ANALYSIS OF THE FRANCHISES FOR THE CONSTRUCTION OF DAMS BY THE
LEGISLATURE—Continued.

Individual Grantees.

Citation.	Grantee.	Stream, Location, County.	Duration of grant.	Purposes.
'80,103	Atley Peterson et al.	Kickapoo river. N. W. qr of N. E. qr. Sec. 31,T.11 N., R. 3 W. Crawford Co.	No limit..........	Hydraulic and facilitate log driving.
'89,144 '81,142	A. D. Lunt.......	Elk river. N.W. qr of N. W. qr. Sec. 31, T. 38, R. 2 E. Price Co.	No limit..........	Facilitate log driving.
'80,151	Thomas B. Scott	Prairie river. Sec. 13, T. 32, R. 7 E. Lincoln Co. Sec. 14, T. 33, R. 8 E. Lincoln Co.	No limit..........	Facilitate log driving.
'80,168	Peter B. Champagne.	Wisconsin river. N. E. qr. Sec. 30, T. 33, R. 6 E. Lincoln Co.	No limit,..........	None specified...
'80,171	William A. Rust.	Hay creek, (branch of Eau Claire). Clark Co.	No limit..........	Facilitate log driving.
'80,177	Delos Moon......	Otter creek (trib. of Wolf). Clark & Chippewa Cos.	No limit..........	Facilitate log driving.
'80,178	Delos R. Moon...	Muskrat river, (trib. of Eau Claire). Eau Claire Co.	No limit..........	Facilitate log driving.
'80,182	Delos R. Moon...	Wolf river, (trib. of N. fork Eau Claire). S. of N. line T. 29 N., R. 5 W. Chippewa Co.	No limit..........	Facilitate log driving.
'80,184 '82,181	D. P. Simons.....	Butternut creek. Sec. 18, T.40 N., R. 1 W. Price Co.	No limit..........	To regulate water and facilitate log driving.
'80,201	G. W. Gate et al.	Spirit river. Lot 4, Sec. 32. T. 34 N., R. 3 E. Price Co.	No limit..........	Facilitate log driving.
'80,205	A. B. McDonnell	Pine Creek. Sec. 18, T. 40 N., R. 2W. Price Co.	No limit..........	Facilitate log driving.
'83,132 '80,214	John & Halvor Annunson.	Poplar river, (branch of Pine). Sec. 13. T. 38 N., R. 15 E. Oconto Co.	No limit..........	Facilitate log driving.
'80,241	Mathew Wadleigh et al.	Little Elk river, Sec. 24, T. 37 N. R. 1 E. Price Co.	No limit..........	Facilitate log driving.
'80,255	Abel Neff........	Prairie river. W. hf, Sec. 14, T. 33, R. 8. Lincoln Co.	No limit..........	Hydraulic. .....

ANALYSIS OF THE FRANCHISES FOR THE CONSTRUCTION OF DAMS BY THE LEGISLATURE—Continued.

Individual Grantees.

Protection of navigation.	Miscellaneous purposes.	Eminent domain.	Reserve clause.	Fishways.
Side for logs etc.	None....	Not granted....	No................	No.
Side for logs etc.	May collect toll.	Not granted.....	No................	No.
None............	May collect toll.	Not granted.....	No................	No.
Free passage of &c. etc.	None..	Not granted.....	No................	No.
None............	May charge toll	Not granted.....	No................	No.
None............	May charge toll.	Not granted.....	No......	No.
None............	May charge toll.	Not granted.....	No................	No.
None......... ..	May charge toll.	Not granted.....	No................	No.
...e for logs, etc.	May charge toll.	Not granted.....	No.......	Yes.
None............	May charge toll.	Not granted.....	No................	No.
Side for logs, etc	May charge toll.	Not granted.....	No................	No.
Sides for logs.	May collect toll.	Not granted.....	Yes....	No.
Sides for logs.	May collect toll.	Not granted.....	No................	No.
Side for logs, etc	None	Granted..........	No........,......	No.

13

ANALYSIS OF THE FRANCHISES FOR THE CONSTRUCTION OF DAMS BY THE
LEGISLATURE—Continued.

Individual Grantees.

Citation.	Grantee.	Stream, Location, County.	Duration of Grant.	Purposes.
'80,294	James W. Heather, et al.	Deer Tail (branch of Chippewa) authorizes following dams. already erected: Those in Secs. 8, 9 & 16, T. 35, R. 4. Chippewa Co. Sec. 24, T. 35, R. 5. Chippewa Co. Following to be erected: T. 35, R.4. Chippewa Co. T. 35, R. 5. Chippewa Co.	No limit., ...	Facilitate log driving.
'80,296	John Redmand..	Hay Creek. Secs. 16 & 17. T. 31, R. 5 W. Chippewa Co.	No limit........	Facilitate log driving.
'80,303 '83,	Thomas J. LaFlesh.	Black river, E. fork. One at Sec. 14, T. 23, R. 1 E. Wood Co. One at Secs. 5 & 30, T. 23, R. 2 E. Clark Co. One at Sec. 4, T.22 &., R. 2 E. Jackson Co.	10 years........	Facilitate log driving.
'80,76	John H. Knapp, et al.	Red Cedar river. Sec. 13. T. 28, R.13 W.	No limit........	Facilitate log driving.
'81, 41	John P. Jacobson	Wood river. Sec. 23, T. 36 N. R. 18 W. Burnett Co.	15 yrs............	Hydraulic. Facilitate log driving.
'81, 57 '89, 449 (repeals authority to erect dams in T. 26, R. 11)	Frederick R. Newbold et al.	Embarass river. S. branch, T. 26, R. 11, or T. 26, R. 12, Shawano Co.	15 yrs............	Render stream navigable for logs, etc.
'81, 58 '83, 140	Wyota Stromsky	Kewaunee river. S. E. ¼. sec. 14, T. 23, R. 24. Kewaunee Co.	15 yrs............	Facilitate log driving.
'81, 67	A. C. Cushman..	Kickapoo river. N. E. ¼ of S. E. ¼. sec. 24, T. 12, R. 3 W. Vernon Co.	No limit........	Hydraulic and facilitate log driving.
'81, 77	John G. Nelson et al.	Hay Creek. Sec 12, T. 40, N. R. 11 W. Burnett Co.	15 yrs............	Facilitate log driving.
'81, 266	Robert Jackson..	Yellow river. Sec. 1, T. 29 N. R. 6 W. Chippewa Co.	No limit........	None specified...

ANALYSIS OF THE FRANCHISES FOR THE CONSTRUCTION OF DAMS BY THE
LEGISLATURE—Continued.

Individual grantees.

Protection of navigation.	Miscellaneous purposes.	Eminent domain.	Reserve clause.	Fishways.
None.............	May collect toll	Not granted.....	No....	No.
....e	May collect toll.	Not granted.....	No...............	No.
....de for logs, etc	May collect toll.	Not granted.....	No........	No.
....es for logs.	None	Not granted.....	No...............	No.
....es for logs. to pass free.	None..	Not granted.....	No...............	No.
....es for logs.	May collect toll..	Not granted.....	No...............	No.
....es for logs.	May collect toll..	Not granted.....	No...............	No.
....es for logs.	None.	Not granted.....	No...............	
... for logs.	May collect toll.	Not granted.....	No...............	
....es and flood ....s for logs, etc.	None-...........	Not granted.....	No...............	No.

ANALYSIS OF THE FRANCHISES FOR THE CONSTRUCTION OF DAMS BY THE
LEGISLATURE—Continued.

Individual Grantees.

Citation.	Grantee.	Stream, Location, County.	Duration of grant.	Purposes.
'81, 160	John Rose et al..	Pine river. (4 dams). One at sec. 22, T. 31 N, R. 7 E.; one at sec. 9, T. 31 N., R. 8 E. and one at sec. 31. T. 32 N, R. 9 E. Lincoln Co.	No limit.........	Facilitate log driving.
'81, 161 '82, 89	James Hewitt...	Wedges Creek. N. E. ¼ of S. E. ¼, sec. 22, and N. W. ¼ of S. W. ¼, sec. 23, T. 25. N, R. 3 W. Clark Co.	No limit.........	Facilitate log driving.
'81, 164	E. E. Le Claire...	Saylor Creek. T. 39, R. 1 E. Price Co.	No limit.........	Facilitate log driving.
'81, 177	Eugene Shaw et al.	Fisher Creek. (trib. to Chippewa) dam or dams, sec. 34, T. 32 N, R. 6 W. or elsewhere on said creek. Chippewa Co.	No limit.........	Facilitate log driving.
'81, 221	John Duncan....	Silver Creek. Above Wis. Cent. R. R. crossing, Taylor and Price Co.	No limit.........	Facilitate log driving.
'81, 255 '83, 96	Stanton Barnard	Chippewa river. (Dam or dams, between E. line sec. 4, T. 28, R. 8, and W. line, sec. 26, T. 29. R. 8, Chippewa Co.	No limit.........	Facilitate log driving.
'81, 267	R. G. Cory.	Plover river. S. W. frac. ¼ sec. 19, T. 28, N. R. 10 E. Marathon Co.	15 yrs..	Facilitate log driving.
'81, 311	Robert L. Henry et al.	Aminican river. below outlet of upper Aminican Lake, T. 46 N, R. 13 W. Douglas Co., or at other places on said river in said Co. for reservoirs, etc.	No limit.........	Facilitate log driving and improvement of navigation.
'81, 326	Robinson D. Pike et al.	Iron river. (Dam or dams) from mouth in T. 51 N, R. 6 W. to source inc. all tributaries. Bayfield Co.	No limit.........	Facilitate log driving.

ANALYSIS OF THE FRANCHISES FOR THE CONSTRUCTION OF DAMS BY THE LEGISLATURE—Continued.

Individual Grantees.

Protection of navigation.	Miscellaneous purposes.	Eminent domain.	Reserve clause.	Fishways.
...l.s for logs,	May charge toll.	Not granted.....	No................	No.
...de for logs,	May charge toll..	Not granted.....	No................	No.
...des for logs,	May charge toll..	Not granted.....	No................	No.
...l.s for logs,	May charge toll..	Not granted.....	No......, ...	No.
...les for logs,	May charge toll..	Not granted.....	No................	No.
None.............	May collect toll. Act not to interfere with vested rights of other within points above. Given 90 days to lose or acquire improvements existing between said points. Must maintain for four years.	Not granted.....	No................	No.
...m to be kept at all times river at a icg stage.	None.....	Not granted.....	No................	No.
...se gates to navigation ...n dams.	May collect toll..	Granted as per mill dam act.	No................	No.
...s for logs,	May collect toll..	Not granted.....	No................	No.

ANALYSIS OF THE FRANCHISES FOR THE CONSTRUCTION OF DAMS BY THE
LEGISLATURE—Continued.

Individual Grantees.

Citation.	Grantee.	Stream. Location. County.	Duration of grant.	Purposes
'81, 327	Robinson D. Pike et al.	Iron river. (Dam or dams and improvements) from mouth in T 50, R. 9 W. to source inc. all tributories. Bayfield Co.	No limit.........	Facilitate log driving.
'81, 331	John Mooning et al.	Windfall Creek. (Branch of Court Onille river.) Sec. 16, T. 38 N, R. 8 W. Chippewa Co.	No limit.........	Facilitate log driving.
'82, 38	William Smith.	Embarass river. S. E. 4, sec. 9, T. 26 N, R. 14 E. Shawano Co.	No limit.........	Hydraulic and boomage.
'82, 103	Knapp Stout & Co.	Red Cedar river. S. E. 1 of N. E. 4, sec. 21 and lot 3, sec. 22, T. 36, R. 10, Barron Co.	No limit.........	Facilitate log driving.
'82, 106	S. A. Sherman...	Wisconsin river. Bloomer Rapids, Sec. 17, T. 23, R. 8 E. Portage Co.	No limit.........	Facilitate log driving.
'82, 107	Clarence A. Sherman.	Big Plover river. Sec. 26, T. 24, R. 6 E., Portage Co.	No limit.........	Facilitate log driving.
'82, 137	Raymond Ayres et al.	Blane Brook. S. 4 of N. E. 1, sec 35, T. 24 N, R. 12 E. Waupaca Co.	No limit.........	Facilitate log driving
'82 144	Knapp Stout & Co.	Hay river. N. fork. S E. 4 of S W. 4 sec 21, T. 32, R. 13 W. Barron Co.	No limit.........	Facilitate log driving.
'82, 145	S. A. Sherman...	Big Plover river. Sec. 9 T 23, W. Portage Co.	No limit.........	Facilitate log driving.
'82, 182	John E. Glover et al.	Totogatleanse river. Sec. 8, T. 43 N., R. 9 W. Bayfield Co.	15 years..........	Facilitate log driving.
'82, 183	J. E. Glover et al.	Totogatleanse river. Sec. 1, T 53 N. R 10 W. Douglas Co.	15 years..........	Facilitate log driving.
'82, 184	J. E. Glover et al.	Totogatleanse river. Sec. 6, T. 43 N., R. 9 W. Bayfield Co.	15 years..........	Facilitate log driving.

ANALYSIS OF THE FRANCHISES FOR THE CONSTRUCTION OF DAMS BY THE LEGISLATURE—Continued

Individual Grantees.

Protection of navigation.	Miscellaneous purposes.	Eminent domain.	Reserve clause.	Fishways.
Slide for logs, etc.	May collect toll.	Not granted..		
Slides for logs, etc.	May collect toll.	Not granted.....	No.........	No,
Slide for logs, etc.	Subject to mill dam act, (c. 146.)	Granted as per mill dam act.	No...............	No.
Not to obstruct passage of logs.	None.............	Not granted.....	No...............	No.
Not to impede navigation.	Subject to c. 70. R. S.	Not granted.....	No...............	No.
Not to obstruct the passage of logs, etc.	Subject to c. 70. R. S.	Not granted.....	No...............	No.
Slides for logs. etc.	None.............	Not granted.....	No...............	No.
Slides for logs, etc.	None....	Not granted.....	No...............	No.
Slide for logs, etc.	Subject to c. 70. R. S.	Not granted.....	No...............	No.
Slide for logs, etc.	May collect toll.	Not granted.....	No...............	No.
Slide for logs, etc.	May collect toll.	Not granted.....	No...............	No.
Slides for logs, etc.	May collect toll.	Not granted.....	No...............	No.

ANALYSIS OF THE FRANCHISES FOR THE CONSTRUCTION OF DAMS BY THE
LEGISLATURE—Continued.

Individual Grantees.

Citation.	Grantee.	Streams. Location. County.	Duration of grant.	Purposes.
'82, 185	J. E. Glover et al.	Totogatlcanse river. Sec. 11, T. 43 N., R. 10 W. Douglas Co.	15 years.........	Facilitate log driving.
'82, 186	Christian Weber.	Big Eau Pleine river. N. W. ⅟, N. E. ⅟ sec. 13, T. 27 N., R. 3 E. Douglas Co.	No limit.........	Hydraulic.........
'82, 224 '89, 215 '91, 478 '95, 352 Repealed. '03, 25	Joel F. Nason et al.	St Croix river. At St. Croix Falls. Polk Co.	No limit.........	Facilitate log driving.
'82, 228 '87, 253 '93, 143 '95, 272	D. P. Simons.....	Jump river. N. W. ⅟ of S. W. ⅟ sec. 32, T. 34, R. 1 W. Price Co.	No limit.........	Facilitate log driving.
'82, 247*	Edw. E. Brown et al.	Wisconsin river. N. ⅟, sec. 6, T. 36, R. 9 E. Oneida Co.	No limit.........	Facilitate log driving and hydraulic.
'82, 269	Alexander P. Ellenwood.	Babb's creek. N. E. ⅟, sec. (9 T. 12 N., R. 4 E Sauk Co.	No limit.........	Hydraulic.........
'82, 270	Philip Rossman.	Rock creek. S. W. ⅟ of S. W. ⅟ sec. 28, T. 27 N., R. 1 W. Clark Co.	No limit.........	Log driving......
'82, 292	James H. Weed et al.	Spring brook. E. ⅟ of N. E. ⅟ sec. 30, T. 31, N., R. 11 E. Langlade Co.	No limit.........	Facilitate log driving.
'82, 297	C. M. Wells et al.	Little Wolf river. S. W. ⅟ of S W. ⅟ sec. 8, T. 22 N., R. 14 E. Waupaca Co	No limit.........	Facilitate log driving.
'82, 316	Henry Stearms..	Embarrass river. S. W. ⅟, sec. 9, T. 27, R. 12 E. Shawano Co.	No limit.........	Hydraulic and log driving.
'82, 251	Frederick Davis et al.	Wolf river. (Dams and improve west branch) from N. line T. 28 N., R. 14 E. to N. line T. 30 N., R. 13 E.	No limit.........	Facilitate log driving.

* Amend c. 253, '87, c. 143, '93 (gives right of eminent domain); c. 272, '95; c. 280, '07. (toll)

ANALYSIS OF THE FRANCHISES FOR THE CONSTRUCTION OF DAMS BY THE
LEGISLATURE—Continued.

Individual Grantees.

Protection of navigation.	Miscellaneous purposes.	Eminent domain.	Reserve clause.	Fishways.
Slides for logs, etc.	May collect toll.	Not granted.....	No................	No.
Slides for logs, etc.	None.............	Granted as per mill dam act.	No................	No.
Not to impede navigation or to interfere with water power.	May collect toll.	Granted as per mill dam act.	Yes	No.
Slides and flood gates for logs, etc.	May collect toll.	Not granted.. ..	Yes...............	No.
Slides for logs. etc.	None.......	Granted..........	Yes...............	No.
None.	None.............	Granted..........	No................	No.
Slide for logs. etc.	May collect toll.	Not granted.....	No................	No.
Not to impede navigation.	Subject to Ch. 70. R. S.	Not granted.....	Yes...............	No.
Slides for logs. etc.	May collect toll.	Not granted.....	Yes...............	No.
Slides for logs. etc.	None.	Not granted.....	No................	No.
Slide for logs. etc.	May collect toll.	Not granted.....	Yes...............	No.

ANALYSIS OF THE FRANCHISES FOR THE CONSTRUCTION OF DAMS BY THE LEGISLATURE—Continued.

Individual Grantees.

Citation.	Grantee.	Streams. Location. County.	Duration of grant.	Purposes.
'82, 260	W. Culver........	Brunett river. (Branch of Chippewa) dam and improve.	No limit..........	Facilitate log driving.
'82, 278 '83, 224	J. A. Humbird et al.	Bad river. White river & tributaries of said rivers. Dam and otherwise improve. Ashland and Bayfield Cos.	No limit..........	Facilitate log driving.
'82, 277	Charles H. Moss	Black river. N. E. ¼ of S. E. ¼ sec. 27, T. 32, R. 1 E. and N. ½ of S. E. ¼, sec. 26, T. 32, R. 1 E. Taylor Co.	No limit....	Hydraulic and boomage.
'83, 3	Knapp Stout & Co.	Red Cedar river. Lots 2 and 6, sec. 6, T. 28, R. 12 W. Dunn Co	No limit..........	Hydraulic and facilitate log driving.
'83, 209 '85, 88 Repealed '93, 111	Jas. Hewitt......	Black river. 600 ft. from where Oneill's creek enters Clark Co.	No limit..........	Hydraulic and boomage.
'83, 170	J. F. Ellis et al..	Copper river. N. W. ¼ of N. E. ¼, sec. 1, T. 31 N., R. 5 E. Lincoln Co.	No limit..........	Hydraulic flooding and booming.
'83, 113	Hector McRae et al.	Duncans's creek. City of Chippewa Falls. Chippewa Co.	No limit..........	None specified..
'83, 75	Erick Lundholm	Dunnum's creek. Lot 3, sec. 28, T. 38 N., R. 17 W. Burnett Co.	15 years..........	Hydraulic and facilitate log driving.
'83, 347	Wm. Irvin.......	Fisher river. Chippewa Co.	No limit.........	Facilitate log driving.
'83, 198	Jas. Morrison et al.	Hay creek. S. W. ¼ of S. W. ¼ sec. 27, T. 36, R. 1 E.	No limit..........	Facilitate log driving.
'83, 289 '87, 377	E. R. Urquhart et al.	Little Black river. S. W. ¼ of S. W. ¼, sec. 1, T. 30 N., R. 1 E. Taylor Co.	No limit..........	Hydraulic and facilitate log driving.
'83, 93	Joseph Mayer.	Little EauPleine river, sec. 34, T. 27 N. R. 2 E. Marathon Co.	No limit........	None specified..

ANALYSIS OF THE FRANCHISES FOR THE CONSTRUCTION OF DAMS BY THE LEGISLATURE. -Continued.

Individual Grantees.

Protection of navigation.	Miscellaneous purposes.	Eminent domain.	Reserve clause.	Fishways.
None	None.............	Not granted....	Yes..............	No.
Shall not impede navigation.	May collect toll.	Granted..........	Yes..............	No.
Not to impede navigation.	Subject to chs. 70 and 146 R. S.	Granted as per mill dam act.	No...............	No.
Slides for logs. etc.	None.............	Not granted....	Yes..............	No.
Slides for logs. etc. to pass free.	None.............	Not granted.....	Yes..............	No.
Slides for logs. etc.	May collect toll.	Not granted.....	Yes..............	No.
None............	None.............	Not granted.....	Yes..............	No.
Slides for logs. etc.	None............	Not granted.....	Yes..............	No.
None............	May charge toll.	Not granted.....	Yes..............	No.
Slides for logs. etc.	None............	Not granted	Yes..............	No.
Slides for logs. etc.	May charge toll.	Not granted	Yes..............	No.
Slides for logs. etc.	None............	Not granted.....	Yes..............	No.

ANALYSIS OF THE FRANCHISES FOR THE CONSTRUCTION OF DAMS BY THE
LEGISLATURE—Continued.

Individual Grantees.

Citation.	Grantee.	Stream, Location, County.	Duration of grant.	Purposes.
83, 88	J. D. Witter et al.	Little Yellow river, secs. 19, 29, 30 and 32, T. 21 N. R. 3 E.	No limit..........	Facilitate log driving.
'83, 224	J. A. Humbird.	White river, near C. St. P. M. & O crossing, Bayfield Co.	No limit..........	Facilitate log driving.
'83, 222	Knapp. Stout & Co.	Long Lake river, (tributary of Red Cedar) S. W. ¼ of N. W. ¼ sec. 24, T. 37, R. 11, W. Burnett Co.	No limit..........	Hydraulic........
'83, 335	Robert Ritchie.	Marengo river, S. ¼ S. E. ¼ sec. 27, T. 45 N. R. 5 W. Bayfield Co.	No limit..........	Facilitate log driving.
'83, 11	Anthony J. Hayward.	Nama Kogan, sec. 27, T. 41, R. 9 W. Ashland Co.	No limit.........	Facilitate logging.
'83, 230	Marshall Miller et al.	Oneil Creek, sec. 29, T. 31 R. 8 W. Chippewa Co.	No limit...	Facilitate log driving.
'83, 130	Thomas Kerns.	Pine Creek, sec. 15, T. 30 N. R. 1 W. Taylor Co.	No limit..........	Facilitate log driving.
'83, 317	H. R. Mills.	Robinson Creek. Dam and otherwise improve in Jackson Co.	No limit..........	Facilitate log driving.
'83, 355	John Arpin et al.	St. German creek two flooding dams) one at sec. 30, T. 40, N. R. 8 E. Lincoln Co. One at sec. 18, T. 39 N, R. 8 E. Lincoln Co.	No limit..........	Facilitate log driving.
'83, 65	Geo. Grimmer, et al.	Scarbro creek, S. W. ¼ of S. E. ¼, sec. 25, T. 24, R. 23 E. Kewaunee Co.	No limit..........	Hydraulic and facilitate log driving.
'83, 259	Louis Navotney.	Spring Brook, W. ¼ of N. E. ¼ of N. W. ¼, sec. 29, T. 31 N., R. 11 E. Langlade Co.	No limit..........	none............ .
'83, 21	Nelson Larson, et al.	Straight river, lot 1, sec. 20, T. 36, R. 16 W. Polk Co.	10 years..........	Facilitate log driving.

ANALYSIS OF THE FRANCHISES FOR THE CONSTRUCTION OF DAMS BY THE
LEGISLATURE—Continued.

Individual Grantees.

Protection of navigation.	Miscellaneous purposes.	Eminent domain.	Reserve clause.	Fishways.
Free passage for logs.	None.............	Granted	Yes...............	No.
Slides for logs, etc.	May collect toll..	Not granted.....	Yes...............	No.
Slides for logs. etc.	Act to be accepted within 30 days by grantee.	Granted..........	Yes...............	No.
Slides for logs. etc.	May collect toll	Not granted.....	Yes...............	No.
None.............	None.............	Not granted......	Yes...............	No.
Slides for logs. etc.	May collect toll	Granted...... ...	Yes..............,	No,
Slides for logs. etc.	May collect toll	Granted as per mill dam act.	Yes..........	No.
None......... ...	May collect toll	Not granted.....	Yes...............	No.
Slides for logs. etc.	May collect toll	Not granted.....	Yes...............	No.
Slides for logs. etc. to pass free.	None............	Not granted.....	yes..........	No.
Not to obstruct navigation.	Subject to Ch. 70, R. S.	Granted..........	No	Yes.
Slides for logs. etc.	May collect toll	Not granted....	Yes...............	No.

ANALYSIS OF THE FRANCHISES FOR THE CONSTRUCTION OF DAMS BY THE LEGISLATURE—Continued.

Individual Grantees.

Citation.	Grantee.	Stream, Location, County.	Duration of grant.	Purposes.
'83, 33 Repealed '87, 108	Isaac Staples et al.	Straight River, one at N. E. of W. ½ sec. 18. T. 36, R. 16 W. Polk Co. One at S. ½ of N. E. ¼ sec. 20, T. 36, R. 16 W. Polk Co One at S. W. ¼ of N. E ¼, sec. 34. T. 36, R. 16 W. Polk Co.	10 years.........	Facilitate log driving.
'83, 344	S. L. Cowan, et al.	Totogata con s e river, S. W. ¼ sec. 30, T. 43, R. 10 W Douglas Co.	No limit.........	Facilitate log driving.
'83, 213	Chas. S. Taylor et al.	Yellow river, S. E. ¼ sec. 27, T. 34 N, R. 12 W. Barron Co.	No limit.........	Hydraulic boomage.
'83, 326	J. E. Ellis.	Yellow river, T. 31 N. R. 4 W. Taylor Co.	No limit.........	Facilitate log driving.
'85, 43	Anthony J. Haywood.	Narakugon river.	No limit.........	Facilitate log driving.
'85, 70	A. Fetzer, et al.	Ahnapee river, E. ¼ of S. W. ¼, sec. 29, T 26, R. 25. Door Co.	No limit.........	Hydraulic.........
'85, 75 amend '87, 154 (as to tolls) Repealed '01, 177	Jacob Bean et al.	Namakagan river, sec. 35, T. 41 N, R. 10 W. Washburn Co.	No limit.........	Improvement of navigation.
'85, 100	Knapp, Stout & Co.	Hemlock Creek, (trib. of Red Cedar) W. ½, N. W. ¼, sec. 26, T. 36, R. 9 W. Chippewa Co.	No limit.........	Facilitate log driving.
'85, 104	Knapp, Stout & Co.	Elm Creek (trib. Red Cedar) lot 4, sec. 10, T. 37, R 9 W. Sawyer Co.	No limit.........	Facilitate log driving.
'85, 158	N L. Bensley, et al.	Wisconsin river, sec. 8, T. 22, R 6 E.	No limit.........	Facilitate log driving.
'85, 180	Jefferson Heath, et al.	Sand Creek, N. ½ sec. 17, T 36, R. 14 W. Barron Co.	No limit.........	Hydraulic and facilitate logdriving.
'85, 231	Knapp Stout & Co.	Miller creek, S. W ¼ Sec. 26, T. 36, R 13. Barron Co.	No limit.........	Facilitate log driving.

ANALYSIS OF THE FRANCHISES FOR THE CONSTRUCTION OF DAMS BY THE LEGISLATURE—Continued.

Individual Grantees.

Protection of navigation.	Miscellaneous purposes.	Eminent domain.	Reserve clause.	Fishways.
Slides for logs. etc.	May collect toll	Not granted......	Yes..............	No.
Slides for logs, etc.	May collect toll	Not granted.....	Yes..............	No.
Slides for logs, etc.	Subject to Ch. 146. R. S.	Granted as per mill dam act	Yes..............	No.
Slides for logs, etc.	None............	Not granted.....	Yes..............	No.
Slides for logs, etc.	None............	Not granted.....	Yes..............	No.
Slides for logs, etc.	Subject to Ch. 70 and 146, R. S.	Granted as per mill dam act.	Yes..............	No.
Slides for logs, etc.	May collect toll	Granted..........	Yes..............	No.
Slides for logs, etc.	None............	Granted..........	Yes..............	No.
Slides for logs, etc.	None...........	Granted..........	Yes..............	No.
Slides for logs. etc.	None............	Not granted.....	Yes..............	No.
Slides for logs. etc.	None............	Granted..........	Yes..............	No.
Slides for logs. etc.	None............	Granted. Mill dam act.	Yes..............	No.

ANALYSIS OF THE FRANCHISES FOR THE CONSTRUCTION OF DAMS BY THE
LEGISLATURE—Continued.

Individual Grantees.

Citation.	Grantee.	Stream, Location, County.	Duration of grant.	Purposes.
'85, 236	Knapp, Stout & Co.	Little Bear creek (Trib. of Red Cedar.) S. W. qr of N. W. qr. sec. 23, T. 36, R. 12 W. Barron Co.	No limit..........	Facilitate log driving.
'85, 235	E. J. Homme....	Embarras river, N. hf of N. W. qr, Sec. 10, T. 27, R. 1, 1 E. Shawano Co.	No limit..........	Hydraulic ....
'85, 254	John C. Schneider.	Apple river. S. hf of N. E. qr Sec. 12. T. 32, R. 17. Polk Co.	No limit..........	Hydraulic........
'85, 255	Carl J. Berg, et al.	Embarrass river, N. W. qr of N. E. qr, Sec. 23, T. 27. R. 12 E. Shawano Co.	No limit..........	Hydraulic and facilitate log driving.
'85, 278	R. C. Lyons.. ...	Wisconsin river. Sec. 18, T. 22 N., R. 6 E.	No limit..........	None specified...
'85, 280	G. W. Hahn......	Red river. N. W. qr, Sec. 3, T. 27 N., R. 14 E. Shawano Co.	No limit..	Hydraulic and boomage.
'85, 281	John Sieber, et al.	Embarrass river. E. hf of S. W. qr, Sec. 15, T. 27. R. 13 E. Shawano Co.	No limit..........	Hydraulic and boomage.
'85, 282	Theodore Buettner.	Embarrass river. N. W. qr, Sec. 23, T. 26. R. 13 E. Shawano Co.	No limit..........	Hydraulic and facilitate log driving.
'85, 283	John C. Schneider.	Apple river. S. E. qr of N. E. qr. Sec. 11, T. 32 N., R. 17 W. Polk Co.	No limit..........	Hydraulic........
'85, 363	Henry Huson....	Sheboygan river. S. E. qr. Sec. 13. T. 16 N., R. 20 E. Sheboygan Co.	No limit..........	Improve navigation.
'85, 367	Geo. W. Mason..	Popple creek. Sec. 28, T. 38, R. 2 E. Price Co.	No limit..........	Facilitate log driving.
'85, 371	Oliver Darwin...	Lewis creek. T. 21, R. 2. 3 and 4 W. Jackson Co.	No limit..........	Facilitate log driving.
'85, 372	M. G. Harlow, et al.	Deer brook (trib to Eau Claire) S. W. qr of N. E. qr. Sec. 30, T. 32 N., R. 11 E. Langlade Co.	No limit..........	Facilitate log driving.

ANALYSIS OF THE FRANCHISES FOR THE CONSTRUCTION OF DAMS BY THE LEGISLATURE—Continued.

Individual Grantees.

Protection of navigation.	Miscellaneous purposes.	Eminent domain.	Reserve clause.	Fishways.
Slides for logs, etc.	None............	Granted..........	Yes...............	No.
Slide for logs, etc.	None............	Not granted....	Yes...............	No.
Slides for logs, etc.	None............	Not granted.....	Yes...............	No.
Slides for logs, etc.	None,	Not granted.....	Yes...............	No.
Slides for logs, etc.	None............	Not granted.....	Yes...............	No.
Slides for logs, etc.	Subject to mill dam act.	Granted as per mill dam act.	Yes...............	No.
Slides for logs, etc.	Subject to mill dam act.	Granted as per mill dam act.	Yes...............	No.
Slides for logs, etc.	None............	Not granted.....	Yes...............	No.
Slide for logs, etc.	None............	Not granted.....	Yes...............	No.
None............	None............	Not granted.....	Yes...............	No.
Slides for logs, etc.	May collect toll.	Not granted.....	Yes...............	No.
Slides for logs, etc.	May collect toll.	Not granted.....	Yes...............	No.
Slides for logs, etc.	May collect toll.	Not granted.....	Yes...............	No.

14

ANALYSIS OF THE FRANCHISES FOR THE CONSTRUCTION OF DAMS BY THE
LEGISLATURE—Continued.

Individual Grantees.

Citation.	Grantee.	Stream, Location, County.	Duration of grant.	Purposes.
'85, 402	Canute Anderson.	Wood river. S. E. qr of S. E. qr. Sec. 28, T. 38 N. R. 18 W. Burnette Co.	No limit..........	Hydraulic and flooding.
'85, 412	H. M. Wadleigh.	Plover river. N. E. qr of S. W. qr. Sec. 19, T. 25 N., R. 10 E. Marathon Co.	No limit..........	Facilitate log driving.
'87, 12	W. H. Bradley...	Wisconsin river. Sec. 10, T. 34. R. 6 E. Lincoln Co.	No limit..	Hydraulic. flooding and boomage.
'87, 41	C. D. Hammond, et al.	Tomahawk river.	No limit..........	Hydraulic "and other."
'87, 68	Benj. Heinemann.	Montreal river. Any point on river. Iron Co.	No limit..........	Facilitate log driving.
'87, 70	W. H. Richards.	Big Eau Pleine river. N. W. qr of S. E. qr, Sec. 4, T. 27 N., R. 3. Marathon Co.	No limit.....	None specified...
'87, 85	John England...	Tea river. On Sec. 3, T. 41 N., R. 6 W. or on Sec. 34, T. 42 N., R. 6 W. Sawyer Co.	No limit..........	Facilitate log driving.
'87, 113	Wm. Wilson, et al.	Apple river. On Sec. 28 or 33, T. 33 N., R. 16 W. Polk Co.	No limit..........	Facilitate log driving.
'87, 117	M. P. Beebe......	Tamarack creek. Dam add otherwise improve. Oneida Co.	No limit..........	Facilitate log driving.
'87,118*	Wausau Boom Co.	Wisconsin river, authority to maintain dam or other improvements on sec. 13, 23 and 26, T. 29, R. 7 E. Marathon Co,	No limit..........	Facilitate log driving.
'87,135	S. W. Campbell..	Apple river, N, W. qr of N. E. qr, sec. 11, T. 31, N, R. 18 W. St. Croix Co,	No limit..........	Hydraulic........
'87,176	J. W. Taylor.....	Yellow river, N. W. qr sec. 27 T. 34 N. R. 12 W. Barron Co.	No limit..........	Hydraulic and boomage.

* Amends c. 45, 71 (authority to maintain booms) see also 256, 73; 96. 81 and 204, 83.

ANALYSIS OF THE FRANCHISES FOR THE CONSTRUCTION OF DAMS BY THE
LEGISLATURE—Continued.

Individual Grantees.

Protection of navigation.	Miscellaneous purposes.	Eminent domain.	Reserve clause.	Fishways.
Slides far logs, etc.	Subject to mill dam act.	Granted as per mill dam.	Yes..............	No.
Slides for logs, etc.	None............	Not granted.....	Yes..............	No.
Slides for logs, etc.	None............	Granted.........	Yes..............	No.
Slides for logs, etc.	May collect toll	Granted.........	Yes..............	No.
Slides for logs, etc.	May collect toll.	Granted.........	Yes............	No.
Slides for logs, etc.	Subject to mill dam act.	Granted as per mill dam act.	Yes..............	No.
Slides for logs, etc.	May collect toll.	Not granted.....	Yes..............	No.
Slides for logs, etc.	May collect toll.	Granted.........	Yes..............	No.
None.............	None............	Granted.........	Yes............	No.
Not to obstruct navigation.	None............	Not granted......	No..............	No.
Slides for logs, etc.	None............	Granted	Yes..............	No.
Slides for logs, etc.	Subject to mill dam act.	Granted per mill dam act.	Yes..............	No.

ANALYSIS OF THE FRANCHISES FOR THE CONSTRUCTION OF DAMS BY THE
LEGISLATURE—Continued.

Individual Grantees.

Citation.	Grantee.	Stream, Location, County.	Duration of grant.	Purposes.
'87,177	Frederick Patterson,	Trade river, W. hf of N. W. qr. sec. 23. T, 37 N. R. 18W.	No limit..........	Hydraulic and boomage.
'87,178	Samuel Harriman, et al.	Blakes lake, sec. 26. T. 35 R. 16, Polk Co.	No limit..........	None specified...
'87,202	Jacob Leinenkugel.	Duncan creek, (city of Chippewa Falls) N. W. qr of N. E. qr sec. 6. T. 28, R. 8 W. Chippewa Co.	No limit...........	None s. ecified...
'87,273	Malcolm Doble...	Devil's creek....	No limit..........	Facilitate log driving.
'87,218	J. C. Schneider...	Rice bed stream. (fork of Apple river) N. W. qr of N. E. qr. sec. 6. T. 34, R. 15 W. Polk Co.	15 years..........	Facilitate log driving.
'87,223	C. A. Torinus....	Tatogatic river. sec. 12, T. 42 N. R. 12, W. Washburn Co.	20 years..........	Hydraulic........
'87,251	Hugh B. Mills....	Robinson creek. T. 20, R. 1, 2, 3 a·d 4 W. Jackson Co.	No limit..........	Facilitate log driving.
'87,299	Jacob Bye........	N. fork of Eau Claire river, sec 28, T. 29 N, R. W. Clark Co.	No limit.,........	Facilitate log driving.
'87,320	Chas. Henry.....	Bear Creek.(trib. of N. fork Flambeau) secs. 1 and 2. T. 40, R. 4 E. Vilas Co.	No limit..........	Facilitate log driving.
'87,339	D. H. Johnson, et al.	Big Rib river, between S. W. qr sec. 8, T. 29 N. R. 5 E. and mouth of Black creek, Marathon Co.	No limit....,.....	Facilitate log driving.
'87,346	Daniel J. Arpin, et al.	Tomahawk river. sec. 28, T. 35, R. 6 E. Lincoln Co.	No limit..........	Facilitate log driving.
'87,386	James Quall et al.	Squd (creek. dam and mprove) from mouth to sec. 16. T. 38 N. R. 1 E. Price Co.	No limit..........	Facilitate log driving.
'87,407	Daniel C. Fifield	Montreal river, W. branch. sec. 34, T. 46 N. R. 2 E. Ashland Co.	No limit..........	Facilitate log driving.

ANALYSIS OF THE FRANCHISES FOR THE CONSTRUCTION OF DAMS BY THE LEGISLATURE—Continued.

Individual Grantees.

Protection of navigation.	Miscellaneous purposes.	Eminent domain.	Reserve clause.	Fishways.
None	None.............	Granted..........	Yes...............	No.
Slides for logs etc.	None	Granted..........	Yes...............	No.
Not to unreasonably obstruct natural flow.	Not to interfere with other dams above and below.	Not granted.....	Yes.....:	No.
Slides for logs, etc.	May collect toll.	Granted..........	Yes..............	No.
Slides for logs, etc.	May collect toll.	Not granted.....	Yes........,.....	No.
Slides for logs, etc.	Subject to c. 146, R. S.	Granted as per mill dam act.	Yes...........,.....	No.
None.......s....	May collect toll.	Not granted.....	Yes...............	No.
Slides for logs. etc.	None............	Not granted.....	Yes..............	No.
None	None.............	Granted..........	Yes...............	No.
Slides for logs, etc.	None............	Not granted.....	Yes...............	No.
Slides for logs, etc.	None............	Granted as per mill dam act.	Yes...............	No.
None	None.............	Not granted......	Yes....	No.
Slides for logs. etc.	May collect toll	Not granted.....	Yes...............	No.

ANALYSIS OF THE FRANCHISES FOR THE CONSTRUCTION OF DAMS BY THE
LEGISLATURE—Continued.

Individual Grantees.

Citation.	Grantee.	Stream, Location, County.	Duration of grant.	Purposes.
'87.434	J. D. W. Heath..	Squirrel river. T. 39 N. R. 5 E.	No limit.........	Facilitate log driving.
'87.438	D. J. Spaulding, et al.	Black river, N. hf. sec. 22, T. 21, R. 4 W. Jackson Co.	No limit.........	None specified .
'87.444	Geo. H. Hall....	Peshtigo river. sec. 28 or 33, T. 37. R. 15, Forest Co.	No limit.........	Hydraulic "and other."
'87.448	C. J. Akerlind....	Trade river. s. E qr of S. E. qr. sec.. 16. T. 37 N. R. 18 W. Burnett Co.	No limit....... .	Hydraulic "and other."
'87.449	Chas. H. Henry..	Flambeau river. (N. fork.) T. 42, R. 5 E. Oneida Co.	No limit.........	Facilitate log driving.
'87.512 '89.270 Granting power of eminent domain.	Leander Choots, et al.	Eagle river, sec. 31, T. 40. R. 10 E. Oneida Co.	No limit.........	Facilitate log driving.
'87.532	J. P. Underwood, et al.	Eagle river. S hf sec. 5, T. 39. R. 11 E.	No limit.........	Facilitate log driving.
'87.539	Samuel Shaw...	Peshtigo river. secs. 25, 35 or 36. T. 37, R. 13 E. Forest Co.	No limit.........	Hydraulic "and other."
'87.254	W. J. Vincent, et al.	Clam river. T. 39 N.. R. 16 W. County.	No limit	Facilitate log driving.
'89.366	Joel Richardson,	Beaver Brook S. W. ¼ of N E. ¼ & N. W ¼ of S. E. ¼ sec. 5, T. 33 N.. R. 15 W.	No limit.........	Hydraulic and boomage.
'89.445 '97.97	James Wright...	Little Chief river. T. 41 N.. R 7 W. Sawyer Co.	No limit.........	Facilitate log driving.
'89,449	Herman Schwanke, et al.	Embarrass river. Secs. 13 & 10 T. 26, R. 11 E. Shawano Co.	No limit.........	Facilitate log driving.
'89,372	Henry J. Rogers, et al.	Fox River. Lots 6 & 7. sec. 24. S of river. to lots 2 & 3, sec. 22 N. of river. T. 21 N.. R. 18 E. Outagamie Co.	No limit.........	Hydraulic.....
'89,485	John T. Cosgriff.	Little Bear creek. S. W. ¼ of S. E ¼, sec. 7. T. 41. R. 5 E. Oneida Co.	No limit	Facilitate log driving.

ANALYSIS OF THE FRANCHISES FOR THE CONSTRUCTION OF DAMS BY THE
LEGISLATURE—Continued.

Individual Grantees.

Protection of navigation.	Miscellaneous purposes.	Eminent domain.	Reserve clause.	Fishways.
None...............	May collect toll.	Granted...........	Yes...............	No.
Slides for logs. etc.	None...............	Not granted......	Yes...............	No.
Slides for logs, etc.	None...............	Granted...........	Yes...............	No.
None...............	None...............	Granted...........	Yes...............	No.
Slides for logs, etc.	May collect toll.	Granted...........	Yes...............	No.
Slides for logs, etc.	May collect toll.	Granted...........	Yes...............	No.
Slides for logs, etc.	May collect toll.	Not granted......	Yes...............	No.
Not to obstruct navigation.	None...............	Not granted......	Yes...............	No.
Slides for logs, etc.	May collect toll.	Granted...........	Yes...............	No.
Slides for logs, etc.	Subject to mill dam act.	Granted...........	Yes...............	No.
Slides for logs, etc.	May collect toll.	Not granted......		
Slides for logs, etc.	May collect toll.	Granted...........	Yes...............	No.
Slides for logs, etc.	Subject to mill dam act.	Granted as per mill dam act.	Yes...............	No.
Slides for logs, etc.	May collect toll.	Not...............	Yes...............	No.

ANALYSIS OF THE FRANCHISES FOR THE CONSTRUCTION OF DAMS BY THE
LEGISLATURE—Continued.

Individual Grantees.

Citation.	Grantee.	Stream, Location, County.	Duration of grant.	Purposes.
'89,446	Wm. Sauntry....	Moose River Dam & improve. Below where same crosses E. line T. 45 N., R. 13 W., St. Croix river, dam & improve between where same crosses W. line sec. 6. T. 44. N., R 11 W. and W. line T. 43 N., R. 13 W. Douglas Co.	No limit.........	Facilitate log driving.
'89,23	John Nohr, Sr., et al.	Pigeon river. S. E. ¼ of S. E. ¼, sec. 15, T. 25 N., R. 13 E. Waupun Co.	No limit.........	Hydraulic.......
'89,45	Aug. G. Schmidt.	Red river. N. W. ¼ of N. E. ¼, sec. 3, T. 27, R. 14 E. Shawano Co.	No limit.........	Hydraulic and boomage.
'89,44	Charles & August Kruger.	Red river. S. E. ¼ of S. W. ¼ & S. W. ¼ of S. E. ¼, sec. 8, T. 27, R. 15 E. Shawano Co.	No limit.........	Hydraulic and boomage.
'89,215 '91,478 '95,352	Amos F. Jefferson, et al.	St. Croix river. Some point between S. line of T. 35, R. 19 W. & N. line T. 36 N., R. 20 W. Polk Co.	30 yrs............	Improve navigation.
'89,405	Geo. W. Mason, et al.	Skinner Creek. Dam & improve. secs. 9, 15 & 19, T. 36, R. 2 W. Price Co.	No limit.........	Facilitate log driving.
'89,83	Leroy Herrick, et al.	Squam creek. N. W. ¼ of S. E. ¼, sec. 28, T. 40 N., R. 4 E. Oneida Co.	No limit.........	Facilitate log driving.
'89,481	John & Daniel Arpin.	Tomahawk river. Sec. 21, T. 36 N., R. 6 E. Oneida Co.	No limit.........	Log driving......
'89,252	David M. Banjamin.	Tomahawk river. Secs. 10 & 15, T. 39 N., R. 6 E. Oneida Co.	No limit.........	Improve navigation.
'89,394	John S. Owen....	White river. Long Lake branch. Dam & improve above E. line sec. 13, T. 45 N. R. 7 W. Bayfield Co.	No limit.........	Hydraulic and facilitate.

ANALYSIS OF THE FRANCHISES FOR THE CONSTRUCTION OF DAMS BY THE LEGISLATURE—Continued.

Individual Grantees.

Protection of navigation.	Miscellaneous purposes.	Eminent domain.	Reserve clause.	Fishways.
slides for logs, etc.	May collect toll.	Granted...... .	Yes.............	No.
Slides for logs, etc.	None............	Not granted......	Yes.............	No.
slides for logs, etc.	Subject to mill dam act.	Granted.........	Yes.............	No.
slides for logs, etc.	Subject to mill dam act.	Granted as per mill dam act.	Yes.............	No.
slides for logs, etc.	May collect toll.	Granted.........	Yes.............	No.
slides for logs, etc.	May collect toll.	Not granted......	Yes.............	No.
slides for logs, etc.	None............	Not granted......	Yes.............	No.
slides for logs, etc.	None....	Not granted......	Yes.............	No.
slides for logs, etc.	None............	Granted.........	Yes.............	No.
slides for logs, etc.	None............	Granted.........	Yes.....	No.

ANALYSIS OF THE FRANCHISES FOR THE CONSTRUCTION OF DAMS BY THE
LEGISLATURE—Continued.

Individual Grantees.

Citation.	Grantee.	Stream. Location. County.	Duration of grant.	Purposes.
'89,53	Thomas E. Nash	Wisconsin river (2 dams). T. 21 N., R. 5 E. Wood Co.	No limit..........	Hydraulic ....
'89,283	Geo. A. Whiting, et al.	Wisconsin river. Sec. 8. T. 23 N., R. 8 E. Portage Co.	No limit.	Hydraulic ....
'89,407	Theodore A. Taylor, et al.	Wisconsin. Sec. 8, T. 23, R. 8. Portage Co.	No limit..........	Hydraulic ....
'89,236 '93,209	Geo. S. Biron, et al.	Wisconsin. Sec. 34, T. 23 N., R. 6 E. Wood Co.	No limit..........	Hydraulic, flooding, boomage.
'89,316	Frank Garrison, et al.	Wisconsin river. Sec. 24, T. 22 N., R. 5 E. Wood Co.	No limit..........	Improve navigation.
'89,49 Repeal '95,27	Wm. Chalmers ..	Yellow river. Dams (one at sec. 27, T. 39 N., R. 12 W., Burnett and Washburn Co.; One at sec. 7, T. 40 N., R. 16 W. Burnett & Washburn Cos. One at sec. 20, T. 39 N., R. 14 W. Burnett and Washburn Cos. One at sec. 10, T. 38 N., R. 13 W. Burnett & Washburn Cos.	No limit..........	Facilitate log driving.
'89,235	C. M. Upham, et al.	Wolf river. Sec. 25 or 36, T. 27, R. 15 E. Shawano Co.	No limit..........	Hydraulic "& other".
'89, 398	John Woodlock.	Little Somo river Sec. 37. T. 35 N. R. 5 E. Lincoln Co.	No limit	None specified ..
'91, 110 Repealed '07, 356	Wm. Sauntry.	Spruce river N. W. ¼ of N. E. ¼ sec. 32, T. 44 N. R. 15 W. Douglas Co. One at S. W. ¼ of N. W. ¼ sec. 27, T. 44 N. R. 15 W. Douglas Co. One at N. W. ¼ of S. E. ¼ Sec. 22, T. 44 N, R. 15 W. Douglas Co. And one at S. W. ¼ of S. W. ¼ Sec. 14 T. 44 N. R. 15 W. Douglas Co.	No limit..........	Facilitate log driving.

ANALYSIS OF THE FRANCHISES FOR THE CONSTRUCTION O
LEGISLATURE—Continued.

Individual Grantees.

Protection of navigation.	Miscellaneous purposes.	Eminent domain.	
Slides for logs, etc.	May sell or lease the right to use water power or water.	Not granted......	Yes.........
Slides for logs, etc.	None.............	Granted..........	Yes.........
Slides for logs, etc.	None.............	Granted..........	Yes.........
Slides for logs, etc.	None.............	Granted..........	Yes.........
Slides for logs, etc.	None.............	Granted.........	Yes.........
Slides for logs, etc.	May collect toll. Subject to mill dam act and Sec. 1777 R. S.	Granted..........	Yes..........
Slides for logs, etc.	None.............	Granted..........	Yes..........
Slide for logs, and lock for boats 40 ft. long.	None.............	Not granted.....	Yes..........
Slides for logs, etc.	May collect toll.	Granted..........	Yes..........

ANALYSIS OF THE FRANCHISES FOR THE CONSTRUCTION OF DAMS BY THE LEGISLATURE—Continued.

Individual Grantees.

Citation.	Grantees.	Stream, Location, County.	Duration of grant.	Purposes.
'91, 104	Wm. Sauntry...	Tomarac river, sec. 6, T. 42 N, R. 15 W. Burnett Co.	No limit.........	Facilitate log driving.
'91, 111 Repealed '07, 293	Wm. Sauntry,..	Moose river 3 dams between mouth and point where E. line of T. 45 N, R. 13 W. crosses said river. Douglas Co.	No limit.........	Improve navigation.
'91, 140	C. C. Van Deusen et al.	Flambeau river, S. fork, Lot 8, sec. 6, T. 39 N. R. 1 E. Price Co.	No limit.........	None specified..
'91, 142	H. C. Payne....	Yellow river, Town of Babcock, T. 21 N, R. 3 E. Wood Co.	No limit........	Hydraulic.......
'91, 148	Carl E. Peterson.	Trade river. sec. 36. T. 37, R. 19 W. Burnett Co.	30 years..........	Hydraulic........
'91, 149 Repealed '95, 28	Wm. Chalmers..	Spring Brook. S. ½ of S. W. ¼ sec. 6, and N. ½ of N. W. ¼, sec. 7, T. 39, R. 11 W. Washburn Co.	No limit.........	Facilitate log driving.
'91, 150	E. W. Dierks.....	Oconomowoc river. N. E. ¼ of N. W. ¼, sec. 25, T. 9. R. 18 E. Washington Co.	No limit..........	Hydraulic........
91, 170	Joseph Lindemann.	Oak creek, N. W. ¼ of S. E. ¼ and N. E. ¼ of S. W. ¼ sec. 2, T. 5 N., R. 22 E. Milwaukee Co.	No limit..........	To create.........
'91, 175	G. W. Huhn......	Red river. N. ½, S. W. ¼ of S. E. ¼, sec. 2, T. 27, R 14 E. Shawano Co.	No limit..........	Hydraulic and boomage.
'91, 177	Dan Graham et al.	Wisconsin river. Sec. 36, T. 40 N. R. 9 E. Oneida Co.	No limit..........	Improve navigation.
'91, 186 Repealed '99, 177	James Meiklejohn et al.	Little Wolf river. N. W. ¼ of S. W. ¼, sec. 15, T. 23 N., R. 13 E. Waupaca Co.	No limit..........	Hydraulic and facilitate log driving.
'91, 222	P. Hynes.........	Iron river and tributaries. Dam and improve river	No limit..........	Facilitate log driving.

ANALYSIS OF THE FRANCHISES FOR THE CONSTRUCTION OF DAMS BY THE LEGISLATURE—Continued.

Individual Grantees.

Protection of navigation.	Miscellaneous purposes.	Eminent domain.	Reserve clause.	Fishways.
Slides for logs. etc.	May collect toll.	Granted..........	Yes...............	No.
Slides for logs. etc.	May collect toll.	Granted..........	Yes...............	No.
Slides for logs. etc.	None.............	Not granted....	Yes...............	No.
None............	None.............	Not granted.....	Yes...............	No.
None.	None.............	Not granted.....	Yes...............	No.
Slide for logs. etc.	May collect toll.	Granted..........	Yes...............	No.
None............	None.............	Not granted.....	Yes...............	No.
None.......	None.............	Granted..........	No...............	No.
Slide for logs. etc.	Subject to mill dam act.	Granted as per dam act.	Yes...............	No.
Slides for logs. etc.	None......... ...	Granted..........	Yes...............	No.
Slide for logs. etc.	May collect toll.	Not grante	Yes...............	No.
Slides for logs. etc.	May collect toll.	Not granted.....	Yes...............	No.

ANALYSIS OF THE FRANCHISES FOR THE CONSTRUCTION OF DAMS BY THE LEGISLATURE—Continued.

Individual Grantees.

Citation.	Grantees.	Stream, Location. County.	Duration of grant.	Purposes.
'91, 229	Henry Collette et al.	Pine river. N. branch. Forest Co.	No limit..........	Facilitate log driving.
'91, 238	Bertin Ramsey et al.	Pine river. N. branch. Forest Co.	No limit..........	Facilitate log driving.
'91, 242	George Clayton et al.	Eau Claire river. Sec. 7, T. 27 N., R. 10 E. Marathon Co.	No limit..........	Hydraulic........
'93, 373	A. Vang Jr........	Shioc creek. S W. ¼ of N. E. ¼ sec. 25, T. 25, R. 16 E. Shawano Co.	No limit..........	Hydraulic........
'91, 313	Wm. F. Bailey et al.	Chippewa river. Between Eau Claire and Chippewa Falls, Eau Claire and Chippewa Cos.	If not constructed in 3 yrs. rights cease.	Facilitate log driving.
'91, 395 '07, 437 *	A. W. Whitcomb et al.	Little Wolf river. Near where line crosses, between sec. 23 and 26, T. 25, R. 12 E. Waupaca Co.	No limit..........	Hydraulic........
'91, 396	James McCrosses et al.	Montreal river. W. branch between Island lake and N. line. Sec. 27, T. 46 N., R. 2 E.	No limit..........	Facilitate log driving.
'93, 111	M. C. Ring........	Black river. Any point between mouth of Oneills creek and railroad right of way across said river. Clark Co.	No limit..........	Hydraulic and boomage.
'93, 221	John Arbuckle..	Clam river. S. E. ¼ of N. E. ¼ sec. 5, T. 37 N., R. 14 W. Burnett Co.	No limit..........	Facilitate log driving.
'93, 264	John Arbuckle..	Clam river. N. W. ¼ sec. 30, T. 38 N., R. 14 W. Barron Co.	No limit..........	Facilitate log driving.
'93, 50	Carl Kleinschmidt.	Devil creek. E. ¼ of N. E. ¼ sec. 20, T. 30 N., R. 6 E. Lincoln Co.	No limit..........	Facilitate log dirving.

* Alters description of location.

ANALYSIS OF THE FRANCHISES FOR THE CONSTRUCTION OF DAMS BY THE
LEGISLATURE—Continued.

Individual Grantees.

Protection of navigation.	Miscellaneous purposes.	Eminent domain.	Reserve clause.	Fishways.
Side for logs. etc.	May collect toll.	Not granted.....	Yes..............	No.
None.............	May collect toll.	Not granted.....	No............	No.
slide for logs, etc.	None.............	Not granted.....	Yes..............	No.
slide for logs, etc.	None.............	Granted as per mill dam act.	Yes..............	No.
Not to materially obstruct naviga- tion.	May collect toll.	Not granted.....	No................	No.
Side for logs, etc.	None.............	Not granted.....	Yes..............	No.
Side for logs, etc.	May collect toll.	Granted..........	Yes...............	No.
Slides for logs, etc.	None.............	Not granted.....	Yes..............	Yes.
Slides for logs, etc.	May collect toll.	Granted..........	Yes..............	No.
Slides for logs, etc.	May collect toll.	Not granted.....	No................	No.
Slide for logs, etc.	None.............	Not granted.....	No................	No.

ANALYSIS OF THE FRANCHISES FOR THE CONSTRUCTION OF DAMS BY THE
LEGISLATURE—Continued.

Individual Grantees.

Citation.	Grantee.	Stream. Location. County.	Duration of grant.	Purposes.
'93,203	James Spaulding	Comet river. Sec. 21, T. 28 N., R.11E, also Sec. 34, T. 28 N., R. 11 E. Shawano Co. Also Sec. 12, T. 25 N., R. 11 E. Waupaca Co.	No limit..........	Facilitate log driving.
'93,194	Chas. W. Hanson	Eldee creek. Sec. 19, T. 31, R.4 W. Taylor Co.	No limit..........	Facilitate log driving.
'95,154	Thomas Christy.	Little Rice river. W. hf of N. E qr. Sec. 23. T. 36 N., R. 5 E.	No limit..........	Facilitate log driving.
'93,122	Frederick Maneele.	Hay Meadow creek. S. E. qr of S. W. qr. Sec. 7, T. 32 N., R. 8 E. Lincoln Co.	No limit..........	Hydraulic......
'93 191	N. H. Brakam, et al.	Oconto river. Lot 1. Sec. 25, T.28 N., R. 19 E. Oconto Co.	No limit..........	Hydraulic........
'93,129	Wm. Sommers...	Pecar brook. N. E. qr of N. E. qr, Sec. 18, T. 29. R. 17 E. Oconto Co.	No limit.....	Hydraulic and facilitate log driving.
'93,169	Paul Browne et al.	Pelican river. Secs. 8, 9 or 16, T. 36 N., R. 9 E.	No limit........	Hydraulic, boomage, and furnishing electric light.
'93,302	Edward J. Thompson.	Sand river. Bayfield Co.	No limit..........	Facilitate log driving.
'93,266	J.N. Catter, et al.	Prairie river. Sec. 1, T. 31 N., R. 6 E. Lincoln Co.	No limit..........	Hydraulic & facilitate log driving.
'93,99	Geo. Danielson, et al.	White river. N. hf of N. E. qr, Sec. 6, T. 46 N., R. 4 W. Ashland Co.	No limit..........	Hydraulic and boomage.
'93,210 '95,82	B. G. Chandos...	Wisconsin river. At Grand Rapids. Wood Co.	No limit..........	Hydraulic and improvement of navigation.
'93,96 Repealed. '03,155	J. D. Ross, et al.	Wisconsin river. T. 28 N. Marathon Co.	No limit..........	Hydraulic & facilitate log driving.
'93,196	Jas. Desert,et al.	Wisconsin river. T. 27 E., R. 7 E. Marathon Co.	No limit..........	Hydraulic & facilitate log driving.
'93,265	Jacob Searls, et al.	Hemlock creek. Wood Co.	No limit..........	To supply canal.
'95,172	Finney, F. E....	Black river. T. 26 N., R. 2 W. Clark Co.	No limit.....	Hydraulic......

ANALYSIS OF THE FRANCHISES FOR THE CONSTRUCTION OF DAMS BY THE
LEGISLATURE—Continued.

Individual Grantees.

Protection of navigation.	Miscellaneous purposes.	Eminent domain.	Reserve clause.	Fishways.
slides for logs, etc.	May collect toll.	Granted..........	Yes..............	No.
slides for logs, etc.	May collect toll. Mill dam act applies.	Granted as per mill dam act.	Yes..............	No.
slide for logs, etc	May collect toll.	Not granted......	Yes..............	No.
slides for logs, etc.	None..............	Not granted......	Yes..............	No.
slides for logs, etc.	Mill dam act applies.	Granted as per mill dam act.	No..............	No.
None..............	None..............	Not granted.	Yes..............	No,
slides for logs, etc.	None..............	Granted..........	Yes..............	No.
slides for logs, etc.	May collect toll.	Granted..........	Yes..............	No,
slides for logs, etc.	May collect toll.	Not granted.....	No..............	No.
slides for logs, etc.	Mill dam act applies.	Granted as per mill dam act.	Yes..............	No.
slides for logs, etc.	—May sell or lease right to use water power or water.	Granted..........	Yes..............	No.
slides for logs, etc.	None..............	Granted..........	Yes..............	No.
slides for logs, etc.	None..............	Granted..........	Yes..............	No.
None..............	None..............	Not granted......	No..............	No.
slides for logs, etc.	None..............	Granted..........	Yes..............	Yes.

15

ANALYSIS OF THE FRANCHISES FOR THE CONSTRUCTION OF DAMS BY THE LEGISLATURE—Continued.

Individual Grantees.

Citation.	Grantee.	Stream, Location, County.	Duration of grant.	Purposes.
'95,210	J. F. McMillen..	Big Eau Pleine, T. 29 N., R. 2 E. Marathon Co.	No limit.........	Hydraulic & facilitate log driving.
'95,357	Warren Flint, et al.	Fisher river. Sec. 34. T. 32 N., R. 6W. Also Sec. 4, T. 31 N., R. 6 W. Chippewa Co.	No limit.....	Facilitate log driving.
'95,340	G. L. Rogers.....	Chippewa river. E. fork. Sec. 12, T. 42 N., R. 2 W. Ashland Co.	No limit.........	None specified. .
'95,60	Henry Sherry, et al.	Turtle river. At any point in Iron Co,	No limit.........	Hydraulic & facilitate log driving.
'95,234	Frank E. Cook...	Peshtigo, middle branch. Sec. 28, and 33, T. 37. R. 13 E. Forest Co.	No limit....... .	Hydraulic "and other."
'95,251	N. G. Nelson.....	Litt'e Wolf river. Sec. 21, T. 23, R. 13 E. Waupaca Co.	No limit.	Hydraulic.......
'95,99	D. J. Arpin et al.	Hemlock creek. Secs. 17-19 or 20, T. 22, R.4 E. Wood Co.	No limit.........	Feed canal ... ...
'95,77	L. M. Alexander	Wisconsin river. Sec. 36, T. 22 N., R. 5 E. Wood Co.	No limit.........	Hydraulic.....
'95,58	Chas. M. Upham	Wolf river. Secs. 1 or 13, T. 27, R. 15 E. Shawano Co.	No limit.....	Hydraulic and boomage.
'95,59	Ole Johnson	Hay river. N. hf of N. E. qr. Sec. 20, T. 33 N., R. 13 W. Barron Co.	No limit.........	Hydraulic and boomage.
'95,114	Ole Matson	Trade river. Sec. 34. T. 37. R. 18 W. Burnett Co.	20 years..........	Hydraulic.......
'95, 134 '01, 294	L. B. Ring.	Black river between Quarter line E. and W. through sec. 22, T. 24 N, R. 2 W, and qr. line E. and W. through sec 26, T. 24 N, R.2 W. Clark Co.	No limit.........	Hydraulic and boomage.
'95, 101 Repealed '97, 141	Abe Johnson.	Yellow river. one in sec 7. T. 40 N. R. 16 W. Burnett Co. One in sec. 20, T. 39 N, R. 14 W. Burnett Co.	No limit.........	Facilitate log driving.

ANALYSIS OF THE FRANCHISES FOR THE CONSTRUCTION OF DAMS BY THE LEGISLATURE—Continued.

Individual Grantees.

Protection of navigation.	Miscellaneous purposes.	Eminent domain.	Reserve clause.	Fishways.
None.............	None.............	Not granted.....	No	No.
None.............	None.............	Not granted.....	No.............	No.
...e for logs.etc	None.............	Not granted.....	Yes.............	Yes.
...es for logs.	May collect toll.	Granted.........	Yes.............	No.
...es for logs.	None.............	Granted.........	Yes.............	No.
...es for logs.	None.............	Not granted.....	Yes.............	No.
None.............	None.............	Granted.........	No.............	No.
...e for logs, etc	May sell or lease the right to use water power.	Not granted.....	Yes.............	No.
...e for logs. etc	None.............	Granted.........	Yes.............	No.
...es for logs.	May collect toll.	Granted as per mill dam act.	Yes.............	No.
None	None.............	Not granted.....	Yes.............	No.
...es for logs.	None.............	Not granted.....	Yes.............	No.
...es for logs.	May collect toll.	Granted.........	Yes.............	No

ANALYSIS OF THE FRANCHISES FOR THE CONSTRUCTION OF DAMS BY TE
LEGISLATURE—Continued.

Individual Grantees.

Citation.	Grantee.	Stream. Location. County.	Duration of grant.	Purposes.
'97, 206	J. F. Hamilton, et al.	Beaver creek, sec. 33, T. 19 N, R. 2 E. Juneau Co.	No limit..........	None specified.
'97, 207	Sidney H. Waterman.	Cranberry creek, sec. 15, T. 38 N, R. 15 W. Burnett Co.	No limit..........	None specified.
'97, 143	W. G. Curtis.	Hay river, N. ½ sec. 18, T. 35 N, R. 13 W. Barron Co.	No limit	Hydraulic a maintain wate of Beaver Da Lake uniform.
'97, 266	Thos. Kirby, et al.	Middle river, sec. 10, T. 47 N. R. 12 W. or at any point north to mouth of said river, Douglas Co.	No limit..........	Facilitate l driving.
'97, 145 '03, 114 (as to height of dam)	G. W. Volk, et al.	Oconto river, lots 1 and 3, sec. 23, T. 28 N. R. 19 E. Oconto Co.	No limit..........	Hydraulic at boomage.
'97, 240	Geo. Beyer, et al.	Oconto river.	No limit..........	Hydraulic....
'97, 211 '01, 122	Wm. Fellows	Rat river, S. E. ¼ of S. E. ¼, sec 25, T. 36 N, R. 14 E. Forest Co., also S. E. ¼ of N. E. ¼, sec. 32, T. 36 N. R. 14 E. Forest Co.	No limit..........	Facilitate l driving.
'97, 234	M. H. Wilcox....	Spring brook, trib. of Gilbert Creek, S. E. ¼ of N. E. ¼, sec. 26, T. 28 N. R. 14 W. Dunn Co.	No limit..........	Fisciculture...
'97, 190 Repealed '05, 483	W. J. Walsh et al.	Wisconsin river, lot 7 and 8, sec. 36, T. 40 N. R. 9 E. Vilas Co.	No limit..........	Hydraulic t improvement navigation.
'99, 134	James E. Rork ..	Elk creek, N. W. ¼ of N. E. ¼, sec. 12, T. 27 N, R. 11 W. Dunn Co.	No limit	Hydraulic....
'99, 144	Frank W. Epley, et al.	Apple river, S. E. ¼ of S. E. ¼, sec. 35, T. 31 N. R. 19 W. St. Croix Co.	No limit..........	Hydraulic l improvement navigation.
'99, 172	F. W. Epley.....	Apple river, S. W. ¼, sec. 26, T 31 N, R. 19 W. St. Croix Co.	No limit..........	Hydraulic improvement navigation.

ANALYSIS OF THE FRANCHISES FOR THE CONSTRUCTION OF DAMS BY THE LEGISLATURE—Continued.

Individual Grantees.

Protection of navigation.	Miscellaneous Purposes.	Eminent domain.	Reserve clause.	Fishways.
None............	None............	Not granted.....	Yes...............	No.
...les for logs.	Subject to mill dam act.	Granted..........	Yes...............	No.
None............	Subject to mill dam act.	Granted..........	Yes...............	No.
...es for logs.	May collect toll; may sell water for power and other purposes.	Granted..........	Yes...............	No.
...es for logs.	Subject to mill dam act.	Granted..........	Yes...............	No.
...es for logs.	Mill dam act applies.	Granted as per mill dam act.	No...............	No.
...les for logs.	Subject to mill dam act.	Granted..........	Yes...............	No.
None............	None............	Not granted.....	No............ ...	No.
...les for logs.	None............	Granted..........	No...............	No.
None............	None............	Granted..........	Yes...............	No.
None............	None............	Not granted......	Yes...............	No,
None............	None............	Not granted.....	Yes...............	No.

ANALYSIS OF THE FRANCHISES FOR THE CONSTRUCTION OF DAMS BY THE LEGISLATURE—Continued.

Individual Grantees.

Citation.	Grantee.	Stream, Location, County.	Duration of grant.	Purposes.
'99, 177	W. H. Hatton et al.	Little Wolf N. W. ¼ of S. W. ¼. sec. 15. T. 23 N. R. 13 E. Waupaca Co.	no limit., ...	Hydraulic and boomage.
'99, 195	R. N. Roberts et al.	Waupaca river, lots 124 and 125, Waupaca, Waupaca County.	no limit..........	Hydraulic.......
'99, 209	A. J. McGilvray	Chippewa river. sec. 30. or on 29 and 30. T. 30 N, R. 7 W.	no limit..........	Hydraulic.....
'99, 227	J. P. Ausman....	Elk creek N. E. ¼ of N. W. ¼, sec. 12. T. 27 N, R. 11 W. Dunn Co,	no limit..........	Hydraulic....
'99, 261	Hieronymus Zech.	Peshtigo river, sec. 1. T. 32 N, R. 18 E. Marinette Co.	no limit..........	Facilitate driving logs.
'09, 320	Abbie Sherry et al.	Flambeau. lots 4 and 5. sec. 13. R. 1 W. Price Co., also lot 6. sec. 25. T. 40 N, R. 1 W. Price Co.	no limit..........	Hydraulic.....
'99, 331	H. W. Wright...	Manitowish river. sec. 14. T. 41 N, R. 6 E. Vilas Co.	no limit.....	Facilitate l driving.
'01, 55	Emil Thomas....	Prairie river, sec. 12. T. 32 N. R. 7 E. Lincoln Co.	no limit..........	Hydraulic an boomage.
'01, 185 '05, 220 (as to location).	F. W. Epley.....	Apple river. S. W. ¼ of N. E. ¼, sec. 31. T. 31 N. R. 18 W. St. Croix Co.	No limit..........	Hydraulic and improvement stream.
'01, 196	Caspar Faust ...	Little Wolf. N. W. ¼ of N. E. ¼. sec. 8, T. 22 N. R. 14 E.	No limit..........	Hydraulic and boomage.
'01, 260	A. P. Nelson. ..	Wood river. N. W, ¼ of N. W. ¼. sec. 22. T. 38 N, R. 19 W. Burnett Co.	25 yrs.............	Hydraulic an flooding.
'01, 261	Horace E. Horton.	Big Plover river. Village of McDill. Portage Co. (Legalizes dam previously constructed)	No limit..........	Hydraulic....

ANALYSIS OF THE FRANCHISES FOR THE CONSTRUCTION OF DAMS BY THE LEGISLATURE—Continued.

Individual Grantees.

Protection of navigation.	Miscellaneous Purposes.	Eminent domain.	Reserve clause.	Fishways.
slides for logs. etc.	None..............	Not granted....	Yes..............	No.
Slides for logs. etc.	None..............	Granted........	Yes..............	No.
Slides for logs. etc.	May sell or lease right to use water or power.	Granted..........	Yes..............	No.
None..............	None..............	Granted..........	Yes...............	No.
Slides for logs. etc.	None..............	Not granted.....	No................	No.
Slides for logs. etc.	Mill dam act applies.	Granted as per mill dam act.	Yes..............	No.
slides for log driving.	None..............	Granted..........	Yes..............	No.
Slides for log driving.	None..............	Not granted.....	No................	Yes.
None.............	None	Not granted.....	Yes..............	Yes.
slides for logs. etc.	None	Not granted.....	Yes..............	No.
slides for logs. etc.	Mill dam act applies.	Granted as per mill dam act.	Yes..............	No.
slides for logs. etc.	May sell or lease right to use water power.	Not granted.....	Yes..............	No.

ANALYSIS OF THE FRANCHISES FOR THE CONSTRUCTION OF DAMS BY THE
LEGISLATURE—Continued.

Individual Grantees.

Citation.	Grantee.	Stream, Location, County.	Duration of grant.	Purposes.
'01, 264	W. H. Dick	Embarass river. N. E. ¼ of N. W. ¼, sec. 36, T. 27, R. 12 E, also N. W. ¼ of N. E. ¼, sec. 7, T. 26, R. 14 E. Shawano Co.	No limit	Facilitate log driving.
'01, 292 '03, 112 *	A. J. McGilvray	Flambeau river. Sec. 35, T. 36 N. R. 6 W. Chippewa Co.	Operations to commence within 2 years,	Hydraulic
'01, 365	Walter Alexander.	Trapp river, Sec. 12 and 13, T. 30 N, R. 8 E. Marathon Co.	No limit	Hydraulic and improve navigation.
'01, 455	Chas. R. Smith et al.	Flambeau. Dam or dams, one at N. ¼, sec. 30 N, T. 35 E, R. 3 W. One at frac. lot 7 and frac. lot 1, sec. 2 T. 34 N, R. 6 W. Chippewa Co.	No limit	Hydraulic
'01, 462	William Gunther et al.	Wisconsin river. Lot 4, sec. 4, T. 13 N, R. 6 E. Sauk Co.	No limit	Hydraulic and improve navigation.
'03, 340	E. T. Harman	Chippewa. Sec. 23 and 26, T. 38 N, R. 7 W. Sawyer Co.	No limit	Improve navigation and hydraulic.
'03, 364	John Woodlock	Tomahawk. S. W. ¼ sec. 18, T. 39 N, R. 6 E. Vilas Co.	No limit	Hydraulic.
'03, 365	H. M. Seaver	Little Wolf river. N. E. ¼ sec. 34, T. 24, R. 13 E.	No limit	Improve navigation and hydraulic.
'03, 62 '07, 123 (height of dam, etc.)	O. E. Pederson et al.	Flambeau river. Lots 2 and 7, sec. 18, T. 34 N, R. 6 W. Rusk Co.	No limit	Hydraulic.
'03, 145	Edward Bradley et al.	Wisconsin. Dam or dams in secs. 3 and 10, T. 33 N, R. 6 E. Lincoln Co.	No limit	Improve navigation and hydraulic.
'03, 153	G. D. Jones et al.	Wisconsin. Secs. 13 or 14, T. 30 N, R. 7 E. Marathon Co.	No limit	Improve navigation and hydraulic.

* Repeals time for commencement of operations. c. 675, laws of 1907.

ANALYSIS OF THE FRANCHISES FOR THE CONSTRUCTION OF DAMS BY THE LEGISLATURE—Continued.

Individual Grantees.

Protection of navigation.	Miscellaneous purposes.	Eminent domain.	Reserve clause.	Fishways.
Slides for logs. etc.	May collect toll..	Not granted.....	Yes..............	Yes.
Slides for logs, etc.	May sell or lease right to use water and power.	Not granted.....	Yes,.............	No.
Slides for logs, etc.	None.............	Granted..........	Yes..............	Yes.
Slides for logs, etc.	None.............	Granted..........	Yes..............	Yes.
None.............	Subject to mill dam act.	Granted 1777 and 1777e R. S.	Yes..............	Yes.
Slides for logs. etc.	None.............	Granted..........	Yes..............	Yes.
Slides for logs, etc.	None.............	Granted..........	Yes..............	Yes.
Slides for logs. etc.	None.............	Not granted.....	Yes..........	Yes.
Slides for logs. etc.	None.............	Granted..........	Yes..............	Yes.
Slides for logs. etc.	May sell or lease surplus water or power or use same for mfg. business, electric lighting, street railway operating. etc.	Granted	Yes..............	Yes.
Slides for logs, etc.	May use. sell or lease power for mfg.. electric lighting, operating street railways, etc.	Granted..........	Yes..............	Yes.

ANALYSIS OF THE FRANCHISES FOR THE CONSTRUCTION OF DAMS BY THE LEGISLATURE—Continued.

Individual Grantees.

Citation.	Grantee.	Stream, Location, County.	Duration of grant.	Purposes.
'03, 154	Alexander Stewart et al.	Wisconsin. Dam or dams, secs. 19, 20, 29, 30 and 31, T. 33 N, R. 6 and secs. 6, T. 32 N, R. 6 E. Lincoln Co.	No limit.........	Improve navigation and hydraulic.
'03, 155	J. D. Ross et al..	Wisconsin river. (Dam formerly owned and operated by J. D. Ross and W. C. Silverthorn) T. 28 N, R. 7 E. Marathon Co.	No limit..	Improve navigation and hydraulic.
'03' 156	C. J. Winton......	Wisconsin. Secs. 32 and 33, T. 26 N. R. 7 E. Marathon Co.	No limit..... ...	Improve navigation and hydraulic.
'03, 172	David R. Davis et al.	Chippewa river. Dams, one at S. ¼, sec. 30, T. 30 N, R. 7 W. Chippewa Co. One at lot 1, sec. 29, T. 30 N. R. 7 W. Chippewa Co.	No limit.	Hydraulic........
'03, 174	A. P. Bixly, et al.	Apple river. Sec. 30, T. 32 N., R. 17 W. Polk Co.	No limit.........	Hydraulic.......
'03, 181 Repealed '07, 31	Alvin A. Nuck...	Brule river. Sec. 22, T. 47 N., R. 10 W. Douglas Co.	No limit.........	Improve navigation and hydraulic.
'03, 209	Robert Gregnon.	Pecar brook. N. E. qr of N. E. qr Sec. 18, T. 29, R. 17. Oconto Co.	No limit.........	Facilitate log driving.
'03 21	Daniel C. Baldwin, et al.	Red Cedar river. Sec. 8, T. 29 N., R. 11 W, Dunn Co	No limit.........	Hydraulic. Supplying municipalities and their inhabitants with light, heat and power.
'03, 223	Personal representatives of Richard Schen.	Copper river. N. E. qr of S. W. qr. Sec. 4, T. 31 N., R. 5 E. Lincoln Co.	No limit.........	Facilitate log driving.
'03, 231	John W. Thomas.	Chippewa. Secs. 1 and 2, T. 29 N., R. 8 W. Chippewa Co.	No limit.........	Hydraulic.......
'03, 239	E. S. Shepard, et al.	Wisconsin. T. 36 N., R. 8 E. Oneida Co.	No limit.........	Hydraulic improvement of navigation.

ANALYSIS OF THE FRANCHISES FOR THE CONSTRUCTION OF DAMS BY THE
LEGISLATURE—Continued.

Individual Grantees.

Protection of navigation.	Miscellaneous purposes.	Eminent domain.	Reserve clause.	Fishways.
Slides for logs, etc.	May use, sell or lease power for mfg., electric lighting, operating street railways, etc.	Granted..........	Yes..............	Yes.
Slides for logs. etc	May use, sell or lease power for mfg., electric lighting, operating street railways, etc.	Granted....... ..	Yes..............	Yes.
Slides for logs. etc.	May use. sell or lease power for mfg., electric lighting, operating street railways, etc.	Granted....... ..		
Slides for logs. etc	Not to interfere with other water power owners on river.	Granted..........	Yes..............	Yes.
Slides for logs. etc.	None........	Granted..........	Yes..............	Yes.
Slides for logs, etc	May use, sell or lease power, work to be commenced within 4 yrs.	Granted..........	Yes..............	Yes.
None....	None.............	Granted..	Yes..............	Yes.
Slides for logs, etc.	May use. sell or lease power.	Granted..........	Yes..............	Yes.
Slides for logs, etc.	None	Granted..........	Yes..............	Yes.
Slides for logs. etc.	None.............	Granted..........	Yes..............	Yes.
Slides for logs. etc.	None.............	Granted..........	Yes..............	No.

ANALYSIS OF THE FRANCHISES FOR THE CONSTRUCTION OF DAMS BY THE
LEGISLATURE—Continued.

Individual Grantees.

Citation.	Grantee.	Stream, Location, County.	Duration of grant.	Purposes.
'08, 243	C. C. Sniteman..	Black river. N. line city of Neillsville. Clark Co.	No limit...... ...	Hydraulic. (Supply hydraulic and electric power to operate machinery, electric plant, pumping work, electric railways, etc.
'03, 244	J. H. Palmer.....	Long Lake creek. (Dam and other improvements) T. 43 and 44 N., R. 3 E. Iron Co.	No limit...:.....	Facilitate log driving.
'03, 288	A. C. Weber.....	Red river. Secs. 21 or 22, T. 27, R. 15 E. Shawano Co.	No limit..........	Hydraulic and facilitate log driving.
'03, 308	Powell Stackhouse.	Menomonie river. Lot 2 or 3 or both. Sec. 22, T. 38, R. 21 E. Marinette Co.	No limit..........	Hydraulic........
'03, 310	Frank J. Kipp...	White river. Sec. 24, T. 18 N., R. 10 E. and Sec. 19. T. 18 N., R. 11 E. Waushara Co.	No limit..........	Hydraulic......
'03, 385	E. F. Decker.....	Embarrass river. S. W. qr Sec. 5, T. 25 N., R. 15 E. Waupaca County. (Dam built and owned by Palmer 1856, hereby validated.)	No limit..........	Hydraulic.... ..
'08, 400	G. W. Henika, et al.	Kickapoo river. Village of Reedstown. Vernon Co. (Dam built in 1901, hereby validated.)	No limit..........	Hydraulic........
'05, 350	Dick, W. H.......	Embarrass, two dams. One at E. hf. S. E. qr, Sec. 32, T. 28 N., R. 13 E. Shawano Co. And one at S. E. qr of N. W. qr. sec. 15, T. 27 N., R. 13 E. Shawano Co.	No limit..........	Improve navigation and hydraulic.

ANALYSIS OF THE FRANCHISES FOR THE CONSTRUCTION OF DAMS BY THE LEGISLATURE—Continued.

Individual Grantees.

Protection of navigation.	Miscellaneous purposes.	Eminent domain.	Reserve clause.	Fishways.
Not to retard log driving.	None............	Not granted......	Yes..............	Yes.
Slides for logs, etc.	May collect toll.	Granted..	Yes..............	Yes.
Slides for logs, etc.	None............	Granted..........	Yes..............	Yes.
Must get consent of Menomonee River Boom Co. Slides, etc. for logs.	None............	Not granted......	Yes..............	Yes.
None............	Work to commence within 4 yrs.	Granted..........	Yes..............	Yes.
Slides for logs, etc.	None............	Granted..........	Yes..............	Yes.
None............	May use, sell or lease water or power.	Not granted......	Yes..............	Yes.
Slides for logs, etc.	*	Granted..........	Yes..............	Yes.

* Charges for power let or sold for public or for lawful private purpose, to be reasonable. Arbitrators to fix price in case of disagreement. Refusal on part of owner of power to submit question of reasonable price or to furnish at price fixed by arbitrators, if power not needed for other use, forfeits charter. Refusal on part of lessee to accept award of arbitrators, cancels lease. Suspension of operation, pursuant to any agreement in violation of Wis. or U. S. law forfeits charter. Act becomes operative only upon written acceptance of conditions hereof being filed with secretary of state. After completion of dam operations must not cease for more than two years.

ANALYSIS OF THE FRANCHISES FOR THE CONSTRUCTION OF DAMS BY THE
LEGISLATURE—Continued.

Individual Grantees.

Citation.	Grantee.	Stream, Location, County.	Duration of grant.	Purposes.
'03, 353 '05, 290	E. G. Boynton, et al.	Black river. Sec. 3, T. 22 N., R. 3 W. Jackson Co.	No limit..........	Improve navigation and hydraulic.
'05, 398	W. E. Brown, et al.	Pelican river. S. hf of S. E. qr, Sec. 4 or N. hf of N. E. qr, Sec. 9, T. 36 N., R. 10 E. Oneida Co.	No limit..........	Improve navigation and hydraulic.
'05, 399	Stephen Stevenson.	La Crosse river. S. W. qr, Sec. 33, T. 17 N., R. 6 W. LaCrosse Co.	No limit..........	Hydraulic.........
'05, 400 '07, 361*	Chas. A. Gesell..	Flambeau. W. hf Sec. 4, T. 41 N., R. 2 E. Iron Co.	No limit..........	Improve navigation and hydraulic.
'05, 401	P. M. Parker, et al.	Red Cedar river. E. hf of N. E. qr. Sec 32, T. 35 N., R. 11 W. Barron Co.	No limit..........	Improve navigation and hydraulic.
'05, 407	D. E. Dawson, et al.	Wisconsin. Lots 3 and 5. Secs. 19 and 20. T. 31 N., R. 7 E. Lincoln Co.	No limit..........	Improve navigation and hydraulic.
'05, 409 Repealed. '07, 243	John T. Casgriff.	Jump river. Sec. 28, T. 33, R. 5 W. Gates Co.	No limit,.........	Improve navigation and hydraulic.
'05,410	J. B. Mathews...	White river. Sec. 1, T. 46 N., R. 5, W.	No limit..........	Improve navigation & hydraulic.
'05,411	G. E. Newman ...	Main creek. Sec. 31, T. 34 N., R. 5 W. Gates Co.	No limit	Improve navigation "& other."
'05,415 '07,359 (Adds to purpose extends time to construct.)	E. W. Hopkins...	Pine river. Sec. 28, T. 30 N., R. 18 E. Florence Co.	No limit..........	Improve navigation & hydraulic.
'05,457	E. H. Van Ostrand et al.	Wolf river. E. hf of S. W. qr Sec. 10, T. 31 N., R. 14 E. Langlade Co.	No limit..........	Improve naviga tion & hydraulic
'05,397	John S. Van Nortwick et al.	Fox river. Lower rapids city of Kaukauna. Outagamie Co.	No limit..........	Hydraulic.......

*Transferred to State Land and Power Co. Time extended 2 years.

ANALYSIS OF THE FRANCHISES FOR THE CONSTRUCTION OF DAMS BY THE
LEGISLATURE—Continued.

Individual Grantees.

Protection of navigation.	Miscellaneous purposes.	Eminent domain.	Reserve clause.	Fishways.
Slides for logs, etc.	+	Granted..........	Yes.......	Yes.
Slides for logs, etc.	Sec. 350, '05, to be constructed within 4 yrs.	Granted..........	Yes..............	Yes.
None.............	Sec. 350, '05, to be constructed within 4 yrs.	Not granted......	Yes..............	Yes.
Slides for logs, etc.	Sec. 350, '05. To be constructed within 6 years.	Granted..........	Yes..............	Yes.
None.............	Sec. 350, 05. To be constructed within 4 yrs.	Granted..........	Yes..............	Yes.
Slides for logs, etc.	Sec. 350, '05. To be constructed within 4 years.	Granted.	Yes..............	Yes.
Slides for logs, etc.	Sec. 350, '05. Grant to W. H. Dick. To be constructed within 4 years.	Granted..........	Yes..............	Yes.
None.............	Sec. 350, '05. Grant to W. H. Dick. To be constructed within 4 yrs.	Granted..........	Yes..............	Yes.
Slides for logs, etc.	Sec. 350, '05. Grant to W. H. Dick. To be constructed within 4 yrs.	Granted.........	Yes..............	Yes.
Slides for logs, etc.	Sec. 350, '05. Grant to W. H. Dick. To be constructed within 6 yrs.	Granted., ...	Yes..............	Yes.
Slides for logs, etc.	Sec. 350, '05. Grant to W. H. Dick. To be constructed within 4 yrs.	Granted..........	Yes..............	Yes.
None.............	Sec. 350, '05. Grant to W. H. Dick. To be constructed within 4 yrs.	Granted..........	Yes..............	Yes.

+ See note on preceding page.

ANALYSIS OF THE FRANCHISES FOR THE CONSTRUCTION OF DAMS BY THE
LEGISLATURE—Continued.

Individual Grantees.

Citation.	Grantee.	Stream. Location, County.	Duration of grant.	Purposes.
'05, 444 '07, 328	E. T. Harmon et al.	Wisconsin river. Sec. 30. T. 33 N., R. 6 E. Lincoln.	No limit..........	Improve navigation hydraulic.
'05, 485	Wm. C. Zachon.	Oconto river. Lots 1 & 8, Sec. 33, T. 28 N., R. 18 E. Oconto Co.	No limit..........	Improve navigation & hydraulic.
'07, 380	Chas. R. Smith..	Chippewa. N. E. qr Sec. 23, T. 36 N., R. 7 W. Rusk Co.	No limit..........	Improve navigation & hydraulic.
'07, 158	Arthur Van Order.	Big Plover. N. E. qr of S. E. qr Sec. 1, T. 24 N., R. 8 E. Portage Co.	No limit..........	Hydraulic ....
'07, 286	Jacob Svetlik et al.	Yellow river. S. E. qr of N. E. qr Sec. 31, T. 29, R. 6 W. Chippewa Co.	No limit..........	Hydraulic........
'08, 416	F. M. Moffat et al	Little Wolf. S. E. qr of S. W. qr Sec. 22, T. 25 N., R. 12 E. Waupaca Co.	No limit..........	Improve navigation & hydraulic.
'07, 284	John C. Young..	Jump river. Sec 34, T. 33 N., R. 5 W. Rusk Co.	No limit..........	Improve navigation & hydraulic.
'07, 404	Edward P. Sherry.	Wolf river. S. hf of S. hf Sec. 25, T. 31 N., R. 14 E. Langlade Co.	No limit..........	Hydraulic........
'07, 409	Max Sells........	Menominee river Sec. 2 or 12, T. 39, R. 19 E. Florence Co.	No limit..........	Hydraulic........
'07, 489	R. C. Schultz.....	Trout creek. S. W. qr of S. W. qr Sec. 14, T. 41 N., R. 6 E. Vilas Co.	No limit..........	Hydraulic........
'07, 514	C. F. Stout et al.	Silver creek. Sec 12, T. 33 N., R. 1 E. Taylor Co.	No limit..........	Improve navigation & hydraulic.
'07, 384	James J. Pontbriand.	Brule river. Secs. 9, 10 & 14 & 15. T. 40 N., R. 18 E. Florence Co.	No limit..........	Hydraulic........

ANALYSIS OF THE FRANCHISES FOR THE CONSTRUCTION OF DAMS BY THE
LEGISLATURE—Continued.

Individual Grantees.

Protection of navigation.	Miscellaneous purposes.	Eminent domain.	Reserve clause.	Fish-ways.
Slides for logs, etc.	Sec. 350, '05. Grant to W. H. Dick. To be constructed within 4 yrs.	Granted..........	Yes...............	Yes.
Slides for logs, etc.	Sec. 350, '05. Grant to W. H. Dick. To be constructed within 4 yrs.	Granted..........	Yes...............	Yes.
Slides for logs, etc.	Sec. 350, '05. Grant to W. H. Dick. To be constructed within 4 yrs.	Granted..........	Yes...............	Yes.
None............	None............	Granted..........	Yes...............	Yes.
Slides for logs, etc.	Sec. 350, '05. W. H. Dick. Construction to be commenced within 2 yrs.	Not granted.....	Yes...............	Yes.
Slides for logs, etc.	Sec. 350, '05. Construction to be commenced within 4 yrs.	Granted..........	Yes...............	Yes.
Slides for logs, etc.	Sec. 350, '05. W. H. Dick. Construction to be commenced within 4 yrs.	Granted..........	Yes...............	Yes.
Slides for logs, etc.	Sec. 350, '05. Construction to be commenced within 4 yrs.	Granted...... ...	Yes...............	Yes.
Slides for logs, etc.	Sec. 350, '05. Construction to be commenced within 4 yrs.	Granted..........	Yes...............	Yes.
Slides for logs, etc.	Sec. 350, '05. Construction to be commenced within 4 yrs.	Granted..........	Yes...............	Yes.
Slides for logs, etc.	Sec. 350, '05. Construction to be commenced within 4 yrs.	Granted...... ...	Yes...............	Yes.
Slides for logs, etc.	None.......	Not granted.....	Yes...............	Yes.

16

ANALYSIS OF THE FRANCHISES FOR THE CONSTRUCTION OF DAMS BY THE
LEGISLATURE—Continued.

Individual Grantees.

Citation.	Grantee.	Stream. Location. County.	Duration of grant.	Purpose.
'07, 381	Wells M. Ruggles et al.	Bad river. Sec. 30, T. 45 N., R. 2 W. Ashland Co.	No limit	Hydraulic....
'07, 449	Soren C. Frost...	Oconto river. N. qr of S. W. qr Sec. 10, T. 31 N., R. 16 E. Oconto Co.	No limit........	Hydraulic........
'07, 285	John C. Young..	Jump river. W. hf of N. E. qr Sec. 25, T. 33 N., R. 5 W. Rusk Co.	No limit.........	Improve navigation & hydraulic.
'07, 1333	A. P. Christianson.	Neenah creek. Lot 5, Sec. 9, T. 13 N., R. 9 E. Columbia Co.	No limit.........	Hydraulic........
'07, 189	J. S. Tripp et al..	Wisconsin. Sec. 25, T. 10. R. 6 E. Sauk & Columbia Cos.	No limit.........	Improve navigation & hydraulic.
'07, 383	Chas. E. Pollins, Jr.	Peshtigo river, lots 1, 2, 3 and 4, sec. 15, T. 32N, R. 19 E. Marinette Co.	No limit	Hydraulic.....
'07, 591	Franklin J. Wood	Chippewa river. sec. 36, T. 37N., R. 7 W., Sawyer Co.	No limit	Improve navigation and hydraulic.
'07, 329	Wausau Lumber Co.	Big Rib river, flooding dams, sec. 30, T. 31 N, R. 4E, Lincoln Co., and sec. 28, T. 32 N, R. 3E., Taylor Co.	No limit	Facilitate log driving.
'07, 335 '09, 361 (Provide bridge.)	Wis. Valley Improvement Co.	Tributaries of Wisconsin, north of the south line, T. 34 N.	No limit	Improve navigation of Wis. and Tomahawk rivers by system of reser.
'07, 405	Crivitz Pulp & Paper Co.	Peshtigo river, sec. 24, T. 32 N., R. 19 E. Marinette Co.	No limit	Improve navigation and hydraulic.
'07, 549	Watertown Gas & Electric Co. (Successors of Calvin and Jos. Benton, p. 37, 1844.)	Rock river. W. ½ sec. 3, T. 8, R. 15, Jefferson Co.	No limit	Hydraulic......
07, 626	John Arpin Lbr. Co.	Chippewa. sec. 10, T. 37 N., R. 7 W. Sawyer Co.	No limit	Improve navigation and hydraulic.

ANALYSIS OF THE FRANCHISES FOR THE CONSTRUCTION OF DAMS BY THE
LEGISLATURE—Continued.

Individual Grantees.

Protection of navigation	Miscellaneous purposes.	Eminent domain.	Reserve clause.	Fishways
None	Sec. 350, '05. Construction to be commenced within 4 yrs.	Granted	Yes	Yes.
None	Sec. 350, '05. Construction to be commenced within 4 yrs.	Granted	Yes	Yes.
Slides for logs. etc.	Sec. 350, '05. W. H. Dick. Construction to commence within 4 yrs	Granted	Yes	Yes.
Free boat passage	None	Granted as per mill dam act.	Yes	Yes.
Slides for logs. etc.	Sec. 350, '05. W. H. Dick. Construction to commence within 4 yrs.	Granted	Yes	Yes.
Slides for logs, etc.	Sec. 350, '05. Construction to commence within 4 years.	Granted	Yes	Yes.
Slides for logs, etc.	Sec. 350, '05. Must begin work within 2 years.	Granted	Yes	Yes.
None	None	Not granted	Yes	Yes.
Slides for logs. etc.	May collect toll, take over all dams, etc. Exceptions stated.	Granted	Yes	Yes.
Slides for logs. etc.	See sec. 350, '05. Construction to commence within 4 years.	Granted	Yes	Yes,
Slides for logs. etc.	See sec. 350, '05. Approval of city of Watertown prerequisite.	Granted	Yes	Yes.
Slides for logs. etc.	See sec. 350, '05. Work to be commenced within 2 years.	Granted	Yes	Yes.

ANALYSIS OF THE FRANCHISES FOR THE CONSTRUCTION OF DAMS BY THE
LEGISLATURE—Continued.

Individual Grantees.

Protection of Navigation.	Miscellaneous purposes.	Eminent domain.	Reserve clause.	Fishways.
Slides for logs, etc.	See sec. 350. '05. (Reasonable price question to be decided by a jury in circuit court.) Instead of by arbitrators as in sec. 7, ch. 350 laws of 1905.	Granted..........	Yes...............	Yes.

ANALYSIS OF THE FRANCHISES FOR THE CONSTRUCTION OF DAMS BY THE
LEGISLATURE—Continued.

Individual Grantees.

Citation.	Grantee.	Stream, Location, County.	Duration of grant.	Purposes.
'07. 644	Beans Eddy Power Co.	Wisconsin. secs. 6, 7 and 8, T. 26 N. R. 7 E. Marathon Co.	No limit	Improve navigation and hydraulic.

EXHIBIT 4.

SUMMARY OF ANALYSIS OF THE FRANCHISES FOR THE CONSTRUCTION OF DAMS BY THE LEGISLATURE OF WISCONSIN.

Figure 1.

Period.	Total granted.	*Improve navigation. Facilitate log driving. Improve navigation and facilitate log driving.	Hydraulic.	Improve navigation and hydraulic.	Facilitate log driving and hydraulic.	‡Other.
'36-'40	5	....	5	....	....	....
'40-'50	58	3	49	4	....	2
'50-'60	105	14	66	3	1	21
'60-'70	50	23	15	....	6	6
'70-'80	101	63	20	....	11	7
'80-'90	181	107	22	....	40	12
'90-1900	77	25	20	5	17	10
1900-'09†	88	9	30	40	4	5
Totals.........	665	244	227	52	79	63

Figure 1—Shows, in ten year periods, the total number of privileges granted to erect dams and the purpose or purposes for which such dams were to be erected.
*Combined as being for the purpose to improve navigation.
†No privileges were granted in the year 1909.
‡Includes grants to erect dams to feed canals, for pisciculture, to create ponds, to flow cranberry marshes, for the "public good", for general municipal purposes, and include 44 grants in which no purpose is specified—the context being indefinite no purpose is given.

EXHIBIT 5.

SUMMARY OF THE ANALYSIS OF THE FRANCHISES FOR THE CONSTRUCTION OF DAMS BY THE LEGISLATURE.

Figure 2.

Period	Improve navigation Facilitate log driving Improve navigation and log driving.				Hydraulic.				Improve navigation and hydraulic.				Facilitate log driving and hydraulic.				*Other.			
	A	B	C	D	A	B	C	D	A	B	C	D	A	B	C	D	A	B	C	D
'30–'40	1				2	5		3												
'40–'50	6	3		1	38	35		12	3	3		4					1	2		1
'50–'60	12	1	1		28	17		8	2			2					6	2		1
'60–'70	12		4		7				2			2	1				2		1	1
'70–'80	30	64	21		13	18							4				3			
'80–'90	16	20			14	16							18	22	8		3	6		2
'90–1900	8	11		10	12		1	1	3	4			10	15	1	1	4	5		1
1900–'09					22	26		23	37	40		40	1	3	1	3	5	5		5
Totals	85	100	26	11	136	117	1	47	47	47		48	34	40	3	4	24	20	1	11

A.—Eminent domain. B.—Reserve clause. C.—Limitations. D.—Fishways.

Fig. 2. Under the respective purpose or purposes for which the privilege to construct dams was granted, shows the number of grants in ten year periods, in which the right of eminent domain is attendant; the reserve clause is found; a time limit is inserted; and in which fishways are provided for.

* See note to Figure 1.

EXHIBIT 6.

ANALYSIS OF THE FRANCHISES FOR THE CONSTRUCTION OF THE LEGISLATURE OF WISCONSIN.

Figure 3.

Period.	Totals Granted.	Eminent domain.	Reserve Clause.	Limitation
'36-'40	5	2	5	..
'40-'50	58	43	43	..
'50-'60 ....!	105	42	20	1
'60-'70 ....|	50	24	..	5
'70-'80 ....|	101	32	2	21
'80-'90 ....|	181	65	110	2
'90-1900 ....'	77	45	60	1
1900-'09 ....|	88	73	85	1
Totals	665	326	325	31

Figure 3—Shows in 10 year periods, the total number of privileges grant
number of grants in which the right of eminent domain was granted, tl
clause was inserted, a time limit is found and in which fishways are provid

By Whom Built (Present Dam)	Purpose of Dam	Remarks
United States in 1845-6 & 7	Navigation and Water Power	Original dam was built by private parties for hydraulic purposed. About 1866 it was purchased by the United States under Condemnation proceedings for $2,000 of the above amount is included in cost.
	Water Power	Owned by Neenah & Menasha Water Power Co. but should be controlled by United States though not a part of Navigation System
United States in 1873 & 4	Navigation	Original dam built by Fox & Wisconsin Improvement Co. for navigation purposes.
Private Parties	Water Power	This dam was built by Water Power Users for power purposes about 1880.
United States in 1869	Navigation	Original dam built by Fox & Wisconsin Improvement Co. for navigation purposes
do in 1878	do	Original dam built by Fox & Wisconsin Improvement Co for navigation purposes about 1850.
do in 1878	do	Original dam built by Fox & Wisconsin Improvement Co for navigation purposes about 1854
Green Bay & Miss. Canal Co.	Water Power	Built by Green Bay & Mississippi Canal Co
United States in 1878.	Navigation	Original dam built by Fox & Wisconsin Improvement 6. for navigation purposes about 1854.
Private Parties	Water Power	
United States in 1878	Navigation	Original dam built by Fox & Wisconsin Improvement 6. for navigation purposes in 1849 Power developed but not used.
do 1878	do	Original dam built by Fox & Wisconsin Improvement 6. for navigation purposes in 1867. Preparing to use power.
do	do	Original dam built by Fox & Wisconsin Improvement 6. for navigation purposes. about 1854.

U.S. Engr discharge of 200,000 cu. ft per minute

low water head at dams.

- Orbison Eng 6 and reduced to basis taken in this schedule.
- undeveloped or lost between dams.

ment was transferre
company called th
valuable lands at a

del tonnage Annually			Ea
	down	Both	An

records gave the tonnage
Report numbered and d
from the down rvoir Tr
very & mostly the more
The following is taken fr

ear	Tonnage	Ma
89	366,675	18
90	383,291	19
91	262,078	19
92	291,300	19
93	202,443	19
94	298,624	19
95	229,103	19
96	148,110	19
97	191,235	19
98	211,725	19

Note : Statistics we
in tonnage prese

practically none at
bats running exce
mall passenger c
igh Water

running to Cedar
ry aside from
renue of 89. or

nt was transfered to the Fox and Wisconsin
mpany, called the Green Bay & Mississippi Canal Co.
iable lands at an appraised valuation of $140,000, the

tonnage velly		Earlier tonnage		Remarks
lown	Both	Amount	Year	
				9 Dams, 17 Locks. Total fall 167 feet.

ords give the tonnage of Fox and
iyers combined and does not separate
from the down river traffic. On the
ing it specify the marine of logs.
Following is taken from enost statistics.

7 Dams 9 Locks. Total fall 35 feet

Tonnage	Year	Tonnage
346,478	1899	290,681
389,281	1900	309,600
262,078	1901	263,719
291,300	1902	265,297
202,443	1903	300,867
290,624	1904	201,372
229,109	1905	263,588
148,110	1906	316,040
191,238	1907	280,732
211,745	1908	266,580

te ' Statistics were not recorded
n Tonnage previous to 1899.

The tabulation showing the annual tonnage on the
Fox & Wolf Rivers combined indicates little variation
from an average of 300,000 annually for the past
20 years, but previous to 1900 the logs were the
principal item and as these have fallen off
greatly since that year the package freight and
coal have considerably increased.
   The record of lockages show a very decided
increase in traffic due to passenger boats and pleasure
yachts. A maximum was reached in 1902 then it
fell off until 1900 and again reached in 1905. Then
gradually increased and in 1908 was 100% greater
than in 1903 due largely to pleasure yachts.
   The merchantile tonnage on the Wolf River is
insignificant excepting the movement of logs
which also will cease within a few years. Twenty
five to thirty years before Railroads were built there
was heavy traffic on this river

tically none at present. No
running excepting occasionally
l passenger craft during
Water

Verycomsiderable traffic on Wisconsin River
25 years ago and earlier.

ring to Cedars Dam, about to the total power on the Lower Fox
aside from other powers owned by individuals is estimated
ue of 8% on this amount.

11	12
Quantity of power (as given in Column 6) not used.			Price per horse power of quantity sold	Amount of proceeds per annum of power sold.

River Valley Knitting Co.

or Whitman Machine Co.

asha Mfg Co

ton Chair Co

n Toy & Furniture Co

eton Paper & Pulp Co

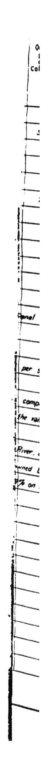

9		12
Quantity of power (as given in Column 6) not used.	Price per horse power of quantity sold	Amount of proceeds per annum of power sold

$$\frac{E}{,2}$$

	10		11	12
of (as in f) net	Power used.		Price per horse power of quantity sold	Amount of proceeds per annum of power sold
	Quantity Approximate	By whom.		
Nee	1435	Kimberly & Clark Co.		
The out	771	Neenah Paper. Co.		
	963	Bergstrom Paper Co.		
	86	Robert Jamison		
	113	Wulff. Clousen Co.		
	432	Krueger & Loehmann		
	36	Neenah Boot & Shoe Mfg. Co.		
A		Rovine Mill		
U.S	1953	Lincoln Mill Fox River Paper Co.		
		Fox River Mill		
	88	Marston Spoke & Hub Co.		
	13	Appleton Machine Co.		
	43	Appleton Woolen Mill		
	26	4th Ward Planing Mill		
E 2	30	Mansur Renner & Co.		
	748	Patton Paper Co.		
	19	A. Spiering		
	428	Telulah Paper Mill Telulah		
	831	Paper Mill Paper Co.		
	20	Eagle Mfg Co		
	43	Valley Iron Works Mfg Co.		
Co	See Sheet 2 4348	Combined Locks Paper Co.		
M	781	Lindaver Pulp Co.		
A	552	Thilmeny Pulp & Paper Co.		
	750	Outagamie Paper Co		

EXHIBIT 7.

TABLES FURNISHED BY THE U. S. ENGINEER'S OFFICE, OSHKOSH, WIS.,

TO THE

LEGISLATIVE COMMITTEE

ON

WATER POWERS, FORESTRY AND DRAINAGE.

---

1. Water Powers on Lower Fox River, Wisconsin.
2. Fox River and Wisconsin Improvement—Wisconsin.
3. Statement Concerning Water Power at Existing Government Dams—Fox River, Wis.
4. Statement Concerning Water Power at Existing Government Dams—Fox River, Wis.
5. Statement Concerning Water Power at Existing Private Dams—Fox River, Wis.

EXHIBIT 8.

BEING ANSWERS TO QUESTIONS PUT TO WATER
POWER OWNERS. MANUFACTURERS, ETC., ON FILE
WITH THE WISCONSIN LEGISLATIVE REFERENCE LI-
BRARY AT THE STATE CAPITOL.

"EXHIBIT 9."

BRIEF NUMBER 16.

SUBMITTED BY GEORGE P. HAMBRECHT

ON

THE SLIDING SCALE OF RETURNS TO PUBLIC UTIL-
ITY CORPORATIONS

TO

THE WISCONSIN LEGISLATIVE COMMITTEE

ON

WATER POWERS, FORESTRY AND DRAINAGE.

———————

(Authorities compiled by M. C. Riley.)

"EXHIBIT 9"

THE SLIDING SCALE OF RETURNS TO PUBLIC UTILITIES

In its application to the commodity or service supply by public utilities the sliding scale system works as follows:

Starting with a fixed normal rate of return upon capital and a fixed normal rate of charge for the service rendered, dividends are allowed to increase in a fixed ratio to the reduction in rates and vice versa.

A noted authority in England defined the sliding scale thus:

"A standard selling price for the gas and a standard rate of dividend being given, it is provided that for every penny of a reduction in the price of gas below the standard, the company are empowered to pay ¼ per cent. above the standard dividend, or 1 per cent. for a reduction of 4d., and *vice versa* if the selling price of the gas is raised." Minority report Mass. Special Committee to consider the London sliding scale of prices and dividends as applied to gas companies, p. 57.*

THEORY OF THE SLIDING SCALE SYSTEM.

"The theory of the sliding scale is that it will substitute a sort of partnership or co-operative relation between the corporations and their customers in place of the present antagonism growing out of the desire of the public to secure both reductions in rates and limitations in dividends without reference to the effect of either upon the other. The objection to high or exorbitant dividends, rests. presumably, upon the proposition that they necessarily involve high or exorbitant rates. If this relation between

---

* The minority report of this Committee was accepted and its recommendations were shaped into law.—See Ch. 422 Mass. Laws, 1906.

the two can be changed, presumably the antagonism referred to can be eliminated. If every increase of return
upon investment is accompanied with a corresponding
reduction in rates, no legitimate objection to such increase
remains. The so-called London sliding scale aims to secure
these results. In its application to the gas business of
England it has met with a large measure of success in that
respect." Report of substitute committee on London sliding scale as applied to Electricity. Report of committee
on public policy, June 1907, p. 31.

ORIGIN AND PROGRESS OF THE SLIDING SCALE SYSTEM.

The germ of the sliding scale of returns to public utilities
is found in the proposed Sheffield (Eng.) Gas Act of 1855.
According to this act dividends to the stockholders might be
increased to a certain maximum rate if accompanied by certain
prescribed reductions in price. Between the years 1855 and
1875, although there was considerable agitation on the part of
the consumers to have gas companies generally adopted the
sliding scale system, there was no legislation along this line.
This was due to the strenuous objections raised by the companies to the system.* The adoption of the system in England
is optional with the companies. However, after the year 1875
there was a marked change of sentiment on the part of the
companies and the adoption of the sliding scale became quite
general. By the year 1880 there were 51 gas companies operating under one form or another of the system. Since 1875 the
system has been extended to 211 companies out of 437 scattered
throughout Great Britain and Ireland. At the beginning of the
year 1904, 39 per cent. of all gas companies had adopted the
sliding scale and these companies were selling 68 per cent. of
the total amount of gas sold in the British Isles. (W. H. Gardi-

---

* Most of the companies objected to any kind of a sliding scale,
mainly on the ground that such a system would not, in the nature of
things, be permanent, and that the public would not be content to see
the companies earn more than 10 per cent, (the maximum return
allowed gas companies on their investment) even if the additional dividends were accompanied by a proportionate reduction in prices. Some
of them were very strong in their opposition to the sliding scale, one
of the directors of the Imperial Company going so far as to charac-
terize the proposal as "ridiculous," "dishonest," and "unfair." Another
company official said that it would be impossible to reach a 12 per
cent dividend under the sliding scale as intimated by the questions of
counsel for the Metropolitan Board of Works. W. H. Gardner, Jr., A.
Paper. etc., P. 82. N.

ner, Jr., a paper read before the National Electric Light Association, Atlantic City, 1906, p. 88.)

The following table shows the increase in the number of standard companies (those operating under the sliding scale) in the different parts of Great Britain from 1875 to 1903, inclusive:

	1875	1883	1893	1903
England and Wales....	1	72	157	192
Scotland	—	—	1	4
Ireland	—	2	5	7

In 1904, of the 10 companies incorporated by Parliament, 8 went under the sliding scale, making 211 sliding scale companies at our latest information. Minn. report Mass. Committee, p. 70.

ARGUMENTS PUT FORTH BY THOSE FAVORING THE ADOPTION OF THE SYSTEM.

Sir George Livesey, President of the British Association of Gas Managers, in his annual address before the association on June 9th, 1874, suggested that a sliding scale would furnish a system and regulation more satisfactory to the companies and consumers than any that had yet been tried. The portion of his address which relates to this matter reads as follows:

"It is now universally admitted that the supply of gas must be a monopoly, of which we are the fortunate possessors; but the objections to all monopolies are so great that nothing but necessity can justify them. It is, therefore, of the utmost importance, if we would retain our position. that our customers be satisfied, which I unhesitatingly contend is possible of attainment. * * * "

"It ought to be possible to frame a scheme, to be embodied in a general act, that should cause the interests of gas companies and their consumers to run side by side; to make the consumers, in a sense, partners in the gas company. whereby both should participate in any improved or more economical working, giving the companies a slightly increased dividend for every reduction in price below a certain minimum standard; and, to be perfectly fair, the companies would have to submit to a reduction of dividend if their prices exceeded a maximum limit. It would be unsatisfactory to fix an exact figure and permit full dividends at such a price, with more or less for every variation from it; but to a'low a range of, say, *1s.* would give companies a chance when unexpected difficulties arose, and, moreover, would give them something to work for in the other direction. Suppose a company to be charging *4s.* for its gas, then if the price went beyond *4s. 6d.*, there would be a reduction of dividend; and, on the other hand, the company might, by reducing below *3s. 6d.*, obtain an increased dividend. I throw this out more as an illustration than a suggestion, for there are several plans where the object might be attained; and I ho'd it to be most strongly to the interests of gas shareholders, directors, and managers to heartily assist in carrying out some system whereby they might have their customers with them, some easily workable self-acting arrangement that would put an end to the cat-and-dog life, and make them live and work in peace with each other,—in fact, make it really to the interest of gas companies and gas managers to do the best they can for the consumers.''

At the parliamentary session of 1875 an argument of council for the Metropolitan Board of Works set out the advantage of the system as follows:

''As we have not got in this trade the general check of the stimulus of supply and demand, we must attempt to replace it by some other motive; and the contention seems to lie between the existing machinery, which is a revision by gentlemen as competent as can be found, and that proposed by the bill—that is to say, a fine if they charge a high price, and a reward if they charge a low price. * * * And the idea before my mind as a man of business is that the general stimulus and interest in conducting a trade—that is to say, getting a larger profit, or appearing to incur a smaller profit—would be a greater stimulus to very good management (which is what is wanted in business) than the visits or inquiries of outsiders would be a check against bad management. * * * ''

''The consumer offers now by this sliding scale to give up a portion of that which is his under legislation—give it up to the company, and let the company have a share of

17

it—in the hope that this inducement to the company
having a share of it will lead to the total being made
larger by the care and diligence bestowed, which will then
be partly for the consumer and partly for the company
themselves. I am giving up, as a consumer, what is my
right by legislation at present; I am giving up half to the
company. I say everything over 10 per cent is mine, and
you—the company—have no right to alter that. I will
sacrifice that position, I will give the company half
of it. * * * ''

"This rise never can take place for the benefit of the
company without being accompanied with a lower price
to the consumer. The consumer will feel sensibly in himself the benefit directly the company feels it. The company can not get more than 10 per cent, the consumer
getting a diminution of his gas bill. It is a very important thing for the consumers to be pleased with the prosperity when they are sharers in that prosperity. * * * ''

"It makes it perfectly secure to the consumers and to
the company that new capital should be raised at the
lowest possible amount; and then by the sliding scale the
consumers and the company will share any benefit derived
from the new capital being raised at the low rate. Of
course, the lower the rate at which capital is raised, the
larger would be the profit upon the amount of capital which
stands at the present time. And that it seems to me to
make the matter perfectly fair without the slightest difficulty.''

At the parliamentary session of 1876, during the progress
of an investigation, the advantages of the sliding scale were
pointed out by Mr. Farrer, speaking for the Board of Trade in
the following words:

"The sliding scale is an endeavor to make it the interest of the companies to act as other trading companies,
by giving them a share in the profits which result from
economy. * * * ''

"The effect of the sliding scale is to make it the interest of the companies to have as small a capital as possible,
because the smaller the capital which they have, the larger

the increase of dividend which they will be able to get by
reducing the price.   *   *   *   ''

"The holders of the existing capital will be unwilling
to increase their capital, because every new increase of
capital involves a division of the profits amongst a larger
amounts of stockholders.   *   *   *   ''

"The smaller the amount of capital, the larger the
amount which would go to the holders of that capital;
and, consequently, in my view, the sliding scale makes it
to the interest of the shareholders not to have more capital
than is necessary.   *   *   *   ''

"The sliding scale will make it the interest of the companies to charge as low a price as possible.''

The board of trade, July 25, 1876, speaking of the agreement reached with the companies to adopt the auction clause
of the sliding scale, said:

"If the dividend should increase, the price of gas, it must
be remembered, will at the same time diminish, and in that
case it is not likely that there will be any desire on the
part if the consumer to purchase (the plants). A dividend
at 14 per cent under the sliding scale would carry with it
a price of 2s. 5d. per thousand feet of gas, and at such a
price there is not likely to be discontent or agitation.
*   *   *   ''

"Under this scheme it will be the interest of the gas companies, as it is the interest of ordinary trading companies,
to manage their concern with economy in order to increase
the profits of their shareholders; and to whatever extent
they may do so the consumer will share in the profit in the
shape of reduction of price. It will also be to their interest
to raise as little additional capital as possible, since existing shareholders will no longer receive a premium upon his
shares, and their dividend will be diminished by the addition of fresh capital.''

CONDITIONS NECESSARY TO MAKE A SCHEME OF A SLIDING SCALE JUST AND EFFECTUAL.

Views of the board of trade, dated May 31, 1875. (The view of the board of trade were solicited by the Parliamentary com mittee to which all bills having to do with the sliding scale wer submitted).

"To make a scheme of a sliding scale of price and divid end just and effectual, the following conditions appear t be necessary:

"1. That the initial price and quality of gas shall t fairly fixed, having regard both to the immediate existin interests of the companies and the consumers and to tl prospects of both under the new system.

"2. That the price and dividend shall vary inversely i certain fixed proportions without limit, so that on the o hand the price may be raised without limit as the dividen diminishes, and so that the dividends may be increas without limit as the price diminishes. Such a plan, if pra ticable, would be beneficial to the companies; for it wou protect them against the contingency of such increase expense in manufacture as would make the price of 1860 i sufficient to produce the requisite dividend and it wou enable them to share with the consumer any amount profit that may arise from diminution in expense of man facture or increased consumption. It would be beneficial the consumer, because it would, without immediate increa of price, give to the companies, who alone possess the quisite knowledge and power, a strong interest to redu expenditure, whether of capital or income, in lieu of present system under which they have an interest in incre ing the expenditure of capital, and no interest in keepi down the expenditure of income."

THE FACTORS OF THE SLIDING SCALE.

W. H. Gardiner, Jr., A Paper read before the National El tric Light Association, Atlantic City, 1906, p. 10.

"The basic factors of the London Sliding Scale are:
(a) The standard dividend and net earnings.
(b) The initial price and reductions.

(c) The ratio of increase in net earnings to decrease in price.

The Standard Dividend.

"Consideration of the standard dividend really involves the entire question of capitalization.

The capital liabilities of the older English lighting companies show a much more complex situation than here exists even under recent conditions. * * * Suffice it to say here that in England new investments in new lighting enterprises are at the start allowed to earn ten per cent on the investment. * * *

The essential point in the determining of the standard dividend is that it shall yield a dividend commensurate with the investments in the business and a fair return from the conduct of the business as a going concern under present conditions.

Starting with this interest rate as a basis, or first lowering its rate but not its amount by a capital conversion, additional increments of net earnings are allowed to be paid upon the regular or other stock by increasing the rate of allowable dividend thereon and conversely as the price is subsequently reduced or raised from the standard or initial price. For instance, for each reduction of one per cent per kilowatt-hour below a standard list price, of, say, 22 cents per kilowatt-hour, an increase of dividend is allowed equal in amount to, say, one per cent on the capital, and conversely. This necessitates the establishment of a price starting point—a standard or initial price."

The Initial Price and Reductions.

"The uniform practice seems to have been to fix the initial price a very little above the price that would be necessary to but exactly meet in amount the interest and dividend charges under the old or new capitalization. The initial sliding scale price is thus usually raised by a slight increase above the old price. The object of so fixing the initial price may be found in the desire of the public and its officials to induce lighting companies to adopt the sliding scale system because it works so well to the public good. Therefore, the initial price may be set at a slight advance over

the former price so that the company may forthwith make a
reduction therefrom and consequently increase the amount
of its dividends." W. H. Gardiner, Jr., A Paper, etc.,
p. 11.

Report of sub-committee on the London sliding scale as applied to electricity. Report of committee on public policy, 30th
convention, June, 1907, p. 33:

"The fixing of the initial rate of dividend, on the one
hand, and the initial schedule of charges, on the other, is of
course, a matter of great delicacy and importance. Theoretically, both should primarily depend upon the fair value
of the investment. The rates charged should be sufficient,
and only sufficient, to yield a fair return upon a reasonable
investment, for the purpose in hand, with due allowance
for depreciation, contingent funds, surplus accounts, and
so forth. All these matters were carefully worked out in
the Massachusetts act above referred to. (Ch. 422 L. 1906.)
The capital of the Consolidated Gas Company was fixed at
the aggregate amount of the capital stocks and permanent
debts of the companies consolidated. That capital having
been thus fixed, the rate of seven per cent was specified for
dividends, with gas at 90 cents per thousand cubic feet.
This dividend may be increased to eight per cent when the
price of gas is reduced to 85 cents per thousand feet, and
so on."

Report (Majority) Mass. Com., p. 45:

"Application of the sliding scale necessarily involves the
fixing of a standard price and a standard rate of dividend,
not for companies generally, but for each individually. The
standard price varies in different companies, and the principle upon which Parliament has fixed the standard price
in the many cases before it is not very clearly apparent.
There is reason to believe that after a hearing the price is
fixed at a point mutually acceptable to Parliament and the
company. The intention apparently is that it shall be high
enough to permit the payment of the maximum dividend
already fixed, whether 10 or 7 per cent, and low enough to
allow no increase above the dividend already payable except
after a reduction in price. In practice we believe the price

has most frequently been fixed at the price existing at the date of the act."

THE RATIO OF INCREASE IN NET EARNINGS TO DECREASE IN PRICE.

The practice in this connection has been to allow the company to increase the rate of its dividends by a constant and predetermined amount for each reduction of stated size from the initial price and conversely.

For example in England the ratio adopted for gas companies is a variation in dividends of one per cent for every change of 4d. in price. This ratio—the "Standard Sliding Scale"—was adopted in 1875. Maj. Rept. Mass. Com., p. 27.

In Massachusetts the initial price for gas was set at 90 cents per thousand cubic feet; a so-called standard rate of dividends of 7% was fixed, and the rate of dividend may be increased at the rate of one per cent for each reduction of five cents per thousand cubic feet. Ch. 422, Mass. Laws, 1906.

EFFECT OF THE ADOPTION OF THE SYSTEM IN ENGLAND.

In a report by Nathan Matthews to the Boston Consolidated Gas Company, on the public regulation of gas companies in Great Britain and Ireland, (for reprint of report see W. H. Gardiner, Jr., A Paper, etc., p. 33 et seq.), the effect of the sliding scale on dividends and prices is indicated by statistical comparison, as follows:

"That the sliding scale has operated to increase the profits of the companies is apparent from an inspection of the annual returns to Parliament. Taking the figures for 1903, we find that in that year two companies were paying 10½ per cent, one 10¾ per cent, two 11 per cent, eight 11½ per cent, two 12 per cent, two 12¼ per cent, three 12½ per cent, six 13 per cent, one 13¼ per cent, one 13⅔ per cent, two 14½ per cent, and one 17 per cent.

The companies in this list include some of the largest in the United Kingdom, and the results obtained would, of course, not have been possible under the system for which the sliding scale was substituted; for in no case has Parliament permitted a maximum dividend company to declare more than ten per cent."

Mr. Matthews states that due to the gradual decrease in the prices charged for gas by all compainies, those operating under the sliding scale as well as those operating as maximum dividend companies, the precise effect of the sliding scale is difficult of ascertainment. Continuing, he said:

"Sufficient data exist, however, to enable us to make certain comparisons of more or less value. These comparisons may be divided into two classes—those which contrast the reductions in price effected by sliding scale companies before they adopted the sliding scale with the reductions made by the same companies after its adoption, and those which contrast the reductions effected by sliding scale companies with those effected by maximum dividend companies.

(1) Comparison for the London companies before and after the adoption of the sliding scale:

It would seem that a comparison of the fifteen years which elapsed between 1860 and 1875 with the fifteen years which elapsed between 1875 and 1890—a comparison, that is to say, of the course of prices charged by the same companies —would give a fair indication of the effect of the sliding scale upon prices. It may be assumed that four-fifths was the average price at which gas was sold in 1860 by the thirteen companies then in operation; at the time of the adoption of the sliding scale in 1875-76 the average price was about 3/8; and in 1890 the average price was about 2/5. We thus had a drop of 9d., of 17 per cent, in the fifteen years preceding the adoption of the sliding scale as compared with a reduction of 1/3; or 34 per cent, in the period of fifteen years immediately succeeding the adoption of the sliding scale; and, when we consider how much easier it is to take 9d. off 4/5 than the same amount off 3/8, the great reduction of 1/3 in the second period is strong presumptive evidence that the sliding scale was in the case of these particular companies a powerful factor in effecting the reduction of prices which took place between 1876 and 1890.

(2) In the report of the Parliamentary committee of 1899 there are to be found tables, furnished by the board of trade, showing the reductions in price effected by certain companies between 1882 and 1897. Taking these tables as they stand, we have rearranged the data contained

in them so as to show the respective reductions in price
effected by the ten maximum dividend companies, the seventeen sliding scale companies, and the twelve corporations
during the fifteen years covered by the figures. The result is that the average reduction in price per company
during this period was 2/7 for the maximum dividend companies, 5/9 for the sliding scale companies, and 6/6 for
the corporations; while the maximum dividends paid were
10 per cent for the fixed dividend companies and 15 per
cent for the sliding scale companies. These figures do not
show the average reduction in price per thousand, but per
company, and include, as do those given in (1), the operations of the Gas Light and Coke Company.

(3) Comparisons between the reductions in price effected
between 1880 and 1903, as disclosed in the returns to Parliament, by the maximum dividend companies, and the reductions effected by those companies which were either
. under the sliding scale in 1880 or had adopted it by 1903:

Taking, for the sake of shortening the computation, only
those companies selling 100,000,000 feet of gas per annum,
and dividing them into three groups, we have worked out
the following results:

Of the companies selling between 100,000,000 and 500,-
000,000 feet of gas in 1903 there were thirty-eight maximum dividend companies which had reduced the price of
gas on the average 9/7, and thirty-nine sliding scale companies which had reduced the average 11/4. Of the companies selling between 500,000,000 and 1,000,000,000 feet there
were six maximum dividend companies which had reduced
on the average 5/1, and five sliding scale companies which
had reduced on the average 8/6. Of the companies selling
over 1,000,000,000 feet the four maximum dividend companies showed an average reduction of 5/7, and the eight
sliding scale companies an average reduction of 7/3. The
results for all the companies selling over 100,000,000 feet in
1903 are that during the twenty-three years between 1880
and 1903 the forty-eight maximum dividend companies had
effected an average reduction per company of 8/8, while
the fifty-two sliding scale companies had effected an average
reduction of 10/5.

These comparisons indicate that the sliding scale has been more effective in reducing prices than either the maximum dividend system or the official revision system."

The minority report of the Massachusetts committee summarizes the effect of the sliding scale on gas prices as follows: (See p. 63.) It will be noticed that the report shows for comparison the decrease in prices charged by certain companies both before and after the adoption of the sliding scale).

"With the adoption of the sliding scale by the 3 large metropolitan companies in 1875–76, the strife between the companies and the consumers which had been waged for many years ceased.

In 1876 the 3 companies were charging as follows for gas, to-wit:

Gas Light and Coke Company, 3s. 9d. (90 cents).
South Metropolitan Company, 3s. 0d. (72 cents).
Commercial Company, ...3s. 9d. (90 cents).

Prices steadily decreased during the next fourteen years, and in 1889 were more nearly uniform than at any other time, viz.:

Gas Light and Coke Company, 2s. 6d. (60 cents).
South Metropolitan Company, 2s. 3d. (54 cents).
Commercial Company, ... 2s. 4d. (56 cents).

The reduction in the price of gas from 1869 to the adoption of the sliding scale, a period of seven years, is shown by the following:

Gas Light and Coke Company,.2.92d. (6 cents).
South Metropolitan Company..5.06d. (10 cents).
Commercial Company, ... 4.27d. (9 cents).

The reduction from the adoption of the sliding scale to 1890, a period of fourteen years, is shown as follows:

Gas Light and Coke Company, 13.57d. (27 cents, 13½ cents in each period of seven years).

South Metropolitan Company, 13.88d. 28 cents, 14 cents in each period of seven years).

Commercial Company, 16.77d. (34 cents, 17 cents in each period of seven years.)

From 1889 to 1894, owing to labor troubles, the high price

of coal and causes which operated all over Great Britain, all the companies raised their prices. There was no general complaint from the consumers against any company but the Gas Light and Coke Company, which in 1894 was charging a higher price than any other company. The highest prices charged by the 3 London companies in that year were as follows:

Gas Light and Coke Company, 3s. 1d. (74 cents).
South Metropolitan Company, 2s. 5d. (58 cents).
Commercial Company, ... 2s. 7d. (63 cents).

Owing to the agitation by the consumers of the Gas Light and Coke Company, and threatened parliamentary investigation by them, it reduced its price in that year to 2s. 10d. (68 cents).

In 1898 and 1899 the price of the Gas Light and Coke Company had again risen, while the two other metropolitan companies had reduced their prices. The prices charged in 1899 were as follows:

South Metropolitan Company, 2s. 2d. (52 cents).
Commercial Company, ... 2s. 6d. (60 cents).
Gas Light and Coke Company, 3s. 0d. (72 cents).

This variation in price led to the appointment of a committee of the House of Commons, presided by Sir James Rankin, "to inquire into the powers of charge conferred by Parliament on the Metropolitan gas companies, and to report as to the method in which these powers have been exercised, having regard to the differences in price charged by the various companies."

The result of the investigation of the committee of 1899 was a finding of mismanagement on the part of the Gas Light and Coke Company, and a complete endorsement of the sliding scale, with, however, recommendations for a reduction of the standard price and a secondary sliding scale."

The following summary, taken from Rostron's "Powers of Charge of the Metropolitan Companies," published in 1900, shows the amounts which in 1899 had been received by the companies and their consumers from the operation of the sliding scale, viz.:

1. The Gas Light and Coke Company.—This company has

received about £2,100,000 in increased dividends, and has given about £13,000,000 in reductions of price.

2. The South Metropolitan Company.—This company has received £469,901 in increased dividends, and has given £3,072,355 in reductions of price.

3. The Commercial Company.—This company has received £396,783 in increased dividends, and has given £1,965,385 in reductions of price.

OPINION EVIDENCE AS TO THE OPERATING OF THE SLIDING SCALE.

1. *From the Standpoint of the Public.*

"From the public standpoint there appears to be no disposition to criticise the operation of the standard sliding scale. There have been no gas agitations and no Parliamentary investigations since its adoption in 1875, except in the case of the Gas Light and Coke Company in 1899." (Explained *supra.*)   W. H. Gardiner, Jr., A Paper, etc., p. 100.

"The system is now and for many years has had the cordial support of the consumers and the companies in London, of both houses of British Parliament, the London county council and the board of trade, and of the wage earners and the representatives,—in fact of the overwhelming majority of all classes and conditions.

While other causes operating during the past thirty years have tended somewhat to reduce the cost of manufacturing gas and consequently to reduce the price, we believe that the sliding scale has been largely influential in attaining a great reduction in price which began at the time of its establishment in England."   Minority report, Massachusetts Committee, p. 58.

The conclusion reached by the Parliamentary committee of 1889 commendatory of the sliding scale system is confirmed by comparisons, based on "Fields Analysis" of all companies in England, between the sliding scale companies and companies working under the maximum system, so called, that is, companies organized under acts which limit both price and dividend and permit revision by the public authorities. The number of companies operating under each system is nearly equal, there being 459 companies at the date at which figures for this comparison are taken (1904), of which over 200 operated under the sliding scale. This comparison establishes:—

a. That the sliding scale companies on an average sell gas at a lower price than do the latter, and pay larger dividends to the stockholders.

b. That the sliding scale companies (excluding the metropolitan companies in this comparison on account of their size) produce more gas and do more business than the maximum companies, to-wit: the average quantity of gas sold per company by the maximum companies, employing an avearge capital per company of £70,894, is 118,528,000,000 cubic feet; and by the sliding scale companies, employing an avearge capital per company of £73,429, is 152,628,000,000 cubic feet.

c. That the average rate of reduction in the price of gas of the standard or sliding scale companies, when fairly in operaton, has been greater than of the maximum companies.

II. *From a Standpoint of the Companies.*

"We believe that the partnership principle of participation in profits and losses by the companies and consumers, upon which the sliding scale system rests, has proved an inducement to the gas companies in Great Britain to manage their business prudently, skillfully and economically, resulting in more progressive and careful business methods, more judicious and economical expenditure of money, greater diligence in the profitable disposition of residuals, and a safer rate of dividend to the stockholders, than any method before known in connection with the gas business in that country; and that it has surpassed all others in establishing respect and confidence between the companies and their consumers and employes in London." Min. Rept. Mass. Com., p. 58.

"No company having once come under the system has asked to be relieved of its provisions." Id. p. 70.

III. *From a General Standpoint.*

One great advantage of the sliding scale in its relation to public regulation and control is that it has a decided tendency to make that regulation and control in a large measure automatic. The initial rate of dividend and charge being once fixed, the future application of the principle of the sliding scale requires only an ascertainment of certain facts and their relations to each other. Even the increase of capital, whether in the form of stocks, bonds or other evidences of indebtedness, which, logically, should be made dependent upon the approval of the public board or commission above suggested, will be principally independent upon facts equally easy of ascertainment. Whether or not the company needs new capital, and, if so, to what extent, is dependent upon physical, business and financial conditions of little if any complexity. Rept. Com. Public Policy, 1907, p. 34.

"The advantages both to the public and to the stockholders, of the sliding scale system for regulating the price of gas and the rate of dividends have been conclusively established in England. The system has stood the supreme test of an experience continued upon an extensive scale during a period of thirty years. The conditions under which it was so tested were necessarily widely divergent; for the sliding scale has been applied to over two hundred companies, differing from one another in capitalization and managerial skill, and operating in communities which varied greatly in character, location and population. It has proven that the conditions of success for the sliding scale system are not local or peculiar in character. Its success results from the nature of the gas business and that of man,—from human nature." Minn. Rept. Mass. Com., p. 71.

Nathan Matthews in his report on the public regulation of gas companies in Great Britain and Ireland, after thoroughly going into the history and workings of the sliding scale system, concludes as follows:—

"So far as it is competent for a stranger to form an opinion, it would seem that the fact that gas is sold in England for prices very much less than anywhere else in the world, the fact that for the past thirty years, notwithstanding the large dividends of from 10 to 15 per cent, the relations between the companies and the public have, with one conspicuous exception, been eitirely harmonious and satisfactory, the statistical comparisons available, the general trend of professional opinion in England,

and the great inducement which the system holds out to
invested capital to introduce new and progressive methods
of manufacture, use and sale—it would seem to the writer
that these facts can lead to but one conclusion: namely,
that the chief though by no means the only cause of the
wonderfully prosperous condition of the English gas industry at the present time, and of the extraordinary low
prices enjoyed by the consumer, has been the standard
sliding scale, operating either directly upon the companies
which have adopted it, or indirectly upon the companies
which have not, but which have felt obliged to meet the
methods introduced and the results achieved by those which
have.''

Report of the committee of parliament 1899 (to investigate
the difference in prices charged for gas by different companies).

"This arrangement (the sliding scale) has, on the whole,
had an excellent effect upon the companies, and has given
them a strong motive to keep down the price of gas, and has
also operated to the advantage of the consumers. * * *
Since the introduction of the sliding scale the prices
charged for gas have at no period been as high as the standard price permitted to each company, and in every case
have fallen considerably below the prices charged before
the introduction of the sliding scale.   In saying this we do
not wish it to be inferred that the whole of the reductions
which have taken place in the price of gas since 1876 are to
be attributed to the operation of the sliding scale. * * *
The auction clauses,* which compel the companies to sell
their stock and their loans to the highest bidders, have had
the effect of enabling the companies to obtain their capital
at a much less rate than if the stock had been offered to
each shareholder at par, which was the usual custom before
1876, and thus the charge for interest has been largely reduced.   Expert evidence upon this matter seems to be entirely in its favor.

"Your committee have no hesitation in coming to the
conclusion that the principle of the sliding scale, coupled

---

* For an explanation of the Auction Clauses also of the Neutral Zone
System, see page following.

with the auction clauses, is an excellent one, and should be maintained; they will, however, have some remarks to make and suggestions to offer later on upon the figures of the present rate * * *

" * * * Your committee have come to the conclusion that the arrangements known as the sliding scale as applied to dividend and price in conjunction with auction sales of stock have had a beneficial effect upon the gas undertakings, especially as far as the consumer is concerned, and they have received no evidence to induce them to propose any alteration in the system."

THE NEUTRAL ZONE SYSTEM.

This system provides "a 'neutral zone' in the standard price, within which no rise or fall in *dividends* can take place."

The reason for this variation in the sliding scale system is that it gives the company a chance to increase the price of gas when rendered necessary by a strike or high price of coal, etc., to a limited extent, without involving a contemporeous necessity for reducing dividends, while, as soon as the danger ground is passed, the company and the consumers reap the full benefit of the sliding scale.

Its earliest appearance is in the Newcastle Gas Act, 1879, and is found all told in but thirteen different acts. The Neutral Zone appears to be more favored by the companies than by the consumers or by Parliament. Nathan Matthews, Appendix A, p. 95, W. H. Gardiner, Jr., A. Paper, etc.

THE AUCTION CLAUSES.

In 1876 provisions known as the "auction clauses" were imposed by Parliament upon two London companies, providing that *new issues* of stock be sold at public auction, as a prevention of stock watering. Since that date the auction clauses have been compulsorily imposed upon all companies coming to Parliament. Min. Rept. Mass. Com., p. 62.

"The common form for the auction clauses provides that the company may either sell the new issues of stock by public acution or by tender, that is, by advertising for proposals. In the latter case an upset price must be fixed and communicated under seal to the Board of Trade. If the stock is offered at public auction, it goes for whatever it may bring. If offered by tender and the upset price is not realized, it must then be offered to the company's stockholders at the upset price..

The premiums received are to be applied exclusively to those expenditures which would otherwise be charged to capital." W. H. Gardiner, Jr., A. Paper, etc., p. 52.

THE SLIDING SCALE SYSTEM IN THE UNITED STATES.

Pursuant to a resolve of the Massachusetts legislature of 1905 (Chap. 101, Resolves of that session), a committee composed of the member of the Board of Gas & Electric Light Commissioners and two others investigated the London Sliding Scale system. The minority (2) members of the committee reported as follows:

"We are of opinion that it is expedient to apply the sliding scale system, with modifications above suggested, to the companies doing business in Boston and Brookline, or at least to the Boston Consolidate Gas Company." Rep of Committee, p. 76.

"We are of the opinion, if the sliding scale is to be applied to the Boston Consolidated Gas Company:

a. That the standard price will be fixed at ninety cents, i. e. the present price.

b. That the standard dividend will be fixed at 7 per cent. per annum.

c. That for every five cents reduction in price, the rate of dividend may be increased 1 per cent."

This minority report of the committee was accepted and its recommendations were enacted into law. See chapter 422, Massachusetts Law, 1906.

The adoption of the system is made optional with the companies. Section 11 of the law. At the end of ten years the state board of gas and electric light commissioners may, upon petition of the company, or upon petition of the mayor of any city or the selectment of any town in which the company is supplying gas to consumers, lower or raise the standard price per one thousand cubic feet, to such extent as may justly be required by changes in conditions effecting the general cost of the manufac-

18

ture or distribution of gas (Section 9). The law provides for
the sale of all issues of additiona! stock by the company at public
auction (Section 7).

EFFECT OF THE ADOPTION OF THE SYSTEM IN MASSACHUSETTS.

"This system has already given to Boston 80 cent gas,
although Boston is located many hundred miles from the
mines which supply its coal. Eighty cents is a lower price
for gas than is actually enjoyed by other cities in the United
States, except a few within the coal and oil region, like Cleve-
land or Wheeling, and Redlands and Santa Ana, Cal. Even
in those cities the price is not lower than 75 cents,—a price
which Boston may reasonably expect to attain soon. For,
during the two years ending July 1' 1907, four reductions
in price of 5 cents each have been made. To have reduced
the price of gas 20 per cent. during that period of general rising prices in labor and material is certainly a notable
achievement. The most recent reductions in price were the
wholly voluntary acts of the company, made under wise laws
framed in the interest of both the public and of the stockholders. The saving of the gas consumer by these reductions was in the first year $265,404.55, in the second year
$565,725.60, and will be in the third (the current) year
about $800,000.

That this saving to the consumer was not attained by a
sacrifice to the interests of the stockholders may be inferred
from the market price of the stock of the association which
controls the gas company. In the two years following the
legislation of 1905, a period in which most other stocks de-
preciated largely, the common stock of the Massachusetts
gas companies rose from $44\frac{1}{2}$ to $57\frac{1}{2}$; and even in the severe
stock depression of late September, 1907, this stock was
firm at 52.

Compare with the results of the Boston experiment the
attempt in New York city made about the same time to reduce the price of gas, from $1 to 80 cents by legislative fiat
and the compulsory orders of the state commission. The
New York company contended that the law was unconstitutional; the federal court issued an injunction; the consumer still pays about $1 for each 1.000 cubic feet of gas. and

the market price of the stock of the Consolidated Gas company of New York during the same period of two years from 200 to 118, and in late September, 1907, to 96¾.

But Boston has reaped from the sliding scale system as applied under President Richard's administration of the company far more than cheaper gas and higher security values. It has been proven that a public service company may be managed with political honesty, and yet successfully, and that its head may become a valuable public servant. The officers and employees of the gas company now devote themselves to the business of making and distributing gas, instead of dissipating their abilities, as heretofore, in lobbying and political intrigue. As a result, gas properties which throughout the greater part of twenty years had been the subject of financial and political scandals, developing ultimately bitter hostility on the part of the people, are now conducted in a manner so honorable as to deserve and to secure the highest public commendation.'' Louis D. Brandeis, Rev. of Rev., Nov., 1907.

APPLICATION OF THE SLIDING SCALE SYSTEM TO OTHER PUBLIC SERVICE COMPANIES.

The sliding scale system in England was first applied to gas companies. The system has been extended to two electric light companies. See The Walker & Wallsend Union gas companies, (electric lighting) Act, 1899. The City of London Electric Lighting Company, (Orders 1890–1891, Acts 1893 and 1900).

As to electric power companies, while no general law has been passed and no common form of sliding scale adopted, Parliament has in most charters held out, by means of the sliding scale, some inducement to the companies to provide energy as cheaply as possible.

Thus the North Metropolitan Electric Power Supply Act, 1900, and the Lancashire Electric Power Act, 1900, provides that when during an entire year the prices charged have been 11¼ per cent. or more below the maximum price, the dividend may be increased above the standard rate by ¼ of 1 per cent. for every complete 1¼ per cent. reduction in price. The company may make up deficiencies in the standard dividend allowed; and, whenever the dividends actually paid exceed the standard rate, except for the purpose of making up deficiencies, the price to be reduced 1¼ per cent. for each complete ¼ of 1 per cent. increase in dividend. It will be seen that the scheme of these acts is a sliding scale working upwards in favor of the companies, but not downwards in favor of the consumers.

The South Wales Electric Power Distribution Company's Act, 1900, contains a sliding scale working both ways, like the standard sliding scale in the gas acts.

The North-western Electricity and Power Gas Act, 1903, provides that the surplus profits of the company in any year, above the sum sufficient to pay a dividend of 10 per cent., shall be applied one-third to a reserve fund until the same amounts to £100,000, one-third to a reduction in price, and one-third to an additional dividend. After the reserve fund amount to £100,000, the surplus is to be applied to a reduction in price and one-half to an increase in dividends.

All these acts contain a provision that the standard price and the ratio between dividends and price may be revised by the Board of Trade upon application of either the company or the consumers at periodic intervals, usually ten years.

By the Shepton-Mallet Gas Act, 1905, the company was authorized to go into the business of electrical distribution on the basis of maximum prices of 1¾d. and 8d. per unit, according to consumption, a standard price of 6d. per unit, a standard rate of dividend of 7 per cent. and a sliding scale of ¼ of 1 per cent. in the dividend rate for every ¼ of 1d. variation in the price per unit.

W. H. Gardiner. Jr., in his paper read before the National Electric Light Association, Atlantic City, 1906, after discussing the application of the sliding scale to gas and electric light companies, said

"These principles might be applied with equal justice and benefit to railroads, traction and other forms of public service."

THE COMPANIES SHOULD HAVE THE RIGHT TO ASSENT TO OR REJECT THE DETAILED PLAN PROPOSED.

The sub-committee on the London Sliding Scale as applied to electricity, in its report to the Committee on Public Policy, National Electric Light Association, with respect to the adoption or rejection by the companies of detailed plans, reported as follows:

"The difficulty in any if not most cases of determining, under actuallly existing conditions, the fair value of the lighting investments in this country, and thus the fair initial dividend and initial rates for service, is so great that fair dealing demands that the particular company involved shall have the right to assent to or reject the plan proposed in every case. The inducement to the company to adopt the system is so great that it can reasonably be trusted to assent to any conditions of its application that it is not unduly hazardous or burdensome."

R. S. OWEN.

POWERS OF THE LEGISLATURE.

The legislature of the State of Wisconsin possesses constitutional power to require gas companies and other public service corporations to furnish their products or service at reasonable prices and profits, and such corporations are bound to submit to reasonable legislative requirements on these subjects. A legislative act, embodying the principles of the sliding scale system, and providing for the adoption and application of such system, would be within legal principles well recognized and maintained by our state and federal courts of last resort.

BIBLIOGRAPHY.

General.

Civic Federation Reports.

Ex-Comptroller Dawes—Sat. Evening Post, Jan. 25, 1905.

Gardiner, W. H., Jr.—"Making of Rates"—29 Annual Report Western Gas Association. May, 1906.

Report of the Special Committee on the London Sliding Scale for Gas. (Massachusetts) 1906.

Senate Document. (U. S.) 696.

Gardiner, W. H., Jr.—London Sliding Scale for Gas— National Electric Light Association, 29th Convention —1906.

Decision—R. R. Comm. of Wisconsin—Madison case.

Standards for gas and electricity—Wis. R. R. Comm. Decision July 24, 1908. Nov. V.—21.

New Legislation of Interest to Gas and Electric Light Companies. 1906 Massachusetts.

"Equitable Sliding Scale for Rates of Electric Power, Gordon. J. B.—Engineering News, April 7, 1910.

"Reasonable Rates" for Gas and Electricity, as determined by Wis. R. R. Comm.—Eng. News, March 11, 1910.

London Sliding Scale for Gas—Marks, Wm. D.—Progressive Age, Jan. 15, 1909.—(Refer to files of this Magazine—see indices.)

Premium System—American Machinist.

Premium System—Commons, Prof. John R.—Book on Trade Unionism.

Meeting of American Gas Institute, Oct., 1909—Farstall, A. E.

List of Parliamentary Publications, P. S. King.

English Blue Books.

Parliamentary Index.

American Report, British Board of Trade on "Sliding Scale."

Additional Business Scheme—Gardiner, Wm. H., Jr., Acts of Parliament.

General Laws:

Companies Clauses, Consolidation Act, 1845, 8& 9 Victoria.

Companies Clauses, Consolidation Act, 1862, 26 & 27 Victoria.

Lands Clauses. Consolidation Act, 1845, 8 & 9 Victoria.

Gas Works Clauses Act, 1847, 10 & 11 Victoria.

Gas Works Clauses Amendment. 1871, 34 & 35 Victoria.

Gas & Water Works Facilities Act, 1870, 33 & 34 Victoria.

Gas & Water Works Facilities Amended, 1873, 36 & 37 Victoria.

Public Health Act, 1870, 38 & 39 Victoria.

Burghs Gas Supply (Scotland) Act, 1876, 38 & 40 Victoria 49.

Metropolitan Act.

Metropolis Gas Act, 1860, 23 & 24 Victoria 125.

City of London Gas Act. 1868, 31 $ 32 Victoria 125.

Metropolis Gas .(Prepayment to meter) Act, 1900, 63 & 64 Victoria 272.

Private Acts.

Commercial Gas Act, 1875, 38 & 39 Victoria 200.

Commercial Gas Act, 1902, 7 Victoria C137.

Gas Light & Coke Act, 1876, 39 & 40 Victoria 225.

Gas Light & Coke Act, 1898, 61 & 62 Victoria 172.

Gas Light & Coke Act, 1903, 3 Ed. VII.—41.

South Metropolitan Gas Act, 1876, 39 & 30 Victoria 229.

South Metropolitan Gas Act, 1896, 59 & 60 Victoria 226.

South Metropolitan Gas Act, 1900, 63 & 64 Victoria 142.

South Metropolitan Gas Act, 1901, Ed. VII. I—189.

See Appendix a—Gardiners—London Sliding Scale—National Electric Light Association, 1906 for further references.

1. Debates in Parliament 1875 and 1876.
2. The Return of the Revision Commission appointed under the City of London Gas Act of 1868—Parliamentary Document, 1874, No. 132.
3. Annual reports to Parliament of the Authorized Gas undertakings, both companies and corporations, 1881 to date.
4. Address delivered June 9, 1874, by Mr. (now Sir) Geo. Livesey, as President of the British Association of Gas Managers.
5. The Journal of Gas Lighting, Water Supply and Sanitary Engineering, published weekly since 1848.
6. Law of the London Gas Companies—Th. J. Barnes, 1900.
7. Precedents in Private Bill Legislation affecting Gas and Water under-takings—By G. W. Stevenson, 1878.
   - E. H. Stevenson and E. K. Burstal, 1879—1890.
   - E. H. Stevenson and E. K. Burstal, 1891—1901.
8. Power of charge of the Metropolitan Gas Companies —By L. U. S. Rostron, 1900.
9. Law relating to gas and water—By Michael and Will, 5th Ed. 1901.

10. Complete gas and water acts by Joseph Reeson, 1902.

11. Historic Sketches of the London Companies.

Report of the Board of Trade, July 25, 1876.

Report of the Board of Trade, April, 1899.

· Report of the Committee of Parliament, 1899.

Michael & Will, 5th Ed. pp. CXIX–CXXIX.

Rostron's Power of Charge, pp. 1–56.

A History of the South Metropolitan Gas Company.

Statistics.

1. Annual reports of the Authorized Gas Undertakings, both companies and corporations, 1881 to date.

2. The analysis of Accounts of Gas Undertakings—Published by the ''Gas World.''

3. The Gas World Book, published annually.

4. The Gas Works Directory and Statistics—Published annually since 1877.

5. Report of Consumers Gas Company, Toronto—1907.

6. Uniform Classification of Accounts in Gas Utilities—R. R. Comm. of Wisconsin, November, 1908.

7. Field's Analysis of Accounts of Principal Gas Undertakings—Published yearly.

BRIEF NUMBER 15.

R. S. OWEN

SUBMITTED BY GEORGE P. HAMBRECHT

—ON—

THE NATURE OF A PUBLIC UTILITY.

—TO—

THE WISCONSIN LEGISLATIVE COMITTEE

—ON—

WATER POWERS, FORESTRY AND DRAINAGE.

———

(Authorities compiled by M. C. Riley.)

I.

THE NATURE OF A PUBLIC UTILITY.

Any business or vocation affected with a public interest is a public utility. Lord Hale in his treatise De Portibus Maris, 1 Harg. Law Tracts, 78.

The doctrine laid down by Lord Hale is the common law foundation for the regulation and control of public utilities. It was definitely accepted for this country and applied in the case of Munn v. Ill. 94 U. S. 113. Waite, C. J. said:

"When, therefore, one devotes his property to a use in which the public has an interest, he, in effect, grants to the public an interest in that use, and must submit to be controlled by the public for the common good to the extent of the interest created." p. 126.

In the case cited a law regulating the charges for storing grain in elevators was sustained.

II.

WHAT BUSINESSES OR VOCATIONS ARE AFFECTED WITH A PUBLIC INTEREST.

What circumstances will affect a business or vocation with a public interest is not clear. At common law (omitting those kinds of businesses which are subjected to special control in the interest of peace, safety, health and morals) the following classes of business were held to be affected with a public interest and were therefore regulated and controlled:

1. The carrier.
2. Innkeeper.
3. Ferryman.
4. Wharfinger.
5. Miller—Freund Pol. Power, p. 381.

By statute, and in addition to the common law, regulation and control has been extended to the business of the

1. Railroad,—
   R. R. Co. v. Fuller, 17 Wall. 560;
   Olcott v. Supervisors, 16 Wall. 678;
   See note—9 Rose's Notes U. S. Reports p. 27 and
   Cooley's Const. Lim. (7th Ed) p. 873.

2. Railroad Terminals,—
   Ryan v. Louisville Term. Co., 102 Tenn. 119.

3. Telegraph & Telephone,—
   Western Union Tel. Co. v. Pendelton, 95 Ind. 102;
   Chesapeake etc., Tel. Co. v. Tel. Co., 66 Md. 399;
   Brown v. Tel. Co., 6 Utah 236;
   State v. Tel. Co., 47 Fed. 633;
   State v. Tel. Co., 93 Mo. App. 358.

4. Turnpikes,—
   Kemper's Lessee v. Turnpike Co., 11 Ohio 292.

5. Canals,—
   Gue v. Tidewater Canal Co., 24 How. 257.

6. Bridges & Toll Roads,—
   Drawbridge Co. v. Shepherd, 21 How. 112.

7. Improvement of Navigation,—
   In re So. Wis. Power Company, 122 N. W. (Wis.) 801.

8. Irrigation,—
   Wheeler v. Irrigation Co., 10 Colo. 589—590;
   White v. Canal Co., 22 Colo. 198.

9. Corporations created for the purpose of constructing and maintaining a pipe line in an oil district for the conveyance or transportation of petroleum for the public generally,——
   W. Va. Trans. Co. v. Oil & C. Co. 5 W. Va. 382.

10. Corporations for constructing and maintaining pipes for the conveyance of natural gas to consumers,—
    Gas Co. v. Elk Co., 181 Pa. St. 465;
    Roch. Natl. Gas Co., v. Richardson, 63 Barb. 437.

11. Corporations for gathering and distributing news* and market quotations,—
   Inter Ocean Co. v. Associated Press, 184 Ill. 148;
   Stock Exch. v. Board of Trade, 127 Ill. 122.

12. Theatres and other places of amusement,—
   People v. King, 110 N. Y. 428;
   Civil Rights Cases, 109 U. S. 42;
   U. S. v. Taylor, 9 Biss. 473;
   Greenberg v. W. Turf Assn., 140 Calif. 361.

13. Storage of tobacco,—
   Nash v. Page, 80 Ky. 547.

14. Storage of Grain,—
   Munn v. Ill., 94 U. S. 113;
   Brass v. No. Dak., 153 U. S. 399;
   Peo. v. Judd. 117 N. Y. 18.

15. Stock Yards,—
   Coting v. Kansas City etc., Yds., 82 Fed. 852.

16. Supply of Water,—
   Knoxville v. Knoxville Co., 107 Tenn. 671;
   Kennebec W. D. v. Watterville, 97 Me. 201;
   Spring Valley W. W. v. Schottler, 110 U. S. 354;
   Mobile v. Bienville, etc., Co., 130 A. Ia. 384.

17. Supply of Light, Heat and Gas,—
   Denning v. Recorders Court, 145 Calif. 641;
   State v. Col. G. L. Co., 34 Ohio St., 572;
   In re Pryor, 55 Kan. 730;
   Rushville v. Gas Co., 132 Md. 575;
   Shepard v. Milw. Gas Lt. Co., 6 Wis. 526;
   Madison v. Gas & El. Co., 129 Wis. 249;
   Indiana, etc., Co. v. Gas Co., 158 Ind. 519.

18. Insurance,—
   Eagle Ins. Co, 153 U. S. 446;
   State v. Stone, 118 Mo. 388;
   Chgo. Life Ins. Co., v. Needles, 113 U. S. 574;
   People v. Formosa, 131 N. Y. 478.

---

* As to corporations for gathering and distributing news, see Contra State v. Associated Press, 159 Mo. 410.

19. Banking,—
    Baker v. State, 54 Wis. 373.

20. Corporations for developing and improving the mining industry,—
    Rv. Co. v. Mont. U. R. Co. 16 Mont. 304 (Allowed to exercise Eminent domain).

21. Furnishing and sale of power originated or created by a dam on a navigable stream,—
    Wis. River Imp. Co. v. Pier, 137 Wis. 325;
    Light & Power Co., v. Hobbs, 72 N. H. 531, at 534;
    Minn. C. & P. Co. v. Koochiching, 97 Minn. 429 at 451;
    See also Power Co. v. Pratt, 101 Minn. 197;
    McMecking v. Cent. C. P. Co., 80 So. Car. 512.

Contra to the Wisconsin, New Hampshire, Minnesota and South Carolina cases, and to the effect that the business of generating such power for sale for manufacturing purposes is not affected with a public interest, see:
    Brown v. Gerald, 100 Me. 372;
    Fallsburg Co. vs. Alexander, 101 Va. 98;
    Berrien Springs W. P. Co. v. Judge, 133 Mich. 48;
    State v. Power Co., 39 Wash. 648;
    See also Atty Gen'l v. Eau Claire, 37 Wis. at 437;
    Gaylord v. S. D. of Chicago, 204 Ill. 576;
    Howard Mills Co. v. Schwartz, 77 Kan. 599;
    Robert Avery v. Vt. El. Co., 75 Vt. 235, to the effect that the generation of power by an individual to supply a railroad with power not a public use.
    Water cannot be taken for the purpose of furnishing mechanical power, In re. W. P. Co. 62 Vt. 27 see Smith v. Barre W. Co., 73 Vt. 310.

For cases in which the business of generating power for manufacturing and other purposes is held to be affected with a public interest, see
    Shasta Power Co., v. Walker, 149 Fed. 568 affmd 160 Fed. 856 (Power for municipal and Mfg. Purposes);
    Helena P. T. Co. v. Spratt, 35 Mont. 108. (Power for irrigation and mfg. purposes);
    Hollister v. State, 71 Pac. 541, and Jones v. No. Ga. El.

Co. 125 Ga. 618, (Municipal and mfg. purposes) ;

D. P. & I. Co. v. D. R. G. Co., 30 Col. 204; (Mfg. Irrigation and other purposes) ;

In re Niagara Co., 97 N. Y. Supp. 853.

Lewis Em. Dom. p. 551 Vol. 1, (3d Ed) says:

"Sawmills and grist mills, carding and fulling mills, cotton gins and other mills, which are regulated by law and obliged to serve the public, are undoubtedly a public use." *Citing* Saddler v. Langham, 34 Ala. 311; McCulley v. Cunningham, 96 Ala. 583; State v. Edwards, 86 Mo. 102; Harling v. Goodlet, 3 Yerg. 41 ; Varner v. Martin, 21 W. Va. 534.

This seems to be the grounds upon which the court based its decision in Wis. River Imp. Co. v. Pier, 137 Wis. 325 Justice Timlin said:

"By the statute above quoted (Public utility law) the **pub**lic are entitled to use and enjoy the power created, **by this** dam, not as a mere favor or by permission of the owner **but** by right. The charges of the power company are to be **rea**sonable and to be regulated by the public authorities. **These** are the tests of a public use."

No one common characteristic is found in the preceding enumeration of business held to be effected with a public interest. The different businesses have to do with transportation, finance, necessaries of life and with the staple **products of** the community. Many of such businesses require **and operate** under a special grant or privilege from the sovereign—such **as a** grant of corporate existence, a delegation of the sovereign prerogative of eminent domain, or a grant of a franchise **to use** streets and other public places. Many of such businesses **are of** a monopolistic character, creating either a legal or a virtual monopoly.

III.

THEORIES ADVANCED JUSTIFYING A HOLDING THAT CERTAIN BUSINESSES ARE AFFECTED WITH A PUBLIC INTEREST.

Various theories have been advanced by the courts and legal profession as to the principles which justify public control, or which justify a holding that a certain class of business is affected with a public interest.

1. Corporate existence.

A mere grant of corporate existence is not sufficient to justify special control or regulation. L. S. & M. S. Ry. Co. v. Smith, 173 U. S. 684, 689.

> "The power to enact legislation of this character cannot be founded upon the mere fact that the thing affected is a corporation even when the legislature has power to amend or repeal the charter thereof."

See also People v. Budd, 117 N. Y. 1 (1889).

An individual conducting any public utility is subject to exactly the same regulation as is a corporation in the same business and under similar conditions.

The power of Eminent Domain.

The basis for imposing special regulation and control is not the delegation of this power. It is true that public utilities are generally given this power. However, innkeepers, hackmen, bankers, owners of stockyards, those who gather and distribute market quotations and warehousemen* enjoy no such power, and yet all are subject to regulation.

3. The grant of a franchise.

Most pursuits subject to regulation and control, operate or exist by virtue of a franchise. Such for example as the telegraph, telephone, gas, electric light and water companies, the street railway and others which are granted the right to use public streets and places. But hackmen use the streets only as do private in-

---

* Warehousemen enjoy this right in Minnesota.

dividuals; innkeepers, warehousemen and others seldom enjoy
any special grant and yet all are admittedly engaged in occupations subject to regulation.

d. *It is suggested that the right to regulate and control is justified by the failure of competition to regulate: that the only businesses or pursuits that can lawfully be specially regulated or controlled are legal or virtual monopolies.*

In Munn v. Ill. 94 U. S. 113, the law regulating the charges
of grain elevators was sustained because of the monopolistic character of the business.

In Shepard v. Milw. Gas Light Co., 6 Wis. 526, the gas light
company was held subject to regulation because of the extent of
the business and the lack of competition.

In People v. Judd, 117 N. Y. 1, the court emphasized the monopolistic feature of the business (grain elevators). However,
in this case the court saw several reasons for justifying regulation. The court said:

"We rest the power of the legislature to control and regulate elevator charges on the nature and extent of the business, the existence of a virtual monopoly, the benefit derived
from the canal creating the business and making it possible,
the interest to trade and commerce, the relation of the business to prosperity and welfare of the state and the practice
of legislation in analogous cases."

In affirming the right of a municipality to regulate the rates
charged for gas by the city gas company, the supreme court of
Ohio discussed the grounds upon which the right is based. Defendant insisted that property devoted to a public use, or business affected with a public interest, means property or business
devoted to the transportation or care of the persons or property
of others. The court said:

"It is true that the public has not the use of the property
of a gas company as it has of a ferry, nor, probably, as it has
of a warehouse, yet a gas company controls and supplies a
public want in a position that gives it, or may do so, a virtual monopoly of the supply. * * * It is the virtual
monopoly of the want that gives to the public the right to regulate the prices demanded for it.

Zanesville v. Gas Light Co., 47 Ohio St. at 33. To the same effect Rushville v. Gas Co. 132 Ind. 575 and Shepard v. Milw. Gas Light Co., 6 Wis. 526.

In the stockyard case the business of handling and yarding stock was held to be affected with a public interest and subject to regulation as to rates because "many people are compelled to become their patrons." Coting v. Kansas City, etc. Yards, 82 Fed. 852.

The Colorado court compelled an irrigation company to furnish water to an applicant at the rate fixed by law because such companies are generally monopolies along the line of their canals. "Its vocation, together with the use of its property, are closely allied to the public interest, and its conduct in connection therewith naturally affects the community at large."

> Wheeler v. Irrigation Co., 10 Colo. 589—590;
> White v. Canal Co., 22 Colo. 198.

For other decisions expressing the monopoly theory for regulation and control, see:

> State v. Edwards, 86 Mo. 105;
> State v. Loomis, 115 Mo. 329;
> State v. Col. G. L. Co., 34 Ohio St. 572;
> In re Pryor, 55 Kan. 730;
> Bolt v. Stennet, 8 Term Rep. 606;
> Allnutt v. Inglis, 12 East. 527;
> The case of monopolies, 11 Coke 85;
> Spring Valley W. W. v. Schottler, 110 U. S. 347;
> Sinking Fund Cases, 99 U. S. 700, 747;
> R. R. Co. v. Ill. 118 U. S. 557;
> 4 Bl. Comm. pp. 158—60;
> Salt Co. v. Guthrey, 35 Ohio St., 666;
> Cloth Co. v. Cloth Co., 14 N. Y. S. 277.

MONOPOLY THEORY WEAKENED.

The force of the decision in the Munn case, in so far as it held to the monopoly feature as the ground for control, was considerably weakened by a decision of the same court in Brass v. No. Dak. 153 U. S. 399. The New York case, People v. Judd, laid by far less stress upon the monopoly feature of the grain elevator business than did the court in the Munn case, but in the

19

North Dakota case the theory that only monopolistic businesses could be regulated was about abandoned. In the Munn (Ill.) case elevators in the city of Chicago (14 in number) only were affected by the law sustained, while in the No. Dakota case elevators throughout the state,—(some 600 owned by about 125 different persons or concerns) were affected. The absence of the monopolistic feature was very strongly urged upon the court, but the law, by a divided court, was sustained.

In Ladd v. So. Cotton Press Co., 53 Tex. 172 it was held that there may exist a virtual monopoly not subject to special control. (Cotton pressing establishment. In the absence of legislation declaring the business affected with a public interest the court refused to fix rates to be charged.)

Coal mining was held not to be a public use
    Millet v. Peo. 117 Ill. 294.

The courts refused to apply the Munn doctrine to a live stock market, although its transactions were upon a vast scale.
    Am. Live Stock Co. v. Exchange, 143 Ill. 239.

or the manufacture of watch cases as carried on by a monopoly.
    Deuber, Etc., Co. v. Havard, etc., Co., 66 Fed. 645.

COMMENT ON CASES.

In commenting upon the foregoing cases, Mr. Rose in his notes on the United States reports, Vol. 9, p. 32, says:
    "But apart from the fact that so many cases have accorded weight to the monopoly feature in deciding this question, rendering it at least a circumstance of the first importance, it not a criterion, it is to be borne in mind that even the North Dakota elevators still present certain of the features of a monopoly in the broad sense of the term. While individual owners thereof have no monopoly, the business itself is such in the sense that grain growers are compelled to resort thereto in moving their crops to market, in much the same way that railroads are a monopoly though paralleling one another and competitors for business, in the sense that the individual must resort thereto in supplying his ordinary

wants, and pursuing his ordinary business vocations. This
same element of monopoly is present in every municipal
gas or water company, in telegraph and telephone companies,
and the like though there be a dozen competing concerns.
The individual is powerless to obtain the service which they
afford without resort to them. All of these doubtless present
the monopoly element in more pronounced form than the
grain-warehousing business, a consideration which suggests
the observation, that the supreme court will probably not
carry the doctrine any further than the limits marked by the
grain elevator cases, stock exchange v. Board of Trade, 127
Ill. 158. 11 Am. St. Rep. 107."

c. *Finally, that the right to control rests upon the nature of the
business itself.*

Under this theory are included and merged all of the foregoing. This theory is broader than all the others combined. In addition to the classes of business enjoying the right of eminent domain, those operating by virtue of a franchise and those of a monopolistic character, it is contended there are others of such a
nature that they may lawfully be specially regulated and controlled. The business of the hackman, of the insurance company and
of the banker are given as examples. The principle underlying
this theory is that if any business is of such a character or is operated under such conditions that there is danger of oppression
of the people, special regulation and control may be invoked. In
other words where there is no other way of protecting the people
in their rights—no other way in which the welfare of the people
can be promoted the government exercising its police power may
step in and regulate in such a way as not to transcend constitutional rights of property or contracts. Of course the opportunity to oppress is most often present because of some form of monopoly, but the business of the hackman, the banker and of the
insurance company are but very remotely, if at all, of a monopolistic character.

In sustaining a law regulating the charges and services of
hackmen, the Massachusetts Court said:

"These regulations are a reasonable exercise of the authority conferred upon the mayor and aldermen by the Gen.
Sts. * * * They are manifestly intended to secure the
use of suitable hackney carriages and the services of compe-

tent drivers for the accommodation of public travel within
the city, at the rates thereby established."

Com. v. Page, 155 Mass. 227;

See also Com. v. Duane, 98 Mass. 1;

Com. v. Gage, 114 Mass. 328.

In stock Exch. v. Board of Trade, 127 Ill. 158, the question
was as to the right of the court to compel the board of trade to
furnish its market quotations to plaintiff, it being shown that it
was in the habit of furnishing them to all other applicants. It
was argued that the defendant was a private corporation and in
nowise subject to public control. But the court held that its
market quotations, while perhaps private property originally, had
through the methods of their use become affected with a public
interest, and, therefore, subject "to such regulation of the legislature and courts as is necessary to prevent injury to such public
interest."

Freund, in his work on Police Power, p. 389, after dwelling
upon the basis for control and discussing the monopoly theory in
connection with others, says:

"A possible solution of the difficulty may be found in the
application of equality * * * Under the principle of
equality the classes so singled out should have some relation
to the possibility of oppression. The justification for regulating charges in some particular business would usually be
that it constitutes a de jure or a defacto monopoly or enjoys
special privileges; but it may also be that the commodity selected is a necessary of life, or that it is essential to the industrial welfare of the community, or that it has been im-
memorially the subject of regulation."

IV.

CONCLUSION.

Reviewing the cases there seems to be no doubt that a business which (1) enjoys special privileges by way of use of public streets and property or (2) has had delegated to it the power of eminent domain* or (3) a business that constitutes a virtual monopoly is affected with a public interest and may on any one of these three grounds, or on a combination of such grounds, be made subject to control under proper circumstances, although neither special privilege nor monopolistic character seems absolutely essential to subject a business to government control. The extent of the public interest will measure the extent of the public control.

V.

PRIMARILY A LEGISLATIVE QUESTION.

Whether or not a business hitherto deemed to be private has become affected with a public interest and therefor subject to special regulation and control, is primarily a question for the legislature.

The supreme court of Illinois in announcing this principle, said:

"It is not claimed that the keeping or doing of business in a market of this character is one of the employments which the common law declares to be public, nor is it pretended that it has been made so by statute. Ordinarily the adoption of new rules of policy, or the application of existing rules to new subjects, is for the legislature and not for the courts. Accordingly it may be held to be a general rule, though perhaps not an invariable rule, that the question whether a

---

*Contra see State v. Ass'd Press, 159 Mo. 410. Ass'd Press Company enjoyed right of eminent domain, but court held that in the absence of legislation to that effect, it, the court, would not declare the company's business to be affected with a public interest.

particular business which has hitherto been deemed to be
private, is public and impressed with a public use, is for the
legislature." Am. Live Stock Co. v. Exch. 143 Ill, 210 at
238.

The court in the case cited, at page 238, gives the following
reasoning for its holding:

"Apart from the consideration that the extension and application of even existing rules of law to subjects not heretofore within their purview is legislative in its nature, the
determination by the courts as to the precise point at which
a mere private business reaches that stage of growth and
expansion which is sufficient to render it *juris publici,* would
be surrounded with very great difficulties, and would present questions for which the courts unaided by legislation,
would be able to find no just or satisfactory criterion or
test. But when the legislature, acting upon a competent
state of facts, has interposed and declared the business to
be *juris publici,* all difficulty is removed."

With reference to the power of the legislature the court at
page 240 said:

"The business which is here sought to be subjected to a
public use was, at its commencement, confessedly private and
private only, and the public use is sought to be impressed
upon it, not by virtue of any voluntary grant to the public,
but simply because, by mere process of growth and expansion, the business has reached such magnitude as to effect
public interests because of its magnitude alone. *These facts
would doubtless be sufficient to warrant the legislature, in
the exercise of its legislative discretion, in declaring a public
use, and placing said business under legal control and super-
vison, but such power, in our opinion does not rest with the
courts."*

The supreme court of Texas has adopted the rule laid down
in the Illinois case.

Ladd v. Southern Cotton Press Mfg. Co. 53 Tex. 172.

"We know of no authority, and none has been shown us,
for saying that a business strictly *juris privati* will become
juris publici, merely by reason of its extent. If the magnitude of a particular business is such, and the persons affect-

ed by it are so numerous, that the interest of society demands that the rules and principles applicable to public employment should be applied to it, this would have to be done by the legislature, (if not restrained from doing so by the constitution), before a demand for such use could be enforced by the courts."

See to the same effect State v. Ass'd Press, 159 Mo. 410, 462 et seq.

ULTIMATELY A JUDICIAL QUESTION.

Whether or not the legislature has transcended its constitutional powers is a judicial question, but every intendment will be in favor of the constitutionality of the legislative act.

Of the propriety of legislative interference within the scope of legislative power, the legislature is exclusive judge, hence if under any circumstances, the Illinois legislature might have declared the Chicago grain warehouses public warehouses, it must be presumed in favor of the act, that such circumstances existed.

Munn v. Ill., 94 U. S. 113 at 132 & 133—The court said:
"For our purpose we must assume that, if a state of facts could exist that would justify such legislation, ('regulating charges of elevators) it actually did exist when the statute now under consideration was passed. For us the question is one of power not of expediency. If no state of circumstances could exist to justify such a statute, then we may declare this one void, because in excess of the legislative power of the state. But if it could, we must presume it did. Of the propriety of legislative interference within the scope of legislative power, the legislature is the exclusive judge."
See also State v. Mfg. Co., 18 R. I. 16, 35;
Antoni v. Greenhow, 107 U. S. 775;
Owen v. Sioux City, 91 Ia. 190, 196, 197;
State v. Wilson, 7 Kan. App. 428, 437.

"EXHIBIT 11"

Brief Number 11.

SUBMITTED BY GEORGE P. HAMBRECHT

ON

THE NATURE OF A FRANCHISE. DOES A FRANCHISE
DIFFER FROM A PERMIT?

TO

THE WISCONSIN LEGISLATIVE COMMITTEE

ON

WATER POWERS, FORESTRY AND DRAINAGE.

———————

(Authorities compiled by M. C. Riley.)

"EXHIBIT 11."

THE NATURE OF A FRANCHISE. DOES A FRANCHISE DIFFER FROM A PERMIT?

DEFINITIONS.

A franchise is a particular privilege conferred by grant from a sovereign or a government, and vested in individuals or a corporation.

> Chgo. Mun. Gaslight & Fuel Co. v. Town of Lake, 130 Ill. 42, 53 (1889).

A franchise is a particular privilege conferred by the grant of government and vested in individuals—a branch of the King's prerogative subsisting in the hands of a subject.

> State v. Pittsburg, Y. & A. R. Co., 5 Ohio St. 239 (1885);
> Araphce Co. Comrs. v. Printing Co., 15 Colo. App. 189 (1900);
> Wilmington, etc., Ry. Co. v. Downward, 14 Atl. (Del.) 720 (1888);
> Young v. Webster, etc., Ry. Co., 75 Ia. 140 (1888);
> Milhau v. Sharp, 27 N. Y. 611 (1863);
> Miller v. Com., 112 Ky. 404 (1901);
> Crum v. Bliss, 47 Conn. 592, 602 (1880).

A branch of the sovereign power of the state, subsisting in a person or a corporation by a grant from the state.

> Rochester, etc., Ry. Co. v. N. Y. etc. Ry. Co.,, 44 Hun. 206, 212, Affmd. 110 N. Y. 128 (1888).

A franchise is a special privilege conferred by the government on individuals, and which does not belong to the citizens of the country generally of common right.*

> Sellers v. U. L. Co., 39 Wis. 525, 527 (1876);

---

* The expression "common right" employed in the foregoing definition is intended to mean a right which pertains to citizens by the common law, the investiture of which is not to be looked for in any special law, whether established by a constitution or an act of the legislature.
> 19 Cyc. p. 452;
> Spring Valley W. W. v. Schottler, 62 Calif. 69, 107 (1882);
> Augusta Bank v. Earle, 13 Pet. 519, 575 (1839);
> Curtis v. Leavitt, 15 N. Y. 9, 170 (1857).

Spring Valley v. Schottler, 62 Calif. 69, 106 (1882);
Bank of Augusta v. Earle, 38 U. S. 517, 595 (1839);
R. R. Co. v. Memphis R. Co., 77 U. S. 38, 50 (1869).

A privilege or immunity of a public nature which cannot
legally be execised without legislative grant."
>   State v. Portage City Water Co., 107 Wis. 441 (1900);
>   Thompson v. People, 23 Wend. 537, 569 (1840).

A special privilege existing in an individual by grant of the
sovereignity, and not otherwise exercisable.
>   Mayor of Detroit v. Moran, 44 Mich. 602, 604 (1880).

A franchise ''is a right such as cannot be exercised without the
xpress permission of the sovereign power—a privilege or immunity of a public nature which cannot be legally exercised
without legislative grant.''
>   State v. Minn. Thresher Mfg. Co., 40 Minn. 213 (1889).

A right belonging to the government which is conferred upon
a citizen.
>   Lasher v. People, 183 Ill. 226 (1899).

Immunities and privileges belonging to the public and conferred on private individuals or on corporations.
>   Com. v. Frankfort, 13 Bush. (Ky.) 185 (1877).

THE ESSENTIALS OF A FRANCHISE.

(a) It is essential to the character of a franchise that it
should be a grant from a sovereign power.*
>   State v. Portage City W. P. Co., 107 Wis. 441 (1900);
>   Sellers v. Union Lbrg. Co., 39 Wis. 525 (1876).

---

* In some states the rule prevails that the legislature cannot grant
to any other body, such as a municipality, the power to grant franchises. In such jurisdiction grants from municipalities authorizing
the use of streets by railway, telephone, electric light and water works
companies, are construed to be mere licenses or contracts.
>   Chicago Municipal Gas. Lt. Co. v. Lake, 130 Ill. 42 (1889);
>   Peo. v. Detroit Gaslight Co., 38 Mich. 154 (1878);
>   Com. El. Lt. Co. v. Tacoma, 17 Wash. 661 (1897);
>   Cain v. City of Wyoming. 104 Ill. App. 538 (1902).

(b) A franchise must be supported by a consideration.

"The older English authorities (as Finch) define franchises to be 'branches of the royal prerogative existing in the hands of a subject by grant from the king:' 3 Cruise, Dig. 278. They regarded such franchises as being mere donations of the sovereign, to be treated strictly and jealously. In their day, they commonly were so. But the advance of liberty, of commerce, and the arts and conveniences of life have given to franchises a higher character of public utility. They have become contracts between the sovereign power and the private citizen, made upon valuable consideration, for purposes of public benefit as well as private advantage."

Thompson v. People, 23 Wend. 537, 578 (1840).

"Franchises are privileges conferred by grant from government, and vested in private individuals. They contain an implied covenant on the part of the government not to invade the rights vested and, on the part of the grantees, to execute the conditions and duties prescribed in the grant."

3 Kent. Comm. 458.

" * * * franchises spring from contracts between the sovereign power and private citizens, made upon a val-

---

In Main. permissive rights given by statute, 1885, "regulating the erection of posts and lines for the purpose of electricity" granted no franchise. Prior to 1885 the legislature kept the granting of franchises in its own hands.

Twin Village Water Co. v. Gas Lt. Co., 98 Me. 325 (1903).

In Nebraska, the right of a street railway company to occupy streets, when granted by a vote of the electors, is, if nothing more, a license coupled with an interest.

Lincoln St. Ry. v. Lincoln, 61 Neb. 109 (1901).

In Wisconsin, the state may indirectly grant franchises, acting through the agency of a municipality.

State v. Portage City Water Co., 107 Wis. 441 (1900);
Ashland v. Wheeler, 88 Wis. 607 (1894);
State v. Madison St. Ry. Co, 72 Wis. 612 (1888).

But the power of municipalities to grant franchises in Wisconsin is dependent upon statute. In State v. Milwaukee Independent Telephone Co., 133 Wis. 588 (1907), it was held that the city of Milwaukee had no power to grant a franchise to a telephone company. An ordinance was there held invalid as an attempt to confer a franchise.

See also Wis. Tel. Co. v. Milwaukee, 126 Wis. 1 (1905).

uable consideration, for purposes of public benefit, as well
as of individual advantage."

Thompson, Corporations, Vol. 4, Sec. 5335.

A franchise is a contract within the protection of the constitutional provision against the impairment of the obligation
of contracts. Of these the doctrine is well settled that whenever
the sovereign power for the time being, within its legitimate
sphere of action acting under the authority derived from the
constitution or statute law of the state, grants to a body of co-
adventurers the franchise of being a corporation, or any other
species of franchise in the nature of property, and the grantees
accept the grant, such franchise is within the constitutional
protection, in such a sense that it cannot thereafter, in the absence of a reserved power of repeal or amendment, be revoked
or repealed by any form of state action.

State v. C. & N. W. Ry. Co., 128 Wis. 449 (1906).

A franchise is a grant by or under the authority of government, conferring a special and usually a permanent right to
do an act or series of acts of public concern; and, when accepted, it becomes a contract, and is irrevocable. unless the
right to revoke it is expressly reserved.

Trustees v. Jessup, 162 N. Y. 122 (1900) ;
Bank of Augusta v. Earle, 38 U. S. 519, 595 (1839) ;
California v. Pac. Ry. Co., 127 U. S. 1 (1887) ;
Wheeling R. Co. v. Triadelphia, 58 W. Va. 487 (1906) ;
So. West. Mo. Lt. Co. v. Joplin, 113 Fed. 817 (1902) ;
Water Co. v. Austin, 206 Pa. St. 297 (1903) ;
Capitol City L. & F. Co. v. Tallahassee, 168 U. S. 401
    (1897) ;
Underground Ry. Co. v. New York, 116 Fed. 952 (1902) ;
Sunset. Tel. Co. v. Medford, 115 Fed. 202 (1902) ;
El. Lt. Co. v. Hot Springs, 70 Ark. 300 (1902) ;
See also: Fletcher v. Peck, 10 U. S. (6 Cranch.) 87
    (1810) ;
Dartmouth Coll. v. Woodward, 4 Wheat. 518 (1819) ;
People v. Cent. U. Tel. Co., 232 Ill. 260 (1908) ;
Mitchell v. Tulsa Water Co., 95 Pac. (Okl.) 961 (1908).

(c) The grant must be of special privileges which do not belong to the citizens of the country generally of common right.

This qualification (by Chief Justice Taney, in Bank of Augusta v. Earle, 13 Pet. 519, 595 (1839.) " 'which do not belong to the citizens of the country generally of common right' is an important one and constitutes the distinguishing feature of a franchise. What is meant by this qualification is made clear by Mr. Justice Bradley, in a recent case decided by the supreme court of the United States. * * * He says 'no private person can establish a public highway, public ferry or railroad, or charge tolls for the use of the same, without authority from the legislature, direct or derived. These are franchises. Corporate capacity is a franchise. California v. Central Pacific Rd. Co., 127 U. S. 1. * * *. Of course, as the learned judge says, the list might be continued indefinitely. But this quotation clearly illustrates the nature of a franchise. Over all public property, highways, navigable rivers and seas, over everything that belongs to the sovereign, the power of the government is absolute, whether that power is derived from the common law or from the state, or the national constitution. When, therefore, the state grants the right thus belonging to the government, and not to the citizens generally, as a matter of right, it is the grant of a franchise." State v. Scougal, 3 S. Dak. 55 (1892).

> "In this country it is a special privilege granted by the state, which does not belong to the citizens of the country generally by common right. This is the distinguishing feature of a franchise. A right which belongs to the government when conferred upon a citizen is a franchise. No one can exercise the right of eminent domain, or establish a highway or railway and charge tolls for the same, without a grant from the legislature. Such rights as inhere in the sovereign power can only be exercised by the individual or corporation by virtue of a grant from such sovereign power, and when the state grants such a right it is a franchise."
> Lasher v. People, 183 Ill. 226, 23 (1899).

> "The attempt to grant, confer, and delegate rights and privileges constituting franchises and public functions of

the state, * * * is an act beyond the authority of the city. They pertain to a class of powers which are public in their nature and which do not belong of common right to persons generally.''

State v. Milw. Ind. Tel. Co., 133 Wis. 588, 595 (1907).

A FRANCHISE IS PROPERTY.

Sellers v. Union Lbrg. Co., 39 Wis. 525, 526 (1876);

State v. Anderson, 90 Wis. 550 (1895);

Chapman Valve Mfg. Co. v. Oconto Water Co., 89 Wis. 264 (1895);

Fond du Lac Water Co. v. Fond du Lac, 82 Wis. 322 (1892);

Oakland R. Co. v. Ry. Co., 45 Calif. 365, 373 (1872);

Porter v. Rockford, etc., Ry. Co., 76 Ill. 561, 577 (1875);

Norwich Gaslight Co. v. Gas Co., 25 Conn. 19, 36 (1856);

R. R. Co. v. Downward (Del.), 14 Atl. 720, 721 (1888).

The grant of a franchise is in the nature of a vested right of property, subject, however, in most cases, to the performance of conditions and duties on the part of the grantees.

Calif. etc. Tel. Co. v. Tel. Co., 22 Calif. 398, 422 (1863).

A franchise is a vested right peculiar in its nature, and is a quasi property.

Tome v. Crathers, 87 Md. 569 (1898).

Although, technically speaking, franchises are property, they are property of a peculiar character, arising only from legislative grant, and are not in ordinary cases subject to execution or to sale and transfer, even in payment of the debts of the corporation.

Randolph v. Larned, 27 N. J. Eq. 557, 560 (1876).

Yellow River, etc. Co., v. Wood county, 81 Wis. 554 (1892).

While franchises are usually conferred on corporations, they are essentially corporate—they may be granted to individuals as well.

Block River Imp. Co. v. Holway, 87 Wis. 584 (1894);

Atty. Gen'l v. R. R. Cos., 35 Wis. 425 (1874).

A franchise, like other property, must have a certain owner; it can exist only by grant, and a certain grantee is essential to a grant.

> Sellers v. Union Lbrg. Co., 39 Wis. 525 (1876).

PARTICULAR FRANCHISES.

The license to keep a saloon confers no special privilege or right upon the holder, but is merely one of the means adopted by the legislature for regulating the sale of intoxicating liquors; and such a license is not, therefore, within the legal definition of a franchise.*

> Martens v. Rock Island Co. Atty., 186 Ill. 314 (1900).

The term "franchise" does not embrace the right of a corporation to receive money on general or special deposit, to lend money on security, or to discount or purchase bills, notes, or other evidence of indebtedness, as the right to carry on such a business belongs to all citizens of common right.†

> International Trust Co. v. Am. L. & T. Co., 62 Minn.
>   501 (1895);
> State v. Scougal, 3 S. D. 55 N. W. 858 (1892).

But the power or privilege of a bank to issue notes to circulate as money is a franchise.

> Int. Trust Co. v. Am. L. & T. Co., 62 Minn. 501 (1895);
> Atty. Gen'l v. New York, 3 Duer. (N. Y.) 119 (1854);
> Dearborn v. Bank, 42 Ohio St. 617 (1885).

---

* Under a Kansas decision the right of licensing the sale of intoxicating liquors as a beverage, and the extction of a tax or charge therefor, is a franchise or privilege which no city has the power to exercise. State v. Topeka, 30 Kan. 653, 661 (1883).

In Alabama the right to operate a dispensary for the sale of liquors is held to be the exercise of a franchise.

    Uniontown v. State, 145 Ala. 471 (1906);
    State v. Wilburn, 39 So. (Ala.) 816 (1905).

So in Kentucky such a license is held to be a franchise.
    Miller v. Com., 112 Ken. 404 (1901).

† In an early case in Alabama it is said, that since the adoption of the constitution in that state, the right to exercise banking powers constitutes a franchise.
    State v. Stebbins, 1 Stew. (Ala.) 209 (1828).

The privilege of doing business as an insurer is a franchise subject to legislative regulation.

People v. Loew, 44 N. Y. Supp. 42, 43 (1896).

Whenever any citizen or corporation receives the right to construct a railroad upon the land of another without his consent by virtue of the right of eminent domain, such individual or corporation has a franchise of eminent domain.

Knoup v. Bank, 1 Ohio St. 603, 613 (1853).

The privilege conferred upon corporations are the most usual franchises.

Sellers v. U. L. Co., 39 Wis. 525 (1876).

The right to build in and on a public road or way is a franchise.

Penn. R. Co. v. Belt Line Co., 10 Pa. Co. Ct. R. 625, 631 (1892).

The term "franchise" is properly applied to a grant to a corporation of a right to lay out, construct, and operate a railroad.

Driscoll etc. R. R. Co., 65 Conn. 230 (1894).

The grant of an exclusive right to construct and operate a street railway in a city is a franchise.

Denver etc. St. Ry. Co. v. Ry. Co., 2 Colo. 673, 682 (1875). (1875).

The right to construct and maintain water works, gas works, electric light plants or a public market, is a franchise. So is the right to collect tolls upon logs put into a public river.

State v. Portage City W. Co., 107 Wis. 441 (1900) ;
Purnell v. McLean, 98 Md. 589 (1904) ;
Maestri v. Assessors, 110 La. 517 (1902) ;
Sellers v. U. Lbrg. Co., 39 Wis. 525 (1876).

Resolutions of the trustees of a town, which give a person liberty to make a roadway and erect a bridge, and which are passed in the exercise of governmental power conferred by

20

charter in colonial days, create a franchise rather than a license or an easement.

> Trustees v. Jessup, 162 N. Y. 122 (1900).

The right to construct and maintain a public bridge is a franchise.

> Comrs. v. Chandler, 96 U. S. 215 (1877);
> Davis v. Mayor of New York, 14 N. Y. 506, 523 (1856).

The Federal Supreme Court, in Covington Drawbridge Co. v. Shepherd, 21 How. 112, 123 (1858), said: "The corporation had conferred on it a public right of partially obstructing the river, which is a common highway, and which obstruction would have been a nuisance if done without public authority. This special privilege, conferred on the corporation by the sovereign power, of obstructing the navigation, did not belong to the country generally by common right and is therefore a franchise."

A right to establish and maintain a public ferry is a franchise. Bridges and ferries are of the same nature.

> People R. R. v. R. R., 10 Wall. 38 (1869);
> Tuscaloose Co. v. Foster, 132 Ala. 392, 399 (1901);
> Bell v. Clegg, 25 Ark. 26 (1867);
> Atty. Gen'l v. Boston, 123 Mass. 478 (1878);
> McRoberts v. Washburne, 10 Minn. 23 (1865);
> Milhau v. Sharp, 27 N. Y. 611 (1863);
> Hudspeth v. Hall, 111 Ga. 510 (1900);
> Crusen v. Chapin, 31 Wis. 209 (1872).

Authority granted to certain persons by act of the legislature to build and maintain a dam across Rock river upon lands owned by them and to use or to sell or lease the right to use, the water of the river for power, with limitations and conditions as to the height of the dam. etc., is a franchise within the meaning of sec. 3466, statutes 1898. (Law relative to quo warranto—providing for actions to be brought against one who "shall usurp, intrude into or unlawfully hold or exercise * * * any franchise within the state.")

> Atty. Gen'l v. Norcross, 132 Wis. 534, 548 (1907);

See also

Dudley v. Berrien Springs W. P. Co., 128 Mich. 280
(1901);
In re So. Wis. Power Co., 140 Wis. 245 (1909).

The term "franchise," in Constitution, Art. 3, Sec. 18, forbidding the granting of any franchise, except to promote the public welfare, includes an exclusive right of one person of fishing in any part of the Hudson river, and therefore such privilege cannot be granted. Such privilege is a private, exclusive monopoly of a public right, and is manifestly a franchise.

Slingerland v. International Com. Co., 60 N. Y. Supp. 12, 17 (1899).

The certificate of authority issued to a foreign insurance company to do business in a state confers on such company a privilege or right not possessed by citizens generally, and not conferred upon it by its original franchise. This right or privilege so conferred is in this sense a franchise.

N. W. Mut. L. Ins. Co. v. Lewis & Clarke Co., 28 Mont. 484 (1903).

It follows from the foregoing that the following elements are essential to the existence of a franchise.

1st. A legislative grant (either direct or indirect in Wisconsin).

2nd. Based upon a valid consideration (which makes a franchise a contract and property, and indefeasible in the absence of a reserved power to alter or repeal or upon the breach of condition by the grantee).

3rd. Of a special privilege to an individual which does not belong to the citizens of the country generally of common right.

Does a Franchise Differ From a Permit.

Definitions.

The word "permit" with an infinitive is defined as meaning to authorize or give leave.

McHenry v. Winston, 105 Ky. 307 (1898).

"Permit is in one sense synonymous with 'suffer' or 'allow,' but when affirmative action is implied, it is equivalent to 'give leave,' 'license' or 'authorize.' * * * ."
  Coon v. Fremont, 49 N. Y. Supp. 305, 306 (1898).

A license is a grant of permission or authority.
  C., M. & St. P. Ry. Co. v. McFetridge, 56 Wis. 256 (1882).

Where, then, affirmative action is implied, the words "permit" and "license" are synonymous.

In so far as a franchise implies bare leave, license or authority to do some certain thing, the three words, "permit," "license" and "franchise" are synonymous.

IN PRACTCE THE WORDS LICENSE, PERMIT AND FRANCHISE ARE SYNONYMIZED.

In the Wisconsin public utility law, for example, the term "indeterminate permit" is defined as "every grant, directly or indirectly from the state to any corporation, etc., of power, right or privilege to own, operate, etc., any plant or equipment, etc., within this state for the production, etc., of heat, light, water, or power, either directly or indirectly, to or for the public," etc. Sub-sec. 5. 1797m—1, Wis. R. S.

Section 1797t—2, synonymizes the three words, providing that "every license, permit or franchise hereafter granted to any street railway company shall have the effect of an indeterminate permit," etc. Similar effect is given such words in section 1797t—3, where it is declared that "any street railway company operating under an existing license, permit or franchise shall, upon filing at any time prior to the expiration of such license, permit or franchise, with the clerk of the municipality which granted such franchise and with the commission, a written declaration legally executed that, it surrenders such license, permit or franchise, receive by operation of law in lieu thereof, an indeterminate permit as provided in this act."

Distinctions between a License or Permit and a Franchise.

Taking the words literally, every franchise may be said to be a license or permit,—an authorization,—but every license or permit is not a franchise.

A franchise is supported by a consideration; a license or permit may not be. A bare license or permit granted by the state is similar to a license or permit granted by an individual; either is revocable at the will of the grantor.

Chapin v. Crusen, 31 Wis. 209 (1872).*

Thompson in his commentaries on corporations, Vol. 3, Sec. 2668, differentiating between a franchise and a license, says:

"Generally speaking, a franchise must be supported by a consideration. This consideration may take the form of an implied undertaking by the grantee to perform duties beneficial to the public, or it may merely amount to an express agreement to do or not to do, a designated act. It is in this respect that the difference between a franchise and a mere license is most marked; a bare license is not supported by any consideration and is revocable by the granting power."

However, a license or permit may become a contract. An arrangement between A and B to the effect that A may use the premises of B for certain purposes, is a license or permit from B to A. Support this arrangement by a valid consideration, and such license or permit becomes a contract with all the rights incident thereto. A license or permit from a municipality or the state to an individual or corporation may, in like manner and in the absence of a power reserved, become an irrevocable contract.†

Belleville v. The Citizens' Horse Ry. Co., 152 Ill. 171 (1894);

Chapin v. Crusen, supra.

---

* The court in State ex rel. Nor. Pac. R. Co. v. R. R. Comm., 140 Wis. 145, 165 (1909), per Kerwin, J., said: "In Chapin v. Crusen, 31 Wis. 209, the case grew out of a ferry franchise which was held to be a mere license. * * *."

† In Illinois it is held that the legislature cannot grant power to a municipality to grant a franchise. Therefore a privilege of the use

But being a grant from the sovereign power and based upon a consideration, is not sufficient to constitute the grant a franchise. The grant, to constitute a franchise, must confer some special privilege which does not belong of common right to persons generally. Sellers v. Union Lbrg. Co., 39 Wis. 525, 527 (1876); State v. Milw. Ind. Tel. Co., 133 Wis. 588, 595 (1907), and cases supra. If this latter element is missing, such a grant is a mere contract, and although within the protection of the clause of the Federal Constitution relative to the impairment of the obligation of contracts, and, therefore irrevocable in the absence of a reserved power to revoke, it is not a franchise.

SUMMARY.

A bare license, or permit, granted by the legislature (or by a municipality in Wisconsin, dependent upon statute) and not based upon a consideration, has but one of the elements essential to a franchise, and that is the grant from a sovereign power. It differs from a franchise in that it is not supported by a consideration, and in that it does not confer a special privilege which does not belong of common right to persons generally.

A license or permit granted by the legislature (or by municipality in Wisconsin, dependent upon statute), and supported by a consideration, has but two of the elements essential to a franchise, and those are the sovereign grant and the consideration. It differs from a franchise in that it does not confer a special privilege which does not belong of common right to persons generally.

Any grant of the legislature (or by a municipality in Wisconsin, dependent upon statute) supported by a valid consideration and conferring a special privilege which does not belong to persons generally of common right, whether called a

---

of streets when granted by an ordinance in that state is a license. However such a license may be a valid and binding contract, as where the grant is based upon an adequate consideration and is accepted by the grantee, Chgo. Mun. Gaslight Co. v. Lake, 130 Ill. 42 (1889). It is also determined in Illinois that a municipal grant of a right to a company to use the streets for its poles, etc., is not a franchise, but a license or contract; a binding contract, upon acceptance of the privilege by the company, which cannot be revoked except for cause shown.
Peo. v. Cent., etc., Tel. Co., 192 Ill. 307 (1901);
Peo. v. Chi. Tel. Co., 220 Ill. 238 (1906).

license, permit, grant, an authority or a franchise, will be construed by the courts to be a franchise.

Any grant of the legislature lacking in any one or more of the essentials of a franchise, is a mere license or permit.

"EXHIBIT 12."

BRIEF NUMBER 2.

SUBMITTED BY GEORGE P. HAMBRECHT

ON

DISTINCTION BETWEEN FLOATABLE STREAMS AND
STREAMS WHICH ARE NAVIGABLE IN THE
BROADER SENSE OF THAT WORD.

TO

THE WISCONSIN LEGISLATIVE COMMITTEE

ON

WATER POWERS, FORESTRY AND DRAINAGE.

———

(Authorities compiled by M. C. Riley.)

DISTINCTION BETWEEN FLOATABLE STREAMS AND STREAMS WHICH ARE NAVIGABLE IN THE BROADER SENSE OF THAT WORD.

Several states distinguish between the rights of the public on mere floatable streams and streams which are capable of more extended navigation. Those states hold that the rights of the public are not superior to the rights of the riparian owner in streams which are merely floatable.

In Michigan this distinction is clearly laid down by the supreme court of that state.

Middletown v. Flat River Booming Co., 27 Mich. 533, 534.

Bill in Equity by a number of owners of mills and factories on Flat River, to enjoin the defendants from various acts which it is alleged tend to render the waterpower by which their machinery is operated of little value to them. Defendants urge that they are organized for improvement of the right of navigation and that this is the paramount right on a navigable river, to which the rights of mill owners must be subordinate.

Held, Cooley, J.: "Flat river is a stream valuable for floatage, but not for navigation in the more enlarged meaning of the term. On such a stream it cannot be said that the right of floatage is paramount to the use of the water for machinery. Each right should be enjoyed with due regard to the existence and protection of the other." Complaints averred that their dams were equipped with shutes.

Thunder Bay River B. Co. v. Speechly, 31 Mich. 336.

A booming company built a dam for the purpose of collecting the water of a stream periodically navigable, and sending it down in floods in the dry season, to enable the company to float logs which could not otherwise be floated at that season. Plaintiff complains that the company's activity prevents him from operating his mill and asks damages—for plaintiff below. On appeal defendants contend that Thunder Bay River is a publi

stream, navigable for floatage of logs and that riparian rights
are subservient.   Held Cooley, J.:   That the stream was not a
public highway at those times when in its natural condition it
could not be used as such and the plaintiff rightly recovered.
The stream was held to be navigable for logs at certain periods
of the year.

White River Log, etc., Co. v. Nelson, 45 Mich. 578, 583.
Cooley J.:   "The rights of the public to run logs in the
stream are not subordinate to those of the owner of the bank,
but they are concurrent, and each must be enjoyed reasonably,
and without any unnecessary interference with the enjoyment
of the other, and without negligence."

Buchanan v. Grand River Log Co., 48 Mich. 364, 366.
Cooley, J.:   "It is manifest from this statement of the issue
that the question before the court is one of the reasonable use
of the parties respectively of the waters of Flat River.   Complainants have a right to make use of them for milling purposes,
and their case is that defendants unreasonably interefere with
the enjoyment of this right.   Defendants have a right in common with the whole public to make use of the waters for floating
logs, and they claim that they assert and enjoy this right in a
careful and prudent manner, and with no unnecessary interference with the rights of any one.   The questions presented, at
least on this branch of the case,—are therefore purely questions
of fact.   Defendant has no rights which are paramount to those
of complainant;   * * *   nor have they (complainants) a right
to monopolize the stream to the prejudice of public floatage.
Each right modifies the other and may perhaps render it less
valuable, but this fact, if the enjoyment of the right is in itself
reasonable and considerate, can furnish no ground for complaint.   * * *   Gould v. Boston Duck Co., 13 Gray 425; Snow
v. Parsons, 28 Vt. 459."

Woodin v. Wentworth, 57 Mich. 278.
Plaintiff, owner of two mills propelled by water, recovered
damages against defendant for holding back water by means
of dams for log driving purposes—both were riparian holders.

In Minnesota, Oregon and Wisconsin, it has been held that
riparian owner has a right without license and as appurtaining

to the ownership of the bank to construct across a floatable stream a dam which does not obstruct and interfere with the navigation of the streams for the purpose for which it is navigable.

Kretzschmar v. Meehan, 74 Minn. 211, 214.

Defendant contended plaintiff's dam was an unlawful obstruction of a navigable river.

"It appears from the complaint that plaintiff owned the shore land on both sides of the river at the point where the dam was built; that Red Lake River is navigable only for the purpose of floating logs and lumber; that the dam was properly constructed, and provided with a sluiceway of sufficient capacity, and so arranged as to permit logs and lumber to pass through without any unreasonable delay or hindrance. The statutes of this state permit the building of such dams across floatable streams. This the state has a perfect right to do, at least in the absence of any prohibition on the part of the federal government. The fact that the plaintiff did not obtain any license to build the dam does not render it unlawful. A riparian owner has a right, without license, to construct a dam across a stream which does not obstruct or interfere with the navigation of the stream for the purposes for which it is navigable. This is a right which is appurtenant to the ownership of the bank. Lamprey v. Nelson, 24 Minn. 304."

Hallack v. Suitor, (Ore.) 60 Pac. Rep. 384.

Suit to enjoin defendant from maintaining a dam on plaintiff's premises. River or stream by use of flooding dams is capable of floating logs certain parts of year. (Not during summer.) Defendant erected dam for purpose of facilitating the driving of logs to his mill. Trial court held both might use stream, but that defendant must remove dam. Plaintiff appealed contending stream not navigable.

Held: Stream was navigable for floating of logs. As to right to maintain dam on plaintiff's premises court said:

"The plaintiff, being the riparian owner upon a stream navigable only for the purpose of floating logs, has, as appurtenant to such ownership of the bank, the exclusive

right to dam the stream upon her premises, provided the
floating of logs by others is not obstructed thereby. * *
And she cannot be deprived of such right except by her
voluntary act or by condemnatory proceedings in the mode
prescribed by Law.''

The A. C. Conn Co. v. The Little Suamico Lbr. Co., 74 Wis. 652
   (1889).

This was an action to recover damages for the obstruction of
a navigable river and the consequent delay in driving plaintiff's
logs. Both parties had dams (to aid in driving logs) on the
stream which is non-meandered and all were erected without
legislative authority.

Plaintiff alleges that the Little Suamico is a navigable river
and contends that defendant has no right to dam it without
legislative permission.

Below there was verdict and judgment for defendant, upon
appeal. Held: (after saying that the dam did not materially
affect or abridge the beneficial use of the stream.)

"A distinction may well be made between those streams
which are capable of floating logs and timber only at certain
periods and then for a few days in time of freshet, and
streams which are capable of more extended and constant
navigation. It seems to us that in reason and common
justice a distinction should be made in view of riparian
rights. For if the right of floatage is paramount, so that
no bridge or dam or other obstruction can be placed in or
over the stream by the riparian owner, his use and enjoyment of his property are unnecessarily abridged and restricted.

The right of the riparian owner and of the public are
both to be enjoyed with due regard to the existence and
preservation of the other. The right of floatage of logs is
not paramount in the sense that the using of the water by
the riparian owner for machinery is unlawful so long as he
does not materially or unnecessarily interfere with the public right; but he may use the stream and its banks for every
purpose not inconsistent with the public use.''

Affirmed for the defendant.

Chanley v. The Shawano W. P. & R. Imp. Co., 109 Wis. 563
at 569.

"While it has been the policy of this state to hold all
streams capable of floating logs and timber to be navigable,
yet in streams like this (Wolf near Shawano) that are not
meandered, the land owner and the public have certain
reciprocal rights, which may be enjoyed without the destruction of the other. This is fully set forth in the opinion
of this court in the case of A. C. Conn Co. v. Little Suamico
L. Mfg. Co., 74 Wis. 652, which holds distinctly that a dam
may be built and maintained by a riparian owner, without
legislative permission, in a stream navigable only for the
floating of logs and timber, and is not unlawful if it does not
materially affect or abridge the beneficial use of the stream."

IN STREAMS THAT ARE ONLY FLOATABLE, THE RIPARIAN OWNER
IS ONLY BOUND NOT TO OBSTRUCT ITS REASONABLE USE FOR
THAT PURPOSE.

Morgan v. King, 18 Barb. 277.

Defendants seek to remove injunction which restrains them
from obstructing the Raquette river (a floatable stream) by
means of any dam, pier, booms, logs or otherwise, so as to prevent the passage of the logs of plaintiffs to their mill. Defendants pleaded that plaintiff's logs had been let by their dams
and booms (used to stop logs for their mill) as soon as reasonably could be. Defendants were riparian owners at point where
boom and dam were located.

Held: "If the Raquette river is a public highway, all
impediments to its use, dams, piers, booms, etc., unauthorized by the legislature, are nuisances. * * * But if it
can be used only for certain purposes, the riparian owner
is only bound not to obstruct it in that respect. If it can
be, and is, a highway for the passage of single logs, he may
use the river and its banks for every purpose not inconsistent with that public use." p. 287.

The injunction was ordered modified—holding that defendants
had a right to maintain dam and piers and that inconvenience
to plaintiff was not unreasonable.

See also

Charnley v. The Shawano etc., 109 Wis. 563;
Monroe v. Conn. R. Lbr. Co., 68 N. H. 89;
Kretzschmar v. Meehan, 74 Minn. 211.

All or most of the foregoing cases hold that the right of float-age is not exclusive of the use of the waters for machinery or other reasonable uses by the riparian owner, and that the rights of the public and those of the riparian owners are both to be enjoyed with a proper regard to the existence and preservation of the other.

Houck, in his treatise on rivers, at p. 61 says:

"In Maine, the supposed common law doctrine (reference to the common law definition of navigable streams and the ownership of the beds thereof) has been asserted repeatedly; and it is held in that state that there is a distinction between navigable rivers, technically so called, and rivers which have sufficient capacity to float boats, rafts, and logs, and are subject to the servitude of the public and which àre therefore denominated public highways."

To substantiate this assertion the author cites Berry v. Carle, 3 Me. 269; Spring v. Russel, 7 Me. 273; Brown v. Chadbourn, 31 Me. 9; Knox v. Chaloner, 42 Me. 150; Strout v. Millbridge Co., 45 Me. 76; and refers to the Maine case, Veazie v. Dwinel, reported in 3 Am. Law Reg., pp. 715–728, and Redfield's note to that case. These cases bear out the author's statement.

In Brown v. Chadbourn, supra, the court said:

"For in this state, the rights of public use have never been carried so far, as to place fresh water streams on the same ground as those in which the tide ebbs and flows, and which alone are considered strictly navigable at common law, and to exclude the owners of the banks and beds from all property in them." P. 21.

This distinction came about as a result of the test of navigability adopted by that court and was recognized and reiterated in many cases up to the year 1907. In that year in the

case of Smart v. Aroostrook Lumber Company, 103 Me. 37, the
distinction referred to by Mr. Houck was abandoned.   The
court in this case at p. 46 said:

"We retain the term "navigable stream" as indicating
one which is subject to public use as a highway for the purpose of commerce and travel.   The tidal test of navigability adopted by the common law has been found inapplicable to the conditions existing in the United States, and
waters are generally declared navigable in a legal sense
if they are in fact navigable.

"Capability of use for transportation is the criterion,
and is a question of fact."

Farther, by way of abandonment of the distinction referred
to, the court at p. 47 said:

"The extended application of the right of the public to
use navigable streams, whether tidal or non-tidal, even
those of inconsiderable size, as highways for transporting
merchandise, rafting and driving logs and propelling
boats, have made the terms "navigable" and "floatable"
practically synonymous."

For extended note, see 15 Va. Law Reg., 705.

"EXHIBIT 13."

Brief Number 1.

SUBMITTED BY GEORGE P. HAMBRECHT

ON

DEFINITION OF NAVIGABLE STREAMS. (a) WISCON-
SIN. (b) FEDERAL.

TO

THE WISCONSIN LEGISLATIVE COMMITTEE

ON

WATER POWERS, FORESTRY AND DRAINAGE.

————————

(Authorities compiled by M. C. Riley.)

21

DEFINITION OF NAVIGABLE STREAMS.

WISCONSIN.

"Waters at the common law were called navigable, only when affected by the ebb and flow of the tide. Of course in this state, bounded on one side by a great fresh water sea, and on the other side by a great river, which with its confluents constitutes perhaps the most extensive inland navigation in the world, and having within it many streams and bodies of water capable of navigation and actually navigated, there is no water subject to the ebb and flow of the tide, or called navigable at the common law. Here therefore, the restricted sense of the word, navigable, at the common law, is wholly inappropriate to the actual condition of things. Waters are here held navigable when capable of navigation in fact, without other condition. And when we use the terms, navigable or unnavigable, we mean capable or incapable of actual navigation."

Diedrich v. N. W. U. Ry. Co., 42 Wis. 248, 263 (1877).

Whether or not a Wisconsin stream is navigable is a question of fact.

"It is the undoubted policy of the state, as manifested in its legislation, to secure the use of all streams within its territorial limits which are navigable as public highways. * * * The real test to determine whether the stream is a public highway is not the fact that it has been meandered and returned as navigable,* but whether it is navigable in

---

* "In respect to meandered streams which were returned by the government surveyors as navigable, the legislature has declared them *navigable so far as the same have been meandered, to the extent that no dam, bridge or other obstruction shall be made in or over the same* without legislative permission; * * * Sec. 1596 R. S." A. C. Conn Co. v. Little Suamico L. M. Co , supra, p. 655. Sec. 1596 has been construed to include all streams navigable in fact as well as those meandered and returned as navigable. Wis. River Imp. Co. v. Lyons, supra, p. 66. But see A. C. Conn Co. v. Little Suamico L. M. Co. and Charnley v. Shawano W. P. & R. I. Co., Supra.

fact, capable of being used and actually used for floating lumber and logs and other products of the country to mill and market.   If it is, it is then a public highway.   So that where a stream is in fact usefully navigable in this manner, to use the language of plaintiff's counsel, all the rights of the public attach,   *   *   *.''

A. C. Conn Co. v. Little Suamico Lbr. Mfg. Co., 74
Wis. 652, 655 (1889).

Navigability is determined by capacity and capacity is a question of fact.

"The rivers of this state, capable of floating the products of the country, such as logs and rafts of lumber, are by the common law public highways."*

Whisler v. Wilkinson, 22 Wis. 572, 576 (1868).

"It was agreed by counsel on the argument that the Yellow river, was,   *   *   *   of sufficient capacity to float logs;   *   *   *   The river was therefore a public highway."

Sellers v. Union Lbrg. Co., 39 Wis. 525, 526 (1876).

"It is the settled law of this state that streams of sufficient capacity to float logs to market are navigable.   Whisler v. Wilkinson, 22 Wis. 572; Sellers v. Union Lumbering Co., 39 Wis. 525; Olson v. Merrill, 42 Wis. 203; Cohn v. Wausau Boom Co., 47 Wis. 324."

Weatherby v. Meiklejohn, 56 Wis. 73, 76 (1882);
See. J. S. Keater Lbr. Co. v. St. Croix B. Co., 72 Wis.
62 (1888).

"The law, as settled by a long line of decisions in this state, is that streams of sufficient capacity to float logs to market are navigable.   Weatherby v. Meiklejohn, 56 Wis. 76, and cases there cited; A. C. Conn Co. v. Little Suamico L. M. Co., 74 Wis. 655.   These cases treat such streams as highways or waterways."

The Falls Mfg. Co. v. Oconto River Imp. Co., 87 Wis.
134 (1894).

* In Wood v. Hustis, 17 Wis. 416 (1863), it is said that a declaration that a stream is a public highway necessarily implies that it is navigable.

"* * * it has been the policy of this state to hold all streams capable of floating logs and timber to be navigable, * * * ."

Charnley v. Shawano W. P. & R. I. Co., 109 Wis. 563 (1901).

"* * * a stream capable of and which has long been used for floating rafts and fleets of lumber and logs, and boats loaded with the products of the country, to mill and market, is a public highway."

Wisconsin River Imp. Co. v. Lyons, 30 Wis. 61, 66 (1872).

It is not essential to navigability that the navigable capacity be continuous throughout the year.

"It is settled in this court, that streams of sufficient capacity to float logs to market are navigable. * * * And we deem it essential to the public interest in the pine growing regions of the state, spoken of in Whisler v. Wilkinson, to adopt the rule collected from the authorities in Angell on Watercourses, sec. 537, and substantially adopted in the charge of the court below: 'Nor is it essential to the public easement that the capacity of the stream, as above defined, should be continuous; or, in other words, that its ordinary state, at all seasons of the year, should be such as to make it navigable. If it is originally subject to periodical fluctuations in the volume and height of its water, attributable to natural causes, and recurring as regularly as the seasons, and if its periods of high water or navigable capacity ordinarily continue a sufficient legth of time to make it useful as a highway, it is subject to the public easement.' " *

Olson v. Merrill, 42 Wis. 203, 212 (1877).

The Oconto river, which in its natural state has a capacity to float logs to market during the spring freshets, which usually lasts about six weeks, is a public navigable waterway, although

---

* It is a valuable and not a continual capacity of use which determines the right." Moore v. Sanborne, 2 Mich. 519, 526 (1853): Brown v. Chadbourn, 31 Me. 9 (1849).

during the remainder of the year it is not practically useful for such purposes without the aid of flooding dams.†

Falls Mfg. Co. v. Oconto R. Imp. Co., 87 Wis. 134 (1894).

Willow river, in St. Croix county, an unmeandered tributary of the Mississippi, capable in times of high water of floating logs and small rowboats,—although at other times rowboats cannot be taken up the stream without dragging or pushing them on the bottom in numerous shallow places, is held to be a public navigable stream.

Willow River Club v. Wade, 110 Wis. 86 (1898).

"Under the uniform holding in this state, public waters include streams of sufficient capacity to float logs in spring or other freshets, though so small that ordinary rowboats cannot be used therein without dragging or pushing the same on the bottom in shallow places."

Bloomer v. Bloomer, 128 Wis. 297, 311 (1906).

"This court has decided that it is the settled law of the state that streams of sufficient capacity to float logs to market are navigable, and that it is not essential to the public easement that this capacity be continuous throughout the year, but it is sufficient that the stream have periods of navigable capacity, ordinarily recurring from year to year, and continuing long enough to make it useful as a highway. Whisler v. Wilkinson, 22 Wis. 572; Sellers v. Union Lbrg. Co., 39 Wis. 525; Olson v. Merrill, 42 Wis. 203."*

A. C. Conn v. Little Suamico L M. Co., supra.

---

† It is not enough that a stream is capable, (during a period in the aggregate of from two to four weeks in the year when it is swollen by the spring and autumn freshets), of carrying down its rapid course whatever may have been thrown upon its angry waters to be borne at random over every impediment in the shape of dams or bridges which the hand of man has erected. To call such a stream navigable in any sense, it seems to us is a palpable misapplication of the term." Munson v. Hungerford, 6 Barb. 215,270 (1849).

* In Michigan it is held that a stream capable of floating logs, etc., only during the spring and fall freshets is navigable and a public highway while such capacity continues, but that its public nature ceases when in its natural condition such capacity for transportation ceases. That such a stream is a public highway only during high states of water. Thunder River Booming Co. v. Speechley, 31 Mich. 336 (1875); Witheral v. Blooming Co., 68., Mich. 48, 58 (1882); Stoffelt v. Estes, 104 Mich. 208, 211 (1895); People v. Horling, 137 Mich. 406, 411 (1904).

Whether or not Wisconsin waters have the quality of navigability, is a question of fact. Our supreme court, basing its holdings upon the common law and the necessities and requirements found to exist in this state, has defined the minimum capacity that must be present in any stream to constitute the same navigable—this is the capacity to float logs. All waters having a capacity equal to or greater than the one so defined are navigable waters of the state of Wisconsin.

The cases afford the following definition of navigable waters :

DEFINITION.

Navigable waters in Wisconsin are such waters as in their natural condition form useful highways—such waters as have capacity, for a reasonable period of time each year or throughout the year, sufficient at least to float logs, rafts of lumber or other products of the country to mill or market.

FEDERAL.

"The doctrine of the common law as to navigability has no application in this country. Here the ebb and flow of the tide do not constitute the usual test, as in England, or any test at all of the navigability of waters."
The Genessee Chief, 12 How. 443 (1851) ;
The Daniel Ball, 10 Wall, 557, 563 (1870) ;
Escanaba Co. v. Chicago. 107 U. S. 678 (1882).

NAVIGABILITY IS A QUESTION OF FACT.

"Those rivers must be regarded as public navigable rivers in law which are navigable in fact."
The Daniel Ball, supra, p. 563;
Packer v. Bird, 137 U. S. 661 ('1891) ;
Rhea v. Newport, etc., Ry. Co., 50 Fed. 16 (1892).

Rivers or streams are navigable in fact "when they are used, or are susceptible of being used in their ordinary condition, as highways for commerce, over which trade and travel are or may be conducted in the customary modes of trade and travel on water."
The Daniel Ball, supra, p. 563;
Packer v. Bird, supra;
Rhea v. Newport, etc., Co., supra.

"The use now actually made of the waterway, its practical dedication to the public, the importance, amount and
nature of its commerce, and the source and destination of
the commodities borne upon it, establish the character of
the navigation."

20 Op. Atty. Gen. 101 (1891).

DEFINITION OF NAVIGABLE WATERS OF THE UNITED STATES.

Such rivers or streams "constitute navigable waters of the
United States within the meaning of the acts of Congress, in
contra-distinction from the navigable waters of the state, when
they form in their ordinary condition by themselves, or by uniting with other waters, a continued highway over which commerce
is or may be carried on with other states or foreign countries in
the customary modes in which such commerce is conducted by
water."

The Daniel Ball, supra;
The Montello, 11 Wall. 411 (1870) ;
The Montello, 20 Wall. 430 (1874) ;
Cardwell v. Am. Bridge Co., 113 U. S. 205 (1885).

(A) "When they form in their ordinary condition by
themselves or by uniting with other waters, a continued
highway over which commerce is or may be carried on with
other states or foreign countries."

"Inland lakes lying wholly within the limits of the state
are not navigable waters of the United States."[*]

Stapp v. Steamboat Clyde, 43 Minn. 192, 193 (1890) ;
The Robert W. Parsons, 191 U. S. 17, 28 (1903).

"If, however, they (rivers) do not thus form such contiguous highways, but are navigable only between places in
the same state, they are not navigable waters of the United
States. but only of the state."

New England Trout & Salmon Club v. Mather, 68
Vt. 338 (1895) ;
The Montello, 11 Wall, 411 (1870).

---

[*] However, if a lake is formed by an enlargement of a river, consti
tuting navigable waters of the United States, or if a lake has an inlet
or outlet navigable in fact and connecting it with navigable waters of
the United States so that commerce in the customary modes can be
carried on thereon, the lake and such connecting waters are navigable
waters of the United States.

(*B*) ''In the customary modes in which such commerce is conducted by water.''

Commerce includes both freight and passenger traffic.
    Henderson v. Weckham, 92 U. S. 259 (1876) ;
    Crandell v. Nevada, 73 U. S. 35 (1867) ;
    Gloucester Ferry Co. v. Penn., 114 U. S. 196 (1884) ;
    McColl v. California, 136 U. S. 104 (1889).

Navigability is not determined by the means of transportation.

''The navigability of a stream for the purpose of bringing it within the terms 'navigable waters of the United States' does not depend upon the mode by which commerce is conducted upon it, as whether by steamers or sailing vessels, or Durham boats, nor upon the difficulties attending navigation, such as those made by falls, rapids, and sandbars, even though these be so great that while they last they prevent the use of the best means, such as steamboats, for carrying on commerce. It depends upon the fact whether the river in its natural state affords a channel for useful commerce.''
    The Montello, 20 Wall. 430 (1874).

''Vessels of any kind that can float upon the water, whether propelled by animal power, by the wind, or by the agency of steam, are or may become, the mode by which a vast commerce can be conducted, and it would be a mischievous rule that would exclude either in determining the navigability of a river.''
    The Montello, 20 Wall. supra, p. 631.

PARTICULAR STREAMS.

In the United States v. Wishkah Boom Co., 136 Fed. 42 (1905), the question as to whether or not the Wishkah river constituted navigable waters of the United States was before the court. The Wishkah river has its source in the state of Washington and empties into the Chehalis river and Grays Harbor (Pacific Ocean). The court at p. 45 said:
    ''We think that the decision of the present case on the

merits must be ruled by the case of the United States v. Bellingham Bay Boom Co., 176 U. S. 211. * * * We find it impossible to distinguish it from that case in any essential particular. The Bellingham Bay Boom Company had established a boom which interfered with navigation on the Nooksack river—a small river situate in Whatcom Co., emptying into Bellingham Bay, and thence into the Pacific Ocean, navigable by light water craft to Lynden, a distance of some 16 miles. In that case, as in this, the logging business was the principal business on the river, and there was the same disparity between its importance and that of the other traffic. In that case, as in this, there was no proof of the actual carriage of goods on the river in interstate commerce. In that case, as in this, groceries, supplies, clothing, and loggers' tools were carried from the mouth of the river to the head of navigation by small steamboats, which on their return trips brought back farmers' produce.''

Both these streams, the Wishkah and the Nooksack, were held to be navigable waters of the United States. The streams were both capable of accommodating small steamboat navigation. The fact that there had been no interstate commerce carried on over the streams does not affect the answer to the question presented, because ''The capability of use by the public for purposes of transportation and commerce affords the true criterion of the navigability of a river rather than the extent and manner of that use.''

The Montello, 20 Wall. 430, 441.

In Leovy v. U. S., 177 U. S. 621, the question was whether or not Red Pass Crevasse—a crevasse which had been made by the overflow of water from the Mississippi river—was navigable waters of the United States. There was some evidence, said the court, ''that small luggers or yawls, chiefly used by fishermen to carry oysters to and from their beds, sometimes went through this pass, but it was not shown that passengers were carried through it, or that freight destined to another state than Louisiana, or indeed, destined for any market in Louisiana, was ever—much less, habitually—carried through it.''

The court after reviewing its prior decisions, said:

"It is a safe inference from these and other cases to the same effect which might be cited that the term 'navigable waters of the United States' has reference to commerce of a substantial and permanent character to be conducted thereon." P. 632.

Referring to the instructions which were given to the jury in the court below, the court said:

"If these instructions were correct, then there is scarcely a creek or stream in the entire country which is not navigable waters of the United States. Nearly all of the streams on which a skiff or small lugger can float, discharge themselves into some other streams or waters flowing into a river which traverses more than one state, and the mere capacity to pass in a boat of any size, however small, from one stream or rivulet to another, the jury is informed, is sufficient to constitute a navigable water of the United States.

Such a view would extend the paramount jurisdiction of the United States over all the flowing waters in the states, and would subject the officers and agents of a state, engaged in constructing levees, to restrain overflowing rivers within their banks, or in regulating the channels of small streams for the purposes of internal commerce, to fine and imprisonment, unless permission be first obtained from the Secretary of War. If such were the necessary construction of the statutes here involved, their validity might well be questioned. But we do not so understand the legislation of congress. When it is remembered that the source of the power of the general government to act at all in this matter arises out of its power to regulate commerce with foreign countries and among the states, it is obvious that what the constitution and the acts of congress have in view is the promotion and protection of commerce in its international and interstate aspect, and a practical construction must be put on these enactments as intended for such large and important purposes." P. 633.

Again at p. 634 the court said: "Indeed the charge necessarily implies that the defendant was guilty if there was a mere capacity for passing from Red River into the Mississippi on any sort of a boat. Very different was the view expressed by Chief Justice Shaw when he said it is not 'every small creek in which a fishing skiff or gunning canoe can be made to float at high water, which is deemed navigable, but in order to give it the character of a navigable stream it must be generally and commonly useful to some purposes of trade or agriculture.' 21 Pick. 344.''

In United States v. Rio Grande Irrigation Co., 174 U. S. 90 (1899), an injunction had issued to prevent the defendant from constructing dams across the Rio Grande river. The bill averred that the Rio Grande river was navigable for steamboats for 350 miles from its mouth up to the town of Roma, Texas; that it was susceptible of navigation above Roma to a point about 350 miles below El Paso, in Texas, and then, after stating that there were certain falls or rapids which there interfered with navigation, it alleged navigability from El Paso to La Joya, about 100 miles above Elephant Butte, the place at which it was proposed to erect the principal dam, and that it has been used between those points for the floating and transportation of rafts, logs and poles. (The bill further alleged that the impounding of the water would injuriously affect the navigable capacity of the river throughout its entire course below the dam.) Later an amended bill was filed bringing in another party defendant. Upon a hearing the District Court of the Territory of New Mexico dissolved the injunction and dismissed the bill on the ground that the Rio Grande was not navigable in New Mexico—the Supreme Court of the Territory affirmed the decree and upon appeal to the United States Supreme Court it was held:

"Examining the affidavits and other evidence introduced in this case, it is clear to us that the Rio Grande is not navigable within the limits of the Territory of New Mexico. The mere fact that logs, poles and rafts are floated down a stream occasionally and in times of high water does not make it a navigable river. * * * Obviously the Rio Grande within the limits of New Mexico is not a stream over which in its ordinary condition trade and travel can be conducted in the customary modes of trade and travel on water. Its use for any purposes or transportation has been and is exceptional, and only in times of high water. The ordinary flow of water is insufficient. It is not like the Fox river, which was considered in the Montello, in which was an abundant flow of water and a general capacity for navigation along its entire length, and although it was obstructed at certain places by rapids and rocks, yet these difficulties could be overcome by canals and locks and when so overcome would leave the stream in its ordinary condition susceptible of use for general navigation purposes.'' (The decree was reversed and the case remanded for further inquiry as to the effect the dams would have upon the general navigable capacity of the river.)

Grand river, a comparatively insignificant water lying wholly within the state of Michigan and emptying into the lake of that name, and only navigable for forty miles from its mouth to Grand Rapids, for a boat of one hundred twenty-three tons burden, is a navigable water of the United States and subject to its control as a highway of commerce, interstate and foreign, on account of its junction with Lake Michigan.

The Daniel Ball, 10 Wall. 557.

The Illinois and Lake Michigan canal, sixty feet wide and six feet deep, was in ex parte Boyer, 109 U. S. 629, held to be navigable waters of the United States. Mr. Justice Blatchford said:

"Navigable waters situated as this canal is, used for the purposes for which it is used, a highway for commerce between parts and places in different states, carried on by vessels such as those in question here, in public water of the United States, * * *. Even though the canal is wholly within the body of a state and subject to its ownership and control."

The Erie canal, wholly within the state of New York, but connecting navigable waters of the United States, is navigable waters of the United States.

The Robert W. Parsons, 191 U. S. 17 (1903).

The Fox River in Wisconsin is navigable waters of the United States. The Montello, 20 Wall. 430 (1874). So is the Chippewa. Pound v. Turck, 95 U. S. 459, 462 (1877).

Waters do not lose their navigability because intercepted by falls or rapids, when above and below the obstructions the same can be used for purposes of commerce:

> "Preliminary, it may be said that the Mississippi River at the point in question is a navigable stream. In order to be navigable, it is not necessary that it should be deep enough to admit the passage of boats at all portions of the stream. One witness for the plaintiff in error said that in its natural state the river at this point was not navigable at ordinary stages of the water for half a mile below St. Anthony Falls, and in its natural state above Nicollet Island. He also stated that when he said the Mississippi River was not navigable at these falls, he meant that it was not navigable for boats; that boats could not go up and down in its natural condition; that it was always used for logs with chutes that are artificially prepared. It was navigable below the rapids and above the rapids, and that the dam made it so. It was navigable above the rapids for the purpose of running shallow boats and floating logs."

> St. Anthony Falls W. P. Co. v. Water Comrs. 168 U. S. 349, 359 (1897);
> See also Montello, 20 Wall. 430 (1874);
> Spooner v. McConnell, 1 McLean, 337 (1838);
> State Reservation Comrs., 37 Hun 537 (1885);
> Broadnox v. Baker, 94 N. C. 675 (1886).

Summary—Federal.

The Federal Courts have defined the term "navigable waters of the United States," as follows: All waters constitute navigable waters of the United States, in contradistinction from the navigable waters of the state, when they form in their ordinary condition, by themselves or by uniting with other streams, a continued highway over which commerce is or may be carried on with other states or foreign countries, in the customary modes in which such commerce is conducted by water.

This definition has been iterated and reiterated by the Federal Courts for about a century. The definition is clear with the exception of its reference to "commerce in the customary modes." No difficulty is encountered when applying the definition to such waters as the Great Lakes, the St. Lawrence, the

Ohio, the Mississippi, and other great rivers upon which transportation in large boats is carried on. A difficulty is encountered however, when attempting, by an application of the definition, to ascertain the minimum capacity of waters that will be held to be navigable waters of the United States.

The cases make it plain that whether or not certain waters satisfy this definition does not depend upon the nature of the craft used for transportation thereon. They hold that capacity for carrying on commerce is the criterion, and they hold, too, that this commerce must be of a substantial and permanent nature. It follows then that a stream or body of water will not be held to be navigable waters of the United States unless it be shown that commerce of a substantial and permanent nature is, or may be, carried on thereon. The mere capacity to float logs or to accomodate small boats such as skiffs, luggers, or rowboats, the cases hold, will not constitute a stream "navigable waters of the United States."

"EXHIBIT 14."

Brief Number 3.

SUBMITTED BY GEORGE P. HAMBRE

ON

THE RELATION OF THE UNITED STATES, S
OF THE INDIVIDUAL TO THE NAVIGABLE
OF THE STATE OF WISCONSIN

TO

THE WISCONSIN LEGISLATIVE COMMI

ON

WATER POWERS, FORESTRY AND DRA

(Authorities compiled by M. C. Riley.)

I.

The Act of 1787 Creating the Northwest Territory Reserved Certain Rights to the People in the Navigable Rivers and Lakes of Said Territory.

The act provides as follows:

"The navigable waters leading into the Mississippi and St. Lawrence, and the carrying places between the same shall be common highways, and forever free, as well to the inhabitants of the said territory, as to the citizens of the Unted States, and those of any other states that may be admitted, into the confederacy, without any tax, impost, or duty therefor."

Art. IV, Ordinance 1787.

This provision is found also in the Wisconsin enabling act, page 49 Wis. R. S. and also in Art. IX of the Wis. constitution.

Applicability to Wisconsin.

The following cases discuss the application of this provision of the ordinance of 1787, to the states formed out of the territory comprising the northwest territory.

Escanaba Co. v. Chicago, 107 U. S., 878 (1882).

This was an action to enjoin the city of Chicago from keeping bridge draws closed for certain times mornings and evenings and to compel removal of piers from the Chicago river.

The plaintiff was a transportation company on Lake Michigan and on navigable waters connecting with it, and the requiring Chicago river bridge draws to be closed (as per city ordinance for certain time each morning and evening) obstructed the navigable waters of the United States which plaintiffs contended was in conflict with the laws of the United States. Plaintiff contended that congress had interfered with the state's right to control by acts recognizing the act of 1787. The lower court held this contention untenable. Upon appeal it was held:

"The ordinance was passed July 13th, 1787, one year and nearly eight months before the constitution took effect * * * and although the act of April 18th, 1818, chapter 67, enabling the people of Illinois territory to form a constitution and state government, and the resolution of congress of December 3rd, 1818, declaring the admission of the state into the union, referred to the principles of the ordinance according to which the constitution was to be formed, its provisions could not control the authority and power of the state after her admission.

Whatever the limititations upon her powers as a government whilst in a territorial condition, whether from the ordinance of 1787, or the legislation of congress, it ceased to have any operative force, except as voluntarily adopted by her, after she became a state of the union. On her admission she at once became entitled to and possessed all the rights of dominion and sovereignity which belonged to the original states. She was admitted, and could be admitted, only on the same footings with them. The language of the resolution admitting her is "on an equal footing with the original states in all respects whatever." Equality of constitutional right and power is the condition of all the states of the union, old and new. Illinois therefore, as was well observed by counsel, could afterward exercise the same power over rivers within her limits that Delaware exercised over Black Creek and Pennsylvania over the Schuylkill River."

See also Pollard's Lessee v. Hagan 3 How. 212;
Permoli v. First Municipality 10 How. 589;
Strader v. Graham, 10 How. 82.

The act for the admission of the state of Wisconsin into the union reads in part as follows:

"Section 1. Be it enacted by the senate and house of representatives of the United States of America in congress assembled, That the state of Wisconsin be and is hereby admitted to be one of the United States of America, *and is hereby admitted into the union on an equal footing with the original states in* all respects whatever." etc.

22

II.

THE ORIGINAL STATES HAD THE POWER TO AUTHORIZE OBSTRUC-
TIONS IN AND ACROSS NAVIGABLE STREAMS WITHIN THEIR
BOUNDARIES.

The state of Delaware had authorized the building of a dam
across the Blackbird creek, a small stream, in which the tide
ebbed and flowed, and defendants being the owners of a sloop
regularly enrolled and licensed according to the navigation
laws of the United States, tore down the dam for the purpose
of effecting a passage. It was held that the state had power to
authorize the dam in the absence of any action by congress in
execution of the power to regulate commerce, and that the defendants were trespassers.

Willson v. Blackbird Creek Marsh Co., 2 Peters, 245.

The state of Pennsylvania authorized the construction of a
bridge thirty feet above the waters of the Schuylkill river, a
tidal stream entirely within the state. The plaintiff was a
citizen of another state, and was the owner of valuable dock
property on the river above the proposed bridge. The majority
of the court maintained the legality of the proposed structure,
holding upon the authority of the Blackbird Creek case, that,
as congress had not acted on the precise subject, the state had
concurrent jurisdiction over it.

Gilman v. Philadelphia, 3 Wallace, 713.

Here it was said that the police power of the state extends
to the closing of navigation upon a tidal river lying wholly
within its own territory, by means of a bridge or dam.

The Passaic Bridges, 3 Wallace 782.

In Cardwell v. Bridge Co., 113 U. S., 205, at 210 the court
said:

"The act enabling the people of Wisconsin territory to
form a constitution and state government, and for admission into the union, contains a similar clause (similar to
the one interpreted in Escanaba Co. v. Chicago) and yet,

in Pound v. Turck, which was before this court at October
term, 1877, it was held, that a statute of that state which
authorized the erection of a dam across a navigable river
within her limits, was not unconstitutional, in the absence
of other legislation by congress bearing on the case.   The
court does not seem to have considered the question as
effected by the clause in the enabling act.   That clause is
not, it is true, commented on in the opinion, but the section containing it is referred to, and the declaration, that
navigable streams within the state are to be common highways, must have been in the mind of the court.   It held,
however, that the case was governed by the decisions in
the Delaware and Pennsylvania cases, observing that there
were in the state of Wisconsin, and other states, many
small streams navigable for short distances from their
mouths in one of the great rivers of the country, by steamboats, but whose greatest value, in water carriage, was as
outlets to saw-logs and lumber, coal and salt, and that,
in order to develop their greatest utility in that regard,
it was often essential that dams, booms and piers should be
used, which are substantial obstructions to general navigation, and more or less so to rafts and barges; but that
to the legislature of the state the authority is most properly
confided to authorize these structures where their use will
do more good than harm, and to impose such regulations
and limitations in their construction and use as will best
reconcile and accommodate the interest of all concerned.
And the court added that the exercise of this limited power
may all the more safely be confided to the local legislatures
as the right of congress is recognized to interfere and control the matter whenever deemed necessary.''

III.

No Such Restrictions as are Found in the Provision of the
Northwest Ordinance (Art. IV) Were Placed Upon
the Original States.

To the effect that all states must be admitted on an equal
footing, and that territorial laws and provisions creating cer-

tain territories do not apply to states subsequently formed out
of such territory, see also:

Pollard's Lessee v. Hagan, 3 How. 212;

Permoli v. First Municipality, 3 How. 589;

Strader v. Graham, 10 How. 82;

Shively v. Bowlby, 152 U. S. 34;

Ward v. Race Horse, 163 U. S. 513;

Stockton v. Powell, 29 Fla. 45;

Grand Rapids v. Powers, 89 Mich. 102;

People v. Thompson, 155 Ill. 473;

Commissioners v. Board of Public Works, 39 Ohio St.
628;

State ex rel. Attorney General v. Cunningham, 81 Wis.
440 at 511 (op. of Pinney, judge).

Huse v. Glover, 119 U. S. 543 at 547.

Justice Field in the course of his opinion said, "Since the decision in the Escanaba case, we have had our attention repeatedly called to the terms of this clause in the ordinance of 1787.
A similar clause as to their navigable rivers is found in the acts
providing for the admission of California, Wisconsin, and Louisiana.   The clause in the act providing for the admission of California was considered in Cardwell v. American Bridge Company,
113 U. S. 205. *We there held that it did not impair the power
which the state could have exercised over its rivers had the clause
not existed; and that its object was to preserve the rivers as highways equally open to all persons without preference to any, and
unobstructed by duties or tolls, and thus prevent the use of the
navigable streams by private parties to the exclusion of the public, and the exaction of toll for their navigation.* The same
doctrine we have reiterated at the present term of the court in
construing a similar clause in the act for the admission of
Louisiana. Hamilton v. Vicksburg, Shreveport & Pacific Railroad, ante, 280. As thus construed the clause would prevent
any exclusive use of the navigable waters of the state—a possible
farming out of the privilege of navigating them to particular individuals, classes, or corporations, or by vessels of a particular
character. That the apprehension of such a monopoly was not
unfounded, is evident from the history of legislation since. The
state of New York at one time endeavored to confer upon Livingston and Fulton the exclusive right to navigate the waters

within its jurisdiction by vessels propelled in whole or in part by steam.

The exaction of tolls for passage through the locks is as compensation for the use of artificial facilities constructed, not as an impost upon the navigation of the stream. The provision of the clause that the navigable streams should be highways without any tax, impost, or duty, has reference to their navigation in their natural state. It did not contemplate that such navigation might not be improved by artificial means, by the removal of obstructions, or by the making of dams for deepening the waters, or by turning into the rivers waters from other streams to increase their depth. For outlays caused by such works the state may exact reasonable tolls. They are like charges for the use of wharves and docks constructed to facilitate the landing of persons and freight, and the taking them on board, or for the repair of vessels.

The State is interested in the domestic as well as in the interstate and foreign commerce conducted on the Illinois river and to increase its facilities, and thus augment its growth, it has full power. It is only when, in the judgment of Congress, its action is deemed to encroach upon the navigation of the river as a means of interstate and foreign commerce, that that body may interfere and control or supersede it. If, in the opinion of the state, greater benefit would result to her commerce by the improvements made, than by leaving the river in its natural state—and on that point the state must necessarily determine for itself—it may authorize them, although increased inconveniences and expense may thereby result to the business of individuals. The private inconvenience must yield to the public good. The opening of a new highway, or the improvement of an old one, the building of a railroad, and many other works, in which the public is interested, may materially diminish business in certain quarters and increase it in others; yet, for the loss resulting, the sufferers have no legal ground of complaint. How the highways of a State, whether on land or by water, shall be best improved for the public good is a matter for State determination, subject always to the right of Congress to interpose in the cases mentioned. Spooner v. McConnell, 1 McLean, 337; Kelloff v. Union Co., 12 Conn. 7; Thames Bank v. Lovell, 18 Conn. 500; S. C. 46 Am. Dec. 332; McReynolds v. Smallhouse, 8 Bush, 447.''

IV.

THE FOLLOWING CASES INTERPRET THE PROVISIONS OF THE ENABLING ACT AND OF THE CONSTITUTION OF WISCONSIN, WHICH ARE IDENTICAL WITH THAT FOUND IN THE ORDINANCE OF 1787 :

J. S. Keator Lbr. Co. v. St. Croix Boom Co., 72 Wis. 62.

Action for damages to plaintiff's boat. The gravaman of the complaint is that the defendant, assuming to proceed under its charter, had wholly obstructed the navigation of the St. Croix river and had thereby injured plaintiff to his damage without authority of law. Defendant justifies all it did under the acts of the territory and state of Minnesota constituting its charter and authority to construct booms in said St. Croix river which forms the boundary line between Minnesota and Wisconsin.

Plaintiff contends Minnesota had no power to grant such right to defendant, maintaining that congress had by the provisions in the ordinance of 1787 (incorporated also into the acts of congress enabling Minnesota and Wisconsin to organize state governments, and into the constitution of such states) interfered with the state's powers over such river. Nonsuit and appeal.

Held: "This clause was not intended to prevent obstructions to the navigation of such waters, but to prohibit the levying of a tax on such navigation. And in the absence of other legislation by congress such states may authorize the construction of booms in such waters, even though they will materially interfere with steamboat navigation or other water crafts." (Reversed on other grounds.)

See also State v. District Board, 76 Wis. at 207;

Falls Mfg. Co. v. Oconto R. Imp. Co., 87 Wis. at 152.

In re Southern Wis. Power Co., 140 Wis. 245, (1909).

"The clause in the constitution, providing that the navigable waters therein referred to 'shall be common highways and forever free,' etc., does not refer to physical obstructions of these waters, but refers to political regulations which would hamper the freedom of commerce.''

Williamette Iron Bridge Co. v. Hatch, 125 U. S. 1.

Plaintiff brought bill to restrain the defendants, assignees of the Portland Bridge Co., which had been authorized by law to erect a bridge, from erecting said bridge; proofs being taken a decree was made in favor of complainants for perpetual injunction and for an abatement of the portions already built because the same were, and the bridge would be, an obstruction to navigation contrary to the act of congress of 1859 admitting Oregon as a state. (Same as provisions in Wisconsin enabling act.) The supreme court in reversing the holding of the lower court said:

"According to the construction given by this court to the clause in the act of congress relied upon by the court below, it does not refer to physical obstructions but to political regulations which would hamper the freedom of congress.'' p. 19.

Cardwell v. Bridge Co., 113 U. S. 205.

Bill in equity for removal of a bridge. The complaint states that defendant erected a bridge over a branch of the Sacremento river which is entirely within the state of California, but which, due to its connection with other waters, is navigable waters of the United States. The bridge being low prevented the plaintiff from using his steamboat for hauling grain and quarry products to market. A demurrer to the bill was sustained. Plaintiff on appeal quotes the California enabling act (similar to Wis.) and contends the construction of the bridge is contrary to the provisions of said enabling act in that it obstructs the common highway therein provided for.

Held: That provision aims to prevent the use of navigable streams by private parties to the exclusion of the public, and the exaction of tolls for their navigation.

"The court below held that the clause contains two provisions, one that the navigable waters shall be a common highway to the inhabitants of the state as well as to citizens of the United States; and the other, that they shall be forever free from any tax, impost, or duty therefor; that these provisions are separate and distinct, and that one is not adjunct or amplification of the other. * * * But upon the mature and careful consideration, which we have given in this case to the language of the clause in the act admitting California, we are of opinion that, if we treat the clause as advisable into two provisions, they must be construed together as having but one object, namely, to insure a highway equally open to all without preference to any, and unobstructed by duties or tolls, and thus prevent the use of the navigable streams by private parties to the exclusion of the public, and the exaction of any toll for their navigation; and that the clause contemplated no other restriction upon the power of the state in authorizing the construction of bridges over them whenever such construction would promote the convenience of the public."

See also Rea v. Newport, etc., R. Co., 50 Fed. 20;
Osborne v. Knife Falls Boom Co., 32 Minn. 412.

The following cases generally overruled are contra to what has preceded:

Sweeney v. The C. M. & St. P. Ry. Co. 60 Wis. 60 at 67.

In an action to recover for damages to a raft of logs by defendant's bridge, the defendant pleads that in so far as the bridge was built under the direction of the U. S. Secretary of War, and that Sec. 1605 R. S. and 1837 R. S. had not been followed by that official, it, the defendant was not liable. The court by justice Taylor said:

"It is clear that the legislature could not have intended to relieve a railroad company, or any other company or person, for any *unreasonable* or *unnecessary* obstruction of the navigable waters of the Wisconsin river, either by the erection of bridges over the same, or by maintaining any other structures on or over the same; and if it had so intended, it is equally clear that such action or intent of the legislature would not justify such obstruction. The right of the citizen to navigate the waters of the Wisconsin river upon such part of it as is in fact useful for navigation, is secured by a higher authority than the legislature of this state. The right was first secured by Art. IV of the ordinance of 1787, which among other things, provides that 'the navigable waters leading into the Mississippi and St. Lawrence, and the carrying places between the same, shall be common highways, and forever free, etc.' This provision of the ordinance was adopted as a part of the constitution of this state in the identical words of the ordinance. See Sec. 1, Art. IX, Const.

The navigability of the waters of the Wisconsin river, so far as the same are navigable in fact, is protected not only by the common law of the country, but by an express constitutional provision. There can be no contention, therefore, that the legislature has the power to entirely obstruct the navigation of said river. That the legislature has the power to authorize the building of bridges across the navigable waters of the Wisconsin, notwithstanding the ordinance, the provisions of our constitution and the common law, must also be admitted. But that power must be subordinate to the rights of navigation, and bridges so authorized must be so constructed and maintained as not to materially or unnecessarily obstruct such navigation."
(See cases cited on page 68. this case.)

See Alaby v. Mauston El. Svc. Co., 135 Wis. 345 which seems by way of dicta to hold that this provision of the ordinance of 1787 is still operative in Wisconsin.

Also Jolly v. Terre Haute Drawbridge Co. 6 McLean (U. S.) 237.

Also Cox v. State, 3 Blackf. (Ind.) 193, where a statute authorizing the erection of a mill dam in a navigable river which is an obstruction to its navigation, is held to be in violation of the ordinance of 1787 and void. (The Ind. Enabling act, sec. 4, declares, that the articles of the ordinance of 1787, are irrevocable, and that the constitution and state government of the territory when formed should not be repugnant to those articles; and the ordinance of Indiana, June 29, 1816 accepts the propositions and conditions of the enabling act.)

V.

WHAT IS NAVIGABLE WATER?

Wisconsin Rule—Statutory and Judicial.

Statutes.

Lakes. Wis. R. S. Section 1607a.

"All lakes wholly or partly within this state which have been meandered and returned as navigable by the surveyors employed by the government of the United States or which have been so meandered and are navigable in fact are hereby declared to be navigable and public waters," etc.

Streams. Wis. R. S. Section 1596.

"All rivers and streams which have been meandered and returned as navigable by the surveyors employed by the government of the United States are hereby declared navigable so far as the same have been meandered to the extent that no dam, bridge or other obstruction shall be made in or over the same without the permission of the legislature;" etc.

See Sec. 1607 R. S. "Rivers and streams declared navigable."

Section 1596 declares navigable only such streams as are meandered and returned as navigable by the surveyors of the United States.

Judicial.

A statute cannot make a stream navigable which in fact is not navigable.

Jones v. Pettibone, 2 Wis. 308;

People v. Elk River Mill, etc. Co. 107 Calif. 221.

The fact that a stream has not been meandered and returned navigable is not the test of its navigability.

Falls Mfg. Co. v. Oconto R. Imp. Co., 87 Wis. 134.

"Those streams capable of floating the products of the country such as logs and rafts of lumber to mill are common public highways." (This was a meandered stream.)
Whisler v. Wilkinson, 22 Wis. 572.

The rule laid down in the preceding case applied to the Kickapoo river (not meandered) Sellers v. Union Lumbering Co., 39 Wis. 525, and to Lewis Creek (not meandered), Weatherby v. Meiklejohn, 56 Wis. 73.

Where a stream is usefully navigable all the rights of the public attach.
A. C. Conn Co. v. Little Suamico, 74 Wis. 652;
See also Cohn v. Wausau Boom Co., 47 Wis. 314;
Black Riv. Imp. Co v. La Crosse, etc. Co., 54 Wis. 659.

"Under the uniform holding in this state, *public waters* include streams of sufficient capacity to float logs in spring, or other freshets, though so small that ordinary rowboats cannot be used therein without dragging or pushing the same on the bottom in shallow places."
Willow River Club v. Wade, 100 Wis. 86;
See also Bloomer v. Bloomer, 128 Wis. 297;
Allaby v. Mauston El. Svc. Co., 135 Wis. 345;
In re So. Wis. Power Co., 140 Wis. 245.

Summary of Wisconsin rule.

There seems to be two classes of navigable streams in Wisconsin; 1st, those declared by section 1596 to be such, and 2nd, those which are not meandered and returned by the surveyors as navigable, but which are navigable in fact.
Wood v. Hustis, 17 Wis. 416.

The legislature seems to have control over either class:
Whisler v. Wilkinson, 22 Wis. 572;
Olson v. Merrill, 42 Wis. 203;
Boorman v. Sumnichs, 42 Wis. 233;
Deleplaine v. Chicago, etc. Ry. Co., 42 Wis. 214;
Wis. R. Imp. Co. v. Lyons, 30 Wis. 61;
Sellers v. Union Lumbering Co., 39 Wis. 525;
Stevens Point B. Co. v. Reilly, 46 Wis. 237;
Weatherby v. Meiklejohn, 56 Wis. 73;
Falls Mfg. Co. v. Oconto R. I. Co., 87 Wis. 134, 145, 150.

See Allaby v. Mauston El. Service Co., 135 Wis. 345, where the Wisconsin rules as to navigability are discussed and where the doctrine of public highways as applied to streams is dwelt upon.

UNITED STATES RULE.

Judicial.

"Such waters as those which form in their ordinary condition, by themselves or in connection with others, highways over which commerce is, or may be carried on with other states or foreign nations in the customary modes, are navigable waters of the United States."

> The Daniel Ball, 16 Wall. 557;

See also
> Miller v. New York, 109 U. S. 385;
> The Montello, 11 Wall. 411;
> Neiderhouser v. State, 28 Ind. 257.

VI.

JURISDICTION OF UNITED STATES OVER NAVIGABLE WATERS OF WISCONSIN.

The power of Congress extends only to *Navigable Waters of the United States.*

> The Daniel Ball, 16 Wall. 557.

The mere capacity to permit passengers in a boat of any size, however small, or to float logs only is not sufficient to constitute a stream navigable waters of the United States. Therefore the Fox and Wolf rivers above Oshkosh are not navigable waters of the United States.

> Moore v. Home Ins. Co., 30 Wis. 496;

See also
> Leovy v. U. S., 177 U. S. 621;
> Manigault v. Wood, 123 Fed. 707;
> Duluth Lbr. Co. v. St. L. B. I. Co., 5 McCrary 382.

It follows that there are streams in Wisconsin, navigable according to the Wisconsin interpretation of that term, which

empty into navigable waters of the United States, and which
do not come under the general jurisdiction of the United
States.

The Federal government may, however, prohibit the erection and maintenance of any obstruction in any such stream,
if such obstruction will hold back the waters thereof to such
an extent as to destroy or impair the navigation of any navigable waters of the United States.

> U. S. v. Rio Grande Dam & I. Co., 184 U. S. 416.

Until Congress, by virtue of its power under the commerce
clause, acts the power of the state over its navigable waters is
plenary.

> Willson v. The Blackbird Ck. M. Co., 2 Pet. 245;
> Gilman v. Philadelphia, 3 Wall. 713;
> Cummings v. Chicago, 188 U. S. 410 at 427.

The right to erect a structure in a navigable river of the
United States, *wholly within the limits of a state,* depends upon
the concurrent or joint consent of the state and federal governments.

> Montgomery v. Portland, 190 U. S. 89;
> Calumet Grain, etc., Co. v. Chicago, 188 U. S. 431;
> Cummings v. Chicago, 188 U. S. 410.

VII.

Ownership of Navigable Waters.

Bed or soil under water:

In Wisconsin the owners of the banks of a navigable stream
own to the middle or thread of such stream.

> Jones v. Pettibone, 2 Wis. 308;
> Walker v. Shepardson, 2 Wis. 483;
> Mariner v. Schulte, 13 Wis. 692;
> Arnold v. Elmore, 16 Wis. 509;
> Wis. River Imp. Co. v. Lyons, 30 Wis. 61;
> Wright v. Day, 33 Wis. 260.
> Olson v. Merrill, 42 Wis. 203;

Norcross v. Griffiths, 65 Wis. 599;

Janesville v. Carpenter, 77 Wis. 288;

Kaukauna W. P. Co. v. G. Bay & Miss. Canal Co., 142 U. S. 254.

The riparian proprietor upon navigable *lakes* and *ponds* in Wisconsin, however, take the land only to the water's edge.

Boorman v. Sumnich, 42 Wis. 233;

Roberts v. Rust, 104 Wis. 619;

Mendota Club v. Anderson, 101 Wis. 479–492;

Pewaukee v. Savoy, 103 Wis. 271.

The bed of navigable streams, although the title is in the riparian holder, is held by the people of the state in their character as sovereign in trust for public uses for which they are adapted.

McLennan v. Prentice, 85 Wis. 427;

Nee-pee-Nauk Club v. Wilson, 96 Wis. 290;

Willow River Club v. Wade, 100 Wis. 86;

Ill. Cent. Ry. Co. v. Ill., 146 U. S. 387.

Any attempt by the state to convey absolutely lands submerged by navigable waters so as to abrogate its trusteeship in respect to the same would be void on its face, or subject to revocation.

McLennan v. Prentice, 85 Wis. 427;

Priewe v. Wis. State L. & I. Co., 95 Wis. 534;

Ill. Cent. Ry. Co. v. Ill., 146 U. S. 387.

Water.

The riparian owner has no property in the particles of water flowing in the stream more than it has in the air that floats over his land. His rights in that respect are confined to their use and to preserving their purity while passing.

Lawson v. Mowry, 52 Wis. 234, 235;

Willow River Club v. Wade, 100 Wis. 86.

The waters of a navigable stream, or other navigable body of water, are so far the property of the state that the state may *control them for public use,* in their flow or otherwise, without

making any compensation to riparian owners upon the borders
of such streams or bodies of water.

Rundle v. Del. & R. Canal Co., 14 How. 80;

Willson v. Blackbird C. M. Co., 2 Pet. 250;

Trans. Co. v. Chicago, 9 Otto (U. S.) 635;

Fay v. Aqueduct Co., 111 Mass. 27;

Commissioners v. Withers, 29 Miss. 21;

Imp. Co. v. Trans. Co., 54 Wis. 659;

Cohn v. Boom Co., 47 Wis. 314;

Field v. Driving Co., 67 Wis. 569;

People v. Canal Appraisers, 33 N. Y. 461;

Spangler's Appeal, 64 Pa. St. 387.

"Neither sovereign nor subject can have any greater
than a usufructuary right in running water. All such interest in such water is simply an easement of fixed appropriation or conversion. But the use is always subject to
the control of the state for the purposes of navigation and
improvement thereof."

Smith v. Rochester, 92 N. Y. 463.

In Rossmiller v. State, 114 Wis. 169, the law prohibiting the
cutting of ice on meandered lakes for shipment out of this
state except by those permitted to do so by a license to be paid
for, was held unconstitutional on the theory that the right to
take ice is a possession of all the people of the state, and that
a law treating some persons within the state differently than
others, in respect to the enjoyment of public waters, violates
the fourteenth amendment of the national constitution.

The court, by Justice Marshall, discusses at length the interests of the individual and of the state in the navigable waters
of this state. Justice Marshall, in his syllabus to the case,
condenses the law as follows:

"The title to the beds of navigable lakes within the state
of Wisconsin is vested in the state in trust to preserve the
same for the enjoyment of the people. The state has no
proprietary right in such beds or in the water above the
same, nor in the fish that inhabit such water or the fowls
that resort thereto, or the ice that forms thereon, which it
can deal in by sale or otherwise."

"The power of the state over navigable waters within

its boundaries is limited to the enactment and enforcement of such reasonable police regulations as may be deemed necessary to preserve the common right of all to enjoy the same for navigation by boat or otherwise, and all incidents of navigable waters, including the taking of ice therefrom for domestic use or sale.''

"The rights of the people in the navigable waters of the state are the same as those incident to tidal waters at common law. They are beyond the power of the state to interfere with, except by reasonable police regulation, as before indicated.''

"The state has no greater right to sell ice that forms upon navigable lakes than to sell the water thereof in a liquid state or the fish that inhabit the water. It can do neither, the whole beneficial use of public waters being in the people of the state as a class.''

CONTROL OF STATE OVER NAVIGABLE WATERS AND STATE POLICY TOWARD SAME AS OUTLINED BY THE CONSTITUTION, STATUTES AND JUDICIAL DECISION.

Wisconsin constitution.

Art. 1, Sec. 13. "The property of no person shall be taken for public use without just compensation.''

The *riparian right* is property.

Gates v. Milwaukee, 77 U. S. 497.

Riparian right.

The right to use the flow and fall of water is inseparably connected with and inherent in the ownership of land.

G. B. & M. Canal Co. v. K. W. P. Co., 70 Wis. 635;

Same case, 142 U. S. 254;

Kimberly-Clark Co. v. Hewitt, 79 Wis. 334.

Subject to the right of the state to improve or aid navigation the bed of navigable streams cannot be taken for public use without compensation.

Janesville v. Carpenter, 77 Wis. 288–300.

But in aid of navigation the legislature it seems may authorize such a structure or obstruction as will impair or destroy riparian rights.

Cohn v. Wausau Boom Co., 47 Wis., 314; see also Black
River Imp. Co., v. La Crosse, etc. Co. 54 Wis. 659.

Restrictions upon riparian rights.

Dams, booms, and other obstructions that will impair navigation can only be constructed in meandered navigable streams by
legislative permission.

See Statutes 1596 and 1607 Ante.

All obstructions placed in navigable streams are nuisances
and may be abated unless placed there by special authority.

Walker v. Shepardson, 2 Wis. 384—Piles, etc. in Milw. River
Nav. in fact).

Barnes v. Racine, 4 Wis. 454—Bridge over Root River (Nav.
in fact).

Walker v. Shepardson, 4 Wis. 486—Above (Change of venue).

In re Eldred, 46 Wis. 530—Dam across Rock River (Nav.
in fact).

Wis. River Imp. Co. v. Lyons, 30 Wis. 61.

To restrain the erection and maintenance of a dam across the
main channel of the Wisconsin river at Grand Rapids.

The defendant alleges that he is owner of the banks adjacent
to the dam, as well as of the soil and bed of the stream, holding
the same by grant as a water power, and that as such riparian
owner he was justified in the construction of his dam.

The Wis. river at this point is navigable in fact (for logs and
boats loaded with product of the country). The dam is to cross
the navigable portion of the river and is being erected without
permission or license from the legislature. The trial court refused the injunction. Appeal. Held:

"The right of the public to control and regulate navigable streams includes the right to prohibit the erection of
any dam, bridge, or other structure which may operate to
impair the free navigation thereof."

The court further construing sec. 1596 of the statutes (then
sec. 2 Ch. 41 R. S.), said:

"The statute expressly declares, not only such streams
23

as are navigable in fact, but all meandered streams, which includes many that are not so declared for the purpose of the statute, 'that no dam, bridge or other structure may be made in or over the same without legislative permission.' "

"The words of the statute are *no dam* should be made without the permission of the legislature, and it is impossible to evade these words, or to avoid the effect of the prohibition by speculating upon the possibility that the dam, when erected, may not impede or obstruct the navigation, which after all is but mere speculation."

The court discussing the rights of the riparian holder said:
"In holding that the title of the riparian holder extends to the center of the stream, it was also held (Jones v. Pettibone, 2 Wis. 319) that he took subject to the public right of navigation. The easement or right of the public to do anything *within the* banks of the stream which may be considered for the benefit and improvement of navigation is a most extensive and elaborate one." Lower court reversed and injunction ordered.

The preceding case (Wis. River Imp. Co. v. Lyons) in so far as it holds that without legislative permission a dam cannot be maintained in and across a river which has been meandered and returned as navigable by United States surveyors, whether it does or does not interfere with navigation, or is or is not maintained by the riparian owners of both banks, is still law. But, in so far as the case includes in this rule all streams navigable in fact, and not coming within 1596 of the statutes, it has been criticised in the following case:

The A. C. Conn Co. v. The Little Suamico Lbr. Co. 74 Wis. 652 (1889).
This was an action to recover damages for the obstruction of a navigable river and the consequent delay in driving plaintiff's logs. Both parties had dams (to aid in driving logs) on the stream which is non-meandered and all were erected without legislative authority.
Plaintiff alleges that the little Suamico is a navigable river and contends that defendant had no right to dam it without legislative permission.

Below there was verdict and judgment for defendant, upon appeal, Held: (after saying that the dam did not materially affect or abridge the beneficial use of the stream.)

"A distinction may well be made between those streams which are capable of floating logs and timber only at certain periods, and then for a few days in times of freshet, and streams which are capable of more extended and constant navigation. It seems to us that in reason and common justice a distinctoin should be made in view of riparian rights. For if the right of floatage is paramount, so that no bridge or dam or other obstruction can be placed in or over the stream by the riparian owner, his use and enjoyment of his property are necessarily abridged and restricted.

The right of the riparian owner and of the public are both to be enjoyed with due regard to the existence and preservation of the other. The right of floatage of logs is not paramount in the sense that the using of the water by the riparian owner for machinery is unlawful so long as he does not materially or unnecessarily interfere with the public right; but he may use the stream and its banks for every purpose not inconsistent with the public use."

Affirmed for the defendant.

The holding in this case was approved (by way of dictum) in Charnley v. The Shawano W. P. & R. I. Co., 109 Wis. 563 at 568.

The private right is subordinate to and must give way to the public use.

Falls Mfg. Co. v. Oconto River Imp. Co.. 87 Wis. 134.

Action to perpetually restrain defendant from interfering with or interrupting the natural flow of the Oconto river at plaintiff's pulp mill and mill dam so as to impair the usefulness of its water power.

Plaintiff and defendant had both been authorized to erect dams—plaintiff's grant being previous in time and for hydraulic purposes; defendant's grant (later in time) gave him the right to erect a dam above that of plaintiff and was for the purpose of aiding navigation (driving logs).

The lower court found that the Oconto river at this point, in its natural state, was capable of floating logs to market during the spring freshets (about 6 weeks)—that it was therefore a *public highway* for the transportation of logs and that defendant had the right to use it, paramount to plaintiff's (private) right to hydraulic power. Upon appeal it was held: The legislature properly authorized defendant to construct the flooding dam in such stream in aid of navigation and that the plaintiffs had no right of action for any impairment of the efficiency of their water power resulting from the proper use of such flooding dams.

Affirmed for defendant.

Cohn v. The Wausau Boom Co., 47 Wis. 314.

Defendant was granted the exclusive right of constructing booms, for holding, storing, and assorting logs, for a certain distance up and down the Wisconsin river. The grant authorized defendant's works in aid of the boom to extend in the water, up and down the river, fronting its own lands and those of other riparian owners, excluding all other booms within the limits specified.

Plaintiff, a riparian holder, alleging that his property was purchased for mill and booming purposes asks that defendant's booms in front of his property be abated as a nuisance, and for an injunction against further construction or maintenance of booms in front of his property. The original grant (sec. 15, ch. 45, 1871) to defendant gave it preference in the use of the booms. This grant was amended (ch. 256, 1873) so as to give the public equal rights. The injunction prayed for was granted below. The supreme court, reversing this holding, said:

"It is well settled in this state that a riparian owner on navigable water may construct in front of his land, in shoal water, proper wharves, piers and booms, in aid of navigation, at his peril of obstructing it, far enough to reach actually navigable water. *This is properly a riparian right, resting on title to the bank, and not upon title to the soil under water.*

A statute may, indeed, in the exercise of legislative discretion, take away the exercise of the private right, which is a quasi intrusion upon the public right,—is subservient to it, and exists only by public sufferance. But this can be properly done only in the enforcement of the paramount public right, and a statute granting an exclusive right to one riparian holder, for a *private* use, could not be supported as a valid prohibition of the right of adjacent riparian owners. Such a provision would not be an assertion of the paramount public right, but the subordination of one private right to another; would not be in aid of public use, but of a quasi monopoly of a private use. As between several riparian owners such a provision would have effect to give one owner's land somewhat of the nature of a dominant estate, and the land of the others somewhat of the nature of servient estates. This could not be upheld as a valid exercise of the legislative control over the private riparian right.

The controlling question in this case, therefore, is whether the franchises of the appellant are granted for a public or for private use.

As they stood under Chap. 45 of 1871, it would be difficult to consider the appellant other than a private corporation, for private use; for section 15 of that statute gives a preference to the members of the corporation over the general public, in the use of the works authorized. But the amendment of 1873 takes away the preference, and gives an equal right in the use of the works to all the world; and the question here must be determined under the latter provisions.

In this state, navigable water includes all water capable of actual navigation (Diedrich v. Ry. Co., 42 Wis. 248), and the capacity of floating logs to market is sufficient to make water navigable within the rule (Olson v. Merrill, 42 Wis. 203). Whether or how far navigable for other purposes, the capacity of floating logs to market appears to be the chief navigable value of the Wisconsin river, as the legislation relating to it and numerous cases in this court abundantly show. Whatever equally aids this use of the river by all having occasion for it, is of public purpose (Wis. R. I. Co. v. Manson, 43 Wis. 235); and the utility, indeed the necessity, of booms at convenient points for receiving, assorting and distributing logs, such as the appellant is authorized to construct, is so universal on

such rivers that it is judicially recognized as entering into
the law governing their use.

The appellant must therefore be held to be a quasi
public corporation, an agent of the state for the improvement of the river and its franchises granted for a public
use.

Of course, private property of others could not be in
any way appropriated or used by the appellant in aid of
the public purpose, without authority of law, upon just
compensation. *But the land of the respondent is neither
taken nor used; the works of the appellant neither touch
nor overflow it. The statutes under which the appellant
acts authorize no such interference with the property of
others. They only aid the public use for which the appellant is chartered, by restraining the exercise of a private
right, which the legislature appears to have considered inconsistent with it; a right which the respondent, as other
riparian owners, held only by implied public license—as it
were, as tenant by sufferance of the state; a right of which
the exercise might always be prohibited by public law, in
aid of public use. The private use is a quasi intrusion
upon the public right, tolerated only in private aid of navigation, and gives way, ex necessitate rei, to public measures
in aid of navigation.''*

Rights as Between Riparian Owners.

The riparian owner has the right to use the water of a navigable stream in any way compatible with the use of the stream
for navigation, provided he does not abridge corresponding
rights of other riparian owners.

> Lawson v. Mowry, 52 Wis. at 235;
> Walker v. Shepardson, 4 Wis. 436;
> Greene v. Nunnemacher, 36 Wis. 50;
> Delaplaine v. Railway Co., 42 Wis. 214;
> Diedrich v. Railway Co., 42 Wis. 248.

In Miller v. Miller, 9 Pa. St., 74, it was held that a supra
riparian owner is liable to the owner of the land below him
for every material diminution of the flow of the water by a
diversion from the stream, whether for irrigation or other purposes; and this, though no actual injury may have suffered

To the same effect see:

Tyler v. Wilkinson, 4 Mason (U. S.) 397;
Mayor v. Appold, 42 Md., 442;
Tillotson v. Smith, 32 N. H., 90;
Parker v. Griswold, 17 Conn., 288;
Harding v. Water Co., 41 Conn. 87; ·
Gleason v. Mfg. Co., 101 Mass. 72;
Clinton v. Myers, 46 N. Y. 511.

In Sampson v. Hoddinot, 87 Eng. Com. L., 590, it was held that the detention of water in that case by one of several riparian owners, for irrigation, was such that an action would lie for the injury, and that every proprietor of lands on the banks of a natural stream has a right to use the water, provided he so uses it as not to work any material injury to the rights of the proprietors above or below him in the stream.

In Miner v. Gilmour, 12 Moore, p. c. c. 156, Lord Kingsdown stated the law thus:

"Every riparian proprietor has a right to what may be called the ordinary use of the water flowing past his land." He also has the "right to the use of it for any purpose, * * * provided that he does not thereby interfere with the rights of other proprietors, either above or below him. * * * He has no right to interrupt the regular flow of the stream, if he thereby interferes with the lawful use of the water by other proprietors, and inflicts upon them a sensible injury."

In McCalmout v. Whittaker, 3 Rawle (Pa.) 90, Gobson, C. J., thus tersely states the law:

"The water power to which the riparian owner is entitled, consists of the fall in the stream *when in its* natural state as it passes through his land or along the boundary of it; in other words, it consists of the difference of level between the surface where the stream first touches his land, and the surface where it leaves it."

Approved in Brown v. Bush, 45 Pa. St., 66.

Where parties have equal rights, as riparian owners, upon a navigable stream, neither of them can so use his land as to impair the rights of the other.

Walker v. Shepardson, 4 Wis. 486.

The *state*, however, may control the waters of a navigable stream for improvement of navigation, to the disadvantage of the riparian owner without making compensation to such riparian owner.

> Imp. Co. v. Trans. Co., 54 Wis. 659;
> Cohn v. Boom Co., 47 Wis. 314;
> Field v. Driving Co., 67 Wis. 569;
> People v. Canal Appraisers, 33 N. Y. 461;
> Spangler's Appeal, 64 Pa. St. 387.

Stevens Point Boom Co. v. Reilly et al., 46 Wis. at 242 et seq

Ryan, C. J., discussing the rights of the riparian owner in navigable waters (the point in issue) said in part:

"It is difficult to understand how serious disagreement should have arisen in the construction of the opinion of this court on the former appeal. Stevens P. B. Co. v. Reilly, 44 Wis. 295. Following Diedrich v. The N. W. U. Railway Co., 42 Wis. 248. which in its turn followed Dutton v. Strong, 1 Black, 23, and Atlee v. Packett Co., 21 Wall. 389, it was held that the appellants might 'lawfully, *until prohibited by statute, construct*, in front of their land, proper booms to aid in floating logs, so as not to violate any public law or obstruct the navigation of the river by any method in which it may be used, *or infringe upon the rights of other riparian owners. * * ** In any case it must not construct the free navigation of the river by floating logs to market or otherwise.' *Subject to these conditions*, the appellants appear to have a right, as riparian owners, to construct a proper boom from their own premises on the bank of the river.'

It seems to be apprehended by the respondents, that the form of order submitted by the appellants to the court below would, under the rule so given, have authorized the appellants, in the exercise of their riparian right on both banks of the river, to maintain booms completely crossing the river. This question was not in the former appeal. But the right suggested is expressly excluded by the opinion. No form of order could have that effect. Such boom or connecting booms would more or less obstruct the navigation of the river, and would violate public law. R. S. 1858,

Ch. 41, Sec. 2; R. S. 1878 Sec. 1596; Barnes v. Racine, 4 Wis., 454; Enos v. Hamilton, 24 Wis., 658. This is not a question of materially impeding navigation, under color of legislative grant, as under Ch. 399 of 1876. *The general statute forbids any obstruction of the river without permission of the legislature.* Booms erected by riparian owners, in aid of navigation, through shoal water far enough to reach actually navigable water, are not within the statute. Such do not obstruct the river, but aid its use.

This private right of the riparian owner, as declared in Diedrich v. Railway Co., quoted in the opinion on the former appeal, is subordinate to the public use of a navigable river, and is always exercised at peril of obstructing navigation. This subjection of the private right to the public use may sometimes impair the private right or defeat it altogether. But the public right must always prevail over the private exercise of the private right. The legislature may indeed, upon public considerations authorize such an exercise of the private right across the river as will not materially obstruct navigation. But, without legislative permission, the exercise of the private right entirely across the stream is forbidden by the statute.

It was suggested in the former opinion in this case, that the riparian right of constructing a boom was presumably limited by the thread of the stream. That is probably correct. It was a mere limitation, however; and it was unfortunately made, if it led the appellants to believe—as the order proposed by them may suggest—that the right always extends to the thread of the stream. It has always been shown that it cannot so extend to the obstruction of navigation.

The appellants seem to apprehend that the language of this court in Diedrich v. Railway Co., and on the former appeal in this case, as well as in the second clause of the order from which this appeal is taken, renders the riparian right nominal and useless. It is claimed by the learned counsel that the measure of riparian right is restricted to water not navigable, and is unavailing because it cannot reach the point where it would become useful. It is not believed that the language of the federal supreme court in Dutton v. Strong or Atlee v. Packet Co., or of this court in

Diedrich v. Railway Co., or on the former appeal in this case, is properly subject to such hypercriticism. The right sustained in all these cases is a practical right, 'in aid of navigation, through the water far enough to reach actually navigable water' (Diedrich v. Railway Co.) ; 'to aid in floaing logs' (Stevens P. B. Co. v. Reilly). These terms do not imply, the whole tenor of the opinions repels, the construction, that wharves, piers, booms and the like, in aid of navigation, must be constructed within such limits as to make them inoperative. A pier upon Lake Michigan, to aid navigation, must go into the water deep enough to be accessible to vessels navigating the lake. A boom on a logging stream, to aid such navigation, must go into the water deep enough to be accessible to floating logs, must be so constructed as to receive and discharge floating logs. In either case, to reach navigable water reasonably implies reaching it with effect to accomplish the purpose; the word often signifying some penetration of the thing reached. One is not understood to stop outside the limits of a place when he is said to reach it. He is understood to enter it, as far as may be necessary for his purpose. The right in question implies some intrusion into navigable water, at peril of obstructing navigation. Atlee v. Packet Co.

This intrusion is expressly permitted to aid navigation, and expressly prohibited to obstruct navigation. It is impossible to give a general rule limiting its extent. That will always depend upon the conditions under which the right is exercised; the extent and uses of the navigable water; the nature and object of the structure itself. A structure in aid of navigation which would be a reasonable intrusion into the waters of Lake Michigan, would probably be an obstruction of navigation in any navigable river within the state. A logging boom which would be a reasonable intrusion into the waters of the Mississippi, would probably be an obstruction of navigation in most or all of the logging streams within the state. The width of a river may justify a liberal exercise of the right of intrusion, or may exclude it altogether. Its extent is purely a relative question. And there are no facts in this record to warrant any opinion of the extent to which the appellants may exercise the right in this case, without impairing the public use.

If within these conditions the appellants can construct a useful boom, they may. If not, their defect of right is in the condition of the river and its relation to their property, and not in the law."

Atlee v. Packet Co., 21 Wall. 389 at 394. (1874.)

The Union Packet Co. filed a libel in admiralty, in the District court of Iowa, against Atlee, founded on the sinking of a barge, for which he, Atlee, was charged to be liable, on the ground that it was caused by a collision with a stone pier built by him in the navigable part of the Mississippi River.

Atlee rests his defense solely on the ground that at any place where a riparian owner can make a structure useful to his personal pursuits or business, he can, without license or special authority, and by virtue of this ownership, and of his own convenience, project a pier or roadway into the deep water of a navigable stream, provided he does it with care, and leaves a large and sufficient passway of the channel unobstructed. The District court below sanctioned Atlee's contention saying that he, as a lumber man and owner of a saw-mill on the banks of the river, had not exceeded his riparian rights. This holding was reversed in the circuit court and upon appeal by Atlee it was held:

"No case known to us has sustained this proposition, (Atlee's contention) and we think it's bare statement sufficient to show its unsoundness.

It is true that bridges, especially railroad bridges, exist across the Mississippi and other navigable streams, which present more dangerous impediments to navigation than this pier of Mr. Atlee's and that they have, so far as they have been subjected to judicial consideration, been upheld. *But this had never been upon the ground of the absolute right of the owner of the land on which they abutted to build such structures.* The builders have in every instance recognized the necessity of legislative permission by express statute of the state or of the United States, before they ventured on such a proceeding. And the only question that has ever been raised in this class of cases is, whether a *state* could authorize such an invasion of the rights of per-

sons engaged in navigating these streams. This court has
decided that in the absence of any legislation of congress
on the subject, the state may authorize bridges across
navigable streams by statutes as well guarded as to protect
the substantial rights of navigation. But Mr. Atlee has
no such authority, and pretends to none.

We are of opinion that the pier against which libellant's
barge was thrust was placed in the navigable water of the
Mississippi River, without authority of law, and that he is
responsible for the damages to the barge and its contents."

> See also Ladd v. Foster, 31 Fed. 834;
> The Imperial, 38 Fed. 618;
> St. Louis v. The Knapp Co., 6 Fed. 224.

REVISED STATUTES.

Chapter 70:

Section 1596. Declares streams that have been meandered
and returned as navigable by the U. S. surveyors to be navigable
*"to the extent that no dam, bridge or other obstruction shall be
made in or over the same without permission of the legislature."*

Section 1598. Provides a penalty for the obstruction of any
navigable stream by booms or otherwise *without legislative permission.* See sections 1599 to 1606.

Chapter 86:

Sections 1777 to 1777e, inclusive, grant to corporations the
right to erect booms, flooding dams, and other obstructions in
streams to improve navigation or to drive and handle logs
(above steamboat navigation) without the consent of riparian
owners and the same rights below steamboat navigation when
the consent of the riparian owners on both sides of the stream
is obtained. These sections give the right of eminent domain
(1777c) and, upon reasonable compensation being paid, to flow
the lands of others (1777a) and gives the grantee corporation,
subject to the right of others to demand that their logs be
handled (1777b), the exclusive right to boom and otherwise
obstruct the stream for the purpose of improving it (1777e).

Chapter 146:

Sections 3374 to 3404, inclusive, known as the mill-dam
act of 1840, was repealed in 1850 and re-enacted in 1857. This

chapter gives any person the right to erect upon his own land, and with consent, upon the land of others, a water mill and a dam upon and across any non-navigable stream, provided no injury is done to a mill or mill dam already erected or in process of erection. The chapter grants, upon payment of a reasonable compensation, the right to flow the lands of others.

Section 4570a provides a penalty for throwing mill waste into streams navigable for vessels or steamers.

Section 4570b provides a penalty for materially obstructing (by banking or browing logs therein) any stream navigable for floating logs.

Section 1222i *provides for an annual license fee to be paid by all persons or corporations operating dams, booms, or sluice-ways,—the license fee based upon earnings.*

Section 1775c *provides for forfeiture of dam franchises heretofore granted if work of building has not been begun within four years from passage of act (1905, Ch. 521) and provides further that all franchises hereafter granted shall be forfeited unless work is begun within four years of the granting.*

COURT DECISIONS.

The policy of the state to retain control over the waters therein, as brought out in legislative enactment, has been confirmed by the supreme court in the following cases:

Upholding the constitutionality of the Milldam act.
(Act applies to non-navigable streams.)

Newcomb v. Smith, 2 Pinney 131 (1849).

The question here was whether the milldam act of 1840 (giving the right to flow the lands of others upon payment therefor as an incident to the right to maintain a mill-dam) was constitutional—whether it contravened the provisions of the ordinance of 1787 and of the constitution of the United States relative to the taking of property for public use. It was contended that the land flowed by defendant's mill-dam was taken for a private use. The trial judge held the act unconstitutional. The supreme court reversed this holding on the theory that there is a public interest in the utilization of the water powers of the state to run mills. The milldam act sustained in later cases on Stare Decisis only.

Fisher vs. Horicon I. Co. 10 Wis. 351.

Allaby v. Mauston El. Svc. Co., 135 Wis. 345 (1909).

Plaintiffs are owners of distinct parcels of riparian land and allege that defendants maintain dams at Lemonweir river (non-navigable) by virtue of 176 P. & L. 1856, which was enacted in the interval between the repeal and the re-enactment of the milldam act ch. 146 R. S.). The special act was in general the same as the mill dam act. Plaintiffs complain that defendants are maintaining their dams at a greater height than authorized by the act and allege a consequential additional flooding of their lands to their injury. Prayer is for abatement of, and injunction against, the excessive height of the dams. Granted below. Upon appeal it was held:

> "The mill dam acts being based upon the theory that there is a public interest in the utilities of the water power of the state to run mills sufficient to justify the exercise of the power of eminent domain in the flooding and consequent taking of lands of individuals, this dam is lawful and not subject to abatement, the land owners injured being limited to the remedy provided by the statute." Mill dam act applies because by its re-enactment (1857) the legislature intended to codify and revise the law regulating dams which had been erected under special acts.) Justice Siebecker concurring said: "I concur in this decision holding that the dam may be maintained as it is, upon the ground that, under the circumstances shown, the defendant is using the mill site to maintain a grist mill, and an electric power plant devoted to public use."

To the same effect see:

> Pratt v. Brown, 3 Wis. 603;
> Fisher v. Horicon I. Mfg. Co., 10 Wis. 351;
> Newell v. Smith, 15 Wis. 101.

Control for the improvement of navigation.

The legislature has plenary power to authorize flooding dams and other structures in *navigable* streams for the purpose of aiding navigation.

> Wis. River Imp. Co. v. Lyons, 30 Wis. 61;
> Tewksbury v. Schulenberg, 41 Wis. 584;
> Wis. Power Imp. Co. v. Manson, 43 Wis. 255;
> Stevens Point Boom Co. v. Reilly, 44 Wis. 295;
> Cohn v. Wausau Boom Co., 47 Wis. 314;

Black River F. D. Assn. v. Ketchum, 54 Wis. 313;
Black River I. Co. v. La Crosse B. & T. Co., 67 Wis. 463;
Falls Mfg. Co. v. Oconto River Imp. Co., 87 Wis. 134;
Charnley v. The Shawano W. P. & R. I. Co., 109 Wis. 563.

The state may exact a reasonable toll for the use of improvements made by it.
Huse v. Glover, 119 U. S. 543;
Spooner v. McConnell, 23 Fed. Cas. No. 13, 245.

The improvement of streams in aid of navigation under legislative authority granted to individuals is, in effect by the state.
Wis. River Imp. Co. v. Manson, 43 Wis. 255;
Underwood Lbr. Co. v. Pelican Boom Co., 76 Wis. 76.

Where the work of improvement is done by a private person or corporation, compensation is generally fixed by authorizing the collection of tolls.
Sauntry v. Laird Norton Co., 100 Wis. 146;
Black River F. D. Assn. v. Ketchum, 54 Wis. 313;
Tewksbury v. Schulenberg, 41 Wis. 514.

The legislature is, primarily at least, the judge of the necessity of an improvement, and when it delegates the power to a corporation, and the state does not question that the improvement made by the corporation is in conformity with the delegated power, neither the necessity or usefulness of the improvement, nor the manner in which it is made, can be called in question by private parties.
Wis. River Imp. Co. v. Manson, 43 Wis. 255;
Falls Mfg. Co. v. Oconto R. I. Co., 87 Wis. 134;
In Re So. Wis. Power Co., 140 Wis. 245.

Grants for purposes other than the improvement of navigation upheld.
The legislature may authorize the erection of dams across navigable streams, *not materially obstructing navigation*, for a *public purpose* other than the improvement of navigation.

State v. The City of Eau Claire, 40 Wis. 533.

Information for a writ of injunction to restrain the officials of the city of Eau Claire from entering upon the work of constructing a dam for the purpose of furnishing the city with water. The act granted the right to construct a dam for the above purpose and the right to sell surplus power generated by the dam. The act no where purports to make provision for the improvement of navigation. It provides that the dam authorized to be constructed shall not materially obstruct navigation. (See analysis of the act by Ryan C. J. in Atty. Gen. v. Eau Claire 37 Wis. 400 at 434.) It was contended by the attorney general that the legislatuie has no power to authorize the placing of dams or other structures in navigable waters for any other purpose than the improvement of navigation therein. (Contention 40 Wis. at 538.) The supreme court, by Ryan, C. J. as to this point, held: "We did not understand counsel as seriously questioning the right of the legislature to authorize the erection of a dam, on a navigable river, not materially obstructing the navigation, for a public purpose other than the improvement of the navigation." The court then cited: "Stoughton v. State, 5 Wis. 291; Newell v. Smith, 15 Wis. 201; Ward v. Hustis, 17 Wis. 416; Arimond v. Canal Co., 31 Wis. 316; Pumpelly v. Green Bay Co., 13 Wall. 166. We therefore need not consider that question." (The act was upheld and the motion for an injunction dismissed.)

In Wood v. Hustis, supra, a giant for hydraulic purposes (Laws 1845 p. 99) was upheld; a like grant was upheld in Stoughton v. State, supra. To the same effect cases cited by chief justice Ryan and Patten Co. v. Green Bay and Miss. Canal Co., 93 Wis. 283.

See contra Smith v. Rochester (supra).

Generally, however, all grants are based on the fiction that the dam, boom, or other structure is to be constructed in aid of navigation.

The legislature in all grants has carefully guarded against material obstruction to navigation.

Smith et al v. City of Rochester, 92 N. Y. 463.

Plaintiffs are owners of certain premises, on the banks of Honeoye Creek, used and occupied by them for milling purposes, and their mills are operated by the waters of the stream; *said creek is a fresh water*, non-navigable stream, formed by the junction of the surplus waters of those small inland lakes; one of these Hemlock Lake, is about seven miles in length, and one and one-half miles in width; it is to a certain extent navigable and has for many years been navigated for local purposes by those living upon it shores. Under legislative authority defendant (city) constructed a conduit from the said lake to the city, for the purpose of furnishing water for the inhabitants of the city, which conduit draws from the lake 4,000,000 gallons of water daily. The plaintiffs bring this action *to restrain the continued diversion of the surplus waters of the lake from such creek.* Complaint was dismissed below. Upon appeal held: (Conceding that the *lake* was part of the navigable waters of the state and subject to all the rules pertaining to such waters).

"The defense proceeds upon the theory that Hemlock lake being a navigable body of water, as such with its bed belongs to the state, and that the state possessed the consequent right of authorizing the appropriation of the water by its agent or grantees for any public use without regard to the rights of individuals who may have previously acquired proprietary interests therein." (Grant to city all the rights of the state.)

After stating that the state did not own the bed of Hemlock lake the court proceeded:

"We have seen that they (the sovereign rights of the state) constituted an easement over the lands of the riparian owners for limited purposes, and embracing no right to convert the waters to any other uses than those for which the easement was created. It is an elementary principle that all easements are limited to the very purpose for which they were created, and their enjoyment cannot be extended by implication. This right, being founded upon the public benefit supposed to be derived from their use as a highway, cannot be extended to a different purpose inconsistent with its original use. The diversion of these waters

24

for the purposes of furnishing the inhabitants of a large city with that element for domestic uses, and especially to lease them for manufacturing purposes, is an object totally inconsistent with their use as a public highway or the common right of all the people to their benefits.

We concede that such a use is a public one in the sense that enables a municipal corporation to procure the lawful condemnation of property for that object, but we. deny that it is consistent with the purpose upon which the sovereign right is based."

See also Ex parte Jennings, 6 Cow. (N. Y.) 518.

Chanago Bridge Case, 83 N. Y. 178, where it is said:

"The legislature, except under the power of eminent domain, upon making compensation can interfere with such streams only for the purpose of regulating, preserving and protecting the public easement. Further that it has no more power over *fresh water* streams than over other private property."

See also Commissioners v. Kempshall, 26 Wend. 404.

CONTROL OF SURPLUS WATER ACCUMULATED INCIDENT TO IMPROVEMENT FOR NAVIGATION.

In Cooper v. Williams, 4 Ohio 253, the law authorizing the construction of the Miami canal, from Dayton to Cincinnati, empowered the canal commissioners, to dispose of the surplus water of the feeder for the benefit of the state, and their action in so disposing of the water was justified.

Ruling repealed, s. c. 5 Ohio 391.

In Buckingham v. Smith, 10 Ohio 288, it was held that, if the water of private streams should be taken by the state for the mere purposes of creating hydraulic power, and rented to an individual, the transaction would be illegal, and no title would pass as against the owner, but it was intimated that in conducting water through a feeder, a discretionary power must necessarily rest in the agents of the state, and in making provision for a supply, it must frequently occur that a surplus must accumulate, and that such surplus might be subject to lease by the commissioners.

In Little Elevator Co. v. Cincinnati, 30 Ohio St. 629, 643, the right to lease surplus water for private use was recognized as an incident to the public use of a canal for the purpose of navigation.

In Atty. Gen. v. Eau Claire, 37 Wis. 400, it was broadly held that where the city was authorized to erect and maintain a dam for a public municipal use, the legislature might also empower it to lease any surplus water power created by such dam. (The ruling was repeated in State v. Eau Claire, 40 Wis. 533.)

Kaukauna Co. v. Green Bay, etc., Can. Co., 142 U. S. 254.

The case of the plaintiff depends primarily upon the validity of the act of the legislature in 1848, whereby the state assumed to reserve to itself any water power which should be created by the erection of a dam across the Fox river. Justice Brown, delivering the opinion of the court said:

"The improvement of the navigation of a river is a public purpose and the sequestration or appropriation of land or other property, therefore, for such purpose is doubtless a proper exercise of the authority of the state under its power of eminent domain. Upon the other hand, it is probably true that it is beyond the competency of the state to appropriate to itself the property of individuals for the sole purpose of creating a water power to be leased for manufacturing purposes. This would be the case of taking the property of one man for the benefit of another, which is not a constitutional exercise of the right of eminent domain. But if in the erection of a public dam for a recognized *public purpose*, there is necessarily produced a surplus of water, which may properly be used for manufacturing purposes, there is no sound reason why the state may not retain to itself the power of controlling or disposing of such water as an incident of its right to make such improvement. Indeed, it might become very necessary, to retain the disposition of it in its own hands, in order to preserve at all times a sufficient supply for the purposes of navigation. If the riparian owners were allowed to tap the pond at different places, and draw off the water for their own use, serious consequences might arise, not only in connection with the public demand for the purposes of navigation, but between the riparian owners themselves as to the proper proportion each was entitled to draw—controversies which could only be avoided by the state reserving to itself the immediate supervision of the entire supply. As there is no need of the surplus running to waste, there was nothing objectionable in permitting the state to let the use of it to private parties and thus reimburse itself for the expenses of the improvement.

Indeed, it seems to have been the practice not only in New York, but in Ohio in Wisconsin and perhaps in other states, in authorizing the erection of dams for the purposes of navigation or *other public improvement*, to reserve the surplus of water thereby created to be leased to private parties under authority of the state, and where the surplus thus created was a mere incident to securing an adequate amount of water for the public improvement, such legislation, it is believed, has been uniformly sustained.

So long as the dam was erected for the bona fide purpose of furnishing an adequate supply of water for the canal and was not a colorable device for creating a water power, the agents of the state are entitled to great latitude of discretion in regard to the height of the dam and the head of water to be created, and while the surplus in this case may be unnecessarily large, there does not seem to have been any bad faith or abuse of discretion on the part of those charged with the constructoin of the improvement. Courts should not scan so jealously their conduct in this connection if there be no reason to doubt that they were animated by a desire to promote the public interest, nor can they undertake to measure with nicety the exact amount of water required for the purpose of the public improvement. Under the circumstance of this case, we think it within the power of the state to retain within its immediate control such surplus as might incidentally be created by the erection of the dam.''

Approved Patten Paper Co. v. Green Bay, etc. Co., 93 Wis. 433.

"EXHIBIT 15."

BRIEF NUMBER 4.

SUBMITTED BY GEORGE P. HAMBRECHT

ON

CONSTITUTIONAL PROVISIONS RELATING TO
NAVIGABLE WATERS

TO

THE WISCONSIN LEGISLATIVE COMMITTEE

ON

WATER POWERS, FORESTRY AND DRAINAGE.

———————

(Authorities compiled by M. C. Riley.)

CONSTITUTIONAL PROVISIONS RELATING TO NAVIGABLE WATERS.

(Some of the states carved out of the Northwest territory have constitutional provisions securing the free navigation of the streams leading into the Misissippi and St. Lawrence rivers. These provisions do not prohibit the states granting authority to obstruct the navigation of navigable waters within their boundaries.)

Unted States. Art. 1, Sec. 8. The congress shall have power * * * to regulate commerce with foreign nations, and among the several states, and with the Indian Tribes.

Ala. (1901) Art. 1, Sec. 24. That all navigable waters shall remain forever public highways, free to the citizens of the state and the United States, without tax, impost or toll and that no tax, toll, impost or wharfage shal be demanded or received from the owner of any merchandise or commodity for the use of the shores or any wharf erected on the shores, or in or over the waters, of any navigable stream, unless the same be expressly authorized by law.

Arizona Bill or Rights, Sec. 22. All streams, lakes and ponds of water capable of being used for the purposes of navigation and irrigation, are hereby declared to be public property; and no individual or corporation shall have the right to appropriate them exclusively to their own private use, except under such equitable regulations and restrictions as the legislature shall provide for that purpose.

Mich. (1850) Art. 15, Sec. 4. No navigable stream in this state shall be either bridged or dammed without authority from the board of supervisors of the proper county under the provisions of law. No such law shall prejudice the right of individuals to the free navigation of such streams or preclude the state from the further improvement of the navigation of such streams.

Miss. (1890) Art. 4, Sec. 8. The legislature shall never authorize the permanent obstruction of any of the navigable waters of the state, but may provide for the removal of such obstructions as now exist, whenever the public welfare demands. This section shall not prevent the construction, under proper authority, of draw-bridges for railroads, or other roads, nor the construction of booms "nd chutes" for logs in such manner as not to prevent the safe passage of vessels, or logs, under regulations to be provided by law.

S. C. (1895) Art. 1, Sec. 28. All navigable waters shall forever remain public highways free to the citizens of the state and the United States without tax, impost or toll imposed; and no tax, toll, impost or wharfage shall be imposed, demanded or received from the owners of any merchandise or commodity for the use of the shores or any wharf erected on the shores or in or over the waters of any navigable stream unless the same be authorized by the general assembly.

S. C. (1895) Art. 14, Sec. 1. The state shall have concurrent jurisdiction on all rivers bordering on this state, so far as such rivers shall form a common boundary to this and any other state bounded by the same; and they, together with all navigable waters within the limits of the state, shall be common highways and forever free, as well to the inhabitants of this state as to the citizens of the United States, without any tax or impost therefor, unless the same be expressly provided for by the general assembly.

Tenn. (1870) Art. 1, Sec. 29. That an equal participation in the free navigation of the Mississippi is one of the inherent rights of the citizens of this state; it cannot, therefore, be concealed to any prince, potentate, power, person, or persons whatever.

WATER FRONTAGES.

Cal. (1880) Art. 15, Sec. 1. The right of eminent domain is hereby declared to exist in the state to all frontages on the navigable waters of this state.

Cal. (1880) Art. 15, Sec. 2. No individual, partnership, or corporation, claiming or possessing the frontage of tidal lands of a harbor, bay, inlet, estuary, or other navigable water in this state, shall be permitted to exclude the right of way to such water whenever it is required for any public purpose, nor to destroy or obstruct the free navigation of such water; and the legislature shall enact such laws as will give the most liberal construction to this provisions, so that access to the navigable waters of this state shall be always attainable for the people thereof.

Cal. (1880) Art. 15, Sec. 3. All tide lands within two miles of any incorporated city or town of this state, and fronting on the waters of any harbor, estuary, bay, or inlet, used for the purposes of navigation, shall be withheld from grant or sale to private persons, partnerships, or corporations.

Art. 290. Riparian owners of property on navigable rivers, lakes, and streams, within any city or town in this state having a population in excess of five thousand shall have the right to erect and maintain on the batture or banks owned by them, such wharves, buildings and improvements as may be required for the purposes of commerce and navigation, subject to the following conditions, and not otherwise, to-wit: Such owners shall first obtain the consent of the council, or other governing authority and of the board of levee commissioners, within whose municipal or levee district jurisdiction such wharves, buildings, and improvements are to be erected, and such consent having been obtained, shall erect the same in conformity to plans and specifications which shall have been first submitted to, and approved by, the engineer of such council, and other governing authority; and when so erected, such wharves, buildings, and improvements shall be, and remain, subject to the administration and control of such council, or other governing authority, with respect to their maintenance and to the fees and charges to be exacted for their use by the public, whenever any fee or charge is authorized to be and is made; and shall be and remain subject to the control of such board of levee commissioners, in so far as may be necessary for the maintenance and administration of the levees in its jurisdiction. The council, or other governing authority, shall have the right to expropriate such wharves, buildings, and improvements, whenever necessary for public purposes, upon reimbursing the owner the cost of construction, less such depreciation as may have resulted from time and decay: such imbursement, however, in no case to exceed the actual market value of the property: Provided, That nothing in this article shal be construed as effecting the right of the state, or any political sub-division thereof, or of the several boards of levee commissioners to appropriate without compensation such wharves, buildings, and improvements, when necessary for levee purposes.

WATER RIGHTS AND IRRIGATION.

Cal. (1880) Art. 14, Sec. 1. The use of all water now appropriated, or that may hereafter be appropriated, for sale, rental, or distribution, is hereby declared to be a public use, and subject to the regulation and control of the State, in the manner to be prescribed by law: Provided, That the rates or compensation to be collected by any person, company, or corporation in this state for the use of water suplied to any city and county, or city, or town, or the inhabitants thereof, shall be fixed annually, by the board of supervisors, or city and county, or city, or town council, or other governing body of such city and county, or city or town, by ordinance or otherwise, in the manner that other ordinances or legislative acts or resolutions are passed by such body, and shall continue in force for one year and no longer. Such ordinances or resolutions shall be passed in the month of February of each year, and take effect on the first day of July thereafter. Any board or body failing to pass the necessary ordinances or resolutions fixing water rates, where necessary, within such time, shall be subject to peremptory process to compel action, at the suit of any party interested, and shall be liable to such further processes and penalties as the legislature may prescribe. Any person, company, or corporation

collecting water rates in any city or county, or city, or town
in this state, otherwise than as so established, shall forfeit the
franchises and waterworks of such person, company, or corporation to the city and county, or city, or town, where the same
are collected, for the public use.

Cal. (1880 Art. 14, Sec. 2.   The right to collect water rates
or compensation for the use of water supplied to any county,
city and county, or town, or the inhabitants thereof, is a franchise, and can not be exercised except by authority of and in the
manner prescribed by law.

Colo. (1876) Art 16, Sec. 5.   The water of every natural
stream, not heretofore apropriated, within the state of Colorado,
is hereby declared to be the property of the public, and the same
is dedicated to the use of the people of the state, subjct to appropriation as hereinafter provided.

Colo. (1876) Art. 16, Sec. 6.   The right to divert unappro
priated waters of any natural stream to beneficial uses shall
never be denied.   Priority of apropriation shall give the better right as between those using the water for the same purpose; but when the waters of any natural stream are not suffi
cient for the services of all those desiring the use of same, those
using the water for domestic purposes shall have the preference
over those claiming for any other purpose, and those using the
water for agricultural purposes shall have preference over those
using the same for manufacturing purposes.

Colo. (1876) Art. 16, Sec. 7.   All persons and corporations
shall have the right of way across public, private and corporate
lands for the construction of ditches, canals and flumes, for the
purpose of conveying water for domestic purposes, for the irrigation of agricultural lands, and for mining and manufacturing
purposes, and for drainage, upon payment of just compensation.

Idaho (1889) Art. 15, Sec. 1.   The use of all waters now appropriated, or that may hereafter be apropriated for sale, rental
or distribution; also of al water originally appropriated for private use, but which after such apropriation has heretofore been.

or may hereafter be sold, rented, or distributed, is hereby declared to be a public use, and subject to the regulation and control of the state in the manner prescribed by law.

Idaho (1889 Art. 15, Sec. 3. The right to divert and appropriate the unapropriated waters of any natural stream to beneficial uses, shall never be denied. Priority of appropriation shall
give the better right as between those using the water; but when
the waters of any natural stream are not sufficient for the
service of all those desiring the use of the same, those using the
water for domestic purposes shall (subject to such limitations
as may be prescribed by law) have the preference over those
claiming for any other purpose; and those using the water
for agricultural purposes shall have preference over those using
the same for manufacturing purposes. And in any organized
mining district, those using the water for mining purposes or
milling purposes connected with mining, shall have preference
over those using the same for manufacturing or agricultural purposes. But the usage by such subsequent appropriators shall
be subject to such provisions of law regulating the taking of
private property for public and private use, as referred to in
section fourteen of article 1, of this constitution.

Idaho (1889) Art. 15, Sec. 4. Whenever any waters have
been, or shall be, appropriated or used for agricultural purposes, under a sale, rental or distribution thereof, such sale,
rental or distribution shall be deemed an exclusive dedication
to such use; and whenever such waters so dedicated shall have
once been sold, rented or distributed to any person who has
settled upon or improved land for agricultural purposes with the
view of receiving the benefit of such water under such dedication, such person, his heirs, executors, administrators, successors, or assigns, shall be thereafter, without his consent, be
deprived of the annual use of the same, when needed for domestic purposes, or to irrigate the land so settled upon or improved, upon payment therefor, and compliance with such equitable terms and conditions as to the quantity used and times of
use as may be prescribed by law.

Idaho (1889) Art. 15, Sec. 5. Whenever more than one person has settled upon, or improved land with the view of re-

ceiving water for agricultural purposes, under a sale, rental, or distribution thereof, as in the last preceding section of this article: Provided, As among such persons priority in time shall give superiority of right to the use of such water in the numerical order of such settlements or improvements; but whenever the supply of such water shall not be sufficient to meet the demands of all those desiring to use the same, such priority of right shall be subject to such reasonable limitations as to the quantity of water used and times of use as the legislature, having due regard, both to such priority of right and the necessities of those subsequent in times of settlement or improvement, may by law prescribe.

Idaho (1889) Art. 15, Sec. 6. The legislature shall provide by law the manner in which reasonable maximum rates may be established to be charged for the use of water sold, rented or distributed for any useful or beneficial purpose.

Mont. (1889) Art. 3, Sec. 15. The use of all water now appropriated, or that may hereafter be appropriated for sale, rental, distribution or other beneficial use and the right of way over the lands of others, for all ditches, drains, flumes, canals and acqueducts, necessarily used in connection therewith, as wel as the sites for reservoirs necessary for collecting and storing the same, shall be held to be a public use. Private roads may be opened in the manner to be prescribed by law, but in every case the necessity of the road, and the amount of all damage to be sustained by the opening thereof, shall be first determined by a jury, and such amount together with the expenses of the proceeding shall be paid by the person to be benefitted.

N. Dak. (1889) Art. 17, Sec. 210. All flowing streams and natural water courses shall forever remain the property of the state for mining, irrigating and manufacturing purposes.

Okla. (1907) Art. 16, Sec. 3. The legislature shall have power and shall provide for a system of levees, drains, and ditches of irrigation in this state when deemed expedient. and provide for a system of taxation on the lands affected or benefitted by such levees, drains and ditches and irrigation, or on crops produced on such land, to discharge such bonded indebtedness or expenses necessarily incurred in the establishment of such improvements; and to provide for compulsory issuance of bonds by the owners or lessees of the lands benefitted or affected by such levees, drains and ditches or irrigation.

Utah (1896) Art. 17, Sec. 1. All existing rights to the use of any of the waters in this state for any useful or beneficial purpose, are hereby recognized and confirmed.

Wash. (1889) Art. 21, Sec. 1. The use of the waters of the state for irrigation, mining and manufacturing purposes shall be deemed a public use.

Wyo. (1889) Art. 8, Sec. 1. The water of all natural streams, springs, lakes or other collections of still water, within the boundaries of the state, are hereby declared to be the property of the state.

Wyo. (1889) Art. 8, Sec. 2. There shall be constituted a board of control, to be composed of the state engineer and superintendents of the water divisions; which shall, under such regulations as may be prescribed by law, have the supervision of the waters of the state and of their apropriation, distribution and diversion, and of the various officers connected therewith. Its decisions to be subject to review by the courts of the state.

Wyo. (1889) Art. 8, Sec. 3. Priority of appropriation for beneficial uses shall give the better right. No appropriation shall be denied except when such denial is demanded by the public interests.

Wyo. (1889) Art. 1, Sec. 31. Water being essential to industrial prosperity, of limited amount, and easy of diversion from its natural channels, its control must be in the state, which, in providing for its use shall equally guard all the various interests involved.

"EXHIBIT 16."

BRIEF NUMBER 5.

SUBMITED BY GEORGE P. HAMBRECHT

ON

DOES THE ORDINANCE OF 1787 MAKE NAVIGABLE
RIVERS IN WISCONSIN PUBLIC FOR ALL PUR-
POSES. EFECT OF THIS ORDINANCE ON WATER
POWERS IN WICONSIN.

TO

THE WISCONSIN LEGISLATIVE COMMITTEE

ON

WATER POWERS, FORESTRY AND DRAINAGE.

———————

(Authorities complied by M. C. RILEY).

1. DOES THE ORDINANCE OF 1787 MAKE NAVIGABLE RIVERS IN WISCONSIN PUBLIC FOR ALL PURPOSES?

2. EFFECT ON WATER-POWERS.

I.

The act of 1787 creating the northwest territory reserved certain rights to the people in the navigable rivers and lakes of said territory. The act provides as follows:

"The navigable waters leading into the Mississippi and St. Lawrence, and the carrying places between the same, shall be common highways, and forever free, as well to the inhabitants of the said territory, as to citizens of the United States, and those of any other states that may be admitted into the Confederacy, without any tax, impost or duty therefor."

The ordinance of 1787 has no binding effect or force on the states carved out of the Northwest Territory.

The United States Supreme Court in Escanaba Co. v. Chicago, 107 U. S. 878 (1882) held the provisions of the Ordinance of 1787 inapplicable to the state of Illinois. The court in the ocruse of its opinion stated:

"The ordinance was passed July 13th, 1878, one year and nearly eight months before the constitution took effect * * * and although the act of April 18th, 1818, chapter 67, enabling the people of Illinois territory to form a constitution and state government, and the resolution of congress of December 3rd, 1818, declaring the admission of the state into the union, referred to the principle of the ordinance according to which the constitution was to be formed, its provisions could not control the authority and power of the state after her admission.

Whatever the limitations upon her powers as a government whilst in a territorial condition, whether from the ordinance of 1787, or the legislation of congress, it ceased to have any operative force, except as voluntarily adopted by her, after she became a state of the union. On her admission she at once became entitled to and possessed all the rights of dominion and sovereignity which belonged to the original states. She was admitted, and could be admitted, only on the same footing with them. The language of the resolution admitting her is "on an equal footing with the original states in all respects whatever." Equality of constitutional right and power is the condition of all the states of the union, old and new. Illinois therefore, as was well observed by counsel, could afterward exercise the same power over rivers within her limits that Delaware exercised over Black Creek and Pennsylvania over the Schuylkill River."

The act admitting the state of Wisconsin into the union is in part as follows:

"Sec. 1. Be it enacted by the senate and house of representatives of the United States of America in congress assembled, That the state of Wisconsin be and is hereby admitted to be one of the United States of America, and is hereby admitted into the union on an equal footing with the original states in all respects whatever," etc.

No such restrictions as are found in the provisions of the Northwest Ordinance (Art. IV) were placed upon the original states.

To the effect that all states shall be admitted into the union on equal footing, and that laws creating certain territories do not apply to states subsequently carved out of such territories, see:

Pollard's Lessee v. Hagan, 3 How. 252 (1845);
Permoli v. First Municipality, 3 How. 589 (1845);
Strader v. Graham, 10 How. 82 (1850);
Shively v. Bowlby. 152 U. S. 34 (1893):
Ward v. Race Horse, 163 U. S. 513 (1895);
Stockton v. Powell, 29 Fla., 45 (1892);
Grand Rapids v. Powers. 89 Mich. 102 (1891);
People v. Thompson, 155 Ill. 473 (1895);
Comrs. v. Board of Public Works, 29 Ohio St. 628 (1884);
Atty. Gen'l v. Cunningham, 81 Wis. 440, 511 (1892).

25

Identical provisions in the Wisconsin Enabling Act and Constitution.

However, provisions almost identical with the one quoted from the Northwest Ordinance are found in the Wisconsin Enabling Act and the Wisconsin Constitution.

The provision in the Wisconsin Enabling Act,—an act to enable the people of Wisconsin Territory to form a constitution and state government, and for the admission of said state into the union,—reads as follows:

"That the said state of Wisconsin shall have concurrent jurisdiction on the Mississippi and all other rivers and waters bordering on the said state of Wisconsin, so far a the same shall form a common boundary to said state and any other state or states now or hereafter to be formed or bounded by the same; and said river and waters, and the navigable waters leading into the same, shall be common highways and forever free, as well to the inhabitants of said states as to all other citizens of the United States without any tax, duty, impost or toll therefore." Wis R. S. Vol. 1, p. 49.

The provision in the Wisconsin Constitution reads as follows " * * * and the river Mississippi and navigable waters leading into the Mississippi and St. Lawrence, and the carrying places between the same shall be common highways and forever free, as well to the inhabitants of the state as to the citizens of the United States, without any tax, impost or duty therefor."

Construction placed upon such clauses.

(a) Northwest Ordinance.

The clause in the Northwest Ordiance was intended to disable the territory or individuals thereof from the infliction of a public injury. The people of the United States were not to be deprived of the use of the water course highways in the Northwest Territory by any unjust or wanton exercise of power over them.

Spooner v. McConnell, 1 McLean 337–338 (1838).

The purpose of the clause is to prohibit political regulation of such streams which will hamper the freedom of commerce.

J. S. Keator Lbr. Co. v. St. Croix Boom Co., 60 Wis 60 (1884).

The clause secures to the public the right to navigate the waters specified.

> Sweeney v. C. M. & St. P. Ry. Co., 60 Wis. 60 (1884).

(b) Enabling Act.

"Since the decision in the Escanaba Case, we have had our attention repeatedly called to the terms of the clause in the Ordinance of 1787. *A similar* clause as to their navigable rivers is found in the acts providing for the admission of California, Wisconsin, and Louisiana. The clause in the act providing for the admission of California was considered in Cardwell v. American Bridge Co., 113 U. S. 205. We there held that it did not impair the power which the state could have exercised over its rivers had the clause not existed; *and that the object was to reserve the rivers as highways equally open to all persons without preference to any, and unobstructed by duties or tolls, and thus prevent the use of the navigable streams by private parties to the exclusion of the public, and the exaction of toll for their navigation.* The same doctrine we have reiterated at the present term of the court in construing a similar clause in the act for the admission of Louisiana. Hamilton v. Vicksburg, Shreveport v. Pacific Railroad. Ante, 280. As thus construed the clause would prevent any exclusive use of the navigable waters of the state—a possible farming out of the privilege of navigating them to particular individuals, classes. corporations, or by vessels of a particular character. That the apprehension of such a monoply was not unfounded, is evident from the history of legislation since. The state of New York at one time endeavored to confer upon Livingston & Fulton the excluisve right to navigate the waters within its jurisdiction by vessels propelled in whole or in part by steam." Per Justice Field, in Huse v. Glover, 119 U. S. 543, 547 (1886).

In Cardwell v. Bridge Co., 113 U. S. 205 (1884), the court construing the clause in the act for the admission of California into the union, from the viewpoint that the clause contains two provisions, said:

"That court (trial court) held that the clause contains

two provisions, one that the navigable waters shall be a
common highway to the inhabitants as well as to the citi--
zens of the United States; and the other, that they shall
be forever free from any tax, impost, or duty therefor;
that these provisions are separate and distinct, and that
one is not an adjunct or amplification of the other. * * *
But upon the mature and careful consideration, which we
have given in this case to the language of the clause admitting California, we are of opinion that, if we treat
the clause as divisable into two provisions, they must be
construed together as having *but one object, namely, to
insure a highway equally open to all without preference
to any, and unobstructed by duties or tolls, and thus prevent the use of the navigable streams by private parties
to the exclusion of the public, and* the exaction of any
toll for their navigating * * * ."

In Williamette Iron Bridge Co. v. Hatch: 125 U. S. 1 (1887),
Mr. Justice Bradley construed the clause as a prohibition
against the imposition of duties for the use of navigable waters
specified therein and any discrimination denying to citizens
of other states the equal right to such use. In other words as
guaranteeing the free use of the stream when in their natural
state, as public highways.

(c) Wisconsin Constitution.
    "The object of the Constitution, so far as it guarantees
that the Mississippi, and navigable waters leading into that
river and the St. Lawrence and the carrying places
between the same, should be common highways and forever free, was to prevent the imposition of any tax, impost
or duty for the use of the stream and carrying places in
their natural state."
    Wis. River Imp. Co. v. Manson. 43 Wis. 255, 262 (1877) ;
    In re Southern Wis. Power Co. v. 140 Wis. 245 (1909).

*The Ordinance of 1787. The Wisconsin Enabling Act or the
Wisconsin Constitution did not alter the common law relative to navigable waters.*
    The Ordinance of 1787 did not change the common law rela-
tive to navigable waters and the rights of the public and the
riparian holders therein.

The Wisconsin Supreme Court has repeatedly held that navigable waters in the state of Wisconsin have all the incidents of tidal (navigable)'waters at common law.

Rossmiller v. State, 114 Wis. 169 (1902);
Ill. Steel Co. v. Bilot, 109 Wis. 418 (1901);
Pewaukee v. Savoy, 103 Wis. 271 (1889);
Willow River Club v. Wade, 100 Wis. 86, 106 (1898).

Sec. 1597 Wis. R. S. provides: "The boundaries of lands adjoining waters and the rights of the state and of individuals in respect to all such lands and waters shall be determined in conformity to the common law so far as applicable."

In the state of Massachusetts where the great ponds are held by the state for all public purposes (due to the Ordinance of 1641—47) it is expressly held that the common law relative to navigable waters and riparian rights has been modified or set aside, and this by the Ordinance just referred to; Watuppa Reservoir Co. v. City of Fall River, 147 Mass. 548 (1888). No case can be found giving a construction to the clause in the Wisconsin Enabling Act or Constitution such as given in the Ordinance of 1641—47 by the Massachusetts courts.

II.

EFFECT ON WATER-POWERS.

Neither the clause of the Ordinance of 1787, of the Wisconsin Enabling Act or the Wisconsin Constitution in any wise affect the legal status of natural water-powers. These provisions (the two latter only being in effect in this state) guarantee rights to the public and individuals. No court has construed any of such provisions as in any manner changing the law of riparian rights. Our supreme Court has held, and our statutes expressly provide, that the status of natural water-powers shall be determined in conformity to the common law—supra.

These provisions do not prevent the legislature granting authority to erect and maintain dams and other obstructions in and across navigable streams. They refer to political regulations and not to physical obstructions.

> In re So. Wis. Power Co., 140 Wis. 245 (1909) ;
> Williamette I. B. Co. v. Hatch, 125 U. S. 1 (1887) ;
> Pound v. Turck, 95 U. S. 459 (1877) ;
> Willson v. Blackbird Creek Marsh Co., 2 Pet. 245 (1829) ;
> Gilman v. Philadelphia, 3 Wall. 713 (1865) ;
> Monongohela Nav. Co. v. U. S. 148 U. S. 312 (1892) ;
> Montgomery v. Portland, 190 U. S. 89 (1902) ;
> J. S. Keator Lbr. Co. v. Boom Co., 72 Wis. 62 (1888).

They do not prevent the levying of toll for the navigation of any of the waters specified when in an improved state—the prohibition applies to streams in their natural condition. **Huse.** v. Glover, 119 U. S. 543 (1886) ;

> Wis. River Imp. Co. v. Manson, 43 Wis. 255 (1877) ;
> Underwood Lbr. Co. v. Pelican Boom Co., 76 Wis. 76 (1890) ;
> Sauntry v. Laird N. Co., 100 Wis. 146 (1898) ;
> - Tewksbury v. Schulenberg, 41 Wis. 514 (1877).

SUMMARY.

The Ordiance of 1787 has ceased to have any binding effect in the state of Wisconsin.

The clauses found in the Wisconsin Enabling Act and the Wisconsin Constitution to the effect that the Mississippi, the St. Lawrence and the navigable waters leading into the same. "shall be common highways and forever free," have been given a most natural construction. The cases hold that the purpose of the clauses is to secure to the public the enjoyment of these public highways—to prevent the levying of toll for the right to navigate the navigable waters specified when such waters are in their natural state. The purpose of these clauses was and is to guarantee or secure to the public a common law right—not to alter the common law.

The Ordinance of 1787 does not make navigable rivers in Wisconsin public for all purposes. Neither do the identical provisions found in the Wisconsin Enabling Act and Constitution; nor do the provisions of the Ordinance of 1787 or of the

Enabling Act or Wisconsin Constitution effect the legal status of natural water-powers in this state, or deny to the legislature the power to grant authority to develop power on navigable waters that lead into the Mississippi and the Great Lakes with the St. Lawrence as their outlet.

The navigable waters of Wisconsin are public for such purposes only as are such waters under the common law.

BRIEF NUMBER 6.

SUBMITTED BY GEORGE P. HAMBRECHT

ON

ES THE "RIGHT OF NAVIGATION" MEAN THE RIGHT OF PASSAGE OVER NAVIGABLE RIVERS FOR PURPOSES OF COMMERCE AND PROFIT, ONLY OR DOES IT INCLUDE AS WELL THE RIGHT OF PASSAGE OVER SUCH RIVERS FOR PLEASURE AND RECREATION?

TO

THE WISCONSIN LEGISLATIVE COMMITTEE

ON

WATER POWERS, FORESTRY AND DRAINAGE.

(Authorities compiled by M. C. Riley.)

DOES THE "RIGHT OF NAVIGATION" MEAN THE
RIGHT OF PASSAGE OVER NAVIGABLE RIVER
FOR PURPOSES OF COMMERCE AND PROFIT
ONLY, OR DOES IT INCLUDE AS WELL THE RIGHT
OF PASSAGE OVER SUCH RIVERS FOR PLEASURE
AND RECREATION?

A NAVIGABLE RIVER IS A PUBLIC HIGHWAY.

(A)   At common law.

"At common law a navigable river is a public highway,
navigable by all his Majesty's subjects in a reasonable way
and for a reasonable purpose."

Coulson v. Forbes, Law of Waters, pp. 81 & 82;
Original Hartlepool Colliers v. Gibbs, 5 Ch. D. 71
   (1877);
Williams v. Wilcox, 8 A. & E. 314 (1838).

Public right of passage over such highway extends to the
whole of the navigable channel, Williams v. Wilcox, 8 A. & E.
314 (1838), which, it appears, may be used as a highway by the
public whenever it suits their convenience, whether such navigation be valuable or not.

A.—G. Lonsdale, L. R. 7 Eq. 377 (1868).

(B)   In Wisconsin.

In Wisconsin the public have a common right of navigation
in streams which have capacity for a reasonable time each year
or throughout the year, sufficient at least to float logs, lumber
or other products of the country to mill or market.

Diedrich v. N. W. U. Ry. Co., 42 Wis., 248 (1877);
A. C. Conn Co. v. Little Suamico Lbr. Mfg. Co., 74 Wis.
   652 (1889);
Whisler v. Wilkinson, 22 Wis. 572 (1868);
Sellers v. Union Lbrg. Co., 39 Wis. 525 (1876);
Cohn v. Wausau Boom Co., 47 Wis. 324 (1879);

Wis. River Imp. Co. v. Lyons, 30 Wis. 61 (1872) ;

Weatherby v. Meiklejohn, 56 Wis. 73 (1882) ;

J. S. Keator Lbr. Co., v. St. Croix B. Co., 72 Wis. 62 (1888) ;

The Falls Mfg. Co., v. Oconto River Imp. Co., 87 Wis. 134 (1894) ;

Charnley v. Shawano W. P. & P. I. Co., 109 Wis. 563 (1901) ;

Olson v. Merrill, 42 Wis. 203 (1877) ;

Willow River Club v. Wade, 100 Wis. 86 (1898) ;

Bloomer v. Bloomer, 128 Wis. 297 (1907).

The court in this state has adopted as a gauge or test of navigability the capacity to float logs. This capacity being present in any stream, such stream is navigable water of the state of Wisconsin and as such has all of the incident of navigable (tidal) water at common law.

Willow River Club v. Wade, 100 Wis. 86, 106 (1898) ;

Pewaukee v. Savoy, 103 Wis. 271, 274 (1889) ;

Illinois Steel Co., v. Bilot, 109 Wis. 418, 425 (1901) ;

Rossmiller v. State, 114 Wis. 169. 186 (1902) ;

Navigable waters in the state of Wisconsin, such waters having all of the incidents of navigable waters at common law, are public highways. In many of the Wisconsin cases "where the extreme doctrine of public rights in trifling bodies of water was discussed, the character of the stream was described not by navigability but by the expression 'public highway', or 'public waterway.'

(Whisler v. Wilkinson, 22 Wis. 572;

Sellers v. Union L. Co., 39 Wis. 525)"

Allaby v. Mauston El. Svc. Co., 135 Wis. 245 (1908).

The use of water highways in Wisconsin is not confined to passage for purposes of commerce and profit.

The use of such public highways is not restricted to the floatage of logs. In the case of Willow River Club v. Wade, supra, defendant was sued in trespass for taking fish from the Willow river. The evidence showed, first, that the Willow river at the place in question is navigable according to the Wisconsin definition of that word, and second, that defendant committed no trespass upon plaintiff's lands in getting onto the stream. It was held that the right of fishery in the navigable waters of this state is common to all, and that the defendant was not answerable in damages to the plaintiff. Justice Marshall in a concurring opinion, p. 104, said:

"In my judgment the right of fishing in navigable waters is common to all, and exerciseable, so far as it can be done without trespass on the banks thereof, whether the person exercising such right be at the time navigating the stream in a boat or otherwise floating upon the surface of the water, or travelling upon the bed in the shallows, or anywhere in any manner, between the lines of ordinary high water mark."

This case distinguishes between the right of navigation and the right of fishery. It holds that the right of fishery is not an incident to the right of navigation, but that it is a common right in navigable waters in this state as it is in tidal waters at common law. It recognizes in the public the right to navigate the navigable waters of this state for purposes of recreation and pleasure. It places water highways, in this respect, on the same basis with highways on land. See also Mendota Club v. Anderson, 101 Wis. 479 (1899).

Justice Marshall, in his syllabus to the case of Rossmiller v. State, 114 Wis. 169 (1902), says:

"The power of the state over navigable waters within its boundaries is limited to the enactment and enforcement of such reasonable police regulations as may be deemed necessary to preserve the common right of all to enjoy the same for navigation by boats or otherwise, * * *"

The courts in other jurisdictions have held that those using navigable waters for the purpose of pleasure, have equal rights with those who use the same for purposes of commerce and profit.

In West Roxbury v. Stoddard, 7 Allen, 158, 171 (1863), the court in the course of its opinion, said:

"The purpose of the navigation is immaterial * * *, and those who pass upon the water for the purpose of pleasure, fishing, or fowling have equal rights with those who navigate for business, trade or agriculture.''

In State v. Club, 100 N. C. 477 (1888) it is said:

"Navigable waters are natural highways—so recognized by government and the people—and hence it seems to be accepted as part of the common law of this country, arising out of the public necessity, convenience and common consent, that the public have the right to use rivers, lakes, sounds and parts of them though not strictly public waters, if they be navigable in fact, for the purpose of a highway and navigation, employed in travel, trade or commerce. Such waters are treated as *publici juris* insofar as they may be properly used for such purposes in their natural state.''

See also State v. Twiford, 136 N. C. 603, 607 (1904.)

The same court, in State v. Baum, 128 N. C. 600, says:

"The rule now most generally adopted, and that which seems best fitted to our own domestic conditions, is that all water courses are regarded as navigable in law which are navigable in fact, that is, that the public have the right to the unobstructed navigation, as a public highway for all purposes of pleasure and profit, of all water courses, whether tidal or inland, that are in their natural condition capable of such use.''

The Supreme Court of Massachusetts in Atty. Gen'l v. Woods, 108 Mass. 436, 439 (1871), in the following language, very definitely holds that the right to navigate for pleasure is equally as sacred as the right to navigate for commerce and profit:

"It is also denied that the stream is navigable, although it is about two feet deep at low water, because it is not proved to be used for purposes of navigation except with pleasure boats. The case of Rowe v. Granite Bridge Co., 21 Pick. 344, 347; is cited to sustain this position. Chief Justice Shaw there says: 'It is not every small creek in which a fishing skiff or gunning canoe can be made to float at high water, which is deemed navigable. But in order to have this character it must be navigable, for some purpose useful to trade or agriculture.' The same thing in substance is stated in Charlestown v. Co. Comrs., 3 Met. 202, and Murdock v. Stickney, 8 Cush. 113, 115. But this language is applied to the capacity of the stream, and is not intended to be as strict enumeration of the uses to which it must be applied in order to give it this character. Navigable streams are highways; and a traveller for pleasure is as fully entitled to protection in using a public way, whether by land or by water, as a traveller for business.''

Michigan follows the rule laid down in the preceding Massachusetts case:

"It (Grand River) has never been navigable for boats, except for canoes and *bateaux*, above Lyons, and no steamboats have been above the rapids at Grand Rapids for many years. Small steamboats have run between the mouth and the city of Grand Rapids, and with the aid of government appropriations, the river below the rapids at that city may be a water-way of great commercial utility; but above the rapids it has nearly served its usefulness as a navigable stream, except for small pleasure boats. The running of logs, lumber and timber upon it is no longer of consequence, on account of the exhaustion of the forest supply of easy access to its tributaries. But it will ever be an important stream, and its navigability for pleasure is as sacred in the eye of the law as its navigability for any other purpose.''

Grand Rapids v. Powers, 89 Mich. 94 (1891).

Farnham, in his treatise on Waters and Water Rights, p. 131 asserts that

"Every one has an equal right to the reasonable use of the water for all legitimate purposes of travel and transportation. Again at p. 134 the author says: "The use of the stream is not confined to purposes of commerce if it is in fact navigable, but it may be used for pleasure as well as business.''

Angell on Water Courses, p. 701 asserts in language similar to that used by Farnham, that the right of navigation for commerce and profit and for pleasure are equal in the eyes of the law. At section 537 it is said: "If a stream is naturally of suf-

ficient size to float boats or mill-logs, the public have the right to
its free use for those two purposes, unincumbered with dams,
etc." To substantiate this assertion the following cases are
cited:

> Wadsworth v. Smith, 2 Fairf. (Me.) 278;
> Brown v. Chadbourne, 31 (Me.) 9;
> Moore v. Sanborne, 2 Gibbs, (Mich.) 519;
> Morgan v. King, 18 Barb. 277; s. c. 31 Barb. 9;
> Barclay v. R. R. Cos., 39 Penn. St., 194.

In Minnesota it is held that navigable lakes, if navigable for
purposes of pleasure, are navigable within the reason and spirit
of the common law rule.

"Most of the definitions of 'navigability' in the decided
cases seem to convey the idea that the water must be capable
of some commerce of pecuniary value, as distinguished from
boating for mere pleasure. But if, under present conditions
of society, bodies of water are used for public uses other
than mere commercial 'navigation,' in its ordinary sense,
we fail to see why they ought not to be held to be public
waters, or 'navigable' waters if the old nomenclature is pre-
ferred. Certainly we do not see why boating or sailing for
pleasure should not be considered navigation as well as
boating for mere pecuniary profits. Many, if not most, of
the meandered lakes of this state are not adopted to, and
probably will never be used to any great extent for, commercial navigation; but they are used, and, as population increases and towns and cities are built up in their vicinity,
will be still more used, by the people for sailing, rowing,
fowling, bathing, skating, fishing, taking water for domestic,
agricultural and even city purposes, cutting ice, and other
public purposes which cannot be enumerated or even anticipated. To hand over all these lakes to private ownership, under any old or narrow test of navigability, would
be a great wrong upon the public for all time, the extent of
which cannot perhaps be now even anticipated."
Lamphrey v. State, 52 Minn. 181 (1893).

Justice Marshall in the Rossmiller case, supra, states that
the public have the right to use navigable waters for every legitimate purpose.

"It has been universally supposed, we venture to say,

that the right of every person within the state to its pub!.
waters for every legitimate purpose, * * * which do
not wrongfully interfere with the right of any other pers!
to like enjoyment, subject only to such mere police regula
tions as the legislature in its wisdom prescribe to preser:
the common heritage of all, is a constitutional right of a.
persons within the state.''

Navigable waters must not be obstructed—Exceptions.

Any obstruction placed in or over navigable waters by an.
person, firm, etc, without legislative permission, is a nuisance.

Barnes v. Racine, 4 Wis. 454 (1854);
Hale v. Carpenter, 68 Wis. 165 (1887);
In re Eldred, 46 Wis. 530 (1879);
Wis. River Imp. Co. v. Lyons, 30 Wis. 61 (1872);
Charnley v. Shawano, etc. Imp Co., 109 Wis, 563 (1901
Conn. Co. v. Little Suamico, etc. Co., 74 Wis. 65
(1889).

*The legislature has no power to authorize the placing of im
  passible obstructions in navigable waters except for the im
  provement of the navigation thereof.*

The state of Wisconsin holds title to the navigable water
within its boundaries in trust for the people. The public has
all the rights in navigable waters of Wisconsin that are inc:
dent to such waters at common law—among others, and para
mount to all, is the public right of navigation or passage t
and fro thereon To protect and enhance this right is 'L
main object of the trusteeship. Therefore, the state, throug'
the legislature, has no power to authorize impassible obstru
tions to be placed in navigable waters so as to destroy thi
paramount public use thereof. This limitation upon the legis
lative power does not, however, deny to that body the rig:
to authorize the placing of impassible obstructions in su!
waters for the improvement of navigation thereof. (See Co::
mittee brief ''Has Congress or the state legislature power t

* Our supreme court holds that an obstruction may be placed !
streams merely floatable and not within Sec. 1596 Wis. R. S., withou
legislative permission, if such obstruction does not materially at·
or abridge the beneficial use thereof. A. C. Conn Co. v Little Suam'r
L. M. Co., 74 Wis. 652 (1889); Charnley v. Shawano W. P. & R. I. Co
109 Wis. 563 (1901).

authorize the erection and maintenance of any bridge, dam or other obstruction in, over or across any navigable waters of this state so as to totally obstruct the navigation thereof. Exhibit 21 of this report.'')

Any *impassible* obstruction placed in a navigable stream in this state, unless placed there with the permission of the legislature and for the purpose of improving the navigation thereof, is a public nuisance, and, as such, may be abated by public prosecution, or upon the motion of a private party, if such nuisance at the same time obstructs, hinders or invades unreasonably some well defined private right of such individual. Wood on Nuisances, (3rd Ed.) Vol. 2, p. 960.

Summary.

The navigable waters of this state are common highways. As such they are subject to the use of the public generally for purposes of travel and commerce in the same manner as are highways on land. An impassible obstruction placed in a public highway is an injury to the public generally—as well to the traveller for pleasure as the traveller on business; both have equal cause for complaint when the public way is barred.

In Wisconsin, it seems, any impassible obstruction placed in a navigable stream, other than one erected and maintained for the improvement of navigation, is a public nuisance and abateable.

The ''right of navigation'' means the right of the public generally to pass to and fro on navigable waters for all legitimate purposes, as well for pleasure and recreation as for commerce and profit.

26

"EXHIBIT 18."

Brief Number 7.

SUBMITTED BY GEORGE P. HAMBRECHT

ON

THE DOCTRINE OF RIPARIAN RIGHTS

TO

THE WISCONSIN LEGISLATIVE COMMITTEE

ON

WATER POWERS, FORESTRY AND DRAINAGE.

———————

(Authorities compiled by M. C. Riley.)

THE DOCTRINE OF RIPARIAN RIGHTS.

(A) ON NON-NAVIGABLE WATERS.

Basis and character of right.

At common law, in England, the owner of land abutting non-navigable stream, or through which a non-navigable stream courses, has certain well defined rights in the waters there. These rights emanate from the ownership of the bank or bank and are a natural incident of such ownership.

The rights of such riparian holder are different than those belonging to the public generally.

"The rights of a riparian proprietor, so far as they relate any natural stream exist *jure naturae*, because his land has by nature the advantage of being washed by the stream; * * *. Lyon v. Fishmongers' Co., 1 App. C. 662 (1876).

"The right to the use of the flow of the water in its natural course, and to the momentum of its fall on the land of the proprietor, is not what is called an easement, because it is inseparably connected with and inherent in the property in the land; it is parcel of the inheritance and passes with it."

Angell on Watercourses, pp. 96, 98.

Phear, Rights of Water, p. 39.

Scope of the right.

The riparian right in non-navigable streams was well defined in the case of Chasemore vs. Richards, 7 H. L. C. 349, 35 (1859). Lord Wensleydale in this case, said:

"The subject of the right to streams of water flowing on the surface has been of late years freely discussed, and by a series of carefully considered judgments placed upon a clear and satisfactory footing. It has been now settled that the right to the enjoyment of a natural stream of water on the surface, *ex jure naturae*, belongs to the proprietor of the adjoining lands, as a natural incident to the right of the soil itself, and that he is entitled to the benefit of it, as he is to all the other natural advantages belonging to the land of which he is the owner. He has the right to have it come to him in its natural state, in flow, quantity and quality, and to go from him without obstruction; upon the same principle that he is entitled to the support of his neighbour's soil for his own in its natural state. His right in no way dependes upon prescription. or the presumea grant of his neighbour.''

See also
Embrey v. Owen, 6 Ex. 353 (1851);
Mason v. Hill, 5 B. & A. 1 (1833).

"By the general law applicable to running streams, every riparian proprietor has a right to what may be called the ordinary use of water flowing past his land—for instance, to the reasonable use of the water for his domestic purposes and for his cattle; and without regard to the effect which such use may have in case of a deficieney upon proprietors lower down the stream.

But every riparian proprietor has also a further right to the use of the water for any purpose, or what may be deemed that *extraordinary* use of it, provided he does not interfere thereby with the rights of other proprietors either above or below. Subject to this condition he may dam it up for the purpose of a mill. (Belfast Rope Works v. Boyd. 21 L. R., Ir. 560; Ward v. Robbins, 15 M. & W. 237) or divert the water for the purpose of irrigation. But he has no right to interrupt the regular flow of the stream, if he thereby interferes with the lawful use of the water by other proprietors and inflicts upon them a sensible injur.y''
Miner v. Gilmour, 12 Moo. P. O.

See also
French v. Hoek Comrs. v. Hugo, 10 app. C. 336 (1885);
Chasemore v. Richards, supra.

. riparian right is property.
"It was at one time contended that a title to the use of running water was not a right or property; but that water was *publici juris,* and, as such, the right to use it could only be acquired by occupancy. This view seems to have been favored by Blackstone, (2 Black, Com. 402) and there

are dicta in some of the earlier cases (Williams v. More land), 2 B. & G. 913 (1824); Ligging v. Inge, 7 Bing. 69: (1831) to the effect that by the law of England the possessor who first appropriates any part of water flowing through his land to his own use, has a right to use so much as he has appropriated as against the world. The cases of Mason v. Hill. 5 B. & A. 1, and Embrey v. Owen. 6 Ex. 353 have now, however, finally negatived this contention." Coulson v. Forbes, Law of Waters, p. 118.

In Mason v. Hill, 5 B. & A. 1, at p. 17, Denman, C. J., said "The proposition of the defendant is, that the right to flowing water is *publici juris,* and that the first person who can get possession of the stream, and apply it to useful purpose, has a good title to it against all the world, *including* the proprietor of the land below, who has no right of action against him, unless such proprietor has already applied the stream to some useful purpose also, with which the diversion interferes; and in default of his having done so may altogether deprive him of the benefit of the water. P. 18. "The position that the first occupant of running water for a beneficial purpose, has a good title to it, is perfectly true in this sense, that neither the owner of the land below can pen back the water, nor the owner of the land above divert it to his prejudice. In this, as in other cases of injury to real property, possession is a good title against a wrong doer; and the owner of the land who applied the stream that runs through it. to the use of a mill newly erected, or other purposes, if the stream is diverted or obstructed, may recover for the consequential injury to the mill: The Earl of Rutland v. Bowler, Palm.; 290. But it is a very different question. whether he can take away from the owner of the land below, one of its natural advantages. which is capable of being applied to profitable purposes, and generally increases the fertility of the soil, even when unapplied and deprive him of it altogether by anticipating him in its application to a useful purpose. If this be so. a considerable part of the value of an estate. which, in manufacturing districts particularly is much enhanced by the existence of an unappropriated stream of water with a fall within its limits, might at any time be taken away; and by parity of reasoning, a valuable mineral or brine spring might be abstracted from the proprietor in whose land it arises, and connected to the profit of another.

The right to the flow of running water, without diminution or alteration, being common to all those through whose land it flows, any unauthorized interference with or use of the water, to the prejudice of one entitled to its use, is the subject of an action for damages, and may be restrained by injunction." Coulson v. Forbes, Law of Waters, p. 116. Citing Grand Jct. Canal v. Shugar, L. R. 6 Ch. 483.

The foregoing quotations and citations establish broadly the proposition of law that a riparian owner in England may use the water of a non-navigable stream flowing through or by his land in any manner he may see fit, provided, in so doing, he does not unreasonably affect riparian holders or owners above or below him; and establish too that the right of the riparian proprietor is property.

(B) Riparian Rights on Navigable Waters.

"It is manifest that the property of riparian owners may exist on the banks of tidal navigable rivers as well as on non-navigable streams.   Riparian owners on the former have similar rights and natural easements to those belonging to riparian proprietors above the flow of the tide, underlying and controlled, though not extinguished, by the public right of navigation." Coulson v. Forbes, p. 111, Citing No. Shore Ry. v. Pion. 14 App. 612 (1889); Booth v. Ratto, 15 App. C. 188 (1889); Lyon v. Fishmongers' Co., 1 App. C. 662.

In Lyon v. Fishmongers' Co., supra, the question of whether or not a riparian holder on navigable streams possessed the natural rights possessed by a riparian proprietor on non-navigable streams was considered and decided. The Lord Chancellor (Cairns) with reference to a statement by Lord Justice Mellish in a previous case, to the effect that the Lords Justices had been unable to find any authority for holding that a riparian proprietor where the tide flows and reflows has any rights or natural easements vested in him similar to those which have been held in numerous cases to belong to a proprietor on the banks of a natural stream above the flow of the tide, said:

"With much deference for the Lords Justices I should have thought that some authority should be produced to show that the natural rights possessed by a riparian proprietor, as such, on a non-navigable river are not possessed by a riparian proprietor on a navigable river. The difference in the rights must be between rivers which are navigable and those which are not; and not between tidal and non-tidal rivers; for as Lord Hale observes (De Jur Mar. Part 1. C. 3.) the rivers which are *public juris*, and common highways for men or goods, may be fresh or salt, and may flow or reflow or not; * * *. A riparian owner on a navigable river has, of course superadded to his riparian rights, the right of navigation over every part of the river, and on the other hand his riparian rights must be controlled in this respect, that whereas, in a non-navigable river, all the riparian owners may combine to divert, pollute, or diminish the stream, in a navigable river the public right of navigation would intervene, and would prevent this being done. But the doctrine would be a serious and alarming one, that a riparian owner on a public river, and even on a tidal public river, had none of the ordinary rights of the riparian owner, as such, to preserve the stream in its natural condition for all the usual purposes of the land ; but that he must stand upon his right as one of the public to complain only of a nuisance or on interruption to the navigation." P. 672, 673. Continuing at page 674, Lord Cairns said: "My Lords, I cannot entertain any doubt that the riparian owner on a navigable river, in addition to the right connected with navigation to which he is en-entitled as one of the public, retains his rights, as an ordinary riparian owner, underlying and controlled but not extinguished by, the public right of navigation."

Lord Chelmsford, in the same case, p. 677, said there were two questions for determination. After stating the first, which has to do with the powers of the conservators of the River Thames, he continued:

"*2ndly.* Whether there is any individual right or privilige in the owner or occupier of Lyon's wharf peculiar to his river frontage, distinct and different from the right of all the Queen's subjects in the highway of the river.

Upon this second question the Lords Justices, said they were "unable to find any authority for holding that a riparian proprietor where the tide flows and reflows has any rights or natural easement vested in him similar to those which have been held in numerous cases to belong to a riparian proprietor on the banks of a natural stream above the flow of the tide. But, with great respect, I find no authority for the contrary proposition, and I see no sound principle upon which the distinction between the two descriptions of natural streams can be supported. And it appears to me that cases have been decided which are strongly opposed to it. Why a riparian proprietor on a tidal river should not possess all the peculiar advantageous which the position of his property with relation to the river affords him, provided they occasion no obstruction to the navigation, I am at a loss to comprehend. If there were an unauthorized interference with his enjoyment of the rights upon the river connected with his property, there can, I think, be no doubt that he might maintain an action for the private injury.''

Lord Selbourne, same case, p. 682, said:

"Upon principle, as well as upon those authorities, (the Duke of Buccleuch v. The Metropolitan Board of Works, Law R. 5 H. L. 418; Rose v. Groves, 5 M. & G. 613; The Atty. Genl. v. Conservators of the Thames, 1. H. & M. 1), I am of opinion that private riparian rights may, and do, exist, in a tidal navigable river. The most material differences between the stream above and the stream below the limit of the tides are, that in an estuary or arm of the sea there exist, by the common law, public rights in respect of navigation and otherwise, which do not generally (in this country) exist in the non-tidal parts of the stream; and that the *fundus* or bed of the non tidal parts of the stream belongs, generally, to the riparian proprietors, while in the estuary it belongs to the Crown. But the rights of a riparian proprietor, so far as they relate to any natural stream, exist *jure naturae*, because his land has, by nature, the advantage of being washed by the stream; and if the facts of nature constitute the foundation of the right, I am unable to see why the law should not recognize and follow . the course of nature in every part of the same stream. Water which is more or less salt by reason of the flow of the tide may still be useful for many domestic and other purposes, though there are no doubt some purposes which fresh water only will serve. The general law as to riparian rights is not stated by any authorities, that I am aware of, in terms which require this distinction, and, if there is any sound principle on which it ought to be made, the burden of proof seems to me to lie on those who so affirm.

As for the public right of navigation, it may well so exist with private riparian rights, which must of course be enjoyed subject to it; just as where there is no navigation, each riparian proprietors right is concurrent with, and is so far limited by, the rights of other proprietors.''

In England the riparian holder has rights and natural easements in tidal navigable waters similar to those which belong to a riparian owner on a non-tidal or non-navigable stream. These rights and natural easements, in tidal navigable waters, are held subject to the right of the public to navigate such waters. In other words the riparian proprietors on tidal navigable waters in England may use, occupy or appropriate such waters in so far as such use, occupation or appropriation does not unreasonably affect riparian proprietors above or below him, or unreasonably affect the public right of navigation. This has been the settled law of England since the judgment rendered in the Fishmongers' Case in 1876.

WISCONSIN.

The English law with reference to riparian rights as laid down in the Fishmongers' Case has been embodied in the law of Wisconsin; Delaplaine et al. v. C. & N. W. Ry. Co., 42

Wis. 214 (1887). The court after dwelling upon the law of
riarian rights, said:

"This whole subject is so forcibly discussed and illustrated in the opinions of the law lords in Lyon v. Fishmongers' Co., 1 App. Cas. 662, that we cannot more
clearly express our views upon it than by quoting some
of their remarks. One question considered in the case was
whether a riparian proprietor on the bank of a tidal navigable river had rights or natural easements similar to those
which belong to a riparian proprietor on the bank of a
natural stream above the flow of the tide; and whether
such proprietor, whose frontage and means of access to such
tidal river is cut off by an encroachment from adjoining
land into the stream, súffers a loss or abridgement of any
private right belonging to him as a riparian proprietor, or
is only damnified in common with the rest of the public."

The court then quotes with approval the remarks of Lards
Cairns, Chelmsford and Selbourne as found on pp. 672, 673,
674 and 682 of the Case, (supra this paper) and to the effect
of the rights of the riparian proprietor on a navigable stream,
are subject to the public right of navigation, the same as those
possessed by such a proprietor on a non-navigable stream.
The question before the Court in the Delaplaine Case was
pertaining to the riparian right of access. The Court by
J. Cole, said:

"But while the proprietor only takes to the water line,
it by no means follows, nor are we willing to admit, that
he can be deprived of his riparian rights without compensation as proprietor of the adjoining land, and as connected with it, he has the exclusive access to and from the
waters of the lake at that particular place; he has the right
to build piers and wharves in front of his land out to
navigable waters, not interfering with the public use.
These are private rights incident to the ownership of the
shore, which he possesses, distinct from the rest of the
public. All the facilities which the location of his land
with reference to the lake affords, he has the right to enjoy
for the purposes of gain or pleasure; and they oftentimes
give property thus situated its chief value. It is evident
from the nature of the case, that these rights of user and

exclusion are connected with the land itself, grow out
its location, and cannot be materially abridged or destroy(
without inflicting an injury upon the owner which t!
law should redress. It seems unnecessary to add the r
mark, that these riparian rights are not common to t!
citizens at large, but exist as incidents to the right of t!
soil adjacent to the water. In other words, according
the uniform doctrine of the best authorities, the foundatic
of riparian rights, *Ex vi termini*, is the ownership of t!
bank or shore. In such ownership they have their orig?
They may and do exist though the fee in tne bed of t!
river or lake be in the state. If the proprietor owns t!
bed of the stream or lake, this may possibly give him son
additional right; but his riparian rights, strictly speakin
do not depend on that fact.''

Another Wisconsin case, Chapman v. O. & M. River R.]
Co., 33 Wisconsin 629 (1873) is in accordance with the Fisl
mongers' case. In this case plaintiffs owned certain city lo?
fronting on a navigable stream and were accustomed to u?
their river front in hitching logs, putting in rafts and shippin
lumber. Defendant by permission of the legislature built
bridge over the river (Fox at Oshkosh) and the bridge an
embankment necessary for the same caused an interruption o
breakage of the river front which obstructed plaintiff's acces
The Supreme Court held the obstruction to the access of th
river ground for a claim for compensation.

The court by Cole, J., at p. 636 held:
    "Fox river where the railway bridge is built. is a nav
    igable stream, and the bridge was created under charter
    which authorized the structure. And it said that th
    plaintiffs had no property in the river front, which th
    legislature could not destroy without making compen
    sation therefor. The plaintiffs, it is said, own the fe
    in the soil only to ordinanry high water mark. and be
    yond the line they had no private property in the wate
    of the river. or in the shore between high and low wate
    mark, which entitled them to recover damages, even i
    their river frontage is cut off or destroyed. There are
    authorities which support this position. Gould v. Th?

Hudson Ry., 6 N. Y. 522; Tomlin v. The Dubuque, B. & M. Ry., 32 Iowa 106. But it seems to us that the doctrine of those cases is unsound. We prefer the rule laid down by Mr. Justice McLean in Bowman's Devises v. Walthen, Where speaking of riparian rights on navigable streams he says: 'On navigable streams, the riparian right, we suppose, cannot extend beyond high water mark. For certain purposes, such as the erection of wharfs, and other structures, for the convenience of commerce, and which do not obstruct the navigation of the river, it may be exercised beyond the limit. But in the present case this inquiry is not important. It is enough to know that the riparian right on the Ohio river extends to the water, and that no supervening right over any part of this space can be exercised or maintained without the consent of the proprietor. *He has the right of fishing, of ferry, and every other right which is properly appurtenant to the soil. And he holds every one of these rights by as sacred a tenure as he holds the land from which they emanate.* The state cannot, either directly or indirectly, divest him of any one of those rights, except by a constitutional exercise of the power to appropriate private property to public purposes. And any act of the state, short of such an appropriation which attempts to transfer any of these rights to another, without the consent of the proprietor, is inoperative and void.'' 2 McLean's R., 376–382.

Following are other Wisconsin cases recognizing riparian rights on navigable waters similar to those enjoyed on nonnavigable waters:

Janesville v. Carpenter, 77 Wis. 288. Bill to enjoin defendant from erecting a building in or continuing piers or piles in the bed of Rock river within the limits of his property line. Reliance was placed upon Ch. 423, Laws of 1887, which purports to give a cause of action for putting obstructions in Rock river. The law provided that it shall be unlawful and presumptively injurious to persons and property to drive piles, build piers, etc., in such river within Rock county and provides that the doing of any such act may be enjoined at the suit of any taxpayer without proof of injury or danger.

The court held the law unconstitutional because, among oth
things, it deprived the reparian owner of his property with
due process of law. The court at p. 300, said:

"That Thomas Lappin, the owner in fee of this groun
has the right to use and enjoy it to the center of the riv
in any manner not injurious to others and subject to tl
public right of navigation, has been too often decided l
. this Court and other Courts to be questioned.   As
riparian owner of the land adjacent to the water, he ov r
the bed of the river *usque ad filum aquae,* subject to tl
public easement if it be navigable in fact, and with *dh*
regard to the rights of other riparian proprietors.   I
may construct docks, landing places, piers and wharve
out to navigable waters if the river is navigable in fa·
and if not so navigable he may construct anything I
pleases to the thread of the stream, unless it injures sor
other riparian proprietor or those having the superi·
right to use the water for hydraulic purposes.   Jones '
Pettibone, 2 Wis. 308; Arnold v. Elmore, 16 Wis. 50"
Yates v. Judd. 18 Wis. 118; Walker v. Shepardson. 4 W·
486; Wis. R. Imp. Co. v. Lyons, 30 Wis. 61; Delaplai·
v. C. & N. W. Ry. Co., 42'Wis. 214; Cohn v. Wausau B. Co
47 Wis. 314; Stevens Point Boom Co. v. Reilly, 46 W·
314; Hazeltine v. Case, 46 Wis. 391.   Subject to these r·
strictions, he has the right to use his land under water tl
same as above water. It is his private property und·
the protection of the constitution, and it cannot be tak··
or its value lessened or impaired, even for public u··
'without compensation or due process of law.' and ·
cannot be taken at all for any one's private use."
See G. Bay & Miss. Canal Co. v. Kaukauna W. P. C.
90 Wis. at 399.
Priewe v. Wis. S. L. & L. Co., 93 Wis. at 546.
McCarthy v. Murphy, 119 Wis. 159.

The Fox river Flour and Paper Co. v. Keeley & others. 7·
Wisconsin 287, 293 (1887).
Action to restrain defendants from using any water, par··'
of a certain water power on the Fox river, city of Appleton.
in hostility to the title of the plaintiff, without leasing or pur·
chasing the same from the plaintiff.

"This case involves questions relating to riparian

rights; and it may be well, at the outset, to refer to some
elementary doctrine which defines or states what there
rights are. In Head v. Amoseag Mfg. Co., 113 U. S. 9–23,
Mr. Justice Gray says: 'The right to the use of running
water is *publici juris*, and common to all the proprietors
of the bed and banks of the stream from its source to its
outlet. Each has a right to the reasonable use of the
water as it flows past his land, not interfering with a
like reasonable use by those above or below him. One
reasonable use of the water is the use of the power inherent in the fall of the stream and the force of the current
to drive mills. That power can not be used without
damming up the water and thereby causing it to flow
back.' In Bates v. Weymouth Iron Co., 8 Cush. 548–552.
Chief Justic Shaw says: 'The relative rights of land-
owners and mill-owners are founded on the established
rule of the common law that every proprietor through
whose territory a current of water flows on its course
towards the sea, has an equal right to the use of it for all
reasonable and beneficial purposes, including the power
of such stream for driving mills, subject to a like reasonable and beneficial use by the proprietors above him and
below him on the same stream. Consequently, no one can
deprive another of his equal right and beneficial use by
corrupting the stream, by wholly diverting it, or stopping
it from the proprietor below him, or raise it artificially
so as to cause it to flow back on the land of the proprietor
above.' Chancellor Kent says: 'Every proprietor of lands
on the banks of a river has naturally an equal right to the
use of the water which flows in the stream adjacent to
his lands, as it was wont to run (currero solebat), without
diminution or alteration. No proprietor has a right to
the use of the water to the prejudice of other proprietors
above or below him, unless he has a prior right to divert
it, or a title to some exclusive enjoyment. He has no
property in the water itself, but a simple usufruct while
it passes along. *Aqua currit et debet currere ut currere
solebat*, is the language of the law. Though he may use
the water while it runs over his land as an incident to
the land, he cannot unreasonably detain it or give it an-

other direction, and he must return it to its ordinary channel when it leaves his estate. Without the consent of the
adjoining proprietors, he cannot divert or diminish the
quantity of water which would otherwise descend to the
proprietors below, not throw the water back upon the
proprietors above, without a grant, or an uninterrupted
enjoyment of twenty years, which is evidence of it.' 2
Kent's Comm. star page 439. The authorities might be
multiplied indefinitely which define the right in substantially the same language, but it is unnecessary. In Lawson v. Mowry, 52 Wis. 219, the same doctrine is recognized and applied, and many cases cited which enforce it.

Applying this doctrine to the case before us, and it is
plain that in the absence of any grant, or of a title acquired by adverse user, the defendants as riparian proprietors only have the right to the natural flow of the
water of the river by their lot; also, as incident to their
ownership of the lot, they have the right to utilize any
fall in the stream in its natural state, as it passes by their
lot, for the purpose of a water power. This is the full
extent of their rights as riparian proprietors owning the
lot on the river below the water power.'' See West v. The
Fox River Paper Co., 82 Wis. at 655 & 656 (1892).

Green Bay & Miss. Canal Co. v. Kaukauna W-P Co., 70 Wis.
652 (1888).

''It is further claimed on behalf of the defendants that,
by locating the south end of the dam upon lot 5, building
an embankment thereon and on lots 6 and 7, and appro-
priating the whole water power created by the dam, the
state took the property of the owners of these lots, and
that the laws of the state made no adequate provision for
compensating them therefor. A riparian owner upon a
navigable stream has no right, without legislative consent, to build a dam across such stream for any purpose.
Wis. R. Imp. Co. v. Lyons, 30 Wis. 61. He has a right,
however, to pass from his land to the river, and from the
river to his land, and to utilize the waters of the river
upon his land for any purpose not interfering with the
navigation of the stream or the rights of other riparian
owners. That the construction of the Kaukauna dam and

improvement *by the state,* and its appropriation of the water power thereby created, take the property of the owner of lot 5, and deprive him of his riparian rights just mentioned (which are also property), does not seem to admit of doubt or controversy. Such owner has never been compensated for his property so taken; neither has he released his right thereto."

"The rule is elementary that, unless affected by license, grant, prescription, or public right or the like, every proprietor of land on the bank of a stream of water, whether navigable or not, has the right to the use of the water as it is wont to run, without material alteration or diminution." Lawson v. Mowry, 52 Wis. 219; quoted with approval in The Kimberly & Clark Co. v. Hewitt & others, 79 Wis. 334 at 337.

"The doctrine we suppose to be well established, that persons who are bounded by the center or thread of the stream, own the land under the stream, to their boundary. If the stream is navigable in fact, the public have the right to use it for the purpose of navigation, and the right of the owner is subject to the public easement. But, with this exception, the right of the owner to use the land as he pleases, is perfect." Jones v. Pettibone, 2 Wis. 308 at 321.

"The right of the riparian owner to have the water of a navigable stream flow past his land adjoining the same as they were accustomed to flow, is as perfect against everybody except the state, or some person or corporation standing in its stead, as it is in the case of unnavigable streams; * * * ." Black Falls Imp. Co. v. La Crosse, etc., Co., 54 Wis. 659 at 691 (1884).

Lawson v. Mowry, 52 Wis. 219 at 235 (1881).
"Were it conceded that the lots extend not only to the center of the river, but also to the center of the canal, and that Mowry had all the rights in the canal and in its waters of any riparian owner, then undoubtedly he would have had the right to use the land in any way compatible

27

with the use of the canal for navigation, provided he did
not abridge corresponding rights of other riparian owners. Walker v. Shepardson, 4 Wis. 486; Green v. Num-
memacher, 36 Wis. 50; Deloplaine v. Railway Co., 42 Wis.
214; Diedrich v. Railway Co., 42 Wis. 248.''

Kaukauna Co. v. Green Bay, etc., Canal Co., 142 Wis. 254, 271
(1891).

"It is the settled law of Wisconsin, announced in repeated decisions of its supreme court, that the ownership
of riparian proprietors extends to the center or thread
of the stream, subject, if such stream be navigable, to the
right of the public to its use as a public highway for vessels. Jones v. Pettibone, 2 Wis. 308; Walker v. Shepardson, 2 Wis. 384; Norcross v. Griffiths, 65 Wis. 599.''

Text writers, too, assert that the rights of riparian proprietors on navigable and non-navigable waters are similar, differing only because of the public right of passage if the waters
be navigable in fact.

Farnham, Waters and Water Rights, p. 278:

"In all states where the common law has not been
changed, the owners of land abutting on bodies of water
are accorded certain rights by reason of their adjacency
which are different than those belonging to the public
generally, and are comprehended within the general term
'riparian rights.' The principle upon which these rights
are founded is equally applicable upon all bodies of
water, whether large or small, tidal or non-tidal;
* * *.''

(Sec. 1597, Wis. Revised Statutes, provides: "The boundaries of lands adjoining waters and the rights of the state and
of individuals in respect to all such lands and waters shall be
determined in conformity to the common law so far as applicable.'')

Gould on Waters, p. 297:

"The distinction between tide waters and fresh, or between public and private waters, is not necessarily a ma-

terial consideration in determining questions relating to riparian rights, since riparian rights proper depend upon the ownership of land contiguous to the water, and are the same whether the proprietor of such land owns the soil under the water or not.''

P. 300: ''Riparian rights exist on the banks of navigable waters as well as of unnavigable streams.''

SUMMARY.

Riparian rights were first recognized on non-navigable waters. Such waters the riparian proprietor may use as he sees fit provided in so doing he does not inflict sensible injury upon the riparian proprietor above or below him. These rights are property. Later it was held that these rights exist as well on navigable as on non-navigable waters. The use of navigable waters by the riparian proprietor, however, is subject to the public right of passage, and other public rights thereon. These rights of the public are paramount to but do not extinguish the private rights of the riparian on such waters.

Floatable Streams.

Several states, among them Wisconsin, distinguish between the relative rights of the public and the individual and on mere floatable streams and streams which are capable of more extended navigation. These states hold that in streams which are merely floatable the rights of the public and of the individual must be enjoyed with due regard to the preservation of the other.

Michigan.

Middleton v. Flat River B. Co., 27 Mich. 533;

Thunder Bay Co. v. Speechly, 31 Mich. 336;

White River Co. v. Nelson, 45 Mich. 578;

Buchanan v. Grand R. L. Co., 48 Mich. 364;

Woodin v. Wentworth, 57 Mich. 278.

Minnesota.

Kretzschmar v. Meehan, 74 Minn. 211.

Oregon.

Hallack v. Suitor, 60 Pac. (Ore.) 384.

Wisconsin.

The A. C. Conn. Co. v. The Little Suamico Lbr. Co., 74 Wis. 652 (1898). The Court said:

''A distinction may well be made between those streams

which are capable of floating logs and timber only at certain periods and then for a few days in time of freshet, and streams which are capable of more extended and constant navigation. It seems to us that in reason and common justice a distinction should be made in view of riparian rights. For if the right of floatage is permanent, so that no bridge or other obstruction can be placed in or over the stream by the riparian owner, his use and enjoyment of his property are unnecessarily abridged and restricted.

The right of the riparian owner and of the public are both to be enjoyed with due regard to the existence and preservation of the other. The right of floatage of logs is not paramount in the sense that the using of the water by the riparian owner for machinery is unlawful so long as he does not materially or unnecessarily interfere with the public right; but he may use the stream and its banks for every purpose not inconsistent with the public use.''

See also Charnley v. The Shawano W. P. & R. Imp. Co.

"EXHIBIT 19".

OWEN.

BRIEF NUMBER 8.

SUBMITTED BY GEORGE P. HAMBRECHT

ON

IN WHAT WAY DID THE ARID STATES IN THE PER-
FECTION OF THEIR IRRIGATION AND MINING
LAWS EVADE THE DOCTRINE OF RIPARIAN
RIGHTS?

TO

THE WISCONSIN LEGISLATIVE COMMITTEE

ON

WATER POWERS, FORESTRY AND DRAINAGE

———————

(Authorities compiled by M. C. Riley.)

IN WHAT WAY DID THE ARID STATES IN THE PER-FECTION OF THEIR IRRIGATION LAWS EVADE THE DOCRINE OF RIPARIAN RIGHTS?

GENERAL STATEMENT OF DOCTRINE OF RIPARIAN RIGHTS.

Every proprietor of land on the banks of a natural stream has an equal right to have the water of the stream continue to flow in its natural course as it was wont to run, without diminution in quantity or deterioration in quality, except so far as either of these conditions may result from the reasonable use of the water for irrigation or other lawful purposes by upper proprietors. He may himself use the water for necessary purposes in a reasonable manner, having due regard to the rights and needs of other proprietors, provided he returns to its natural channel, before it leaves his estate, all the waters not necessarily consumed in his own lawful use.* The rights of the riparian

---

*Union Mill & Min. Co. v. Ferris, 2 Sawy. 176, F. Cas. No. 14,371 (1872); Union Mill & Min. Co. v. Dangberg, 2 Sawy. 450, Fed. Cas. 14, 370 (1872); Ferres v. Knipe, 28 Cal. 340 (1865); Lux v. Haggin, 69 Cal. 255, 10 Pac. 674 (1886); Stanford v. Felt, 71 Cal. 249, 16 Pac. 900 (1886); Hargrave v. Cook, 108 Cal. 72, 41 Pac. 18 (1887); Gould v. Eaton, 117 Cal. 539, 49 Pac. 577 (1897); Elliott v. Fitchburg R. Co., 10 Cush. (Mass.) 191, 57 Am. Dec. 85 (1852); Vansickle v. Haines, 7 Nev. 249 (1872); Hayden v. Long, 8 Ore. 244 (1880); Coffman v. Robbins, 8 Ore. 278 (1880); Rhodes v. Whitehead, 27 Tex. 304 (1863).

The following passage from Chancellor Kent (3 Kent. Comm. 439) has met with universal approval as a correct statement of the law:

"Every proprietor of lands on the banks of a river has naturally an equal right to the use of the water which flows in the stream adjacent to his lands, as it was wont to run ('currere solebat'), without diminution or alteration. No proprietor has a right to use the water, to the prejudice of other proprietors, above or below him, unless he has a prior right to divert it, or a title to some exclusive enjoyment. He has no property in the water itself, but a simple usufruct while it passes along. 'Aqua currit et debet currere ut currere solebat' is the language of the law. Though he may use the water while it runs over his land as an incident to the land, he cannot unreasonably detain it, or give it another direction, and he must return it to its ordinary channel when it leaves his estate. Without the consent of the adjoining proprietors, he cannot divert or diminish the quantity of water which would otherwise descend to the proprietors below, nor throw the water back upon the proprietors above, without a grant, or an uninterrupted enjoyment of twenty years, which is evidence of it. This is the clear

owner is limited to a simple usufruct in the water as it passes along, and does not include the proprietorship in the water itself.*

Where in force.

The doctrine of riparian rights as above defined prevails in Great Britain and in all of the states and territories in the United States, with the exception of seven within the arid region. Long on irrigation, Sec. 10, p. 21.

Right of riparian owner at common law to use water of natural stream for irrigation.

A riparian proprietor has the right at common law to make a reasonable use of the waters of a natural stream for irrigation puposes. This principle is well established in England and the United States.†

---

and settled doctrine on the subject, and all the difficulty that arises consists in the application. The owner must so use and apply the water as to work no material injury or annoyance to his neighbor below him, who has an equal right to the subsequent use of the same water; nor can he, by dams or any obstruction, cause the water injuriously to overflow the grounds and springs of his neighbor above him. Streams of water are intended for the use and comfort of man; and it would be unreasonable, and contrary to the universal sense of mankind, to debar every riparian proprietor from the application of the water to domestic, agricultural, and manufacturing purposes, provided the use of it be made under the limitations which have been mentioned; and there will, no doubt, inevitably be, in the exercise of a perfect right to the use of the water, some evaporation and decrease of it, and some variations in the weight and velocity of the current. But 'de minimis non curat lex,' and a right of action by the proprietor below would not necessarily flow from such consequences, but would depend upon the nature and extent of the complaint or injury, and the manner of using the water. All that the law requires of the party by or over whose land a stream passes is that he should use the water in a reasonable manner, and so as not to destroy, or render useless, or materially diminish or affect the application of the water by the proprietors above or below on the stream."

* Vernon Irr. Co. v. City of Los Angeles, 106 Cal. 237, 39 Pac. 762 (1895); Hargrave v. Cook, 108 Cal. 72, 41 Pac. 18 (1895); Gould v. Eaton, 117 Cal. 539, 49 Pac. 577 (1897); Rhodes v. Whitehead, 27 Tex. 304 (1863); Rigney v. Tacoma Light and Water Co., 9 Wash. 576, 38 Pac. 147 (1894). See Riverside Water Co. v. Gage, 89 Cal. 410, 26 Pac. 889 (1891).

† England: Embrey v. Owen, 8 Exch. 355 (1851); see also Strutt v. Bovingdon, 5 Esp. 56 (1803); Greensdale v. Halliday, 6 Bing. 379 (1830); Hall v. Swift, 6 Scott, 167 (1838); Earl of Sandwich v. Gt. Nor. Ry. Co., 10 Ch. Div. 707 (1878); Miner v. Gilmour, 12 Moore, P. C. 131 (1858).

United States: Union Mill & Min. Co. v. Ferris, 2 Sawy. (U. S.) (1872); Union Mill & Min. Co. v. Dangberg, Id. 450.

Alabama: Ulbricht v. Eufaula Water Co., 86 Ala. 587 (1888).

The use must be reasonable.

No precise rule can be laid down as to what constitutes a reasonable use of the waters of a natural stream for irrigation purposes. In England, it seems that any perceptible diminution of the water of the stream would give a right action in favor of a lower proprietor. Embrey v. Owen, supra. In the Eastern states, the general trend of the decisions is to the effect that any substantial or essential diminution of the stream is unreasonable, and not permissible, but even in those states the main inquiry seems to be whether the lower proprietor is materially injured or not. Gillett v. Johnson, 30 Conn. 180 (1861); Blanchard v. Baker, 8 Greenl. (Me.) 253 (1832); Eliot v. R. R. Co., 10 Cush. (Mass.) 191 (1852); Arnold v. Foot, 12 Wend. 330 (1834). The upper riparian owner has no right to exhaust the entire flow of the stream. Id.

Irrigation and the doctrine of riparian rights in the arid and subhumid states and territories.

Radically different climatic conditions necessitating more extensive system of irrigation in the arid and subhumid states and territories of the United States, has resulted in some of such states and territories in a modification and in others in an abrogation of the common law doctrine or riparian rights.

States and territories embraced in the arid and subhumid regions.

The arid region, or region in which irrigation is absolutely essential to successful cultivation of the soil, embraces, either wholly or in part, the following states and territories, namely: Arizona, California, Colorado, Idaho, Montana, Nevada, New Mexico, Oregon, Utah, Washington and Wyoming. In the subhumid region, or region in which the rainfall is in some seasons

---

Connecticut: Gillet v. Johnson, 30 Conn. 180 (1861).

Maine: Blanchard v. Baker, 8 Greenl. 253 (1832); Davis v. Getchell, 50 Me. 602 (1862).

Massachusetts: Weston v. Olden, 8 Mass. 136 (1811); Anthony v. Lapham, 5 Pick. 175 (1827); Elliott v. Fitchburg R. Co., 10 Cush. 191 (1852).

New Jersey: Farrell v. Richards, 30 N. J. Eq. 511 (1879).

New York: See Garwood v. N. Y. C. & R. R., 83 N. Y. 400 (1881).

Nevada: Jones v. Adams, 19 Nev. 78 (1885).

Oregon: Hayden v. Long, 8 Ore. 244 (1880); Coffman v. Robbins, 8 Ore. 278 (1880).

Pennsylvania: Randall v. Silverthorn, 4 Pa. St.; 173 (1846); Miller v. Miller, 9 Pa. St. 74 (1848); Messinger's Appeal, 109 Pa. St. 285 (1885).

sufficient, and others insufficient for agricultural purposes, are embraced parts of Kansas, Nebraska, North and South Dakota and Texas. Census report of agriculture by Irrigation, 1890, pp. VII, 257.

Two systems of Irrigation Laws have been adopted in the states enumerated.

While the absolute necessity for irrigation has been recognized in all the arid and some of the subhumid states, two different views prevail as to the nature and extent of the rights of the irrigation growing out of this necessity. The result is that two entirely distinct systems of irrigation law have grown up side by side, based upon principles fundamentally different, yet overlapping each other in many important details. The older system, has prevailed from an early date in California, and which may be called the "California System," rests upon and is consistent with the doctrine of riparian rights. The other system, which originated in California, but which was first applied to private lands in Colorado, and is therefore known as the "Colorado System." is based upon an entirely new principle in the law of water rights, known as the doctrine of "appropriation"

THE "CALIFORNIA SYSTEM."

The California, rule as to the use of waters of natural streams for irrigation, is tersely laid down in the case of Harris v. Harrison, 93 Cal. 676 (1892). In this case plaintiffs alleged that they were entitled to all the water of a certain stream for purposes of irrigation, and defendants denied that they were entitled to any of it. The court found that plaintiffs were entitled to a portion of the water only, and that to make the water available for irrigation it was necessary that a full flow of the stream to be used at once. It was held further, thtt the trial court did not err in apportioning by its degree to plaintiffs the full flow of water during one-half of each week, and to defendants the flow during the remaining half of such week. The court observed:

"According to the common-law doctrine of riparian ownership, as generally declared in England and in most of the American states, upon the facts in the case at bar, the plain-

tiffs would be entitled to have the waters of Harrison cannon
continue flow to and upon their land as they were naturally
accustomed to flow, without any substantial deterioration in
quality or diminution in quantity. But in some of the
western and southwestern states and territories, where the
year is divided into one wet and one dry season, and irrigation is necessary to successful cultivation of the soil, the
doctrine of riparian ownership has by judicial decision been
modified, or rather enlarged, so as to include the reasonable use of natural water for irrigating the riparian land,
although such use may appreciably diminish the flow down
to the lower riparian proprietor; and this must be taken
to be the established rule of California, at least where irri
gation is thus necessary. Lux v. Haggin, 69 Cal. 394, 10
Pac. Rep. 674. Of course, there will be great difficulty in
many cases to determine what is such reasonable use; and
'what is such reasonable use is a question of fact, and depends upon the circumstances appearing in each particular
case.' Lux v. Haggin, supra. The larger number of riparian proprietors whose rights are involved, the greater the
difficulty of adjustment. In such case, the length of the
stream, the volume of water in it, the extent of each ownership along the banks, the character of the soil owned by
each contestant, the area sought to be irrigated by each—
all these and many other considerations must enter into
the solution of the problem; but one principle is surely establish, namely, that no proprietor can absorb all the
water of the stream, so as to allow none to flow down to
his neighbor. In the case at bar only the rights of two
riparian proprietors are to be considered. None other involved. And the amount of water in the stream is so small
that it is apparent that defendants could not use it
for any useful irrigation without practicaly absorbing it
all, and leaving none to flow down to plaintiff's land. There
was sufficient evidence to warrant the finding of the court
that in order to irrigate, 'it is necessary that the full flow
of the stream be used at once.' But defendants, as well
as plaintiffs, were entitled to reasonable use of the water
for irrigation; and the rights of either could be declared
or preserved by an atempted division of the flow of the
water without reference to time. The only way, therefore,

to preserve these rights, and to render them beneficial, was to decree to the parties the use of the full flow of the stream during alternate periods of time; and we do not see why the court could not decree a division of the OWEN, water according to that method, when there was no othei method by which it could be done. And that the division as a just one, and not erroneously determined upon, seems clear. The evidence showed that the arable and irrigable lands of each party was about equal in area; and there was no contention that the division was not equitable, provided that all other facts were correctly found by the courts." See also Lux v. Haggin, supra.

In Oregon where waters flow in a well defined channel through the lands of several persons, each riparian owner has the right to have it continue to flow in its natural course without diminution, *except so far as it may be legally used by others, while passing through their respective premises for irrigation and other purposes.* Coffman v. Robbins, 8 Ore. 278 (1880).

The two preceding cases establish that the general doctrine as to the right of the riparian proprietor to use the water of a natural stream for irrigation is the same in the states which follow the 'California System" as at common law and in the moister regions, except that a somewhat more liberal policy as to the permissible extent of such use—as to what is a reasonable use —has been adopted in view of the greater need for irrigation in such states. As was previously stated the system of irrigation laws developed by California, Montana, Oregon and Washington, the states following the "California System," is not inconsistent with the common law doctrine of riparian rights. In those states the doctrine of riparian rights still prevails.* (As to the doctrine of prior appropriation in the above states and the extent to which riparian rights are thereby affected, see post, p. 8).

* California: Conger v. Weaver, 6 Calif. 548 (1856); Lux v. Haggin, 69 Calif. 255 (1866).
Montana: Smith v. Denniff, 24 Mont. 20 (1900).
Oregon: Simmons v. Winters, 21 Ore. 35 (1891); Kaler v. Campell, 13 Ore. 596 (1886); Hayden v. Long, 8 Ore. 244 (1880); Coffman v. Robbins, Id. 278.
Washington: Isaacs v. Barber, 10 Wash. 124 (1894); Benton v. Johncox, 17 Wash. 277 (1897).

THE "COLORADO SYSTEM."

The Colorado system of irrigation is based upon the doctrine of prior appropriation. This doctrine prevails in Arizona, Colorado, Idaho, Nevada, New Mexico, Utah and Wyoming. The doctrine, limited in its application, prevails in all the other arid and in the subhumid states and territories. See Post, p. 8.

General statement of the doctrine of prior appropriations.

In reference to the right to flowing water prior **appropriation** means the right which the first or original appropriatior thereof has as against the riparian proprietor and all others. Drake v. Earhart, 2 Idaho 750 (1890).

"According to the doctrine of the appropriation a right to the use of the water of natural streams, not already appropriated by others, may be acquired by simple apropriation, irrespective of the ownership of the lands through which the stream may flow, or any other consideration."

Long on Irrigation, Sec. 22, p. 23.

"The doctrine of "prior appropriation" confers upon a riparian proprietor, or one having title to a water right by grant from him, the right to a use of the waters of a stream which would be unreasonable at the common law, and to this extent the doctrine of prior apropriation may be said to have abrogated the common law rule." Smith v. Denniff, 242 Mone. 20, 23 (1900).

In what states and territories in force.

In most of the arid and subhumid states it is provided by constitution or statute or both, that the unappropriated water of natural streams shall be subject to apropriation for irrigation and other useful purposes.*

* Arizona: Rev. St., 1887, secs. 3201, 3205, 3215; Act Apr. 13, Acts 1893, p. 119.
California: Civil Code, secs. 1410–1422.
Colorado: Con. Art. 16, sec. 6.
Idaho: Con. Art. 15, sec. 3.
Kansas: Gen. Stats. 1899, sec. 3519.
Montana: Civil Code 1895, secs. 1880–1885.
Nebraska: Comp. Stats. 1899, sec. 5486.
Nevada: Comp. Laws 1900, secs. 354–359.
New Mexico: Comp. Laws 1897, secs. 1–63.

The doctrine of appropriation in the states following the "California System."

While the doctrine of appropriation prevails in all of the *arid* states, the extent to which it is carried is not everywhere the same. The doctrine is wholly contrary to and inconsistent with the common law doctrine of riparian rights, and hence, in these states in which the latter doctrine prevails, the doctrine of appropriation applies only where the common law doctrine is inapplicable—that is, to streams in which no riparian rights have attached. It is accordingly held in those states that doctrine of appropriation applies to, and only to, the water on the public lands, belonging either to the state† or to the United States, and the right to water for irrigation cannot be acquired by prior apropriation, where the land has been reduced to private ownership.‡ The right of appropriation cannot be exercised in these states against a riparian proprietor.§

The doctrine of riparian rights prevails in the subhumid states.

In the subhumid states the doctrine of prior appropriation has not supplanted the doctrine of riparian rights.¶

North Dakota: Laws 1899, secs. 1–10.
Oregon: App. for pub. use and upon compensation, Hill's Ann. Laws 1892, secs. 1, 2 and 8.
Texas: Sayles Civ. St. Arts. 3117–3119, 3122.
Utah: Rev. St. 1898, secs. 1261–1284.
Washington: Code 1897, sec. 4091–99.
Wyoming: Con. Art. 8, sec. 3.
† Lux v. Haggin, 69 Calif. 255 (1896).
‡ In California, the statutes authorizing the appropriation of water expressly provides that the rights of riparian owners shall not be affected by its provisions. Civ. Code Calif. sec. 1422.
In Texas, the statute provides that the unappropriated waters of rivers and natural streams within the arid portions of the state, may be appropriated; provided, however, that the water may not be diverted so as to deprive riparian proprietors of the use of the water for domestic purposes. Supp. Sayles Civ. St. Art. 3000a, secs. 1 and 3.
§ California: Lux v. Haggin, 69 Calif. 25, (1896); Santa Cruz v. Enright, 95 Calif. 105 (1892); Irr. Co. v. Los Angeles, 106 Calif. 237 (1895); Hargrave v. Cock, 108 Calif. 72 (1895).
Montana: Smith v. Denniff, 24 Mont. 20 (1900).
Oregon: Kaler v. Campbell, 13 Ore. 596 (1886); Simmons v. Winters, 21 Ore. 35 (1891).
Washington: Thorpe v. Ditch Co., 1 Wash. 566 (1890); Geddis v. Parish, 1 Wash. 587 (1890); Benton v. Johncox, 17 Wash. 277 (1897); Offield v. Ish, 57 Pac. 809 (1899).
¶ Kansas: City of Emporia v. Seden, 25 Kan. 588 (1881).
Nebraska: Clark v. Cambridge, etc. Co., 45 Neb. 798 (1895).
North Dakota: Bigelow v. Draper, 6 N. D. 152 (1896).
Texas: McGhee v. Hudson, 25 Tex. 591 (1860); Barrett v. Metcalf, 12 Tex. Civ. App. 247 (1896).

The doctrine of prior appropriation in the states and territories following the Colorado System.

In Arizona, Colorado, Idaho, Nevada, New Mexico, Utah and Wyoming, the states and territories following the "Colorado System," the doctrine of riparian rights is not recognized.* Hence in those states and territories there is no restriction upon the exercise of the right of appropriation, so far as the character of the land to be irrigated (riparian or remote), or from which the water is to be taken is concerned; but the right extends to the unappropriated water of all streams within the state, whether the land by or through which they flow be private or a part of the public domain. Coffin v. L. H. Ditch Co., 6 Colo. 443 (1882); Hammond v. Rose, 11 Colo. 524 (1888); Mahoney v. Neisanger (Idaho) 59 Pac. 561 (1899).

Constitutionality or statutory and constitutional provision authorizing appropriation.

The precise point upon which the constitutionality of such provisions would most naturally be assailed is that, in abrogating the common law rule doctrine of riparian rights, they may authorize the taking or damaging of private property for other than a private or a public use and without compensation.

At common law riparian rights are property.

At the common law the right of a riparian proprietor to the flow of the water of a natural stream is property, which when vested, can be destroyed or impaired only in the interest of the general public, for a public use—upon just compensation and in accordance with established law.†

---

* Arizona: Clough v. Wing, 17 Pac. 453 (1888); Oury v. Goodwin, 26 Pac. 376 (1891); Austin v. Chandler, 42 Pac. 483 (1895).
  Colorado: Oppenlander v. Left Hand Ditch Co., 18 Colo. 142 (1892).
  Idaho: Drake v. Earhart, 2 Idaho 716 (1890).
  Nevada: Reno Smelting Works v. Stevenson, 20 Nev. 259 (1889).
  New Mexico: Trambley v. Luterman, 6 N. M. 15 (1891). See Millheiser v. Long, 61 Pac. 111 (1900).
  Utah: Stowell v. Johnson, 7 Utah 215 (1891).
  Wyoming: Moyer v. Preston, 44 Pac. 845 (1896); Farm Investment Co. v. Carpenter, 61 Pac. 258 (1900).
  † See Committee brief—The Doctrine of Riparian Rights. Clark v. Cambridge & A. Imp. Co., 45 Neb. 798 (1895); 64 N. W. 239; Bigelow v. Draper, 6 No. Dak. 152 (1896); Lux v. Haggin, 69 Calif. 285 (1886).
  Riparian rights exist on navigable as well as on non navigable streams. See brief above cited.
  It is not deemed necessary here to dwell upon the extent to which this right or property is qualified by the rights of other riparian pro-

. (A) STATUTORY PROVISIONS.

A state legislature has no power by a general law authorizing the appropriation of water by private persons to deprive a riparian proprietor of his vested rights.† And it has been held in Nebraska that the act of that state of 1889, as amended in 1893, providing for the acquisition of a right to the use of running water by appropriation, with a proviso that, in all streams not more than twenty feet in width, the rights of the riparian proprietor should not be affected by the act, is unconstitutional. The court proceeded upon the ground that riparian rights had become vested in all of the streams of the state prior to the passage of the act, which was therefore an invasion of private rights, within the prohibition of the constitution.‡

(B) CONSTITUTIONAL PROVISIONS.

Nor can such rights be divested by constitutional provisions. The North Dakota Constitution provides that "All flowing streams and natural water courses shall forever remain the property of the state for mining, irrigation and manufacturing purposes." Sec. 210. This provision was construed by the court in Bigelow v. Draper, 6 N. D. 152 (1896). The court at p. 163, said:

> "These doctrines of the common law were in force in the Territory of Dakota at the time of the adoption of the constitution of this states. By virtue of them, the riparian owners in the territory were vested with the specified property rights in the bed of all natura' water course . and in the water itself. Such rights were under the protection of the fourteenth amendment of the federal constitution, which protects property against all state action that does not constitute due process of law. It follows that sec. 210 of the

---

prietors in the flow of water in navigable and non-navigable streams, and by the rights of the public if such property or right be on a navigable stream.

† Lux v. Haggin, 69 Calif. 255 (1886); Barrett v. Metcalf, 12 Tex. Civ. App. 247 (1896); Watuppa Reservoir Co. v. Fall River, 154 Mass. 305 (1891).

‡ Clark v. Cambridge & A. Irr. & Imp. Co., 45 Neb. 798 (1895), 64 N. W. 239.

state constitution would itself be unconstitutional so far as it attempted to destroy those vested rights of property, if it should by construction be given a scope sufficiently wide to embrace such matters. For this reason, we feel constrained to hold despite its broad language, that sec. 210 was not framed to divest the rights of riparian owners in the water and bed of all natural water courses in the state." The stream in question was non-navigable. See also Mill & El. Co. v. Irr. Co., 26 Colo. 47 (1899 ;

Armstrong v. Larimer Ditch Co., 1 Colo. App. 49 (1891).

No objections to statutes or constitutional provisions authorizing appropriations where no riparian rights have vested.

But these objections to the statutes and constitutional provisions authorizing appropriation cannot prevail where no riparian rights have vested. As previously stated the states and territories following the 'Colorado System," even though all have adopted the common law in so far as applicable to their society and conditions, do not recognize the doctrine of riparian rights. These states and territories hold that the common law relative to the rights of riparian owners never was in force within their boundaries, and, proceeding accordingly, have either by constitutional or statutory provision, or by judical construction, repudiated the common law doctrine and substituted in lieu thereof the doctrine of appropriation.

Folowing are the statutory or constitutional provisions and the court decisions in the different "Colorado System" states and territories adopting the doctrine of prior appropriation instead of the common law doctrine of riparian rights.

Arizona.

Common law abolished.

Rev. St. 1887, sec. 3198. "The common law doctrine of riparian water rights shall not obtain or be of any force in this territory."

Streams public property.

Sec. 3198. "All rivers, creeks and streams of running water in the territory of Arizona are hereby declared public, and applicable to the purposes of irrigation and mining, as hereinafter provided."

Sec. 2863. "All streams, lakes and ponds of water capable of being used for the purposes of navigation or irrigation are hereby declared to be public property; and no individuals or corporation shall have the right to apropriate them exclusively to their own private use, except under equitable regulations and restrictions as the legislature shall provide for that purpose. (Bill of Rights sec. 22)."

"* * * the common law has no application whatever to the use of water with us. Not even the common law doctrine of riparian right is acknowledged by us, but it is expressly repudiated by section 3198 Rev. St. So the common law can furnish no aid in the adjustment of water rights in this territory." Austin v. Chandler (Ariz.), 42 Pac. 483 (1895).

In Clough v. Wing (Ariz.) 17 Pac. 453 (1888), the court holds that riparian rights have never been recognized in Arizona.

"The legislature of Arizona at its first session in 1864, enacted that (C. L. 3240). 'All rivers, creeks, and streams of running water are hereby declared public and applicable to the purposes of irrigation and mining; (3242) all the inhabitants who own or possess arable and irrigable lands shall have the right to construct public or private *acequias* (canals) and obtain the necessary water for the same from any convenient river, creek or stream or running water; (3243) and prohibits the obstruction of such canals, as the right to irrigate the fields shall be preferable to all others.' Up to about a third of a century ago, and but recently before this enactment, the territory of Arizona had been subject to the laws and customs of Mexico, and the common law had been unknown; and that law has never been, and is not now, suited to conditions that exist here, so far as the same applies to the use of water."

Colorado.

Water public property.

Con. Art. 16, Sec. 5. "The water of every stream not heretofore appropriated, within the state of Colorado, is hereby declared to be the property of the public, and the same is dedicated to the use of the public of the state, subject to appropriation as hereinafter provided."

In Oppenlander v. Left Hand Ditch Co., 18 Colo. 142 (1892),
the court after discussing the differences between water rights at
common law and under the state constitutional provision,
said:

"Thus it appears that the constitution has, to a large
extent, obliterated the common law doctrine of riparian
rights and substituted in lieu thereof the doctrine of appropriation."

The same court in Coffin v. Left Hand Ditch Co., 6 Colo. 443
(1882), holds that the doctrine of appropriation was adopted in
that state and territory, prior to the vesting of ripraian rights,
and that the doctrine of riparian rights is inapplicable to that
state. The court in the course of its opinion, stated:

"It is contended by counsel for appellants that the com
mon law principles of riparian proprietorship prevailed in
Colorado until 1876, and that the doctrine of priority of
right to water by priority of appropriation thereof was
first recognized and adopted in the constitution. But we
think that the latter doctrine has existed from the date of
the earliest appropriations of water within the boundaries
of the state. * * * We conclude, then, that the common
law doctrine giving the riparian owner a right to the flow
of water in its natural channel upon and over his lands,
even though he makes no beneficial use thereof, is inapplicable to Colorado."

Idaho.

Con. Art. 15 Sec. 1. makes the use of water for sale, etc., a
public use and subject to legislative regulation. Sec. 3 provides for the right to appropriate water. No statute or constitutional provision expressly refers to the doctrine of riparian
rights or makes streams or water public poperty.

The court in Drake v. Earhart, 2 Idaho 750 (1890), with reference to the doctrine of riparian rights, says:

"The important question, for the settlement of which
this appeal was chiefly brought, is what, if any, rights the appellant has to any of that water as a riparian proprietor.
His claim is not based upon prior or any appropriation
under our territorial laws, but upon the fact that the
stream in question flows by its natural channel through

his land; hence, that he is entitled to the use thereof allowed by the common law. * * * While there are questions growing out of the water laws and rights not fully adjuciated, this phantom of riparian rights, based upon facts like those in this case, has been so often decided adversely to such claim, and in favor of the prior appropriation, that the maxim, 'First in time, first in right,' should be considered the settled law here. Whether or not it is a beneficient rule it is the lineal descendant of the law of necessity. When, from among the most energetic and enterprising classes of the east, that enormous tide of emigration poured into the west, this was found on arid land, which could be utilized as an agricultural country, or made valuable for its gold, only by the use of its streams of water. The new inhabitants were without law, but they quickly recognized that each man should not be a law unto himself. Accustomed, as they had been, to obedience to the laws they had helped make, as the settlements increased to such numbers as justified organization, they established their local customs and rules for their government in the use of water and land. They found a new condition of things. The use of water to which they had been accustomed, and the laws concerning it had no application here. The demand for water they found greater than the supply, as is the unfortunate fact still all over this arid region. Instead of attempting to divide it among all, thus making it unprofitable to any, or instead of applying the common-law riparian doctrine, to which they had been accustomed, they disregarded the traditions of the past, and established as the rule suitable to their situation that of prior appropriation. This did not mean that the first appropriator could take all he pleased, but what he actually needed, and could properly use without waste. Thus was established the local custom, which pervaded the entire west, and became the basis of the laws we have today on that subject. Very soon these customs attracted the attention of the legislatures, where they are approved and adopted, and next we find them undergoing the crucial test of judicial investigation.''

Nevada.

Water property of state.

Comp. Laws 1900, sec. 354. "All natural water courses and natural lakes, and the waters thereof, which are not held in private ownership, belong to the state, and are subject to regulation and control by the state."

Sec. 359 et seq., authorize appropriation.

In Reno Smelting Works v. Stevenson, 20 Nev. 269 (1889), the court holds that the common law only in so far as applicable was adopted in Nevada, and that therefore the riparian never had any common law water rights in that state. The court said:

> "Plaintiff upon this appeal neither claims nor disclaims a right by virtue of a prior appropriation, but urges an affirmance of the judgment upon the sole ground that it is a riparian proprietor, and as such, is entitled to the natural flow of the water through its land."

After stating the common law doctrine of riparian rights and declaring that Nevada adopted the common law by legislative act, the court proceeded to show that the adoption of such law was to the extent only that the same is applicable to the habits and conditions of Nevada society, and in harmony with the genius, spirit and objects of Nevada institutions, and therefore, that the doctrine of riparian rights never prevailed in the jurisdiction. By way of conclusion the court said:

> "Our conclusion is that the common law doctrine of riparian rights is unsuited to the condition of our state, and that this case should have been determined by the application of the principles of prior appropriation."p. 282.

Reno Smelting Works v. Stevenson, 20 Nev. 269 (1889).

New Mexico.

Comp. Laws 1897 secs. 1–63 declare waters public property and authorize appropriations.

The two cases following hold that the doctrine of riparian rights does not now and never prevailed in New Mexico.

> The " common law, as to the rights of riparian owners, is not in force in this territory, nor in California (?), Nevada and other Pacific states." Trambley v. Luterman, 6 N. M., 15 (1891).

"It is clear that the law of prior appropriation governs in this territory, and water rights must be determined by it. In 1876 the legislature enacted a law which provided: 'all currents and sources of water, such as springs, rivers, ditches and currents of water flowing from natural sources in the territory of New Mexico, shall be and they are by this act declared free'. Comp. L. 1897 sec. 2. By this act private ownership of water in the public streams of the territory was prohibited, and a right to the use of such waters for beneficial purposes was given to those who appropriated and applied them to such uses. Millheiser v. Long, (N. M.) 61 Pac. 111 (1900)."

The court then quoted from U. S. v. Rio Grande Dam & Irr. Co., 174 U. S. 690, 704 (1898) to the effect that the doctrine of riparian rights never prevailed in New Mexico.

Utah.

Rev. St. 1898, secs. 1261 et seq, authorize appropriation. The Supreme Court of Utah holds that:

"Riparian rights have never been recognized in this territory, or in any state or territory where irrigation is necessary; for the appropriation of water for the purpose of irrigation is entirely and unavoidably in conflict with the common-law doctrine of riparian proprietorship. If that had been recognized and applied to this territory, it would still be a desert; for a man owning ten acres of land on a stream of water capable of irrigating a thousand acres of land or more, near its mouth, could prevent the settlement of land above him. For at common law the riparian proprietor is entitled to have the water flow in quantity and quality past his land as it was wont to do when he acquired title thereto, and this right is utterly irreconcilable with the use of water for irrigation. The legislature of this territory has always ignored this claim of riparian proprietors, and the practice and usuages of the inhabitants have never considered it applicable, and have never considered it applicable, and have never regarded it." Stowell v. Johnson, 7 Utah 215, 25 (1891).

Wyoming.

Water property of state.

Con. Art. 8, sec. 1. "The water of all natural streams, springs, lakes or other collections of still water wherein the boundaries of the state are hereby declared to be property of the state."

"The common law doctrine relating to the rights of a riparian proprietor in the water of a natural stream, and the use thereof is unsuited to our requirements·and necessities, and never obtained in Wyoming. So much only of the common law as may be applicable has been adopted in this jurisdiction. * * * We incline strongly to the view expressed by the supreme court of Colorado, to the effect that such right and the obligation to protect it (i. e. the right of appropriation) existed anterior to any legislation upon the subject."

Mayer v. Preston, (Wyo.) 44 Pac. 845, 847 (1896);

See also, Farm Invest. Co. v. Carpenter, (Wyo.) 61 Pac. 258 (1900).

The doctrine of prior appropriation is founded upon Spanish-Mexican law, custom and necessity.

The doctrine of prior appropriation, as contradistinguished from the doctrine of riparian rights, is founded upon Spanish-Mexican laws, custom and necessity. The law best adapted to conditions was adopted by custom by the early miners and agriculturists settling in the west, and later the same, by constitutional provision, statutory law and judicial decision, became the paramount law of those states and territories in which the "Colorado system" is followed.

The Nebraska court, in the recent case of Meng v. Coffey, 67 Neb. 500 (1903), has made an elaborate examination of the foundation of the rule of prior appropriation,—how it supplanted the doctrine of riparian rights,—and makes the following statement as to its origin and extent:

"The doctrine of prior appropriation arose in California at a time when government and law were not yet established, when there was no agricultural population and *were no riparian owners,* and when streams could be put to no use except for mining. From the necessities of the case, there being no law applicable, the miners held meet-

ings in each district or locality and adopted regulations
by which they agreed to be governed. As at that time,
streams could be put to no use except for mining, and as
the use of large quantities of water was essential to mining operations, it became settled as one of the mining customs or regulations that the right to a definite quantity of
water, and to divert it from streams or lakes, could be acquired by appropriation. This custom acquired strength;
rights were gained under it, and investments made, and it
was soon approved by the courts and by local legislation;
and, though not originally available against the general
government or its patentees, was made so available by the
act of Congress in 1866." Sec. 9, U. S. Comp. Stats. 1901,
p. 1437.*

Farnham, in this treatise on Waters and Water Rights, Vol.
III, pp. 2018, 2019, accounts for the doctrine of appropriation
in the following language:

"When the land (i. e. that included within the arid
states) was ceded by Mexico to the United States, the title
to all land within the section passed to the United States
government, and it possessed largely the character of a
common. The United States had conferred none of the
titles of the former residents and had *made no grants to
its own citizens,* so that gold seekers treated the land as belonging to no one, and, by a tacit understanding among
themselves, the one who would first take possession of a
parcel was regarded as the rightful owner while his possession continued. The same rule was made to apply to
the other flowing in the streams. It had no owner except
the government, and therefore the one who first took possession of it and applied it to a beneficial use was regarded

<hr>

*This Act provides: Whenever, by priority of possession, rights to
the use of water for mining, agricultural, manufacturing or other purposes have vested and accrued, and the same are recognized and acknowledged by the local customs, laws and the decisions of courts, the
possessors and owners of such vested rights shall be maintained and
protected in the same; and the right of way for the construction of
ditches and canals for the purposes herein specified is acknowledged
and confirmed; but whenever any person, in the construction of any
ditch or canal, injures or damages the possession of any settler on the
public domain, the party committing such injury or damage shall be
liable to the party injured for such injury or damage. (Act July 26,
1866.)

as having a right to continue the enjoyment of it so long as he continued his beneficial use. This was an application. not only of the Mexican law, but was the rule which must, of necessity, be applied by settlers of a country where there was no private titles and each one was at liberty to take possession of what he could find unoccupied. For eighteen years, from 1846 to 1866, the regulations and customs of miners, as enforced and molded by the courts and sanctioned by the legislation of the states, constituted the law governing property in mines and the water on the public mineral lands. Jennison v. Kirk, 98 U. S. 453 (1878).

When Congress undertook to make provision for the granting of titles to settlers it found that improvements had been made and money expended upon the faith of the conditions which the settlers had founded, and therefore, it made provision for the confirmation of titles which had their origin under the consent or custom rule of the settlers, and provided that any grants which should be made by the government should be subject to rights which had accrued under such customs. Act July 26, 1866, 14 Stats. at L. 253 Chap. 262 U. S. Comp. Stats. 1901, p. 1437. The legislation of Congress, however, applied only to the public land and had no application to riprarian owners under the laws of the state, which were formed out of the public territory.

When the states were formed and were confronted with the problem as to what the rights of flowing waters should be, *they were at liberty to make such rules as seemed best.* Most of the states, by general statutory provisions established the common law rules as their law. A few incorporated in their constitutions provisions reserving to the public the ownership of public waters, and made it subject to appropriation by individuals. Broder v. Natoma Water & Min. Co., 101 U. S. 274 (1879). And the courts of other states held that the statutory adoption of the common law did not include the doctrine of riprarian rights, because it was inapplicable to local conditions and therefore declared the doctrine of prior appropriation to be the rule in the state."

The United States supreme court in Atchison v. Topeka, 20 Wall. 507 (1874), dwells upon the necessity for the change in the common law relative to water rights in the arid states and holds that no riparian rights vested during the early settlement in those states because of a reservation of mineral lands from sale. The court held:

"This quality of right among all the proprietors on the same stream would have been incompatible with any extended diversion of the water by one proprietor, and its conveyance for mining purposes to points from which it could not be restored to the stream. *But the government being the sole proprietor of all the public lands, whether bordering on streams or otherwise, there was no occasion for the application of the common law doctrine of riparian proprietorship with respect to the waters of those streams.* The government by its silent acquiescence, assented to the general occupation of the public lands for mining, and to encourage their free and unlimited use for that purpose, reserved such lands as were mineral from sale and the acquisition of title by settlement. And he who first connects his own labor with property thus situated and open to general exploration does, in natural justice, acquire a better right to its use and enjoyment than others who have not given such labor." Atchison v. Topeka, 20 Wall. 507 (1874).

The doctrine of prior appropriation prevailed in Mexico.

"When pioneers first began settling in the territory along the Western boundary of the United States, they found in force the laws of Mexico, by which the title to the water in all streams was in the public, and the water was subject to use by any one who could gain access to it for purposes necessary to the support of life; and the Mexican government possessed the power of retaining the water in its natural channel or of conveying the exclusive use of portions of it to individuals upon such terms and conditions and with such limitations as it saw fit to establish by law." Lux v. Haggin, 69 Calif. 255 (1886).

Finding the title of the water in the public, the settlers proceeded to expand the use of it so as to include the acquisition of a supply for mining purposes 'or for the irrigation of such small crops as they wished to plant. This use grew into cus-tom, Drake v. Earhart, 25 Idaho 750 (1890), so that when the states were subsequently organized, with constitutions adopt-ing the common law as far as it was applicable to the existing conditions, many water rights were held by custom and few or none under claim of riparian ownership. The result was that, so far as these customary rights existed, they were recog-nized as establishing a good title. Crawford Co. v. Hathaway, 61 Neb. 317 (1901). And as other states were formed, pro-vision was made for the establishment of the right to acquire water rights by appropriation rather than by riparian proprie-torship. Ft. Morgan Land & Canal Co. v. So. Platte Ditch Co., 18 Colo. 1 (1892).

The states and territories had power to say to what extent the common law should apply within their respective bound-aries.

In a recent case in the United States supreme court it was held that the power to change the common law rule, and per-mit the appropriation of water of the streams within its domain, undoubtedly belongs in each state, and possibly to a territory as well, but that to this power there are two limitations: First, that in the absence of specific authority from Congress, a state cannot by its legislation, destroy the right of the United States, as the owner of lands bordering on a stream, to the continued flow of its water, so far, at least, as may be necessary for the beneficial uses of the government property; and, Second, that it is limited by the superior power of the general government to secure the uninterrupted navigation of all navigable streams constituting navigable waters of the United States. U. S. v. Rio Grande D. & I. Co., 174 U. S. 690 (1898).

SUMMARY.

Two systems of irrigation laws have been perfected or de-veloped by the arid states and territories:

One is consistent with and does not abrogate the common law doctrine of riparian rights. To meet the necessities of irri-gation the states and territories (California, Montana, Oregon and Washington) adopting this system, modified the common law by allowing a more liberal use of the water for that purpose than is allowed in England and in the humid states of the United States. The doctrine of appropriation, in so far as it prevails in the states and territories folowing this system, applies only to waters upon the public lands—state or federal— and therefore does not affect the rights of the private riparian. The riparian proprietor enjoys substantially all his common law rights in these states and territories

The other system is founded upon the doctrine of prior appropriation which is clearly inconsistent with and abrogates ·the common law doctrine of riparian rights. In Colorado, Idaho and Wyoming constitutional provisions declare prior appropriation to be the paramount law. In Arizona, Nevada, New Mexico and Utah this result is accomplished by statute. In all the states and territories adopting this system it is held that no riparian rights had vested or were recognized within their respective jurisdictions prior to the taking effect of such statutes and constitutional provisions, and, therefore, that all riparian lands subsequently acquired were acquired subject to the rule of property therein contained. These states and territories adopted the common law rule in so far as applicable to their conditions, etc., but all hold that because of the Spanish-Mexican law which was in force when the first settlements were made in the west, and because of necessity and custom, this adoption of the common law did not include the inapplicable doctrine of riparian rights. The United States supreme court sanctions this holding.

It will be noticed that the extreme doctrine of appropriation has been adopted by the wholly arid states and territories, and that the common law doctrine of riparian rights, in a slightly modified form, has been adopted in these states which are only in part arid. In two of the subhumid states, North Dakota and Nebraska, laws authorizing appropriation and declaring the waters of natural streams to be the property of the state, have been declared unconstitutional as depriving the riparian owner of his property without due process of law. (See also McGhee I. D. Co. v. Hudson, 25 Tex. 591 (1860) and Barrett v. Metcalf, 12 Tex. Civ. App. 247 (1896).

The states and territories which have repudiated the doctrine of riparian rights, evaded the application of the provision of the federal constitution relative to the deprivation of private property without due process of law, by holding that riparian rights never existed within their respective jurisdiction.

"EXHIBIT 20."

Brief Number 9

SUBMITTED BY GEORGE P. HAMBRECHT

ON

THE LAW GOVERNING THE GREAT PONDS Ol
MASSACHUSETTS.

TO

THE WISCONSIN LEGISLATIVE COMMITTEE

ON

WATER POWERS, FORESTRY AND DRAINAGE

(Authorities compiled by M. C. Riley)

THE LAW GOVERNING THE GREAT PONDS OF MASSACHUSETTS.

"It is a settled rule of law in this state (Maine) and Massachusetts that all great ponds,—that is, ponds containing more than ten acres,—are owned by the state. This is a rule of law peculiar to this state and Massachusetts. It is said to have been derived from the Colonial Ordinance of 1641-7." Auburn v. Union Water Co., 90 Me. 576, 584.

The Colony Ordinance of 1641-1647 provides that "every inhabitant who is an householder shall have free fishing and fowling in any great ponds, bays, coves and rivers so far as the sea ebbs and flows within the precincts of the town where they dwell, unless the freemen of the same town or the General Court have otherwise appropriated them. Provided, that no town shall appropriate to any particular person or persons, any great pond, containing more than ten acres of land, and that no man shall come upon another's propriety without their leave, otherwise than as hereafter expressed. The which clearly to determine, it is declared that in all creeks, coves, and other places about and upon salt water, where the sea ebbs and flows, the proprietor of the land adjoining, shall have propriety to the low water mark, where the sea doth not ebb above a hundred rods, and not more wheresoever it ebbs further, provided, that such proprietor shall not by this liberty have power to stop or hinder the passage of boats or other vessels in or through any sea, creeks or coves to other men's houses or lands. And for great ponds lying in common, though within the bounds of some town, it shall be free for any man to fish and fowl there, and may pass and repass on foot through any man's propriety for that end, so that trespass not upon any man's corn or meadow." Anc Chart, 148.

By amendment probably adopted in 1647 great ponds are defined to be those covering more than ten acres of land, and it is provided that no town shall appropriate any great

pond to any particular person or persons. Body of liberties—8 Mass. Hist. Soc. Coll., 3rd series, 219.

Construction of the ordinance.

"Although fishing and fowling are the only rights named
in the ordinance, it has always been considered that its .object
was to set apart and devote the great ponds to public use, and
that 'with the growth of the community, and its progress in
the arts, these public reservations, at first set apart with reference to certain special uses only, become capable of many
others which are within the designs and intent of the original
appropriation. The devotion to public use is sufficiently
broad to include them all, as they arise.' West Roxbury v.
Stoddard, 7 Allen 158."· Watuppa Reservoir Co. v. Fall River,
147 Mass. 548, 557.

"Under the ordinance the state owns the great ponds as
public property, held in trust for public use. It has not only
the *jus privalum;* the ownership of the soil, but also, the *jus
publicum,* and the right to control and regulate the public uses
to which ponds shall be applied. The littoral proprietors of
land upon the ponds have no peculiar rights in the soil or in
the waters, unless it be by grant from the legislature. Hittinger v. Eames, 121 Mass. 539, Gage v. Steinkrauss, 131 Mass.
222." Watuppa Reservoir Co. v. Fall River, supra, at p. 557.

The ordinance has been held to be broad enough to justify
the state in granting authority to a certain commission, to
forbid the public navigating the waters of a great pond set
aside as a reservoir for water supply. Defendant denied the
right of the commissioners to keep him off.

Held: "There is no doubt that the control of the great
ponds in the public interest is in the legislature that represents the public. It may regulate and change these
public rights or take them away altogether to serve some
paramount public interest. * * * The legislature having seen fit to devote the water of the lake to a public
use for the benefit of the inhabitants of the metropolitan
water district, it was in its power to deprive the general
public of the right to go upon it with boats or otherwise,
on the ground that a safe and advantageous use of the
water for drinking, and for other domestic purposes would

be best promoted by terminating this former public right
and putting the property in the control of the water
board." Sprague v. Minon, 195 Mass. 581, 583.

The state under this ordinance could even lease one of those
great ponds to an individual and give the individual the exclusive right of fishery therein. Com. v. Vincent, 108 Mass.
441.

The court in the last cited case, at p. 459 said:

"The defendant contends that the Tisbury great pond
is within the ebb and flow of the tide, (in other words
that it is navigable) and therefore not within the purview of the statute. It is true that most of the great
ponds which have heretofore been the subject of judicial
decision have been above the flow and ebb of the tide.
Cummings v. Barret, 10 Cush. 186. West Roxbury v. Stoddard, 7 Allen 158. Berry v. Raddin, 11 Allen 577. And
if this pond had been accessible in vessels or boats from
the sea, there would be great force in the objection that
the legislature could not have intended by this statute
to put it so far under the control of the commissioners
as inland fisheries as to authorize them to lease it. * * *
And it appears by the facts stated in the report that this
pond is not connected with the sea except by a narrow
channel, partly natural and partly artificial, not suited
to any other use than the passage of fish, not always sufficient for that purpose without being artificially cleaned,
and not a navigable stream within the definition of the
statute itself. The court is of opinion that such a pond
is a great pond, within the meaning of the statute, of
which, as it is twenty acres in extent, the commissioners
may make a lease."

To the same effect see Com. v. Tiffany, 119 Mass. 300.

The waters of great ponds being by virtue of the ordinance
public waters may be devoted to any legitimate public use.
In the case of Watuppa Reservoir Co. v. Fall River, 147 Mass.
548, the city of Fall River was authorized by the legislature
to draw daily one million five hundred thousand gallons of
water from the North Watuppa pond (a great pond) and to
"apply the water taken under this act to all domestic uses,

the extinguishment of fires, and to the public use of the city.''
Plaintiffs are the owners of manufacturing establishments on
the only outlet of the pond and are owners also of the bed and
land on either side of the stream; were incorporated for the
purpose of constructing a reservoir in the pond; had at great
expense acquired flowage rights all around the pond, built a
dam, raised the water of the pond and were maintaining their
reservoir. The draw off by the city caused actual injury to
plaintiffs who contended that the statute authorizing such
withdrawal of the water without compensation to plaintiffs
was unconstitutional.

Held: ''These are all public purposes. The legislature, acting on the conviction that an abundant supply
of pure water to the people is of paramount importance,
has deemed it to be a wise policy to appropriate the waters
of this pond to those public uses without making compensation to those who, owning land on the natural stream
flowing from it, have been accustomed to use the water,
for power as it flows through the stream. Such owners
have no vested rights in the waters of the pond, and a
majority of the court is of the opinion that the commonwealth may thus appropriate the waters by its direct
action, or may authorize a city or town to do so, without
being legally liable to pay any damages to the littoral
owners on the pond or on the stream.''

After the decision was given in the foregoing case, certain
additional facts were incorporated in the agreed statement of
facts and the case came again before the court in 154 Mass.
305. It then appeared that the original grantors of whom the
plaintiff was the successor in title had acquired by deed a
title to the land on both sides of the outlet, and the whole of
South Watuppa Pond, and a large part of but less than half
of North Watuppa Pond, and that the original grant was not
to a town but a sale of land to private individuals for a substantial sum of money, and antedated the application to the
pond in question of the ordinance of 1647. Hence the court
held that the pond having been appropriated to private rights
before the ordinance went into effect, those rights remained
unaffected afterward, and that the city of Fall River could be
enjoined from drawing off the water.

29

Farther as to the construction of the ordinance and as to the power and authority of the state over great ponds, the court in Attorney General v. Herrick, 190 Mass. 307 at 309 says:

"The law of Massachusetts * * * has treated great ponds as of a character nearly resembling tide waters * * * the title in which and the lands under them was not the subject of private property, unless by special grant from the legislature." Paine v. Woods, 108 Mass. 160, 169. "Great ponds are public property, the use of which for taking water or ice, as well as for fishing, fowling, bathing, boating or skating, may be regulated or granted by the Legislature at its discretion * * *. The pond and the water therein belonged not to the petitioners, but to the public." Fay v. Salem & Danvers Aqueduct, 111 Mass. 27. 28. "By the law of Massachusetts, great ponds, not appropriated before the Colony Ordinance of 1647 to private persons, are public property, the right of reasonably using and enjoying which * * * is common to all." Hittinger v. Eames, 121 Mass. 539, 546. "No question is made, that, under the laws of this Commonwealth, Spy Pond is a great pond." It is therefore public property," etc. Gage v. Steinkrauss, 131 Mass. 222. "The great ponds of the Commonwealth belong to the public, and, like the tide waters and navigable streams, are under the control and care of the Commonwealth." Attorney General v. Jamica Pond Aqueduct, 133 Mass. 361, 364. "Under the ordinance, the State owns the great ponds as public property, held in trust for public uses." Watuppa Reservoir Co. v. Fall River, 147 Mass. 548, 557. "They (the colonists) reserved to the Colony the property in the ponds themselves, the better to regulate these and other kindred public rights for the common good." "The ordinance secures to the Commonwealth, in great ponds, the same kind of ownership in the water than an individual purchaser of the entire area of a small pond would get by a perfect deed, or by an original grant from the government without restrictions." Minority opinion in the last case, pages 564, 566. "The Commonwealth was the owner of the great pond before the taking." Proprietors of Mills v. Commonwealth, 164 Mass. 227, 229,

Basis for State Control and Ownership of Great Ponds.

The great ponds of Massachusetts are not subjected to public control and are not owned by the state because of their navigable qualities, as is the case at common law and in about all the states of the United States. Massachusetts follows the English test of navigable waters, namely, the tide, and only tidal waters are public in that state. Therefore the colonial assembly when it passed the ordinance of 1641-7 were not legislating with reference to navigable waters.

"The term 'navigable waters,' as commonly used in the law, has three distinct meanings: 1st, as synonymous with 'tide waters,' being waters, whether salt or fresh, wherever the ebb and flow of the tide from the sea is felt; or 2nd, as limited to tide waters which are capable of being navigated for some useful purpose: or, 3d (which has not prevailed in this Commonwealth), as including all waters, whether within or beyond the ebb and flow of the tide, which can be used for navigation. Commonwealth v. Chapin, 5 Pick. 199. Rowe v. Granite Bridge Co., 21 Pick. 344. Murdock v. Stickney, 8 Cush. 113, 115. Attorney General v. Woods, ante, 436. Waters v. Lilley, 4 Pick. 145, 147. Genesse Chief v. Fitzhugh, 12 How. 443. The Daniel Ball, 10 Wallace, 557." Com. v. Vincent, 108 Mass. 441, 447.

The great ponds not being navigable, the soil underneath them and the ponds themselves, would, if the English law were followed, except in case of inland seas, be private property.

Phear, Right of Water, p. 1;
Woolrych. p. 121;
Bristowe v. Cormican, 2 App. C. 641.

It was to avoid private ownership of great ponds that the ordinance was passed. The ordinance no where refers to the right of navigation in great ponds. The ordinance simply retained to the colony and future state a part of its domain— the state owns the great ponds for all public purposes.

Affect of ordinance upon vested property rights.

The ordinance did not extinguish property rights acquired in those ponds, their outlets and inlets, before its passage.

Watuppa Reservoir Co. v. Fall River, 154 Mass. 305.

The ordinance affected only those who acquired property on
those great ponds after its going into effect—about 1641.   At
that time the colony owned about all the land within its boundaries.   All who subsequently purchased land abutting on
great ponds took the same subject to this law or ordinance.

> Cummings v. Barrett, 10 Cush. 186;
> West Roxbury v. Stoddar, 7 Allen, 158;
> Paine v. Wood, 108 Mass. 160, 169, 173;
> Com. v. Vincent, 108 Mass. 441, 446;
> Fay v. Salem v. Danvers Aq., 111 Mass. 27.

A purchase of land abutting a great pond takes the land with
only such rights in the waters as the state sees fit to allow him.

*Riparian rights and rights of the public in great ponds are dif-
ferent from common law riparian rights and the rights of
the public in tide waters.*

Riparian and public rights in great ponds in Massachusetts
are not the same as riparian and public rights on ordinary navigable streams—whether navigable according to the English test
or navigable in fact.

The Massachusetts court has held that the common law rules
as to riparian rights and as to the character of water is not the
same in great ponds as in tidal (navigable) waters.

> Paine v. Wood, 108 Mass. 161 at 169.

"But the law of Massachusetts from a period reaching back
almost to the first settlement of the colony, has treated great
ponds as of *a character nearly resembling tide waters,* the enjoyment of which for fishing and fowling and other uses was
common to all, and the title in which and the lands under them
was not the subject of private property, unless by special grant
from the legislature."   Citing

> Body of Liberties of 1641, Art. 16;
> Ord. 1647;
> Anc. Charter, 148, 149;
> West Roxbury v. Stoddard, 7 Allen, 158;
> Com. v. Vincent, 108 Mass. 441.

The court, in enjoining the city of Fall River from with-
drawing water from a great pond to the injury of riparian

owners who had acquired their property—riparian rights prior
to the ordinance taking effect as to that certain pond, held that
at common law the riparian owners had certain property—
riparian rights that could not be destroyed in that way.
Watuppa Reservoir Co. v. Fall River, 154 Mass. 305.

The court in this same case in 147 Mass. 548 held that because
of the ordinance the riparian owner had no rights to destroy.

At common law and in about all of the states, especially in
Wisconsin, Fall Mfg. Co. v. Oconto, etc., Co., 87 Wis. 134;
Black R. Falls Imp. Co. v. La Crosse, etc., Co., 54 Wis. 659;
Cohn v. Wausau Boom Co., 47 Wis., 314, the right of navigation in navigable waters is paramount to all other rights.   In
Massachusetts, and contrary to the common and general state
law, this right of navigation is subservient to the right to authorize a city to use a great pond as a reservoir for a water supply. Sprague v. Minon, 195 Mass. 581.

Farther to the effect that riparian rights in Massachusetts,
because of the ordinance of 1641—7, are different than at common law, and in other states, the court in Watuppa Reservoir
Co. v. City of Fall River, 147 Mass. 548, 557 and 559, said:

"In view of the rights and powers of the state in and
over the great ponds, it seems clear that the rights of proprietors owning land either on the pond or on any stream
flowing from it *cannot be decided by the rules of the common law applicable to ordinary streams. They must be determined with reference to the ordinance and the rules of
property established by it, and we are of opinion that they
must be regarded as subordinate and subject to the paramount rights of the public declared by the ordinance. All
who take and hold property liable to be affected by this
rule of property take and hold under and in subordination
to it. Each grant carries with it an implied reservation.
of these paramount rights,* unless the terms of the grant
exclude such reservational so that the grant from the state
of land upon a stream flowing from a great pond did not
convey an unqualified fee with the right to enjoy the usual
and natural flow of the stream, but a qualified right, subject to the superior right of the state to use the pond and

its waters for other public uses, if the exigencies of the
public for whom it holds the pond in trust demand it."

At p. 559—

*"As this case depends upon the effect of the Colony Or-
dinance, the decisions in England cannot be of assistance
to us. They depend upon the common law, which as we
have said, is changed by the ordinance.* This may be said
of the decisions in the other states of this country, most
of which are governed by the rules of the common law.
* * * "

*The basis for the Massachusetts holdings is peculiar to Massa-
chusetts and does not exist except in that state, Maine and
the state of Washington where constitutional provision has
the same effect as the ordinance of 1641–7.*

The riparian and public rights on navigable waters at common law and in other states are broader than those rights on
great ponds in Massachusetts. Any law passed by a state legislature at this time, or even any amendment to a state constitution, attempting to restrict the riparian right as the Massachusetts courts have held the right restricted by the ordinance of
1641–7, would be in violation of property rights and would be
unconstitutional. A state law or constitutional amendment to
the same effect as the ordinance of 1641–7, in so far as it will
not affect vested rights and will only affect rights that come
into existence in the future, as is the effect of the ordinance of
1641–7, would be constitutional.

"EXHIBIT 21."

BRIEF NUMBER 10.

SUBMITTED BY GEORGE P. HAMBRECHT

ON

TO WHAT EXTENT HAS CONGRESS OR THE STAT
LEGISLATURE POWER TO AUTHORIZE TH
INTERFERENCE WITH OR OBSTRUCTION O
NAVIGATION IN NAVIGABLE STREAMS?

TO

THE WISCONSIN LEGISLATIVE COMMITTEE

ON

WATER POWERS, FORESTRY AND DRAINAGE.

(Authorities compiled by M. C. Riley.)

HAS CONGRESS OR THE STATE LEGISATURE POWER
TO AUTHORIZE THE ERECTION AND MAINTE-
NANCE OF ANY BRIDGE, DAM OR OTHER STRUC-
TURE IN, OVER OR ACROSS ANY NAVIGABLE
WATERS OF THIS STATE SO AS TO TOTALLY OB-
STRUCT THE NAVIGATION OF THE SAME?

COMMON LAW· POWERS OF THE SOVEREIGN OVER NAVIGABLE
WATERS.

In England the crown, although vested, as the representative
of the public, with the right of property in all tidal—navigable
waters, cannot authorize obstructions to be placed in such
waters.

> Hale de jure maris, p. 22;
> Hargrave, Law Tracts, p. 36;
> Peo. v. N. Y. etc., Co., 68 N. Y. 71, 76;
> Williams v. Wilcox, 8 A. & E. 314.

Although "the right of property in the sea, etc., is, prima
facie, vested in the King as the representative of the public,
and that form him all liberties in contemplation of law are
primarily derived, yet it cannot be construed that the King
has legal tenure in the rights of fishing and navigation other
than belong to him in the character of protector of public and
common rights.   And hence, it is that the King has no authority either to grant the exclusive liberty of fishing in any arm
of the sea, or to do anything which will obstruct its navigation."

> Angell Tide Waters, 33;
> Warren v. Matthews, 6 Mod. 73;
> Atty. Gen'l v. Parmeter, 10 Price 378.

The public right in such waters can only be abridged by act
of Parliament, by writ *ad quod damnum*, followed by an inqui-

sition, or by natural causes—such as the recess of the sea, or the accumulation of mud.

> Rex v. Montague, 4 B. & C. 598;
> Wiliams v. Wilcox, 8 A. & E. 314;
> Hargraves, Law Tracts, p. 36;
> Angell on Tide Waters, p. 33;
> Flanagan v. City of Philadelphia, 42 Pa. St. 219, 232;
> Woolr. on Ways, 60;
> Abraham v. Ry. Co., 16 Q. B. Rep. 586.

Power of the states.

When the revolution took place, the people of each state, became themselves sovereign, and, in that character, hold the absolute right to all the navigable waters and the soil under them for their own common use.

> Martin et al. v. Waddell, 16 Pet. 410;
> Pollard's Lesee v. Hagan, 3 Howd. 230;
> Gibbons v. Ogden, 9 Wheat. 203.

Upon admission to the union, Wisconsin· became vested with the title to all its navigable waters to hold the same in trust for the people.

> McLennan v. Prentice, 85 Wis. 427;
> Priewe v. Wis. etc., Co., 93 Wis. 534;
> Willow River Club v. Wade, 100 Wis. 86 at 106;
> Pewaukee v. Savoy, 103 Wis. 271, 274;
> Illinois Steel Co. v. Bilot, 109 Wis. 418, 425;
> Rossmiller v. State, 114 Wis. 169, 186;
> Barney v. Keokuk, 94 U. S. 324;
> Ill. Cent. Ry. Co. v. Ill., 142 U. S. 387.

Restrictions upon state powers.

(A) The states, by the Federal Constitution (Art. 1 Sec. 8) delegated to Congress the power "to regulate commerce with foreign nations and among the several states * * *."

(B) Art. IX, Sec. 1 Wisconsin State Constitution provides:

"* * * : And the river Mississippi and the navigable waters leading into the Mississippi and St. Lawrence, and the carrying places between the same shall be common highways and forever free, as well to the inhabitants of the state as to the citizens of the United States, without any tax impost or duty therefor." (This same provision is found in the Northwest Ordinance, Art. IV, Ordinance 1787, and in the Wisconsin Enabling Act, Wis. R. S. p. 49).

(C) The state of Wisconsin holds the title to all navigable waters within its borders in trust for the people and it cannot constitutionally impair such trust.

Effect of these restrictions upon state's powers.

(A) The powers of Congress under the commerce clause extend only to navigable waters of the United States.

> The Daniel Ball, 16 Wall. 557;
> Miller v. New York, 109 U. S. 385;
> The Montello, 11 Wall. 411;
> Neaderhouser v. State, 28 Ind. 257.

Such waters as those which form in their ordinary condition by themselves or in connection with others, highways over which commerce is, or may be carried on with other states or foreign nations in the customary modes, are navigable waters of the United States.

> Id.

The mere capacity to permit passengers in a boat of any size, however small, or to float logs is not sufficient to constitute a stream navigable waters of the United States. Therefore the Fox and Wolf rivers above Oshkosh are not navigable waters of the United States.

> Moore v. Home Ins. Co., 30 Wis. 496;
> Same effect, see Leovy v. U. S., 177 U. S. 621;
>> Manigault v. Ward, 123 Fed. 707;
>> Duluth Lbr. Co. v. St. Louis B. & I. Co., 5 McCrary 382.

It follows that there are streams in Wisconsin, navigable according to the Wisconsin interpretation of that term, which empty into navigable waters of the United States and which do not come under the general jurisdiction of the Federal Government. (The Federal Government may however, prohibit the erection and maintenance of any obstruction in any such stream, if such obstruction will hold back the waters thereof to such

in extent as to destroy the navigation of any navigable waters
of the U. S.   U. S. v. Rio Grande Dam & I. Co., 184 U. S. 416).

Until Congress by virtue of its powers under the commerce
clause acts, the power of the state over its navigable waters, even
though the same form a highway for interstate commerce, is
plenary.

Willson v. The Blackbird Creek M. Co., 2 Pet. 245;
Gilman v. Philadelphia, 3 Wall. 713;
Cummings v. Chicago, 188 U. S. 410 at 427.

Justice Barnes of the Wisconsin Supreme Court in In re
Southern Wisconsin Power Co., 122 N. W. 801, having examined
cases bearing upon the powers of Congress and the states over
navigable waters wholly within the limits of a state, but forming part of a highway for interstate commerce, said:

"These decisions establish the following propositions:

(a)   Under the commerce clause of the federal constitution the Congress of the United States has jurisdiction
over all navigable waters therein.

(b)   As to navigable streams entirely within the borders
of a single state, such state has plenary power in the absence
of congressional action, but Congress is not concluded by
anything that the state, or individuals by its authority, may
have done from assuming entire control over such streams,
and abating any erections that may have been made, and
preventing others from being made.

(c)   In the absence of legislation by Congress on the
subject a statute of a state which authorizes the construction
of a dam across a navigable river wholly within such state
is constitutional.

(d)   There must be a direct statute of the United States
in order to bring within the scope of its laws obstructions
and nuisances in a navigable stream wholly within a state."
Page 807.

(B)   "The clause in the constitution, providing that the
navigable waters therein referred to 'shall be common highways
and forever free,' etc., does not refer to physical obstructions of

these waters, but refers to political regulations which would
hamper the freedom of commerce.''

> In re Southern Wis. Power Co., Supra. page 8Q7, citing
> > Williamette I. B. Co., v. Hatch, 125 U. S. 1;
>
> Pound v. Turck, 95 U. S. 459;
>
> Willson v. Blackbird Creek Marsh Co. 2 Pet. 245;
>
> Gilman v. Philadelphia, 3 Wall. 713;
>
> Monongohela Nav. Co. v. U. S., 148 U. S. 312;
>
> Montgomery v. Portland, 190 U. S. 89;
>
> See also Cardwell v. Bridge Co., 113 U. S. 205.
>
> J. S. Keator Lbr. Co. v. St. Clair Boom Co. 72 Wis. 62;
>
> Huse v. Glover 119 U. S. 543 at 547.

The limitations of the Northwest Ordinance upon the territory of Wisconsin ceased to have any operative force after she
become a state of the union. (Even though this were not the
case, that clause of the Ordinance under examination has received the same construction as announced by Justice Barnes
to be placed upon the identical provision found in the Wisconsin Constitution. (See cases cited by Justice Barnes.)

> Pollard's Lessee v. Hagan, 3 How. 212;
>
> Permoli v. First Municipality, 10 How. 589;
>
> Strader v. Graham, 10 How. 82;
>
> Huse v. Glover, 119 U. S. 543.

(C) Our Supreme Court has said that the state upon its
admission to the union became vested with title in all of its
navigable waters to hold the same in trust for the people, ''and
that the state never has and never can constitutionally impair
the trust,'' Rossmiller v. State, 114 Wis. 169, 186 (1902; ''Which
trusteeship is inviolable, the state being powerless to change the
situation by in any way abdicating the trust,'' Pewaukee v
Savoy, 103 Wis. 271. 274 (1898), and that this title vested in
the state ''in trust to hold the same so as to preserve to the
people forever the enjoyment of the waters of such lakes, ponds
and rivers.'' Ill. Steel Co. v. Bilot, 109 Wis. 418, 425 (1901).

Justice Marshall in his syllabus to the Rossmiller Case defines
the power of the state over its navigable waters as follows:

> ''The power of the state over navigable waters within
> its boundaries is limited to the enactment and enforcement

of such reasonable police regulations as may be deemed
necessary to preserve the common right of all to enjoy the
same for navigation by boats or otherwise, and all incidents
of navigable waters, including the taking of ice therefrom
for domestic use or sale."

"The rights of the people in the navigable waters of the
state are the same as those incident to tidal waters at common law. They are beyond the power of the state to interfere with, except by reasonable police regulations, as before
indicated."

Rossmiller v. State, 114 Wis. 169.

There seems to be no case directly in point on this question.
However, the dicta found in several cases lead to the conclusion
that legislative power is limited to the protection and enhancement of the public rights in the navigable waters of the state,
and that it has no authority or power to destroy such rights.
The public right to navigate such waters being paramount to all
other rights therein, and the state being trustee of such right
for the people, the legislature, by authorizing impassible obstructions to be placed in such waters, would be acting beyond
its powers as trustee.

Following are quotations to the effect that it would be beyond
the legislative function to obstruct the passage along any navigable waters, and to the effect that the power of the legislature
over the navigable waters of this state are restricted as are the
powers of the crown over the navigable waters of England.

"In Priewe v. Wis. S. L. & I. Co. 93 Wis. 534, 67 N. W.
918, and again in the same case in 103 Wis. 548, 79 N. W.
780, it was held, in effect, that the state has no such interest in the beds of navigable lakes that it can treat the same
as a subject for bargain and sale or grant the same away to
private owners under the guise of police power or otherwise;
that it is a mere trustee of the title thereto, under a trust
created before the state was formed, to which it was appointed as trustee by its admission into the Union; that
it has no active duty to perform in respect to the matter,
or power over the same, except that of mere regulation to
preserve the common right of all; that its power over the
res is limited by the original purpose of the trust; that it

is, in effect, a mere trustee of an express trust, a trustee
with duties definitely defined. Those principles are too
firmly established to admit, at this late day, of being seriously questioned." Rossmiller v. State, Supra at p. 187.

"This court has repeatedly said that the navigable waters of the state have substantially the incidents of tidal
waters at common law; that the title to the beds of such
waters was reserved for the state by the Ordinance of
1787, and vested in it at the instant it was admitted into the
Union, to preserve the public character of such waters with
all such incidents; and that the state never has and never
can constitutionally impair the trust. McLennan v. Prentice, 85 Wis. 427, 444, 55 N. W. 764; Willow River Club v.
Wade, 100 Wis. 86, 113, 76 N. W. 273; Priewe v. Wis. S.
L. & I. Co. 93 Wis. 534, 550, 67 N. W. 918; Priewe v. Wis.
S. L. & I. Co. 103 Wis. 537, 79 N. W. 780; Pewaukee v.
Savoy, 103 Wis. 271, 274, 79 N. W. 436 Mendota Club v.
Anderson, 101 Wis. 479, 78 N. W. 185; Illinois S. Co. v.
Bilot, 109 Wis. 418, 84 N. W. 855, 85 N. W. 402, Att'y Gen.
ex rel. Askew v. Smith, 109 Wis. 532, 85 N. W. 512. In
McLennan v. Prentice, quoting from the opinion of Mr.
Justice Field in Illinois Cent. R. Co. v. Illinois, 146 U. S.
387, 13 Sup. Ct. 110, the court said:
'The right which the state holds in these lakes is in virtue
of its sovereignty and in trust for public purposes of nav-
igation and fishing. The state has no proprietary interest
in them, and cannot abrogate its trust in relation to them.' "
Id. p. 186.

"The wisdom of the fathers in securing to the whole
people the right to enjoy the navigable waters of the state,
with all their common-law incidents, beyond the possibility
of any rightful prejudicial governmental interference therewith, and the consistent and vigorous defense of such right
by the judiciary, will be more and more appreciated as time
goes on. The right is deemed to be so strongly intrenched
that all assaults upon it must fail."
Id. p. 188.

In Sweeney v. C. M. & St. P. Ry. Co., 60 Wis. at 67, the court said:

"The navigability of the waters of the Wisconsin river, so far as the same are navigable in fact, *is protected not only by the common law of the county*, but by an express constitutional provision. (Sec. 1, Art. IX—The prov. construed in In re So. Wis Power Co. Case and held not to apply to physical obstructions). There can be no contention, therefore that the legislature has the power to entirely obstruct the navigation of said river. That the legislature has the power to authorize the building of bridges across the navigable waters of the Wisconsin, notwithstanding the ordinance, the provisions of our constitution and the common law, must also be admitted. But that power must be subordinate to the rights of navigation, and bridges so authorized must be so constructed and maintained as not to materially or unnecessarily obstruct such navigation."

Continuing, the court at p. 70, said:

"In Blanchard v. W. U. Tel. Co., 60 N. Y., 510, the court of appeal says: 'In furtherance of commerce and travel, slight obstructions, and such as may temporarily interrupt the passage of vessels or occasion a cursory inconvenience, but which do not materially impair navigation, are made lawful and tolerated by reason of the great public good that results from these inconsiderable disturbances of the right of the public to the free and uninterrupted use of navigable streams. Upon this principle the bridging of streams, the building of wharves, and other like acts, are permitted; the necessary obstruction in every case being reduced to its minimum. If there is an unnecessary interference with the navigation, the act becomes unlawful by reason of the excess of the limits within which obstructions are allowed in the interest of the public.' The rule above stated is sanctioned by this court in Barnes v. Racine, 4 Wis. 454, 466."

There are decisions which tend, at least, to hold that the state legislature may authorize obstructions to navigation—that the legislative power over navigable streams, subject to the power delegated to congress to regulate commerce, is as extensive as the power of parliament over the navigable waters of England.

U. S. v. Bedford Bridge, 1 Woodbury & Minot (U. S.) 401;

Flanagan v. City of Philadelphia, 42 Pa. St. 219, 231;

People v. N. Y. & S. I. F. Co., 68 N. Y. at p. 78.

Farnham, in his work on waters and water rights, says:

"The question (as to whether or not the state has the power to authorize obstructions) depends altogether upon the importance of the navigation as compared with the interest that would be promoted by sacrificing it." P. 398.

"The limit of this power is the necessity of the case; and until the injury greatly exceeds the public benefit the obstruction will not be interfered with by the courts." P. 399.

"It is primarily for the legislature, and not for the courts, to determine between the conflicting interests and the necessity of requiring the navigation right to yield, and its discretion will not be interfered with by the courts. except in cases of a plain and gross abuse of discretion." P. 399.

Unless it be shown that the state of Wisconsin holds its navigable waters in trust for all public purposes, instead of for the purpose of navigation, fishing, taking ice and other rights recognized by the common law as belonging to the public in such waters, Farnham's conclusion is antagonistic to the trust theory announced by our Supreme Court. The Wheeling Bridge Case, 13 Howard 518 at 577, repudiates the doctrine enunciated by Farnham that the lawfulness of an obstruction to navigation is to be ascertained by a comparison between the injuries and benefits produced. The case on the authority of King v. Sir John Morris, 1 Barn v. Adol. 441 and King v. George Henry Ward, 4 Ad. & Bl. 384, holds that the injury cannot be balanced against the benefits secured.

Houck, in his treatise "on rivers," pp. 123 to 136, after considering effects of the commerce clause and the ordinance of

1787 upon the relative rights of the United States and the state over navigable waters, concludes:

"1. That the states are the absolute owners of the navigable rivers, their beds and shores. 2. That the states continue to exert all powers over the sovers granted to congress. 3. That the state can authorize obstructions to navigation, although no subordinate body acting under it can exert the same power. 7. That the ordinance of 1787 has no binding force on the states carved out of the Northwest territory." P. 136.

Conclusion 1, to the effect that the states are the absolute owners of the navigable rivers, is out of harmony with the law of Wisconsin, where it is held that the state is merely vested with title thereto to hold in trust for the pepole, and as a result conclusion 3, to the effect that the state may authorize obstructions in such waters, is inapplicable to this state.

The legislature may, however, for certain purposes and under certain conditions, grant authority to erect and maintain dams, bridges and other structures in or over navigable waters.

The legislature has power to authorize the erection and maintenance of dams or other works in and across navigable waters for the purpose of improving the navigation thereof.

Technically such a dam or such works does not act as an obstruction but as an improvement of the navigation of such waters. And this even though such dam or works constitute a barrier to passage at the particular location.

"The dam here permitted to be erected is authorized in aid of navigation, and the power of the Legislature is plenary to empower individuals to construct dams in navigable streams of the state for such purpose. Falls Mfg. Co. v. Oconto River Imp. Co., 87 Wis. 134, and cases cited on page 150 of the opinion, 58 N. W. 257, 261; in re Dancy Drainage District, 129 Wis. 129, 139, 108 N. W. 202 "

In re Southern Wis. Power Co., 122 N. W. (Wis.) 806, at 807.

See also Wis. Riv. Imp. Co. v. Manson, 43 Wis. 255;

Black River F. D. Ass'n v. Ketchum, 54 Wis. 313;

30

Black River Imp. Co. v. LaCrosse B. & T. Co., 54 Wis. 659;

J. T. Keator Lbr. Co. v. St. Croix Boom Corp., 72 Wis. 62.

This power to authorize dams or other works to be placed in navigable waters for the purpose of improving the navigation thereof, is very broad.

'It is next urged that, while the act specifies that its purpose is to improve the navigation of the Wisconsin river above the dam, such dam is in fact an obstruction to navigation, extending as it does from bank to bank, and being 15 feet in height, that its real purpose is to create hydraulic power and that the navigation of the river cannot be obstructed for any such purpose. *It has been held that the Legislature is at least primarily the judge of the necessity for the proposed improvement, and that when it delegates such a power, and the state does not question that the improvement made is in conformity with the power delegated, neither the necessity nor the usefulness of the improvement, nor the manner in which it is made, can be called in question by private parties.*''

In re Southern Wis. Power Co., supra, pp. 807, 808.

Citing: Wis. River Imp. Co. v. Manson, 43 Wis. 255, 265;

Falls Mfg. Co. v. Oconto River Imp. Co., 87 Wis. 134, 151;

Underwood Lbr. Co. v. Pelican B. Co., 76 Wis. 76, 85;

J. S. Keator Lbr Co. v. St. Croix B. Corp, 72 Wis. 62, 81;

Cohn v. Wausau Boom Co., 47 Wis. 314, 326;

Black River Imp. Co. v. La Crosse B. & T. Co., 54 Wis. 659, 686.

The Legislature has power to authorize the erection and maintenance of dams or other works in and across navigable waters for a public purpose other than the improvement of navigation.

To this effect Ryan, C. J., in State v. City of Eau Claire,
40 Wis. 533 at 541, said:

"In the former case, speaking of the power granted to
the city to construct water works, we had occasion to say:
'That is so essentially a public and municipal purpose,
that it is obvious that the city can take any legitimate
power in aid of it. For that purpose, the Legislature could
unquestionably grant, and the city take, power to construct
and maintain a dam, *not obstructing the navigation of a
public river, or violate other rights, public or private.*"

The legislature may grant authority to a riparian proprietor
to erect and maintain a dam or other works in navigable waters,
provided, the same does not materially affect the navigation of
such waters, and, provided, that the erection and maintenance
of such dam or works does not inflict sensible injury upon other
riparian proprietors above or below him. (The legislature, of
course, cannot authorize one riparian proprietor to take the
property of another, by flowing his lands or otherwise, without providing that just compensation be paid therefor, and,
in no case, can the legislature grant such authority unless the
property be taken for a public purpose.)

The Territorial Legislature, 1843, granted to one Stoughton
and another authority to erect and maintain a dam across the
Rock River, on any land they might own in certain sections
named. This grant authorizing the damming of the Rcok River
for the purpose of creating hydraulic power, gave the grantees
power to sell or lease the right to use said power. The act
provided that the dam be equipped with a lock of certain
dimensions, slides and chutes, and with a fishway.

The constitutionality of this act being drawn in question, the
court in Stoughton v. State, 5 Wis. 296, said:

"We have-stated that the legislature had competent authority to authorize the erection of the dam. This appears
to us to be clear beyond dispute, *so far as the public or
state is concerned.* The legislative authority extended to
all 'rightful subjects of legislation;' and we cannot doubt
that it extended so far, as to allow of the erection of the
dam in question. It is a very common exercise of legislative power to authorize such obstructions to be placed

in rivers, the legislature taking care to annex such conditions as it may deem essential, to protect the public from injury. Our state constitution did not repeal any of the acts of the territorial legislature, except such as were repugnant to its provisions; and we see nothing in it which can be regarded as repugnant to the act in question."

See also

Cobb v. Smith, 16 Wis, 662;
Newell v. Smith, 15 Wis. 101.

Section 1596, Wis. R. S., declares streams that have been meandered and returned as navigable by the United States surveyors to be navigable *"to the extent that no dam, bridge or other obstruction shall be made in or over the same without permission of the legislature."*

This section applies only to the streams that have been meandered and returned as navigable by the United States Surveyors, and makes the right to erect an obstruction in navigable waters contingent upon gaining legislative permission therefor.

Floatable Streams. (Navigable according to Wis. definition).

Our supreme court has held that a riparian proprietor has the right, without legislative permission, to erect a dam in and across a floatable stream not thereby materially affecting the beneficial use of such stream. A. C. Conn v. The Little Suamice Lbr. Co., 74 Wis. 652 and Chornley v. The Shawano W. P. & R. I. Co., 109 Wis. 563. In this latter case the court at p. 596 said:

"While it has been the policy of this state to hold all streames capable of floating logs and timber to be navigable, yet in streams like this (Wolf near Shawano) that are not meandered, the land owner and the public have certain reciprocal rights, which may be enjoyed without the obstruction of the other. This is fully set forth in the opinion of this court in the case of A. C. Conn. v. Little Suamico L. Mfg. Co., 74 Wis. 652, which holds distinctly that a dam may be built and maintained by a riparian owner without legislative permission, in a stream navigable only for the floating of logs and timber, and is not unlawful if it does not materialy affect or abridge the beneficial use of the stream."

Powers of Congress to Obstruct.

Congress has absolute power and control over all the navigable waters of the United States in the interest of commerce, and the right to declare what may or may not, constitute obstruction thereof. U. S. v. North Bloomfield G. M. Co., 81 Fed. 243.

> "The authority is given to congress for the purpose of aiding and not destroying navigation and commerce, so that although authority over the stream is absolute in execution of the trust imposed upon it, whatever obstruction it authorizes must be for the purpose of improving the navigation of the stream, or of facilitating commerce." Farnham, Waters and Water Rights, p. 60.

Citing Depew v. Wabash and E. Canal, 5 Ind. 8.

SUMMARY.

1. Wisconsin holds the title to the navigable waters within its boundaries in trust for the people. The people have all the rights in navigable waters of Wisconsin that are incident to such waters at common-law—among others, and paramount to all, is the public right of navigation. To protect and enhance this right is the main object of the trusteeship. Therefore the state, through the legislature, has no power to authorize impassable obstructions to be placed in navigable waters so as to destroy this paramount public use thereof.

2. However, the legislature may authorize dams and other works to be erected and maintained in such waters for the improvement of the navigation thereof, and the legislative power in granting such authority is very broad.

3. The legislature may grant authority to erect and maintain dams or other works in, over or across navigable waters *not materially affecting the navigation thereof.* If the grant be for public purpose, the right of eminent domain may also be given. If the grant be to a riparian proprietor and for a private purpose, the grantee cannot be given power to inflict insensible injury upon any other riparian proprietor above or below him.

4. In floatable, non-meandered streams the riparian proprietor, without legislative permission, may erect and maintain

dams or other works in, over or across the same not materially affecting the beneficial use thereof.

Congress, by the commerce clause is delegated power to regulate interstate commerce and for such purpose is given absolute authority over interstate navigable waters. The powers of congress extend to the improvement and not destruction of navigation.

P. S. OWEN,

"EXHIBIT 22."

BRIEF NUMBER 12

SUBMITTED BY GEORGE P. HAMBRECHT

ON

HAS THE LEGISLATURE POWER TO DESTROY THE
NAVIGATION OF A NAVIGABLE STREAM IN THE
INTEREST OF DRAINAGE OF SUBMERGED OR
SWAMP LANDS.

TO

THE WISCONSIN LEGISLATIVE COMMITTEE

ON

WATER POWERS, FORESTRY AND DRAINAGE.

———————

(Authorities compiled by M. C. Riley.)

HAS THE LEGISLATURE POWER TO DESTROY THE NAVIGATION OF A NAVIGABLE STREAM IN THE INTEREST OF DRAINAGE OF SUBMERGED OR SWAMP LANDS?

The above question has never been ideally presented to our supreme court for decision. However, dicta is found in cases decided within the past three or four years indicating what the Wisconsin holding will be should the question be so presented. These cases interpret the Wisconsin drainage laws, and afford a discussion of the power of the legislature over the navigable waters of the state.

In the case of In re Dancy Drainage District, 129 Wis. 129, 138 (1906), Cassoday C. J., stated the question before the court as follows:

"The important question presented is whether the trial court was justified in holding that the commissioners, by the 'drainage system' so reported, had no power to 'destroy and wipe out of existence the body of water shown and designated on the map as Rice Lake,' nor to 'impair the navigability of the Little Eau Pleine river,' and that it was 'beyond the power of the court to grant to' such commissioners any such power."

After holding that the power to destroy any navigable lake or river is not expressly conferred upon the commissioners by the drainage laws, and that they therefor had no such power notwithstanding Sec. 1379—31 which provides that the drainage laws shall be liberally construed to promote the public health and welfare by reclaiming wet and overflowed lands, etc., Justice Cassoday said:

"It is undisputed that Rice Lake is a meandered body of water and navigable in fact, and is also undisputed that the Little Eau Pleine river is a navigable stream, which has been used for driving and rafting logs for many years,

and that the lake is an enlargement of the river, and that
in and upon both the river and the lake fish and game
abound.   This court has repeatedly held that the title to
the bed of a meandered lake navigable in fact 'is in the
state in trust for legitimate public uses, such as fishing,
navigation and the like'; and that 'the state cannot convey it away for private uses, nor can it abdicate the trust.·
Atty. Gen'l ex rel. Askew v. Smith, 109 Wis. 432, 539,
and cases there cited.''

In the Horicon Drainage District Case, 136 Wis. 227 (1908),
the proposed scheme of drainage embraced within the limits
ordered contemplated the destruction of Hustisford dam built
across Rock river by authority of law more than forty years
ago. and which has since maintained a pond or enlargement or
the river.   This pond at some seasons of the year is capable of
floating small craft.   By the proposed scheme it would be necessary to destroy the pond and decrease the volume of water
in the Rock river and otherwise materially alter the physical
condition of the river, and impair if not destroy many of the
common law incidents of navigation.   Op. p. 235.   The court,
by Justice Kerwin, in the course of its opinion, said:

"Having determined that Rock river is navigable, the
next question is, does the drainage law authorize its impairment.   The power conferred upon drainage commissioners under sec. 1379—22, stats.   (1898), was the same
as the power given them under sec. 18, Ch. 419, and Laws
of 1905.   And it will be seen that no authority is conferred
upon them to appropriate or impair navigable waters.   If
the legislature has the power in any case to authorize the
commissicners to appropriate or impair navigable waters,
the authority must be conferred in the most plain and un-
ambiguous terms.'' p. 234.

"The policy of the legislature of this state has been to
preserve navigable waters of the state from impairment,
and this court has held it the duty of the legislature to
do so.   In re Horicon D. Dist. 129 Wis. 42, 108 N. W.
198, and cases cited.'' p. 235.

"The policy of this court as shown by a long line of
decisions has been to scrupulously protect the navigable

waters of the state from impairment. Ne—pee—Nauk Club v. Wilson, 96 Wis. 270, * ' * *; Willow river Club v. Wade, 100 Wis. 86, * * *; Mendota Club v. Anderson, 101 Wis. 479, * * * ; Pewaukee v. Savoy, 103 Wis. 271, * * * ; Rossmiller v. State, 114 Wis. 169, * * * ." P. 334.

Justices Marshall and Siebecker concurring in the above opinion said:

"This case goes upon the ground that the injurious interference with navigable waters is, at least, of such doubtful policy that nothing short of unmistakable language in a legislative enactment authorizing the same should be held to have been so intended, and applying that to the law in question no such intention is expressed. There is no need of going further, but it is proper to say in passing that whether the legislature could authorize the destruction of a navigable lake is so very doubtful that it were better not to say anything liable to be construed as suggesting the existence of such power. Generally speaking, a trustee can never rightfully destroy the subject of the trust even by the consent of the *cestui que trust* if thereby the dominant purpose of the donor would be defeated. Why the great trust under which the public waters of the state are held is not governed by that rule is difficult to perceive.

The most significant reason in my judgment why the drainage scheme in question is not legitimate is that it contemplates the destruction of a navigable lake."

Justices Bashford and Timlin, dissenting, were of the opinion that neither Rock river at the place in question nor the mill pond is navigable in fact, and that mere legal or artificial navigability is not sufficient to defeat the beneficient purposes of the drainage statutes.

In Johnson v. Eimerman, 140 Wis. 327 (1909), the drainage system planned necessitated the destruction of a pond created by an enlargement of Waterloo Creek (non-navigable). The mill-dam creating the pond was built some sixty years ago and had been maintained ever since. The pond is about a mile and a half long and varies in width from a few feet at the upper end to 200 or 300 feet at the lower end,—covering in all about 150 acres, and has a depth of eight feet at the dam, which gradually lessens until it does not exceed two or three feet at the upper end. The evidence showed that the pond was navigated by rowboats; that it was used as a reserve for fire protection for the village of Marshall; that it furnished the supply of ice for said village; that it was resorted to for fishing, and that farmers in its immediate vicinity might transport their grist to the mill over the same if they saw fit (although no evidence was offered to show that they had done so or were ever likely to do so). The court, per Justice Barnes, held :

> "Slight as is the showing of navigability in this case, still we think it is sufficient to sustain the finding of the trial court that this pond is in fact navigable and is water in which the public has acquired rights, * * * . It is true that the body of water found to be navigable in this case is small, but if it is navigable in fact and constitutes a public highway the rights of the public therein are as sacred and as much entitled to protection as they would be in a more pretentious watercourse."

Then, after holding that the case is ruled by the Horicon D. Dist. Case, supra, the court continued:

> "In the Horicon Drainage Case the court does not decide that the legislature may not authorize the destruction of bodies of water navigable in fact, but it does decide that the act we are considering did not authorize any such destruction, and it is at least strongly intimated in some of the decided cases that such an act could not be upheld. In re Dancy D. Dist. supra; Priewe v. Wis. S. L. & I. Co., 93 Wis. 534, * * * ."

The above cases adhere to the trust doctrine.

The above cases reiterate the trust doctrine adopted and unqualifiedly adhered to by the Wisconsin supreme court. The court—

> · "has repeatedly said that the navigable waters of the

state have substantially the incidents of tidal waters at
common law; that the title to the beds of such waters was
reserved for the state by the ordinance of 1787 and vested
in it the instant it was admitted into the Union to preserve
the public character of such waters with all such incidents;
and that the state never has and never can constitutionally impair the trust." Rossmiller v. State, 114 Wis. 169,
189 (1902).

"The title to the beds of all lakes and ponds and of
rivers navigable in fact as well up to the line of ordinary
high-water mark within the boundaries of the state became vested in it at the instant of its admission into the
Union, in trust to hold the same so as to preserve to the
people forever the enjoyment of the waters of such lakes,
ponds, and rivers to the same extent that the public are entitled to enjoy tidal waters at common law."
Ill. Steel Co. v. Bilot, 109 Wis. 418, 425 (1901)

"Upon the admission of the state into the Union the
title to such lands (under navigable waters) by operation
of law, vested in it in trust to preserve to the people of the
state forever the common rights of fishing and navigation,
and such other rights as are incident to public waters at
common law, which trusteeship is inviolable, the state being
powerless to change the situation by any way abdicating its
trust." Pewaukee v. Savoy, 103 Wis. 271, 274 (1889).

*Navigable rivers and lakes, large and small, are alike affected
by the trust doctrine.*

Navigable rivers are as much affected by this trust doctrine
as are navigable lakes. This is made plain by the protection
afforded the Rock and Little Eau Pleine rivers in the Horicon
and Dancy D. Dist. cases, supra. The Johnson v. Eimerman
case, supra, makes plain that small bodies of water, if navigable in fact, are as much affected by this trust doctrine as are
more "pretentious" watercourses.

SUMMARY.

The three cases,—In re Dancy D. Dist.; Horicon D. Dist.; and Johnson v. Eimerman, supra,—in connection with the other Wisconsin cases enunciating, iterating and reiterating the trust doctrine over navigable waters in this state, are opposed to any contention to the effect that the legislature has power to destroy the navigation of a navigable stream or lake in the interest of drainage of submerged or swamp lands.

See also Committee Brief—"Has Congress or the state legislature power to authorize the erection and maintenance of any bridge, dam or other structure in, over or across any navigable water of this state so as to totally obstruct the navigation thereof?" "Exhibit 21" of this report.

"EXHIBIT 23."

Brief Number 13

SUBMITTED BY GEORGE P. HAMBRECHT

ON

LEGISLATIVE CONTROL OVER PRIVATE AND QUASI-
PUBLIC CORPORATIONS

TO

THE WISCONSIN LEGISLATIVE COMMITTEE

ON

WATER POWERS, FORESTRY AND DRAINAGE.

———

(Authorities compiled by M. C. Riley.)

LEGISLATIVE CONTROL OVER PRIVATE CORPORA-
TIONS.

In attempting to ascertain the extent of the legislative control over private corporations, much that is elementary and of
common learning must be gone over. The different sources of
legislative power over these artificial bodies, both before and
after their creation, have been worked out by the courts in innumerable cases. It is the purpose of this brief, to ascertain
these sources of legislative power found to exist by the courts
as well as the powers reserved by express law, and to point out
as nearly as possible the nature, extent and application of the
power of control emanating and developed from such sources
and such law. The application of these powers of control to
the two general classes of private corporations and to corporations that are to be formed or created and to those already in
existence will be considered.

Two classes of corporations are included in the term private
corporations,—those formed or organized for the purpose of
conducting businesses of a purely private nature, and these
formed or organized for the purpose of conducting businesses
affected with a public interest and known as quasi-public corporations. The creation of either class—of any corporation—
is a legislative function.

> State v. Bradford, 32 Vt. 50, 52 (1859);
> Stowe v. Flagge, 72 Ill. 297, 401 (1874).

INITIAL CONTROL—CREATION OF PRIVATE CORPORATIONS.

The practice was formerly for the Wisconsin legislature, in
its discretion, to grant special charters of incorporation to any
association applying therefor, but since 1871 this legislative
function can be exercised by enactment of general law only,
Wis. Con., Sec. 1, Art. XI and Sec. 31, Art. IV. Pursuant to
these provisions the legislature of this state enacted general

statutes under which a number of persons, by complying with certain conditions, may become a corporation for certain specified purposes.

The legislature is the sole judge as to whether or not corporations shall be created. This being so it follows that the legislature has power to dictate the terms and conditions under which corporations may be formed.

"The granting of the rights and privileges which constitute the franchises of a corporation being a matter resting entirely within the control of the legislature, to be exercised in its good pleasure, it may be accompanied with any such conditions as the legislature may deem most suitable to the public interests and policy."

Horn Silver Mining Co. v. New York, 143 U. S. 305 (1891).

"It is fundamental that a corporation can only be created and exist by sanction of the legislature." (or of Congress).

Schuetzen Bund v. Agitations Verein, 44 Minn. 313 (1880) ;

Indiana Bond Co. v. Ogle, 22 Ind. App. 593 (1899) ;

Hoadley v. Essex Co., 105 Mass. 519 (1870) ;

Franklin Bridge Co. v. Wood, 14 Ga. 80 (1853) ;

Stowe v. Flagg, 72 Ill. 397 (1874).

"A corporation is the creature of the law, and none of its powers are original. They are precisely what the incorporating act has made them, and can only be exercised in the manner which the act authorizes. In other words, the state prescribes the purposes of the corporation and the means of executing those purposes. The purposes and means are in the state's control."

Waters Pierce Co. v. Texas, 177 U. S. 28, 43 (1899).

A corporation "being the mere creature of law, it possesses only those properties which the charter of its creation confers upon it, either expressly, or as an incident to its very existence."

Dartmouth Coll. v. Woodward, 4 Wheat. 518 (1819) ;

31

Waters Pierce Co. v. Texas, 177 U. S. 28, 43 (1899) ;

Dillard v. Webb, 55 Ala. 468 (1876) ;

Ex parte Conway, 4 Ark. 302 (1842) ;

Utley v. Mining Co., 4 Colo. 369 (1878) ;

Coite v. Savings Soc., 32 Conn. 173 (1864) ;

Deringer v. Deringer, 5 Houst (Del.), 416 (1878) ;

State v. Stormont 24 Kan. 686 (1881) ;

Miller v. Ewer, 27 Me. 509 (1847) ;

Swan v. Williams, 2 Mich. 427 (1852) ;

Horback v. Tyrell, 48 Neb. 514 (1896) ;

Curtis v. Leavitt, 15 N. Y. 9 (1857) ;

McCandless v. Richmond, etc., R. Co., 38 So. Car. 103 (1892) ;

Waterbury v. Laredo, 60 Tex. 519 (1883) ;

Richards v. Clarksburg, 30 W. Va. 491 (1887) ;

Green's Brices Ultra Vires, p. 23.

The Wisconsin legislature, then, may by general law prescribe the purposes for which corporations may be formed ; the
method of procedure preliminary to incorporation; whether or
not as well as the purpose or purposes for which stock and
bonds may be issued;* the conditions as to denomination of
shares of stock and their transferability; that stock and bonds
shall be issued under the supervision of a commission only ; the
amount of stock that shall be subscribed and paid in as a condition precedent to the doing of business by the corporation;
that the stock issued shall be sold for cash only, or that the
same may in part be exchanged for property or services, and
that the same shall be sold at not less than par. The legislature may dictate the amount of indebtedness that may be incurred by the corporation; that bonds may be issued in amount
only to a certain proportion of the capital stock actually paid
in, and that the bonds bear only a certain rate of interest. It
may prescribe the purpose or purposes for which additional or

---

* The power to issue stock or bonds will not be implied as an incident to corporate existence, Cooke v. Marshall, 191 Pa. St. 315 (1899) ;
Salem Mill Dam Corp. v. Ropes, 6 Pick. 23 (1827); Farrington v. Tenn
95 U. S 679 (1877); Crandall v. Lincoln, 52 Conn. 73 (1884); State v.
Fire Assn. 23 N. J. L. 195 (1851).

new stock or other securities may be issued;† the price for
which the same shall be sold; that the same shall be sold at
public auction, and that the issue shall be under the supervision of a commission. In short, the legislature may by general
laws dictate that the issue of securities by any corporation to
be formed shall represent actual investment in its property.

In like manner the legislature may fix the personal liability
of the stockholders; prescribe the number and method of election of directors; dictate the scheme of management of the
corporation and the system of accounting to be adopted; require that the business and all transactions of the corporation
be given the utmost publicity, and may dictate any other terms
or conditions it may see fit. The general incorporation laws of
Wisconsin, in so far as corporations to be formed are concerned,
may be amended or reconstructed so as to embrace any or all
of the foregoing suggestions. The corporators must accept all
terms and conditions provided, dictated and required or aban-
don incorporating as an alternative.

As to all corporations of either class, therefore, the legislature has an almost unlimited power of initial regulation, Dodge
v. Woolsey, 18 How. 331 (1855). The charter offered by the
state, if accepted, constitutes a contract between the state and
the corporators. Dartmouth College Case, 4 Wheat. 518 (1819).

CONTROL OVER PRIVATE CORPORATIONS ALREADY IN EXISTENCE.

The constitutionality of legislation affecting existing private
corporations.

Constitutional prohibitions:

Sec. 10, Art. 1, U. S. Con., provides that "no state shall
* * * pass any * * * law impairing the obligation of
contracts."

The Fourteenth Amendment, U. S. Con., provides that no

---

† In the absence of express authority from the state a corporation
has no power whatsoever to increase or reduce its capital stock. Sco-
ville v. Thayer, 105 U. S. 143 (1881); Sutherland v. Olcott, 95 N. Y. 100
(1884); Grangers, etc. Ins. Co. v. Kamper, 73 Ala. 325 (1882); Moses v.
Oroe Bank, 1 Lea (Tenn.) 398 (1878); Ferris v. Ludlaw, 7 Ind. 517
(1856); Lathrop v. Knelland, 46 Barb. (1866); Kampman v. Farver, 87
Tex. 491 (1895); Laredo Imp. Co. v. Stevenson, 66 Fed. 633 (1895).

state shall "deprive any person of life, liberty, or property without due process of law, nor deny to any person within its jurisdiction the equal protection of the laws."

Sec. 13, Art. 1, Wis. Con., provides that "the property of no person shall be taken for public use without just compensation therefore."

That a charter of incorporation is a contract between the state and the corporators, and that a corporation is a person, so as to bring the charter and the corporation within the protection of Sec. 10, Art. 1, and the Fourteenth Amendment, U. S. Con. respectively, is too well settled to require citation of authority. However, these rules do not confine the legislative power over private corporations to initial regulation and control. In other words corporations now in existence—those that have acquired vested rights under and by virtue of existing charters—are still within certain limits, subject to be controlled and regulated by the legislature.

THE POLICE POWER AS A SOURCE OF LEGISLATIVE CONTROL OVER PRIVATE CORPORATIONS.

(a) Protection of the lives, health, property and morals of citizens.

All rights, corporate and individual, are held subject to the police power of the state. The doctrine that a charter is a contract does not exempt corporations from future legislation enacted for the protection of the lives, health and property of the citizens of the state, or for the maintenance of good order and the preservation of the public morals. A railroad company cannot therefore set up its charter to escape the operation of a law compelling it to adopt certain safeguards such as the construction of bridges, building of fences, improvement of crossings, erection of danger signals, regulation of speed, and others. calculated to prevent accident, Kan. Pac. Ry. Co. v. Mower, 16 Kan. 573 (1876); Thorpe v. Rutland, etc. Ry. Co., 27 Vt. 140 (1854); Galena, etc., Ry. Co. v. Appleby, 28 Ill. 283 (1862); Ind. Ry. Co. v. Kercheval, 16 Ind. 84 (1861); C. M. & St. P. Ry. Co. v. Milwaukee, 97 Wis. 418 (1897); the charter rights of an electric company to place its wires under the streets of a city are subject to reasonable municipal regulation as to the method of exercising that right; Gaslight Co. v. Murphy, 170 U. S. 78 (1897); the legislature may, in justice to miners, require coal mining companies to weigh coal before it is screened, Woodson v. State, 69 Ark. 521 (1900); under this power the legislature may limit the hours of work of women and children, even as against corporations, Conn. v. Hamilton Mfg. Co., 120 Mass. 383 1876), and the charter of a lottery or a brewing company does not prevent subsequent legislation to suppress lotteries or the manufacturing of intoxicating liquors. Stone v. Miss. 101 U. S. 514 (1879); Boston Beer Co. v. Mass., 97 U. S. 25 (1877).

The court in Pearsall v. Gt. Nor. Ry., 161 U. S. 646, 666 1896) in speaking of the police power said:

> "So important is this power, and so necessary to the public safety and health, that it cannot be bargained away by the legislature, and hence it has been held that charters for purposes inconsistent with a due regard for the public health or morals may be abrogated in the interests of a more enlightened public opinion."

b) Publicity of corporate transactions and financial condition.

The legislature may under the police power require corporations at stated times or periods to make and file with some public official of the state or county, reports of their business transactions and financial condition for a state preceding period. Elliott, Priv. Corps. Sec. 92. The supreme court of Illinois recently held that the state had power to compel a corporation created for a purely private purpose to make such reports, and to declare that failure so to do would be prima-facie evidence of non-user and sufficient to authorize a forfeiture of the charter, and that such a requirement was not objectionable as impairing the obligation of contracts. People v. Rose, 207 Ill., 352 1904).* The United States Supreme Court has held that the power to require such reports is implied in every charter of incorporation. Chicago Life Ins. Co. v. Needles, 113 U. S. 574 1884); Eagle Ins. Co. v. Ohio, 153 U. S. 446 (1893). To the

---

*The power to require reports was in this case based upon the power to tax and to procure the necessary information to properly exercise that power.

same general effect, see State v. Eagle Ins. Co., 50 Ohio St. 272 (1893) ; Pearsall v. Gt. Nor. Pac. Ry. Co., 161 U. S. 666 (1895); Louisville R. R. Co. v. Kentucky, 161 U. S. 697 (1895). The same doctrine is recognized in Wisconsin as applied to the visitorial power of the state over corporations:

"The visitorial or superintending power of the state over corporations created by the legislature will always be exercised, in proper cases, through the medium of the courts of the state, to keep those corporations within the limits of their lawful powers, and to correct and punish abuses of their franchises. To this extent the courts will issue writs of *quo warranto mandamas* or injunction, as the exigencies of the particular case may require; will inquire into the grievance complained of, and, if the same is found to exist, will apply such remedy as the law prescribes. Every corporation of the state, whether public or private, civil or municipal, is subject to this superintending control, although in its exercise different rules may be applied to different cases of corporations." The state ex rel. Cuppeil v. Milw. Chamber of Commerce, 47 Wis. 670, 679 (1879); see also Wis. Keeley Ins. Co. v. Milw. Co., 95 Wis. 153, 158 (1897).

This power of the legislature to require periodic reports is a natural concomitant of the power to regulate the charges and services of quasi-public corporations, but the power extends to corporations of either class.

(C) CONTROL OVER THE CHARGES AND SERVICE OF PRIVATE CORPORATIONS.

"When * * * one devotes his property to a use in which the public has an interest, he, in effect, grants to the public an interest in that use and must submit to be controlled by the public for the common good, to the extent of the interest he has thus created. He may withdraw his grant by discontinuing the use, but so long as he maintains the use he must submit to the control."

Munn v. Ill., 94 U. S. 113.

In the preceding case the question was as to the power of
the legislature of Illinois to fix by law the maximum of charges
for the storage of grain in warehouses at Chicago and other
places in the state having not less than 100,000 inhabitants, and
to require persons doing business as private warehousemen to
take out a license for such business, and to declare the business
to be that of public warehousemen. The constitutionality of
such legislation was sustained on the theory that "where private property is devoted to the public use it is subject to public regulation."

Following the Munn and other cases, commonly called the
"Warehouse Cases," came the "Granger Cases" involving a
consideration of the charters of different railroad companies
and the extent of the power of the legislature to control their
charges. These cases decided that railroads are subject to the
supervision and control of the legislature like all carriers at common law, and under the decision in the Munn Case, that they
are subject to legislation as to their rates of fare and freight
and their service, unless protected by their charter; that in the
absence of charter-contracts the charges by railroad companies
for services within the state may be limited by the legislature;
that where the state constitution reserves a right of alteration
or repeal, the legislature may prescribe a maximum rate of
charge, although the charter authorizes such charges as are reasonable.

> Chicago B. & R. R. R. Co. v. Iowa, 94 U. S. 155 (1876) ;
> Peik v. C. & N. W. Ry. Co., Ibid. 164 ;
> C. M. & St. P. Ry. Co. v. Ackley, Ibid. 179 ;
> Winona & St. P. Ry. v. Blake, Ibid. 180 ;
> Stone v. Wis., Ibid. 181 ;
> Ruggles v. Ill., 108 U. S. 526 (1883).

The "Railroad Commission Cases," 116 U. S. 307 (1885),
affirm the "Granger Cases" and go beyond them, sustaining
the validity of a statute regulating rates of transportation and
creating a state board of commissioners to supervise and enforce the same. The court holds that the creation of such a
board does not violate the charter rights of the corporation to
manage its affairs through its own directors; that statutes regulating rates of charges do not deprive corporations of their

property without due process of law; but declares that the power
of regulation is not power to destroy,—that limitation is not
equivalent to confiscation. This power of regulation is declared
to be one that cannot be bargained away except by express grant.

The legislative control over corporations thus maintained is
based upon the nature of the business carried on, and the legislative power is, therefore, left to the combined determination
of the legislative and judicial authority as to the nature of the
business. Since the decision in the Munn Case, the courts, both
Federal and state, have gradually added to the classes of business subject to this control and regulation.

The cases hold that a business which (1) enjoys special privileges by way of use of public streets and property, or (2) has
had delegated to it the sovereign prerogative of eminent domain,* or (3) a business that constitutes a virtual or legal
monopoly, is affected with a public interest and may, on any
one of these three grounds or on a combination of such grounds,
be subjected to unusual regulation and control. A review of
the cases, however, leads to the conclusion that neither special
privilege nor monopolistic character is absolutely essential to
subject a business to this governmental supervision. The nature of the business seems to be the criterion. The principle
underlying this theory is that if any business is of such a character or is operated under such conditions that there is danger
of oppression of the people, special regulation and control may
be invoked.†

Corporations engaged in a business of a purely private nature are not subject to this unusual regulation and control.

---

* For an exception see State v. Ass'd Press, 159 Mo. 410, where the
court held that in the absence of legislation to that effect, it, the court,
would not declare the Press Company's business to be affected with a
public interest even though the company had delegated to it the power
of eminent domain.

† For a compilation of businesses that have been held to be affected
with a public interest and therefore to be subject to this unusual regulation and control, see Committee Brief—The Nature of a Public Utility.

CONTROL UNDER THE POWER OF EMINENT DOMAIN.

The legislature may exercise the power of eminent domain to authorize the taking of the property of corporations, including their franchises, upon due compensation.

W. River Bridge Co. v. Dix. 6 How. 507 (1848);
Richmond etc. R. R. Co. v. Louisa R. Co. 13 How. 71;
Greenwood v. Frt. Co. 105 U. S. 13 (1881);
N. O. G. L. Co. v. La. etc. Co., 115 U. S. 650 (1884).

The Constitution of the U. S. cannot be so construed as to take away this power from the state. The charter is a contract with the state, but like all other property is subject to this sovereign prerogative—to be taken for a public purpose. W. River Bridge Co. v. Div. 6 How. 507 (1848).

This principle places the most valuable and exclusive rights and franchises of corporations under legislative control, whenever the *public interests* appears to the legislature to require that new corporations should be organized and that constantly developing necessities of growing and progressive communities be aided by new corporate undertakings. The practical operation of this principle is to keep the limits of the field of corporate exertion under the constant supervision of the legislature, and to leave to the determination of the representatives of the people the question whether that field should be enlarged or restricted at any particular period. Under the power of eminent domain this end is subserved, and corporations which have acquired vested rights and interests receive just compensation for whatever is taken from them.

CONTROL UNDER THE POWER TO TAX.

"There are, in general, four methods of taxing corporate interests. These are, first, by tax on the franchise; second, on the capital stock; third, on the real estate and personal property of the corporation; fourth, by a tax on the shares of stock in the hands of the stockholders." Cook Corporations, Vol. 3, Sec. 56, Citing, 2 Redf., Railw. (3d. Ed.), p. 453; Ottawa Glass Co. v. McCaleb, 81 Ill. 556 (1876); Louisville, etc., R. R. Co. v.

State, 8 Heisk (Tenn.) 63, 795 (1875). (A fifth method is
sometimes adopted—a tax on corporate dividends; but this is
construed to be only a method of valuing the franchise on capital stock, and can hardly be called a fifth method.)*

Where the matter is not regulated by the state constitution,
it is entirely within the discretion of the legislature to say which
of these four methods of taxation shall be adopted. It is also
within the discretion of the legislature to tax the corporation
in two or more of these ways—to levy a double, treble or quad-
ruple tax thereon.†

(a) Taxation on shares of stock.

(a) The right of the state to tax resident stockholders of a
resident corporation on their shares of stock is undoubted.

(b) On the principle of law that shares of stock are personal
property and follow the domicile of their owner, resident stockholders in a non-resident or foreign corporation may be taxed
on their shares of stock.

>Bradley v. Bander. 36 Ohio St., 28 (1880);
>Seward v. Rising Sun, 79 Ind. (1881);
>Dyer v. Osborne, 11 R. I. 321 (1876);
>McKeen v. North Hampton Co., 49 Pa. St. 519 (1865);
>Dwight v. Boston, 94 Mass. 316 (1866);
>Worth v. Comrs., 82 N. C. 420 (1880).

(c) Non-resident stockholders in resident or domestic corporations may be taxed on their shares of stock. To avoid the
common law rule relative to the situs of personal property, the

---

* Economists differ in their classifications of the methods of taxing
corporations. Mr. Cook's classification is inclusive. Seligman classi-
fies as follows: Taxation on the value of the property, on the capital
stock at par value, on the capital stock at market value, on the capital
stock plus bonded debt, on the capital stock plus total debt, on gross
earnings, on dividends, on capital stock according to dividends, on net
earnings, on franchise, on loans and on business.

† Aside from constitutional restrictions it is within the power of the
legislature to levy, not only a double tax, but even a treble or quad-
ruple tax, if it so chooses. Salem Iron, etc. Co. v. Danvers, 10 Mass.
514 (1813); Belo v. Forsyth Comr's., 82 N. C 415 (1889); Hasely v.
Ensley, 82 N. E Rep. 809 (Ind. 1907); Toll Bridge Co. v. Osborne, 35
Conn. 7 (1868); Hannebal, etc. R. R. v. Shacklett, 30 Mo. 550, 560
(1860); see Cooley on Taxation, Vol 1, p. 387 et seq.; Frozer v. Siebern.
16 Ohio St. 614 (1866).

state in creating a corporation may in its charter give to the shares of stock a situs at the location of the corporation.

> Ottawa Glass Co. v. McCaleb, 81 Ill. 556 (1876);
> State v. Mayhew, 2 Gill (Md.) 487 (1845);
> Whitnay v. Ragsvale, 33 Ind. 107 (1870);
> Tallman v. Butler Co., 12 Ia. 531 (1861);
> Corry v. Mayor, etc., 96 Md. 310 (1903);
> St. Louis National Bank v. Patin, 21 Fed. 203 (1876).

The method of enforcing the payment of this tax may be by compelling the corporation to pay it and giving it a lien therefore on the stock, authorizing it to deduct the tax from the non-resident stockholders' dividends. Such tax may be levied under the reserved right to amend the charter.

> Corry v. Baltimore, 196 U. S. 466 (1905);
> Ottawa Glass Co. v. McCaleb, supra.

In the case of St. Albans v. National Car Co., 57 Vt. 68 (1884), it was held that the statute giving shares of stock a situs at the location of the corporation may be passed after incorporation and that *mandamus* lies to compel the corporation to pay the tax. The state may prescribe that resident stockholders shall pay a tax where they reside, and that the corporation shall pay a tax based upon the values of the shares of stock held by non-residents, and that the corporation shall have a lien on the stock of such stockholders for such tax so paid. State v. Travelers Ins. Co., 70 Conn. 590 (1898). Cooley, Taxation (2nd Ed.), 433, clearly upholds the rule that the state may levy a tax on shares of stock and compel the corporation to pay it. Numerous cases are there cited to substantiate this proposition.

CONTROL UNDER THE POWER OF FORFEITURE.

"A private corporation created by the legislature may loss its franchises by a misuser or nonuser of them; and they may be resumed by the government by a judicial judgment upon a *quo warranto* to ascertain and enforce the forfeiture. This is the common law of the land, and is a tacit condition to the creation of every such corporation."

> Terrett v. Taylor, 9 Cranch, 51 (1815);
> State v. Milw. L. S. & W. R. Co., 45 Wis. 579 (1878);

State v. Madison St. Ry., 72 Wis. 612 (1888) ;
Weight v. Milw. E. R. & L. Co., 95 Wis. 29 (1897) ;
.Peo. v. No. River Sugar Ref. Co., 121 N. Y. 582 (1890);
Chgo. Life Ins. Co. v. Auditor, 101 Ill. 82 (1881) ;
Distilling Co. v. People, 156 Ill. 448 (1895) ;
Peo. v. Pullman Pal. Car Co., 175 Ill. 125 (1898).

(a) Forfeiture for misuser.

Ultra vires acts* and usurpations of franchises are acts which
constitute a misuser.

In People v. Pullman Pal. Car Co., supra, the charter of the
Car Co. which was incorporated to manufacture railroad cars
was forfeited because the company laid out a town around its
works; built 2,200 homes to lease to its employees; built a hotel,
saloon, theatre, gas plant, a system of waterworks, and a brick
plant, and operated a farm for supplies to sell to its employees.

In People v. Nor. River Sugar Ref. Co.. supra, the charter
of the corporation whose stockholders had entered into a
"trust" with the stockholders of competing corporations, for
the purpose of forming a monopoly to raise the price of sugar,
was, at the instance of the attorney general, forfeited. Like
treatment was accorded a corporation formed to purchase sub
stantially all the distilleries in the country. Distilling, etc., Co.
v. Peo., 156 Ill. 448 (1895). The state may forfeit a charter for
the failure of the officers to file the annual report and of the
stockholders to pay in the capital stock as required by statute.
Peo. v. Buffalo, etc., Co., 131 N. Y. 140 (1892). A waterworks
charter may be forfeited where the corporation willfully and
persistently charges more for water than its charter specifies.
State v. New Orleans, etc., Co., 107 La. 1 (1901). See s. c. 336.
Where a railroad leases its line in violation of a constitutional
provision, prohibiting the consolidation of parallel lines, it is
subject to forfeiture. So also where it issues "watered stock"
in violation of the constitution. State v. Atchison, etc., R. R..
24 Neb. 143 (1888) ; see s. c., 38 Neb. 437. The charter of a
plank-road company for failure to keep the road in repair was
forfeited in the case of Peo. v. Detroit, etc., Co., 131 Mich. 30
(1902). A street railroad company's charter may be forfeited

---

* Not every ultra vires act constitutes a misuser.

for failure to keep tracks in a condition required by the charter. State v. Madison St. R. R., 72 Wis., 612 (1888). It has
been held to be misuser to file a false certificate that the capital
stock has been paid up; Eastern, etc., Co. v. Regina, 22 Eng.
Law & Eq. 328 (1853). The issue of fictitiously paid-up stock,
with a view of defrauding the public may constitute misuser
of the corporate rights and franchises. In such a case it has
been held that the state may forfeit the charter of the corporation and that a palpable case of fraud will justify such forfeiture. State v. Webb, 97 Ala. 111 (1893). In Holman v. State,
105 Ind. 569 (1886), the state caused the charter to be forfeited because the subscribers for stock were insolvent at the
time of subscribing, thereby perpetrating a fraud on the public.*

,b) Forfeiture for non-user.

Non-user of a franchise is a cause for forfeiture where a corporation is possessed not only of its franchise to be a corporation, but also other franchises, such as a right of way which
the public are interested in having kept in active use. Where
a charter required a street railway company to lay its tracks
on certain streets, and the company did so on a part of such
streets, and then removed them, and for many years operated
no cars thereon at all, the court held that the charter might be
forfeited at the instance of the state. Peo. v. Broadway R. R.,
126 N. Y. 29 (1891). A suit for forfeiture lies where a railroad company takes up part of its tracks. State v. West, etc.,
R. R. Co., 34 Wis. 197 (1874), s. c. 36 Wis. 466 (1874). A
street railway grant from the city may be forfeited at the instance of the state where a company runs but one car a day
in order to hold its franchise. It may also be forfeited for
failure to construct the entire line within time specified by
statute. People v. Sutter St. Ry. Co., 117 Cal. 604 (1897).
(holding also that the court may impost a fine instead of forfeiting the charter).

Turning to purely private corporations which do not exercise any great public franchises, it is the rule here too that for
a non-user quo warranto will lie. The state may forfeit a char-

---

* For additional citations and examples of misuser which justify forfeiture, see Cook Corporations, Vol. 2, sec. 633, and note.

ter for wilful non-user, although the corporation is a private one. Peo. v. Milk Exchange, 133 N. Y. 565 (1892). **Edgar Coll. Inst. v. Peo.**, 142 Ill. 363 (1892); where a river-improvement company has received a grant from the state for the purpose of improving the river and has long ceased operations, and the parties interested in it have departed, a dissolution at the instance of the state may be obtained. State v. Cannon, etc., Assoc.. 67 Minn. 14 (1896).

In Peo. v. National Savings Bank, 11 N. E. Rep. 170 (Ill. 1887), a corporate charter was revoked for failure to complete subscriptions as required in the charter. In Eastern, etc., Co. v. Regina, 22 Eng. L. & Eq. 328 (1853), a charter was forfeited for failure to pay in capital stock as prescribed therein.

CONTROL UNDER THE RESERVED POWER TO ALTER' OR REPEAL CORPORATE CHARTERS.

The power to alter or repeal corporate charters is reserved to the legislature of the state of Wisconsin by Sec. 1, Art. 11, Wis. Con. The provision reads: "All general laws or special acts enacted under the provisions of this Sec. (relating to the organization of corporations) may be altered or repealed by the legislature at any time after their passage."

As the power to amend and repeal corporate charters would be ample in the state legislature in the absence of the provision of the Federal Constitution prohibiting the impairment of the obligation of contracts, such a reservation of power leaves a state where any sovereignity would be if unrestrained by constitutional limitations.
Detroit v. Detroit, etc. Co., 43 Mich. 140;
Smith v. R. R. Co., 114 Mich. 460.

"A power reserved to the legislature to alter, amend or repeal a charter authorizes it to make any *alteration* or *amendment* of a charter granted subject to it which will not defeat or substantially impair the object of the grant or any rights vested

under it, and which the legislature may deem necessary to secure either that object or any public right.''

> N. Y. & N. E. R. R. v. Birstol, 151 U. S. 556 (1894);
> Sinking Fund Cases, 99 U. S. 700 (1878);
> Hamilton G. & C. Co. v. Hamilton, 146 U. S. 259 (1892);
> Greenwood v. Freight Co., 105 U. S. 13 (1881);
> Dam Co. v. Gray, 30 Me. 547 (1849);
> Shields v. Ohio, 95 U. S. 319 (1877);
> Atty. Genl. v. R. R. Cos., 35 Wis. 425 (1874);
> Tomlinson v. Jessup, 15 Wall. 454 (1872);
> Water Works v. Schottler, 110 U. S. 353 (1883).

Under this reserved power the legislature may *repeal* the
charter altogether, so as to terminate absolutely the existence of
the corporation by the abrogation of ''the organic law on which
the corporate existence depends.''

> Greenwood v. Freight Co., supra;
> Wilmington St. Ry. Co. v. Wilmington etc. Co., 8 Del.
>   Ch. 468 (1900);
> Peo. v. O'Brien et al., 111 N. Y. 1 (1888);   •
> Griffin v. Ry. Ins. Co., 3 Bush (Ky.) 592 (1868);
> So. Bell Tel. & Tel. Co. v. Richmond, 98 Fed. 671 (1899);
> McClaren v. Pennington, 1 Paige (N. Y.) 102 (1828);
> Schurz v. Cook, 148 U. S. 397 (1895);
> Mayor of N. Y. v. Twenty-third St. R. R. Co., 113 N. Y.
>   311 (1889);
> Cook, Corporations, 6th Ed., Vol. 2, Sec. 639;
> Thompson, Law of Corporations, Vol. IV, Sec. 5417.

The power to *alter or repeal* corporate charters may be exercised at the pleasure of the legislature.

> Pratt v. Brown, 3 Wis. 532 (1854);
> Atty. Genl. v. R. R. Cos., supra;
> W. Wis. R. R. Co. v. Trempealeau Co., 35 Wis., 257
>   (1874);
> Greenwood v. Freight Co., supra;
> Hamilton G. & C. Co., v. Hamilton, supra;
> Wilmington St. R. R. Co., v. Wilmington etc. Co., supra;
> Zabriski v. Hackensack, 18 N. J. Eq. 178 (1867).

The power reserved to alter corporate charters is unrestricted save only that under an exercise thereof the legislature may not destroy vested rights of property, nor may the legislature under the guise of alteration change the substantial purposes for which the corporation was created, or transform it from a corporation of one kind into a corporation of another kind, or one the object of which is materially different from that originally created.

The power reserved to the legislature to repeal corporate characters is an unrestricted one, save only that the legislature under an exercise thereof may not destroy vested property rights.*

In New York it is held that the state under the reserved power may compel the acceptance of an alteration of a corporate charter as an alternative for the revocation of the charter.

> The Mayor v. Twenty-third St. R. R. Co., 113 N. Y. 311 (1889).

SUMMARY.

The legislature being the creator of corporations, and there being no inherent or vested right in any person or persons to incorporate, that body has full power to dictate the terms and conditions under which corporations may be created and exist. Laws that will efficiently cope with the trust, watered stock and other corporate problems may be passed for application to corporations to be created. Those states in the union which have succeeded in eliminating most of the evils of the trust and of stcok watering have applied the remedy when creating corporations.

Combinations of domestic corporations as well as the combining of domestic with foreign corporations can be effectively prohibited.

We have the evils of stock watering because of failure to provide that all issues of corporate stocks and bonds shall be under strict supervision of the legislature, or, more effectively, under the strict supervision of a commission created to enforce compliance with wholesome laws relative to the issuing of cor-

---

* See Committee Brief—Power of the Legislature to Alter or Repeal Corporate Charters where the power is expressly reserved.

porate securities. The legislature may enact that corporate securities shall be issued for certain purposes and to a certain
amount, and may invest a commission with ample power to find
as a matter of fact what is a reasonable issue of securities for
such purpose or purposes. Such commission can be given power
to restrict the issue of stocks and bonds to a reasonable amount
for the purpose authorized. In Massachusetts stock watering
has been effectively eliminated. The remedy there is a prohibition against the issue of any stock or bonds for *property* until
after commissioners have passed upon the proposed issue. In
other states the same result is obtained by prohibiting the issue
of stock except for a money consideration. As a further remedy
against stock watering the legislature may provide for the fullest publicity of the transaction and financial condition of all corporate bodies, and with the ideal condition of restricting the issue of securties to an amount not to exceed the value of the property of the issuing corporation, both the investing and the consuming public will be protected—the investing public in the
purchase of the original and subsequent issues of corporate
stocks or bonds, and the consuming public in the rates charged
by public service companies. Protection of the investing public, in-so-far as the manipulation of stocks already issued is concerned, is without the scope of this paper.

The foregoing suggestions are but examples of the initial control and power over private corporations by the legislature.
These examples can be multiplied indefinitely—the legislative
control over private corporations to be formed is about unlimited.

With respect to legislative control over corporations already
in existence, a much broader and more complicated question is
presented. It would seem that the legislative control under the
police power, the power of eminent domain, the power to tax,
the power of forfeiture, and under the reserved power to alter
or repeal, would be sufficient for any and all purposes. The
provision of the Federal constitution prohibiting the impairment of the obligation of contracts has been effectually off-set
by the clause in the Wisconsin constitution reserving to the legislature the right or power to alter or repeal corporate charters
at any time after their passage. Were it not for the limitations
placed by the courts upon the legislative power under this re-

32

serve clause to *alter* corporate charters, corporate property, including charters and franchises and the accompanying rights and privileges, would be subject to subsequent legislation as are the property and rights of individuals.

Under the legislative powers enumerated future stock watering by existing corporations can be effectually prohibited.

There are four methods of issuing watered stock, viz.: 1, by part cash payment; 2, by taking property at over-valuation in exchange for stock; 3, by an invalid stock dividend, and 4, by consolidation.

1. An issue of paid-up stock for cash, upon payment of only part of the par value of the stock, is not often made, in as much as the real nature of the transaction is readily discovered and easily remedied. Sometimes the corporation makes the issue under a contract with those receiving it that no more than a certain percentage of the par value will be called for. Again, a release is sometimes made by a resolution of the directors or stockholders, after subscriptions have been made and partly paid, discharging the subscribers from any future liability on such subscriptions. The proceedings are generaly spread upon the corporate records; certificates are issued, asserting on their face that they are paid-up, and all inquiries at the corporation office are answered by a substantiation of that assertion.

2. Stock watering by taking property at an over-valuation in exchange for stock, is the method most frequently applied and is the most difficult to prove and the least easy to remedy.

3. If the capital stock and the actual property of the corporation are not increased to the extent of the par value of the stock distributed as a dividend, then the issue of stock by such dividend is irregular, and under certain circumstances fraudulent. A stock dividend may take the shape of an issue of stock for cash at less than the par value.

4. The fourth method of issuing watered stock is by the consolidation of two or more corporations or by the sale of all the property and assets of one corporation to another. (The latter, the sale of one company's assets to another company in considertion of the full paid stock of the latter, is but a method of issuing stock for property). If all stockholders consent and creditors are not injured, such a sale, if the corporation is purely private and there is no law to the contrary, is legal.

These methods of getting fictitious stock on the market, or of issuing such stock, can be blocked. In most existing corporate charters provisions allowing and providing for the increase of capital stock are found. Under the reserved power to alter corporate charters these provisions may be so altered as to thoroughly regulate such new or additional issues. The alteration may provide that new stock or bonds shall be sold for cash only; that the same be sold at a certain price, at par for example, or at public auction, and that in all cases no new stock shall be issued except under the supervision of a commission.

The present remedy in this state to prohibit the issuance of watered stock is ineffective. Sec. 1753, Wis. R. S., provides that "No corporation shall issue any stock or certificates of stock except in consideration of money or labor or property, estimated at its true money value actually received by it, equal to the par value thereof, nor any bonds or other evidence of indebtedness except for money, labor or property estimated at its true money value, actually received by it, equal to seventy-five per cent of the par value thereof, and all stocks and bonds issued contrary to the provisions of this section and all fictitious increase of the capital stock of any corporation shall be void; * * * ." The provisions of this section are so sweeping in effect and so disastrous to innocent holders that the courts are reluctant to enforce it. Many states of the union have enacted a similar law. Cook, in his work on corporations, Vol. 1, Sec. 47, after discussing the injustice that would accompany a strict enforcement of such a law, says: "Except in Alabama and Missouri, it may be said that the courts have construed away the language and purpose of the provision." Watered stock when in the hands of innocent holders will not be interfered with by the courts. To remedy the evils resultant from the issue of watered stock, all issues of stock should be regulated in detail by law, and should be issued and sold as supervised by a commission invested with as broad powers as possible.*

---

* Penn. prohibits issue of stock by railroads except for cash at par. The Attorney General, by the statute, is obliged to enforce the same whenever any stockholder or two reputable citizens make out a prima facie case. Act of May 7, 1887 P. L. 94.

In Conn. if stock is paid for otherwise than in cash, a majority of the directors must make and sign on the records of the corporation a statement showing particularly the property received and that it has

Under the police power, the power to tax and the reserved power publicity of all corporate transactions and the financial condition of corporations can be required. Publicity along these lines will effectively aid the legislature or a commission in enforcing laws passed to prohibit issues of watered stock.

Stock watering may be discouraged, at least, by a proper application of the state's power to tax. This can be done by levying a tax on the excess of stocks and bonds issued over and above the tangible property of the corporation.

---

an actual value equal to the amount for which it was received. **Conn. L. 1903, Chap. 194, Sec. 13.**

In Illinois provision is made for the appraisement of property taken for stock. Hurd Rev. St. 1906, Chap. 32, Sec. 4.

In Massachusetts only manufacturing and mercantile corporations are allowed to issue shares for anything except cash, and that since 1875, Ch. 177, L. 1875. Under certain conditions water and aqueduct companies may take property in payment for shares. Ch. 380, L. 1894. In 1852 railroads were expressly prohibited issuing stock for less than its par value, Ch. 303, L. 1852, and a few years later the same restriction was placed upon all corporations. Chs. 167 L. 1858 and 104 of 1859; Gen'l. Stats. 1860, Ch. 68, Sec. 9. In 1851 the general incorporation act for manufacturing corporations had prohibited these companies from issuing stock for less than par. Ch. 133 L. 1851. This requirement was strengthened by subsequent legislation expressly prohibiting stock and scrip dividends. Chs. 310 L. 1868, 389 L. 1871 and 350 L. 1894, and by creating state commissions to supervise public service industries and enforce compliance with the laws. The average capitalization of street railways in the United States in 1902 was $96,287 per mile of track; in Mass. it was $45,600. Rept. on street and electric Railways, 1902, p. 51. Street Railways in Mass. are permitted to consolidate subject to the approval of the railroad commissioners; and the law provides that in the process there shall be no increase in the aggregate issues of stocks and bonds. Ch. 463 L. 1906, Pt. II, Secs. 52 and 53. The law governing consolidation of railroads and gas and electric companies are somewhat similar. Ch. 392 L. 1906 and 463, Part 1, Sec. 67.

The laws of Mass. provide that no corporation shall issue bonds bearing more than 7% interest. Rev. L. Ch. 73, Sec. 3, and the further restriction of gas and electric companies to bonds paying not more than 6% per annum. Rev. L. Ch. 121, Sec. 10. Gas companies are expressly forbidden to issue bonds at less than their par value, Idem., but the statutes do not prohibit other corporations from issuing bonds at a discount. The borrowing power of corporations is limited—the limitation is on the permanent debt. This provision relative to manufacturing corporations is found in Ch. 53 L. 1829 (R. S. Ch. 38, Sec 5) and requires that the debts of such companies shall not exceed the capital paid in. A similar law applicable to railroads was passed. Ch. 386 L. 1854. Similar restrictions were subsequently placed upon other public service corporations. Telegraph or telephone companies may not contract debts exceeding one-half of their capital stock, Ch. 217 L. 1851. (R. S. Ch. 122, Sec. 7); gas and electric light companies may not issue bonds in excess of their capital actually paid in, Ch. 346, L. 1886, Sec. 3; Ch. 371, L. 1890; (R. S. 121, Secs. 10 and 12), and railroads and street railways may not issue "bonds, coupon notes, or other evidence of indebtedness, payable at periods of more than 12

The Wisconsin legislature has under the powers enumerated sufficient control over both classes of private corporations to prevent combinations resulting in trusts and monopolies, to prohibit issues of watered stock, and to regulate the rates and service of public service companies. Under the reserved power, the police power and the power to tax, affirmative remedies can be applied. Under the reserved power or the power of forfeiture the corporate life, upon failure to comply with these affirmative remedies, may be extinguished. Under the power

months from the date thereof," to an amount exceeding their paid-up capital stock, Ch. 463, L. 1906, Pt. II, Sec. 48, and Pt. III, Sec. 108.

The Mass. Commissions have control of the amount of securities that public service corporations can issue for any or all purposes. Only such amounts of stock and bonds can be issued as the commissions may determine to be "reasonably necessary" for the purpose for which they are authorized. Railroads and street railways must apply to the railroad commission; gas and electric light companies, to the gas and electric light commission, and telephone, telegraph, aqueduct, and water companies, to the commissioner of corporations.

To determine the amount of securities "reasonably necessary" in any case, the railroad commission is expressly empowered whenever "the public interests require" it, to "employ competent experts to investigate the character, cost, and value" of the property of any company. Chs. 450, 453 and 462, L. 1894; 337, L. 1897; 463, L. 1906. Corporations are explicitly prohibited from applying the proceeds of stocks and bonds "to any purpose not specified" in the certificate obtained from the commissions. Directors, officers and agents who knowingly issue securities in violation of the statute are liable to punishment by fine or imprisonment or both. In the theory of the law the purposes for which stocks and bonds may be issued are determined by law; and this implies that the commission, in passing upon applications by the companies, shall withhold their consent in any case where the securities are for a purpose not authorized by law. The statutes define in very general terms the purpose for which securities may issue leaving a great deal to the discretion of the commission. Thus street railways are authorized to increase their stock and bonds for sixteen specific objects, and "for other similarly necessary and lawful purposes." Ch. 463, 1906.

From 1871 to 1873 railroads, street railway and gas companies were required to offer all new shares of stock at public auction. Ch. 392, L. 1871. In 1878 and 1879 these laws in so far as railroads and street railways are concerned, were repealed. Ch. 84, L. 1878 and Ch. 90, L. 1879, but the act relating to gas companies is still in force.

Other "anti-stock watering laws" provide that when a public service corporation increases its capital stock the new shares shall be offered to stockholders at a price to be determined by the appropriate commission. Rev L. Ch. 189, Secs. 30 and 31; Ch. 463, L. 1906, Pt. II, Secs. 69 and 70. This price was to be "not less than the market value" of the shares, and in determining it the commissions were required to take "into account previous sales of stock of the corporation and other pertinent conditions." In no case, however, were shares to be issued for less than par. In case any part of any issue was not subscribed for by the stockholders at the price thus fixed, the corporation was authorized to sell such shares to the highest bidder at public auction, but at not less than par.

of eminent domain all rights and privileges granted to a corporation may be taken for a public purpose, upon just compensation being paid therefor.   .

BRIEF NUMBER 14.

SUBMITTED BY GEORGE P. HAMBRECHT

ON

POWER OF THE LEGISLATURE TO ALTER, AMEND OR REPEAL CORPORATE CHARTERS WHERE THE POWER IS EXPRESSLY RESERVED. EFFECT ON ACQUIRED PROPERTY UNDER CHARTER

TO

THE WISCONSIN LEGISLATIVE COMMITTEE

ON

WATER POWERS, FORESTRY AND DRAINAGE.

(Authorities compiled by M. C. Riley.)

POWER OF THE LEGISLATURE TO ALTER OR REPEAL CORPORATE CHARTERS WHERE THE POWER IS EXPRESSLY RESERVED.

The Dartmouth College case, 4 Wheat. 518 (1819), enunciated the doctrine that the charter of a corporation is a contract, and therefore that any material alteration of such charter by legislative enactment, is a law impairing the obligation of contracts within the meaning and prohibition of Art. 1, Sec. 10, of the Federal Constitution.

Mr. Justice Story at the conclusion of his concurring opinion in the above named case, at p. 712, said:

"In my judgment it is perfectly clear that any act of the legislature which takes away any powers or franchises vested by its charter in a private corporation or its corporate officers, or which restrains or controls the legitimate exercise of ,them, or transfers them to other persons without their assent, is a violation of the obligation of that charter. If the legislature mean to claim such an authority, it must be reserved in the grant."

As the meaning and practical consequences of this decision became known throughout the Union, steps were taken to avoid its future effect. In accordance with the suggestion of Mr. Justice Story, the different states, by means of the so-called reserved clause, retained the power or right to alter or repeal all corporate charters thereafter granted. In some states the right or power was reserved—as in Wisconsin—by a constitutional provision; in others by general statute. In most cases the language used in reserving the power was to "alter, amend or repeal" the charter. In Massachusetts and Connecticut "at the pleasure of the legislature" was added. In Georgia it was simply "to withdraw the franchise;" in Delaware it consisted in the prohibition to create corporations except "with a reserved power of revocation by the legislature." In some states the power is unconditional; in others conditional.

See appendix for compilation of the reservations in the different states.

The power to alter or repeal corporate charters is reserved to the legislature of Wisconsin by Section 1, Article XI, Wis. Con., in the following words:

> "Corporations may be formed under general laws, but shall not be created by special act, except . . . All general laws or special acts, enacted under the provisions of this section, may be altered or repealed by the legislature at any time after their passage."

The United States Supreme Court, and the Supreme Court of this State, in all cases have held that such a reservation of power either in the constitution or general statutes becomes a part of all charters—contracts between the states and the corporators—subsequently granted as if expressed in the charter itself.

> Tomlinson v. Jessup, 15 Wall. 456 (1872);
> Sinking Fund Cases, 99 U. S. 700 (1878);
> Hamilton G. L. & C. Co. v. Hamilton City, 146 U. S. 258, 270 (1892);
> Waterworks v. Shattler, 110 U. S. 353 (1883);
> N. Y. etc. Ry. Co. v. Bristol, 151 U. S. 556, 567 (1893);
> Pratt v. Brown, 3 Wis. 532 (1854);
> Atty. Genl. v. R. R. Cos., 35 Wis. 425 (1874).

Sec. 1768 Wis. R. S. provides: "The legislature may at any time limit or restrict the powers of any corporation organized under any law, and' for just cause annul the same, and prescribe such mode as may be necessary for the settlement of its affairs." This section of the statute cannot abridge the powers conferred upon the legislature by the constitution.

By virtue of Sec. 1, Art. XI, Wis., Con., and the judicial construction of that clause, all corporate charters granted by the legislature of the state of Wisconsin contain the provision that the legislature may alter or repeal the same at any time after their passage. Two essentially different and distinct rights are reserved, 1, to alter, and 2, to repeal, the state's contract with the corporators constituting the corporate charter. All cases recognize and distinguish these two rights or powers.

Being essentially different, the courts have placed different limitations upon these two powers. It is necessary therefore in determining their scope and limitations to consider them separately. However, the legislative power under this so-called reserve clause must necessarily be restricted by the purpose for which the same was invented. In this connection the clause as an entirety must be considered.

These restrictions and limitations upon the reserve power to alter or repeal corporate charters will, therefore, be treated in the following order: 1st, with respect to the power to alter corporate charters; 2nd, with respect to the power to repeal corporate charters, and, 3rd, with respect to the restrictions and limitations upon the powers of the legislature under this clause found in the purpose or purposes for which the same was made a part of our constitution.

(1) WITH RESPECT TO THE POWER TO ALTER CORPORATE CHARTERS.

A corporate charter is a contract between the state and the corporators. Such a contract is not different than one between individuals—this is the holding in the Dartmouth College Case. The sovereign nature of the state avails it nothing in its contract with corporators. This contract is subject to the ordinary rules relating to legal agreements, including the necessity of assent of both parties, and the presence of a consideration moving from each party to the contract. In Wisconsin, as has been seen, every charter of incorporation contains the provision that the legislature, one of the contracting parties, may alter or repeal the contract or charter at any time after its passage. The power thus retained is a power to alter or recall only that which the state has given in the charter, and only those rights which the corporation gets from the state. State v. C. & N. W. Ry. Co., 128 Wis. 449 (1906). It is the reservation of an authority or right to alter or withdraw a particular contract. It in no sense creates a new or distinct power that will entitle the legislature to deprive a corporation of its property or of the equal protection of the law in violation of the 14th amendment of the federal constitution, or Sec. 13, Art. 1, Wis. Constitution, nor does the reserve clause empower the legislature to legislate so as to impair or affect contracts between the corporation and third parties, except in so far as the alteration or repeal of its own contract indirectly máy affect such other contracts.

Atty. Genl. v. R. R. Cos., supra;

State ex rel. Nor. Pac. R. R. Co. v. R. R. Comms. of Wis., 140 Wis. 145 (1909);

State v. C. & N. W. Ry. Co., supra;

Greenwood v. Freight Co., 105 U. S. 13 (1881);

Sinking Fund Cases, supra;

People v. O'Brien, 111 N. Y. 1 (1888);

Detroit v. D. & H. P. R. Co., 43 Mich. 140 (1880).

Alteration under the reserve clause of the contract of incorporation—the franchises and immunities derived directly from the state—does not violate private property rights.

C. J. Ryan, in Atty. Gen. v. R. R. Cos., supra, at p. 578, very fully discusses the effect of the alteration of a corporate charter under the reserve clause upon its property, he said:

"It was said that ch. 273 (fixing rates of tolls) violates the rights of property of these defendants. We cannot perceive that it does. Whether it will lessen the income of their property, we cannot foresee. We only know that it does lessen their rates of toll. But it does not wrongfully touch their property. As far as the franchise is to be considered, it was subject to this very limitation; and the limitation is the exercise of a right over it, which does not violate it. The right of limitation entered into the property and qualified it. And the act does not at all meddle with the material property, distinct from the franchise. It acts only on the franchise, not at all upon the material property. And it is sufficient to say that they acquired the material property, as distinct from the franchise, subject to the alteration of the franchise under the reserved power. That was a condition under which they chose to hold their property; and they have no right to complain when the condition is enforced. Their rights in their material property are inviolate, and shall never be violated with the sanction of this court. But they are no more violated by this act and its enforcement, than by foreclosure of a mortgage or ejectment by paramount title. It is a right over property which is enforced, not a wrong to right in property."

See also Sinking Fund Cases, supra;

Holyoke v. Lyman, 15 Wall. 500 (1872);

New Jersey v. Yard, 95 U. S. 104 (1877);

Tomlinson v. Jessup, 15 Wall. 454 (1872);

R. R. Co. v. Maine, 96 U. S. 499 (1877);

R. R. Co. v. Georgia, 98 U. S. 359 (1878).

Nor does such an alteration impair the obligation of contracts between the corporation and third parties.

"Persons making contracts with a private corporation know that the legislature, even without the assent of the corporation, may amend, alter or modify their charters in all cases where the power to do so is reserved in the charter or in any general antecedent law in operation at the time the charter was granted. * * * Such contracts made between individuals and the corporation do not vary or in any manner change or modify the relation between the state and the corporation in respect to the right of the state to alter, modify or amend such a charter, as the power to pass such law depends upon * * * some reservation made at the time, as evidenced by some pre-existing general law or by an express provision incorporated in the charter. * * * It is a mistake to suppose that the existence of such a contract between the corporation and an individual would inhibit the legislature from altering, modifying, or amending the charter of the corporation by virtue of a right reserved to that effect * * * if, in view of all the circumstances, the legislature should see fit to exercise that power."

Penn. Coll. Cases, 13 Wall. 190 (1871).

"Surely it cannot rationally be contended that because the alteration of charters with respect to the latitude of the franchises granted may or does operate unfavorably upon executory contracts made by or under the corporations, the charters must remain unaltered in this respect and the reserved power in the legislature be reduced to a power in name only."

Macon & Bermingham R. R. Co. v. Nibson, 85 Ga. 1 (1890).

See also Atty. Genl. v. R. R. Cos., supra;
Storrie v. R. R. Co., 92 Tex. 129 (1898);
Louisvill Water Co. v. Clark, 143 U. S. 1 (1891).

However, this power of alteration is by the very definition of
the word "alter" a limited power.

The court in Atty. Gen. v. R. R. Cos., supra, at pp. 576, 577,
defines and lays down in the following words a general limitation upon this power:

> "The power to alter depends on the meaning of the
> word, alter.   To alter is to make different, without destroy-
> ing identity (Crabb); to vary without entire change
> (Webster and Imp. Dict.).   A corporate charter of one
> kind cannot be altered to a charter of an entirely differ-
> ent kind.   But a corporate charter may be altered so as
> to make it different in detail, so long as the general iden-
> tity of the corporation remains; so that it is varied, with-
> out entire change.   This is the obvious meaning to lawyer
> or layman."

This limitation is well stated in Zabriski v. Hackensack, 18
N. J. Eq. 178, 192 (1867):

> "Again, the power of the legislature has its limits.   It
> can repeal or suspend the charter; it can alter or modify
> it, it can take away the charter; but it cannot impose a
> new one, and oblige the stockholders to accept it.   It can
> alter or modify the old one; but power to alter or modify.
> anything can never be held to imply a power to substitute
> a thing entirely different.   It is not the meaning of the
> words in their usually received sense.   Power to alter a
> mansion-house would never be construed to mean a power
> to tear down all but the back kitchen and front piazza, and
> build one three times as large in its place.   In anything
> altered, something must be preserved to keep up its iden-
> tity; and a matter of the same kind, wholly or chiefly new,
> substituted for another, is not an alteration; it is a
> change."

It follows from the foregoing general limitation that the
power under the reserve clause to alter a corporate charter depends in each case upon the provisions and scope of the particu-

lar grant. For this reason the cases having to do with the power of alteration are difficult to reconcile. All cases hold that the substitution of powers and privileges may not be carried to the point where a new corporation is practically substituted, and that private property and vested rights cannot be destroyed in the exercise of this power. The courts have been unusually emphatic in expressing these general limitations. The following quotations are examples:

"The power of alteration and amendment is not without limit. The alterations must be reasonable; they must be made in good faith, and be consistent with the scope and object of the Act of incorporation. Sheer oppression and wrong cannot be inflicted under the guise of amendment or alteration." Shields v. Ohio, 95 U. S. 324.

"That this power has a limit no one can doubt. All agree that itcannot be used to take away property already acquired under the provision of the charter, or to deprive the corporation of the fruits actually reduced to possession of contracts lawfully made; * * * ." Sinking Fund Cases, supra, at p. 720.

Like language is found in Holyoke v. Lyman, 15 Wall. 500, 522 (1872); Comrs. of Inland Fisheries, v. Holyoke W. P. Co., 104 Mass. 451 and in Miller v. State 15 Wall. 498 (1872). The court in Holyoke v. Lyman, summarizing the rule laid down in the two latter cases, held:

"Power to legislate founded upon such a reservation is not without limit, but it may safely be affirmed that it reserves to the legislature authority to make any alteration or amendment in the charter granted subject to it, that will not substantially impair the object of the grant, or any right vested under it, * * * . Vested rights, it is conceded, cannot be destroyed or impaired under such a reserved power, but it is clear that the power may be exercised, and to almost any extent to carry into effect the original purposes of the grant and to protect the rights of the public and of the corporators, or to promote the due administration of the affairs of the corporation."

"It has * * * been * * * determined that the reserved right to repeal, alter or amend does not confer mere arbitrary power, and cannot be so exercised as to violate fundamental princip'es of justice by depriving of the equal protection of the laws or of the constitutional guarantee against the taking of property without due process of law;" Stearns v. Minn. 179 U. S. 225 (1900) (Concurring opinion of Mr. Justice White).

"It is impossible to lay down any exact rule as to the lawful extent of the exercise of this reserved legislative power, and each case depends largly upon its peculiar facts. But it is universally admitted that the power of alteration and amendment is not without limit. The alteration must be just and reasonable. The vested rights of property of corporations must be respected. The power should be confined to reasonable amendments regulating the mode of using and enjoying the franchise granted which do not defeat or essentially impair the object of the grant." Portland & Rochester R. R. Co. v. Deering, 78 Me. 61 (1885).

By far the best exposition of this entire subject is the opinion written by Mr. Justice Field in the so-called Railroad Tax Cases (County of San Mateo v. Southern Pacific R. R. Co., 13 Fed. Rep. 722 (1882); County of Santa Clara v. Southern Pacific R. R Co., 18 Fed. 385 (1883). In this opinion that eminent jurist shows clearly that the reserved power enables the state merely to revoke or alter the rights given by it to the corporation, but that it does not give the state more power over other property of the corporation than it has over similar property of individuals, nor does it give the state power to violate the inhibitions of the Constitution of the United States. The state of California had taxed certain railroad companies in a way that the court in this case held was unfairly discriminatory as compared with the taxation of the property of other corporations and individuals, and that therefore the act denied to these companies the equal protection of the laws and was invalid under the fourteenth amendment. It was argued by counsel that the state had the right to impose such taxes—in fact, to impose any taxes—upon corporations whose charters were subject to the reserved power of alteration, amendment, or repeal. On this point Mr. Justice Field said:

"The state in the creation of corporations, or in amending their charters, * * * possesses no power to withdraw them when created, or by amendment, from the guarantes of the Federal Constitution. It cannot impose the condition that they shall not resort to the courts of law for the redress of injuries or the protection of their property; that they shall make no complaint if their goods were plundered and their premises invaded; that they shall ask no indemnity if their lands be seized for public use, or be taken without due process of law, or that they shall submit without objection to unequal and oppressive burdens arbitrarily imposed upon them; that, in other words, over them and their property the state may exercise unlimited and irresponsible power. Whatever the state may do, even with the creatons of its own will, it must do in subordination of the inhibitions of the Federal Constitution. .

. . Whatever property the corporations acquire in the exercise of the capacities conferred, they hold under the same guarantees which protect the property of individuals from spoliation. It cannot be taken for public use without compensation. It cannot be taken without due process of law, nor can it be subjected to burdens different from those laid upon the property of individuals under like circumstances. The state grants to railroad corporations formed under its laws a franchise, and over it retains control, and may withdraw or modify it. By the reservation clause it retains power only over that which it grants; it does not grant the rails on the road, it does not grant the depots alongside of it; it does not grant the cars on the track, nor the engines which move them, and over them it can exercise no power except such as may be exercised through its control over the franchise, and such as may be exercised with reference to all property used by the carriers for the public. The reservation of power over the franchise—that is, over that which is granted—makes its grant a conditional or revocable contract, whose obligation is not impaired by its revocation or change. * * * The reservation relates only to the contract of incorporation, which, without such reservation, would be irrepealable. It removes the impediment to legislation touching the contract. It places the corporation in the same position it would have occupied had the Supreme Court held that charters are not contracts, but that laws repealing or altering them did not impair the obligation of contracts. The property of the corporation acquired in the exercise of its faculties is held independently of such reserved power, and the state can only exercise over it the control which it exercises over the property of individuals engaged in similar business.''

It is about impossible, even by an analyisis of the cases in which this .power to alter corporate charters is considered, to disclose a basis for arriving at determinate results. The reservations are different in the different states—in some the power to alter or repeal is unconditional; in others an exercise of the power is subject to certain provisos, such as that it can be exercised only ''in such manner * * * that no injustice shall be done to the corporators;'' that the power be exercised ''if they (the legislature) deem it necessary or convenient to the public interest;'' that the power may be exercised ''but not so as to divest or impair any right of property acquired under the same;'' that a corporate charter may be altered or repealed ''when ever in its (the legislature's) opinion it (the corporate charter) may be injurious to the citizens of the state'' and that such power may be exercised ''at any time when necessary for the public good and general welfare.'' These provisos have necessarily made different the holdings in the different states. (To aid in distinguishing these cases, a compilation of the reservations of the different states is hereto annexed).

Other circumstances tend to complicate the holdings and make reconciliation about impossible. Many of the acts upheld by the courts as a proper exercise of the power under the reserve clause, are justified only as a legitimate exercise of the police power. Many of the courts have upheld acts altering corporate charters to the extent of destroying the property rights of the corporation, and this approval is seemingly based upon the theory that the legislature may force upon the incorporation an acceptance of an alteration as an alternative to an exercise of the right to destroy its existence under the power to repeal.

Examples of the extent to which the courts have gone in approving and disapproving exercise of this power to alter corporate charters are afforded in the following cases:

Under the power reserved to alter corporate charters a legis-

33

lative act changing the name of the corporation has been upheld, Phinney v. Trustees of Shepard and Pratt Hospital, 88 Md. 633 (1898). A change of place for the principal office of the corporation was approved, Bryan v. Board of Education, 151 U. S. 639 (1893); Park v. M. W. A., 181 Ill. 214 (1899). The decisions in most of the courts are to the effect that the state may. under its reserved power of amendment, or repeal, regulate and control, either compulsorily or by way of permission to some of the stockholders, the scheme of management of the corporation; that it may change the number and method of election of the directors, Miller v. State, 15 Wall. 478 (1872); Close v. Glenwood Cemetery, 107 U. S. 466 (1882); Looker v. Maywood, 179 U. S. 46 (1900). Changes in the method of voting among the stockholders or the forced introduction of new corporators to voting privileges have been sanctioned, Hyatt v. Esmond, 37 Barb. 601 (1862); Com. v. Bonsall, 3 Whart. (Pa.) 559 (1838); Gregg v. Cranby M. & S. Co., 164 Mo. 616 (1901). Contra see In re Newark Lib. Assn., 64 N. J. L. 217 (1899) and Orr v. Bracken County, 81 Ky. 593 (1884).

In Wilson v. Tesson, 12 Ind. 285 (1859), and act of the legislature was sustained which provided that banking corporations could continue to do business only if they paid all their circulating notes in coin upon demand. In Yates v. The People, 207 Ill. 316 (1904), the court approved an act providing that the charters of all insurance companies which ceased for the period of one year to transact the business for which they were organized should be deemed and held extinct in all respects as if they had expired by their own limitation.

In Railway v. Philadelphia, 101 U. S. 528 (1879), it was stated that the legislature under the reserve clause could raise the license fee for the running of cars by a street railway company. See also Atty. Gen'l ex rel. Hilbert, 72 Wis. 184.

The power to regulate the rates of carriers it is held may be exercised under the reserve clause. Atty. Gen'l v. R. R. Cos., supra.

In Ohio v. Neff, 52 Ohio St. 375 (1895), the legislature attempted to put the affairs of the Cincinnati College, a corporation subject to the reserved power, under the management of the directors of the University of Cincinnati, and to give to the latter control of the funds of the College. The court held the act void, as violating the provision in the state constitution that "private property shall ever be held inviolate."

In Woodward v. Central Vermont Ry. Co., 180 Mass. 599 (1902), the defendant company was incorporated, subject to the reserved power, for the purpose of acquiring, to effect a reorganization, the property of an insolvent corporation which had been foreclosed by a judicial sale. A subsequent statute provided that certain judgments recovered against the former corporation could be collected from the defendant company. It was held that the act was void, as being a confiscation of property.

In Commrs. of the sinking Fund v. Green & Barren River Nav. Co., 79 Ky. 73 (1880), the state of Kentucky leased to the defendant corporation a certain river line of navigation, with all rights and franchises thereto pertaining. Afterwards the legislature sought to revoke the lease and to recall the right to collect tolls which appertained thereto. The court held that this could not be done. The lease had been made subsequently to the incorporation of the company, was a distinct right of property vested in the corporation by the state, was not a franchise of incorporation, and therefore was irrevocable.

In C. M. & St. P. Ry. Co. v. Minn. Cent. R. Co., 14 Fed. 525 (1882), the city of Redwing granted to complainant the right to lay tracks on Levee Street. Later, and after the complainant had begun construction of its line on that street and had expended some $1,500 therein, the city, under a reserved power to alter the grant, passed an ordinance amending the original grant so as to prohibit the laying of tracks along the route previously agreed upon. The complainant asks that the city and the Minn. Cent. R. Co. be enjoined from interfering with the construction of its line.

It was held that the company must submit to such alterations and amendments as were reasonable and necessary to carry into effect the original purpose of the ordinance; but that the reserve clause gave no authority to alter, amend, or repeal the ordinance so as to affect the company's vested rights. The court said:

"The ordinance did not, however, give authority to amend or repeal so as to *affect* essential and vested rights. The common council of the city reserved the right to alter

and amend this ordinance of 1870, within the scope of the
legislative power conferred on the municipality, * * *''

The legislative power under the reserve clause of Minn. may
be exercised ''but not so as to divest or impair any right of
property acquired under the same (the charter).'' The complainant was allowed to complete its line.

In Stearns v. Minnesota, 179 U. S. 223 (1900), an act of incorporation provided that the company should pay 3% of its
gross earnings in lieu of all taxes on property. The power to
alter or repeal was reserved, and the state subsequently passed
an act by which the companies were required, in addition to this
original tax of 3%, to pay on such of their lands not used for
railroad purposes as were theretofore or might thereafter be
granted to them by the state of Minnesota or the United States,
the same taxes as were paid on similar lands by individuals.
The decision is not strikingly clear, but holds the act invalid
apparently as in conflict with the 14th amendment of the Federal
Constitution guaranteeing the equal protection of the law.

In Mayor & Aldermen of Worcester v. Norwich & W. R. R.
Co., 109 Mass. 103 (1871), the legislature passed an act requiring certain railroads to unite in the construction of a union
passenger depot in the city of Worcester at a place to be determined by certain commissioners to be appointed for that purpose,
also requiring these railroad companies to extend their tracks
in that city to this new depot, and then to discontinue specified
portions of their then existing lines. The cost to the companies
was very great. This act was held to be a ''reasonable exercise'' of the reserved power to alter, amend or repeal the charters of the railroad companies concerned.

In Com. v. Eastern R. R. Co., 103 Mass. 254 (1869), the legislature, under the reserve power, required the railroad companies to erect a station at a specified point on the road. The court
approved the requirement.

In Sioux City St. Ry. Co. v. Sioux City, 138 U. S. 98 (1890)
and in Storrie v. Huston City St. Ry. Co., 92 Tex. 129 (1898),
the requirement was that a street railway company should pay
for the paving of the street in which it operated for a certain
distance outside of the rails, although the original act of incorporation had required the company, as the consideration for

the grant of the franchises, which contained the reserve clause, to pave the street merely between the rails. This requirement, too, was approved. See also Fair Haven R. R. Co. v. New Haven, 203 U. S. 372 (1906) ; Marshalltown Ry. v. City of Marshall town, 127 Ia. 637 (1905).

In English b. New Haven & Northampton Co., 32 Conn. 240 (1864), the railroad company was obliged to widen certain bridges over its tracks in the city of New Haven, because its charter was subject to alteration or repeal. See Contra Peo. v. Lake Shore Mich. So. Ry. Co., 52 Mich. 277 (1883), and C. G. I. Ry. Cor. Hough, 61 Mich. 507 (1886).

In Monongohela Nav. Co. v. Coon, 6 Pa. St. 379 (1847) the navigation company erected a dam in the Monongohela River, being thereunto enfranchised by the state. It had been decided in the Supreme Court of Pennsylvania in 1843, same parties, 6 W. & S. (Pa.) 101 (1843), that the building of the dam did not render it liable in damages to Coon, who owned a mill on a branch of the main stream. Subsequently, in 1844 the legislature acting under its powers to amend the charter of the company, passed an act requiring it to pay damages for all injuries done by building the dam. The court held this act valid and that Coon could recover under it—apparently a confiscation.

In Holyoke v. Lyman, 15 Wall. 50 (1872), a manufacturing company was chartered to build and maintain a dam across a river, paying damages for injuries suffered by the owners of fishing rights *above* the dam. The legislature later passed an act requiring the company, at an expense of $30,000, to construct a fishway in the dam so as to protect fishing rights below the dam. This act was held constitutional under the reserve clause. See Com. v. Essex Co., 79 Mass. 239 (1859). Seemingly Contra.)

In Wisconsin a requirement that a senior railroad pay one half the expense of maintaining crossing signals, etc., made necessary by the crossing of its lines by a junior road, was held to be an unauthorized exercise of the reserve clause and a taking of property that had vested in the senior company. State ex rel. Nor. Pac. R. R. Co., 140 Wis. 145 (1909).

To the effect that the power of alteration cannot be exercised so as to substitute a new corporaton for the original. See Atty. Gen'l v. R. R. Cos., 35 Wis. 425 (1874) ;

Zabrieszi v. Hackensack, 18 N. J. Eq. 178 (1867) ;

Treadwell v. Salisbury, 7 Gray, 393 (1856);
Durfee v. Old Colony, etc., Ry. Co., 5 Allen 230 (1862);
Dow v. Nor. Pac. Ry. Co., 67 N. H. 1 (1886).

The foregoing quotations and citations (the compilation of cases is not exhaustive) are presented merely to substantiate the assertion that the cases having to do with the power under the reserve clause to *alter* corporate charters are difficult to reconcile. They bring out distinctly, however, three restrictions upon this power to alter the state's contract with the corporators; first, that property rights independent of the charter cannot, in the exercise of such power, be violated; second, that the reservation does not empower the legislature to deny to corporations or persons the equal protection of the laws, and third, that the power to alter cannot be carried to the point where practically a new contract is foisted upon the corporators.

(2) WITH RESPECT TO THE POWER TO REPEAL CORPORATE CHARTERS.

By the contract of incorporation the power is reserved to the legislature to repeal the corporate charter at any time after its passage. The power thus reserved is a power to recall only that which the state has given in the charter, and only those rights which the corporation gets from the state. The state gives life to a corporation—at least, to the extent of licensing it to do business as a corporation. Therefore, this privilege,—the franchise to exist as a corporation,— may, if constitutional rights are not thereby violated, be recalled; the charter may be repealed, and the word repeal bears but one construction.

C. J. Ryan, in Atty. Gen'l v. R. R Cos., supra, pp. 576 & 577, construing this power, says:

"We are bound, in our construction of it, by the very words used. * * *: The power is limited by its own words only. Any limitation of it must come from these words. * * *: The power to repeal can bear but one construction; for, in this use, the word has but one meaning * * *. Arguments ab inconvenienti cannot weigh against the manifest meaning of the word used; they may go to impeach the wisdom of the power, but not to impair its import."

The repeal, under the reserve clause, of a corporate charter
—of the franchises, privileges and immunities derived directly
from the state—does not violate private property rights.

The court in Greenwood v. Freight Co., supra, p. 17, dwelling
upon this phase of the reserve power, said:

"* * * What is it may be repealed? It is the act of incorporation. It is this organic law on which the corporate
existence depends which may be repealed, so that it shall cease
to be law * * *.

*Personal and real property acquired by the corporation
during its lawful existence, rights of contract, or choses
in action so acquired, and which do not in their nature depend upon the general powers conferred by the charter, are
not destroyed by such a repeal; and the courts may, if the
legislature does not provide some special remedy, enforce
such rights by the means within their power. The rights
of the shareholders of such a corporation, to their interest
in its property, are not annihilated by such a repeal, and
there must remain in the courts the power to protect those
rights."* Id. p. 18 & 19.

Nor does the repeal of a corporate charter containing the
reserve clause impair the obligation of contracts between the
corporation and third parties. After the repeal the corporate
property becomes a trust fund for distribution among creditors
and stockholders.

Mumma v. Potomac Co., 8 Pet. 281 (1834);

Bacon v. Robertson, 18 How. 480 (1855);

Greenwood v. Freight Co., supra.

"It (the reserved power) became, by operation of law, a
part of every contract or mortgage made by the company * * *. The share and the bondholders took their
stock or their securities subject to this paramount condition, and of which they, in law, had notice. If the corporation, by making a contract or deed of trust on its property,
could clothe its creditors with an absolute, unchangeable
right, it would enable the corporation, by its own act, to
abrogate one of the provisions of the fundamental law of
the state."

Peik v. C. &. N. W. Ry. Co., 94 U. S. 164 (1890).

The power to repeal having been exercised was approved in the following cases:

Greenwood v. Freight Company, 105 U. S. 16 (1881.)

Bill by Greenwood, a stockholder in the Marginal Freight Railway Company, praying an injunction to prevent the Union Freight Company from taking over the property of the corporation in which he, Greenwood, was a stockholder.

The Marginal Freight Railway Company was organized by act of the Massachusetts Legislature, April 26, 1867, to build and operate a street railway in Boston. The right of way of this company for part of its route lay over the line of a railway previously granted to the Commercial Freight Railroad Company and the Marginal Company by virtue of a provision in its charter, purchased and paid the Commercial Company for the joint use of its tracks. On May 6, 1872 the Legislature of Massachusetts incorporated the Union Freight Company with authority to run its track through the same streets and over the same ground covered by the Marginal Company, and to take possession of the tracks of the Marginal Company, on payment of compensation. This latter act repealed the charter of the Marginal Company. Plaintiff objects to the repeal of the charter and to the authority to take over the property of his company.

The question before the court was "whether the features of the act to which complainant objects in his bill are beyond the power of the legislature of Massachusetts, or are forbid by anything in the constitution of the United States." p. 16.

After stating that under the unvarying decisions of the United States Supreme Court, the unconditional repeal of the Charter of the Marginal Company was void unless made valid by some reservation of power, the court said:

"The first of these reservations of legislative power over corporations is found in sec. 41 of chap. 68 of the General Statutes of Massachusetts, in the following language: 'Every act of incorporation passed after the eleventh day of March, in the year one thousand eight hundred and thirty-one, shall be subject to amendment, alteration, or repeal, at the pleasure of the legislature.'

It would be difficult to supply language more comprehensive or expressive than this."

"Such an act may be amended; that is, it may be changed by additions to its terms or by qualifications of the same. It may be altered by the same power, and it may be repealed. What is it may be repealed? It is the act of incorporation. It is this organic law on which the corporate existence of the company depends which may be repealed, so that it shall cease to be a law; or the legislature may adopt the milder course of amending the law in matters which need amendment, or altering it when it needs substantial change. All this may be done at the pleasure of the legislature. That body need give no reason for its action in the matter. The validity of such action does not depend on the necessity for it, or on the soundness of the reasons which prompted it. This expression, 'the pleasure of the legislature,' is significant, and is not found in many of the similar statutes in other states.

This statute having been the settled law of Massachusetts, and representing her policy on an important subject for nearly fifty years before the incorporation of the Marginal Company, we cannot doubt the authority of the legislature of Massachusetts to repeal that charter. Nor is this seriously questioned by counsel for appellant; and it may, therefore, be assumed that if the repealing clause of the act of May 6, 1872, stood alone, its validity must be conceded. Crease v. Babcock 23 Pick. (Mass.) 334; Erie & N. E. Railroad Co. v. Casey, 26 Pa. St. 287; Pennsylvania College Cases, 13 Wall. 190; 2 Kent, Com. 306.

The property of corporations, even including the franchises when that is necessary, may be taken for public use under the power of eminent domain, on making due compensation."

See also Thornton v. Marginal Frt. Co., 132 Mass. 32, 34.

Willmington Street Railway Co. v. Willmington Etc. Co., 8 Delaware, Ch. 468 (1900).

The legislature under the reserve clause revoked that portion of complainant's franchise which gave it an exclusive right to operate a street railway system in the city of Wilmington.

The contention of parties (p. 490) raised the question of the precise meaning and effect of the reserve clause in Section 17, Article 2, Del. Con. 1831. With the context this clause reads:

"No act of incorporation except for the renewal of existing corporations, shall be hereafter enacted without concurrence of two-thirds of each branch of the Legislature ; with a reserved power of revocation by the Legislature."

The Court, after referring to difficulties that have arisen in interpreting the more common form of the reserve clause, i. e., to "alter, amend or repeal," says:

"This long review of the authorities shows that there is no decision of any sort in opposition. to the plain, logical interpretation of the phrase, 'reserved power of revocation by the Legislature,' as.meaning the power to revoke, at the pleasure of the Legislature, any or all of the franchises granted to a corporation. the power to recall all the rights, privileges or franchises granted to a corporation or any number less than all, or any single right, privilege, or franchise; that it cannot mean less than this, and that it cannot mean more. * * * "

See also Lathrop v. Stedman, 13 Blotch. 134 (1875) ;

Beer Co. v. Mass. 97 U. S. 25 (1877).

People v. O'Brien et al , 111 N. Y. 1 at 48 (1888).

The Broadway Surface Railroad Company was incorporated under a general law of New York, May 15th, 1884. The corporation was dissolved by legislative act on May 4, 1886.

The Court dwelling upon the constitutionality of this act dissolving the corporation, held:

"It may be assumed in the discussion that the authority of the legislature to repeal a charter, if it has expressed its intention to reserve such power in its grant, constitutes a valid reservation. Parties to a contract may lawfully provide for its termination at the election of either party, and it may, therefor, be conceded that the state had authority to repeal this charter, provided no rights of property were thereby invaded or destroyed." P. 46 Andrews & Earl, J. J., concur with the holding that the annuling act was constitutional and that its effect was only to take the life of the corporation.*

Griffin v. Kentucky Ins. Co., 3 Bish (Ky.) 592 (1868).

The Kentucky Insurance Company was incorporated March 4th, 1865. The legislature, under a power reserved by general law to mend or repeal corporate charters at the will of that body, repealed this charter in 1868. The one question before the court was as to the constitutionality of this repealing act.

Held: After deciding that the reserve clause contained in the general law became a part of complainant's charter, and that the repealing law was constitutional, the court said:

"And, whatever might be thought of the policy of such legislation, or of the policy or justice of the repealing statute, over which the judiciary has no jurisdiction our conclusion, as to the mere power of the repeal, is we think sustained by reason and abundant authority."

So. Bell Telephone & Telegraph Co. v. City of Richmond. 98 Fed. 671 (1899).

The city of Richmond, Va., by ordinance passed June 26, 1884, gave the complainant the right to use the streets of that city for poles and wires of its system. The right was reserved to the council to repeal said entire ordinance at any time, such repeal to take effect twelve months after the adoption of the repealing resolution. On Dec. 14th, 1894, the city re-

---

* Dissolution of the corporation in People v. O'Brien, 111 N. Y. 1, had not the effect to extinguish the franchises to operate a street railway system in New York City. All cases hold that the effect of the repeal of a corporate charter is to deprive the corporators of all the rights, privileges and franchises contained in such charter. In this case the Marginal Co. was incorporated under a general law of New York, May 13, 1884. No franchise to operate a street railway was contained in the articles of incorporation—nor did the legislature ever grant any such franchise to the Marginal Company. The Constitution of New York provided that the city of New York had the exclusive power to grant such franchises and the franchise of the Marginal Company was granted to the company on December 5th, 1884, by the City of New York. A franchise being property, and in this case not being contained in the articles of incorporation repealed, it was property legitimately acquired under its charter and was not destroyed by the extinction of the corporate life. Had this franchise been granted in the charter, or subsequently by the legislature to the Broadway Surface R. R Co., or to another with the reserved right to alter or repeal the same, and the Broadway Surface Co., as transferee, became owner thereof, a different question would be presented.

pealed the ordinance and consequently the complainant one year
from and after that date had no legal right to use the streets
of Richmond for its poles and wires.

The sole question before the court was the validity of this repealing resolution.

Held: "The complainant accepted the terms of the ordinance giving consent, and erected its lines along and over
the streets of the city of Richmond under the provisions of
the same. Having agreed with the city, for reasons of its
own, to the terms, conditions and restrictions of said ordinance, and having for years acquiesced in the same, complainant should not now be permitted to either deny its
validity or escape its requirements. * * * This court
is not to pass upon the propriety of the ordinance of repeal; for the power of the repeal does not depend on
either the necessity for it, or on the soundness of the reasons assigned for it."

McLaren v. Pennington.   1 Paige 102 (1828).

On December 20th, 1824, the New Jersey legislature incorporated the New Jersey Protection and Lombard Bank. The
bank commenced operation June 1st, 1825, after paying an incorporation fee of $25,000 and continued in operation until
November 18, 1825, when it stopped payment. On November
23, 1825, the legislature repealed the charter granted in 1824
and appointed defendants trustees of the assets of the bank.
The original act of incorporation contained the reserve clause.
The validity of the act repealing the charter was called in question.

Held: "If the act repealing the charter of the bank was
unconstitutional, the defendants acquired no rights under
that act, and the notes in controversy, still belong to the
corporation. It is proper, therefore, that, that question
should be first considered. It is a well settled principle
of the common law, and the privileges and franchises
granted to a private corporation become a right vested,
which cannot be divested or altered, except by the consent
of the corporation, by a forfeiture declared by the proper
tribunal, or by act of parliament." . . .

"The validity of the act repealing the charter, must

therefore depend upon the affect that is to be given to the seventeenth section of the original act of corporation. This section, in terms, gives the legislature a right, at any time, to alter, mend, or repeal the act of incorporation. But the counsel for the complainant contends that this section is repugnant to the grant of the franchises contained in the other parts of this act, and is therefore void. The common law principle that a condition repugnant to the grant is void, has no application to this case. The seventeenth section is not condition repugnant to the grant; it is only a limitation to the grant." * * *

"It is not pretended that there is anything in the constitution of New Jersey, or of the United States, which prohibits the reservation of such a power in a legislative grant. * * * The power of repealing the bank charter was therefore legally and constitutionally reserved to the legislature of New Jersey, and this court will not presume it has been improperly or unconscientiously exercised."

The following cases and quotations bear on the power under the reserve clause to repeal corporate charters.

In Mayor of New York v. Twenty-third St. Ry. Co., 113 N. Y. 311 (1889), the court, per Justice Earle, said:

"It (the legislature) may take away its (the company's) franchise to be a corporation, and it may regulate the exercise of its corporate powers. As it has the power utterly to deprieve the corporation of its franchises to be a corporation, it may prescribe the conditions and terms upon which it may live and exercise such franchise." *

In the matter of the petition of the New York Cable Ry. Co., 40 Hun (N. Y.) 1 (1886), in holding that the legislature might repeal the right of the petitioners to acquire the consent of the municipal authorities and property owners to the construction of its railways, the court, per Daniels, said:

"While it is true that the legislature cannot deprive a corporation of any of its property, it may limit, restrict, or withdraw any of its franchises or corporate privileges by means of the power reserved to it by the constitution.

* * * The distinction which has been taken on this
subject warrants the conclusion that it is only where other
rights of a proprietory character have been acquired and
become vested that the interposition of the legislative authority for divesting or forfeiting them has been forbidden.''

In Schurz v. Cook, 148 U. S. 397, 410—411 (1893) the court
after reference to the reserve clause in the constitution and revised laws of New York, said:

"In the case of People v. O'Brien, 111 N. Y. 1, cited by
counsel for the plaintiffs in error, while the court held
that it was not within the power of the legislature to destroy the property rights of a corporation, it was not a
question that the legislature could destroy the existence
of the corporation.'' To this effect the court cites, The
Mayor, etc., of New York v. The Twenty-third St. R. R.
Co., 113 N. Y. 311; Hamilton Gas Light Co. v. Hamilton
City, supra, and Greenwood v. Freight Co., supra.

Cook in his treatise on corporations, 6th Ed. Vol. 2, Sec. 639,
says:

"Where, however, the right of repeal is reserved by the
legislature, then such reservation becomes a part of the contract, and the repeal of the charter rests in the discretion of
the legislature.''

Thompson, in his commentaries on the Law of Corporations,
Vol. IV, Sec. 5417, states:

"If the charter, or an existing constitutional provision
or general law, reserves to the legislature a plenary right
of alteration or repeal, then the co-adventurers, by accepting the charter act and organizing under it, consent that
future legislatures may exercsie that right; and it seems to
be an untenable view that they may repudiate that consent and fly in the face of future legislation which takes
place under a right thus reserved.''

The state may also give to the corporation other franchises,
privileges and exemptions; in so far as it does so it can revoke

or repeal such grants, because they form part of the contract
existing between the state and the corporation, and the state.
has reserved to itself the power to annul or amend the whole or
any part of such contract.   Thus if the state has exempted the
corporation from taxation by the state, such exemption may
be repealed under the reserve clause.

Comrs. v. Bancroft, 203 U. S. 112 (1906) ;
R. R. Co. v. Georgia, 98 U. S. 359 (1898);
Tomlinson v. Jessup, 15 Wall. 454 (1872) ;
Iron City Bank v. Pittsburg, 37 Pa. St. 340 (1860) ;
State v. Commr., 37 N. J. L. 228 (1874) ;
Bank v. Daviess Co., 102 Ky., 174 (1897) ;
West Wis. Ry. Co. v. Trempeleau Co., 35 Wis. 257
(1874).

Not only the franchise to exist as a corporation, but also
the other franchises of the corporation may be resumed by the
state—the franchise to carry on a particular business in which
the corporation is engaged; for example to operate a railroad,
or a street railway, Greenwood v. Freight Co., supra; Hender-
son v. Ry. Co., 21 Fed. 358 (1884) ; or the exclusive privileges
to lay pipes and mains in a public street of a city and supply
the inhabitants with gas, Hamilton G. L. & C. Co. v. Hamilton,
146 U. S. 258 (1892) ; or to transact a banking business, State
v. Society, 11 Ohio 1 (1841), or to collect tolls on a highway,
Zimmerman v. Road Co., 81½ Pa. St. 96 (1873).

The power of eminent domain may be recalled.   Adirondack
Ry. Co. v. N. Y., 176 U S. 335 (1899).

THE RESERVE CLAUSE NEGATIVES ANY LEGISLATIVE INTENTION TO GRANT AN IRREPEARABLE CHARTER.

"A reservation of the right to repeal, alter, or amend the
charter or franchise of a corporation negatives any intention on the part of the state to confer irrevocable rights upon
the corporators.   Under such a restriction, the franchise
must be regarded as simple legal powers, resulting from
an enabling act of the legislature, not as rights secured by
contract with the state."   Morawetz, Priv. Corps. p. 1055.

IT IS VERY DOUBTFUL THAT THE LEGISLATURE, EVEN IF IT SO DESIRES, HAS POWER TO GRANT AN IRREPEALABLE CORPORATE CHARTER.

"The provision of our constitution has taken away from the legislature the power of making such an irrevocable contract with a corporation. It seems to us that this is the decision of this court in the cases of West. Wis. R. Co. v. Trempealeau Co., 35 Wis. 257, 265; Atty. Gen. v. R. R. Cos., 35 Wis. 425, 574 et seq.; and these decisions are sustained by the decisions of the supreme court of the United States. Railroad Co. v. Philadelphia, 101 U. S. 528, 536, 83 Pa. St. 429, 434. In the case of New Jersey v. Yard, 95 U. S. 104, 111, Justice Miller, in speaking of the difference in power of the legislature when there is no constitutional inhibition and when there is such constitutional inhibition, says: 'The case differs from those in which, by the constitution of some of the states, this right to alter, amend, and repeal all laws creating corporate privileges becomes an inalienable legislative power. The power thus conferred cannot be limited or bargained away by any act of the legislature, because the power itself is beyond the legislative control.' " The state ex rel. The Cr. City R. Co. v. Hilbert, 27 Wis. 184, 193 (1888).

THE EFFECT OF THE REPEAL OF A CORPORATE CHARTER.

The court in Greenwood v. Freight Co., supra, discussing the effect of the repeal of a corporate charter, stated:

"What is the effect of the repeal of the charter of a corporation like this?

One obvious effect of the repeal of a statute is that it no longer exists. Its life is at an end. Whatever force the law may give to transactions into which the corporation entered and which were authorized by the charter while in force, it can originate no new transactions dependant upon the power conferred by the charter. If the corporation be a bank, with power to lend money and to issue circulating notes, it can make no new loan nor issue any new notes designed to circulate as money.

If the essence of the grant of the charter be to operate a railroad, and to use the streets of the city for that purpose, it can no longer so use the streets of the city, and no longer exercise the franchise of running a railroad in the city. In short, whatever power is dependant solely upon the grant of the charter, and which could not be exercised by unincorporated private persons under the general laws of the state, is abrogated by the repeal of the law which granted these special rights.''

The legislature under the reserve clause may repeal all or any of the franchises, privileges or immunities granted by the charter.

> Atty. Gen'l. v. R. R. Cos., supra;
> Greenwood v. Freight Co., supra;
> Wilmington St. Ry. Co., v. Wilmington, etc. Co., supra;
> So. Bell Tel. & Tel. Co. v. City of Richmond, supra.

A strict construction of the reserve clause in the Wisconsin constitution would seem to confine the power of alteration or repeal to acts or laws for the formation of corporations, but it has been interpreted broadly by the court and has been held to extend to all legislation affecting corporations, including not only the grant of the franchise to exist as a corporation, but also to all grants of power and privileges, i. e., franchises of corporations—whether granted at the time the corporation comes into existence or at some later date.

> West. Wis. R. R. Co. v. Trempealeau Co., 35 Wis. 257.— 265;
> Atty. Gen'l. ex rel. Hilbert, 72 Wis. 184.

''Corporate charters often contain franchises of the greatest value not only the franchise to be a corporation, but often a franchise to operate a railroad, to erect and maintain a bridge, to establish and maintain a telegraph system, or the like. And while the affirmation to withdraw all this would seem in conflict with the preconceived notions of justice and although it has been argued that such a reservation is inconsistent with the grant and therefore, void, nevertheless it is well settled that these rights may be well swept away where the stipulation has been made, and that the true conception of their nature is as a sort

34

of a license repealable at the option of the power which **grants**
them.''

>Citing: Roses Notes on U. S. Reports, 339.
>State v. R. R. Co., 24 Tex. 125, 126;
>Crease v. Babcock, 23 Pick. 540;
>Bridge Co. v. U. S. 105 U. S. 481.

After repealing the charter of a corporation, the legislature
may charter a new corporation, confering upon it powers similar to those enjoyed by the dissolved company, and authorize
it to take the property of such dissolved company for a public
purpose, upon making due compensation.

>Grenwood v. Freight Co., supra, pp. 22, 23.

(3) WITH RESPECT TO THE PURPOSE FOR WHICH THE RESERVE CLAUSE WAS MADE A PART OF OUR CONSTITUTION.

Although the legislature is the sole judge of the expediency
of altering or repealing corporate charters, Am. Coal Co. v.
Coal Co., 46 Md. 15; Miner's Bank v. U. S., 1 Greene (Ia.)
553; Greenwood v. Frt. Co., supra, and the legislative motive
in exercising this power will not be inquired into by the courts,
id. and Cooley Const. Lim. pp. 257, 260, 300 and cases there
cited, it is, however, proper and within the functions of the
courts to construe or interpret the reserve clause, and to determine by ascertaining the intention of the framers of the constitution, the purpose or purposes for which the same was intended.

The prime purpose of the reserve clause was to do away in
this state with the rule of the Dartmouth College Case. See
supra. But was the intention of the framers of the constitution to give the legislature power to alter or repeal corporate
charters at the will or pleasure of that body, or was the intention that this clause should retain in the legislature a mere
power to regulate and control corporations of its own creation.

This question was discussed in a late Wisconsin case.
State ex rel Nor. Pac. R. R. Co., 140 Wis. 145 (1909). The
question before the court was as to the power of the legislature

under the reserve clause to compel the Nor. Pac. R. R. Co. to bear a portion of the expense occasioned by the crossing of its lines by another company. Under the law objected to, the Railroad Commission and the trial court held that the expense of maintaining the crossing and the cost of construction and maintaining the interlocking, derailing and signal system should be borne one-half by each road. The conclusion is based upon the right of the state to alter or repeal the charter of the complaining company.

The court held that the effect of this law was to take away property which had been become vested under a legitimate exercise of the powers granted to the complaining company by its charter. With respect to the reserve power the court said:

"The right to alter or repeal existing charters is not without limitation when the question of vested property rights under the charter is involved. The power is one of regulation and control, and does not authorize interference with property rights vested under the power granted. The doctrine is well stated in Sinking Fund Cases, 99 U. S. 700, 720, as follows:

'That this power has a limit no one can doubt. All agree that it cannot be used to take away property already acquired under the operation of the charter to deprive the corporation of the fruits actually reduced to possession of contracts lawfully made * * * .'

The reserve power stops short of the power to divest vested property rights, and is embodied in the state constitution for the purpose of enabling the state to retain control over corporations, and must be construed in connection with the other provision of the constitution to the effect that private property shall not be taken for public use without compensation. It follows, therefore, 'that where under power in a charter, rights have been acquired and become vested, no amendment or alteration of the charter can take away the property or rights which have become vested under a legitimate exercise of the powers granted."
Comm. v. Essex Co., supra. "Moreover, the power to alter or amend is a reserved power in the interest of the state to modify or repeal its own contract with the corporation. Tomlinson v. Jessup, U. S. 454; State v. C. & N. W. Ry. Co., 128 Wis. 449, 108 N. W. 594."

In so far as this opinion by Justice Kerwin holds that th
reserve clause reserves to the legislature nothing more than th
right to regulate and control corporations, it was qualified b;
Justice Marshall in his concurring opinion, at p. 175.   Justic
Marshall said:

> '..¹"By oversight, I think, the declaration appears in th(
> opinion that the reserve power in the constitution to alter
> amend, and repeal corporate charters is 'one of regulatioı
> and control.' ''

This qualifying opinion by Justice Marshall evidently nega
tives any contention that the state of Wisconsin has adopteɗ
a "regulation and control" theory. Continuing at p. 175 Jus
tice Marshall said: •

> "The court did not intend to go further than Sinkinɡ
> Fund Case, 99 U. S. 700, cited to the effect that such powei
> does not extend to authority to take away property as
> quired under a corporate charter."

The Wisconsin Supreme Court in Pratt v. Brown, 3 Wis.
532 at 540 (1854), seems to approve of the principle that the
power to alter or repeal may be exercised at the will or pleasure
of the legislature.

> "But is it not obvious, that such corporations may hold
> and exercise such power at the will of the legislature, cir-
> cumscribed either by the fundamental law, or by the par-
> ticular act of incorporation? Sometimes the grant of such
> franchises is in perpetuity; sometimes for a given number
> of years, and sometimes during the pleasure of the sovereign
> grantor. But in whatever mode, or at whatever time, the
> franchise is determinable, it is nevertheless dependent upon
> the sovereign power, and is determinable at its will con-
> stitutionally expressed."

Continuing at p. 40, the court said:

> "Where the power of modification or repeal is reserved,
> either in the one mode or the other (by Con. Prov. or in
> the particular act) it is obvious that the grantees must
> rely, for the perpetuity and integrity of the franchises
> granted to them, solely upon the faith of the sovereign
> grantor. A similar statement is found in Cooley, Const.
> Lim. 7th Ed., p. 547.

The Court in Atty. Gen'l· v. R. R. Cos., at p. 574, holds in the following language to the principle enunciated in the earlier Wisconsin case.

"Subject to this reserved right, and under the rule of the Dartmouth College Case, charters of private corporations are contracts, but contracts which the state may alter or determine at pleasure. Contracts of that character are not unknown in ordinary private dealings; and such we hold to be the sound and safe rule of policy. It is so in England. It is so under the Federal Government itself. The material property and rights of corporation should be inviolate as they are here; but it comports with the dignity and safety that the franchise of corporations should be subject to the power which grants them, that corporations should exist as the subordinates of the state, which is their creator, *durante bene placito.*"

C. J. Cole, in West Wis. R. R. Co. v. Trempealeau Co., supra, at p. 272, said that even though outsiders had invested in the bonds and securities of the company, "The whole charter would still be subject to revocation or alteration at the will of the legislature. * * * ."

The following cases hold that under the reserve clause corporate charters may be altered or repealed "at the pleasure of the legislature;" that the power is broader than that of mere regulation and control. In Greenwood v. Frt. Co., supra, the court laid considerable stress upon the wording of the Massachusetts reserve clause. After dwelling upon the power to alter or repeal, the court at p. 17, said:

"All of this may be done at the pleasure of the legislature. That body need give no reason for its action in the matter. The validity of such action does not depend upon the necessity of it, or on the soundness of the reason which prompted it. This expression. 'at the pleasure of the legislature,' is significant, and is not found in many of the similar statutes in other states."

The same court eleven years later, however, held and adopted the principle that the power so reserved must necessarily be exercised at the pleasure of the legislature.

"The words 'at the pleasure of the legislature' are not

in the clauses of the constitution of Ohio, or in the statutes to which we have referred. But the general reservation of the power to alter, revoke or repeal a grant of such privileges necessarily implies that the power may be exerted at the pleasure of the legislature." Hamilton G. L. & C. C. v. Hamilton City, supra, p. 271.

The court in Wilmington St. R. R. Co. v. Wilmington etc. Co., supra at p. 500, adopts the principle laid down by Justice Harlan in the Hamilton G. L. & C. Co. Case, 146 U. S., at p. 270, in the following language:

"This long review of the authorities shows that there is no decision of any sort in opposition to the plain, logical interpretation of the phrase, 'reserve power of revocation by the legislature,' as meaning the power to revoke, *at the pleasure of the legislature,* any or all of the franchises granted to a corporation, * * * ."

The words, "pleasure of the legislature," are not found in the Delaware reserve clause which reads "and with a reserve power of revocation by the legislature."

Again at p. 494 this same court said:

"It may be considered settled, therefore, beyond the possibility of doubt, that the constitutional reservation of the power of revocation by the legislature became a part of the charter of the Wilmington City Railway Company as if it had been inserted therein *ipissimis verbis,* and that the legislature might exert that power at any time, and for any reasons that might seem sufficient to itself, in other words. at its pleasure."

Zabriske v. Hackensack. 18 N. J. Eq. 178 (1867).

"The provision (reserve clause) is contained in the general act of this state, passed in 1846. (Nix. Dig. 152, Sec. 6) that such charters should be subject to alteration. suspension and repeal, in the discretion of the legislature. This and all similar special and general provisions were intended for the purpose specified; to give to the legislature the clear right, at their pleasure, to alter or repeal the acts of incorporation." P. 185.

See, to this effect, Note to Madison, Watertown, & Milwaukee Plank Road Co. v. Reynolds, 3 Wis. 258 at 266 (1854).

In determining the intention of the framers of the constitution, the state's power over corporations without express reservations should be kept in mind.

Even after the decision of the Dartmouth College Case and before the invention of the reserve clause, the state was not without power to regulate and control corporations.

The state, by proper proceedings instituted in the courts by the attorney general, could forfeit a corporate charter for misuse or abuse.

> State ex rel. Atty. Gen'l v. Milwaukee L. S. & W. R. Co., 45 Wis. 579;
> State v. Madison St. Ry., 72 Wis. 612;
> Wright v. Milwaukee E. R. &. L. Co., 95 Wis. 29;
> Peo. v. No. River Sugar Ref. Co., 121 N. Y. 582;
> Chicago L. Ins. Co. v. Auditor, 101 Ill. 82;
> Distilling Co. v. People, 156 Ill. 125;
> Peo. v. Pullman Pal. Car Co., 175 Ill. 125.

For additional citations, and for the various misuses, abuses and other causes held sufficient to cause a forfeiture of charter, see 2 Morawetz Priv. Corps. Sec. 1018 et seq.

The legislature could have reserved ·in each charter the power to repeal for cause. In Iowa, Massachusetts, Delaware, New York and in the U. S. Supreme Court, it is held that the legislature is the sole arbiter as to whether the condition has happened upon which the power to repeal is contingent.

> Miners' Bank v. U. S., 1 Greene (Ia.) 482 (1846);
> Crease v. Babcock, 23 Pick. 234;
> Del. R. R. Co. v. Thorp, 5 Harr. (Del.) 454 (1854);
> McLaren v. Pennington, 1 Paige 107;
> Bridge Co. v. U. S., 105 U. S. 470 (1881).

In other states even though the legislature reserves this power of repeal for cause, the courts hold that an antecedent judicial finding of the happening of the condition upon which the power to repeal is limited, is necessary. Flint, etc., P. Road Co. v. Woodwell, 25 Mich. 99 (1872).

Tripp v. Plank Road Co., 66 Mich. 1 (1887). An intermediate position is taken in Pennsylvania and Minnesota,
where it is held that the legislature can repeal the charter,
and there is then the presumption that the condition had occurred and that the repeal was valid, but the fact is subject
to a judicial review, the burden being upon the corporation to
show that the repeal was unjustified.

> Erie, etc., R. R. Co., v. Casey, 26 Pa. St. 287 (1856) ;
> Myrick v. Brawley, 33 Minn. 377 (1885).

Quere—did the framers of the constitution by inventing the
reserve clause intend duplicating these powers? Was it their
intention to make more positive this power in the legislature
to alter or repeal by refraining from making exercise of the
power contingent upon misuse or abuse or by limiting it upon
a condition—such as when the public interests require an exercise thereof?

In addition to the above common law control over corporations, there is a power which abides with the state to legislate
so as to affect the corporate powers conferred by charter, although such power be not especially reserved either in the
charter, the constitution, or general law. This is a power to
pass laws for the promotion of the general peace, health, and
good order of the community—and is known as the police
power.

Under the sanction of this power, laws have been enacted
and upheld requiring railroad companies to ring bells at crossings to warn wayfarers—Galena, etc. R. Co. v. Appleby, 28 Ill.
283; to refrain from constructing their tracks so as to prevent
free and safe access to public highways and depot buildings—
Veazie v. Mayo, 45 Me. 560; and to moderate the speed of their
trains—Toledo, etc., Ry. Co. v. Deacon, 63 Ill. 91. It has also
been held competent for the legislature to regulate the carrying rates of railroads—People v. Boston, etc., Ry. Co., 70 N. Y.
569; Blake v. Winona, etc., Ry. Co., 19 Minn. 418. Affirmed
94 U. S. 180; Chicago, etc., Ry. Co., v. Ackley, 94 U. S. 179.
This power was held sufficient to justify the discontinuance
of the use of the burial grounds of a cemetery corporation,
for the purposes of interment; to prohibit the carrying of
lottery schemes by previously chartered corporations—Moore
v. State, 48 Miss. 147; Freliegh v. State, 8 Mo. 606.

In all the cases where the question at issue was the power, under the reserve clause, to repeal corporate charters, it has been held that this power could be exercised at the will or pleasure of the legislature. In Greenwood v. Freight Company; Willmington Street Railway Comppany y. Willmington, etc. Company; People v. O'Brien, et al; Griffin v. Kentucky Ins. Co.; and in So. Bell Tel. & Tel. Co. v. City of Richmond, where a similar question in the law of contracts was at issue, no cause is assigned for the legislative act or act of the common council in repealing the grant to the corporation. In McLaren v. Pennington, although the court declares there was cause for repealing the charter of the bank, it expressly holds that cause need not be shown.

In all cases where it is asserted that the power under the reserve clause is a limited one, the issue before the court was the power to *alter* and not the power to *repeal* corporate charters. Even the declarations or assertions in these cases do not go so far as to hold that the legislative power under the reserve clause cannot be exercised at the will or pleasure of that body. In Shields v. Ohio, supra, the court said: "The alteration must be reasonable; they must be made in good faith * * *. Sheer oppression and wrong cannot be inflicted under the guise of amendment or alteration." Like declara tions can be selected from numerous cases. In many of these cases it is said the power is not without limit. However, if read in connection with the facts of the cases, it will be found that such declarations were made with reference to the rule that the alteration must be consistent with the scope and object of the act of incorporation, and to the rules that private property cannot be taken without due process of law and that the state shall not deny to any person the equal protection of the laws.

The law with respect to the power under the reserve clause to alter corporate charters is unsettled and full of difficulties. These difficulties have brought forth dicta and decision which if applied to the reserved power in all its phases, tend, at least, to complicate. The law with respect to *repeal* is not attended by these difficulties—at any rate not all of them—the word "repeal" has in its application to all charters a definite meaning; the word "alter" has not. The exercise of the power to

alter has been so confusedly approved and disapproved that
it is difficult to define either its limits or purpose. This is not
so of the power to repeal. The court in People v. O'Brien,
supra, p. 48, by way of distinction between these two powers,
said:

> "The authorities seem to be uniform to the effect that
> a reservation of the right to repeal, enables a legislature to
> effect a destruction of the corporate life, and disable it
> from continuing its corporate business (Peo. ex rel. Kim-
> ball v. B. &. A. R. R. Co., 70 N. Y. 569; Phillips v. Wickham,
> 1 Paige 590), and a reservation of the right to alter and
> amend confers power to pass all needful laws for the
> regulation of the domestic affairs of a corporation, freed
> from the restrictions imposed by the Federal Constitution
> upon legislation impairing the obligation of contracts.
> (Munn. v. Illinois, 94 U. S. 113, 125)."

THE CASES HOLD AS FOLLOWS:

The power reserved to the legislature by Section 1, Art. XI.
of the Wisconsin Constitution, to repeal all general or special
acts by which corporations without banking powers are created, is an unrestricted one, save only that the legislature may
not destroy vested rights of property. In no case has the power
of the legislature under the reserve clause to repeal a corporate charter been denied. The power reserved to alter corporation charters is unrestricted save only that the legislature
may not destroy vested rights of property, nor defeat or essentially impair the object of the grant, that is, it may not
under the guise of alteration, change the sustantial purposes for
which the corporation was created, or transform it from a corporation of one kind into a corporation of another kind or one
the object of which is materially different from that originally
created. Nor can the legislature under the guise of alteration
deny to any person the equal protection of the laws. It may
alter or repeal corporate charters at pleasure, and what ever
rights or franchises are given by the legislature may be thus
modified or entirely taken away. All such rights and franchises are received, held and exercised, solely upon the faith
of the granter, and during its pleasure.

It follows that any corporate charter granted pursuant to

Sec. 1, Art, XI, Wisconsin Constitution and under Ch. 86 of the Wisconsin revised statutes or any other general law of the state providing for the incorporation of persons for certain purposes, may be altered or repealed at the pleasure of the legislature. A repeal of the corporate charter not only extinguishes the corporate life, and disables the corporation from continuing its corporate business, but also recalls all rights, privileges and franchises granted in the charter.

APPENDIX TO "EXHIBIT 24."

ALABAMA.

Constitution of 1902 Art. XII, Sec. 229: "The legislature
shall pass * * * general laws under which corporation
may be organized and corporate powers obtained, subject
nevertheless, to repeal at the will of the legislature; and shall
pass general laws under which charters may be altered or
amended. * * * The charter of any corporation shall be
subject to amendment, alteration, or repeal under general
laws."

Idem, Sec. 238: "The legislature shall have the power to
alter, amend or revoke any charter of any corporation now
existing, and revokable at the ratification of this constitution
or any that may be hereafter created, whenever, in its opinion
such charter may be injurious to the citizens of this state; in
such manner, however, that no injustice shall be done to the
stockholders."

ARKANSAS.

Constitution of 1874, Art. XII, Sec. 6: "Corporations may
be formed under general laws, which laws may, from time to
time, be altered or repealed. The general assembly shall have
the power to alter, revoke or annul any charter of any corporation now existing, and revokable at the adoption of the
constitution, or any that may be hereafter created, whenever
in its opinion, such charter may be injurious to the citizens
of this state; in such manner, however, that no injustice shall
be done to the corporators."

Statutes of 1894, Ch. XLVII, Art. 11, Sec. 1358: "The general assembly may at any time for just cause, rescind the
powers of any joint-stock corporation created pursuant to

the provisions of this act, and prescribe such mode as may be necessary or expedient for the settlement of its affairs."

CALIFORNIA.

Constitution of 1879, Art. XII, Sec. 1: "Corporations may be formed under general laws, but shall not be created by special act. All laws now in force in this state concerning corporations, and all laws that may be hereafter passed pursuant to this section, may be altered from time to time or repealed."

Codes and Statutes of 1886; Civil Code, Div. 1, Part IV, Title 1. Ch. 111, Art. 111, Sec. 384: "The legislature may at time amend or repeal this part, or any title, chapter, article, or section thereof, and dissolve all corporations created thereunder; but such amendment or repeal does not nor does the dissolution of any such corporation take away or impair any remedy given against any such corporation, its stockholders or officers, for any liability which has been previously incurred."

COLORADO.

Constitution of 876, Art. XV, Sec. 3: "The general assembly shall have the power to alter, revoke or annul any charter of any corporation now existing, and revocable at the adoption of this constitution, or any that may be hereafter created, whenever, in its opinion, such charter may be injurious to the citizens of the state; in such manner, however, that no injustice shall be done to the corporators."

Statutes of 1891, Ch. XXX, Div. 1, Sec. 634: "The general assembly may, at any time, alter, amend, or repeal this act, and shall at all times have power to prescribe such regulations and provisions as it may deem advisable, which regulations and provisions shall be binding on any and all corporations formed under the provisions of this act."

CONNECTICUT.

Act of June 22, 1903, Sec. 43: "All acts creating or authorizing the organization of corporations, or altering the charters of corporations previously existing, which have been or shall be passed by the general assembly, and the charters of all cor-

porations heretofore granted, and under which no corporations
have been organized, shall be subject to alteration, amendment.
and repeal at the pleasure of the general assembly, unless
otherwise expressly provided in such acts; but no such amendment or repeal shall impair any remedy against any such corporation, or against its officers, directors, or stockholders, for
any liability which shall have been previously incurred.''

DELAWARE.

Act of March 17, 1903, Sec. 140: ''This act may be amended
or repealed at the pleasure of the legislature, but such amendment or repeal shall not take away or impair any remedy
against any corporation under this act, or its officers, for any
liability which shall have been previously incurred. This act.
and all amendments thereof, shall be a part of the charter of
every such corporation, except so far as the same are inapplicable and inappropriate to the objects of such corporations.''

Note: The constitution of 1831 contained a clause reserving
to the legislature power to alter and repeal charters, but there
is no such provision in the constitution of 1897.

FLORIDA.

Note: There does not seem to be any reservation of power
in the legislature to alter or revoke charters, either in the constitution or general statutes of the state.

GEORGIA.

Civil Code of 1895, Title II, Sec. 1880: ''In all cases of private charters hereafter granted the state reserves the right
to withdraw the franchise, unless such right is expressly
negatived in the charter.''

IDAHO.

Constitution of 1889, Art. XI, Sec. 2: ''Any such general
law (for the organization of corporations) shall be subject to
future repeal or alteration by the legislature.''

Idem.., Sec. 3: ''The legislature may provide by law for al-

tering, revoking, or annulling any charter of incorporation existing and revocable at the time of the adoption of this Constitution, in such manner, however, that no injustice shall be done
to the corporators.''

Rev. Statutes of 1887, Part II, Title IV, Ch. 1, Sec. 2641:
''The legislature may at any time amend or repeal this title or
any chapter, articles, or section thereof, and dissolve all corporations created thereunder; but such amendment or repeal
does not, nor does the dissolution of any such corporation, take
away or impair any remedy given against any such corporation,
its stockholders for any liability which has been previously
incurred.''

ILLINOIS.

Act of April 18, 1872, Sec. 9: ''The General Assembly shall,
at all times, have power to prescribe such regulations and provisions as it may deem advisable, which regulations and provisions shall be binding on any and all corporations formed under
the provisions of this act.''

INDIANA.

Act of March 9, 1901: ''This act (for the organization of corporations) may be repealed or amended at the discretion of the
legislature.''

IOWA.

Constitution of 1857, Art. VIII, Sec. 12: ''Subject to the
provisions of this article, the General Assembly shall have power
to amend or repeal all laws for the organization or creation of
corporations   *   *   *   by a vote of two-thirds of each branch
of the General Assembly.''

Code of 1897, Part I, Title IX, Ch. I, Sec. 1619: ''The
articles of incorporation, by-laws, rules, and regulations of corporations hereafter organized under the provisions of this title,
or whose organization may be adopted or amended hereunder,
shall, at all times, be subject to legislative control, and may be,
at any time, altered, abridged, or set aside by law, and every
franchise obtained, used, or employed by such corporation may
be regulated, withheld, or be subject to conditions imposed upon

the enjoyment thereof, whenever the General Assembly shall deem necessary for the public good."

KANSAS.

Constitution of 1859, Art. XII, Sec. I: "Corporations may be created under general laws, but all such laws may be amended or repealed."

KENTUCKY.

Constitution of 1891, Bill of Rights, Sec. 3: "Every grant of a franchise, privilege or exemption shall remain subject to revocation, alteration or amendment."

Statutes of 1894, Ch. LIX, Sec. 1987: "All charters and grants of or to corporations, or amendments thereof, enacted or granted since the fourteenth of February, 1856, * * * shall be subject to repeal at the will of the General Assembly, unless a contrary intent be therein plainly expressed; provided, that whilst privileges and franchises so granted may be repealed, no repeal shall impair other rights previously vested."

LOUISIANA.

Civil Code of 1870, Sec. 447: "A corporation legally established may be dissolved by an act of the legislature, if they deem it necessary or convenient to the public interest; provided, that when the act of incorporation imports a contract on the faith of which individuals have advanced money or engaged their property, it cannot be repealed without providing for the reimbursement of the advances made, or making full indemnity to such individuals."

Note: For a construction of this proviso, see *Asylum v. New Orleans*, 105 U. S. 362 (1881).

MAINE.

Constitution of 1819, Art. IV, Sec. 14: "However formed, they (i. e., corporations) shall forever be subject to the general laws of the state."

Revised Statutes of 1903, Title IV, Ch. XLVII, Sec. 2: "Acts of incorporation passed since March 17, 1831, may be amended, altered or repealed by the legislature, as if express provision therefor were made in them, unless they contain an express limitation.''

MARYLAND.   R. S. OWEN.

Constitution of 1867, Art. III, Sec. 48, par. 2: ''All charters granted, or adopted in pursuance of this section, and all charters heretofore granted and created, subject to repeal and modification, may be altered, from time to time, or be repealed; provided nothing herein contained shall be construed to extend to banks, or the incorporation thereof.''

Public General Laws of 1888, Art. XXIII, Sec. 85: ''Every corporation formed under the provisions of this article, shall be subject to any and all provisions and regulations which may hereafter, by any change in or amendments of the Laws of this State, be made applicable to such corporation.''

MASSACHUSETTS.

Revised Laws of 1902, Title XV, Ch. CIX, Sec. 3: ''Every act of incorporation passed after the eleventh day of March in the year 1831 shall be subject to amendment, alteration or repeal by the General Court. All corporations which are organized under general laws shall be subject to such laws as may be hereafter affecting or altering their corporate rights or duties or dissolving them * * *. Such laws of amendment, alteration, or repeal, or such dissolution shall not take away or impair any remedy which may exist by law * * * against the corporation, its members or officers, for a liabiiity previously incurred.''

MICHIGAN.

Constitution of 1850, Art. XV, Sec. 1: ''All laws passed pursuant to this section (referring to the incorporation of companies may be amended, altered or repealed.''

Idem, Sec. 8: ''The legislature shall pass no law altering or amending any act of incorporation heretofore granted, without the assent of two-thirds of the members elected to each house, nor shall any such act be renewed or extended. This restriction shall not apply to municipal corporations.''

35

Compiled Laws of 1897, Title IX, Part XXVII, Ch. CCXXX, Sec. 20: "Every act of incorporation passed since the twentieth day of April in the year 1839, or which shall be hereafter passed, shall, at any time, be subject to amendment, alteration or repeal at the pleasure of the legislature; provided, that no act of incorporation shall be repealed, unless for some violation of its charter or other default, when such charter shall contain an express provision limiting the duration of the same."

MINNESOTA.

General Statutes of 1894, Ch. XXXIV, Title II, Sec. 2837: "This act (relating to corporations not having the right of eminent domain) may be altered or amended at the pleasure of the legislature, but not so as to divest or impair any right of property acquired under the same."

MISSISSIPPI.

Constitution of 1890, Art. IV, Sec. 88: "The legislature shall pass general laws * * * under which corporations may be created, organized, and their act of incorporation altered, and all such laws shall be subject to repeal or amendment."

Idem, Art. VII, Sec. 178: "The legislature shall have power to alter, amend or repeal any charter of incorporation now existing and revocable and any that may hereafter be created, whenever, in its opinion, it may be for the public interest to do so; provided, however, that no injustice shall be done to the stockholders."

MISSOURI.

Note: In the revised statutes of 1845 and 1855 (Art. 1, Ch. XXXIV, Sec. 7) there was a provision that "the charter of every corporation that shall hereafter be granted by the legislature shall be subject to alteration, suspension and repeal in the discretion of the legislature," but no provision exists in the latest revision, that of 1889.

MONTANA.

Constitution of 1889, Art. XV, Sec. 3: "The legislative assembly shall have the power to alter, revoke or annul any charter of incorporation eixsting at the time of the adoption of this Constitution, or which may be hereafter incorporated, whenever in its opinion it may be injurious to the citizens of the state."

Civil Code, Div. 1, Part IV, Title 1, Ch. 1, Art. 1, Sec. 394: "Every grant of corporate power is subject to alteration, suspension or repeal, in the discretion of the legislative assembly."

NEBRASKA.

Constitution of 1875, Art. III, Sec. 1: "All general laws passed pursuant to this section (relating to incorporation of companies) may be altered from time to time, or repealed."

NEVADA.

Constitution of 1864, Art. VIII, Sec. 1: "Corporations may be formed under general laws, and all such laws may, from time to time, be altered or repealed."

Act of March 16, 1903, Sec. 113: "This act may be amended or repealed at the pleasure of the legislature, but such amendment or repeal shall not take away or impair any remedy against any corporation under this act, or its officers, for any liability which shall have been previously incurred; this act and all amendments thereof shall be a part of the charter of every such corporation except so far as the same are inapplicable and inappropriate to the objects of such corporation."

NEW HAMPSHIRE.

Public statutes of 1891, Title XX, Ch. CXLVIII, Sec. 19: "The legislature may at any time alter, amend or repeal the charter of any corporation of the laws under which it was established, or may modify or annul any of its franchises, duties and liabilities; but the remedy against the corporation, its members or officers, for any liability previously incurred, shall not be impaired thereby."

NEW JERSEY.

Constitution of 1844, Art. IV, Sec. 7, par. 11: "The legislature . . . shall pass general laws under which corporations may be organized and corporate powers of every nature
obtained, subject, nevertheless, to repeal or alteration at the
will of the legislature."

Act of April 21, 1896, Sec. 4: "The charter of every corporation or any supplement thereto or amendment thereof shall
be subject to alteration, suspension, and repeal, in the discretion of the legislature, and the legislature may at pleasure dissolve any corporation."

Idem, Sec. 5: This act may be amended or repealed at the
pleasure of the legislature, and every corporation created under
this act shall be bound by such amendment; but such amendment or repeal shall not take away or impair any remedy
against any such corporation or its officers for any liability
which shall have been previously incurred; this act and all
amendments thereof shall be a part of the charter of every
corporation heretofore or hereafter formed hereunder, except so
far as the same are inapplicable and inappropriate to the objects of such corporation."

NEW YORK.

Constitution of 1894, Art. VIII, Sec. 1: "All general laws
and special acts passed pursuant to this section (relating to
the incorporation of companies) may be altered from time to
time or repealed."

Act of 1895, Ch. 672: "The charter of every corporation
shall be subject to alteration, suspension and repeal, in the
discretion of the legislature."

NORTH CAROLINA.

Constitution of 1868, Art. VIII, Sec. 1: "All general laws
and special acts passed pursuant to this section (relating to
the incorporation of companies) may be altered from time to
time or repealed."

Act of March 11, 1901, Sec. 6: "The charter of every corporation, or any supplement thereto or amendment thereof shall

be subject to alteration, modification, amendments or repeal, in the discretion of the legislature, and the legislature may at pleasure dissolve any corporation."

Idem, Sec. 7: "This act may be amended or repealed at the pleasure of the legislature, and every corporation shall be bound by such amendment; but such amendment or repeal shall not take away or impair any remedy against any such corporation, or its officers, for any liabilities which shall have been previously incurred; this act and all amendments thereof shall be a part of the charter of every corporation heretofore formed, or hereinafter formed hereunder, except so far as the same are inapplicable and inappropriate to the objects of such corporation."

NORTH DAKOTA.

Constitution of 1890, Art. VII, Sec. 131: "The legislative assembly shall provide by general laws for the organization ot all corporations hereinafter to be created, and any such law, so passed, shall be subject to future repeal or alterations."

Revised Code of 1895, Ch. XI, Art. 1, Sec. 2851: "Every grant of corporate power is subject to alteration, suspension, or repeal in the discretion of the legislative assembly."

OHIO.

Constitution of 1851, Art. XIII, Sec. 2: "Corporations may be formed under general laws, but all such laws may, from time to time, be altered or repealed."

OREGON.

Constitution of 1875, Art. II, Sec. 2: "All laws passed pursuant to this section (relating to the incorporation of companies) may be altered, amended, or repealed, but not so as to impair or destroy any vested corporate rights."

PENNSYLVANIA.

Constitution of 1874, Art. XVI, Sec. 10: "The General Assembly shall have the power to alter, revoke or annul any charter of incorporation now existing and revocable at the adoption of this constitution, or that may hereafter be created, whenever in their opinion it may be injurious to the citizens of the Commonwealth, in such manner, however, that no injustice shall be done to the corporators.''

Act of April 29, 1874, Sec. 4: ''The General Assembly reserves the power to revoke or annul any charter of incorporation granted or accepted under the provisions of this act, when ever in the opinion of the said Assembly it may be injurious to the citizens of this Commonwealth, in such manner, however, that no injustice shall be done to the corporators or their successors.''

RHODE ISLAND.

General Laws, 1896, Title XIX, Ch. CLXXVII, Sec. 28: ''Every corporation hereafter created shall be subject to the provisions of this chapter, and its charter or articles of association may be amended or repealed at the will of the General Assembly.''

SOUTH CAROLINA.

Constitution of 1895, Art. IX, Sec. 2: ''The General Assembly shall provide by general laws . . . for the organization of all corporations hereafter to be created, and any such law so passed, as well as all charters now existing, or hereafter created, shall be subject to future repeal or alteration.''

Code of 1902, Part 1, Ch. XLVII, Sec. 1842: ''It shall be deemed a part of the charter of every corporation created under the provisions of any general law, and of every charter granted, renewed or amended by act or joint resolution of the General Assembly (unless such act or joint resolution shall, in express terms, declare the contrary), that such charter, and every amendment and renewal thereof, shall always remain subject to amendment, alteration or repeal by the General Assembly.''

SOUTH DAKOTA.

Constitution of 1890, Art. XVII, Sec. 9: ''The legislature shall have the power to alter, revise or annul any charter of any corporation now existing and revocable at the taking effect

of this Constitution, or any that may be created, whenever in
their opinion it may be injurious to the citizens of this State,
in such a manner, however, that no injustice shall be done
to the corporators."

Revised Code of 1903, Civil Code, Div. II, Part III, Title II,
Ch. III, Art. 1, Sec. 398: "Every grant of corporate power is
subject to alteration, suspension or repeal in the discretion
of the legislature."

TENNESSEE.

Constitution of 1870, Art. XI, Sec. 8: "The General Assembly shall provide by general laws for the organization of
all corporations hereafter created, which laws may, at any time,
be altered or repealed; and no such alteration or repeal shall
interfere with, or divest, rights which have become vested."

Code of 1884, Part 1, Title IX, Ch. III, Art. 1, Sec. 1699:
"The powers conferred on any company incorporated hereunder shall be subject to repeal or amendment at the will of
the legislature."

TEXAS.

Constitution of 1876, Art. 1, Sec. 17: "All privileges and
franchises granted by the legislature or created under its authority, shall be subject to the control thereof."

Revised Statutes of 1895, Title XXI, Ch. II, Art. DCL:
"All charters, or amendments to charters, under the provisions
of this chapter, shall be subject to the power of the legislature
to alter, reform or amend the same."

UTAH.

Constitution of 1895, Art. XII: "All laws relating to corporations may be altered, amended or repealed by the legislature."

VERMONT.

Statutes of 1894, Title XXXV, Ch. CLXIV, Sec. 3686: "Acts
creating, continuing, altering or renewing a corporation or body
public, hereafter passed by the General Assembly, may be altered, amended or repealed as public good requires."

VIRGINIA.

Constitution of 1902, Art. XII. Sec. 154: " . . . Such general laws may be amended or repealed by the General Assembly; and all charters and amendments of charters now existing and revocable, or hereafter granted or extended, may be repealed at any time by special act."

Act of May 21, 1903, Ch. V, Sec. 61: "This act or any part thereof may be amended or repealed at the pleasure of the General Assembly, and every corporation created under this act shall be bound by such amendment; but such amendment or repeal shall not take away or impair any remedy against any such corporation or its officers for any liability which shall have been previously incurred; this act and all amendments thereof shall be a part of the charter of every corporation formed hereunder, except so far as the same are inapplicable and inappropriate to the objects of such corporation."

WASHINGTON.

Constitution of 1889, Art. XII, Sec. 1: "All laws relating to corporations may be altered, amended, or repealed by the legislature at any time."

WEST VIRGINIA.

Code of 1891, Ch. LIII, Sec. 8: "The right is hereby reserved to the legislature to alter any charter or certificate of incorporation hereafter granted to a joint-stock company, and to alter or repeal any law applicable to such company. But in no case shall such alterations or repeal affect the right of the creditors of the company to have its assets applied to the discharge of its liabilities, or its stockholders to have the surplus, if any, which may remain after discharging its liabilities and the expenses of winding up its affairs, distributed among themselves in proportion to their respective interests."

WISCONSIN.

Constitution of 1848, Art. XI, Art. 1: "All general laws or special acts enacted under the provisions of this section (relating to the organization or corporations) may be altered and repealed by the legislature at any time after their passage.''

Revised Statutes, 1898, Part 1, Title XIX, Ch. LXXXV, Sec. 1768: "The legislature may at any time limit or restrict the powers of any corporation organized under any law, and for just cause annul the same, and prescribe such mode as may be necessary for the settlement of its affairs."

WYOMING.

Constitution of 1889, Art. X, Sec. 1: "All laws relating to corporations may be altered, amended or repealed by the legislature at any time when necessary for the public good and general welfare."

Revised Statutes, 1899, Div. II, Title IV, Ch. i, Sec. 3052: ''The legislature may, at any time, amend or repeal this title, but such amendment or repeal shall not take away or impair any remedy given against, or in favor of, any such corporation, its stockholders or officers, for any liability which shall have been previously incurred."

BRIEF NUMBER 17.

SUBMITTED BY GEORGE P. HAMBRECHT

ON

GOVERNMENT REGULATION OF INDUSTRY AND THE
PRICE OF COMMODITIES

TO

THE WISCONSIN LEGISLATIVE COMMITTEE

ON

WATER POWERS, FORESTRY AND DRAINAGE.

(Authorities compiled by M. C. Riley.)

LEGISLATION.

In England as early as the sixteenth century parliament passed laws to regulte various industries and the price to be asked certain commodities. Governmental interference then was much broader than in more modern times.

Examples of such laws follow. The compilation is not exhaustive.

As early as 1533 statutes were enacted regulating the prices of victuals.

25 Henry VIII. c. 2 (1533).

The law provided that the King's counsellors, justices and officers should fix the price of

"cheese, butter, capons, hens, chickens and other victuals necessary for man's sustenance * * * in order to protect the pepolp against the greedy covetousness and appetites of the owners."

The prices fixed must be "reasonable"—the first use of the much used word. It provided, however, that local authorities might also fix prices notwithstanding the general schedule.

A statute enacted a year later (25 Henry VIII. c. 15) was enacted in part to protect the English makers of books. It prohibited the sale of books brought over the sea but provided that if the local dealers or binders enhanced or increased the price, the King's high officers should inquire therein and reform and redress such enhancing of the prices from time to time and "to limit prices as well of the books as for the binding of them" and further provided a penalty for enhancing the prices fixed.

Beer and beer barrels were regulated by a later statute.

(35 Henry VIII. Chap. 8, 1543).

"Every artificer of the mystery of coopers may take for every beer barrel by him sold 10d. and for every been

Kilderkin 6d. * * * No man in London or within two miles compass shall cut or diminish any barrels Kilderkins or firkins but for his own provision. No man shall transport beer in a greater vessel than a barrel upon pain to forfeit 6s. 8d. for every vessel."

(2 and 3 Philip and Mary cv. 16) A. D. 1555 attempted to regulate the watermen operating on the Thames river.

This statute recites that "Whereas * * * watermen being masterless men and single men * * * and many boys being of small age and of little skill and do for the most part of their time use "dyeing, cadding and other unlawful games, etc." and provides that the mayor and aldermen of London shall appoint eight persons as overseers of wherrimen and watermen: That all watermen carrying passengers must have two years experience, must not be single men, must have boats of a certain size and pronounced safe by the overseers; that they must not refuse to furnish service when needed on penalty of two weeks imprisonment and loss of right to row on the river for one whole year and a day; that the mayor and aldermen of London shall fix fares, and rates and cause a schedule "to be written and set up in tables in Guild Hall in the city of London, Westminister Hall and elsewhere" where they shall think convenient. It further provides that any waterman taking any fare in excess of legal rates shall forfeit "40 shillings and shall suffer imprisonment by one-half year."

17 and 17 Car. c. 11 (1664), regulated the price of coal. It provided that the lord mayor of London and the court of aldermen and the justices of the peace of the several counties respectively

"are hereby empowered to set the rates and prices of all such coals as shall be sold by retail as they from time to time shall judge reasonable allowing a competent profit to the said retailer beyond the prices paid by him to the importer and the ordinary charges thereon accruing."

And if the dealer refuses to sell at the rates fixed officers may force entrance to his storehouse, take possession of the coal and sell it out at reasonable prices accounting to the dealer for moneys received.

3 W. & M. C. 12, Sec. 24 (1691) was a brief though complete provision for the regulation of the rates of common carriers.

"And whereas divers waggoners and other carriers by combination among themselves have raised the prices of carriage of goods in many places to excessive rates to the great injury of the trade, be it therefore enacted by the authority aforesaid. That the justices of the peace of every county and other place within the realm of England or dominion of Wales, shall have power and authority and are hereby injoined and required at their next respective quarter or court sessions after Easter day yearly to assess and rate the prices of all land carriage of goods whatsoever, to be brought into any place or places within their respective limits and jurisdictions, by any common wagon or carrier, and the rates and assessments so made to certify to the several mayors and other chief officers of each respective market town within the limits and jurisdictions of such justices of the peace, to be hung up in the same public place in every such market town to which all persons may resort for their information; and that no such common waggoner or carrier shall take for carriage of such goods and merchandise above the rate and price so set upon pain to forfeit for every such offense the sum of five pounds to be levied by distress and sale of his and their goods, by warrant of any two justices of the peace where such waggoner or carrier shall reside, in manner as aforesaid, to the use of the party grieved."

JUDICIAL REGULATION.

The courts have also the right to compel and to a degree control the service to be rendered by a public utility.

As early as A. D. 1450 it was decided by the court that if an inkeeper refused to give entertainment an action would lie. (Anonymous Keelway 50 pl. 4—cases p. 1.) In 1494 it was held that a victualler must sell his victuals if offered the price. (Anonymous Y. B. 10 II. 9 pl. 14—cases p. 283.)

In 1683 it was held that a carrier could not refuse to carry goods (Jackson vs. Rogers, 2 Shower 327—cases p. 1.)

It had been decided again and again that even in the absence of statute the courts will by mandamus compel the public utility to render service.

As early as A. D. 1450 it was held that neither a horse shoer or innkeeper had any right to refuse service. (Keilway, 50, pl. 4, Kings Bench cases 1.)

The American colonies found governmental. interference—regulation necessary.

In fact the colonists had hardly become settled before they found it necessary to curb the rapacity of those engaged in various pursuits—and in some instances the pursuits were not of the sort now deemed public pursuits.

In 1635 Plymouth Colony enacted as follows: (Colonial Law Mass. p. 183).

"For awarding such mischief as may follow by such ill disposed persons as may take liberty to oppress and wrong the neighbors by taking excessive wages for their work or unreasonable prices for such merchandise or other necessary commodities as shall pass from man to man. It is ordered that if any man shall offend in any of said cases he shall be punished by fine or imprisonment according to the quality of the offense as the court to which he is presented upon lawfully trial and conviction shall adjudge."

In 1636 Plymouth Colony limited the price of beer to two pence the quart.

In 1636 the colony regulated ferry tolls and mill tools and laborers' wages and forbade purchase of goods for purpose of enhancing prices. Millers' tools for grinding grain were thereafter repeatedly changed.

In 1642 smiths were compelled to repair all arms promptly at reasonable rates.

Mass. (1655) Colonial Law Mass. p. 185.

Recites abuses in Boston and Charlestown and gives select men power

"to regulate * * * and to state their wages as in their understanding shall be most just and equal and also to determine what persons shall be employed therein."

In 1646 and 1652 Mass. regulated by a schedule the size of the penny white loaf according to the price of wheat and provided for forcible inspection of all bread on hand.

In 1671 the maximum price of rum was fixed at 5 shillings per gallon.

Note that the temporary and local economic conditions were the occasion and justified the measures—for example the law requiring smiths to repair arms, the regulation of the carriers' charges and services, the millers' tolls, the price of coal, etc.

"EXHIBIT 26."

BRIEF NUMBER 18.

SUBMITTED BY GEORGE P. HAMBRECHT

ON

TAXATION OF MANUFACTURING, MERCANTILE TRANSPORTATION AND TRANSMISSION CORPORATIONS IN THE UNITED STATES

TO

THE WISCONSIN LEGISLATIVE COMMITTEE

ON

WATER POWERS, FORESTRY AND DRAINAGE.

(Authorities compiled by M. C. Riley.)

36

TAXATION OF CORPORATIONS.

MANUFACTURING, MERCANTILE, TRANSPORTATION AND TRANSMISSION AND THEIR SHAREHOLDERS AND BONDHOLDERS.

CONTENTS.

TABLES.

TAXATION OF CORPORATIONS.

MANUFACTURING, MERCANTILE, TRANSPORTATION AND TRANSMISSION AND THEIR SHAREHOLDERS AND BONDHOLDERS.

I.

This inquiry deals with the taxation of manufacturing, mercantile, transportation and transmission corporations and their stock and bondholders.

The Purpose.

The purpose of the inquiry is to present in a general way, for analysis and criticism, the systems now in vogue in thirty states selected at random from the New England, Middle Atlantic, South Atlantic, North Central, South Central, Western and Pacific groups, for deriving revenue from the above classes of corporations and their stock and bondholders.

The plan.

Criticism of any taxing system must be based in part upon theory, and in part upon comparison with other systems. In order to afford a comprehensive basis for criticism by comparison, a brief account of the early ·taxation of corporations and the development thereof leading up to the existing systems, is presented. In order to prepare for theoretical criticism, the various systems of corporation taxation in these states will be analyzed so as to bring out the general methods in use.

The former presentation will ·divulge the attempts to make more effective the taxing systems in the different states. These attempts will divulge the present day tendencies toward the attainment of precision, both practical and theoretical, in the exacting of payments for governmental purposes from these legal entities and the holders of their securities.

II.

EARLY TAXATION OF CORPORATIONS.

"During the first two decades of this century, (1800–1900) banks and insurance companies formed the chief examples of corporations, apart from the numerous turnpike and toll bridges.* During the twenties and thirties the development of transportation facilities led to the creation of many canal and railway companies; and it was not long before many other forms of commercial and industrial enterprise followed in the same path of incorporation. The early tax laws make no mention of corporations. But as the general property tax was in vogue throughout all the commonwealths, it was tacitly assumed, that the property of artificial as well as of natural persons was liable. Corporations were new institutions which the legislatures in happy-go-lucky fashion, tried to tax under existing methods, whether they naturally belonged there or

---

* Summary of all the acts of incorporation for private business purposes granted in this country before the year 1800.

(From a contribution by Hon. Simeon E. Baldwin formerly Chief Justice of the Supreme Court of Connecticut, to the Yale Bicentennial Publication, "Two Centuries of American Law, 1701-1901." at p. 312.)

Sttate.	Aid of agriculture	Banks	Bridges	Burying ground	Canals	Commerce	Aid of emigration	Fisheries	Insurance	Land company	Logging	Manufactures	Mining	Improving navigation	Turnpikes	Waterworks	Total
N. Hampshire..									1							1	2
Massachusetts	1	7	25		12	3	1		5		2	5		4	16	7	88
Rhode Island..		2							1								3
Connecticut ...		5	3	1	1				2	1		1	1	1	18	3	37
New York...		4	1		1	1		1	3			4			5	1	21
New Jersey ...												1					1
Pennsylvania .	2	2				1			4			1					10
Delaware		1															1
Maryland		3			2				4						2		11
Virginia		2			3				3					10	2		20
No. Carolina ..					2										2		4
So. Carolina ..	1		1		1				2						3	1	9
Georgia																	0
Vermont			5												3	5	13
Kentucky	1	1													1		3
Tennessee																	0
United States..		2															2
Total	5	23	36	1	21	6	1	1	25	1	2	12	1	26	38	21	225

not. Our Solons had neither the leisure nor the inclination to make a more careful study of the subject.

The first commonwealth law which treated of the taxation of corporations in general was the New York law of 1823. This provided that 'all incorporated companies receiving a regular income from the employment of their capital' should be considered' persons' liable to the general property tax. They were required to make returns to the county officers of all their property and their capital stock, paying the tax themselves and deducting it from the dividends of stockholders. They might, however, commute the tax by paying to the treasurers of the counties where they transacted business ten per cent on their 'dividends, profits, or income,' (which the legislators evidently presumed to be identical). These taxes were paid by the county officers to the state, and were then credited to the counties in proportion to the amount of stock held within each county, after deducting the state tax.

In 1825 and again in 1828 the system was slightly changed so as to conform more closely to the general property tax. The tax was made applicable to "all monied and stock corporations deriving an income or profit from their capital or otherwise." The real estate of these corporations was separately taxed; and in addition, they paid the property tax on their capital stock paid in or secured to be paid in, deducting the amount paid for real estate and the stock belonging to the state and to literary and charitable institutions, manufacturing and turnpike companies paid on the cash value, not on the amount, of the capital stock; turnpike, bridge and canal companies, whose 'net income' did not exceed five per cent of the capital stock paid in, were exempted; while manufacturing and marine insurance companies under the same conditions might commute by paying a five per cent of this net income. It is thus seen that by this law corporations were divided into different classes, and that the system followed was the general property tax, with the exception that if a corporation had no profits it paid no tax on its stock, and that certain classes might commute by paying an income tax to the local officials. This remained the tax system, except for banks and for foreign insurance companies, until the middle of the century.

In 1853 the total exemption of non-profit-paying corporations was abolished and all companies were taxed on their real estate

and on their capital stock, together with their surplus profits
or their reserved funds in excess of ten per cent of the capital, with the same deductions as above. All corporations, however, whose profits did not equal five per cent on the capital
stock might commute by paying five per cent on their 'net annual profits or clear income.' It seems that very few ever
availed themselves of this doubtful privilege, and accordingly
in 1857, the law was again changed. The principle of commutation was abandoned; and since there was no distinction between profitable and unprofitable companies, so far as personal
property was concerned, all corporations were taxed on their
realty, and on the actual value (not the amount) of their capital stock plus the surplus or reserve in excess of ten per cent
of the capital. In addition to the previous deductions a further
abatement was made for the capital invested in taxable shares
of other companies. The remainder was then taxed in the same
manner as the other personalty and realty of the county. This
remained the law of New York, with the exception of some
special provisions as to banks and insurance companies, until
the recent changes in the taxation of corporations. These
changes, however, affect only taxation for state purposes,
leaving the local taxation still governed by the law of 1857.
Foreign corporations, however, are taxable for local purposes,
under a law of 1855, on all sums actually invested in the state.

It appears, then, that the New York system was a taxation of
the real and personal property of corporations by the local
assessors and that the personal property was virtually defined as
the capital stock not invested in real estate. In the other
commonwealths, where corporations were taxed at all they were
included in the general property tax; and most of the laws
lacked even such provisions as those of the New York statute
in reference to the capital stock. A typical enactment of this
kind is the Connecticut law of 1826, which provided simply that
the personal property of a corporation should be taxed in the
place where its principal business was transacted. In Massachusetts, on the other hand, where the first general law was
passed in 1832, only the real estate and machinery of corporations was taxed. In lieu of the tax on personality there was
substituted the property tax on the corporate shares in the
hands of individuals, a proportionate amount being deducted
from each for the part of the capital stock invested in ma-

chinery and in real estate. Even this was still in theory the
general property tax. In the other commonwealths when the
corporation was taxed, the. shares in the hands of individuals
were usually exempt. The only state which from the very outset broke with the principle of the general property tax was
Pennsylvania * * * .

With this one exception, then, the early principle of corporate taxation was the assessment of all real and personal property by the local officials, corporations, in other words, were
taxed by the same method as individuals. This primitive system
has been retained up to the present day by many commonwealths
for almost all classes of corporations; and in eight states, indeed,
the constitutions require that corporate property be taxed in
the same manner as that of individuals.* 'The practical defects
of such a system, however, have led to numerous changes in
many of the progressive states, and the tendency is everywhere
away from the original plan." Essays in Taxation, Seligman.
pp. 137, 141.

III.

DEFECTS OF THE GENERAL PROPERTY TAX.

Economists treat the defects of the general property tax under five heads, namely, inequality of assessment, failure to
reach personalty, incentive to dishonesty, regressivity, and
double taxation. Seligman in his Essays in Taxtion, p. 141,
after elaborating upon the defects enumerated, says:

"As a result of these practical defects many commonwealths have abandoned in part or altogther, the taxation
of corporation property by local officials."

The movement away from the general property tax—the
original position—has taken two directions: (1) the property
of public service companies, especially railroads ,is being assessed
by a special board and according to well defined rules; (2)
certain classes of corporations are being taxed, not on their
property, but on certain elements supposed to represent roughly
their taxable capacity.

---

* Ala., Colo, Fla., Ia. Miss., Nev., Ohio, and So. Car.

Tendencies away from the primitive property tax.

(1) The first of these tendencies has progressed so far that but one of the thirty states herein included, namely, Rhode Island, still applies the primitive methods of the general property tax to steam railroads. That is, in but one of these thirty states is the real and personal property of railroads assessed for state and local purposes by local assessors. Twenty of these states which apply the general property tax to railroads have such property assessed for state purposes by a central body. The tax on such property is imposed at the usual rate of the general property tax; but some of the difficulties of local assessments have been obviated. In a few cases like California and Washington the state boards assess the greater part of the property, such as the roadbed and rolling stock, but leave the remainder to be appraised by the local assessors. In Florida the real estate of railroads is assessed by the local officials. In Massachusetts the real estate and machinery of railroad companies is assessed locally for both state and local purposes. In Ohio railroad property is assessed by the county auditors. In many of the states included in this inquiry, including some of those whch do not apply the general property tax to steam railroads for state revenue, the property, most often the real property only, not specifically used in the exercise of the railway company's franchise, is assessed and taxed locally.

This tendency to have property of corporations assessed by a central body has become general in the case of other transportation and in the case of transmission companies.

In a majority of these states the property of express and car companies is assessed by state boards, and the same is true in the case of transmission companies.*

In six of these states** the property of local utilities is assessed by state boards.

Seven of the states herein included, namely, Connecticut, Deleware, Maine, Minnesota (except in the case of telegraph companies), New York, Pennsylvania and Vermont have broken away from the general property tax on railroads as a source of state revenue. The methods adopted by these states are comprised in the second tendency.

---

* See Post—Summaries of the Three Principal forms of Taxation.
** Ala., N. H , Okl., Ore., Uta., and Wisconsin (The property of street railways and of electric lighting companies operated in connection with such companies is so essessed in Wisconsin.)

(2) The *second tendency* has consisted in subjecting particular classes of corporations to special taxes on other elements than their general property. A brief account of the development of the methods of taxing these particular classes follows.

Railroads.

A full history of the development of railroad taxation would occupy a volume or more; hence, it will be possible here to say but a few words about some of the typical states.

In Pennsylvania, railroads were included in the general tax law of 1840, and were assessed on their personalty and on their dividends. In 1884 the tax on personalty was abandoned, but the general corporation tax on capital and dividends continued with some modification for over two decades. In 1860 a special tonnage tax was levied on transportation companies at the rate of two, three and five cents per ton of freight carried, and an additional tax of three-quarters of one per cent was laid on gross receipts. The former was declared unconstitutional by the federal court, and as a result, by the act of 1874, all transportation companies were taxed only on their capital stock, at the rate of nine-tenths of a mill for each one per cent of dividends, or at the rate of six mills if there were no dividends. In 1879 the dividends and earnings taxes were slightly changed, and the law was passed which, with the amendments of 1885, 1889 and 1891, is in force today.

In New York, railroads were subject to the general property tax until 1880, when a law was enacted which with some modifification is now in force.

In New Jersey, railroads were subject to the property tax until 1873, when a tax was imposed at the rate of one-half of one per cent on their cost, equipment and appendages. Three years later the cost tax was abandoned, and a tax at the same rate was imposed on the true value of the roads. This system prevailed until 1884, when the present method was introduced.

In Connecticut, the law requiring certain stock companies to make returns of the stock owned by individuals was extended in 1846 to railroads. Three years later every railroad that had paid a dividend in the preceding year was required to pay one-half of one per cent on the market value of the shares held by non-residents, but if the railroad was partly out of the state, the tax was to be proportioned to the mileage in the state. This system worked so well that in 1850 it was extended to resident stockholders, and was made one-third of one per cent in lieu of all other taxes.   In 1862 the rate was increased, but the provision was inserted that the stock should not be assessed at less than ten per cent of the par value.   In 1864 the outlines of the present system were drawn by requiring the companies to add to the valuation of the stock the market value of the funded and floating indebtedness less the cash on hand, and to pay one per cent on this valuation in proportion to the mileage in the state.   In 1871 it was provided that if the railroad paid any local tax this might be deducted from the state tax.   In 1881 a deduction was made from the taxable valuation for such portion of its debt as was contracted for stock taken in other roads.   In 1882 the funded and floating debts and bonds were to be valued at par unless the market value was below par.   And in 1887 the present law, with substantially the same provisions was enacted,*

In Vermont, the first attempt to tax railroad real estate, which included roadbed, tracks, and all lands used for railroad purposes, was made in 1874.   An exemption for eight years was allowed from the time regular trains begun to run.

In 1878 began a series of laws on the taxation of corporations culminating in a general law passed in 1882.† Up to this time the method had been to tax certain organizations on their profits and the shares of stock in the hands of the holders. Now the movement was toward taxation of the corporations themselves.   Express and telegraph companies were taxed on their gross receipts.   The general act of 1882 provided for a state tax commissioner and a tax based mainly on the gross receipts of railroad, express, telegraph, telephone, steamboat and car transportation companies.   In 1866 the word "railroads" was held by the tax commission to include street railways. From that time the law on taxation of corporations has remained essentially the same, though with some modifications and revisions,‡ although the gross receipt tax on railroads, etc.,

* Seligman, Essays in Taxation, pp. 153, 154 (1903).
† History of Taxation in Vermont. F. A. Wood (1894).
‡ Report of Com. on Taxation, 1908, p. 18.

has been changed in form to an optional alternative, in order to avoid conflict with the Federal Constitution.†

In Delaware a general passenger tax law applicable to railroads was passed in 1864, but was a few years after declared unstitutional in so far as it affected interstate commerce.‡ In 1869 general laws were passed taxing the net earnings, the rolling stock and the cash value of the capital stock of railroads. A year later the United States circuit court held that the tax on rolling stock was a restraint on interstate traffic, but sustained a portion of the law hich taxed net earnings and capital stock. The United States supreme court affirmed this decision as to the constitutionality of the provisions concerning net earnings and capital stock, that as to the rolling stock not coming before them.

Pending the last mentioned decision, and probably induced by the uncertainity of the outcome, the first of a number of special legislative acts, forming a particular feature of railroad taxation in Delaware were passed. This first act was passed in 1873. It provided that the Philadelphia, Wilmington and Baltimore R. R. Co. should be privileged to pay $40,000 annually in lieu of all state taxes, and further, that the act was not to be construed to repeal or affect the existing law as hereinbefore given, otherwise than to suspend the collection of taxes under them in any year in which the company pays the state the amount specified.

Following this act special measures were passed from time to time until similar privileges were given to all railroads operating within the state.*

In Wisconsin, from 1854 to 1903, the general method of taxing railroads was on the basis of gross receipts. In the beginning this tax was at a flat rate; later at graduated and progressive rates. The Wisconsin gross receipt system had its origin in the desire to do away with the inequalities of *locally* assessed ad valorem taxes on railroads. In 1903 the ad valorem

---

† Railroad Co. v. Railroad Co., 63 Vt. 1 (1890), s. c. 159 U. S, 630 (1895). State v. Ruthland Ry. Co., 71 Atl. 197 (1908).

‡ State Treasurer v. R. R. Co., 4 Houston 158 (1871), Minot v. R. R. Co., 2 Abb. C. C. 333 (U. S. Cir. Ct. 1870).

§ The Delaware R. R. Tax, 18 Wall. 206 (1873).

* Report State Rev. and Tax Com. 1909, p. 26 et seq.

system, assessed by a central body, was adopted for application to these companies. The rate is the average rate on the general property in the state, determind by dividing the total taxes, state, county and local, on the general property in the state by the aggregate value of such property subject to taxation.

The states of Michigan and Washington first taxed railroads on their general property and left the assessment of such property to the local assessors. This primitive system was later abandoned and a tax on the earnings or income was substituted. These two states, like Wisconsin, became dissatisfied with the earnings or income tax and now apply the ad valorem system to railroads, their property being assessed by a central body.

Other Transportation and Tranmission Companies.

The taxation of telegraph and telephone companies has undergone an evolution similar to that of railroads, but not quite so complicated.

In a number of these states telegraph companies are no longer taxed on their property, the original system, but now pay special taxes based on other elements representing their taxable capacity. Here again, as in the case of other corporations the special tax is in some instances applicable only to state taxation, while the local tax is still assessed on property.

Telephone companies are usually taxed as are telegraph companies. However, the tendency toward a special tax is greater in case of telephone companies than in case of the telegraph. For instance, in Minnesota and Wisconsin, telephone companies are taxed on gross receipts,—while telegraph companies are taxed on their property which is assessed by state boards.

Treatment of express and car companies for purposes of taxation have undergone an evolution similar to that of railroad and transmission companies. The tendency toward special taxation is very pronounced in the case of these companies. Many states that retain the general property tax system for corporations generally have made exceptions of these companies which enjoy a large income from a very insignificant outlay in capital.* See Post—Summary of the Three Principal forms of Tax-ation.

Evolution in Wisconsin.

From 1854 to 1899 public service companies generally in Wisconsin were taxed on a basis of gross receipts. In 1899 the gross receipts tax on express companies gave way to a state ad-ministered ad valorem tax. In the same year, freight line com-panies, companies furnishing cars to shippers, dining, buffet, chair, parlor, palace and sleeping car companies were made tax-able on practically the same ad valorem basis. In 1905 the ad valorem system was extended to all other public service com-panies, except telephone companies, which are still taxed on gross receipts. Beginning with the year 1907, telegraph com-panies came under the ad valorem system; street railways and electric lighting companies beginning with the year 1908.

Local Utilities.

The tendency away from the primitive general property tax system is found also in the case of local public service or utility companies. There is a marked tendency to include street rail-ways under the laws providing for the taxation of steam rail-ways. This is the case in six states† where the property of street railway companies is assessed by a central body for state and local purposes. In Massachusetts street and steam rail-way companies are taxed on their "corporate excess" and their real estate and machinery. In Pennsylvania and Florida these companies are placed in the same category with steam rail-railroads. In seven of these states‡ the assessment of street railway companies for state and local purposes is left to the local assessor. In Wyoming such property is assessed for state and local purposes by the county assessors. In the remaining

---

* The inadequacy of the property tax when applied to express com-panies has been strikingly pointed out by the supreme court of the United States. In the so called Ohio Express Co. case (Adams Ex-press Co. v. Ohio, 165 U. S. 194) the court said that it was "unity of use" which enabled $23,400 worth of horses, wagons and safes, in the state to produce $275,446 in a single year.

† N. H. Ala., Okl., Wis., Utah, Oregon and Vermont. In the latter state the tax on such companies is either on gross earnings or on property.

* Calif., Mich., Ohio, Ken., Minn., Neb. and Wash.

twelve states† these companies are taxed for state purposes on elements other than property. However, in some cases this special taxation for state purposes is in addition to the state's portion of the general property tax locally assessed, and in addition to special taxation, either franchise or privilege, for local purposes. In Delaware and New Jersey this special tax for state purposes is based on gross receipts. In Maine it is a franchise tax based on capital stock. In North Carolina and Indiana these companies, in addition to the property tax locally assessed for state and local purposes, pay the "corporate excess tax." In West Virginia they pay a state license tax. In Rhode Island a tax on gross earnings. In New Jersey and Delaware a tax on gross receipts. In Maryland a tax on gross receipts and on the assessed value of their capital stock. In Virginia a state franchise tax based on capital stock and in Mississippi a privilege tax and an additional tax on capital stock.

Electric light companies, unless operated as one system in connection with a street railway, are generally assessed for state and local purposes by the local assessors. However, in a number of states revenue for state purposes is derived from these companies through special taxation. This is the case in Maine, Rhode Island, Connecticut, New York, New Jersey, Pennsylvania, Delaware, and partly the case in Massachusetts.

Manufacturing and mercantile companies have received less attention than the foregoing classes of corporations. In all excepting a few states, like Connecticut, New York, New Jersey an Delaware, where no state revenue is derived through the application of the general property tax, these business corporatins are assessed locally on property, real and personal, for both state and local purposes. In twenty of the states* herein included, special taxes are levied against these companies. These special taxes, either franchise, license or privilege, are in most cases based upon capital stock; in some cases on the par value, in some on the authorized capital stock, and in others on the assessed value thereof. Such is the system in fourteen

---

† Me., R. I., Conn., N. Y., Del., Md., Va., W. Va., N. C., Miss. & Ind. and N. J.

* Me., Vt., Mass., Conn., N. J., Penn., Del., Md., Fla., W. Va., N. C., Ala., Ky., Miss., Okl., Ind , Minn., Utah and Calif.

of the twenty states† levying special taxes on these companies. In Massachusetts, Indiana and Minnesota these companies, in addition to the property tax locally assessed, pay a corporate excess tax. In Delaware a business license tax. In Connecticut a chose in action tax, and in Alabama a privilege tax varying in amount with the nature of the business transacted. In Virginia these companies, in addition to the general property tax and a franchise tax based on capital stock, pay a license tax based on purchases.

IV.

DESCRIPTION OF THE TAXING SYSTEMS IN THIRTY STATES.

Following are presented descriptions of the systems of taxing corporations in thirty states of the United States. The states included are all of those in the New England and Middle Atlantic groups. Eight in the South Atlantic, six in the North Central and two in the Western groups, and three, or all, in the Pacific group. These states have been selected at random.

In presenting these descriptions continuous reference has been made to the report of Corporation Commissioner Knox on the Taxation of Corporations, Washington, D. C., May 17, 1909 and June 6, 1910. In these two reports Commissioner Knox describes the systems of taxing corporations in the New England and Middle Atlantic states. The descriptions herein. for those two groups are taken almost wholly from Commissioner Knox's report. In working out the descriptions for the remaining groups, reference has been made to the constitution. statutes, and tax reports of the different states. Although an unusual effort has been put forth to be accurate in these descriptions, it must be appreciated that a state's system of taxation often differs in practice from what the printed matter would lead one to expect. Commissioner Knox in the preparation of his report interviewed the respective state officials. No such opportunity to attain precision was afforded in the case of the South Atlantic, North Central, South Central, Western and Pacific groups.

---

† The above excepting Mass., Conn., Del., Ala., Ind. and Minn.

NEW ENGLAND.

Maine.

Chief features.   Ո. Ց. OWEN.'

First. A tax upon the par value of the capital stock of corporations generally.

Second. A tax on the transportation and transmission receipts of certain classes of public-service corporations.

Third. A local ad valorem tax.

General property tax.

Corporations generally are taxed locally on property. R. S. 1903, ch. 9, secs. 2, 3, 8; Id. ch. 9, secs. 2, 5, 12, 13. Important classes of corporations reached chiefly through the property tax are gas, water, electric lighting, heating and power companies. Rept. of Tax Com. 1908, p. 44. This tax on property of corporations is modified for railroad, street railway, telephone, telegraph and express companies.

Shareholders and bondholders.

Shares of stock and bonds of domestic and foreign corporations are taxed locally as personal property. Id., ch. 9, secs. 2. 5, 13.' It is important to note, however, that an attempt is made to prevent double taxation in the case of domestic corporations by providing that owners of their corporate shares are exempt from taxation thereon to the extent of their proportional part of the corporation's machinery, goods, and lands taxed within the state. In the case of domestic and foreign railroad, street railway, telegraph and telephone companies doing business in the state, and domestic manufacturing, mining, smelting, agricultural, and stock raising corporations, their shares are not taxed to the holder. Id., ch. 9, sec. 5, as amended by ch. 16, '07.

The General Franchise Tax.

Domestic corporations, except railroads, street railways, palace-car companies, telegraph and telephone companies, express companies and insurance companies, are taxed upon the par value of capital stock in addition to the regular local property tax. Id., ch. 8, sec. 18, as amended by ch. 185, '07.

37

Excise Tax.

Transportation and transmission companies are taxed on gross receipts. This tax is paid to the state for state and local purposes and is called "an annual excise tax." Domestic and foreign railroad, street railway, telegraph, telephone, express, and car companies are subject thereto. Id., ch. 8, sec. 24; id., ch. 9, sec. 4.

Railroads.

Railroad companies pay an excise tax, a local tax on property outside the right of way, and a tax to defray the expenses of the Board of Railroad Commissioners.

The excise tax is paid to the state for state and local purposes and is based upon average gross receipts per mile. The rate of taxation begins at ½ of 1 per cent of such receipts when they do not exceed $1,500 per mile, and increase at the rate of ¼ of 1 per cent for each additional $500 or fractional part thereof, the maximum rate being 4½ per cent. Id., ch. 8, sec. 24; id., ch. 8, sec. 25, as amended by 168, '07.

The above tax is apportioned to the cities and towns to the extent of 1 per cent of the actual value of stock held therein. Id., ch. 8, sec. 24.

All buildings, whether within or without the right of way, and the land and fixtures outside the right of way, are taxed by the cities and towns as other property. Id., ch. 9, sec. 4.

Each railroad company pays to the state treasurer its proportional share of the expense of the Board of Railroad Commissioners, based upon gross transportation receipts. Id., ch. 8, sec. 30.

Telegraph and telephone companies.

Transmission companies pay a tax on gross receipts and a local tax on property.

The gross receipts tax is called "an annual excise tax for the privilege of conducting such business." It is paid to the state treasurer for state and local purposes. The tax is apportioned to the local units as is the excise tax on railroad companies. Id. Ch. 8, sec. 36. This tax is based upon gross receipts—when they exceed $1,000 and do not exceed $5,000 per mile, 1%. The tax increases with the gross receipts, the maximum, however, is 4%. Id. Ch. 8, sec. 37.

The personal property not exempted and the real estate of such companies is taxed locally. But this local property tax is deducted from the excise tax above. Id. Ch. 8, sec. 41.

Express companies.

Express companies pay taxes on gross receipts and locally on property.

The gross receipts tax amounts to 2½% on gross receipts from business done in the state, and is for state and local purposes. Id. Ch. 8, sec. 42, as amended by Ch. 167, '07.

Real estate of express companies is taxed in the municipality where situated, but such tax is deducted from the gross receipts tax. Id. Ch. 8, sec. 44.

Sleeping, etc., car companies.

Sleeping, dining, and parlor car companies pay a tax of 4½% on gross receipts for business done in the state in lieu of all other taxes. Id. Ch. 8, sec. 32, as amended by Ch. 156, '07.

Street railways.

Street railways are taxed on receipts as are railways, but at different (lower) rate. The tax is distributed locally as in the case of railroads. Id. Ch. 8, sec. 31.

Manufacturing and mercantile companies.

These companies are taxed locally on their real and personal property and all stock used in factories, and pay the general franchise tax. Id. Ch. 9, sec. 25, as amended by Ch. 16, '07. Shares of stock therein are not taxed to owners. Id. Their bonds and other securities are taxed. Id. Ch. 9, sec. 5.

Foreign corporations.

There are no general statutes applying especially to foreign corporations. Foreign transportation and transmission companies are taxed on receipts and property in the same manner as are similar domestic corporations.

Administration.

The state's corporation tax laws are administered by the Board of State Assessors, three in number, chosen by the legislature for six years. L. 1909, Ch. 220.

New Hampshire.

Chief features.

The general application of the property tax. This is due to constitutional provision. State v. U. S. & C. Express Co., 60 N. H., 219, 245 (1880).

A payment by all railroad companies to the state of net receipts when the same for any year exceed the average of 10% on its expenditures from the beginning of its operations.

The general property tax.

The general property tax is the only one levied on manufacturing, mercantile. electric light, power and gas companies, the property in the state of such corporations, domestic and foreign. being taxed locally as are individuals. Pub. Stats. 1901, Ch. 56, sec. 9. Laws 1905, Ch. 42, sec. 1; Id. 42, sec. 2. Property is the basis of the tax on steam and street railways, and express, car, telegraph and telephone companies. Id. Ch. 64, secs. 1, 3, 4, 5, 8, 9, 12.

Shareholders and bondholders.

Shares of stock are taxed locally to the holders except where the corporation's property is taxed directly or where, in the case of foreign companies. the stock or property is taxed in the state where they are located. Id. Ch. 55, sec. 7, divs. 2 and 3. The taxable value of such shares is reduced in proportion as the property of the corporation is otherwise locally taxed. Id. Ch. 58, sec. 1.

Railroads and street railways.

Railroad companies, including street railways, domestic and foreign, pay a tax to the state for local and state purposes based upon the value of their road, rolling stock, equipments and franchise, in the state, at a rate as nearly equal as possible to the average rate upon other property throughout the state. Id. Ch. 64, sec. 1. These items of property are valued and assessed and the rate determined by the state board of equalization. Id. Ch. 64, sec. 4.

The real estate of railroads not used in their ordinary business is taxed where situate by the local assessors. Id. Ch. 55, sec. 6, as amended by Ch. 119, '07.

In every year when the net receipts of a railroad company exceed the average of 10% on its expenditures from the beginning of its operations, the excess shall be paid to the state treasurer.   Id. Ch. 157, sec. 9.   (Inoperative.)

Expenses connected with the state board of railroad commissioners is borne by street and steam railways in proportion to gross receipts.

Railroad taxation is distributed as follows:

1. One-fourth to the towns in which railroad is located, to be pro-rated upon the basis of the amount expended by the company in each town for buildings and right of way.

2. Of the remaining three-fourths each town receives a part proportioned to the number of shares held by its residents.

3. Usually an amount still remains, represented by the stock held outside the state, and this remainder is retained by the state for its own use.   Id. Ch. 64, secs. 13–17.

Shares of stock in these companies are not taxed to the holders, Id. Ch. 64, sec. 12, but their bonds are taxable to the holders.   Id. Ch. 53, sec. 7.

Transmission companies.

Telegraph and telephone companies, domestic and foreign are taxed upon their lines in the state, including poles, wires, instruments, apparatus, office furniture and fixtures of all kinds at same rate as railroad company property is taxed.   Their property is valued and the rate fixed by the state board of equalization.   Such taxes are in lieu of all taxes upon the stock of such corporations.   Id. Ch. 64, secs. 3, 4, 5, 8, 9, 12.

Real estate not taxed by the central body is taxed by the towns where located.   Id. Ch. 55, sec. 6, as amended by Ch. 119, '07.

Bonds in these companies are taxed to holders.   Id. Ch. 55, sec. 7.

Express companies.

Express companies, domestic and foreign, are taxed upon property as are railroad and transmission companies.

The board in getting at the value of the property of such companies is guided by the ratio which the value of the companies property in New Hampshire bears to the entire property of the company in and out of the state, determined by the capital stock of the company, and by such other evidence and rules as are necessary to a true valuation. Deduction is made for real estate taxed in the state. This tax in lieu of all other except on real estate, and is for state purposes. L. 1907, Ch. 81.

Shares of stock and bonds in these companies are taxable to the holder. Id. Ch. 55, sec. 7.

Car companies.

The owners or operators of these cars are assessed by the state board of equalization on the value thereof. Same rate as in case of transportation and transmission companies. L. 1907, Ch. 91.

The cars subject to taxation shall be the same proportion of the average number of cars making trips within the state as the number of miles of railroad track over which the same were used in the state bears to the number of miles of track over which they were used within and without the state.

Shares of stock and bonds in these companies are taxable to the holders. Id. Ch. 55, sec. 7.

Manufacturing and mercantile companies.

These companies are assessed and taxed locally on their property. Id. Ch. 56, sec. 9.

Their shares and bonds are taxable to the holders. Id. Ch. 55, sec. 7.

Electric power and light companies.

"Lands, dams, canals, water power, buildings, structures, machinery, dynamos, apparatus, poles, wires, fixtures of all kinds and descriptions owned, operated, and employed by any private corporation" "(domestic or foreign)" or person not a municipal corporation, in generating, producing, supplying, and distibuting electric power or light, shall be taxed as real estate in the town or towns in which said property or any part of it is situated." L. 1905, Ch. 42, sec. 1.

The personal property of these corporations is taxed locally like that of manufacturing and mercantile corporations. Id. Ch. 56, sec. 9.

Shares of stock and bonds in these companies are taxable to the holders. Id. Ch. 55, sec. 7.

Foreign corporations.

The property in the state of foreign corporations and their shares of stock and bonds are taxed like similar domestic cor-porations.

Administration.

Corporation tax laws are administered by the state board of equalization—five members appointed by the supreme court for 2 years. The board assesses and levies corporate taxes in the case of railroad, sleeping, dining, parlor car, telegraph, telephone, and express companies. Id. Ch. 63, secs. 1-9.

Vermont.

Chief features.

First. The "annual license tax" cn capital stock of all corporations doing business in Vermont. Unincorporated associations doing business in Vermont pay this tax on their assets.

Second. Transportation and transmission companies (except express companies, which are taxed on mileage, and palace car companies, which are taxed on capital invested in the state) have the option of being taxed on property or on gross earnings. They also pay the license tax.

All the above taxes are for state purposes.

General property tax.

In Vermont corporations have been for the most part classified and each class subjected to a special tax.

The real and personal estate used in operating a railroad, steamboat, car or transportation company or used in carrying on express, telegraph and telephone business in the state, and shares of stock in domestic telephone, telegraph, steamboat, car and transportation companies, are exempted from the general property tax. Pub. Stats. 1906, sec. 797, as amended by acts of 1908, p. 27.

Real estate of railroads not specifically used in their business, is taxed locally. Id. Sec. 527.

Goods, wares, merchandise, stock in trade, including stock used in the business of the mechanic arts and machinery used in manufacture, if belonging to corporations, are taxed as if belonging to individuals. Id. sec. 510.

Stockholders and bondholders.

Shares of stock in corporations, domestic and foreign, are taxed locally to the owner if he resides in the state. Id. sec. 515. If the owner is a non-resident and holds stock in a domestic corporation, the tax is paid locally by the corporation and a lien on the stock in favor of the corporation is thereupon created. Id. sec. 516.

Deduction is made for all property taxed to manufacturing, mercantile, and trading companies in Vermont or elsewhere. In taxing stock of other corporations deduction is made for real estate taxed in Vermont or elsewhere. Id. sec. 520.

There are exempted from taxation the shares of stock in railroad, Id. sec. 515, domestic "telephone, telegraph, insurance, surety, guaranty, steam-boat, car (not palace car) and transportation companies." Id. sec. 797, as amended by acts 1908, p. 27.

Shares of stock in foreign corporations, when all the stock of such corporations is taxed in the home state, are exempt from taxation in the hands of the holder. Id. sec. 476, Ill.

Bonds, except those of insurance companies, are taxed to the holders as personal property. Id. sec. 494.

Tax on capital stock or "deposit."

Domestic and foreign corporations pay the "annual license tax." For companies having a capital stock this tax is based on the par value thereof, and for those having no capital stock the tax is based on assets ("deposit"). It is collected by the state for state purposes and ranges in amount from $10 to $50 on capital stock or deposit from $10,000 or less up. Id. secs. 752, 753, 754.

Railroads.

Corporations in the railroad business may elect to pay either a property or an earning's tax. Either tax is collected by the state for state purposes.

The commissioner of state taxes biennially appraises railroad property at its fair and just value, including the corporate franchise; and a tax of 1% per annum, payable semi-annually is assessed upon such appraised value. Id. secs. 706–720.

Instead of the above the companies may pay on gross earnings as follows: Two and one-half per cent on such part of the gross earnings derived from all sources as does not exceed $2,000 per mile of the road bed located wholly within the state; 2¾% of such part of such gross earnings as exceeds $2,000 and does not exceed $2,500 per mile, the rate increasing progressively one quarter of one per cent on each additional increment of $500 per mile up to $4,500 per mile; and 4% of such part of the gross earnings as exceeds $4,500 per mile. Id. secs. 714–717.

Shares of stock in such companies are exempt to the holder, Id. secs. 515, 797; bonds are taxable.   Id. sec. 494.

Transmission companies.

Telegraph companies pay to the state a tax assessed at the rate of sixty cents per mile of poles and one line of wire, and forty cents for each additional wire. In lieu of such mileage tax the companies may elect to pay a tax of 3% on gross earnings from business done within the state. Id. secs. 734–736.

Stocks and bonds of telegraph companies are taxed to the owners. Id. sec. 515.

Telephone companies pay to the state a tax of forty cents on the average number of telephone transmitters in use within the state, and thirty cents per mile on the average mileage of wires used in the state, or in lieu thereof 3% of the entire gross earnings collected within the state. Id. secs. 737–739.

Shares of stock in telephone companies are exempt to the holders. Id. sec. 797; their bonds are taxed to the holders.

Express companies.

Express companies pay an annual tax of $8.00 per mile for every mile of the routes or lines within the state over which they transported express matter for hire. Id. sec. 731.

Their shares of stock and bonds are taxed to the holders, Id. sec. 515.

Car companies.

Sleeping, dining and parlor car companies pay an annual franchise tax equal to seven-tenths of one per cent of the capital invested or used in the state, which is deemed to be that portion of the entire capital invested or used in operating such cars which the number of miles of all railroads within **the** state on which such cars have been operated during such **years** bears to the total number of miles of railroad within and **with** out the state over which cars have been operated during **such** year, and such other facts as the commissioner of state **taxes,** who values the investment, deems necessary. Id. secs. 726 - 730.

Shares of stock in the above companies are taxed to **the** holders like other personalty. Id. sec. 515.

Other car, steamboat and transportation companies, **do** mestic, are taxed on their rights, property and franchises **at** fair cash value by the commissioner of state taxes. A tax **of** one per cent is assessed on such appraised value, or in **lieu** thereof the company may pay two and one-half per cent **of its** entire gross earnings. Id. secs. 721–725.

Their shares of stock are exempt to the holder. Id. sec. **787,** their bonds are taxable to the holders. Id. sec. 515.

Street railways.
Electric railroads are subject to the same laws of **taxation** as are steam railroads.

Manufacturing and mercantile companies.
These companies are subject to the "annual license **tax,"** above given, for state purposes, and their real **and personal** property is taxed in the towns where situated. Id. **secs. 503,** 510, 752.

Shares of stock in these companies less the value of **all** property taxed to the corporation are, in theory, taxed to **the** owner. Id. secs. 515, 520; bonds are also taxable. Id. **sec.** 494.

Foreign corporations.
Foreign corporations in Vermont are generally subject **to** the same provisions of corporation taxation as are similar **do** mestic corporations.
Administration.
The administration of the law governing the taxation of cor porations is in the hands of the commissioner of state **taxes** appointed biennially by the governor. Pub. Acts, 1908, p. **167.**

Massachusetts.

Chief features.

Corporations are taxed by the state on the margin of intangible value found by deducting the assessed value of tangible property taxed locally to the corporation from the market value of its capital stock. This is called a tax on "corporate excess" and is known as the "Massachusetts plan."

General property tax.

Domestic corporations are taxed locally upon their real estate and machinery, and foreign corporations are taxed in the same manner, except that they are taxed on their merchandise as well. This property tax is for state and local purposes. R. L., ch. 12, secs. 2 and 3, and Acts of 1903, ch. 437, sec. 71.

Corporations are taxed only upon specific classes of personal property. The theory is that the personal property of natural citizens alone is taxable, and that the personalty of domestic corporations is reached in the tax on corporate excess. Salem Iron Co. v. Danvers, 10 Mass. 514 (1813). When machinery of corporations was made taxable, its deduction from the tax on capital stock (corporate excess) was required.

In order that the local authorities taxing the property of a corporation shall not place a value too high thereon, and thus unduly reduce the amount of corporate excess, it is provided that the tax commissioner may request a corporation to appeal from such valuation. Id., ch. 14, secs. 39, 42.

Stockholders and bondholders.

Shares of stock on domestic corporations, and of those foreign public-service companies doing business within the state and paying the tax on corporate excess, are not taxed in the hands of the holders. Id., ch. 14, sec. 61.

Shares of foreign corporations generally, however, are taxed. Id., ch. 12, sec. 4, as amended by acts 1902, ch. 374, sec. 4, and no deduction from this tax for property taxed within the state is permitted. Dwight v. Boston, 12 Allen, 316 (1866).

Bonds of both foreign and domestic corporations are taxed to the holders. Id., ch. 12, sec. 4, par. 2, as amended by acts 1902, ch. 374, sec. 4; id., ch. 12, sec. 4, par. 5.

General corporation tax on "Corporate Excess."

Domestic corporations and foreign transportation and transmission corporations doing business in Massachusetts are taxed for state and local purposes upon a basis of "corporate excess."

The tax commissioner ascertains the corporate excess from returns made by the different companies. He estimates the entire value of the capital stock of each company. This estimate is called the value of the "corporate franchise." Deduction is made for the value of real estate and machinery taxed locally, and the remainder called the "corporate excess," is taxed at the average rate of taxation for the whole state during the last three years. Id., ch. 14, secs. 37–38, as amended by acts 1906, ch. 271, sec. 9.

Such proportion of the tax collected by the state as corresponds to the amount of stock owned within the state is returned to the towns and cities in which the stockholders reside, in proportion to the number of shares there owned. The portion of the tax which represents the tax on shares of stock held outside of the state goes to the state. Id., ch. 14, sec. 61. About 20 per cent of the entire tax under this arrangement goes to the state. Rept. on the systems of taxing corporations. Dept. of Commerce & Labor, Washington, 1909, part 1, p. 90.

Shares in domestic corporations paying this tax are not taxed to the holders. Bonds are so taxable. Id., ch. 14, sec. 61; id., ch. 12, sec. 4, par. 2, as amended by acts, 1902, ch. 374. sec. 4.

Railroads.

Domestic railway companies are taxed locally on real estate and machinery and foreign companies of this class pay taxes on real estate, machinery and merchandise. Id., ch. 12, secs. 2 and 3, and acts of 1903, ch. 437, sec. 71.

In addition to the above, foreign and domestic railway companies pay the "corporate excess" tax. Provision is made for a proportionate assessment of the tax where the line extends outside the state.

The tax commissioner ascertains from returns or otherwise the true market value of all the shares of every railroad company, which shall be taken as the true value of its corporate franchise. From this is deducted, in the case of both foreign and domestic corporations, so much of the value of its capital stock as is proportional to the length of that part of its lines, if any, lying without the state, and also the value of its real estate and machinery subject to local taxation within the state, for which purpose the assessed value may be taken as the true value, but is not conclusive. Upon the valuation so found the railroad pays to the state a tax at the average rate throughout the state. Acts 1906, ch. 463, part II, secs. 211, 212, 214.

The expenses of the railroad commission are assessed by the tax commissioner upon the gross earnings of railroad and street railways. Id., ch. III, sec. 10.

Shares of stock in railroad companies which pay the corporate excess tax are not taxed. Bonds are taxed to the owners. Id., ch. 12, sec. 4, par. 2, as amended by acts 1902, ch. 374, sec. 4.

Transmission companies.

Telegraph and telephone companies pay the corporate excise tax. Provision is made for division of the valuation of companies doing an interstate business.

The companies make a return to the tax commissioner from which he ascertains a fair cash value of all their capital stock. From this amount he deducts, in case of a telegraph company, so much of the value as is proportional to the length of the line outside of the state, and all real estate and machinery subject to local taxation within the state. If it is a domestic telephone company, there is deducted the value of stock in other corporations held by it upon which a tax has been paid in Massachusetts or any other state during the year. If it is a foreign telephone company, there is deducted so much of the value as is proportional to the number of telephones used or controlled by it outside the state. Upon the net value so found, taxes are assessed by the state at the average rate throughout the state during the last three years. The tax is apportioned as in the case of railroad companies. Id. Ch. 14, secs. 37, 38, 48; Acts of 1906, Ch. 271, sec. 9.

Shares are not taxed in the hands of stockholders; bonds are. Id. Ch. 12, sec. 4, par. 2, as amended by acts 1902, Ch. 374, sec. 4.

These companies are assessed locally on real estate and machinery if domestic and on real estate, machinery and other

personal property if foreign. Id. Ch. 12, secs. 2 and 3, and
Acts of 1903, Ch. 437, sec. 71.

Express companies.

Express companies make returns to the tax commissioner of
the par and market value of their stock and bonds and unfunded debt, of their real estate and personal property, and
the amount of taxes paid on its property locally in the state.
The return also shows the gross earnings in the state and the
total gross earnings, and the securities not liable to taxation.
The tax commissioner then ascertains the true market value of
their stock, bonds, and such part of the unfunded debt as was
incurred for the purpose of construction or permanent equipment or improvement. After deducting the value of real and
personal property taxable within the state and securities not
liable to local taxation, the tax commissioner lays a tax upon
such part of the remainder as represents the ratio of gross
earnings of the company within the state to the total gross
earnings. The rate of taxation and the distribution of the tax
is the same as in case of railroads. Acts 1907, Ch. 586, as
amended by acts 1908, Chs. 194, 615.

Shares and bonds of these companies are taxed to the holders.

The property of these companies is taxed locally, as is that
of transportation and transmission companies. Id. Ch. 12, secs.
2 and 3, and Act of 1903, Ch. 437, sec. 7.

Street railways.

These companies pay the corporate excess tax as do railroads.
Acts 1906, Ch. 463, Pt. III, secs. 125, 126, 128.

If an operating street railway (including such as may have
lines partly outside the state), domestic or foreign, pays during
the year dividends exceeding 8% on its capital stock, it pays
an additional tax equal to the amount of such excess, provided
that the tax is not imposed if from the time the railway commenced business it has not paid in the aggregate dividends
equal to at least six per cent on its capital stock from year to
year. Acts 1906, Ch. 463, sec. 130. This tax is collected and
distributed in the same way as the corporate excess tax.

A "commutation tax" is required locally of street railways,
whether domestic or foreign (including companies whose lines
are partly within and partly without the state). The com-

panies make an annual return to each city and town, stating the length of track operated in public ways and places therein, and the total length of track of such company operated in public ways or places and also the total amount of gross receipts from operation for the year, excluding income derived from other sources, such as sale of power and rental of tracks. The local assessors tax such corporations on an assessed amount equal to such proportion of the percentage of gross receipts named in the act as the length of track in the public ways and places in the city or town bears to the total length of such track operated by the company in public ways and places. Id. Acts 1906, Ch. 463, Pt. III, secs. 133–134. This tax is for the towns and is levied as compensation for the use of public streets.

These companies are taxed locally on property as are railroad companies.

No tax is assessed to stockholders in such companies. Acts 1906, Ch. 463, Pt. III, sec. 131. Bonds of such companies are taxed to the holders.

Business corporations.

Manufacturing and mercantile corporations are assessed locally on property.

In addition to the above they pay the "corporate excess" tax in a somewhat modified form. Acts 1903, Ch. 437, secs. 1, 72, 74; Acts of 1906, Ch. 271, sec. 12.

Shares in business corporations are not taxed to holders, bonds are taxed. Id. Ch. 12, sec. 4, par. 2, as amended by Acts 1902, Ch. 374, sec. 4.

Foreign corporations.

In addition to being taxed, as are similar domestic corporations, foreign corporations in Massachusetts having a usual place of business in the state or engaged in the construction of a building, bridge or railway in the state, pay an excise tax of one-fiftieth of 1% of the par value of their capital stock, the total tax not to exceed $2,000. Acts 1903, Ch. 437, secs. 75 and 76, as amended by Acts of 1907, Ch. 578. This tax is for state purposes.

While domestic corporations are taxed locally on real estate and machinery, foreign companies are taxed on real estate and all personal property.

Shares of stock of foreign corporations (except those foreign transportation and transmission companies which pay the corporate excess tax) are taxed to the holders as personalty. Bonds of such companies are also taxed.

Administration.

The administration of corporation taxes is in the hands of the tax commissioner and commissioner of corporation, both offices being held by the same individual. He is appointed by the governor for a term of three years. Acts 1909, Ch. 490, Pt. III.

Rhode Island.

Chief features.

First. The wide application of the local general property tax to corporations including even steam railroads.

Second. The state taxation of street railways on gross earnings and of express, telegraph and telephone companies on gross receipts.

Third. The exemption of all corporations from taxation of intangible personalty.

Fourth. The deduction of indebtedness from the intangible personalty of domestic corporations only.

The general property tax.

This is assessed locally on the real and personal property of domestic and foreign corporations, except (a) the intangible personalty of all corporations, (b) the entire personal property of all telegraph, telephone and express companies. Rev. Laws (General Laws) 1906, Ch. 29, sec. 6, 12, 13; Laws Jan. 1905, Ch. 1246, sec. 1, last par. and sec. 2 and 4, subdiv. 1st and 6th.

Deductions for debts.

"No * * * bodies corporate resident of this state shall be liable to taxation on personal property except upon the surplus of the ratable personal estate owned by such * * * bodies corporate over and above their actual indebtedness. Laws, Jan. 1905, Ch. 1246, sec. 4, subdiv. 10th.

Deductions for debts are allowed in each town in the proportion that the personal property in such town bears to the total personal property in all towns. Id. subdiv. 11th.

Stockholders and bondholders.

The shares of corporation, domestic and foreign, which are taxed on the value of their real and tangible personalty to an amount equal to the market value of the shares, are not taxed; but if the corporation is taxed for less than this amount the stockholder is taxable for the difference between the market value of each share and the proportionate amount per share at which the corporation was last assessed. Laws, Jan. 1905, Ch. 1246, sec. 4, subdiv. 8th.

Resident holders of bonds of all corporations, foreign and domestic, resident and non-resident, are taxable locally.

Railroads.

Steam railroads are taxed locally under the general property tax—on their real estate and personal property.

Transmission and express companies.

Telegraph, telephone and express companies, domestic and foreign, pay annually to the state for state purposes one per cent of their gross receipts from business done within the state. This takes the place of all other taxes upon the lines and personal property used exclusively in the telegraph and telephone business, and upon the personal property used exclusively in the express business. Rev. 1896, Ch. 29, secs. 12 and 13.

The Providence Telephone Company also pays to that city three per cent of its gross earnings therein. Charter and Special Laws, City of Providence, 1901.

Street railways.

Street railways accepting the provisions of Chap. 580, Laws 1898–99, pay a minimum tax to the state, for state purposes, of 1% on their gross earnings, proportioned to trackage in the state; and whenever the annual dividends is over eight per cent an additional tax rate equal to such a fraction of the excess dividends as the gross earnings in the state are a fraction of the whole yearly gross earnings. This is in addition to all

38

special municipal taxes and local taxes on real estate and personal property. Laws, 1898–99, Ch, 710.

Street and steam railways pay the expenses of the railroad commissioner, including salary. Such expenses are assessed on each of such corporations, one-half in proportion to its gross receipts in the state and one-half in proportion to the length of its main road and branches in the state. The expenses and salary is limited to $4,000 annually. Laws 1900–01, Ch. 754.

The Providence Street Railway Company pays to that city for the use of the public street, etc., five per cent of its gross earnings in that city. Charter and Special Laws, City of Providence, 1901.

These companies pay also the local general property tax on their real and tangible personal property.

Manufacturing and mercantile companies.

These companies pay the local property tax on real and tangible personal property. Laws, Jan. 1905, Ch. 1246, sec 2 and 4, subdiv. 5th and 6th of sec. 4.

See stockholders and bond holders above for tax on shares and bonds of these companies.

Foreign corporations.

The property of domestic and foreign corporations is taxed alike except that deductions for debts is not allowed foreign corporations.

Administration.

The General Treasurer of the state is the principal state tax officer.

Connecticut.

Chief features.

First. The collection of the state taxes independent of the towns, there being no state general property tax.

Second. The privilege to holders of tangible property of paying to the state a low uniform tax thereon instead of the local property tax.

Third. The unique method of estimating the value of steam

and street railway property, on a basis of funded and floating indebtedness and market value of capital stock.

Separation of sources of state and local taxes.

No part of the tax collected locally on real and personal property is paid into the state treasury. State revenue is obtained principally from the special taxation of transportation, transmission, and financial corporations, from the taxation of inheritances, and from the "chose-in-action" tax—a special tax at a low uniform rate on any "bond, note, or other chose in action," a tax optional on the holders thereof, but nevertheless usually paid, being an alternative to paying the much higher local rates. Rev. Stats. 1902, sec. 2325, as amended by acts 1907, Chs. 160, 253.

General property tax.

All corporations doing business in the state, domestic and foreign, except steam and street railways and express companies, are taxed on real estate by the towns. The towns also collect this tax on personal property in the state of all corporations, domestic and foreign, except the entire personal property of steam and street railways, express telegraph, telephone and financial companies, and except that intangible personal property on which the chose in action tax is paid. Id. sec. 2322; Id. sec. 2329, as amended by Ch. 184, '07; Rev. Stats. 1902, sec. 2342; Id. sec. 2415.

Stockholders and bondholders.

No stock is taxed to the stockholder in Connecticut, the assumption being that the stock of foreign corporations is taxed in the home state, and that the property of domestic corporations is taxed to the corporations itself. Id. sec. 2329, amended by Ch. 184, '07.

Bonds of railroads and street railways operating in the state are not taxed to the holders, and the holders of other bonds may pay thereon either the chose in action tax or the much higher general property tax. Osborn v. N. Y. N. H. & H. R. R. Co., 40 Conn. 496 (1873).

Railroads.

Steam railroads, domestic and foreign, pay to the state for state purposes, one per cent of the market value, on a given date, at the capital stock and one per cent of the par value of the railroads funded and floating indebtedness, or if the indebtedness is less than par, then one per cent of the determined value of said indebtedness. Id. sec. 2424. Taxes locally paid upon real estate not used for railroad purposes are deducted. Id. sec. 2424. This tax is in lieu of all other taxes on the franchises, funded and floating debt, and property of railroads in the state. Id. sec. 2424 and see, Osborn v. R. R. Co., supra.

When only part of a railroad lies in the state, the company pays on a fraction of the valuation determined by the ratio of the length of the road in the state to the entire length. Id. sec. 2425. Not unconstitutional, see State v. R. R. Co., 60 Conn. 326 (1891).

The valuation of stock and indebtedness is determined by the state board of equalization.

Transmission companies.

Domestic and foreign telegraph companies pay, for state purposes, an annual tax of twenty-five cents on each mile of wire. This is in lieu of all other taxes on property used exclusively in the telegraph business, except a local tax on real estate. Id. secs. 2437, 2438.

Shares of stock not taxed. Bonds are taxable. Id. sec. 2323.

Telephone companies, domestic and foreign pay, for state purposes, one dollar for each transmittter furnished or rented in the state for telephone purposes, and also twenty-five cents on each mile of wire used in the state. These taxes are in lieu of all other, except the local tax on real estate. Id. sec. 2438, 2439, as amended by Chs. 158, 204 (sec. 1), Laws 1907.

Shares of stock in telephone companies are not taxed; bonds are. Id. sec. 2323.

Express companies.

Domestic and foreign express companies operating on steam railroads pay to the state, for state purposes a tax of five per cent of the gross charges received from business done wholly within the state. Id. sec. 2433, as amended by Acts 1907, Ch. 204, sec. 1. This is in lieu of all other taxes. The companies may pay $10,000 in lieu of the above. Id. sec. 2424.

Such companies operating on electric railways pay a tax of two per cent on gross receipts from business done wholly within the state. Acts 1905, Ch. 264; 1907, Ch. 268.

Shares of stock in express companies are exempt; bonds are taxed to resident owners, R. L. 1902, sec. 2323.

Street railways.

"The existing statutes with regard to the taxation of steam railways shall apply, extend to, and include all street railways of every description." Id., sec. 2432.

Foreign corporations.

The property of foreign corporations of the classes herein treated is taxed in the same manner as domestic corporations.

Administration.

The principal tax officer is the state tax commissioner, and there is the state board of equalization, composed of the treasurer, comptroller, and tax commissioner. The tax commissioner is appointed by the governor for four years. Id , secs. 2413–2414.

MIDDLE ATLANTIC.

New York.

Chief features.

First. A sharp separation between sources of state and local taxes.

Second. Capital stock tax at a varying rate governed by rate of dividends paid, market value of the stock, and financial condition.

Third. Corporations are taxed locally upon property, including "special franchises" (i. e., right to use public streets).

General property tax.

Domestic and foreign corporations are taxed locally on their property like individuals, but for local purposes only. Tax

Law (ch. 60, Consolidated Laws 1909), secs. 2, 3, 11, 12, 32. The assessment of personal property is based upon the total assets of the corporation after deducting property exempt by law (including shares of other corporations), assessed value of th corporation's real estate, debts of the corporation, and surplus if any, up to ten per cent of the capital. Id., sec. 12.

As a part of the general property tax, public service corporations, domestic and foreign, pay a "special franchise tax" for the right to use the public streets. This is a property tax, assessed on incorporated rights and tangible property. Id., secs. 2 and 3 for definitions. The valuation of these "special franchises" is determined by the state Board of Tax Commissioners, but the tax is collected locally, and used for local purposes. Id., secs. 43–45.

Stockholders and bondholders.

Shares of stock in domestic and foreign corporations are exempt from taxation in the hands of holders. Id., sec. 4, subd. 16.

Bonds of corporations, domestic and foreign, except those exempted by payment of recording tax, id., sec. 251, are taxable to the owner as personal property, but for local purposes only.

Capital-stock tax.

"For the privilege of doing business or exercising their corporate franchises" in New York, the general rule is that domestic and foreign corporations pay to the state a tax computed upon the basis of the amount of capital stock employed therein. The measure is such a portion of the issued capital stock as the gross assets employed in business within the state bear to the gross assets wherever employed in business. The rate varies according to dividends paid, market price of the stock, and net assets. For exemplé, 1. Corporations paying dividends of six per cent or more are subject to a state tax of one-fourth of a mill for each one per cent of dividends. This tax is computed on the par value of the capital stock employed within the státe, regardless of the assets or the market price of the stock. 2. Solvent corporations paying dividends of less than six per cent are subject to a tax of one and one-half mills on each dollar of the valuation of the capital stock employed within the state. This same rate applies when the average market price of the corporate stock equals or exceeds par. The taxable value shal not be less than either the net assets of the company or the average price at which such stock sold during the year, the higher valuation of the two being used. There are three other classes. Banks, trust companies, insurance, manufacturing, mining, laundering companies under certain conditions, elevated railways, surface railways not operated by steam; water, gas, electric or steam heating, lighting and power companies are exempt from this tax. Id., secs. 182, 183.

Stock transfer tax.

There is imposed on all sales or transfers of shares of stock, domestic or foreign, in the state, a tax payable by the vendor, of two cents on share of face value of $100 or less. Id., sec. 270.

Transportation and transmission companies.

In addition to the capital-stock tax, transportation and transmission companies, except elevated railways, and except surface railways not operated by steam, pay to the state five-tenths of one per cent on gross earnings, from business beginning and terminating in the state. Id., sec. 184.

These companies pay the local ad valorem tax. Id., secs. 2, 3, 11, 12, 32.

Elevated railways; surface railways not operated by steam.

These companies pay to the state for state purposes one per cent upon gross earnings within the state, and three per cent upon dividends declared in excess of four per cent upon the actual amount of paid-up capital employed. Id., sec. 185.

These companies pay the local ad valorem and the special franchise tax.

Water, light, heat and power companies.

These public utility companies pay to the state for state purposes, five-tenths of one per cent on gross earnings within the state, and three per cent on all dividends declared or paid in excess of four per cent on the actual amount of paid-up capital employed. Id., sec. 186. These companies pay the local ad valorem tax and the special franchise tax.

Manufacturing and mercantile companies.

Business corporations pay the local and ad valorem tax. Shares of stock in such companies are exempt. Id., sec. 12.

Foreign corporations.

Foreign corporations are, for both state and local purposes, taxed practically like domestic corporations.

Administration.

State taxes on corporations are levied and assessed by the comptroller and paid into the state treasury. The state board of tax commissioners value and assess "special franchises." They are also clothed with advisory powers over local assessors. Com. Laws, 1909, v. 5, p. 5939–40.

New Jersey.

Chief features.

First. The "franchise tax," based on the par value of the capital stock of "miscellaneous" corporations, which is paid to the state for the use of the state.

Second. The property tax on railroads and canals, including "privileges."

Third. The property tax on public-service corporations, and their "privileges," using or occupying the streets, highways. or other public places—such as street railways, water, lighting. telegraph, telephone, sewer, and pipe-line companies.

These public-service corporations are taxed also upon the basis of their gross receipts, and this "franchise tax" is distributed among the local taxing districts.

"Miscellaneous" corporations. Franchise tax.

"Miscellaneous" corporations, being domestic corporations in the main not doing business in New Jersey (though many corporations engaged in manufacturing within the state are included), pay for state purposes what is termed an annual license fee or franchise tax, based on the par value of the capital stock issued. The tax or fee is one-tenth of one per cent on all amounts of capital stock issued and outstanding up to $3,000,000; in excess thereof one-twentieth of one per cent up to $5,000,000 and $50 per million in excess of $5,000,000. If at least fifty per cent of the outstanding stock be invested in manufacturing or mining in New Jersey, the corporation is exempted from this tax. Railroad, canal, and banking corporations and corporations not conducted for profit are also exempted therefrom. Laws 196, ch. 19.

General property tax.

Under the general tax law, codified in 1903, the real and personal property of foreign and domestic corporations is taxed locally for local purposes, like that of individuals; and corporations are regarded as residents and inhabitants of the taxing district where their chief office is situated. Laws 1903, Ch. 208, Art. III, par. 16.

Certain property is exempt from taxation under this act, including the personal property of domestic corporations situated out of the state upon which taxes have been assessed and paid anywhere within twelve months; the shares of stock of any corporation of this state, the capital or property of which is made taxable to and against the corporation, and all offices and "franchises," and all property used for railroad and canal purposes, the taxation of which is provided for by any other law of the state. Laws 1903, Ch. 208, Art. I, sec. 3, parts 1. 5, 8.

From the valuation of personal property all debts due to creditors residing in the state may be deducted. Id. Art. III, part 13.

Taxes collected under the general property tax are used entirely for county and municipal purposes.

Shares of stock in corporations paying this tax are not taxed to the holder. Laws 1903, Ch. 208, Art. I, sec. 3, part 5, their bonds are taxable.

Stockholders and bondholders.

Shares of stock of any New Jersey corporation, the capital or property of which is taxed by the state, are exempt from taxation. All other stocks and bonds are by law taxable to the holder as personal property.

Railroads and canals.

Railroad and canal companies are assessed by the state board of assessors on their property, real and personal, and franchises. Gen. statutes (1709–1895), Vol. III, p. 3325, amended March 27, 1888. They are assessed locally on property not specifically used in their business. Id. p. 3324, same amendment.

The tax on real estate of railroad and canal companies is collected by the state, but the entire amount is paid over to the local taxing district, giving each the tax derived from such property situated therein. Laws 1905, Ch. 91. The state retains the tax on the main line, the tangible property, and the franchise. Gen. stats. III, p. 3325, amended March 27, 1888.

Other public service corporations.

In 1900 public utility companies were segregated from "miscellaneous corporations" which pay the franchise tax on capital stock, and a tax upon gross receipts was imposed by the "municipal franchise act," Laws 1900, Ch. 195, sec. 4, for the taxation of all the property and franchises of all persons or corporations (other than municipal or those taxed as railroads and canals) which have the right to use or occupy the streets, highways, etc., in the state, in lieu of all other taxes. This tax, collected by and for the use of the local taxing districts, is in addition to the taxation of real and personal property under the general property tax law.

The companies make returns to the state board of assessors and from these reports gross receipts are determined and the tax assessed thereon. The rate for all companies, except street railways, is two per cent on annual gross receipts; for street railways the rate increases by the year as follows: for 1906 2½%; for 1907, 3%; for 1908, 3½%; for 1909, 4%; for 1910, 4½%; for 1911 and annually thereafter, 5% on annual gross receipts. Laws 1906, Ch. 290.

The state board of assessors annually apportions this tax to the various taxing districts in proportion to the value located in or under the streets of the district and the tax is collected locally. Laws 1906, Ch. 290.

Shares of stock in corporations paying this tax are not taxed to the holder. Laws 1903, Ch. 208, Art. 2, sec. 3, part 5, but bonds are.

Express, parlor car, gas, etc., companies.

A few corporations, though included under the heading "miscellaneous corporations" are not taxed on capital stock. They are not taxed like public-utility corporations, but are reached under a supplement of 1892 to the act of 1884.

These included five express companies not owned by railroads (2% on gross receipts from business done in the state); one parlor-car, etc., company (same tax as on express companies); one gas and electric light company (½ of one per cent upon gross receipts) and five per cent on dividends in excess of four per cent.

The shares of stock of these corporations are not taxable—their bonds are.

Foreign corporations.

Foreign corporations generally are taxed, in and for the benefit of the local taxing districts, upon the amount of capital usually employed in the state and not otherwise taxed on real and personal property.   Laws 1903, Ch. 209, Art. III, sec. 16.

Administration.

The state board of assessors created in 1884 has control of the state taxation of corporations.

Pennsylvania.

Chief features.

First.   State taxes on "capital stock" (practically net assets), on corporate bonds, loans, etc., and on gross receipts, for state purposes.

Second.   An almost complete separation of local and state taxation.

Third.   A tax on real estate and certain personal property of corporations, both domestic and foreign, collected locally, for local purposes.

Local taxation; general property tax.

Corporations, other than public-service, are taxed locally for local purposes upon their real estate and certain personal property, in the same manner as individuals; public service corporations are taxable on so much of their property as is not essential to the exercise of their corporate franchise.

Stockholders and bondholders.

Stocks and bonds are not taxed under the local property tax.

Licenses.

Special taxes and licenses are imposed by certain localities on public service corporations and on some mercantile pursuits. Corporations following such pursuits are liable in the same manner as individuals.

Public service companies.

These corporations, domestic and foreign, are exempt from local taxation on so much of their property, real and personal, as is essential to the exercise of their corporate franchise, except in Philadelphia and Pittsburg. Act April 21, 1858, P. L. 385; Act Jan. 4, 1859, P. L. 828, sec. 3.

Foreign corporations.

Foreign corportions are taxable locally on property situate in this state like domestic corporations.

State taxation.

State revenue from corporations is obtained through three special classes of taxes, namely, the "capital stock tax," the "tax on corporate loans," and the "gross receipts tax on transportation, transmission and electric light companies."

"Capital stock tax."

The meaning of the term "capital stock" as used herein may be stated to be in general the assets of the company less indebtedness. A tax at the rate of five mills upon each dollar of the actual value of the "capital stock" employed within the states is imposed for state purposes upon all domestic and foreign corporations. Act of March 26, 1846, P. L. 179. The following companies are exempted or conditionally included within the taxing act:

(1) Banks, saving institutions, and foreign insurance companies.

(2) Manufacturing companies (except companies engaged in brewing or distilling spirits or malt liquors, and such as enjoy and exercise the right of eminent domain) are exempt in so far as their capital stock is employed in manufacturing within the

state. Act of June 8, 1893. P. L. 353, act of June 7, 1907,
P. L. 430.

(3) Bourse or exchange halls, except when dividends are declared. Act of June 10, 1893, P. L. 430.

Railroad companies whose lines are partly within and partly
without the state are taxed on their capital stock (assets) in
the proportion which the miles of their main track in Pennsylvania bears to their total mileage. Palace car companies, domestic and foreign, are taxable on their ''capital stock'' in the
proportion which the number of miles traveled by their cars
in Pennsylvania bears to the total number of miles traveled by
all their cars. Pullman Car Co. v. Pa., 141 U. S. 18 (1891).

Telegraph companies, domestic. and foreign, are taxed on
their ''capital stock'' (assets) in the proportion which the
length of their lines within the state bears to the total length
of all their lines. Com. v. W. U. Tel. Co., 15 W. N. C. 331
(1884). Companies owning bridges connecting Pennsylvania
with another state are taxable in Pennsylvania on one-half of
their ''capital stock'' only. Com. v. Bridge Co., 9 Am. L. Reg.
(O. S.) 298 (1860). Capital stock of manufacturing companies
invested in bonds, mortgages, and other securities, the same not
being essential to manufacture, is subject to the capital stock
tax; and, like other corporations paying a capital stock tax,
manufacturing corporations are not required to return such securities to local assessors for taxation.

The amount of the tax is fixed by the auditor-general and
state treasurer, upon annual reports made by all companies,
and upon other information. Act June 8th, 1891. P. L. 229.

Brewing and distilling companies.

These companies are not exempted from the capital stock
as are some manufacturing companies. Act June 7, 1907,
amending Act June 3, 1893 P. L. 353.

Distilling companies are taxed, as a separate class, ten mills
per dollars of actual value of their whole capital stock. This
provision applies also to companies wholesaling spirituous
liquors; and does not differ from the general ''capital-stock
tax'' except in the rate. Act July 15, 1897, P. L. 294.

Breweries pay the regular capital stock tax of five mills.

Tax on corporate loans.

The law provides that a treasurer of a corporation, domestic or foreign, when paying the interest on any "scrip, bond, or certificate of indebtedness" of the corporation, shall deduct from such payments four mills on every dollar of the full value of the debt and pay the same into the state treasury. This tax is for state purposes only. The holders of the obligations are then exempt from further taxation thereon. Act June 30, 1885, P. L. 194; Act June 8, 1891, P. L. 229.

The tax is not imposed on obligations owned by corporations paying the capital stock tax, upon those held by banks or charitable institutions, or upon certain other obligations. Act June 7, 1907, P. L. 430; Act June 8, 1891, P. L. 229; Act May 22, 1883, P. L. 39; State Tax on Foreign Held Bonds, 15 Wall. 300 (1872); Mattern v. Calvin, 213 Pa. 588 (1906); Com v. Traction Co., 1 Daup. C. R. 117 (1889).

Tax on gross receipts of transportation, transmission, and electric light Cos.

In addition to the "capital stock" and "corporate loan" taxes, every transportation, oil pipe line, telegraph, telephone, and electric light company doing business within the state pays a tax of eight-tenths of one per cent on gross receipts from business done wholly within the state. Act June 1, 1889, P. L. 420, sec. 23. This tax is payable to the state for state purposes only.

Corporations are not taxable, however, on receipts derived from interstate transportation and transmission. Express companies employing railroads and other companies to do their transportation are not entitled to exemption on the amount of receipts paid for such service, even though the payments enter into the amounts upon which the other companies have paid. Com. v. U. S. Ex. Co., 157 Pa. 579 (1893).

Electric light, heat and power companies are taxable upon receipts from all sources, except such as may not result from the sales of the product of such companies. Com. v. Elec. Co., 5 Daup. C. R. 89 (1902).

Licenses.

In addition to the foregoing state taxes, to which corporations are liable, business taxes and licenses are imposed for state purposes upon the manufacture and sale of liquors, and upon certain mercantile, financial, and other pursuits and occupations.

Stockholders and bondholders.

Shares of stock in corporations liable to the "capital stock tax" or expressly exempted therefrom (principally manufacturing companies) are not taxed in the hands of the holders, act June 8, 1891, P. L. 229, sec. 1, amending act June 1, 1889, P. L. 420, but shares of stock in foreign corporations not paying the capital stock tax in Pennsylvania are taxable as personal property. Makeen v. County of Northampton 49 Pa. 519 (1865).

Bonds in domestic companies are, in theory, taxed to the holder for state purposes only, at four mills on the dollar of nominal value, by the "corporate loan tax," but the tax is usually paid by the corporation. Foreign held bonds are not taxable in Pennsylvania. Bonds of foreign corporations are taxed by the state directly through local tax officers to the holders. Act June 1, 1889, P. L. 420, as amended by Act June 8, 1981, P. L. 229.

Foreign corporations.

Foreign corporations doing business in the state are subject to taxation for state purposes like domestic corporations.

Delaware.

Chief features.

First. A lump-sum commutation of state taxes upon steam railroads in lieu of all other state taxes.

Second. Taxation of many corporations on authorized capital stock.

Third. A sharp separation of the sources of state and local taxation, namely, taxation of corporations for state purposes and a general property tax for local purposes.

General property tax.

All real and personal property is assessed locally at true value. Revised Code 1852, as amended 1893, ch. 10, sec. 11. Real estate of railroads occupied as right of way, or roadbed

is exempt from local taxation.   All other real estate, including
buildings on right of way, is taxed locally like property of
individuals.   Id., p. 115.

The state derives no revenue through the general property
tax, its provisions applying exclusively to county and municipal taxation.

Stockholders and bondholders.

Stocks and bonds held by residents of Delaware are not
taxed; and shares of stock in domestic corporations owned by
persons without the state, under a constitutional provision,
cannot be taxed in the state.   Con., art. IX, sec. 6, as amended,
Laws of Del., vol. 22, ch. 254 (1903).

The following special taxes are all assessed and collected for
   state purposes:
Annual franchise tax.

This tax has two features—a tax on gross receipts, applied,
in theory to certain specified classes of corporations, and a
tax on authorized capital stock.

The tax on capital stock applies only to domestic, mercantile companies, organized after March 10, 1899 (date of act),
and either conducting business wholly without the state or
doing less than fifty per cent of their business within the state.
Laws of Del., vol. 21, ch. 166 (1897), as amended, vol. 22, ch.
15 (1901); vol. 22, ch. 260 (1903); vol. 24, ch. 1 (1906), and
vol. 24, ch. 247 (1907).   The assessed value of real estate and
personal property in the state is deducted from the authorized
capital stock.

The tax on gross receipts from business within the state
applies, in theory, to transmission, certain transportation, insurance (other than life), and light, heat and power companies.   Light, heat and power companies are also, in theory,
taxed on dividends in excess of four per cent; life insurance
companies, on gross premiums and surplus.

Tax on gross earnings.

Domestic and foreign express companies are taxed six per
cent on their gross earnings from business in the state.   Id.,
p. 73, as amended by vol. 25, ch. 13 (1909).

Domestic and foreign telegraph and telephone companies are taxed at a graduated rate on wire mileage within the state, and telephone companies pay an additional tax on each transmitter within the state. Id., p. 72, as amended by vol. 25, ch. 6 (1909).

Heat, light and power companies are taxed on gross receipts. Vol. 25, ch. 7 (1909).

Business license taxes.

A graduated license tax, based on the aggregate cost value of real and personal property located within the state and used in production or manufacture, is imposed on manufacturingg companies. Rev. Code, p. 69, as amended by vol. 22, ch. 17 (1901).

A graduated license tax, based on cost value of articles purchased during the year in the course of purchasing and selling property of any description, is imposed on domestic and foreign mercantile companies. Rev. Code, p. 547.

The Pullman Company, vol. 20, ch. 375 (1897), and express and telephone companies pay annual license fees. Express companies, $250. Rev. Code, p. 73, as amended by vol. 25, ch. 13 (1909). Telephone companies, twenty-five cents on each transmitter. Rev. Code, p. 72, as amended by vol. 25, ch. 6 (1909).

Railroad companies—by specific amounts.

All railroads operating within the state are permitted to pay to the state for state purposes fixed sums in lieu of all state taxes under general laws. Laws Del., vol. 24, chaps. 42, 43, 44 (1907); id., vol. 25, chaps. 10, 11, 12 (1909).

Express, transmission, light, heat, and power companies—gross receipts, mileage and license taxes.

Express, light, heat and power companies pay to the state, for state purposes, a tax on gross receipts; Id., vol. 21, ch. 166 (1899); vol. 22, ch. 15 (1901); vol. 22, ch. 260 (1903); vol. 24. chaps. 1, 47 (1906–7); telegraph, cable, and telephone companies, on miles of wire owned or operated within the state. Id., p. 72, as amended by Laws of Del., vol. 25, ch. 6 (1909). In addition to the above, express and telephone companies pay

39

certain license taxes. Id., pp. 72 and 73, as amended by vol. 25, ch. 6 (1909).

Parlor and sleeping car companies.

The Pullman palace car company, in lieu of a license tax, pays to the state annually $300. Id., vol. 20, ch. 375 (1897).

Manufacturing, mining, and mercantile companies—on property and authorized capital.

Manufacturing and mining companies pay a graduated tax based on the cost value of real and personal property in the state used in manufacture or production; mercantile companies, on the cost value of property purchased by them for sale. All companies of the above-named classes, incorporated since March 10, 1899, having more than fifty per cent, or all, of their capital invested without the state, pay in lieu of this property tax an "annual franchise tax" on authorized capital stock. Vol. 21, ch. 166 (1899); vol. 22, ch. 260 (1903); vol. 24, chaps. 1, 47 (1906-7). Rev. Code, p. 547.

Foreign corporations.

Before doing business in the state, foreign corporations (except insurance companies) pay to the state for the use of the state an initial fee of fifty dollars. Mercantile companies maintaining branch houses in the state are subject to a graduated tax based on the cost value of goods received for sale.

Maryland.

Chief features.

First. A tax based on gross receipts, paid principally by companies of a public service nature.

Second. All corporations (except steam railroads) are taxed by the state and locally upon the total value of shares of stoock, less deductions for real estate taxed. This capital-stock tax is merely the general property tax in its application to corporations.

General property tax.

Corporations, domestic and foreign (except steam railroads), are taxed locally for both state and local purposes upon real property in the same manner as are individuals. Dec. of Rights, art. 15. Personal property of domestic corporations whose capital stock is subject to taxation is exempt. Code, 1904, art. 81, sec. 159. Personal property of foreign corporations is taxable. Dec. of Rights, art. 15.

Steam railroads are not taxed on property for state purposes, but are taxed locally for local purposes on real and personal property in the same manner as individuals. Code, 1904, art. 81, sec. 189.

Stockholders and bondholders.

Shares of stock in domestic corporations (except steam railroads) owned by residents and non-residents are, under the capital-stock tax above described, taxed to the corporation, which may charge the amount of the tax to the stockholder. Stock in foreign corporation is taxed to the holders, as are also bonds and other securities in both domestic and foreign corporations. The shares in domestic and foreign steam railroad corporations subject to the gross-receipts tax and the local property taxes are exempt from taxation. Code, art. 81, secs. 2, 159 and 210; Code, art. 81, sec. 159.

Capital-stock tax.

Domestic corporations (except steam railroads) pay a tax for state and local purposes, based on the assessed value of the entire capital stock of the corporation less exempted property and real estate. This tax may be charged by the corporations to the stockholders. The personal property of a corporation paying it is exempt from further taxation, as is also the stock of such corporations in the hands of the holders. Code, 1904, art. 81, secs. 156, 156, 161; Code, art. 81, secs. 147 and 159.

State tax on gross receipts.

A state tax is imposed upon the gross receipts of business done within the state by domestic and foreign steam railroads, Laws 1906, amending Code, art. 81, sec. 160, oil pipe line, electric light, electric, construction, and gas companies, sleeping-car companies, telegraph, telephone, cable, express, or transportation companies, and certain financial and insurance com-

panies. Laws 1906, ch. 712, amending Code, art. 81, sec. 164.
Foreign fertilizer companies are also taxed under this provision.

Licenses.

In addition to the foregoing, an extensive system of special
taxes and licenses is imposed upon certain businesses and professional pursuits, to which corporations following such occupation are liable in the same manner as individuals.

Foreign corporations.

Real estate and personal property of foreign corporations are
taxed for state and local purposes "as if the same belonged to
a natural person." Code Art. 23, sec. 72, as amended by
Laws 1908, Ch. 240, p. 53. In addition to this, all foreign corporations, except those taxed upon gross receipts, are subject
to a special graduated tax based on capital employed in the
state. Code, Art. 23, sec. 70, same amendment.

Administration.

State taxation is under the supervision of the state tax commissioner, who acts also in an advisory capacity to the local
taxing authorities. Local taxation is administered by the respective boards of county commissioners and the Appeal Tax
Court of Baltimore.

District of Columbia.

Chief features.

First. The broad application of the general property tax.

Second. A special tax on the gross earnings (or receipts)
of certain classes of corporations.

Third. The absence of any tax against the holders of shares
of stock, bonds, or other corporate securities, upon such holdings.

General property tax.

"Hereafter all real estate in the District of Columbia subject to taxation, including improvements thereon, shall be assessed at no less than two-thirds of the true value thereof, and shall be taxed one and one-half per centum upon the assessed valuation thereof. * * * ." 32 U. S. Stat. 616. sec. 5.

"On all tangible personal property, assessed at a fair cash value (over and above exemption provided in this section) * * * , there shall be paid one and one-half per centum on the assessed value thereof." 32 U. S. Stat. 618, par. 2.

Under the two preceding provisions corporations, domestic and foreign, are taxed on their tangible real and personal property like individuals.

Steam·railroad, telegraph, steamboat, canal, express, car and manufacturing companies are taxed only under the general property tax law.

Corporations paying a gross earnings tax (street railway, telephone, electric lighting and gas companies are taxed on gross earnings) do not pay taxes on personalty.

Stockholders and bondholders.

Stocks, bonds, and other securities of domestic and foreign corporations are not taxed to the holders. Tangible personalty only is taxable. 32 U. S. Stat. 618, par. 2.

Gross earnings and gross receipts tax.

Street railways pay four per cent per annum "on their gross receipts and other taxes as provided by existing law." 32 U. S. Stat. 619. The other taxes are on realty and $30,000 per annum in salaries to crossing policemen. Tracks are not taxed. They are regarded as occupying "public space as a franchise, the tax upon which is construed to be included in the personal tax of four per cent per annum on gross receipts." Assessors Report for 1907, p. 9.

Telephone companies are taxed four per cent per annum on gross earnings, 32 U. S. Stat. 619, and in addition upon realty, including overhead wires and supporting poles, assessors Report for 1907, p. 10.

Electric lighting companies pay four per cent per annum on gross earnings, 32 U. S. Stat. 619, and also the general property tax upon real estate, including conduits, poles, lamps, etc.

Gas companies are taxed five per cent per annum on their gross earnings, 32 U. S. Stat. 619, and in addition the real estate owned by them in the district 'shall be taxed as other real estate in said district."

Tax on capital stock.

There is provision made for a tax on capital stock, but it is inoperative. Rept. on systems of corporation taxation, Washington, 1910, Part II p. 102.

Manufacturing and mercantile companies.

These companies are taxed on their tangible real and personal property.

Administration.   •

The tax laws of the District are administered by the assessor and the board of assistant assessors. 19 U. S. Stat. 400; 20 Id. 104; 21 Id. 460; 28 Id. 282, 32 Id. 617. The assessments are finally approved by the commissioner of the District. 28 Id. 284.

SOUTH ATLANTIC.

Florida.

Chief features.

First. The broad application of the general property tax to corporations.

Second. A tax on the gross receipts of sleeping and parlor car companies.

Third. License taxes, for state, county and local purposes, on railroad and other corporations.

General property tax.

All corporations, domestic and foreign, are taxed on their real and personal property for state and local purposes. L. 1907, Act. No. 1, Ch. 5596. All assessments, except of personal property of a few public service companies, are made by the county and local assessors.

Stocks and bonds.

Owners of stock, if the same is returned for taxation by the issuing company, or if the property of such company is taxed, are not taxed thereon. L. 1907, Ch. 5596, (No. 6), sec. 8. Bonds are taxed. Id. sec. 5.

Gross receipts tax.

This tax is collected of sleeping and parlor car companies Id. sec. 47—see below.

License taxes.

About all corporations•are subject to the payment of occupation taxes or license fees, which vary according to the nature of the business transacted. Provisions therefor are contained in Act No. 2, of the laws of 1907.

Railroads and street railways.

Steam and street railways are assessed for taxation by the comptroller, attorney general and state treasurer on all personal property. Items of property assessed at value are: "locomotives, engines, passenger, sleeping, freight, parlor, platform, construction and other cars and appurtenances."

The real property of such companies is assessed by the county assessors. Companies report to both. Value of personalty assessed as above, is apportioned to counties according to mileage, and the tax is collected locally. Id. secs. 46, 49.

In addition to the above all railroads pay a license tax of ten dollars on each mile of track, main, branch and sidetrack, to the state treasurer; one-half for state and one-half for county purposes.

Municipalities may impose license taxes on railroads varying in amount according to population: $10–$250. L. 1907, No. 26, Ch. 5623.

Transmission companies.

Telegraph companies are assessed and taxed on real and personal property as are railroads. Id. sec. 46.

In addition to the above such companies pay a license tax of fifty cents per mile of line; one-half to counties, one-half to state. L. 1907, Ch. 5597 (No. 2).

Telephone companies pay the ad valorem tax and a license tax based on the number of telephones in actual use; twelve and one-half cents per instrument; tax not to exceed fifteen dollars—two hundred dollars according to population. Id.

Express companies.

Express companies, in addition to the ad valorem tax, pay an annual license fee to the state of $7,500, and license fee to municipalities graduated according to the population therein, $6.00–$200.

Sleeping and parlor car companies.

Car companies pay a gross receipts tax of one dollar and fifty cents on each one hundred dollars of gross receipts from business done within the state. Id., sec. 47.

Such companies pay license taxes as follows:

Sleeping and parlor cars, $25.00 per car,
Sleeping and parlor cars, with buffet, $40.00 per car,
Dining cars, $20.00.

Laws 1907, ch. 5597 (No. 2).

Mercantile and manufacturing companies.

This class of corporations pay the ad valorem tax and the license tax, the latter varying according to the nature of the business transacted. Laws 1907, act No. 2, ch. 5597.

Foreign corporations.

There are no provisions which differentiate between foreign and domestic corporation taxation.

Administration.

Boards of county commissioners review and equalize taxes. With the exception of the personal property of steam and street railway and telegraph companies, which is assessed by a local board composed of the comptroller, attorney general and state treasurer, corporation property is assessed by county and local assessors.

Virginia.

Chief features.

First. The broad application of the general property tax.

Second. Franchise taxes based upon capital stock and receipts.

Third. License taxes and charter and registration fees.

Fourth. Absence of tax on shares of stock where the corporation has paid the franchise tax.

General property tax.

Public service companies, excepting car companies, are assessed on their property, tangible and intangible. All corporations, with the above exception, pay the general property tax for state and local purposes.

Stockholders and bondholders.

Shares of stock of companies, other than those which pay the franchise tax, are taxed to the holders as personal property. L. 1902-3-4, ch. 148, sec. 8, par. 8. Bonds are taxable to the holders.

State franchise tax.

Domestic corporations, excepting railway, canal, insurance, banking and security companies and telephone companies having an authorized capital stock of $5,000 or less, in addition to the charter fee, tax on property and income or receipts, license tax, and registration fee, pay an annual state franchise tax to be assessed by the state corporation commission. The tax is based on capital stock and ranges from ten dollars where the capital stock is $85,000, or under, to $200 where the same exceeds $500,000. Tax Laws, sec. 43, as amended by Act, March 14 (1908).

License taxes.

License taxes, varying according to the nature of the business transacted, are collected of corporations and persons.

Charter and registration fees.

All corporations pay charter and registration fees. Charter fees range from twenty-five dollars to five thousand dollars depending upon capital stock; registration fees, based upon the amount of capital stock, range from five dollars to twenty-five dollars. Id. secs. 29-30, 41-42.

Railroad and canal corporations.

Railroad and canal companies are assessed by the state corporation commissioner on the fair value of their tangible and intangible property—twenty cents per one hundred dollar value on tangible and twenty-five cents per one hundred dollar value on intangible property for state purposes, ten cents per one hundred dollar on all property tangible and intangible for support of the free public schools, and five cents per hundred dollars on tangible property for payment of pensions.

In addition to the above property tax railway and canal corporations pay to the state an annual state franchise tax equal to one per centum upon their gross transportation receipts, for the privilege of exercising their franchises in the state. In case of interstate companies the gross transportation receipts in Virginia are determined by ascertaining the average gross transportation receipts per mile over the entire lines of such companies, and multiplying the result by the number of miles operated within the state. Id. secs. 27, 28.

Shares of stock in such companies are exempt from taxation. Id. sec. 28.

Transmission companies.

The tangible and intangible property of telegraph and telephone companies is assessed and taxed as is the same property of railroad and canal companies, and at the same rate for state school and pension purposes.

In addition to the above property tax, transmission companies pay a license tax as follows, to-wit:

Telegraph companies, two dollars per mile of line of poles or conduits, and two per cent on gross receipts.

Telephone companies, a tax on gross receipts based on mileage and gross receipts. Tax ranges from one per cent on gross receipts to two per cent thereon and two dollars per mile of line or conduits. Id. secs. 34, 35, 36, as amended by Act of March 14, 1908.

Shares of stock and bonds in these companies are taxed.

Express, steamboat and ferry companies.

The property, tangible and intangible of these companies, is assessed and taxed as is the same property of railroad and canal and transmission companies.

Steamboat and ferry companies pay, in addition to the property tax, an annual license tax equal to one per centum of their gross receipts.

Express companies pay a license tax of three dollars for every mile of mileage operated in the state, in addition to the property tax. Id. secs. 29, 30, 31, as amended by Act March 11, 1908.

Shares of stock and bonds in these companies are taxed.

Car companies.

Sleeping, parlor and dining car companies operating a mileage in Virginia, pay a license fee or tax of two dollars "for each and every mile of track over which it operates its cars in this state." These companies are not taxed on property. Id. secs. 32 and 33.

Shares of stock and bonds in these companies are taxed.

Local public utilities.

Local public service companies are taxed locally on their real and personal property. In addition thereto they pay the state franchise tax, charter and registration fees and license taxes.

These companies pay the state franchise tax, therefore, their stock is not taxed to the holders. Their bonds are taxable.

Manufacturing and mercantile companies.

These companies are taxed as are local public utilities. Mercantile companies pay to the state a license fee graduated according to purchases—$1,000 purchase. $5—to 30c on each $100 from $2,000 to $50,000, and 10c per $100 in excess of $50,000. L. 1902-3-4, C. 148, sec. 46.

Foreign corporations.

The taxation laws apply about alike to foreign and domestic corporations.

Administration.

Corporation taxation is generally supervised by the commissioner of revenue, and the commissioner of corporations. The latter assesses the property of railroad, express, steamboat, ferry, telegraph and telephone companies.

West Virginia.

Chief features.

First. License taxes on capital stock, on all classes of corporations.

Second. License tax on non-residents domestic, and on foreign corporations greater than those on domestic corporations.

Third. The broad application of the general property tax. General property tax.

All corporations, domestic and foreign, pay taxes on the value of their property for state and local purposes.

Stocks and bonds.

The stock of domestic insurance, transmission and express companies is not taxed. Code, sec. 6, ch. 34, as amended by ch. 35, '05. When the property; stock or capital of any company is assessed to such company, owners of shares are not taxed thereon. See Assessment Laws, sec. 66.

Annual license tax.

Resident domestic corporations pay an annual license tax to the state for state purposes based on capital stock ranging from $10 for $5,000 or under of capital stock to $150 where the capital stock is $1,000,000, etc., up. Code, sec. 126, ch. 32, as amended by ch. 36, '05.

Non-resident domestic corporations pay a license tax to the state for state purposes based on capital stock increasing from $15 for $10,000 of capital stock to $675 where the capital stock amounts to $4,000,000, etc., up. Code, sec. 128, ch. 32, as amended by sec. 36, ch. 128, '05.

Foreign corporations pay a license tax of not less than $100, and up, according to sec. 126, ch. 32, above, if property owned in state exceeds $5,000; if less than that amount, up according to sec. 128, ch. 32, above. Code, sec. 130, ch. 32, as amended by sec. 130, ch. 36, 1905.

Railroad, car, telegraph, telephone, pipe line and bridge companies.

These corporations are taxed on their property, real and personal, for state and local purposes. Assessment by the Board of Public Works. Secs. 85–107a, ch. 35, Acts 1905.

Foreign insurance, telegraph, telephone and express companies.

These companies, in addition to the property and other taxes (assessed and collected as are taxes on railroad companies) pay a license tax as follows: Insurance companies pay a tax

on the total amount of risks written; fire insurance companies
one-fourth of one mill on each dollar; life and accident companies one and one-half mills on each dollar; express companies one dollar and fifty cents per mile of track over which
express is carried; telegraph one dollar per mile of wire over
which messages are sent; telephone companies one dollar per
mile of wire between cities, etc. (local exchange wires not
figured in the mileage). The above tax is for state purposes.
Code, sec. 13, ch. 34, as amended by 107, '01.

Manufacturing and mercantile corporations.

These companies pay the annual license tax based upon capital stock, and are assessed on their property for local purposes.

Foreign corporations.

The state of West Virginia imposes heavier license fees on
foreign than on domestic corporations. It subjects foreign insurance, telegraph, telephone and express companies to a license tax not exacted from domestic companies.

Administration.

Since 1907 West Virginia has a state tax commissioner appointed by the governor for six years.

North Carolina.

Chief features.

First. An annual franchise tax on certain corporations.

Second. A capital stock tax applicable to about all corporations excepting insurance companies.

Third. License taxes.

General property tax.

About all corporations, domestic and foreign, are taxed on
their general (including intangible) property for local purposes. In some cases state revenue is derived through application of the ad valorem system to corporations, but most generally through franchise, capital stock and license taxes.

Shares of stock.

Shares of stock in companies paying the capital stock tax are not taxed to the individual owner. Pell's Revisal, 1908, sec. 5108.

Capital stock tax.

All corporations, domestic and foreign, except insurance companies pay a tax to the state on the actual value of their capital stock,—forty-three cents on each one hundred dollars of actual value thereof. Id. sec. 5108.

Annual franchise tax.

Domestic and foreign corporations, except railroads, banks, building and loan associations, insurance, telegraph and telephone and express companies, pay to the state for state purposes an annual franchise tax graduated according to capital stock. Tax ranging from five dollars to five hundred dollars on capital stock ranging from $25,000 to over $1,000,000. Id. sec. 5190.

Railroads.

Railroad companies are assessed on their tangible and intangible property by the corporation commission. This assessment is for state and local purposes and is apportioned among the counties occording to mileage. Companies pay the state tax directly to the state treasurer. Id. secs. 5288–5294.

In addition to the above railroad companies pay to the state a privilege or license tax graduated according to gross earnings per mile. Roads earning $1,000 or less per mile per year, two dollars per mile; those earning between one and two thousand, three dollars per mile; those earning between two and three thousand, four dollars per mile; those earning in excess of three thousand dollars, five dollars per mile. Id. secs. 5185, 5186.

Transmission companies.

Telegraph companies are subject to local ad valorem taxes and to the privilege tax to the state of two and one-half per cent on gross earnings in the state. Id. sec. 5188.

Telephone companies taxed locally on property and pay to the state as a privilege tax two and one-half per cent of gross receipts in state. This privilege tar decreases in amount as the proportion of the aggregate property of the company invested in North Carolina increases. For example, a company, three-fourths of the' assets of which are invested in North Carolina or North Carolina securities, pays a privilege tax of only one-half per cent of gross receipts.

The property of transmission companies subject to the local ad valorem tax is assessed by the corporation commission and the assessment is certified to the localities. Id., 5284.

Car companies.

Companies owning and operating sleeping, palace, dining and merchandise cars in North Carolina are assessed for state and local purposes on the value thereof by the corporation commission. Assessment is apportioned to the counties according to mileage. Id. secs. 5279–82, 5284, 5287.

Canal and steamboat companies.

Water transportation companies are assessed and taxed as are steam railroads. Id. 5295.

Express companies.

Express companies, in addition to a privilege tax of two and one-half per cent on gross receipts from business in the state for state purposes, pay a local tax on property, Id. sec. 5187.

Street-railway, waterworks, electric-light and power, gas, ferry, bridge, canal and other companies exercising the right of eminent domain.

Report all property, tangible and intangible, to the corporation commission. The value of their entire property is taken to be the value of all shares of stock, plus mortgage indebtedness, minus value of all real estate not specifically used in the general business. From this result is deducted the value of all property subject to local taxation. The assessed valuation by the commission is apportioned among the counties. Companies pay the state tax directly to the state treasurer. Id. sec. 5281–5287.

Manufacturing and mercantile companies.

These companies are subject to· ad valorem taxes and to the capital stock and ·annual franchise tax. Id. secs. 5108, 5190.

Foreign corporations.

Insurance and telephone companies investing their capital
in North Carolina pay a lower privilege tax than other companies. Otherwise domestic and foreign corporations are
treated alike.

Administration.

Corporation commission; three members; elected by the people for six years, acts as state tax commission and administers
the state's taxing laws. Id. Ch. 20, (Vol. 1).

NORTH CENTRAL.

Indiana.

Chief features.

First. Tax on the capital stock, privileges, franchises and
"corporate excess" of certain·domestic corporations.

Second. Unique method of ascertaining the value of the
mileage or property of transmission, express, sleeping and
freight car and pipe line companies.

Third. The application of the general property tax to steam
and street railway companies.

The general property tax.

The general property tax in theory is applied to all corporations, domestic and foreign, excepting foreign insurance companies. R. S. 1908, sec. 10161.

Stocks and bonds.

Shares of stock, other than bank stock, are assessed to the
corporation. R. S. 1908, sec. 10161 and Id. 10208–10215.

Steam and street railway companies.

Steam and street railway corporations list their property,
including capital stock and franchises, with the county auditor,
who reports to the state board of tax commissioners. This
board values the real and movable property of such companies.
The value is apportioned according to mileage in the counties
and other local units. R. S. 1908, Secs. 10236–10249.

Telegraph, telephone, express, sleeping and freight car and pipe line companies. ·

These corporations are assessed by the state board of tax commissioners. The value of their property is taken to be that proportion of the aggregate property of such company (the value of all shares of stock plus mortgages on property minus real estate not specifically used in the general business) as the miles of telegraph or telephone lines, or the mileage of express and car companies' in the state, bear to the entire length of lines or mileage of such companies. The value so ascertained is apportioned according to mileage in the counties and other local units. R. S. 1908, secs. 10217–10230.

Foreign bridge and ferry companies.

These companies pay taxes on their tangible property and on receipts. R. S. 1908, sec. 10232.

Domestic waterworks, gas, manufacturing, mining, road, savings bank, and insurance companies.

Pay taxes on their capital stock, privileges and franchises, and on the excess of capital stock over the value of their tangible property listed for taxation. They are assessed by the county board of review and taxed locally. If no tangible property is listed such companies are assessed on their capital stock at true cash value. In so far as capital stock is invested in tangible property returned for taxation, it is not assessed. Franchises and privileges are assessed at true cash value. If the franchise is represented by the capital stock listed for taxation, then it is not taxed, but in all cases where the franchise is of greater value than the capital stock, then it is assessed at its full cash value. R. S. 1908, secs. 10233–10235.

Manufacturing companies.

These companies are subject to the "corporate excess" tax and are taxed on their capital stock, privileges and franchises. R. S. 1908, secs. 10233–10235.

Administration.

Corporation taxation is administered by the county auditor and by the state board of tax commissioners; three members appointed by the governor for four years. Ch. 93, Acts 1907.

40

Michigan.

Chief features.

First. Application of the ad valorem system to railroad, union station, car, telegraph and telephone companies.

Second. Manner of ascertaining the basis for taxation of express companies.

Third. Exemption of the shares of stock of domestic corporation if property of company is .taxed.

General property tax.

All corporations, in theory at least, are assessed according to the general property tax for state and local purposes.

Shares of stock.

Shares of stock of foreign and banking corporations are assessed locally. All shares of stock of domestic corporations when the property of such companies is not exempt is not taxable thereto, or when the personal property thereof is not taxed, are assessed. C. L. sec. 3831, Subs. 7 and 8.

Railroad and union station companies.

The property of railroad and union station companies excepting real and personal property not used by the companies in the exercise of their franchises, is assessed by the Board of State Tax Commissioners. The property of such companies in Michigan is taken to be the proportion of the aggregate property thereof which the miles of main line in Michigan bear to the entire mileage of main track owned by such corporations. The rate is the average rate of taxation throughout the state on all property upon which ad valorem taxes are levied. Act. 282, 1905, as amended by 49, 1909.

Telegraph and telephone companies.

Transmission companies are assessed as are transportation companies. Id.

Car companies.

Sleeping, dining and other car companies are assessed on the value of the cars owned and operated in Michigan. Such value is ascertained by multiplying the total value of the cars owned by such companies by the number of miles of track over which the same are operated in Michigan and dividing such amount by the number of miles over which such cars are run within and without the state. Id.

Express companies.

The basis of taxation for express companies is found as follows: To the entire amount of the capital stock and the bonded indebtedness of such companies and subtract the actual value of all real and personal property not used in the express business. Divide this result by the total mileage of the company, which gives the value per mile and multiply the value per mile by the number of miles the cars of such companies are operated in the state. To this mileage value is added the value of all real estate of the company in the state.

Mercantile and manufacturing companies.

These corporations are taxed locally as are individuals. Act 206, 1893 as amended by 229, 1895 and 235, 1903.

Foreign corporations.

The laws pertaining to corporation taxation apply in like manner to domestic and foreign corporations.

Administration.

The tax laws relative to public service corporations generally are administered by the Board of State Tax Commissioners— three members appointed by the governor for six years. The governor acts with the board in the assessment of corporate property.

Minnesota. .

Chief features.

First. The gross earnings tax on railroads, telephone, freight line, and express companies, and the gross earnings or ad valorem tax, at the option of the companies, on sleeping car companies.

Second. A separation between state and local taxes.

Third. A tax on the corporate excess of certain companies.

General property tax.

The tax on earnings of public service companies has about supplanted the general property tax in Minnesota, telegraph companies being about the only companies taxed for state purposes on their general property. Street railway, electric-light, gas and water companies are assessed locally for state and local purposes under the general property tax system.

Stock and bondholders. ·

The owners of shares of domestic corporations as well as those holding the shares of foreign corporations certified to do business in Minnesota are not required to list their property, since the property of the corporation is listed and taxed as provided by sec. 838, R. L. 1905. The principle has not been extended to bondholders. Under sec. 816, R. L. 1905 bonds are assessed to the owner the same as other personal property. Corporate excess or franchise tax.

All corporations other than railroad, telegraph, telephone, express, freight line, car, banking and insurance companies, pay a tax on "bonds or stock," which is the differenece between the market or actual value of the shares of stock and the value of the real and personal property. R. L. 1905, sec. 838.

Railroads.

Railroad corporations pay a percentage of their gross earnings (4%) in lieu of all other taxes. The gross earnings and percentage to be paid is ascertained by the railroad and warehouse commission. R. L. 1905, secs. 1003–1011. Tax for state purposes.

Transmission companies.

Telegraph companies are taxed on the true cash value of their lines ascertained by the state board of equalization at a rate not to exceed the average rate on property throughout the state. This tax is in lieu of all others and is for state purposes. R. L. 1905, secs. 1031–1034.

Telephone companies, in lieu of all other taxes, pay to the state three per cent of their gross earnings derived from business within the state. R. L. 1905, secs. 1034–1037.

Car companies.

Freight line companies pay four per cent on "the total gross earnings received from all sources from the operation of such freight lines within the state." For state purposes. L. 1907, Ch. 250, secs. 1–5.

Sleeping car companies are taxed on their gross earnings (4%) or according to the ad valorem system at the option of the companies. L. 1907, Ch. 453, secs. 1–5.

Express companies.

These companies pay six per cent on their gross earnings from business done within the state minus the amount annually paid for transportation. R. L. 1905, secs. 1012–1014.

Local utilities.

Electric light, street railway and gas companies are asesssd locally on their general property for state and local purposes.

Mercantile and manufacturing companies.

Business corporations are assessed and taxed, locally for state and local purposes on real and personal property. In addition thereto these companies pay the corporate excess tax. R. L. 1905, secs. 816, 822, 828, 829 and 838.

Foreign corporations.

The taxation of foreign corporations is carried on in the same way and under the same provisions of law as that of domestic corporations.

Administration.

The state board of equalization and the tax commission (three members appointed by the governor for six years) administer the Minnesota corporation tax laws. L. 1907, Ch. 408.

Nebraska.
Chief features.

First. Broad application of the general property tax.

Second. A franchise tax based upon gross receipts.

General property tax.

The real and personal property of all classes of corporations is taxed for state and local purposes.

Stocks and bonds.

Shares of stock, if the capital stock of the issuing company is not taxed, are assessed against the holder. Bonds are taxable as other personal property. Com. Stats. 1909, sec. 4949.

Railroad and terminal companies.

The property of railroad and terminal companies, including moneys, credits and franchises and all property on right of way, is assessed by the state board of equalization. Other property is assessed and taxed locally. Assessment is apportioned among local units according to mileage. The tax is collected by the county treasurer. Id. secs. 5005–5017; H. R. 215, 1909.

Express, pipe line, telegraph and telephone companies.

Express, pipe line and transmission companies are assessed locally on tangible property (personal), and in addition thereto on gross receipts which shall represent the franchise value and which shall be taken as an item of property and be so listed and levied against as other property. Id. 4997–5004.

Car companies.

Freight car companies are assessed on the value of the cars used in the state. The number and value of cars is ascertained by the state board of equalization from reports furnished. Id. 5018–5021.

Sleeping, palace, etc., car companies are assessed on the value of the cars used in Nebraska. The value of the cars used is that proportion of the total value of the cars of the respective companies running into and through the state, which the number of miles of main track over which such cars were used within the state, bears to the total number of miles of main track over which such cars were used everywhere." 5022–5025.

Manufacturing and mertantile companies.

These companies are assessed and taxed locally on their property. Id. secs. 4965, 4978.

Foreign corporations.

Except in the case of insurance companies, foreign and domestic corporations are taxed the same.

Administration.

The state board of equalization and assessment has general supervision over corporation taxes. However, most assessments, except in case of railroads, are made locally.

Ohio.

Chief features.

First. The broad application of the ad valorem system. .

Second. A tax on all corporations, foreign and domestic other than public service, based on capital stock.

Third. A privilege tax based on gross receipts, earned in the state on all public service corporations, foreign and domestic other than freight line and equipment and sleeping car companies.

Fourth. An excise tax on sleeping, freight car and equipment companies. .

General property tax.

Corporations generally are required to list for taxation all personal property, including within such term all real estate used in the operation of the company as well as all moneys and credits within the state at the actual value thereof. Real estate owned by a corporation but not used in the operation of the business is appraised as real estate decennially. R. S. 2744.

Stock and bond holders.

Shares of stock in domestic corporations are exempt from taxation. R. S. 148c as amended. L. 1904. Shares of stock in foreign corporations whose property is taxed in Ohio, or two-thirds of whose property is taxed in Ohio and the remainder in some other state or states, are also exempt. (97 O. L. 498).

Capital stock tax on corporations other than public service companies.

All corporations, domestic and foreign, other than public service, pay annually one-tenth of one per cent, the domestic upon their subscribed and outstanding capital stock, and the foreign upon the proportion of their authorized capital stock represented by property owned and used and business transacted in Ohio. The tax is collected by the secretary of state and the proceeds used exclusively for state purposes. R. S. secs. 2780—24, 2780—31, inc.

Gross receipts tax on public service companies.

All public service companies, domestic and foreign, engageo in steam or street railway, express, telegraph, telephone, electric light, gas, pipe line, water transportation and certain kindred businesses pay annually one per cent of their gross receipts earned in Ohio for the privileges of operating therein. This tax is for state purposes only. R. S. secs. 2780—17, 2780—23, inc.

Excise tax on freight line and equipment companies.

Such companies report annually to the auditor of state the name and nature of the company, the number of shares, par value and market value of their capital stock, the value of real estate owned within and without the state, the whole length of line over which the company runs its cars, the length of so much of said line as is within and without the state, the number and value of their cars, and such other information as may be required. From these statements the board of appraisers and assessors, consisting of the auditors, treasurer, secretary of state and attorney general, determine annually the amount and value of the proportion of the capital stock of such companies representing the capital and property owned and used in Ohio and upon such value lsss the value of real estate assessed locally the companies pay a tax of one per cent. The tax is for state purposes. R. S. secs. 2780—7, 2870—11 inc.

Excise tax upon sleeping car companies.

This tax is similar to the one on freight line and equipment companies. R. S. secs. 2780—12, 2780—16 inc.

Steam railroads.

These companies are taxed on their real and personal property assessed annually by the several county auditors through whose counties the line of road passes, and the valuation so fixed may be equalized among the various companies of the state by a state board of equalization. R. S. secs. 2770, 2771, 2772, 2773, 2811 and 2812. All the property so valued is treated as personalty, and the amounts ascertained for purposes of taxation are apportioned among the several counties through which the road or any part thereof runs. The local and state tax levy is then applied to such property. R. S. 2774.

In addition to the above tax for state and local purposes, these companies pay the gross receipts tax above described (1%) for state purposes. R. S. 2780—17, 2780—23.

Suburban and interurban electric railways.

These companies are taxed on their property much as are steam railways and pay the same gross receipts tax. R. S. 2776—1, 2776—9 inc. and secs. 2780—17, 2780—23 inc.

Express, telegraph and telephone companies.

These companies have their property valued by a special method. The companies report to the state auditor the number of shares of their capital stock, the par and market value thereof, the real estate owned in Ohio and the value thereoi as assessed for taxation, a full inventory of all personalty, including moneys and credits, and the total value of all real property owned by the company outside of Ohio. In the case of telegraph and telephone companies the whole length of lines and the length of so much theroef as is without and within the state; in the case of telegraph and express companies the entire gross receipts from whatever source for the previous year. From these statements the board of appraisers and assessors fix a value on the property of such companies from this value is deducted the value of their real estate assessed for taxation and the resulting value is apportioned to the different units through which the companies operate. Tax for state and local purposes. R. S. 2777—2780, inc. These companies pay the gross receipts tax (1%) above described.

Car, freight and equipment companies.

These companies are assessed by the board of assessors and appraisers on the proportion of their capital stock representing their capital and property owned and used in Ohio. See excise tax on freight line and equipment companies. The tax is for state purposes. R. S. 2780—7, 2780—11 and 2780—12, 2780—16, inc.

Local utilities.

Local public service companies—street railway, electric light, gas and telephone companies, in addition to a tax on their general property, pay the gross receipts tax on public service companies above described.

Manufacturing and mercantile companies.

These business corporations are taxed on their real property as are individuals. They are taxed on the average value of the personalty had from time to time in their possession during the year. The tax is for state and local purposes. R. S. 2740 and 2742. These companies pay the capital stock tax for state purposes.

Foreign corporations.

Foreign, like domestic corporations, are assessed on their general property in the state. Like domestic corporations they pay the capital stock or the gross receipts tax depending upon the nature of the business conducted.

Administration.

Ohio corporation tax laws are administered by the state and county auditors. Assessment of corporate property is generally made by the county auditors, but such assessments are subject to equalization by the board of appraisers and assessors, consisting of the state auditor, state treasurer, attorney general and secretary of state.

Wisconsin.

Chief features.

First. The broad application of the ad valorem system to all public service companies, except telephone companies.

Second. A tax on the gross receipts of telelphone companies.

Third. The exemption from taxation of shares of stock in Wisconsin corporations which are taxed on their property

General property tax.

All corporations in Wisconsin, with the exeption of those operating a telephone system, are taxed, on their general property. The property of railroad, street railway, of electric light, heat and power companies, when operated in connection with a street railway, of express, car, freight line and equipment companies and of telegraph companies, is assessed by the tax commission. In the case of steam railroads, express, car, freight line and equipment companies and of telegraph companies, the assessment is for state purposes, the local units deriving no revenue from these companies except through a local assessment and tax on certain property not specifically used in the exercise of the companies' franchises. The assessment of street railway and light, heat and power companies is for state and local purposes. See railroads, etc.

R. S. OWEN,

Stock and bond holders.

Shares of stock in Wisconsin corporations which are taxed on their property are exempt from taxation in the hands of the holders. Shares in other corporations are taxed. R. S. (1898) secs. 1034, 1038 and 1040.

Steam railroads

The property of steam railroads is assessed for state purposes by the tax commission. The property included in such assessment is the franchise, right of way, roadbed, tracks, stations, terminals, rolling stock, equipment and all other real estate and personal property used or employed in the operation of the railroad or in conducting its business. The companies are required to make reports to the tax commission, and the commission is given very broad powers in making such assessment.

Real estate not adjoining the track, stations or terminals, grain elevators and coal docks not exclusively used by railroads in the operation of their business are assessed and taxed locally.

The rate of state taxation is the average rate on the general property in the state, determined by dividing the total taxes, state, county, and local, on the general property in the state by the aggregate value of such property subject to taxation. Ch. 315 L. 1903 as amended by Ch. 216, Laws 1905.

Telegraph companies.

The property of telegraph companies, including their franchise, is assessed annually by the tax commission for state purposes. The real estate, personalty and franchise of such companies are included as an entirety in such assessment, much the same as in the case of steam railways. No portion of the tax of these companies is apportioned to the local units. Ch. 494, L. 1905.

Telephone companies.

These companies, for purposes of taxation are treated different than are other public service companies. They are taxed on their gross reciepts—those with gross receipts of $100,000 and over pay a license fee of four per cent on gross receipts. Those with gross receipts of less than $100,000 pay a license fee of two and one-half per cent on their gross receipts. The license fee on eighty-five per cent of the gross receipts is paid to the town, city or village in which the exchange is located. The license fee on the remaining fifteen per cent of the gross receipts is paid to the state for state purposes. Sec. 1222a, Wis. R. S., as amended by Ch. 488, L. 1905.

Express, sleeping car, freight line and equipment companies.

These companies are taxed under the ad valorem system. The basis for taxation is Wisconsin's per mileage share of the value of the company's capital stock, less the value of its real estate situated outside of Wisconsin, and its personal property not specifically used in carrying on its business. The rate is the same as in the case of steam railways. The tax is for state purposes only. Wis. R. S. secs. 111, 112, 113, 114 and Ch. 477 L. 1905.

Street railways.

These companies and electric-light companies operated in connection with a street railway, are taxed on their property and franchises according to valuation thereof in substantially the manner as provided in the act for ad valorem taxation of the property of steam railrods. The board values the property of each street railway company, including its franchise, as an entirety. When the property of a light, heat and power company is operated in connection with that of a street railway, the property of the light, heat and power company and that of the street railway are valued together for taxation purposes as a unit.

Eighty-five per cent of the tax collected from these companies is apportioned among the local units in proportion to the gross earnings of such companies in each. Fifteen per cent of such tax is retained by the state for state purposes. Ch. 493, L. 1905.

Manufacturing and mercantile companies.

Business corporations are assessed and taxed locally for both state and local purposes on their real property and on their tangible and intangible personalty. The state levies no special tax on this class of corporations.

Foreign corporations.

For purposes of taxation foreign corporations are treated as are similar domestic corporations.

Administration.

Wisconsin corporation tax laws are administered by the tax commission composed of three members appointed by the governor for eight years. Ch. 380, L. 1905.

SOUTH CENTRAL.

Alabama.

Chief features.

First. Franchise tax on all companies enjoying public privileges.

Second. License, or privilege taxes based on capital stock of certain companies and in the shape of lump sums from other.

Third. Franchise tax on foreign corporations for state and county purposes.

Fourth. Constitutional provision requiring the general application of the property tax to all property.

General property tax.

The property of private corporations, associations and individuals must forever be taxed at the same rate. Con. sec. 217.

Stocks and bonds.

Shares of stock, except in banking associations, are assessed to the owners. The issuing company pays the tax and gets a lien on the stock or interest in the property of the company. Code 1907, sec. 2082, subd. 9, as amended by act of March 7th, 1907, p. 403, sec. 3. Act of March 4, 1907, exempts shares in public service corporations which pay a franchise tax. Bonds are assessed and taxed as other personalty.

Franchise tax on public service companies.

All corporations which have or exercise, under authority from Alabama or any other state, any exclusive privileges. franchises or friction which is or may be dependent upon the grant of public power or privileges, or which involves the operation of any public utility in Alabama, pay a franchise tax for state and local purposes. The franchise value is taxed at the same rate as other property and is ascertained by the state tax commission as follows:

Companies doing business within the state: from the true value of all shares of stock plus the true value of all indebtedness secured by any mortgage, lien or other charge on property, which is taken to be the value of the entire property, tangible and intangible, of the company, is deducted the value of the entire tangible real and personal property.

Companies doing an interstate business: from the value of the entire property, tangible and intangible, of the company, ascertained as above, is deducted the value of all real and personal property not specifically used in the business of the company. The result is taken as the value of the entire tangible and intangible property specifically used by the company. The value of all such company's property, tangible and intangible, in Alabama, is such proportion of the entire property, tangible and intangible, specifically used in the business as the total lines within the state bear to the total lines both inside and outside the state, or as the total receipts within the state bear to the total receipts without the state. From this amount is deducted the total assessed valuation of all real and personal property within the state. The tax is apportioned among the counties, cities, vilages, etc. Code 1907, secs. 2364—2390.

Franchise tax on foreign corporations.

Every foreign corporation authorized to do business in the state, excepting benevolent, educational, or religious corporations pay a franchise tax based on capital stock for the use of the state, and one-half the amount paid to the state to one county. Code 1907, secs. 2391—2400.

Privilege taxes.

All domestic corporations not otherwise specifically required to pay a license tax shall pay a privilege tax according to capital stock. $10—$500 capital stock $10,000 to $1,000,000 and over. Code 1907, sec. 2361 subd. 26.

Railroad companies.

Railroad corporations are taxed on their franchises in addition to the ad valorem tax which is assessed by the state board of assessments. Code 1907, secs. 2133—2145, 2364—2390.

Telegraph and telephone companies.

Telegraph companies are taxed on their franchise and on their property which is assessed by the state board of assessment. Code 1907, secs. 2141—2145, 2364—2390. In addition to the above such companies pay a license tax to cities and towns and a privilege tax based on mileage to the state. Companies having one hundred and fifty miles or less of line one dollar per mile; those having lines in excess of one hundred and fifty miles, pay five hundred dollars and one dollar per mile. Code 1907, sec. 1085.

Long-distance telephone companies are taxed on their franchise and property as are telegraph companies. In addition to the above such companies pay a privilege tax based on mileage and a license tax to cities and towns. Code 1907, secs. 2143, 2085, 2364—2390. Local telephone companies are taxed on their property and receipts. Code 1907, secs. 2115—2116, and a license tax according to population. Code 1907, sec. 2361, subd. 88.

Electric light, gas, water-works and street railways companies.

These local public utility companies, in addition to the franchise and ad valorem tax, pay a license or privilege tax based on population, to the state. City of 20,000 or more, $200; between ten and twenty thousand, $50; between 5,000 and 10,000, $25; less than 5000, $15. Code 1907, sec. 2361, subdiv. 35; Id. secs. 2364—2390.

Sleeping car companies.

Sleeping, etc., car companies pay to the state a privilege tax of $3,000, in lieu of all other taxes and licenses except $10 to

municipalities authorized to collect a privilege or license **tax.**
Code 1907, sec. 2087.

Express companies.

Each express company, domestic or foreign, pays a privilege tax of $4,000 to the state, and a privilege tax to cities,
etc., based on population. 500 pop., $2.50 to 30,000 pop. $500
per annum. The above and ad valorem taxes in lieu of all
other exactions. Code 1907, sec. 2086.

Manufacturing and mercantile companies.

Nearly all business corporations, domestic and foreign, **pay**
to the state, county, and cities, etc., a license or privilege **tax.**
Code sec. 2361. In addition thereto these companies pay the ad
valorem, and privilege tax.

Water powers.

"To encourage the development of the various unused **water**
powers of the state, the plants and the property, business **and**
franchises, necessary for the production, transportation, **and**
distribution of electric current, of any person, firm, or of any
corporation, organized for the purpose of developing **hydro**
electric power for the use of the public, shall in consideration
of the benefit to be derived by the public from the development and operation of such properties and plants, be **exempt**
from state, county, and municipal property and privilege **tax**-
ation of all description, either under general or local **laws,**
until ten years after the beginning of the construction of **any**
such plant." (Does not include the land upon which **plants**
are erected, or hydro electric plants already developed). **2069**
as amended by act July 27, 1907, p. 520, sec. 5.

Foreign corporations.

In addition to the property and special taxes imposed upon
domestic corporations, foreign corporations pay a franchise **tax**
based on capital stock to the state.

Administration.

The state tax commission, Code 1907, V. 1, secs. 2210—2220,
and the state board of assessment Code 1907, sec. 2135, Acts
1907, p. 354, have general supervision over the taxing laws.

The latter assesses the property of railroad, telegraph and long distance telephone companies. Code 1907, sec. 2144. The former ascertains the franchise value of public utility companies. Code 1907, secs. 2364—2390.

Kentucky.

Chief features.

First. Franchise tax on all public utility and guarantee and security companies.

Second. License tax on all other corporations, excepting foreign insurance and foreign domestic building and loan associations, banks and trust companies.

General property tax.

Corporations are taxed on their real and personal property. In some instances, as in the case of railroads, assessment is made by a central body but generally assessments are made by the local officials. This tax is for state and local purposes.

Franchise tax.

A franchise tax, in addition to ad valorem taxes, is collected from all public utility and guarantee and security companies. The value of the franchise is ascertained by the board of valuation and assessment. The method of ascertaining the franchise value is very similar to that adopted in Alabama (see above). The rate of taxation is the same as that on other property. Stats. of Ken. 1909 (Russell) secs. 6050—6064.

License tax.

All corporations, domestic and foreign, except foreign insurance, foreign and domestic building and loan associations, banks, trust companies and corporations subject to pay the franchise tax above, pay on annual license tax based on capital stock represented by property owned and business transacted in the state, which shall be ascertained by finding the proportion that the property owned and business transacted in Kentucky bears to the aggregate amount of property owned and business transacted in and out of the state. Companies may elect to pay at said rate on their entire authorized capital stock. Id. secs. 6066—6074.

41

· Railroads.

Railroad companies are taxed on their real and personal property assessed by the railroad commission. The total value found by such commission is apportioned to the local units according to mileage. Id. secs. 6097—6105. These companies pay also the franchise tax.

Mercantile and manufacturing companies.

These concerns pay a license tax based on capital stock and are taxed locally on all property. Id. 6066—6074.

Foreign corporations.

Excepting building and loan associations, foreign and domestic corporations are taxed alike.

· Administration.

Corporation taxation is under the supervision of the board of valuation and assessment and the board of equalization and assessment. Ch. 22, Act of 1906.

Mississippi.

Chief features.

First. Privilege or license taxes on about all classes of corporations.

Second. Tax on the capital stock of domestic corporations other than railroads and banks.

Third. The general application of the property tax.

General property tax.

The real and personal property of corporations is taxed for state and local purposes. In some instances assessment is made by a central body, but in most cases assessment and levy are local. Code 1906, secs. 4259–4267, 4382–4391.

Capital stock tax.

The capital stock of all domestic corporations, other than railroads and banks, is listed with the local assessors and taxed. In arriving at the value of the capital stock for taxation, the aggregate value of all real estate, owned by the respective companies and subject to taxation is deducted from the market value of the capital stock. Id. sec. 4267.

Railroads.

Railroad companies are taxed on their real and personal property. The value of such property is ascertained by the members of the railroad commission who constitute the state railroad assessors. The franchise and capital stock of such companies are 'considered in arriving at the value of the property for taxation. The assessed value is apportioned and the taxes collected locally. Id. secs. 4382—4391.

In addition to above, railroad companies, classified by the railroad commission, pay privilege taxes as follows:

Those of the first class, per mile....................$22.50
Those of the second class, per mile................ 16.87½
Those of the third class, per mile.................. 10.00
Those of the fourth class, per mile..(narrow guage) 2.00
Id. sec. 3856.

Transmission companies.

Telegraph and telephone companies are assessed and taxed on their property as are railroad companies. Id. 4384—4391.

In addition to the above transmission companies pay privilege taxes as follows:

Telegraph companies operating 1,000 miles or more of pole line, $2.50: those operating less than 1,000 miles, 25c per mile of pole line.

Telephone exchange companies pay privilege tax according to number of subscribers. 20 subscribers $2.50 to 150 subscribers $50. Long distance companies pay according to mileage. Id. sec. 3856.

Car companies.

Sleeping, parlor and dining car companies are taxed on their property as are individuals. Id. 4384—4391. In addition to the ad valorem tax each such company pays a privilege tax of $300 and 50c per mile of first class and 30c per mile of second, third and fourth class railroad over which their cars are operated. Id. sec. 3867.

Companies operating refrigerator, oil tank, or stock cars in the state, pay, in lieu of all other taxes, a privilege tax of $2.00 on each car operated in the state. Id. 3856.

Express companies.

Express companies pay the ad valorem tax assessed and levied as in the case of railroads. Id. 4384—4391.

In addition to the above such companies pay a privilege tax of $500, and $2.00 per each mile their cars are operated on first class and one dollar per mile on second, third and fourth class railroads. Id. sec. 3810.

Electric light, gas and street railway companies.

These local public service companies are assessed and taxed locally on their property and pay in addition thereto privilege taxes as follows:

Street railway—$20 per mile of line or fraction thereof. Id. sec. 3874.

Electric light—according to population, $25—$75. Id. sec. 3805.

Gas companies—according to population, $50—$100. Id. sec. 3817.

Water works—according to population, $50—$250. Id. sec. 3886.

Manufacturing and mercantile companies.

Business and manufacturing companies are assessed and taxed locally on property. Id. secs. 4259—4267, and pay the tax on capital stock. Id. sec. 4267.

Foreign corporations.

Except in the case of building and loan insurance companies, foreign and domestic corporations are taxed alike.

Administration.

The railroad commission act as a board of railroad assessors and assess the property of railroad and transmission companies. Other corporations are assessed and taxed locally.

Oklahoma.

Chief features.

First. The classification of corporation for purposes of taxation.

Second. Gross revenue tax on public service companies for state purposes.

General property tax.

All corporations pay taxes on their real and personal property, but for local purposes.

The property of public service corporations is assessed by the state board of equalization of all other corporations by the local assessors.   Comp. laws 1909 (Snyder), secs. 7584–7598, 7558–7577.

Stock and bonds.

Shares of stock and bonds seems to be taxed to the owners generally.   Bank pays tax for its shareholders.   Stock in building and loan associations is exempt.   Id. secs. 7558, 7662, 7573, 1511–1512, 7580–7583.

Public service companies.

All public service companies (transportation, including car companies, transmission, gas, electric, light, heat and power, water works and water power companies and all others authorized to exercise the right of eminent domain or to occupy any right-of-way, street, alley or public highway) are taxed locally on their property.   The property of such companies is assessed by the state board of equalization which, through the state auditor, certififies to the county clerk.   The return shows the portions of the property of all public service companies in each county and local unit and the assessed value thereof. The tax is collected locally.   Id. secs. 7584—7598.

In addition to the above ad valorem tax, public service companies pay to the state for state purposes a gross revenue tax · Railroads, one-half of one per cent; car and express companies, three per cent; telephone companies, one-half of one per cent; telegraph companies two per cent; electric light, heat, power and gas companies, one-half of one per cent; water works companies, one-fourth of one per cent of gross receipts from business done in the state.   Id. sec. 7702.

Mining, oil and gas companies.

These companies, like public utilities, are taxed locally on their property and pay to the state a tax of one-half of one per cent on gross receipts for their products.   Id. 7706.

Corporations other than public service.

All corporations, other than public service, report to local assessors and are assessed on all property. Id. 7558—7577.

Many of these companies are subject to the license tax enacted in 1910, Laws 1910, Ch. 57.

Foreign corporations.

Domestic and foreign corporations are taxed alike.

License tax.

Domestic and foreign corporations, other than railroad, car, electric railway, telephone and telegraph, heat, light and power, water-works, and water power companies, insurance, bank and trust building and loan companies, pay license tax as follos:

Domestic companies, 50c for each $1,000 of authorized capital stock.

Foreign companies, $1.00 on each $1,000 of authorized capital stock. Laws 1910, Ch. 57.

Administration.

A state board of equalization administers the tax laws. Board is composed of the governor, state auditor, state treasurer, secretary of state, attorney general, state examiner and inspector, and president of the board of agriculture. Id. sec. 7620.

WESTERN.

Utah.

Chief features.

First. An annual license tax based on the authorized capital stock.

Second. Exemption of corporate stock if the property of issuing companies is taxed.

Third. The broad application of the general property tax.

General property tax.

All corporations, excepting insurance companies, are assessed and taxed on their general property for state and local purposes.

Railroad, street railway, car, telephone, telegraph, electric-light, pipe line, power and express companies.

Are taxed on real and personal property and franchises. If operating in more than one county such property is assessed by the state board of equalization and the assessed value is apportioned among the counties according to value of property of mileage in each of such counties. Lands not used by railroads in the exercise of their franchises is assessed by the county assessors.

The property of all such companies operating wholly within one county is assessed locally. Comp. Laws, 1907, sec. 2513— 2515.

Shares of stock.

Shares of stock in corporations taxed on their property are exempt. Con. Art. 13, sec. 2.

Annual license tax.

Foreign and domestic corporations, other than those formed for charitable or religious purposes and private canal and irrigation and insurance companies, pay an annual license tax based on capital stock. Five dollars for $10,000 to fifty dollars for $200,000 and over of capital stock. Id. secs. 456—6 to 456—10.

Manufacturing and mercantile companies.

These companies pay the annual license tax and ad valorem taxes.

Foreign corporations.

In matters of taxation there is no discrimination between foreign and domestic corporations.

Administration.

The state board of equalization composed of four members appointed by the governor for four years has supervision over corporation taxation. Id. sec. 2583.

Wyoming

Chief features.

First. Tax on the capital stock and surplus, not including real estate in other states, of foreign corporations.

Second. The broad application of the general property tax administered by county assessors and by the state board of equalization.

General property tax.

All corporations, other than insurances and express companies, are taxed on their property. Comp. Stats. 1910 (Mullen) secs. 2330, 2331, 2444—2448.

Tax on capital stock on foreign corporations.

The paid in capital stock and surpluus of all foreign corporations are assessed against them. Shares in the hands of the owners are exempt. Id. sec. 2334.

Shares of national bank stock are assessed to the owners. Id. sec. 2332.

Railroads.

The property, real and personal including the franchises, of railroad corporations, is assessed by the state board of equalization. The assessed valuation is prorated among the counties according to mileage of track. Real and personal property not specifically used in the exercise of their franchise is assessed by the county assessor. Id. secs 2358—2361.

Telegraph and telephone companies.

Transmission companies are assessed and taxed as are railroad companies. Id. secs. 2358–2361.

Express companies.

Express companies, in lieu of all other taxes pay five per cent on their gross receipts from business done in the state. One-half of tax goes to the local units, one-half to state for state purposes. Companies report to state auditor, and state board of equalization from this report and other information ascertains the gross receipts. Id. secs. 2444–2446.

Car companies.

Railroad companies hauling private cars (other than sleeping etc.) report to state auditor total number of miles made in Wyoming by the cars of the different companies. State board of equalization ascertains the number of cars necessary to make such reported mileage and fixes a value thereon. Value is apportioned to the different counties according to mileage. Id. secs. 2362-2366.

Sleeping, etc., car companies are taxed on the value of the cars used in Wyoming. The cars are listed for taxation by the person in charge thereof and are assessed as are other cars. Id. sec. 2358.

Manufacturing and mercantile companies.

These companies are taxed on their general property by the county assessor.

Foreign corporations.

Sec. 2334 comp. stats. 1910, provides for a tax on the paid in capital stock and surplus of all foreign corporations. Domestic companies are expressly exempted. Otherwise foreign and domestic corporations receive similar treatment.

Administration.

There is a commissioner of taxation in Wyoming, but the state board of equalization does the assessing of what corporate property is assessed by other than the county assessors. Laws 1909, Ch. 66 (Comr. of Taxation).

Washington.

Chief features.

First. Privilege taxes on private car and express companies in addition to the property tax.

Second. Application of the general property tax to railroad and telegraph companies.

Third. Telephone companies are taxed on real and personal property by local assessors.

General property tax.

The property real and personal, of all corporations is taxed under the general property tax for state and local purposes.

Stocks and bonds.

The stock of all banks is assessed to holder where bank is situated. Bank pays the tax and gets lien on the shares. Deduction is made for assessed value of all real estate of bank. L. '07, p. 61, sec. 1. Where the property of corporations is assessed it is held to be double taxation and illegal to assess shares of stock against the owners. Red Path v. Spokane Co., 23 Wash. 436.

Railroads and street railways.

All property of railroads, including franchises, right-of-way, road-bed, tracks, terminals, rolling stock equipment, etc., is assessed by the state board of tax commissioners. Real estate not adjoining its tracks, stations and other buildings are asssessed locally. L. '07, p. 132. The value of such property is apportioned to the counties according to mileage. The tax is collected locally. Id. p. 139, sec. 11.

Transmission companies.

Telephone companies pay taxes on their real and personal property assessed by the county assessor. Companies make reports to such assessor. P. C. sec. 8632.

Telegraph companies pay taxes on all their real and personal property which is assessed as is railroad property by the state board of tax commissioners. The items of property are: Franchises, right-of-way, poles, wires, cables, devices, appliances, instruments and all other property used or employed. The value is apportioned to the counties according to mileage. The tax is collected locally. L. '07, p. 243.

Car and express companies.

Private cars operated for transportation of merchandise are subject to a privilege tax of seven per cent on gross receipts for business done within the state. L. '07, p. 46, sec. 1.

Express companies pay a privilege tax equal to five per cent of gross receipts for business done within state. L. '07, p. 79, sec. 1.

The privilege tax on private car and express companies is in addition to the general property tax.

Manufacturing and mercantile corporations.

These two classes of corporations are assessed locally on their real and personal property as are individuals. P. C. 8612.

Foreign corporations.

For purposes of taxation there is no difference between foreign and domestic corporations.

Administration.

The administration of the taxing laws of Washington is in the hands of a state board of tax commissioners. Three members appointed by the governor for four years.

PACIFIC.

California.

Chief features.

First. The license tax on all corporations, domestic and foreign, based upon capital stock for state purposes.

Second. The broad application of the general property tax to all corporations.

Third. The absence of any tax on shares of stock, other than those of national banks, on the theory that the same possess no intrinsic value over and above the actual market value of the corporation which they represent.

General property tax.

All corporations are taxed on their general property for state and local purposes. Pol. Code, secs. 2641, 3663, 3628.

Stock and bond holders.

Shares of stock, other than national bank stock, are not taxed. Id. secs. 3608, 3609. Bonds are taxed. Id. 3629.

License tax.

All corporations, domestic and foreign, pay an annual license tax authorizing the transaction of business. The tax is based upon capital stock and increases from ten dollars on a company having a capital stock of not exceeding $10,000 to a tax of two hundred and fifty dollars if the capital stock exceeds $5,000,000, L. 1907, Ch. 347.

Railroads.

Railroads are taxed on their property for state and local purposes. Assessment is by the state board of equalization. The items of property assessed include the franchise, roadway, roadbed, rails and rolling stock. Depots, stations, shops, and buildings on and of the right of way are assessed by the county assessors. The valuation found by the state board of equalization is apportioned among the local units in proportion to mileage therein. P. C. secs. 3665, 3668.

Transmission companies.

Telegraph and telephone lines are assessed by the county assessors as personal property and are taxed at a rate per mile. Id. sec. 3663.

Car and express companies.

California has no special method for the assessment of freight car, express and similar transportation companies. They are assessed by the county assessors in the same manner as are other corporations. The Pullman Company is, however, assessed by the state board of equalization as a railroad operating in more than one county. Report of Commissioner on Taxation and Rev., 1906, p. 41.

Local utilities.

Street railways, electric light and gas companies are assessed locally for state and local purposes. These companies, as all others, pay the license tax above described.

Water ditches and toll roads.

Water ditches constructed for mining, manufacturing or irrigation purposes, and wagon and turnpike toll roads must be assessed the same as real estate by the assessor of the county, at a rate per mile for that portion of such property as lies within his county. P. C. sec. 3663.

Manufacturing and mercantile companies.

All business corporations are assessed locally on their real and personal property other than shares of stock. P. C. sec. 3641. These companies pay the license tax.

Foreign corporations.

Foreign corporations, for purposes of taxation, are treated as are similar domestic corporations.

Administration.

The administration of the assessment and levy of railroad taxes, and the general supervision over assessors, is in the hands of one central body—the state board of equalization. The board is composed of one member from each congressional district elected by the people for four years. The state comptroller is *ex officio* a member of this board. P. C. secs. 352, 3700.

Oregon.

Chief features.

First. The general application of the general property tax.

Second. License fee from express, telephone, sleeping car, refrigerator car, and oil companies.

General property tax.

All corporations pay taxes on their real and personal property for state and local purposes. Laws 1909, Ch. 218, sec. 5.

Stocks and bonds.

Stocks and bonds of railroad, sleeping car, union station and depot companies and of electric railway, express, telegraph, telephone, refrigerator car, oil and tank companies, and of heat, light, power, water, gas and electric companies doing business as one system, are considered in arriving at the value of the property of such companies. Id. secs. 6, 7. Shares of national bank stock are assessed to the holders. L. 1907, p. 487. Shares of stock in other banks, trust companies and building and loan associations are assessed to the holders. L. 1907, p. 446. The owners of stock in any company taxed on its capital shall not be taxed as an individual for such stock. L. 1907, p. 490.

Railroad, union depot and station companies, electric and street railway companies, and such heat, light, power, water, gas and electric companies as do business as one system within the state, pay taxes on all their real and personal property having a citus in Oregon for state and local purposes. The tax is assessed and levied by the board of state tax commissioners. All property including franchises of such companies is assessed by said board excepting real estate not occupied in the exercise of its franchise, car and machine shops, grain elevators and warehouses, docks, bridges across boundary of state, and the water craft and real property devoted to navigation. These latter items are assessed by the local assessors. L. 1909, Ch. 218, sec. 5.

Express, telephone, telegraph, sleeping car, refrigerator car, and oil companies, pay the property tax as above and in addition thereto pay a license fee: express companies three per cent of gross receipts; telegraph and telephone companies two per cent of gross receipts received in the state. L. 1907, Ch. 1. Sleeping car, refrigerator car and oil companies three per cent on gross earnings. L. 1907, Ch. 2.

Manufacturing and mercantile corporations.

Manufacturing and mercantile corporations are taxed locally on their real and personal property. L. 1907, Ch. 268, secs. 11, 13, 14, 15.

Foreign corporations.

Foreign corporations are treated the same as similar domestic corporations.

Administration.

The whole state administration of the assessment and levy of corporate taxes, excepting mercantile and manufacturing, is in the hands of the board of state tax commisions composed of two members appointed by the governor, secretary of state and state treasurer who are ex officio members of the board. One holds office for two the other for four years. L. 1909, Ch. 218, secs. 1, 2, 3, 4.

TABLES SHOWING GENERAL METHODS OF TAXING
CERTAIN PUBLIC SERVICE CORPORATIONS IN
THE FOREGOING STATES.

TABLE NO. 1—SHOWING THE GENERAL METHODS OF TAXING

NAME OF STATE.	Taxed for state purposes only.	GENERAL PROPERTY TAX.	
		Assessed by state board.	Assessed by local officials.
Alabama.........		1. Railways. 2. Long distance Telphone. 3. Telegraph. 4. Sleeping Car Co's.	1. Local Telephones. 2. Express Co's.
California.......		1. Railways operating in more than one county.	1. Telegraph.* 2. Telephone.* 3. Express. 4. Car Co's.
Connecticut,....	1. Railways. 2. Telegraph. 3 Telephone. 4. Express Co's.		
Delaware.........	1. Railways. 2. Telegraph. 3. Telephone. 4. Express Co's. 5. Sleeping Car Co's.		
Florida		1. Railways. 2. Telegraph.	1. Telephone.
Indiana		1. Railways. 2. Transmission Co's. 3. Express. 4. Sleeping, etc., Car Co's.	
Kentucky.......		1. Railway. 2. Telegraph. 3. Telephone. 4. Express Cos.	
Maine..........			
Maryland.......	1. Railway. 2. Transmission Cos. 3. Express Cos. 4. Car Cos.		1. Transmission Cos. 2. Express Cos. 3. Car Cos. (On real property only.)
Massachusetts..			1. Railways ‡. 2. Transmission Cos. 3. Express Cos. 4. Car Cos. † Footnote.

*By county assessors.
†Corporations domestic and foreign are assessed locally on real estate and certain specific personal property under the name of machinery.
‡Taxed to defray expenses of railroad commissioners in addition to tax on property.

CERTAIN PUBLIC SERVICE COMPANIES IN THE FOREGOING STATES.

TAX ON CAPITAL.		Tax on gross receipts.	Tax on net earnings.	Specific taxes.
On capital stock.	On capital stock and bonded debt			
		1. Local telephone.		1. Long distance telephones. 2. Telegraph. 37 Express Co's. 4. Sleeping Car Co's.
	1. Railways.	1. Express Co's.		1. Telegraph. 2. Telephone.
1. Railways.**		1. Telegraph. 2. Telephone. 3. Express Co's. 4. Sleeping Car Co's.	1. Railways.	1. Railways. 2. Telegraph. 3. Telephone.
		1. Sleeping Car Co's. 2. Parlor Car Co's.		1. Railways. 2. Telegraph. 3. Telephone. 4. Express Co's.
1. Freight, etc., Car Co.				
	1. Railway. 2. Transmission Cos. 3. Express and Car Cos. + Footnote.			
		1. Railways. 2. Express Cos. 3. Transmission Cos. 4. Sleeping, etc., Car Cos.		
1. Transmission Cos. 2. Express Cos. 3. Car Cos.		1. Railways. 2. Transmission Cos. 3. Express Cos. 4. Car Cos.		
1. Railways. 2. Transmission Cos. 3. Express Cos. 4. Car Cos. (Corporate excess.)				

* Or lump sum.

+ Value of all franchise companies ascertained on a stock and bond basis; assessed value of tangible property then deducted, and remainder apportioned to counties as value of franchise.

TABLE NO. 1.—SHOWING THE GENERAL METHODS OF TAXING

NAME OF STATE.	Taxed for state purposes only.	GENERAL PROPERTY TAX.	
		Assessed by state board.	Assessed by local officials.
Michigan	1. Railways. 2. Express Cos. 3. Sleeping cars. 4. Freight car lines.	1. Telegraph 2. Telephones 3. Railroads 4. Express Cos. 5. Car Cos.	
Minnesota........	1. Railways. 2. Telegraph. 3. Telephone. 4. Express. 5. Car Cos.	1. Telegraph Cos.	
Mississippi.......		1. Railroads 2. Transmission Cos. 3. Car Cos. 4. Express Cos.	
Nebraska........		1. Railways 2. Car Cos. 3 Transmission Cos.	
New Hampshire		1. Railways* 2. Transmission Cos. 3. Car Cos. 4. Express Cos.	
New Jersey......	1. Telegraph 2. Telephone 3. Express 4. Car Cos.	1. Railways 2. Equipment Cos.	
New York.......			
North Carolina..		1. Railways. 2. Transmission Co's 3. Express Co's. 4. Car Co's.	
Ohio.............		1. Railways.† 2. Transmission Co's. 3. Express Co's.	
Oklahoma		1. Railways. 2. Transmission Co's. 3. Express Co's. 4. Car Co's. ‡ Footnote.	
Oregon......		1. Railways. 2. Transmission Cos. 3. Express Co's. 4. Car Co's.	

* Taxed to defray expenses of railroad commissioners in addition to tax on property.
† By county auditors.
‡ For local purposes.

CERTAIN PUBLIC SERVICE COMPANIES IN THE FOREGOING STATES.

TAX ON CAPITAL.		Tax on gross receipts.	Tax on net earnings.	Specific taxes.
On capital stock.	On capital stock and bonded debt.			
		1. Railways 2. Telephone 3. Express 4. Car Cos.		
				1. Railways 2. Transmission Cos. 3. Car Cos. 4. Express Cos.
		1. Telegraph 2. Telephone 3. Express Cos. 4. Sleeping Car Cos.		
1. Railways. 2. Transmission Co's. 3. Express Co's. 4. Sleeping car Co's.		1. Railways. 2. Transmission Co's. 3. Express Co's. 4. Sleeping Car Co's.		
1. Railways. 2. Transmission Co's. 3. Express Co's. 4. Car Co's.		1. Railways. 2. Transmission Co's. 3. Express Co's. 4. Car Co's.		
1. Car Co's.		1. Railways. 2. Transmission Co's. 3. Express Co's.		
		1. Railways, 2. Transmission Co's. 3. Express Co's. 4. Car Co's. * Footnote.		
		1. Transmission Co's. 2. Car Co's. 3. Express Co's.		

*For state purposes.

TABLE NO. 1. –SHOWING THE GENERAL METHOD OF TAKING

NAME OF STATE	Taxed for state purposes only	GENERAL PROPERTY TAX	
		Assessed by state board.	Assessed by local officials.
Pennsylvania....	1. Railways 2. Transmission Cos. 3. Express Cos. 4. Car Cos.		
Rhode Island....	1. Tra smission Cos. 2. Express Cos.		1. Railways
Utah.............		1. Railways 2. Transmission Cos. 3. Car Cos. 4. Express Cos, * Footnote	
Vermont.........	1. Railways 2. Transmission Cos. 3. Express Cos. 4. Car Cos.	1. Railways†	
Virginia		1. Railways 2. Transmission Cos. 3. Express Cos.	
Washington......		1. Railways 2. Telegraph 3. Telephone‡ 4. Car Cos.	
West Virginia...		1. Railways. 2. Transmission Co's. 3. Express Co's. 4. Car Co's.	
Wisconsin	1. Railways. 2. Telegraph Cos. 3. Express Cos. § 4. Car & equipment Cos.	1. Railways. 2. Telegraph Cos. 3. Express Cos. 4. Car and Equipment Cos.§	
Wyoming........		1. Railways. 2. Transmission Cos. 3. Car Cos.	

*If operating in more than one county.
†Alternative with general property tax on railrways and milage tax on transmission Cos.
‡By the county assessors.
§On that portion of their capital stock. estimated at its market value, which the business done in the state bears to the entire business of such company, with a deduction for the value of real estate assessed outside the state; in lieu of all other taxes.

CERTAIN PUBLIC SERVICE COMPANIES IN THE FOREGOING STATES.

TAX ON CAPITAL.		Tax on gross receipts.	Tax on net earnings.	Specific taxes.
On capital stock.	On capital stock and bonded debt			
	1. Railways 2. Transmission Cos. 3. Express Cos. 4. Car Cos.	1. Railways 2. Transmission Cos. 3. Express Cos. 4. Car Cos.		
		1. Transmission Cos. 2. Express Cos.		
1. Car Cos.		1. Railways* 2. Telegraph* 3. Telephone*		1. Express Cos.
		1. Railways 2. Transmission		1. Transmission Cos. 2. Express Cos. 3. Car Cos.
		1. Express Cos. 2. Car Cos.		
				1. Transmission Cos. 2. Express Cos.
1. Express Cos.† 2. Car & equipment Cos.†		1. Telephone Cos.		
		1. Express Cos.		

*Alternative with general property tax on railways and milage tax on transmission cos.

†On that portion of their capital stock. estimated at its market value. which the business done in the state bears to the entire business of such company, with a deduction for a value of real estate assessed outside the state: in lieu of all other taxes

SUMMARIES OF THE THREE PRINCIPAL FORMS OF TAXATION IN VOGUE IN THE THIRTY STATES HEREIN INCLUDED.

THE GENERAL PROPERTY TAX.

Railways.

The general property tax, assessed by a central body ,is the principal tax on railroads in Alabama, California, Florida, Indiana, Misisippi, Michigan, Nebraska, New Hampshire New Jersey, Oregon, Utah, Washington, West Virginia, Wisconsin and Wyoming. In Rhode Island railroads are assessed under the general property tax system by the local assessors. The property tax is applied to railroads in conjunction with other forms of taxation in Kentucky, Massachusetts, North Carolina, Oklahoma, Vermont, (alternative with a gross receipts tax in Vermont) and Virginia.

Summary:

Fifteen states retain the geenral property tax, assessed by a central body, as the prinicpal tax on railroads.

Six states use the general property tax assessed by a central body in conjunction with other forms of taxation for railroads.

One state leaves the assesment of railroad property to the local officials.

Transmission companies.

The general property tax, assessed by a central body, is the principal tax on telegraph and telephone companies in Alabama, California, (assessed by the county assessors) Indiana, Michigan, Mississippi, Nebraska, New Hampshire, Utah, Washington, West Virginia and Wyoming. Telegraph companies are so assessed under the general property tax system in Florida, Minnesota and Wisconsin. The general property tax in conjunction with other forms of taxes, is applied to transmission companies in Kentucky, Maryland, Massachusetts, North Carolina, Ohio, Oklahoma, Oregon and Virginia.

Summary:

Eleven states apply to the general property tax, assessment by a central body, to transmission·companies as the principal tax thereon.

Eight states use the general property tax in conjunction with other taxes on these companies.

Three states apply the general property tax, assessment by a central body, to telegraph companies.

Express companies.

The general property tax, assessment by a central body, is the principal tax on express companies in Colifornia, assessed by county assessors), Indiana, Michigan, Mississipi, New Hampshire, Utah, Virginia, West Virginia, (the two latter lay specific taxes also on these companies) and Wisconsin. This tax in conjunction with others is applied to express companies in Alabama, Kentucky, Maryland (assessed locally on real estate only), Massachusetts, North Carolina, Ohio, Oregon and Oklahoma.

Summary.

Nine states still retain the general property tax, assessment by a central body, as the principal on express componies.

Eight states use this tax in conjunction with others for deriving revenue from this class of corporations.

Car companies.

The general property tax, assessment by a central body, is the chief tax on car companies in Alabama, (specific taxes in addition in Alabama), Michigan, Mississippi, Nebraska, New Hampshire, Utah, West Virginia, Wisconsin and Wyoming. This tax, in conjunction with other taxes is applied to car companies in Indiana, Kentucky, Maryland, Massachusetts (local assessment in Maryland and Massachusetts), New Jersey, North Carolina, Ohio, Oklahoma, Oregon and Washington.

Summary:

Ten states still adhere to the general property tax, assessment by a central body, as the principal means for obtaining revenue from car companies.

Ten of these states use the general property tax in conjunction with other forms of taxation for car companies.

THE GROSS RECEIPTS TAX.

Railroads.

The gross receipts tax is the principal tax on raillroads in Maine, Maryland, Minnesota and Vermont. It is used in conjunction with other taxes in New York, North Carolina, Oklahoma, Ohio, Pennsylvania and it has recently been introduced in Virginia. It was the principal tax on railroads in Michigan and Wisconsin for many years, but has recently been abandoned in those states in favor of the ad valorem tax on property.

Summary:

Four states use the gross earnings tax a the chief tax on railroads.

Five states use the gross earnings tax to supplement other taxes on this class of corporations.

Two states have recently abandoned the gross earnings tax.

One state has recently adopted the gross earnings tax for railroads.

Transmission companies.

The gross receipts tax is the principal tax on transmission companies in Delaware, Maine, New Jersey, Rhode Island and Vermont. It is applied to these companies in conjunction with other forms of taxes in Maryland, New York, North Carolina, Ohio, Oklahoma, Oregon, Pennsylvania and Virgina. It is applied to telephone companies in Minnesota and Wisconsin.

Summary:

Five states apply the gross earnings tax as the chief tax on transmission companies.

Eight states apply this form of taxation to transmission companies to supplement other forms of taxation.

Two states tax telephone companies on their gross earnings.

Express companies.

The tax on earnings is the chief tax on express companies in Connecticut, Delaware, Maine, Minnesota, New Jersey, Rhode Island and Wyoming. It is used in conjunction with other taxes in Maryland, New York, North Carolina, Ohio, Oklahoma, Oregon, Pennsylvania and Washington.

Summary:

Seven states use the gross earnings tax as the principal tax on express companies.

Nine states use the gross earnings tax to upplement other taxes on express companies.

Car companies.

The gross earnings tax is the main tax on car companies in Delaware, Florida, Maine, Minnesota and New Jersey. This form of taxation is used in conjunction with others for deriving revenue from car companies in Maryland, New York, North Carolina, Ohio, Oklahoma, Oregon, Pennsylvania and Washington.

Summary:

Five states use the gross earnings tax as the principal source of revenue from car companies.

Eight states use the gross earnings tax in addition to other taxes on car companies.

TAX ON CAPITAL STOCK.

Railroads.

The tax on capital stock is applied to railroads in conjunction with other forms of taxation, in Delaware (and net earnings), Massachusetts (and real estate and machinery locally assessed for state and local purposes), New York (and gross receipts), and in North Carolina (and ad valorem and gross receipts).

Summary:

Four states apply the capital stock tax in conjunction with other forms of taxations to railways.

Transmission companies.

The tax on capital stock in conjunction with other forms of taxation, is applied to transmission companies in Maryland (and ad valorem locally assessed and gross receipts), Massachusetts (and real estate locally assessed), New York (and gross receipts) and in North Carolina (and ad valorem and gross receipts).

Summary:

Four states apply the capital stock tax, in conjunction with other forms of taxation to transmission companies.

Express companies.

The tax on capital stock, in conjunction with other taxes is collected of express companies in Maryland, Massachusetts (and real estate locally assessed for state and local purposes), New York (and gross receipts), and North Carolina (and ad valorem and gross receipts).

Summary:

Four states apply the tax on capital stock in conjunction with other forms of taxation to express companies.

Car companies.

The tax on capital stock is the chief tax applied to car companies in Ohio.   This tax, in conjunction with others, is applied to these companies in Indiana (and ad valorem), Maryland and Massachusetts (and real estate locally assessed), New York (and gross receipts), and in North Carolina (and ad valorem and gross receipts).

One state applies the capital stock tax as the principal tax on car companies.

Five states apply this tax in conjunction with other forms of taxation to car companies.

TAX ON CAPITAL STOCK AND BONDED DEBT.

Connecticut derives its revenue from railways through a tax on capital stock and bonded and floating indebtedness.

Pennsylvania taxes railways and transmission, express and car companies on their capital stock, bonded debt and gross receipts.

Kentucky levies a franchise tax based on stock and bonds on railway, transmission, express and car companies.

SPECIFIC TAXES.

Specific taxes in the shape of taxes on miles of wire and on instruments, telegraph and telephone, are levied on telegraph and telephone companies in Connecticut, Delaware, Virginia, Vermont and West Virginia, and in other forms on these companies in Alabama, Florida, and Mississippi.

Specific taxes are levied on railroads in Delaware, Florida and Mississippi.

SUMMARY OF THE FOREGOING ANALYSIS OF RAILROAD TAXATION.

1. A tax based on capitalization, of which the Connecticut tax is the best example.

2. A tax based on an appraisal of property, of which Michigan and Wisconsin furnish examples.

3. A tax based on gross earnings, of which there are two distinct types.

(a) Like that of Maine, where all gross earnings of a given road or system, both in and out of the state, are apportioned; the state taxing its proportion of the whole.

(b) Like that of Minnesota, where only the gross earnings of interstate traffic are apportioned; the state taxing all *intrastate* earnings and its proportion of interstate earnings.

THE GENERAL METHODS IN VOGUE FOR THE TAXATION OF CORPORATIONS.

The preceding description show the chaos of principle in which the whole subject of corporation taxation is involved. They disclose no less than thirteen important methods of taxing corporations, not counting the various combinations of methods which are practiced in some states. These thirteen methods include the following:

1. *Value of the property,* i. e., the realty plus the visible and invisible personalty. This was originally the universal method and it is still the practice in the majority of cases.

2. *Cost of the property.* This method is still practiced in isolated cases, as in New York in the local taxation of telegraph companies.

3. *Capital stock at par value.* This is true of the taxation of manufacturing and mercantile companies in New Jersey.

4. *Capital stock at market value.* This is true of the general corporation law in Massachusetts and in New York when applied to corporations where the dividends are less than six per cent. It is also the custom in local taxation in many states.

5. *Capital stock plus bonded debt at market value.* This is true of all corporations in Pennsylvania, and Maryland, with certain restrictions. In Maryland only the surplus over the value of the real estate is taxable as capital stock.

6. *Capital stock plus total debt, both funded and floating.* This is true of railroads in Connecticut.

7. *Bonded debt or loans.* This is true of all corporations in Maryland and Pennsylvania. In all cases however, it is only supplementary to the tax on capital stock.

8. *Business transacted.* This is true in several states where telephone companies are taxed on the number of telephone transmitters in use; in some states where car companies are taxed according to the number and mileage of cars and in Michigan of mining and smelting companies taxed on tonnage.

9. *Gross earnings.* This is true of transportation and other public utility companies taxed on gross receipts.

10. *Dividends.* This is true of gas and electric light companies in New Jersey.

11. *Capital stock according to dividends.* This is true in New York of all corporations, when the dividends are at least six per cent.

12. *Net earnings.* This is true of railroads and other public service companies in a few states.

13. *Franchise.* This is true of a large number of cases; but the term *franchise*, denotes nothing definite, and the value of the franchise is measured by each one of the preceding twelve tests except that of property.

CRITICISMS OF THE THIRTEEN GENERAL METHODS
OF TAXING CORPORATIONS.

Seligman, in his Essays in Taxation, at pp. 192—202, offers
the following criticisms of these thirteen general methods of
taxing corporations:

"First, *the general property tax,* or the taxation of the
corporate realty plus its visible and invisible personalty at
its actual value. It will not be necessary to show the inadequacy of this primitive plan; all the actual reforms are
moving away from it. We have seen in the previous chapter that the standard of taxation is ability to pay, and
that this ability is no longer proportional to the general
mass of property. The general property tax is today an-
tiquated. When as a state tax it is levied by the local
assessors, it becomes especially unjust; and even when assessed by a separate state board it is inexact, and exhibits
all the defects of the general property tax on individuals.
We may conclude, therefore, with the railroad tax commission of 1879, that as a system it is open to almost every
conceivable objection. [1]

The cost of the property, as a basis for taxation, is even
less defensible than the value of the property. For no
one would assert that the original cost of corporate property bears any necessary relation to the present value,
much less to its present earnings capacity. This method is
so obviously unjust as to deserve no further mention.

The capital stock at its market value. This plan is open
to several vital objections. The idea is that the market value
of the stock will be practically equivalent to the value of
the property, or, as it is put by some of our state courts,
that the entire property of a corporation is identical with
its stock. As has already been observed, heavily bonded
corporations would in this way entirely escape taxation;
because in such cases—and they are the great majority—
the capital stock alone would represent the value of the

[1] Taxation of Railroads and Railroad Securities, by C. F. Adams,
W. B. Williams and J. H. Oberly, p. 8.

property. Secondly, even in the case of corporations without any bonded debt, the tax is unjust, because it does not
necessarily bear any relation to the earning capacity. If
a company without bonded debt pays dividends, the value
of the stock is indeed a fair index to earning capacity, its
value would represent the capitalized earnings. But if
there are no dividends, the value of the capital stock is
wholly uncertain and largely speculative, depending on
happens that non-dividend-paying stock fluctuates in value
happens that non-dividend-paying stock fluctates in value
from thirty to fifty per cent within one year. A standard
of taxation which in such large classes of cases bears no
proportion to the earning capacity of productiveness of
the property clearly cannot be successfully defended. We
can again agree with the railroad tax commission in their
conclusion that the tax on the value of the capital stock
is "clumsy and devoid of scientific merit." that it "would
admit of evasions in a most obvious way," and that "it
is impossible of any general application."[2]

The New York Statute which governs the taxation of
corporations for local purposes requires the capital stock
to be assessed "at its actual value in cash." In determining the "actual value." the assessors may take "book
value," i. e. a value obtained by estimating the assets
separately and deducting from the aggregate the total
amount of the liabilities, actual or contingent.[3] The latter
method is employed when the market value of the stock
is fictitious or artificially inflated, but in principle is open
to precisely the same criticisms as the other method. In
fact, the objections are rather stronger; for, whereas in the
case of the tax on capital stock according to market value
the bonded indebtedness is not taxed at all, in this case the
bonded indebtedness is actually deducted. Under the
New York law it has been recently decided that "capital
stock" does not necessarily mean share stock, but the capital owned, the fund required to be paid and kept intact
as the basis of the business enterprise. When the capital

---

[2] Report, etc. p. 7. Cf. the report on the Valuation and Taxation of
Railroads, to the Pennsylvania Tax Conference, written by Mr. Joseph
D. Weeks.
[3] 107 N. Y. 541.

is undisclosed, the assessor may consider the market value of the shares as an aid in discovering the capital, but not as the thing to be valued and assessed.

The capital stock at its par value. This method is open to all the objections of the preceding and to many more in addition. Moreover, it is peculiarly liable to evasion. For example, in New York it is a common practice for corporations to evade the organization tax by issuing a nominally small capital, but selling it to the stockholders at a premium of several hundred per cent; the market value of the stock is thus at once many times the par value. The sole recommendation of this plan is the facility of fixing a basis for assessment, but this does not compensate for its obvious defects. The par value of stock is certainly no gauge either of the real worth of the property or of its earnings capacity. This is perhaps the least defensible of all the methods.

The capital stock plus the bonded debt at the market value. The justification for adding to the value of the stock the value of what the company owes, in the shape of its funded debt, is the simple fact that the existence of this indebtedness makes the stock worth just so much less. The sum of the two elements is a far better index to the value of the property than the capital stock alone. This method is much preferable to any that has yet been discussed, because is prevents the exemption of heavily bonded companies; and yet it is not entirely free from objections. Owing to the complications of interstate policy, the proceeds of the tax, in all cases where the stock and bonds of a corporation are owned outside of the commonwealth, will accrue not to the state of the owner's residence, but to the state where the corporate property is situated. Secondly, when the tax is on bonds as well as on stock it will be inadequate, because applicable only to the bonds owned by the residents of the state. If the tax is, however, levied not on the bonds, but on a valuation equal to the stock plus bonds. this objection may be obviated. * * * Thirdly and principally in all those cases where the corporation pays no dividends and its stocks nevertheless possesses a speculative value for the reason adduced above, will not necessarily bear any relation to the earning capacity of the company. In short, while this method is far better than the taxation of capital stock, it does not avoid the objections that have been urged against the latter.

. There remain thus only the taxes on earnings, on business, on dividends and on profits.

The gross earnings. This tax was the one recommended by the railroad tax commission. It possesses many undeniable advantages. It is certain, easily ascertained and not susceptible of evasion. But it has one fatal defect; —it is not proportional to the real earning capacity, it taxes no account of the original cost, nor does it pay any regard to the current expenses, which may be necessary and just. For example, when the cost of building a railroad is great, its gross earnings must be correspondingly large in order to enable its owners to realize any fair return on the investment. A tax on gross earnings does not recognize this distinction. It discriminates unfairly between companies, and makes a line built at great expense and with great risk pay a penalty for the enterprise of its constructors. Again, a gross earnings tax takes no account of expenses. Of two corporations which have equally large gross receipts, one may be in a naturally disadvantageous position which unduly increases the cost of operation or managament. Clearly its ability to pay is not so great as that of its rival in possession of natural advantages. In short the gross receipts tax is like the old tithe, the most primitive of all land taxes.

These defects in the proportional earnings tax are so apparent that several commonwealths, as we know, have introduced, in the case of railroads at least, the graded gross earnings tax, the rate per cent increasing with the earnings. But this system removes the objection only in part, for the graduation takes place only up to a certain point. Above all, there is no guarantee that the increase of net receipts will correspond with the increase of the gross receipts. There is no necessary connection between them. A corporation with gross receipts of five thousand dollars per mile may have actually lass net receipts than one with four thousand dollars per mil. In such case a graded earnings tax would intensify the disadvantages of the first line and augment the injustice. To tax gross earnings, is, therefore, essentially a slip-shod method.

The business transacted. This tax, while closely analogous to the gross earnings tax, does not possess all its advantages. The business may be large but not lucrative. An extensive business does not mean even proportionally extensive gross earnings. The business transacted is an exceedingly rough way of ascertaining the prosperity of a corporation. It affords no accurate test of profits, and fails to take account of the personal equation which may make all the difference between good and bad management. Clearly, the tax on business is but a clumsy device.

The dividends or the capital stock according to dividends. Economically speaking these taxes are the same; but from the legal point of view, at least according to the opinion of the Supreme Court, there is a decided difference. The distinction is brought out in connection with the subject of extra-territoriality, and will be fully discussed below. We are here dealing only with the economic problem.

The dividends tax, it may be said, is good so far as it goes; but it does not go far enough. It is indeed true that some of the objections are slight. Thus it has been contended that this tax fails to reach the profits which are not divided but which are simply put in a reserve fund; and some commonwealths have even sought to obviate the supposed difficulty by providing that the tax should apply to the dividends, whether declared or merely earned and not divided. This objection, however, is not of great importance, for even if the undivided earnings are not taxed, they go into the reserve surplus fund; and as this increases the corporate capital, it must in the long run lead to increased earnings on the larger capital. Since the surplus cannot be increased indefinitely, it will ultimately find its way to the shareholders as dividends, and thus become liable to the tax.

Another objection which might be urged is that a corporation may devote a portion of its earnings to new construction or to new equipment. This expense may be

defrayed out of profits, instead of from the capital or
construction fund. The dividends in such a case, it might
be said, do not represent the actual earnings capacity of the
enterprise. While this is true temporarily, the improvements made by the corporation necessarily enchance the
value of the property, and ultimately lead to increased
dividends, so that in a long run a tax on dividends would
still reach the corporation.

The real objection to the dividends tax is of quite a different character. It is utterly inadequate when applied to
those corporations which have bonded indebtedness. Thus
one corporation having no bonds may earn enough to pay
dividends of five per cent on its stock, while another, with
the same earnings, may have devoted half to the payment
of interest on bonds, and only half to the payment
of dividends. A tax on dividends, while nominally just,
would be actually most unjust, for one corporation would
pay just twice as much as the other. The objection has
been recognized in American legislation, but only once.
The United States internal revenue law of 1864 provided
for a five per cent tax (raised from three per cent in 1862),
which in the case of railroads, canals, tunpike, navigation
and slackwater companies, was imposed on all dividends, as
well as on coupons or on all interest, on evidence of indebtedness and on all profits carried to the account of any fund.
In the case of those companies which were not presumed to
have bonded debts, like banks, trust companies, savings
institutions and insurance companies, the tax was imposed
only on dividends and surplus. The federal law, indeed,
violated strict consistency in imposing a gross earnings tax
on transportation and on certain insurance companies: but
the correct implication in the law was the inadequacy of a
tax on dividends alone. In fact, the objections to the dividends tax are closely analogous to those which we found in
the capital stock as compared with the tax on stock plus
debt. Its great defect is that it reaches only a part of the
corporate earning capacity.

We thus come finally to the tax on *net arnings*, or
rather on net receipts, profits or income. This is the most
logical form of corporate taxation. The tax is not, like the

gross earnings tax, unequal in its operation. It holds out
no inducement, like the general property tax, to check improvements.   It is just; it is simple; it is perfetly proportional to productive capacity.   In short it satisfies requirements of a scientific system.

There are two possible objections to a tax on net receipts.
One is that the accounts may be "cooked" by paying unduly large salaries to the officers; that is, the profits may
be divided as nominal expenses, thereby leaving very insignificant net recepits or none at all.   This objection, however, would not apply at all to the vast majority of corporations whose stock or bonds are held by outside parties,
who will not consent to see their dividends or interest
curtailed by any practices of this nature.   The danger can
be real only in respect to the few corporations in which
the stock is owned entirely by the managers.   But these are
chiefly manufacturing corporations, which, as we know,
are usually exempted from the general corporation tax
Even here, however, the danger is not very great.   We
hear of no complaints on this score in the American Commonwealth where the net receipts tax prevails; and in
Europe, where this method of taxation is well-nigh universal, the objection has never been raised.   It may be
thus pronounced of little importance.

Secondly, it may be contended that the tax is impracticable in the case of great railroad corporations which
having leased lines in other states, are interested in so
manipulating the traffic that the heavily mortgaged leased
lines will earn little or nothing above fixed charges.   Such
cases are very common.   The commonwealths in which such
leased lines are situated will, it is argued, be robbed of
the whole benefit of the tax; since the proceeds acrue to
the state of the parent company.   In realty, this objection
arises simply from a quibble about words.   Of course net
recepits must be strictly defined.   The logical basis of corporate taxation is the total annual revenue from all sources
minus all actual expenditures except interest and taxes.
The reason for not deducting fixed charges, 1. e., interest
on the bonds, is the same as that which leads some of the
states to levy the railroad tax on capital plus debt, and

which made the federal government tax coupons as well
as dividends. Both together represent earning capacity.
Although the interest on the funded debt is known by the
name of fixed charges, it is really part of the profits which.
in the absence of funded debt, would go to the shareholders as dividends. It would obviously be suicidal so to frame
the definition of net receipts as to exclude this interest on
bonds. Net receipts of a corporation mean gross receipts
minus actual current expenses. Any other definition would
confuse the whole conception.

In several commonwealths some very dubious arbitrary
distinctions have been attempted. The Minnesota courts
have held that "earnings" means only receipts from operation. Under the New York law it has been held that "income" means gross income, and that "profits" means gross
profits; but this decision was owing to some peculiarities
of the statutory phraseology. From the standpoint of the
science of finance we understand by "income," net income.
and by "profits," only net profits. So in Pennsylvania
and Alabama it has been held that income, gains or net
earnings means the whole product of the business deducting
nothing but expenses. The Thurman law, indeed, which
regulates the relations of the federal government to the
Pacific railroads defines net earnings in a different way,
viz., as the gross earnings, deducting "the necessary expenses actually paid within the year in operating the lines
and keeping the same in a state of repair, and also deducting "the sums paid by them in discharge of interest on
their first mortgage bonds," but "excluding all sums paid
for interest on any other portion of their indebtedness."
The explanation of this arbitrary definition, lies not in any
principle but in a particular legislative provision whereby
the first mortgage bonds are given precedence over the
government liens. The Supreme Court has held that "net
earnings" as here used exclude expenditures for new construction and new equipment. The Interstate Commerce
Commission makes a distinction between earnings and income, including in earnings only receipts from transportation, and designating as income the receipts from property
owned but not operated. The aggregate it calls total earnings and income. While this separation of earnings is cor-

rect, the nomenclature is on the whole confusing since the term *income* should be reserved for the conception net profits. In Virginia the net income of corporations is ascertained by "deducting from gross receipts the costs of operation, repairs, and interest on indebtedness." So also by the federal law of 1894 the income tax was levied only on corporate dividends; but this, as we have seen, is economically incorrect. Interest on bonds should not be exempted.

If it be desired to obtain in the case of railroad companies a more exact definition of net receipts or income, the following would be a sound method or procedure: Gross receipts consist of all earnings from transportation of freight and passengers, receipts from bonds and stocks owned, rents of property and all miscellaneous receipts from ancillary business enterprises or otherwise. From these aggregate gross receipts we should deduct what are classified by the Interstate Commerce Commission as operating expenses, that is, expenses for conducting transportation, for maintenance of roadway, structures and equipment, and for general expenses of management. No deduction should be made for fixed charges, i. e., for taxes or for interest on the debt, or for the amount used in new construction, in betterments, in investments, in new equipment, or for any of the expenditures that find their way into profit and loss account.

The method here suggested would lead to the abolition of one of the serious abuses of American railway management—that of putting all possible expenses into the construction account. The railways, for example, frequently fail to charge the maintenance of their rolling stock to current expenses. When the equipment has become unserviceable, new stock is bought and charged to the construction or to the profit and loss account. In the meantime the nominal earnings of the railway seem large, and the managers reap whatever temporary benefit they may desire. he taxation of net profit in the sense that has been indicated would tend to check this practice, since deductions would be allowed for maintenance, but not for new equipment. A tax on net receipts. thus, would possess not only a financial, but also a wider economic advantage."

Economists, generally, agree with the above criticisms of the general methods in vogue for taxing corporations. They generally agree that the only just and scientific method for taxing transportation and transmission companies is on their receipts. See H. C. Adams, Public Finance, p. 449, et seq.

DIVERSITIES IN METHODS OF TAXING CORPORATIONS ARE CAPABLE OF EXPLANATION.

The great diversity in methods of taxing corporation is dwelled upon at length by Corporation Commissioner Knox. Illustrative of the diversity of methods in the New England States, he has compiled the following two tables showing the systems applied to manufacturing and mercantile and to railroad companies and the holders of their securities in those states:

TABLE NO. II.—TAXATION OF MANUFACTURING CORPORATIONS, THEIR STOCKHOLDERS, AND THEIR BONDHOLDERS.

(Unless otherwise specified, statements apply to both domestic and foreign corporations.)

State	Tax to the corporation.				Tax to resident stockholders?	Tax to resident bondholders?
	On real estate?	On tangible personalty?	On moneys and net credits?	On capital stock?		
Maine	Yes	Yes	No	Yes[1]	No[2]	Yes
New Hampshire	Yes	Yes	Yes[3]	No	No[4]	Yes
Vermont	Yes	Yes	Yes[3]	Yes[5]	Yes[6]	Yes
Massachusetts	Yes	Yes[7]	No	Yes[8]	No[1]	Yes[9]
Rhode Island	Yes	Yes	No	No	Yes[10]	Yes
Connecticut	Yes	Yes	Yes[8]	No	No[11]	Yes

[1] This is true of domestic corporations only.
[2] From stockholders in a foreign corporation a tax is due, but there is a deduction for a proportional part of the assessed value of machinery, goods, and real estate. Few returns are made, however.
[3] Few returns are made, however.
[4] On condition that the corporation pays either in New Hampshire or in its home state taxes on stock or on the property represented by it—a condition assumed to exist in all cases.
[5] But not to exceed $50.
[6] But the value of property taxed is deducted; and the stock of a foreign corporation is wholly exempt when the whole stock is taxed in the home state.
[7] On machinery only of a domestic corporation.
[8] A domestic corporation pays on corporate excess, namely, the market value of the stock, less the value of the taxed tangible property and of tax-exempt securities, but a foreign corporation pays one-fiftieth of one per cent on the par value of authorized capital, the tax not to exceed $2,000.
[9] Unless bonds are secured by an adequate mortgage on Massachusetts real estate.
[10] But only on the difference between the market value of each share and the proportionate value per share on which the corporation was last assessed; and, in practice, few returns are made.
[11] The exemption is conditioned on the taxation of the corporation's whole property by Connecticut of some other states; but this condition is, or is assumed to be, invariably satisfied.

TABLE NO. III.—TAXATION OF STEAM RAILROAD CORPORATIONS, THEIR STOCKHOLDERS AND THEIR BONDHOLDERS.

(Unless otherwise specified, statements apply to both domestic and foreign corporations.)

| State | TAX TO THE CORPORATION. | | | | | Tax on resident stock-holders ? | Tax on resident bond-holders ? |
	On real estate?	On tangible personalty?	On moneys and net credit?	On capital stock?	On gross receipts?		
Maine...............	No[1]	No	No	No	Yes[2]	No	Yes
New Hampshire...	Yes[3]	Yes[3]	Yes[3]	No[4]	No	No	Yes
Vermont...........	No[5]	No[6]	No[6]	Yes[7]	Yes[5]	No[8]	Yes
Massachusetts.....	Yes[9]	Yes[10]	No	Yes[11]	No	No[12]	Yes
Rhode Island......	Yes	Yes[13]	No	No	No	Yes[14]	Yes
Connecticut........	No[15]	No[15]	No	Yes[16]	No	No	No[17]

[1] But buildings are taxed, and lands and fixtures outside the right of way.
[2] On the average gross transportation receipts per mile within the state.
[3] Not by towns, but included in the state's valuation.
[4] The value of stock is, however, considered in the state's valuation.
[5] Real estate used for railway purposes is not taxed if the corporation elects to pay the tax on gross receipts. (See note [6].) Real estate not used for railway purposes is taxed locally.
[6] There is a tax of one per cent on the whole property, unless the corporation elects to pay the tax on gross receipts, and the practice is to pay the latter tax.
[7] But not to exceed $50.
[8] But the stock of foreign railway corporations not operating in Vermont is taxable unless taxed in the home state.
[9] There is an exemption of the right of way and of railway buildings thereon: but property thus exempted is really taxed under corporate excess.
[10] On machinery only: and machinery outside of the right of way is exempt, save as reached under corporate excess.
[11] On corporate excess. All railways operating in Massachusetts are incorporated there.
[12] The exemption does not extend to stock in foreign corporations not operating in Massachusetts.
[13] Not enforced as to rolling stock.
[14] But only on the difference between the market price and the proportionate amount per share at which the corporation was last assessed; and in practice few returns are made.
[15] But property not used for railway purposes is taxed.
[16] On Connecticut's fraction of the entire value of stock and bonds, deducting taxed real estate and deducting securities issued to pay for property outside the state or for property taxed in the state for securities of other railways.
[17] The exemption does not extend to the bonds of railways not doing business in Connecticut.

Diversities are capable of explanation.

These diversities, Mr. Knox contends, are capable of explanation. In his report of May 17, 1909 at p. 6, he says:

"Inevitably the first impression gained from such diversities as are indicated by the tabular views is that the methods of corporate taxation are so chaotic as to be almost incapable of explanation and of classification. Investigation, however, will show that the diversities in the system of corporate taxation are not accidental or irrational, but that they largely flow from diversities in the general theories of taxation and from the peculiar problems attending the taxation of corporations and of the holders of corporate securities."

THE GENERAL THEORIES OF TAXATION.

Economists generally favor the theory that taxes should be paid in accordance with ability to pay. They adhere to this faculty or ability theory, and maintain that any taxing system which is not founded upon this theory, is theoretically, at least, wrong. Mr. Knox, in the above report (May 17, 1909, p. 7, et seq.,) expounds the two general theories of taxation, and concludes that in practice neither theory can consistently be followed, and that each jurisdiction necessarily follows partly one theory and partly the other.

He says:

"The theories of taxation date back to Adam Smith's Wealth of Nations, published in 1776. For practical purposes, the theories are two—(1) the theory that taxes are paid for governmental protection and are assessed according to the value of the protection enjoyed, and (2) the theory that taxes are paid as a mode of securing for all society governmental protection, and that the payer pays not in proportion to the protection, but in proportion to his own ability to aid in securing for society the really inestimable benefits of government. Neither of these theories is followed consistently either as to natural persons or as to corporations. On the contrary, each jurisdiction follows partly one theory and partly the other. The theory of payment in proportion to the value of the protection enjoyed is incapable of complete adoption. One difficulty—and it is radical and fatal—is that the value of governmental protection to the poor is really greater than the value of governmental protection to the rich, for government bestows upon rich and poor alike the benefits of education, peace, and wholesome surroundings, and those benefits—equally indispensable for all—are largely obtainable by the rich at their own personal expense but by the poor are obtainable in no other way than through government. Hence, the preference is commonly given to the theory that each person, natural or artificial, should contribute to governmental support according to his ability,[*] and yet this

---

[*] The ability theory is favored by most economists. R. T. Ely, Outlines of Economists, Rev. Ed. 1909. p. 614.

theory in turn is practically incapable of thorough adoption. What is to be done with the skilled surgeon who neglects to earn the income which his skill places easily at his disposal Is he to be taxed according to his ability to earn and thus to pay? Nothing of this sort has been attempted in the case of private individuals. On the contrary, they are taxed not upon the basis of their ability to earn, but upon the basis of their savings or actual income. The result of the impossibility of applying perfectly either of the two theories is, as has been said, that each is adopted partially. Thus the owner of land is taxed at the place where the land is, on the theory that this is the place where governmental protection is received, although, clearly enough, the ability to pay taxes is a purely personal quality and exists only at the owner's residence. On the other hand, taxes or the support of the schools and of the police and the like are apportioned to the payers wealth, his ability—quite irrespective of the possibility that he may have no occasion to use the schools, or that his wealth, being in unimproved land, requires no protection from the police.

Every tax system combines more or less of each of the two general principles, and is largely affected by the practical question of ascertaining and locating the property to be taxed.

Any system must be a compromise between what theoretically ought to be and what practically can be. In establishing or criticising any system this practical factor must be kept in the foreground.''

THE PECULIAR PROBLEMS ATTENDING THE TAXATION OF CORPORATIONS—THEIR PROPERTY AND THE HOLDERS OF CORPORATE SECURITIES.

Mr. Knox, in the same report at p. 8 et seq., further accounts for the diversity of method by analyzing the difficulties arising from the subject matter of taxation. His analyses and observations are as follows:

"Perhaps the source of the difficulties or diversities will be better understood if the various subjects of taxation

are examined. Let us, then, notice the most important
kinds of property which are made the basis of taxation,
whether owned by natural persons or by corporations, and
let us notice that when we come to corporate taxation the
theoretical and practical difficulties increase and thus explain the diversities of treatment.''

Real estate as a subject of taxation—little difficulty.

''Problems as to taxation have various degrees of complexity.
The simplest problem of all has to do with real estate, including improvements. No one doubts that the land owner should
contribute toward the support of government. Few doubt that
the contribution must be estimated with reference either to the
value of the land including the improvements, or to the income
actually received. Even the advocate of the single tax suggests no very different starting point for the estimating of the
land tax, for his theory simply takes the value of the land, not
including improvements, and makes an argument as to the
proper amount of the contribution to be exacted. There are,
then, to repeat, only two practical foundations for a tax on
real estate, and, in truth, one of these, namely, the income derived, is not favored in the United States, so that practically
we find only one foundation, namely, the value. Further, as
to the place where the tax should be payable, there is no difference in opinion, or at least in practice. The land owner pays
the tax where the land is. The land seems to be personified.
It itself is said to be liable to the tax and to pay the tax. Even
if th non-resident land owner were to be taxed at his residence
on the income derived from his land, it would not be urged
that the tax on the land at its situs should be abolished or reduced.

As to land there is no practical difference of opinion either as
to the place of taxation or as to the value to be taken as a basis,
and still less is there difference of opinion upon the question
whether land should be taxed at all. As to the place of taxing
land, by the way, it is obvious that we find firmly the theory
that taxes are based upon benefits received, and should be
paid at the situs of the benefit.

Tangible personalty—greater difficulty.

"What has just been said of land is largely applicable to tangible personalty. The owner of this is taxed without hesitation, and he is taxed upon its value, rather than upon the income derived from it, and he is taxed at the situs of the property. Yet some difficulties have been caused by the doctrine that movables are supposed to follow their owner—*monila siquinter personam;* and consequently there are not wanting instances in which there is still an attempt to tax the owner both at his residence and at the situs of the property.

Thus taxation as to tangible personalty is a somewhat more complex problem than taxation as to realty."

Intangible personalty—still greater difficulty.

"Passing to intangible personalty, one finds a much greater perplexity. There is no perfect agreement on the elementary question whether intangible personalty should be taxable at all. The reason for this is partly that intangible personalty is difficult to trace ,and partly that intangible personality—a creditor's claim or a shareholder's stock, for example—usually represents, in fact, though perhaps not in law, a mere right to share in property which, whoever now owns the title to it must be conceded to be, whenever and wherever existant, the subject matter of adequate taxation already. To state the matter in a more concrete form, the typical case of intangible personalty is a claim by a creditor against a debtor, and this claim is valuable and ultimately enforceable merely because this debtor, or some debtor of his, has, or is to have, tangible wealth which can be used, directly or indirectly for the satisfaction of the claim. The whole wealth of a nation consists obviously enough of tangible property and of those mental and physical abilities and conditions which may result in the production of other tangible property. Abilities are theoretically an ideal basis for taxation; but * * * there is usually no attempt to tax them. If, on the one hand, intangible personalty represents anything except a claim secured in affect by tangible property already existant, intangible personalty represents a mere claim against the ability of some potential producer, and hence represents what is not in practice taxed. If, on the other hand, intangible personalty represents ultimately a claim against existant tangible property, it represents what is taxed already; and it need hardly be repeated that there is an objection to double taxation and that there is a tendency to shape the law in such a way as to respect this objection. These are the reasons—besides the impracticability, already mentioned, of tracing intangible personalty—for the view, frequently found, that intangible personalty should not be made a subject of taxation, or at least that intangible personalty should be exempt in cases where double taxation is obvious. When it is decided that the owner of intangible personalty should be taxed, it is common to deduct the debts owed by him, for it is recognized that only the resultant of such subtraction represents his actual power to share in the country's wealth. Further, after this deduction is made there remains the question in what locality the resultant should be taxed. The answer usually is that it should be taxed where the owner resides, or in this instance it is not repugnant to reason to say *mobile sequinter personam*. Yet embarrassing questions arise in cases where intangible personalty is represented by promissory notes, drafts, bonds, or even bank deposits, or there is a growing tendency to treat claims thus evidenced and secured as analogous to tangible property.

It is clear, that the taxation of intangible personalty is a much more complex subject than the taxation of tangible property, whether realty or personalty.''

Corporate property—A combination of difficulties.

''Questions of taxation involving corporations are much more intricate than questions of taxation as to individuals. Corporations are owners—large and growing owners, in fact—of all these kinds of property, and hence the difficulties explained in making these kinds of property the basis of taxation of natural persons apply with at least equal force when we attempt to tax corporations.

In the case of corporations there is the additional and invariable element that there are at least two classes of persons interested in the corporate property. The first class is composed of the corporations themselves, considered as separate legal entities. The second class is composed of the stockholders —those natural persons who stand behind those creatures of the law. There is also frequently a third class of persons interested in the corporate property—a class composed of bond-holders and other creditors.   Should the corporation's property be made the basis of taxation to the corporation itself, or to the stockholders alone, or to both?   Obviously a tax on the corporation is really a tax upon its stockholders, for otherwise than as a matter of legal reasoning a corporation and its stockholders are one.   Hence the question whether both the corporation and the stockholders shall be taxed is an interesting problem to double taxation.

Further, that same question as to the simultaneous taxation of corporation and stockholder has another and even more puzzling aspect.   The corporation's property is commonly in one place and the stockholder in another.   If the theory be that taxation is to be measured by protection received, the proper place for taxation is the situs of the corporation's property. If the theory be that taxation is to be measured by ability to pay, the proper place is the residence of the stockholders.   On no one theory can both places be chosen.   When the corporation's property is in one country and the stockholder in another, no one is shocked by taxation, in each place.   When the corporation's property and the stockholder is in the same town, county, or state, no one fails to perceive that there should be but one taxation.   What shall be done when the corporation's property is in one of the states and the stockholder in another? For this purpose should the states be treated, *inter se*, as separate countries, or as something like counties of the same country?   The systems of corporate taxation indicate a difference of opinion upon this question, and the diversity of results is natural and reasonable, corresponding to a difference, perhaps a change, in the attitude of the minds of our legislators.

Another source of difficulty is that corporations are very likely to possess in diverse jurisdictions property of which the value is chiefly due to the whole inseparable undertaking as one great machine, a going concern—a railway, for example— and as to which, obviously, taxation should be exacted by each jurisdiction neither upon the entire value of the machine nor upon the value of the local part considered as severed and comparatively valueless.

Again, there is the additional difficulty that the system of taxation adopted must neither conflict with that exclusive power to regulate interstate commerce which resides in the federal government nor transgress the inhibition of the fourteenth amendment against a state's taking property without due process of law or denying to any person the equal protection of the laws.

Further, there is a great difference in corporations. A manufacturing corporation—its property being situated in one place, the business being not of a quasi public nature, and no practical monopoly being enjoyed—is much more like a natural person or a partnership than is a corporation engaged in railway business; and the diversities between corporations lead properly to diversities in methods of taxation.''

DOUBLE TAXATION.

The exacting of two or more payments from one person or from two or more persons by reason of the same piece of property or other source of ability to pay taxes is double taxation.

"There are in reality no less than five different forms of double taxation in the case of corporations:—

1. Double taxation of property and of debts, or of income and of interest on debts.

2. Double taxation of property and of income.

3. Double taxation of property and of stock.

4. Double taxation arising from conflicts of jurisdiction.

5. Double taxation of the corporation and of the holders of stock or bonds." Seligman, Essays in Taxation, 1903, p. 213.

Duplicate taxation of corporations due to conflicts of jurisdiction, is properly arranged under four chief headings:

1. Interstate taxation of corporate property.

2. Interstate taxation of stock and bonds or of dividends and interest.

3. Interstate taxation of non-resident stockholders or bondholders.

4. Interestate taxation of corporate receipts or income.

TAXATION OF INTANGIBLE PERSONALTY.

The problem of how to tax what is known as "intangible personalty," including rights, credits, corporate securities, and money at interest, is still unsolved.

Shall intangible personalty be exempt entirely from taxation, on the theory that otherwise there is double taxation? Shall it be taxed with a low uniform rate? Or shall further attempts by way of doomage and the like be made to collect the local general property tax thereon?

Connecticut is the only state that specifically and directly taxes intangible personalty to the holders thereof other than by the local general property tax. There, stockholders are not taxed, nor are holders of bonds of a railroad company operating in the state. The holders of other bonds, notes, choses in action, deposits in national banks, etc., may elect to pay either the local general property tax thereon, averaging about $20 a thousand, or a low uniform rate of $4 a thousand to the state treasurer. This optional plan is unique, and the receipts under it are increasing every year.

In Rhode Island no intangible personalty is taxable to a corporation; and a few returns are made by the corporations taxable on such property in Maine, New Hampshire, or Vermont. In all these five states individuals are subject to the local general property tax on their bank deposits, credits (except mortgages sometimes), bonds, and to some extent, on their stock, but the attempt to collect has resulted in the usual failure.

The reasons of this failure can be stated thus: First, intangible personalty can be readily concealed; second, the temptation to conceal it is great, because a general property rate of $20 a thousand often amounts to half the income from the intangible personalty; third, when found, such property is taxed at its true cash value, while real estate is usually undervalued; and, fourth, holders of such property go where they will be taxed the lowest.

The Massachusetts Tax Commission (1908) recommend that a uniform tax at the rate of $3 a thousand be levied on this class of property, and the Massachusetts constitution be amended in accordance with the recommendation, in case the

Massachusetts supreme judicial court should decide that the proposed low rates are not "proportional," and hence are unconstitutional. That court did so decide.[*]

The Maine Tax Commission of 1908 recommend that their legislature give serious consideration to the plan for a low uniform rate on intangibles, stating that the collection of such a low tax would be "aided by a strong favorable public sentiment, so necessary in the proper and easy administration of any law."

The Vermont Tax Commission of 1908 recommend a low uniform tax rate on intangibles, while the New Hampshire Tax Commission of 1908 recommend that "money and securities" be dropped from the taxable list.

Summarizing, it is seen that the "low uniform rate" method is popular in New England. It already exists in Connecticut, where it is giving satisfaction, while commissions in three other states of this group recommend it.

COMPARISON OF THE RESULTS OBTAINED BY THE DIFFERENT SYSTEMS OF TAXING CORPORATIONS IN THE NEW ENGLAND AND MIDDLE ATLANTIC STATES.

The states embraced in the New England and Middle Atlantic groups apply about all of the different methods of taxation heretofore outlined and discussed to corporations. We have in these two groups examples of the general property tax, assessed by local officials and by central bodies, of the gross receipts tax, of the tax on capital stock, of the tax on capital stock and funded and floating indebtedness, and of the special and specific taxes found elsewhere in use.

The following two tables, compiled by Corporation Commissioner Know (Rept. of June 6, 1910, p. 16), give complete financial results of the application of these different systems in these two groups of states.

---

[*] Opinion of the Justices, 195 Mass. 607 (1908).

TOTAL STATE TAXES, AND AMOUNTS AND PERCENTAGES CONTRIBUTED BY CERTAIN SPECIFIED SOURCES OF TAXATION: NEW ENGLAND AND MIDDLE ATLANTIC GROUPS.

(The figures for the first group are mainly for 1908; for the second, mainly for 1909.)

State.	Corporation tax.	General property tax.	Inheritance tax.	Liquor tax.	Miscellaneous tax receipts.	Total state taxes.
New England Group.						
Maine	$1,258,649	$153,859	$68,001	$5,900	$91,430	$2,296,439
New Hampshire	295,214	437,723	180,409			894,476
Vermont	978,942	18,661	68,025	50,200		1,018,818
Massachusetts	4,706,743	4,000,000	772,469	839,367		10,818,009
Rhode Island	826,770	766,989		$137,855	124,896	1,898,462
Connecticut	2,884,274		278,371		439,338	3,622,008
Middle Atlantic Group.						
New York	9,442,903		6,992,615	5,140,550	*7,737,084	•29,283,188
New Jersey	6,791,794		569,430			7,361,244
Pennsylvania	16,899,333	1,042,780	1,730,853	1,741,180	1,996,697	23,359,798
Delaware	292,506		3,444		177,822	473,772
Maryland	1,108,405	1,255,810	257,089	372,772	453,816	3,447,442
District of Columbia	903,195	4,298,308		464,898	116,014	5,782,415

44

PER CENT OF TOTAL STATE TAXES.

State.	Corporation tax.	General property tax.	Inheritance tax.	Liquor tax.	Miscellaneous tax receipts.	Total state taxes.
New England Group.						
Maine	35	37	4		4	100
New Hampshire	35	55	[2]10			100
Vermont	86	2	7	5		100
Massachusetts	46	39	7	8		100
Rhode Island	45	41		[3]7	7	100
Connecticut	70		8		13	100
Middle Atlantic Group.						
New York	32		24	[3]18	[4]26	100
New Jersey	92		8			100
Pennsylvania	72	5	7	[2]7	9	100
Delaware	62		1		37	100
Maryland	32	37	[1]7	11	13	100
District of Columbia	16	[5]74		8	2	100

[1] Legacy and succession tax.
[2] Includes some taxes other than those on liquors.
[3] Receipts for five months only.
[4] Of this amount, $3,385,540.16 came from the stock transfer tax and $1,844,827.45 from mortgage tax, which is included under corporation tax. The
[5] Certain public-service corporations paid $968,590 general property tax in addition to this amount. The total general property tax is $1,571,888, or about 70 per cent of the District taxes.

Reference to these tables will show that New Jersey with its general property tax on railways, assessed by a central body, and a gross receipts tax on transmission, express and car companies, derives a greater percentage of state taxes from these corporations than does any other state in these two groups. It should be noted in this connection that in New Jersey the tax on railroads, although assessed by a central body, is for both state and local purposes.

The other states of these groups, with reference to the percentage of state taxes paid by corporations, rank as follows:

Second—Connecticut with its tax on the capital stock and funded and floating indebtedness of railways, gross receipts tax on express and car companies, and mileage tax on transmission companies.

Third—Pennsylvania with tax on the capital stock and gross receipts of all these companies.

Fourth—Delaware with its tax on the capital stock of railways, or a lump sum in lieu thereof (the lump sum is paid), and gross receipts and specific taxes on transmission, express and car companies.

Fifth—Maine with a gross receipts tax on all these companies.

Sixth—Massachusetts with its tax on capital stock and real estate and "machinery" of all these companies.

Seventh—Rhode Island with its primitive general property tax on railways and a gross receipts tax on express and transmission companies.

Eighth—New Hampshire with an ad valorem tax, central assessment, on all these companies.

Ninth—New York with taxes on the gross receipts and capital stock of all these companies.

Tenth—Maryland with a tax on the gross receipts of railways, transmission, express and car companies, and a capital stock and local property tax on the three last classes.

The above comparisons by no means are conclusive to the effect that the state deriving the greatest percentage of state taxes from corporations has the most perfect system for taxing these bodies. It is possible that a system of taxation theoretically imperfect and equitable unjust may be an unusual revenue producer. It is possible also that a system of taxation theoretically perfect in form, may, because of inefficient administration, work badly from the view point of revenue.

The system of taxing these companies on their income or receipts is the one favored by economists generally. Maine has adopted a system of taxing corporations on a basis of their gross receipts and that state ranks fifth in the above list.

The effectiveness of any system of corporation taxation, from the revenue view point, at least, depends to a very great extent upon efficiency in the administration of the taxing laws. The effectiveness of any taxing system from the view point of equity and justness depends wholly upon the form of the system.

TENDENCIES.

The foregoing analysis, tables and discussions divulge the following tendencies:

First—Starting from the original position of taxing corporations on their general property, assessment by local officials, the first and most pronounced tendency, is away from that system, and although still in favor of a tax on the corporate property, assessment thereof is made by central or special bodies under well defined rules.

Second—The second tendency, not quite as general as the first, is away from the original position altogether and in favor of a tax not on property but on other elements supposed to better represent taxable capacity.

Third—A general and pronounced tendency toward a separation of the sources of state and local taxation—the taxation of certain corporations, with which is usually found grouped revenue from inheritance for state purposes, and the general property and special and specific taxes for the minor units.

Fourth—Due to a growing hostility to double taxation, a tendency away therefrom by the exempting of shares of stock in companies which are taxed on their property.

Fifth—By way of an effort to solve the problem of ferreting out and taxing intangible personalty, a tendency toward the exemption of the same from the application of the general property tax laws and to leave the taxation of the same to the state at a low and uniform rate.

VI.

The Franchise Tax.

One of the chief sources of governmental income from corporations is the so called franchise tax. As was stated previously the term franchise denotes nothing more; and the value of the franchise is, for the purpose of taxation, measured by various tests—such as the capital stock at par value, capital stock at market value, capital stock plus bonded debt, capital stock plus total debt, business, gross earnings, dividends, capital stock according to dividends and net earnings. The meaning of "franchise tax" is thus something wholly indefinite. What is called a franchise tax in one state may be absolutely unlike that in the adjoining state.

There are certain restrictions upon the power of the state to tax corporate franchises. In the case of a foreign corporation, the state which has not given the franchise cannot tax it. With a domestic corporation the franchise or right to exist and transact certain business is something separated and apart from the property of the corporation, and is capable of being taxed *—the right to exist and the right to transact business, in the case of a domestic corporation, are inextricably bound together. But as regards a foreign corporation, the two things are distinct, and the state can tax only the privilege of carrying on the business within its borders. The corporate franchise has no existence apart from the laws of the state which created it. In order to avoid legal entanglements, therefore, the tax on foreign corporations is usually imposed on the business transacted, but is very often termed a franchise tax.

The denial of the right to tax the franchises of a foreign corporation applies equally to corporations chartered by the United States which are not legally foreign corporations.†
Even national banks cannot be subjected to license or privilege

---

* Nothing is better settled than that the franchise of a private cor_ poration * * * is property and of the most valuable kind, as it cannot be taken for public use without compensation." Wilmington R. R. v. Reed, 13 Wall. 264, 268 (1871).

† California v. So. Pac. Ry. Co., 127 U. S. 40 (1887).

taxes.‡ Some fairly recent cases in Pennsylvania have even held that the tax on capital stock is invalid as to stock invested in a patent right, because such taxation involves a property right which depends for its existence exclusively on the federal constitution and on an act of congress.§ Subject to these restrictions and to the further restriction that no state may impose a franchise tax to interfere with interstate commerce, the taxation of corporate franchises seems to have no limitation, except the discretion of the taxing power.**

What is the real significance of the franchise tax? Why is it desirable that such a hard and fast line should be drawn between the property tax and the franchise? What is the meaning of the distinction?

The answer is very plain. In the first place, according to the constitution of several of the states, the taxes on property must be uniform. If, however, the corporation tax is held to be a franchise tax, there is no necessity of such uniformity between the tax on individuals and that on corporations. Secondly, according to the principles of the property tax, deductions, are allowed for certain classes of exempt or extra-territorial property. If the tax is a franchise tax, such exemptions cannot be claimed. Thirdly, if the tax is a franchise tax, and not a tax on property, or earnings, it may be upheld as not interfering with interstate commerce. Finally, if the tax is a franchise tax, many of the objections to double taxation would be removed, * * * Every commonwealth imposing a franchise tax, for instance, could assess the entire capital of a corporation, although only a very small portion might be located or employed within the state. We can hence readily understand the persistence with which the corporations seek to uphold the distinction and to have the charge declared to be not a franchise, but a property tax.'' Seligman, Essays in Taxation, pp. 186 and 187.

The question has arisen almost exclusively in connection with the taxation of capital stock or of earnings.

Whether or not the taxation of capital stock is the taxation

---

‡ Mayor v. Natl. Bank of Macon, 59 Ga. 648 (1877).
§ Com. v. Westinghouse Co., 151 Pa. St., 265 (1892); Com. v. Air Brake Co. id. 265; Com. v. Lehigh C. & I. Co., 162 Pa. 603 (1894).
** Delaware R. R. Tax Case, 18 Wall. 231 (1873); California v. So. Pac. R. R. Co., 127 U. S. 41 (1887).

of the corporate property, is not definitely agreed upon by all the courts. That capital stock is in one sense property cannot be denied; but whether the tax on capital stock is tantamount to a tax on general property is an entirely different question. In several states it has been held that capital stock practically represents the property, and that the two are in all intents and purposes inter-changeable terms.[1]   As regards the tax on capital stock in general, other states have decided, and the federal courts have affirmed the decision, that it is not a tax on the property. Thus, it has been held that the Delaware railroad tax of one-quarter of one per cent on the actual cash value of the capital stock is a tax not on the property or on the shares of individuals, but on the corporation, measured by a certain percentage on the value of its shares.[2]   In like manner the Massachusetts taxes on the whole value of the corporate shares and on the capital stock in excess of the value of the real estate and machinery have been pronounced taxes on the franchise.[3] In a recent case it has been held that this tax, although nominally upon the shares of capital stock, is in effect a tax upon the organization on account of property owned or used by it, and therefore valid. It is an excise tax, and not a property tax, and therefore not limited by the constitutional restrictions as to uniform taxation of all property.[4]   On the other hand the Connecticut courts have held that a tax on capital stock and debt is not a tax on franchise, but on property;[5] and older cases in Alabama and Missouri were similarly decided.[6]

Secondly, in the case of capital stock as measured by dividends, the courts of Pennsylvania and New York have arrived at diametrically opposite conclusions. In Pennsylvania a long series of cases has consistently maintained the doctrine that this tax is one on property.[7]

---

[1] Burke v. Rad'am, 57 Calif 594 (1881); New Orleans v. Canal Co., 29 La. A. R. 851 (1877); Whitney v Madison, 23 Ind. 351 (1864); Co. Comrs. v. Natl. Bank, 48 Md 117 (1877).
[2] Delaware R. R. Tax Case, 180 Wall 206 (1871).
[3] Com. v. Hamilton Mfg. Co, 94 Mass. 298 (1866); Portland Bank v. Apthorp, 12 Mass. 252 (1815).
[4] Western Union Tel. Co. v. Mass. 125 U. S. 530 (1837).
[5] Nichols v. R. R. Co., 42 Conn. 103 (1875).
[6] State v. Ins. Co., 89 Ala. 335 (1889); State v. Ry. Co., 37 Mo. 265 (1865).
[7] Fox's Appeal, 112 Pa. 319 (1886); Comr. v. Standard Oil Co., 101 Pa 119 (1882); Phoenix Iron Co. v. Com., 59 Pa. 104 (1868); Catawissa Appeal, 78 Pa. St. 59 (1875).

The New York and New Jersey courts on the other hand have held the tax on capital stock to be a 'franchise tax.[1] The New York case was carried in last instance to the federal court. Of course the fact that the statute expressly declares the tax to be a franchise tax is of no weight—no importance attaches to mere nomenclature. But the United States supreme court had already shown the tendency of its thought in the Massachusetts and Delaware decisions just cited. In a subsequent case the court said, that the new York tax was "a franchise tax in the nature of an income tax."[2] Finally, in a later case, the tax was definitely pronounced to be on franchise, the court holding that the tax was not upon the capital stock nor upon any bonds of the United States composing a part of that stock; but that reference was made to the capital stock and dividends only for the purpose of determining the amount of the tax to be exacted each year.[3]

The third case in which the question of a franchise tax is of importance is in connection with interstate commerce. In a Maine case, involving the constitutionality of the Maine Excise tax law, the United States supreme court held that a tax on gross receipts, as a measure of a company's ability to pay an excise tax, is valid.[4] A tax on the gross receipts from business done wholly within the state by a foreign corporation, is valid. See Constitutionality of Tax on Corporations Engaged in Interstate Commerce.

THE CONSTITUTIONALITY OF A TAX ON CORPORATIONS ENGAGED IN INTERSTATE COMMERCE.

Of the several provisions of the federal constitution intended jointly to safeguard "the freest interchange of commodities among the people of the different states." Justice Miller, in Cook v. Penn., 97 U. S. 566, 574 (1878), the one chiefly relied upon in connection with the taxation of carriers engaged in in-

---

[1] People v. Home Ins. Co., 92 N. Y. (1883); Singer Co. v. Hoppen. heimer, 25 Vroom 439 (1892).

[2] Mercantile Bank v. New York, 134 U. S. 594.

[3] Home Ins Co. v. New York, 134 U. S. 594 (1889).

[4] Maine v. Grand Trunk Ry. Co., 142 U. S. 217 (1891); Ratterman v. W, U. T. Co., 127 U. S. 411 (1888).

terstate commerce is paragraph 3, of section 8, art. 1, which confers upon congress the power: ''To regulate commerce with foreign nations and among the several states and with the Indian tribes.''

The difficulty of drawing a sharp line between the federal powers and the state powers in the matter of the taxation and regulation of these great agencies of commerce, like the railways and the telegraph, which extend from one end of the country to the other, has troubled the courts since 1872. It is only recently that the problem has been solved.

While the greater part of each of the two fields in which each of the two great divisions of our government may respectively exercise its powers is clear enough, yet the boundary of one seems to merge almost imperceptibly into that of the other at places. This has resulted in much litigation, and the decisions of the supreme court on some of the most vital points have occasionally seemed contradictory. In not a few instances the court has apparently reversed itself.

However, the following points seem now to be settled:

A. *As to the taxation of interstate carriers on an ad valorem basis:*

1. A state may tax the property, within its bounds, of railroad companies and other persons or corporations engaged in interstate commerce.

R. R. Co. v. Peniston, 18 Wall. 5 (1873) and later cases based thereon.

2. It may tax both the tangible and intangible property of the carriers, provided only, that it may not tax a federal franchise. Cent. Pac. Ry. Co. v. Calif., 162 U. S. 91 (1895).

3. A state may value the property by the ''unit rule,'' i. e., make a valuation of the entire property of the ''system'' of a given corporation engaged in interstate business, and tax that proportion of the entire property which the mileage in the state bears to the total mileage operated or what is the same thing, may make the apportionment of the basis of business done.

State R. R. Case, 92 U. S. 575 (1875);

W. U. Tel. Co. v. Taggert, 163 U. S. 1 (1895);

Adams Exp. Co. v. Ohio, 165 U. S. 194 (1896);

4. It may arrive at a valuation by the following methods:

(a) By adding the market or fair cash value of the shares of capital stock and the market or par value of the various kinds of funded indebtedness. State. R. R. Tax Case, 92 U. S. 575 (1875).

(b) By considering one or more of several elements, or evidences of value, as: the cost of constructing or equipment, the market value of the outstanding securities, the gross earnings and the net earnings, and all other matters appertaining thereto. Indiana R. R. Case, 154 U. S. 425, 439 (1893).

5. The court has recognized the fact that the value of property of this class depends largely upon earnings. In some of the decisions already referred to this is made clear. Thus in the Indiana Railroad Case at p. 445 it was said:

"The rule of property taxation is that the value of the property is the basis of taxation. It does not mean a tax upon the earnings which the property makes, nor for the privileges of using the property, but rests solely upon the value. But the value of the property results from the use to which it is put and varies with the profitableness of that use, present and prospective, actual and anticipated. There is no pecuniary value outside of that which results from such use. The amount and profitable character of such use determines the value, and if property is taxed at its actual cash value, it is taxed upon something which is created by the uses to which it is put. In the nature of things it is impossible—at least in respect to railroad property—to divide its value and determine how much is caused by one use to which it is put and how much by another. Take the case before us; it is impossible to disintegrate the value of that portion of the road within Indiana and determine how much of that value springs from its use in doing interstate business and how much from its use in doing business wholly within this state. An attempt to do so would be entering upon a mere field of uncertainty and speculation. And because of this fact it is something which an assessing board is not required to attempt."

B. *As to the taxation of carriers or of interstate business by methods other than the property or ad valorem tax:*

1. A state may not levy a tax as a prerequisite in carrying on interstate business.

In Osborne v. Mobile, 16 Wallace, 479 (1872), the supreme court decided that this could be done. But fifteen years later that case was overruled in Leloup v. Mobile, 127 U. S. 640 (1877). The trenchant part of this decision reads:

"A great number and variety of cases involving the commercial power of congress have been brought to the attention of this court during the past fifteen years which have frequently made it necessary to re-examine the whole subject with care; and the result has sometimes been that in order to give full and fair effect to the different clauses of the constitution, the court has felt constrained to refer to the fundamental principles stated and illustrated with so much clearness and force by Chief Justice Marshall and other members of the court in former times, and to modify in some degree dicta and decisions which have occasionally been made in the intervening period. This is always done, however, with great caution, and an anxious desire to place the final conclusion reached upon the fairest and most just constructions of the constitution in all its parts."

The conclusion was therefore (p. 648) "that no state has the right to lay a tax on interstate commerce in any form, whether by way of duties layed on the transportation of the subjects of that commerce, or on the receipts derived from that transportation, or on the occupation or business of carrying it on, and the reason is that such taxation is a burden on that commerce and amounts to a regulation of it, which belongs solely to congress."

See also: Webster v. Bell, 68 Fed. 183 (1895);
McCall v. Calif., 136 U. S. 104 (1889);
R. R. Co. v. Penn., 136 U. S. 114 (1889);
Crutcher v. Kentucky, 141 U. S. 47 (1890).

2. A state may levy a license tax on local business performed by interstate carriers.
Osborne v. Florida, 164 U. S. 650 (1896);
Postal Tel. Co. v. Adams, 155 U. S. 688 (1894).

3. A state may not tax freight, in interstate commerce, nor interstate telegraph messages.
State Freight Tax Case, 15 Wall. 2323 (1872);
Telegraph Co. v. Texas, 105 U. S. 460 (1881).

4. A state may levy a tax in proportion to the gross receipts from interstate commerce under certain conditions and in certain forms. But may not tax the receipts as such.

The earliest case involving this point seems to be one decided in 1872, at about the same time that the State Freight Tax Case, above referred to, was decided. This is known as "The State Tax on Gross Receipts," 15 Wall. 284 (1872).

The state of Pennsylvania levied a three-fourths of one per cent tax on gross earnings of every railroad incorporated under its laws and the tax was held valid, even when it covered the earnings of a state railroad on coal carried out of the state. This case was distinguished from the State Freight Tax Case on the ground that not everything which effects commerce amounts to a regulation of it within the meaning of the constitution. The court said, in words that often reappear in the latter decisions on the same point, after showing that the states have authority to tax the *property,* real and personal, of all corporations whether engaged in interstate commerce or not:

"We think also that such a tax may be laid upon a valuation, or may be an excise, and that in exacting an excise tax from their corporations the states are not obliged to impose a fixed sum upon the franchises or upon the value of them, but they may demand a graduated contribution; proportional either to the value of the privilege granted, or to the extent of the exercise, or to the results of such exercise. There certainly is a line which separates that power of the Federal Government to regulate commerce among the states, which is exclusive, from the authority of the states to tax a person's property, business or occupation, within their limits. The line is sometimes difficult to define with distinctions. It is so in the present case; but we think it may safely be laid down that the gross receipts of railroad or canal companies, after they have reached the treasury of the carriers, though they may have been derived in part from transportation of freight between states, have become subject to legitimate taxation."

In commenting on these decisions, Mr. Judson, an authority on the taxation of interstate carriers, says:

"It seems to have been conceded that a state can levy a tax upon net earnings, and the court said that it is difficult to state any well founded distinctions between a state tax on net earnings and one on gross earnings, that net earnings are a part of the gross receipts, and that gross receipts are a measure of approximate value.

Neither of these cases have been overruled; but the authority of the decision in the case of the State Tax on gross receipts for a time was seriously impaired by decisions of the court apparently inconsistent with the broad statement therein of the right to tax gross receipts, on the ground that they have passed into the treasury of the company and lost their distinctive character.as freight.''

See Steamboat Co v. Penn. 122 U. S. 326 (1886);
Fargo v. Mich., 121 U. S. 230 (1886).

''It will be noticed that the mileage rule of apportionment of interstate properties was not suggested or considered in the case of the State Tax on Gross Receipts. The case presented was that of a railroad whose line was entirely within the state, but which did an interstate business through its connection with other lines leading out of the state.''

We come now to a series of cases in which a state tax on gross receipts from interstate trade has been held invalid. The first is Fargo v. Mich., 121 U. S., 230 (1886). The Merchants' Despatch Transportation Company, a New York corporation, owned certain cars which it leased to the railroad companies which operated them. The state of Michigan assessed a tax on the gross receipts of that company in the state measured by the unit rule and based on receipts from the transportation of freight from points without to points within the state and from points within to points without, but did not tax the receipts from business passing entirely through the state. This case was distinguished from the Railroad Gross Receipts Case (which it did not distinctly overrule) on the grounds (1) that the Merchants' Despatch was not a Michigan corporation, and (2) that in the Pennsylvania Case the money was in the treasury of the company in that state, while in the Michigan case the money for the freight was probably never in that state and hence not property subject to taxation.

In the next term of the court the theory that gross receipts could not be taxed was more fully developed in the case of the Philadelphia Steamship Co., v. Pennsylvania, 122 U. S. 326. In this case Pennsylvania had attempted to impose a tax on the gross receipts of railroads, canal, steamboat and other transportation companies. The steamship company in question was a Pennsylvania corporation running between Philadelphia and Savannah and from New Orleans to foreign ports. The court held that interstate commerce carried on by ships at sea is national in character and must be covered by one general rule. The court said:

"If, then, the commerce carried on by the plaintiff in error in this case could not be constitutionally taxed by the state, could the fares and freights received for transportation in carrying on that commerce be constitutionally taxed? If the state cannot tax the transportation, may it, nevertheless, tax the fares and freights received therefor? Where is the difference? Looking at the substance of things, and not at mere forms, it is very difficult to see any difference. The one thing seems to be tantamount to the other. It would seem to be rather metaphysics than plain logic for the state officials to say to the company: 'We will not tax you for the transportation you perform, but we will tax you for what you get for performing it.' Such a position can hardly be said to be based on a sound method of reasoning.

No doubt a ship owner, like any other citizen, may be personally taxed for the amount of his property or estate, without regard to the source from which it was derived, whether from commerce, or banking or any other employment. But that is an entirely different thing from laying a special tax upon his receipts in a particular employment. If such a tax is laid, and the receipts taxed are those derived from transporting goods and passengers in the way of interstate or foreign commerce, no matter when the tax is exacted, whether at the time of realizing the receipts, or at the end of every six months or a year, it is an exaction aimed at the commerce itself, and is a burden upon it, and seriously affects it. A review of the question convinces us that the first ground on which the decisions in State Tax on

Railway Gross Receipts was placed is not tenable; that
it is not supported by anything decided in Brown v. Maryland; but on the contrary, that the reasoning in that case
is decidedly against it.''

On the basis of these decisions the state courts quite generally held that gross receipts of carriers in interstate commerce
could not be taxed.

But there is another line of decisions which seem to modify
the effect of the line running from Fargo v. Michigan without
expressly overruling them. These connect with the cases sanc-
tioning the taxation of property. But so far as they affect the
question of the actual measurement of a state tax by the gross
receipts, including an equitable portion of the receipts from interstate commerce, they are more recent than the other line and
have ended in such emphatic re-assertion that they seem absolutely conclusive.

In 1881 Maine inaugurated a tax on each railroad in the state
entitled ''an annual excise tax, for the privileges of exercising
its franchise and the franchises of its leased roads in the state.''
This tax ''is in the place of all taxes upon such railroad, its
property and stock.'' The amount of this tax was calculated
on the basis of the average gross receipts per mile of road. It
is important to note that the tax was payable in April and was
computed on the basis of gross receipts for the year ending June
30th in the preceding year. The following provisions covered
interstate railroads:

>''When a railroad lies partly within and partly without
>the state or is operated as a part of a line or system ex-
>tending beyond the state, the tax shall be equal to the same
>proportion of the gross receipts in the state, as herein pro-
>vided, and its amount shall be determined as follows: the
>gross transportation receipts of such railroad, line or sys-
>tem, as the case may be, over its whole extent, within and
>without the state, shall be divided by the total number of
>miles operated to obtain the average gross receipts per mile,
>and the gross receipts in the state shall be taken to be the
>average gross receipts per mile, multiplied by the number
>of miles operated within the state.''

The Grand Trunk Railway, a Canadian corporation, operated
a road in Maine, which it leased, and became subject to this

tax. The railroad opposed the tax on the ground that the case of the State Tax on Gross Receipts had been overruled by the case of Fargo v. Michigan, and this contention was sustained by the lower United States court. On appeal to the supreme court the decision of the lower court was reversed and the tax was held to be valid. The court said:

"The tax, for the collection of which this action is brought, is an excise tax upon the defendant corporation for the privilege of exercising its franchise within the state of Maine. It is so declared in the statutes which impose it; and that a tax of this character is within the power of the state to levy there can be no question. The designation does not always indicate merely an inland imposition or duty on the consumption of commodities, but often denotes an impost for a license to pursue certain callings or to deal in special commodities, or to exercise particular franchises. It is used more frequently, in this country, in the latter sense than in the other. The privilege of exercising the franchises of a corporation within a state is generally of value, and often of great value, and the subject of earnest contention. It is natural, therefore, that the corporation should be made to bear some proportion of the burdens of government. As the granting of the privilege rests entirely in the discretion of the state, whether the corporation be of domestic or foreign origin, it may be conferred upon such conditions, pecuniary or otherwise, as the state in its judgment may deem most conducive to its interests or policy. It may require the payment into its treasury, each year, of a specific sum, or may apportion the amount exacted according to the value of the business permitted, as disclosed by its gains or receipts of the present or past years. The character of the tax, or its validity, is not determined by the mode adopted in fixing its amount for any specific period or the time of its payment. The whole field of inquiry into the extent of revenue from sources at the command of the corporation is open to consideration of the state in determining what may be justly exacted for the privilege. The rule of apportioning the charge to the receipts of the business would seem to be eminently reasonable, and likely to produce the most satisfactory results, both to the state and the corporation taxed.

The court below held that the imposition of the taxes was a regulation of commerce, interstate and foreign, and therefore in conflict with the exclusive power of congress in that respect; and on the ground alone it ordered judgment for the defendant. This ruling was founded upon the assumption that a reference by the statute to the transportation receipts and to a certain percentage of the same in determining the amount of the excise tax, was in effect the imposition of the tax upon such receipts, and therefore an interference with interstate and foreign commerce. But a resort to those receipts was simply to ascertain the value of the business done by the corporation, and thus obtain a guide to a reasonable conclusion as to the amount of the excise tax which should be levied; and we are unable to perceive in that respect any interference with transportation, domestic and foreign, over the road of the railroad company, or any regulation of commerce which consists in such transportation. If the amount ascertained were specifically imposed as the tax, no objection to its vilidity would be pretended. And if the inquiry of the state as to the value of the privilege were limited to receipts of certain past years instead of the year in which the tax is collected, it is conceded that the validity of the tax would not be affected; and if not, we do not see how a reference to the results of any other year would affect its character. There is no levy by the statute on the receipts themselves, either in form or fact; they constitute as said above, simply the means of ascertaining the value of the privilege conferred.

The case of Philadelphia and Southern Steamship Company v. Pennsylvania, 122 U. S. 326, in no way conflicts with this decision. That was the case of a tax, in terms, upon the gross receipts of a steamship company, incorporated under the laws of the state, derived from the transportation of persons and property between different states and to and from foreign countries. Such tax was held, without any dissent, to be a regulation of interstate and foreign commerce, and, therefore, invalid. We do not

question the correctness of that decision, nor do the views
we hold in this case in any way qualify or impair it."
  Maine v. Grand Trunk Ry., 142 U. S. 217, 228 (1891).

From the above decision four justices dissented, which was
regarded as slightly impairing its authority. But in Erie R.
R. Co. v. Pennsylvania, 158 U. S. 431, the same principle was
reaffirmed. See also Lehigh Valley R. R. Co. v. Penn., 145
U. S. 192 (1891), and W. U. Tel. Co. v. Taggert, 163 U. S. 1
(1895).

The most recent case on the subject is Wis. & Mich. Ry. Co.
v. Powers, 191 U. S. 379. The right of the state to levy a tax
on the gross earnings of an interstate carrier was involved in
this case, together with one other point not connected with
our question.

On the point in which we are interested the court said:

  "We need say but a word in answer to the suggestion
  that the tax is an unconstitutional interference with interstate commerce. In form the tax is a tax on 'the property
  and business of such railroad corporation operated within
  the state,' computed upon certain percentages of gross
  income. The prima facie measure of the plaintiff's gross
  income is substantially that which was approached in
  Maine v. Grand Trunk Railroad Co., 142 U. S. 217, 228.
  See also Western Union Telegraph Co. v. Taggert, 163
  U. S. 1. Decree affirmed."

This was a unanimous decision, except that Mr. Justice
White, not having heard the argument, took no part in the
decision. He concurred, however, in the decision in Erie Railroad v. Pennsylvania, a case involving the same points.

It appears, then, that a state tax on the property measured
in various ways as indicated supra, or on the franchise measured by the gross receipts is valid and is not a "regulation of
interstate commerce," in the sense in which the right to regulate commerce is prohibited to the states by the constitution.

VIII.

POWER TRANSMISSION COMPANIES.

The property of hydraulic and power transmission companies is generally taxed, as is the property of individuals, under the general property tax system. This is the case in New Hampshire. L. 1905, Ch. 42, sec. 1. See supra, description of the New Hampshire taxing system. In Alabama, the plants, property, and franchises necessary for the production, transformation, and distribution of electric current of any person, firm or corporation organized for the developing of hydro electric power *for the use of the public*, are, in consideration of the benefits to be derived by the public, exempt from taxation of all description, until ten years after the beginning of the construction of any such plant. (Does not include land upon which plants are already erected, or plants already in operation. These are taxed as are individuals.) Code sec. 2069, as amended by Act July 27, 1907, sec. 5 (p. 520).

The Wisconsin Tax Commission, in its report for the year 1909, pp. 97-102, outlines the system of taxing these companies in Wisconsin, and discusses at some length the feasibility of changing the present system. The outline and discussion covers both river improvement and power transmission companies, and reads as follows:

RIVER IMPROVEMENT COMPANIES.

"There is a class or group of public service corporatinos existing in the state which seems to require separate con sideration. The group includes all that may come under the general designation of river improvement companies Many of them were formed years ago to facilitate the transportation and storage of logs and other forest products on the various streams of the state, having authority under general laws or special acts to make various improvements in streams for such purposes and to charge and collect tolls for the use of such improvements. Some of such companies are no longer active in the exercise of the functions mentioned, and as to most of them their operations and importance to the public have greatly diminished and will go on diminishing with the continued depletion of the forests. But where such corporations have virtually ceased to exercise their original functions, the dams constructed by them and the rights to overflow lands by means of such dams, are for the most part held and maintained for water power purposes when serviceable for such uses. In some instances the opportunity to use such dams by hydraulic power has been utilized while the corporation owning the same continued to exercise its public service function as a river improvement company. Indeed, there are cases in which the right to construct and maintain a dam and over-flow lands has been obtained ostensibly for the purpose of improving the navigability of the stream, when in fact the only substantial use ever made has been the utilization of the water power for private purposes. When the original purpose for which river improvements were authorized and maintained has ceased to have substantial existence, the improvements and rights connected therewith are usually still held, it is believed, in the name of the corporation which used the same in exercising its authority as a public service concern. Changes in ownership and control have been accomplished often and perhaps generally by transference of shares of stock in the corporation. It is probable that there has been a change in control in the majority of cases where the original use was in accordance with the ostensible public service purpose and the later use is primarily or wholly for water power purposes. But where there has been a change in the use of those things which are susceptible of other uses, the new use has not always been for private purposes. Sometimes dams and flowage rights originally employed and exercised in aid of navigation are now utilized for power used in operation of an electric lighting plant or an electric railroad, or both, or in part for some such public service business and in part for some private enterprise.

For some years the state has imposed an excise or license fee tax upon these river companies, the provisions thereof

being contained in sections 1222h and 1222i of the statutes. The amount of revenue accruing from this source
for the entire state is relatively unimportant and has
greatly diminished in recent years, as the following figures
will show:

Year ending September 30, 1899..... $1,886
                              1900..... 1,292
                              1901..... 1,578
Nine months ending June 30, 1902...   779
Year ending June 30, 1903.........   558
                              1904.........   395
                              1905.........   316
                              1906.........   346
                              1907.........   289
                              1908.........   252

But the license tax mentioned is not in lieu of other
forms of taxation. The property and franchises of such
corporations are taxable by local authorities under the general assessment laws, and the amount of taxes thereby imposed may be deducted from the amount of license fees
otherwise chargeable. Some phraseology in section 1222l
might be taken as implying that the local assessment may
be made in disregard of the unit rule referred to, but it
is not considered that the courts would adopt such construction in view of the ruling made in respect to one of
such companies in one of the earlier cases in which the
unit rule was declared.*

It may be doubted whether it is good policy to continue
the taxation of this class of public service corporations by
the two methods just mentioned, in view of the relatively
small amount of revenue produced by the license fee tax
and its continued diminution. If the unit rule for ad
valorem assessment of the property and franchises of these
corporations is to be adhered to, adequate provisions should
be made for working details, and consideration should be
given to the question whether it is practicable for local
assessors, to make such assessment. The various dams and
other structures and works, and the real estate items which

* Yellow River Imp. Co. v. Wood county, 81 Wis. 554.

make up the physical property of such companies are often
widely separated one from another and frequently located in
assessment districts far apart.† It would be impracticable
for the assessors of the different districts to get together, to
say nothing of their difficulty in agreeing either upon the
valuation of the unit or the basis for apportionment of revenues. The principal office of such companies is not usually
located in the district in which any considerable portion oi
the physical property is situated or in which the company's
franchises are chiefly exercised, except in the case of some
of the corporations operating a local boom system for storing and sorting logs. In advising a working plan adequate provisions must be made for those cases in which the
property of such companies is now to some extent devoted
to uses for private purposes.

POWER TRANSMISSION COMPANIES.

Similar in some respects to some of the public service corporations mentioned above are the companies engaged in the
converting of water power into electric energy and the
transmission thereof to points at greater or less distance
for various purposes. Most of such enterprises are of recent origin, but the number has been increasing in recent
years and doubtless will continue to increase until the
available unused water powers of the state have been utilized. In respect to some of them the enterprise represents quite large investments of capital and the power
plants and transmission lines are valuable and important
properties, demanding, or at least justifying, careful consideration in any scheme of property taxation. Whether
the situation, character and uses of such properties are
such as to warrant or render advisable any special method
for their taxation, is the problem for consideration.

There are many purely private manufacturing concerns.
usually incorporated, which derived the power used in

---

† A conspicuous example of wide spread activities and widely scattered physical properties is afforded in the case of the river improvement company whose authority and jurisdiction are in part set forth
in chapter 335, laws of 1907.

their manufacturing establishments from water power plants, the hydraulic power being converted into electric current and transmitted by wire to motors in the factory. In such cases, where the manufacturing company owns the power and transmission plant, the conversion and transmission of the power is merely a feature of the company's business, and the power plant itself is simply a part of the property employed in manufacture. There would seem to be hardly more reason for a special method of assessing and taxing water power plants thus used than there would be in respect to the ordinary steam power plants in mills and factories, unless the existence of a transmission line, often extending into more than one district, affords ground for distinction.

But the case is quite different where the development and transmission of power and its sale to consumers is undertaken as a business by itself, or as the chief business of the company engaging therein. In some of such cases the purchasers of the power are engaged in operating lighting plants or other public utilities, and when this is the situation it gives the power-transmission company the semblance at least of a public service concern. Sometimes the power-transmission company is itself directly in operating some public utility requiring the use of a portion of its power, being to that extent clearly a public service company. Indeed it is believed there may be found almost every shade of difference in the character of the activities of power-transmission companies, ranging from the case of those which use the greater portion of their own power in the direct operation of a public utility or some private enterprise conducted by the same company, to the case of those who do nothing more than to develop, transmit and sell power for such price as may be obtainable without reference to the character of the use to which it may be devoted. Like some of the other corporations mentioned in this chapter, the physical property and the activities of these transmission companies often extend into several assessment districts. In some instances they extend beyond the borders of the state. The power developing plant is usually located in a district which may

be anywhere from a few miles to fifty or more miles from
the place or places where the power is delivered to consumers, and the connecting transmission line may, and
often does, extend across a large number of assessment
districts. Some of these properties are of great magnitude, representing an investment of millions of dollars in
a single plant, and most others are of very considerable
importance. It seems wholly unnecessary to attempt any
statement of the practical difficulties which confront local
assessors in undertaking to value the property of these
transmission companies, whether assessed under the unit
rule or otherwise, in view of what has been said on the
same subject respecting the other corporations mentioned.
Enough has been said, it is believed, to indicate the need
of devising a more practical and scientific method than now
afforded under the general assessment laws if it can be
done by acts not repugnant to constitutional restrictions.

The commission has been unable, within the time available, to work out any definite plan for better methods for
the taxation of the properties mentioned in the foregoing
discussion. It seeks only to present the situation sufficiently to indicate the importance of the subject and the
need for legislation adequate to overcome the faults in
the law now applicable thereto. An effort will be made
during the coming legislative session to devise and formu-
late such plan as will seem efficient to that end upon further study and investigation.''

EXHIBIT 27.

STORAGE RESERVOIRS AT THE HEADWATERS OF THE WISCONSIN RIVER AND THEIR RELATION TO STREAM FLOW.

By C. B. STEWART, Consulting Engineer, of Madison, Wisconsin.

The following paper is an abstract of the results of an investigation and report on the above subject to the Wisconsin State Board of Forestry, prepared by C. B. Stewart, Consulting Hydraulic Engineer, Madison, Wisconsin.

Storage reservoirs controlled by the Wisconsin Valley Improvement Co.

The headwaters of the Wisconsin River are located in the northern part of Wisconsin in Vilas and Oneida counties in numerous lakes and swamps. Plate 1 shows these counties and the main lakes and their tributory drainage areas in which the main branches at the headwaters of the river have their source. About 19 of these natural lakes having a total area of water surface of about 58 square miles, and a tributory drainage area of about 580 square miles as shown in the table have been made into storage reservoirs by means of dams at the outlets of the lakes and are at present used by the Wisconsin Valley Improvement Company for storage of flood waters.

The operation of these storage reservoirs throughout the year is about as follows: In the spring of the year as soon as the natural flow of the river below the reservoirs is sufficient to supply the needs of the power plants nearest the headwaters, the gates at the outlets of the lakes are closed and water collected. When the summer drought begins the gates are slightly opened and the stored water used to increase the summer flow in the river. During the fall of the year the natural flow of the river again increases as a result of the fall rains, the gates are closed and the reservoirs partially refilled. This storage and any remaining from the summer period is gradually used during the late fall months and winter, the longer period of drought, when the precipitation is slight and being stored in the form of snow.

On the shores of some of the more attractive lakes, summer homes and summer resorts have been built and in order to obtain the use of these lakes for storage purposes it has been necessary to limit the range of fluctuation of these lakes in the summer months. On a few of the lakes during the summer season and on all during the winter season the water is gradually lowered and the lakes with their outlets allowed to resume a condition of nature as nearly as possible, the gates being left wide open and natural flow occurring. The effect of regulation by gates and holding spring floods until a later period of the summer is to shorten the summer period of low lake level and keep higher at least to some extent the low water that would occur under conditions with a natural outlet. The question of regulating and keeping up the lake levels during the summer season on the lakes where the summer resorts interests were suffering has been carefully investigated during the recent summer season of 1910. The lack of rainfall on the upper Wisconsin River during this season has been unprecedented so far as record shows, and resulted in lowering the levels of the lakes considerably below normal low water, where they have been allowed to resume a condition of nature with gates wide open. This condition would probably not occur more often than once in ten years, but in order to avoid such contingency in the future, new low water limits in certain cases have practically been agreed on. These low water limits are at least as high as normal low water level. It was found possible in these cases to raise the high water limits slightly so that the allowable range of fluctuation of lake level remained the same. In other cases the thoroughfares between the lakes were the cause of complaints and harmony has been brought about by a combination of raising the low water limits slightly and an agreement for the dredging of the thoroughfares, the cost of dredging to be divided equally between the interested parties, the Wisconsin Valley Improvement Company and the summer resort interests. In

Plate I.

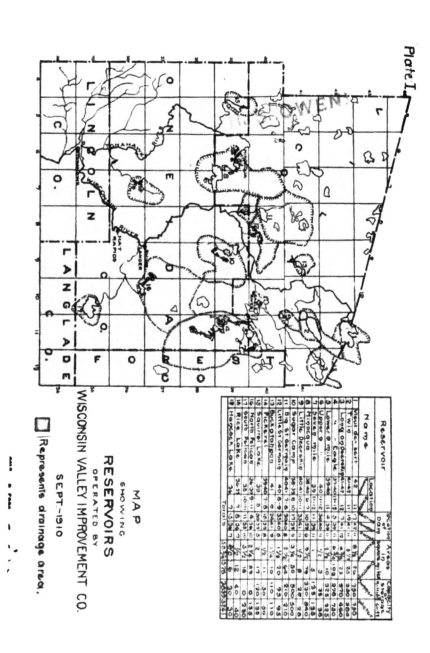

MAP
SHOWING
RESERVOIRS
OPERATED BY
WISCONSIN VALLEY IMPROVEMENT CO.
SEPT.-1910

☐ Represents drainage area.

this matter it should in justice be stated that the results of investigation have shown that the Wisconsin Valley Improvement Company have been acting in good faith, have in all cases investigated, lived strictly within their legal rights and have shown willingness to co-operate equally with the Summer resort interests in the matter of expense incident to main taining suitable boating conditions on these lakes and thorough-fares.

Table 1, following, is an approximate estimate of the amount of money invested on the various lakes under control by the Wisconsin Valley Improvement Company for private homes, and Summer resorts, also the number of guests that can be accommodated and number of gasoline launches.

TABLE 1.

Name of Lake.	No. of private homes.	No. resorts and clubs.	Guests accommodated in resorts and clubs.	No. gasoline launches.	Investment in buildings.
Vieux des Sert............	3	2	40	2	$11,000
Twin	2	2	130	16	18,500
Long on Deerskin.............	....	2	60	7	16,000
Long on Eagle...............	40	7	125	80	42,000
Minocqua	40	8	270	150	125,000
Sugar Camp................	....	1	15	....	2,500
Big St. Germain.............	2	3	85	1	14,000
Little St. Germain...........	....	3	30	....	6,000
Buckatahpon............	....	1	15	....	2,000
Squirrell	1	1	35	2	9,000
N. Pelican	2	1	45	1	14,000
S. Pelican	36	2	110	30	35,000
Totals	126	33	960	239	$295,000

The total number of private homes, clubs and resorts is seen to be about 160, and the number of guests which can be accommodated about 1000 and the money invested in building about $300,000. In July, 1910, the resorts were about one-fourth filled, the reason of the absence of guests in most cases was considered to be due to scare from fire, though in a few cases low water conditions were claimed to be the cause.

While there is an apparent conflict between the summer resort interests and the water power interests in that the former desires the minimum fluctuation during the summer season, while the latter desires the maximum, yet by limiting the low water levels and the dredging of thoroughfares as proposed, conditions quite favorable to the summer resort interests will be secured.

When more storage becomes available from additional reservoirs it will be possible to hold up the summer level on the more important lakes until the latter part of the summer season thus accommodating the summer resort interests without material decrease in benefit to the water power interests.

Relation of storage reservoirs to stream flow.

In order to intelligently study the question of benefits resulting from increased uniformity of stream flow and of reasonably high and low water limits for the various lakes it has become necessary to investigate the subject of stream flow of the Wisconsin River in considerable detail. Referring to the river as a whole it would be well to state that the total fall developed and utilized by water power plants at the present time amounts to about 295 feet, while a future development of about an equal amount can be counted on with reasonable certainty. It should be the policy of the state to encourage to the fullest extent possible both the summer resort interest and that of the water powers along the river. Each storage reservoir should if possible have sufficient capacity or allowable range of fluctuation of water levels to hold the flood waters of the spring months in an average year. Actual observed data of these fluctuations have been observed during the past three years and furnish a good guide for dry years. For average and wet years the data are yet incomplete. For these years existing high water marks have been used as indicating the desirable high water limits.

Referring to the watershed of the upper Wisconsin river, the soil of Vilas and Oneida county consists of glacial drift of porus sandy material, varying from pure sand in some places to sand mixed with a slight amount of clay in others. The land is more or less rolling but the slopes are gradual with the variations in elevation not exceeding about one hundred feet. Excepting about three or four per cent of the land which has been cleared the land consists almost entirely of cut over land with second growth of timber, about one-half of the land having been burned over in the last two or three years. The character of the topography and soil together with any lack of noticable erosion indicates that surface flow from rains will not occur except during periods of the early spring when the ground is frozen. Fortunately the distribution of rainfall throughout the year is such that the heavy rains occur during the summer and fall months so that the injurious results of surface flow are greatly reduced. The following table shows the average monthly precipitation in inches on the Wisconsin Watershed above Merrill for 14 years 1896—1909.

January 0.89
February 1.00
March 1.82
April 2.15
May 3.25
June 3.95
July 3.91
August 3.42
September 4.20
October 2.94
November 1.89
December 1.01
                                     ———
                    Total..............30.43

Plate II shows the result of the investigation for determining the yield of the watershed of the upper Wisconsin River. The curves, numbered 2, 3 and 4 are direct results from gage readings of the river at Hat Rapids and Merrill, while curves numbered 1, 5, 6, and 7 are deducted from curve number 2 by allowing for the rainfall and evaporation on the lake surface.

Curve No. 1 shows that for the 4 dry years the average annual runoff for all land surface was about 15 inches on the watershsed. Curve No. 4 at Hat Rapids with a drainage area having about 10 per cent water surface the average annual run off decreased to about 12½ inches. For a drainage area having about 50 per cent water surface the average annual run off would be about 4½ inches. The effect on stream flow of a large percentage of water surface at the headwaters is seen to be very marked.

On the 580 square miles of drainage area under control by the reservoirs of the Wisconsin Valley Improvement Company there are about 84 spuare miles of water surface, thus making about 14 per cent water surface on the drainage area. Curve No. 5 has been drawn to represent the average condition of these lakes under control. The upper line represents the regulated discharge from the reservoirs, represented in cubic feet per second per square mile. The total storage on these lakes is about 5 billion cubic feet giving an average fluctuation of level of about 3 feet. Were these lakes in a condition of nature without dams at their outlets there would be a natural fluctuation of lake level resulting from natural storage. The amount of this natural fluctuation of lake level cannot be known as it would depend on local conditions. Experience from similarily located lakes would indicate that if in a condition of nature there would be a fluctuation of about 1½ feet or about ½ that obtained by regulation. This would give a storage capacity of about 2½ billion cubic feet in excess of natural storage and from which actual benefit would be obtained. In the diagram, curve No. 5, the medial line represents the aproximate discharge that would have occurred were the lakes in a condition of nature. The increase in stream flow in cubic feet per second per square mile can be taken from the diagram for the summer and winter seasons. Table 2 shows the benefits obtained since the summer season 1908.

Plate II.

MASS CURVES

Showing the

YIELD OF THE WATERSHED OF THE UPPER WIS. RIVER

and

EFFECT OF VARIOUS AMOUNTS OF STORAGE

DRY YEARS 1906-1910

Explanation regarding curves

Curve No.	Runoff from watershed located	Approx. drainage area in sq. mi.	Percent water surface	Remarks
1	Between H.R.& Merrill	1530	0	Approx. flow from land surface alone. Deduced from 2
2	" " "	1530	4	From daily gage readings
3	Merrill and above	2600	6 ½	" " "
4	Hat Rapids & above	1070	10	" " "
5	Between H.R.& Merrill	1530	14	Deduced from No.2 less for sp.gr.area under read by R.R.Co.
6	" " "	1530	25	Deduced from No.2
7	" " "	1530	50	" "

Depletion = 3.25" = 20 B cu ft for 12" req at Merrill

1909

1910

950 cu.sec

Inc

Draft diagram

4200 M cu. ft.

Ave. yearly runoff (av.) = 14.95

Ave = 14.1

Ave = 13.5

Ave = 12.6

2.5" depl = 6 ¾ B cu ft

Cub.

Note:-
The mass diagram of ...

... ted by Wis Valley
... q.mi with 14% water sur
... charge without
... ulation
... ly to lake includes
... fall and evaporation
... tself.

TABLE 2.

BENEFITS FROM STORAGE RESERVOIRS OPERATED BY THE WISCONSIN VALLEY IMPROVEMENT CO.

Season.	Storage draft.	Head utilized.	Period of service.	Increase in flow cu. ft. per second.	Water H. P.	Total cost.	Cost per water H. P.
	Million Cu. Ft.		Months.				
Summer 1908....	8,480	198	2½	270	5,900	$7,645	$1.30 for 2½ Mo.
Winter 1908-1909....	2,160	200	4	105	2,380	8,413	3.50 for 4 Mo.
Summer 1909	2,750	235	4	130	3,460	9,470	2.75 for 4 Mo.
Winter 1909-1910	3,290	244	3½	180	4,950	10,680	2.18 for 3½ Mo.
Summer 1910	1,450	276	3½	80	2,500	9,059	3.60 for 3½ Mo.

The increase in water horse power and cost per water horse power for the time of service is also shown. The column "Total Cost" of service is made up of cost of maintenance and 6 per cent interest on the capital invested as shown by reports of the Secretary of Wisconsin Valley Improvement Company.

Plates III, IV and V are hyhrographs of the River and show graphically the effect of increase of stream flow during the summer and winter seasons. The percentage of the increase in flow to the average monthly flow at any time for the three places, Hat Rapids, Merrill and Necedah are readily taken from the diagrams. Experience during the past year in Wisconsin has shown the great importance of increasing the Storage Reservior system. The results of the investigation of the yield of the watershed of the upper Wisconsin River, Plate II shows that for dry years the maximum flow at any point cannot exceed a rate of flow determined from the average annual run off of about 12 inches.

Plate VI shows the run off of the Wisconsin River and relation of stream flow to storage capacity for 12 inch regulation.

The actual economical limits of storage capacity can only be determined after topographical data are available. The stream flow limits however, are an important element in the solution of the problem. The benefit that would result from Reservoir construction on a basis of 12 inch regulation the limits for dry years would be approximately as given in Table 3.

TABLE 8.

INVESTIGATION OF STORAGE RESERVOIRS AND STREAM FLOW ON THE WISCONSIN RIVER.

Amount of add. reservoir capacity in billion cubic feet.	Approx. location and drainage area in square miles.	Present approx. ave. min. flow for portion of dry year cu. ft. per sec.	Approx. min. flow for stated regulation cu. ft. per sec.	Approx. ave. increase in flow for portion of dry year.	Approximate average increase in 24 hour H. P. 300' head.			Probable min. ave. yearly return from sale of storage power @ $5.00 W. H. P.
					Water H. P.	Actual H. P.	Months' service.	
1	Hat Rapids—1,070	565 for 5 months.	645 for 8"	80 for 5 months.	2,730	2,040	5	$13,650
3	Hat Rapids—1,070	580 for 6 months.	775 for 10"	195 for 6 months.	6,683	5,000	6	33,175
6¼	Hat Rapids—1,070	650 for 8 months.	950 for 12"	300 for 8 months.	10,250	7,700	8	51,250
	6¼ Hat Rapids.							
13½	7¼ Tomahawk—1,900	3,070 for 8 months.	1,700 for 12"	650 for 8months.	22,030	16,500	—	110,250
	6¼ Hat Rapids.							
	7¼ Tomahawk.							
20	6½ Merrill—2,600	1,345 for 8 months.	2,310 for 12"	965 for 8 months.	32,700	24,500	—	163,500

46

The rate of five dollars per water horse power for from 5 to 8 months' service per year has been assumed as a probable minimum rate for the sale of storage power and must be taken as subject to change should further investigation show that a higher rate would be necessary to yield a reasonable return on the investment.

It is very important that the state should gain information at an early date in regard to the storage problem on all the main rivers of the state. All natural basins at the headwaters of the rivers and main branches should be carefully investigated and if found more suitable for storage purposes and benefit to the river as a whole than for local power development, the site should be reserved and developed accordingly.

The U. S. Government engineers in their preliminary surveys of the Wisconsin and Chippewa River in 1882 found large storage possibilities but conditions of development along the shores of these lakes and rivers since then have probably progressed to such a point that it will be impossible to obtain one half of what may then have been feasible.

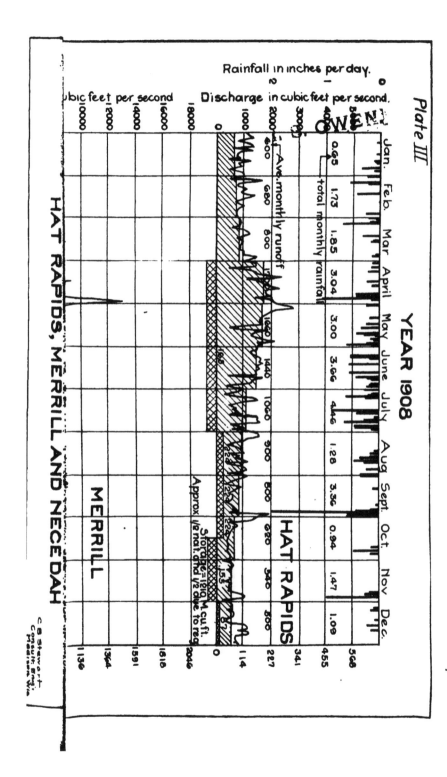

Plate III

YEAR 1908

HAT RAPIDS, MERRILL AND NECEDAH

C. B. Stewart
Consult. Engi.
Madison. Wis.

Plate IV.

YEAR 1909

Rainfall in inches per day.

Discharge in cubic feet per second

Feet per second.

Average monthly runoff

Total monthly rainfall

Regulated flow

Storage = 3460 M. cu. ft.

Storage = 1840 M.cu.ft.

HAT RAPIDS

MERRILL

HAT RAPIDS, MERRILL AND NECEDAH

C. B. Stewart

Jan. Feb. Mar. Apr. May June July Aug. Sept. Oct. Nov. Dec.

0.53 1.26 1.29 2.95 2.11 3.56 5.26 2.41 2.45 1.71 4.48 0.93

Plate V.

Rainfall in inches per day.

Discharge in cubic feet per second.

cond.

16000
18000
20000
22000

0

1000
2000
3000
4000
5000

Jan. Feb. March A ril May June Jul

YEAR 1910

Oct. Nov. Dec.

568
435
841
227
114
0
2500
2272
2046
1610

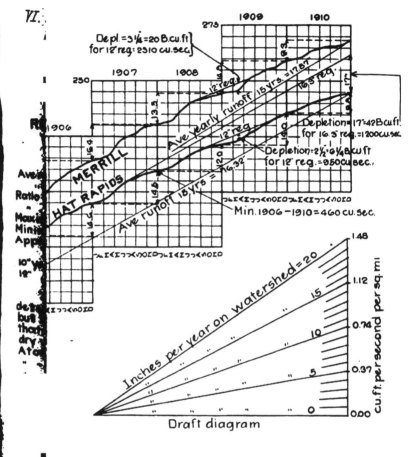

Depl.=3¼=20 B.cu.ft for 12'reg.=2310 cu.sec.

Ave.yearly runoff 15 yrs.=17.87

Depletion=17÷42 B.cu.ft for 16.5'reg.=1200 cu.sec.

Depletion=2½÷6¼ B.cu.ft for 12'reg.=850 cu.sec.

MERRILL

HAT RAPIDS

Ave.runoff 15 yrs.=16.32

Min. 1906-1910 = 460 cu.sec.

Inches per year on watershed = 20

Draft diagram

cu.ft. per second per sq.mi

1.48
1.12
0.74
0.37
0.00

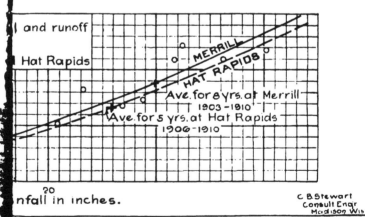

l and runoff

Hat Rapids

MERRILL

HAT RAPIDS

Ave. for 8 yrs. at Merrill
1903-1910
Ave. for 5 yrs. at Hat Rapids
1906-1910

nfall in inches.

C.B.Stewart
Consult.Engr.
Madison Wis

"EXHIBIT 28."

THE INTIMATE RELATION OF FOREST COVER TO STREAM FLOW.

By E. M. GRIFFITH, STATE FORESTER.

1910.

One of the most valuable of Wisconsin's resources is her water powers. As the state has no deposits of coal, the great source of energy for manufacturers, for transportation, for light and heat is in the many water powers that are well distributed over the state. It is of the greatest importance to the industrial interests of Wisconsin that these water powers be developed and utilized to their highest capacity and protected by the construction of reservoirs and the maintainance of a forest cover on all watersheds.

A uniform stream flow is of the utmost importance to the proper utilization of water powers, as the usefulness of a power must be measured largely by its head at low water flow.

It has been a common experience in Wisconsin for many years past, following upon the large lumbering operations in the state, that the thaws of spring have brought on more or less heavy floods and an enormous volume of water has been discharged through our steam channels within a comparatively short period of time and beside the inordinate waste of power and loss of water, a great deal of damage was done by erosion of the banks. By summer the same streams are reduced to a mere trickle and even our largest rivers but thinly cover their erosion-widened channels, while great clogging shoals of sand appear above the surface of the water. The great problem is to save the damaging flood waters of spring to supplement the summer flow.

A great deal can be accomplished by the operation of artificial reservoirs but the maintainance of a forest cover upon the upper watersheds is necessary, even with artificial reservoirs; and with an adequate area under forest cover, artificial reservoirs might be dispensed with.

Many people do not understand just how forests affect the regimen of streams. A comparison of conditions in the forest and in the open will make this clearer. In the spring the snow in the open is melted rapidly by the sun and wasted rapidly by the winds, although much of the moisture is dissipated by evaporation and the water is formed very rapidly by the melting snow and flows off all slopes without hindrance because the frozen ground has a hard impermeable surface. Even in summer there may be similar conditions in the open. The rain will flow quickly over the sunbaked ground, rushing into whatever natural channels are available, not finding permeable soil.

In the forest on the contrary, and especially in the pine forest, the snow is sheltered from the sun's rays and protected from the sweep of drying winds. It melts very slowly and gradually. In the cedar swamps the Indians find snow or ice for their sick far into the summer season. The water formed by the melting snow does not flow off over the surface. It is held by the thick layer of leaves and twigs that forms the forest floor and sinks gradually into the soil underneath which is not only very permeable but contains an intricate network of rootlets and roots along which the water finds its way downward deep into the earth, whence it reappears long afterward through underground streams and springs, forming the small streams that feed our rivers. The summer rains also reach the forest soil gradually through the dense mid-season foliage, which drips water for hours after a rain, and are received into the soil, which yields them up gradually to the stream channels, as they are needed. In the open, the rains flow off rapidly over the ground surface and hard rains on bare ground beat the soil and wash it away, forming little gullies and then larger ones, and clogging the stream channels with detritus. The difference in the same soil in the open and under forest cover can be seen by examining an unsheltered road through a forest and the soil on either side. After a rain the road will be muddy but no matter how saturated the forest soil, it will be porous and grainy and one can walk over it without getting his shoes muddy.

Wisconsin has no mountains and therefore has no need to guard against sudden mountain torrents, with the accompanying loss of surface soil and the burying of fertile valleys under sand and gravel; but the configuration of the state is sufficiently varied to conduce to the production of floods and very serious ones, and the creation of innumerable reservoirs alone could never prevent certain serious evils. Much water might be stored and saved, but reservoirs could never prevent the sudden melting of snow on frozen ground, nor the washing away of soil and the clogging of both stream channels and reservoirs with sand and detritus.

The water that issues from forested watersheds and that flows in forest streams, is remarkably clear. The forest soil is not only porous but it is bound together by the root of trees and undergrowth and the water filters through it instead of beating upon it and carrying portions of it away. Of course the erosive power of water charged with sand and gravel, is very much greater than that of clear water. The Mississippi river is a tragic example of the evils of deforestation, and the United States government has recognized the source of the evil in granting the forestry departments of both Minnesota and Wisconsin a tract of 20,000 acres, so as to bring the upper headwaters of the river under forest cover. No amount of dredging will make a permanent deep water channel. The planting of trees has held the banks intact on limited areas, but with the varying flow, sands are continually shifting, channels widening, and the level of the stream-bed rising, while tons of soil are continually carried out through the mouth of the river.

Our water power resources are not only incalculably benefited by a uniform stream flow, but they become of little value with a widely fluctuating flow and all its accompanying evils, and although the operation of reservoirs will mitigate the evils, it will not cure them. The almost immediate and always disastrous effect upon stream flow when forests upon the headwaters of rivers are destroyed, has long been recognized in all parts of the world where forestry is practiced, but as this beneficial effect of the forest has been denied by certain interests in Wisconsin, the following authorities are quoted and a few examples of the many which might be given.

The theory of the relation of forest cover to stream flow and soil stability is as follows:

Gifford Pinchot says: "Both wide experience and scientific investigation have shown that there are two functions exercised by the forest in relation to stream flow.

1. Its tendency to reduce the difference between high and low water, an influence which is of the utmost importance in the distribution of flood crests, and in maintaining a steady flow of water during the different seasons of the year and during cycles of dry and wet years.

2. Its value as a surface protection against soil erosion, thus reducing the solid burden of storm waters, and decreasing the deposits of sand and silt, which are the causes of shallow and changing channels.

These two functions follow from the very nature of the forest as a soil cover. The roots of trees penetrate through the soil to the underlying rock, where they fix themselves in the crevices, and in this way hold in place the loose soil and prevent slipping and washing. The crowns of the trees break the force of the rain and also protect the soil from being carried away to the lower valleys during heavy storms. The leaves and the branches allow the rain to reach the ground but gradually; after a rain. water continues to drip from the crown for several hours, and the soil is thus enabled to absorb the greater part of it. Screened from the rays of the sun and covered with a surface milch of fallen leaves and humus, the soil remains loose and granular in structure and is therefore capable of imbibing and retaining water with spongelike capacity. It is strewn with fallen leaves, branches and trunks, and traversed by a network of dead and live roots which impede the superficial run off of water after heavy storms. This retardation of the superficial run-off allows more of it to sink into the ground through the many channels left in the soil by decayed roots. Surface run-off of rain water is wasteful and destructive, and unless artificially controlled serves as a rule no useful purpose and may inflict great loss. Sub-surface drainage makes the best use of the total precipitation that reaches the ground. It serves both for the sustenance of plant life and for the flow of streams. Accordingly the agency of the forest cover in increasing the seepage run-off at the expense of the surface run-off is the most important function which the forest performs in relation to the water supply.

A common conception of the effect of forest destruction upon climate is that it reduces the amount of rainfall. Because springs become dry and streams shrink in a deforested region, it is assumed that less rain must fall. Whether or not there be any truth in this assumption (I believe there is), it is certian that the main cause of the observed facts is the profound effect which forest destruction has upon the course which the water takes after it reaches the ground. The greatest influence of the forest is not upon the amount of rain that falls, but on what becomes of the rain after it falls. The water that sinks into the ground passes for greatly varying distances beneath the surface before reappearing, and is thus drawn off gradually from the forested watershed and supplies the brooks with pure water relatively free from detritus.''

B. E. Fernow in ''Economics of Forestry'' says:

''The philosophy of the influence on waterflow rests mainly upon the recognition that the rain and snow waters penetrate more reaily a forest-covered soil than one that is bared of this protective cover. The action here is of a threefold nature; first, the mechanical obstruction which the foliage offers reduces the amount of the water which reaches the soil and lengthens the time during which it can do so; the foliage, together with the loose litter of the forest floor, also reduces the compacting effect of the raindrops and the drying effect of sun and wind, and keeps the soil granular, so that the water can easily percolate; then the mechanical obstruction which the litter, underbrush, and trunks, and possibly here and there moss, offer to the rapid surface drainage of waters, lengthens the time during which this percolation may take place; and thirdly, the network of deeply penetrating roots, live and decayed, offers additional channels for a change of surface drainage into subdrainage. .* * * Particular interest in this connection attaches to the influence of forest cover on the melting of snow masses, which gives rise to spring floods. In the dense forest, the snow in usually less deep, a part being intercepted by the crowns of trees and evaporated, and lies more uniformly, owing to the absence of drifting winds. It is a well-noted experience that it will lie in the shade of the woods from one to two weeks longer. i. e. melt so much more slowly. These elements of distribution in space and time must have an influence upon the rapidity of surface flow, and it the soil is not frozen, time is given for precolation and gradual removal. * * * This forest effect on the run-off of terrestrial waters is naturally greatest and most important in mountainous regions, where the water has the tendency to collect quickly, and to be carried off rapidly, but it also exists in the level plain, where it has the tendency to elevate the general ground-water level and thereby make a reserve available during times of drouth.''

The few following examples are given as showing the effect of forest cover on stream flow:

"Mr. W. B. Greeley of the U. S. Forest Service made a careful investigation of two streams in the Catskills. One, Esopus Creek, was well timbered, having not more than 15 per cent of cleared land upon its basin. The Walkill has 85 per cent. of cleared land and the remaining forest cover was confined to small scattered wood lots, but its topography was such that there could be water storage by natural reservoirs. The difference in the two streams were as follows:

1. The slope of the Esopus basins are twice as steep as those of the Walkill.

2. The fall of the Esopus is six times as rapid as that of the Walkill.

3. The topography of the Esopus basin is much more simple and direct than that of the Walkill.

4. The Esopus has no natural reservoirs, whereas a relatively large percentage of the Walkill basin consists of swamps and ponds.

The question was whether forest cover on the one hand or moderate topography, extensive natural reservoirs, and favorable geological conditions on the other exert the greatest relative influence in storing precipitation and equalizing stream discharge.

It was found that the combined influence of the moderate topography, natural reservoirs, and favorable geological conditions of the Walkill is somewhat stronger in promoting evenness of stream flow than the compact forest cover of the Esopus basin.

At the same time the margin of difference between the regularity of the two streams is so small as to establish beyond doubt that the forest cover of the Esopus does exert a strong conserving and regulating influence upon the flow of that stream. This is especially true when we recall how unfavorable the other factors of topography and geology upon that catchment area are to equable stream flow. The forest cover of the Esopus thus appears to overcome to a large degree the unfavorable effects of steep topography, hard and dense surface rocks, and marked deficiency in natural storage facilities. It reduces the flow of that mountain stream to a regularity almost equal to that of a lowland type of stream where exactly opposite topography conditions prevail.''

Mr. C. C. Vermeule in the report of the State Geologist for New Jersey for 1895 says:

"It is a matter of common observation that at such times rivers continue to flow when rainfall is very much less than the evaporation, and indeed, for long periods when there is no rainfall at all. Anything which tends to increase this amount of water held in the ground, and to regulate its discharge into the streams, tends to give a larger flow, and to shorten the periods of very low water in the streams during droughts, and with this increased capacity of the ground to absorb rain comes also less frequent floods. The more water that is drained out from the soil the more can be absorbed when the heavy rains come at the end of the droughts. Humus in the forest forms a great sponge, and of itself holds a large amount of water, while it and the inequalities caused by tree roots, etc., tend to prevent the water flowing over the surface and the roots of the trees provide channels by which the water percolates into the sub-soil readily. In this way the forest will easily absorb a larger amount of water than open lands. A high state of cultivation also has a tendency to increase the capacity of the ground to absorb water because of constant loosening of the surface and the facilities provided for ready drainage. In this way cultivation, like forests, tends to render floods less frequent, but the effect of the drainage of the soil is that the ground water absorbed is fed out more rapidly to the streams during the early months of a dry period than is the case in forests; consequently, the ground water is sooner exhausted, and the duration of the low stages of the rivers during protracted droughts is thereby lengthened. Barren watersheds offer much less capacity for absorption of rainfall.

There is no humus or other matter on the surface to retain the rain, and the ground becomes hard and resists free percolation. The difference between forested and deforested watersheds is very well illustrated by the Passaic and the Raritan respectively, while some of our small red sandstone watersheds are good types of barren country.

We have, in the following table, contrasted these types, the data being obtained from the Report on Water Supply. This table shows in inches of rainfall the amount of water which would flow off to the several streams from their watersheds for each month, during a drought of such a character that all conditions from rainfall, or depletions from evaporation, to the ground water are suspended, the water here shown being entirely water of drainage.

YIELD OF SPRINGS ON VARIOUS TYPES OF WATER SHEDS DURING DROUGHT, IN INCHES OF RAINFALL.

Month	Passaic type of forest watershed	Raritan type of highly cultivated watershed	Type of barren watershed
First.............................	1.16	1.43	.94
Second	.54	.64	.33
Third.............................	.40	.45	.26
Fourth............................	.33	.35	.20
Fifth.............................	.32	.30	.14
Sixth.............................	.31	.27	.12
Seventh...........................	.30	.25	.10
Eighth............................	.29	.23	.08
Ninth.............................	.28	.22	.07
Total.............................	3.93	4.14	2.29

It will be observed that while the Raritan and the Passaic show nearly the same total amount of drainage, the Raritan gives up this water faster in the early months, and therefore its springs become sooner exhausted and it runs lower toward the last of the drought. The barren ground, having absorbed much less water, has less flow from springs throughout. How important this is upon the dry season flow of these streams becomes apparent from the following table:

FLOW IN GALLONS DAILY PER SQUARE MILE DURING THE LAST EIGHT MONTHS OF THE DRIEST YEAR.

Month	Passaic forested	Raritan cultivated	Barren watershed
April	597,000	754,000	631,000
May	297,000	325,000	145,000
June	272,000	272,000	139,000
July	207,000	134,000	22,000
August	140,000	89,000	22,000
September	139,000	87,000	23,000
October	129,000	84,000	22,000
November	127,000	93,000	23,000

The conditions here shown are believed to be illustrative of the effect of forests upon stream flow, and the comparative effects of cultivation and barrenness. We have found it a rule that the heavier forested catchments furnish a steadier flow, better sustained during dry periods, and that while they are subject once in a great while to severe floods, nevertheless floods not quite so severe are less frequent than upon deforested catchments not highly cultivated. Flood-flow, it must be remembered, however, is largely a matter of topography, and while floods are heavy and frequent upon the deforested Raritan and Neshminy, the same is true of the well-forested Ramapo and Pequannock, while they are extremely light upon the lightly-wooded Pequest. The economic importance of the effect we have noted lies in the greater value of forested streams for water power, and the smaller storage reservoirs needed thereon to furnish a given daily supply of water to cities. Illustrative of this, the Passaic will furnish for 9 months of the year from 100 square miles of watershed, 45 horsepower on 10 feet fall, whereas the Raritan will furnish but 41 and the barren watershed 28 horsepower. During the other 3 months the Passaic will furnish an average of 36, the Raritan 32 and the barren watershed 20 horsepower. To collect 570,000 gallons per square mile of watershed, we shall need storage reservoirs of the following capacity: Passaic 84,000,000, Raritan 110,000,000, and the barren watersheds 126,000,000 gallons. The difference in cost of collecting a supply at the above rate per square mile, therefore, upon the type of streams selected to represent the forested and those representing the barren conditions, would be about $8,400 per square mile. Both the Passaic and Raritan exceed 800 square miles in catchment. For this area the saving would be $6,720,000.

Taking the same area, we find the excess of water power of the forested stream would be for 100 feet fall, 1,360 horsepower. the value of which. at a rental of $35 per horsepower per annum, would be $47,600 or the interest at 5 per cent. on $952,000.

We do not advance these figures as exact measures of the value of forests, but they may be taken as indicative of the possible financial loss which might result in stream flow alone from deforesting such of our water sheds as are not adapted for cultivation.

It will also be seen how amply this effect of forests in increasing the stream-flow for 5 or 6 months during the latter part of a dry period justifies popular opinion as to a falling off of streams when the forests are cut off. Such effect is very much more likely to impress itself upon the popular mind than increase of evaporation, for this would tend to decrease the total run-off for the year without being very apparent to ordinary observation. Being a much more enduring effect, it would also be more noticeable than any change in the very greatest or least rate of discharge.

Most of the portion of the state now in forest is not adapted to cultivation. It should remain in forest, because it will in no other way yield revenue; because it is needed to maintain the equable flow of our streams, and because it renders beautiful what would otherwise be an unsightly waste. Unless the state is prepared to assume the ownership of forest lands, the continued good condition of the forests can only be secured by instructing the owners how they can improve this condition, and, at the same time, increase their revenues. It is especially important that our highlands forests, for the future gathering grounds of our city water supply, shall continue to be preserved and improved, as they undobtedly have improved during the last quarter century."

Says Mr. Charles A. Stone, of the firm of Stone & Webster, Electrical Engineers, Boston, Mass.:

"One of the most important features in the commercial development of a waterpower enterprise is the uniformity or flow of the stream on which the development is undertaken. Where streams are subject to severe drought or great floods, commercial development is practically impossible. Nature has provided for the uniformity of flow by covering the watersheds at the headwaters of these streams with forests. * * * When these forests are cut off, conditions are entirley changed, and great freshets result."

Mr. Theophilus Parsons, a representative of the manufacturing interests of New England, says:

"New England is largely dependent upon her factories run by water power. The flow of the rivers furnishing this power is growing yearly more uncertain. Both floods and droughts are more frequent. It is plenty or famine. This situation is due to the pernicious cutting of woods along the headwaters of the New England rivers.

I have known the Connecticut for over thirty-six years. It drains an area of four thousand square miles. Until recently the wooded hills kept the flow of the river even. Now, in the spring, we have floods, while in the summer the water sometimes will not run our mills.

This is a question in which every manufacturer on the eastern coast of the United States is interested.".

"Snow will lie in the forest more evenly and continuously than on the open, wind-swept areas. Thereby not only the amount finally remaining for drainage is increased, but the soil is presented from freezing, and is kept open for percolation when the snow melts. The retardation of the melting has been determined by Buhler in Switzerland to be from eight to fourteen days."

Honorable Robert M. La Follette said in his message as Governor of Wisconsin in 1905:

"Probably not more than half a dozen states in the Union, are so abundantly supplied wtih natural water power as Wisconsin, and no state in the middle west is comparable to it in this respect. More than one thousand lakes, widely distributed within its borders, form natural reservoirs, furnishing sources of supply to the streams which flow through every section of the state.

We have recently undertaken, at considerable expense, the
establishment of a forestry commission with a view of preserving whatever remains of the forests upon state lands not suited
to agriculture, and the reforesting of these, and such other
lands as can most profitably be used for that purpose. The
state forestry legislation, adopted two years ago, very defective
in many respects, will, it is hoped be so amended as to establish
this important work upon a permanent and efficient basis. It
is referred to in this connection because the preservation of our
forests and the reforesting of lands about the sources and
along the headwaters of our principal streams, are absolutely
essential to the preservation of Wisconsin's splendid water-
powers. The restoration of our forests, and the preservation of
our water powers go hand in hand.''

Governor James O. Davidson in his message in 1909, said:

''Our forest reserve now comprises 300,000 acres of land,
situated in seventeen counties of the state. During the past
two years the state has purchased, through the department,
about 34,000 acres of cut-over lands, an addition to the reserves in Iron, Vilas and Onedia counties, and has entered into
a contract to purchase 1,400 more acres in Vilas county. These
lands, will, in time, be of great value to the state in timber produce, but their greatest value is in protecting the water powers
thereon. The lands preserved by the state are not of value for
agricultural purposes and have been purchased at a small outlay.   The acquiring of other lands for forestry purposes, especially on or near the head waters of our streams, should be
encouraged.''

The governors of all the states at the White House Conference
in May, 1908, adopted the following declaration of principles:

''We urge the continuation and extension of forest policies
adapted to secure the husbanding and renewal of our diminishing timber supply, the prevention of soil erosion, the protection of headwaters, and the maintenance of the purity and
navigability of our streams. We recognize that the private
ownership of forest lands entails responsibilities in the interests of the people and we favor the enactment of laws looking to the protection and replacement of privately owned forests.

We recognize in our waters a most valuable asset of the people

of the United States, and we recommend the enactment of laws
looking to the conservation of water resources for irrigation,
water supply, power and navigation, to the end that navigable
and source streams may be brought under complete control and
fully utilized for every purpose. We especially urge on the
Federal Congress the immediate adoption of a wise, active, and
through waterway policy, providing for the prompt improvement of our streams and the conservation of their watersheds
required for the uses of commerce and the protection of the
interests of our people."

The letter of President Roosevelt transmitting to Congress the
report of the National Conservation Commission contained the
following passage: "I especially commend to the Congress the
facts presented by the Commission as to the relation between
forests and stream flow in its bearing upon the importance of
the forest lands in national ownership. Without an understanding of this intimate relation the conservation of both these
natural resources must largely fail."

The North American Conservation Conference representing
Canada, Mexico and the United States made a declaration of
principles which contained the following:

"We recognize the forests as indispensable to civilization and
public welfare. They furnish material for construction and
manufacture, and promote the habitability of the earth. We regard the wise use, effective protection, especially from fire, and
prompt renewal of the forests on land best adapted to such
use, as a public necessity and hence a public duty devolving
upon all forest owners alike, whether public, corporate or individual.

Forests are necessary to protect the sources of streams,
moderate floods and equalize the flow of waters, temper the
eliment and protect the soil; and we agree that all forests
necessary for these purposes should be amply safeguarded. We
affirm the absolute need of holding for forests, or reforesting,
all lands supplying the headwaters of streams, and we therefore favor the control or acquisition of such lands for the
public."

It is estimated that Wisconsin is blessed with approximately
1,000,000 horsepower in hundreds of water powers widely distributed over the state. Such a wealth of water powers which

in a few years will all be harnessed and made to convey energy
to nearly every city and town, weans everything to the future
of the state, providedthat reasonable, commonsense methods
of stream conservation, which have been tried and long since
proven in old countries, are adopted. The value of our streams
for water power development will rest almost entirely upon the
eveness and uniformity of their flow. Wisconsin is remarkably
fortunate in having such a network of lakes and swamps at the
head-waters of her important rivers, as these catch and hold the
spring freshets and their capacity can be greatly enlarged by
building dams. The lands draining into these lakes at the headwaters of the rivers should be included within the forest reserves
and the forest growth protected.

Fortunately most of these lands are not as valuable for agricultural crops as for timber, and therefore it will not be necessary to keep forests on lands which should be made into farms.

"EXHIBIT 29"·

STATEMENT OF

PROFESSOR D. W. MEAD, OF MADISON, WISCONSIN,

TO

COMMITTEE ON WATER POWERS, FORESTRY AND
DRAINAGE,

OF THE WISCONSIN LEGISLATURE.

. (Revised-1910)

Subjects:

Value of Water Powers.

Forests and Stream Flow.

Water Power Trust.

The Legal Phase.

State Regulation and Control.

Stream Flow Measurements.

Mr. Chairman and Gentlemen: I wish to offer a word of
personal explanation. I come here at your request, to assist
you in any way that I can, and give to you such benefit as I
may of some 25 years of experience in the development of
water resources in many of the United States in the lines of
water supply, water power, drainage, and irrigation. In my
practice, which has been principally that of a civil engineer,
my connection with the University having only extended for
some five years and my professional practice still continuing, I
. 47

have studied these questions very largely in their practical
bearing; but I have endeavored to give them a broad consideration and investigation. I do not appear before you as the representative of any special interests, and I would not consciously
offer any suggestion here that is illogical or in any way in-
equitable. I am here to give you what information I can, let
its effect be what it may on the questions at issue.

Value of Water Powers.

In the consideration of any question, it is important that all
fundamental facts be correctly understood, for deductions based
on misinformation or false promises will necessarily be in error.

I think, therefore, in the consideration of the questions before you it is important that the erroneous impressions which
have been widely circulated in regard to the great value of undeveloped water power should be corrected. In the public
prints statements are frequently made that the undeveloped
water power of this country has a value from $20' to $25 per
horse power per annum. This idea of value is based upon the
general proposition that water running down a stream is energy
going to waste, and the idea is prevalent that he who saves
this waste must necessarily realize richly therefrom.

A rich return would be certain if this energy could be utilized without expense, or if the cost of development were small.
If we could save the vast amount of energy that is going to
waste in the rivers of Wisconsin and apply it to useful purposes without expense of development, a vast economy could
be effected and a rich return would result.

Electrical energy generated from water power is sold in this
country at prices per horse power ranging from $15 at and
near Niagara Falls, New York, to $40 or more in the South and
West, depending on the various conditions under which it is
sold. Whatever its price, that price must represent not only
the earnings of the water power itself but of the invested capital necessary for its development, and the expense incurred in
its generation.

For developed water power to be profitable, the income derived from it must be sufficient to meet all of the following
items of expense:

1. Interest on value of real estate.

2. Interest on cost of plant.

3. Operating expense of plant.

4. Expenses of management, clerical work, sales and collections.

5. Depreciation, repairs, and maintenance.

6. Taxes and insurance.

7. Interest on value or cost of water power rights.

8. A profit commensurate with the risk involved and also commensurate with the returns from other possible investments.

These items, with the exception of the 7th, must be met in every water power installation to make it commercially successful, and the income must be in excess of the sum of all the other items before any value whatever can be attributed to item 7—the water power itself.

It is exceedingly difficult to reach even a general conclusion as to the value of water power, but there are a few data which may afford some indications. Before the installation of the hydro-electric plant of the Chicago Sanitary District, bids were asked for the leasing of the undeveloped power from the drainage canal, and I understand that the maximum rental offered was $5 per horse power per annum. This power it should be remembered is located within forty miles of the City of Chicago. Power partially developed (dams constructed, but no plant) in the state of Wisconsin has been leased for $5 per horse power per annum in the manufacturing territory along the Fox River. Such a value is above what may be considered a fair value of the average undeveloped water power of either the State or of the United States, although under specially favorable conditions, where fuel is high and power expensive, the actual value of water power may occasionally be greater.

The question "What is the value of water power?" cannot be answered categorically. It is as indefinite as the similar question of "What is the value of a house?" The answer to the question depends entirely upon the circumstances surrounding the power in question, the nature of the market, the expense involved in construction, in operation, in maintainance, and all the fixed and operating charges as outlined above. These matters must all be determined before an intelligent answer to the question is possible.

The cost of developing water powers vary exceedingly. The contingencies and conditions in one place are frequently much more severe than in others. In some places the bedrock comes to the surface and a good foundation is readily obtained and the cost of construction is moderate. In other places the foundation may be deep below the water or insecure and unsafe without any precautions, and there may be great extra expense entailed thereby in the cost of foundations. It may be in one place that the banks of the stream are comparatively close together, and the length of the dam is consequently short and the structure comparatively inexpensive. In another place a very long dam must be constructed with consequent extra expense.

The head available is also an important matter. If a dam can be constructed under favorable circumstances at the top of a natural fall, a dam of small height may develop a high head. Such a dam may perhaps develop several times the power that might be developed with a similay dam if the natural fall were not there—and the cost of development will be correspondingly low. The cost per horse power of any development will depend in the first place upon the first cost of the plant, and in the second place upon the amount of power that can be developed and sold. As these points are taken into consideration, it is evident that there will be a wide divergence in the cost of water powers and no general estimate of cost can be safely made.

It may be said in a general way that there are few places in Wisconsin where hydro-elctric plants can be developed below the cost of $100 per horse power. I would not say there are not places where the cost would not be below that amount; but I will make the general statement that the cost will usually be from $100 to $200 per horse power developed.

The expense of water power development may vary all the way from perhaps as low as $40 per horse power, with the high heads available on some of our Wstern streams and power, delivered at the wheels shaft, to as high, uerhaps, as $350 per horse power with low heads and under favorable conditions with power delivered at the switchboard of the consumer at the end of a long transmission line.

Depreciation is not a large item in the annual cost of water power plants. In the best modern plants, one to two per cent on the total plant cost will usually cover the charge, but occasionally the contingencies of operation in some unfavorable locality will increase the estimate somewhat. Repairs and maintenance vary so much with the design and conditions surrounding a plant that the variation may be considerable, but it cught not to exceed the amount allowed for depreciation.

The cost of the operation of a water power plant also varies greatly with the capacity of the plant and the conditions under which it must be operated. The smaller plants are much more evpensive per horse power to operate at attendance is necessary no matter how small the plant, and the expense of labor per horse power in the smaller plants is frequently double what is in the larger plants. The same remarks will also apply to the general expenses of management, etc.

The cost of power depends on a good many technical considerations which I do not know whether I can explain as fully and as clearly as desirable. One of the important considerations is the manner in which the power is used. If the plant is to furnish a certain quantity of power, the time and manner in which it is to furnish it become important and an element in the cost.

Power will cost less provided it is delivered uniformly and continuously, and will cost more if furnished irregularly with great difference between the maximum and minimum demand. There are practically no power customers that are using power all of the time and to the maximum capacity.

While the term "one thousand horse power" may sean definite, it has a varied significance. It may mean that this is the maximum limit or peak of the load, or it may mean that the customer is carrying a fairly uniform load of that amount. In either case the term gives no indication of the time the load is carried which may be ten, twelve or possibly twenty-four hours. The technical measure of the manner of using power is the "load factor" which expresses the relation or ratio between the highest power that is needed and the average load for not only one day, but for the week, the month, and the year —constituting what we call the daily, weekly, monthly or annual load factor. It is evident that the plant must be built to furnish the maximum power ever required while it may be actually delivering—most of the time—very much. less than such maximum power. Take, for example, any of the electric powei. plants built to supply general service in the cities of the state. It would be perhaps a fair statement to say that they have an average load factor of about 33 per cent. This statement means that if the peak load of such a plant is 3,000 horse power that while it must have installation that is able to carry 3,000 horse power, yet the actual average power that it really carries is only 1,000 horse power. So this plant must pay interest, depreciation, and other fixed charges on a capacity that is three times the average capacity of its output. This condition must enter very largely into the consideration of the cost of water power. The water power plant must practically be able to carry the maximum load that is sold unless arrangements are made for the use of auxiliary power (usually steam) for peak loads and low water conditions.

On account of this variable use of power the information is still quite indefinite if we are told that the power actually costs —say $25 per annum per horse power, and it becomes necessary to have much more information before such cost can be compared with a different cost under a different load factor, and before one would actually understand the real cost of the energy that is being developed.

For example, I know of one case where a price was offered of $25 per horse power per annum for power to be furnished to a municipality, a price which seemed much lower than the actual cost at which power was being developed. On inquiry, the engineer found the price named was based on the peak load. This city plant operated on about a 33⅓ per cent load factor, and the price named actually meant that they would have to pay about $75 per horse power per annum for the average horse power actually used.

The whole question of cost and price of power is exceedingly complicated, and it is impossible to make any estimates that will not be modified by the particular conditions under which the power is to be used. All conditions of operation enter into these questions and frequently become exceedingly important and modify, cost and prices proportionately.

The extent to which a power should be developed depends on how that power is to be used. If power is to be used twenty-four hours a day, only sufficient turbines are needed to utilize the continuous flow of the stream. If, however, a pondage or reservoir capacity is available that will hold back the flow during the night when the power is used only in a small way, and makes it possible to use the power at a greater rate during the day, the capacity of the turbines can often be doubled to advantage, and, in many cases where a night load is to be carried only for a few hours and a short and high peak load must be carried, the turbine capacity can be made three or four times the actual continuous horse power of the stream.

There are a great many places where water powers have no storage capacity and where the water runs away to waste when not used. If there is no storage, you cannot save this water. You use it as you can and the rest escapes. There are other places where there is considerable pondage and where if you do not use it at night and the pond is large enough, the water will simply be conserved in the pond, wholly or partially, and can be used during the day time. Such lines of development can be carried on to the extent of large reservoir systems which can catch and hold the flood waters and largely equalize the entire flow of the stream.

Then again the question of development, so far as capacity is concerned, depends on the value of the power. In the East at the present is a stream will develop a certain power for six or eight months in the year, or sometimes even for four months, the power may occasionally be of sufficient value to warrant such expense of development and to warrant the installation of auxiliary power to help the plant over the low water of the balance of the year.

A waterpower in itself is not necessarily a mine of wealth, the popular writer to the contrary not withstanding. It must at the present time be well located, not too far from centers of industry where the cost of power is fairly high it must be capable of development at reasonable cost; it must be able to sell power at fair prices and under reasonable regulations; and many other conditions must be favorable.

It will readily be seen that as a result of the above conditions there are many water powers in the State of Wisconsin, and many water powers in the United States that, so far as the present is concerned, are not worth a dollar. They would not pay to develop under present conditions. There is no market available that would warrant the great expense of their development.

It has been assumed by popular writers that energy generated from water power can be furnished in competition against any other source of power and undersell it. Such a statement is untrue—it is purely fiction. If today the Falls of Niagara existed just outside the city of Gary, Indiana, the Steel Company could not afford to develop them for their own use because the waste gases from the furnaces of the Company afford a source of energy so cheap that the utilization of water power would be impracticable. There could be no competition between the two. Take, for example, within the state of Wisconsin, the saw-mills and the wood-working establishments. They produce a by-product of slabs and of sawdust that enable them to operate by steam power at a cost so low that water power, as a rule, cannot compete. They also, for example, many manufacturing industries of the state in which steam is used for perhaps six or seven months of the year for heating purposes, or where a steam is used in the process of manufacture. As a general proposition at the present day, energy from water power cannot be economically furnished to such institutions at a cost as low as they can produce it from feul. Steam in such plants is a by-product that reduces the cost of the energy which they are generating, and in many cases it is generated so cheaply that it is hopeless to attempt to undersell it with water power. It is certainly impossible where power is generated from an expensive plant and transmitted for long distances.

While the cost of water power plants varies so widely from place to place, and the cost of the power they develop is also so variable that no general estimate can be of much value, yet some idea of the trend of conditions can perhaps be gathered from a few comparative estimates. I have therefore prepared Table I, which shows some comparative figures made by the Ontario Hydro-Electric Power Commission, showing their estimate of the cost of various proposed hydro-electric plants— their head, capacity, and cost per horse power, also the cost per horse power per annum at the plant and delivered at the sub-station some distance away. It should be noted that these cost figures are based on an interest charge of 4 per cent, which is much less than the rate at which any private water power company can secure funds. I have also taken from the same source Table II, which gives the estimate of the Commission on the cost of steam power, generated in units of different sizes and of different degrees of efficiency.

The tables are as follows:

TABLE 1.

ESTIMATES OF ONTARIO HYDRO-ELECTRIC POWER COMMISSION.

Estimated Cost of Water Power.

Location.	Head.	Capacity H. P.	Estimated cost.	Cost per H. P.	Yearly operating charge per H. P.	Length of transmission line, miles.	Yearly cost including transmission losses, etc
Niagara Falls		50,000	$5,788,560	$114	$11.16	88	$16.53
Niagara Falls		100,000	8,681,188	98	8.82		
St. Lawrence River at Iroquois	12	1,200	179,000	149	20.21	27	82.55
High Falls, Ontario	78	2,400	195,000	81	10.35	63	25.68
Dog Lake	810	6,840	619,700	91	8.30	25	12.00
Slate Falls	40	3,686	338,000	97	9.10	16	27.10

TABLE 2.

ESTIMATED COST OF STEAM POWER.

Class.	Power.	Per 10 hour H. P. Per annum.	Per 24 hour H. P. Per annum.	Investment per horse power.
Simple slide valve.........	10	$91.16	$150.76	$:03.00
Simple slide valve.........	50	53.95	106.46	74.00
Simple Corliss	50	50.70	97.73	90.00
Simple Corliss	100	40.55	79.19	89.60
Compound Corliss	100	33.18	60.05	91.40
Compound Corliss	1,000	23.25	43.71	51.00

NOTE.—In this table coal is estimated at $4 00 per ton so that the estimated cost is somewhat higher than the actual cost would be in most Wisconsin cities.

It is hardly possible to arrive at any general expression for the relative value of steam and water power because, as before stated, there are many water powers at the present time in Wisconsin that could not possibly be developed and the power be sold at a profit. This is true under conditions very many of which are adverse so far as steam power is concerned, where coal is high and steam power is expensive, and yet where the water power—which is freely going to waste—cannot at the present time and under the present conditions be turned into power, transmitted, and economically used. There are places where water power is very much more expensive than steam power, and in other places water power may be much less expensive: so that the relation varies from point to point and no generalization of the relation is possible.

If we select a particular locality and either design a water power plant at that place, or consider a plant already designed, investigate the fixed charges, cost of maintenance, cost of production, and cost of transmission, and then compare it with a steam plant of a certain type designed to furnish power for the same general purpose, a comparison could be drawn, and such comparison is drawn every time an intelligent installation of a water power project is attempted. The field must be examined in detail, the possibilities of the power market must be gone into very carefully, and it is only after it is found in the best judg-

ment of those investigating the matter that it will pay to construct a water power plant that such water power plant should
be constructed.

With the many steam and water power plants now in operation throughout the state, it would seem that comparative data
under various conditions might be readily obtained. The cost
of water power and of steam power can be determined—at least
approximately—in all localities, so that a local comparison
would be possible if time and energy can be spared for such an
investigation. As a matter of fact, however, there are comparatively few companies developing and using power today that
know the amount of power they are actually developing, or the
actual cost of the same. As a general thing their information
is inexact and in error. Frequently in estimating the cost they
do not consider interest on the investment, depreciation, etc.,
but only operating expenses, taxes, and money actually expended annually in operation and maintenance. They forget
that machinery is wearing out and will have to be replaced.

The fictitious values that have been placed by popular writers
upon potential or undeveloped water powers have given a false
idea to the public, and the assumption that the water power
owners are necessarily making large and unreasonable profits
on account of their ability to undersell at other sources of
power, is a fiction, or very largely so.

In some favorable locations in the Western States where
fuel is expensive, where water power can be cheaply developed,
where the cost of maintenance is low, and where an active demand for power exists, large profits are possible. There are
undoubtedly places where the returns from investments in
water power have been large. I know of no such plants in the
state of Wisconsin. As a general proposition I do not believe
that investments in the development of water powers today—as
a general rule—except under the most favorable conditions,
compare favorably with opportunities for investment that are
offered in many other lines. I believe moreover that any serious
restrictions upon the development of water powers, or any unfavorable legislation will so discourage investors that it will
make the development of these resources practically impossible.

It will, I think, be admitted without argument, that the income from a water power investment should be equal to the

sum of the first six items mentioned on page 2, and if the seventh item represents an actual cost or rental value, such value must be recognized in the income as well. The eighth item may be questioned but it must be met, or at least the investor must believe that it can be met or no investment will be made. And the anticipation of meeting every one of the items of expense listed above is essential and absolutely necessary if further water power development is to take place in this state. No legislature, no rate commission, can control this law of development.

The legislature can by unjust laws inflict hardships on the existing plants when serving the public which may not be sufficiently unjust to be called by the courts confiscatory but whch may reduce incomes to little more than current interest on the investment. The legislature may even be able to inflict an unjust tax on private powers. The right to tax has been called the right to destroy, but when such unjust taxes are once levied and sustained by the courts, no legislature can compel unprofitable investment, and the development of industries so handicapped, will cease.

Whether or not a water power will be profitable is purely a local question in each particular case. I could name you some waters powers installed in this country that have never paid. I could name you one of the most important water powers in this country that has been built and operated 20 years and has never paid a dividend on its stock as yet. I could name you two large water power plants of recent construction which were financial failures. One, at Messina, New York, was purchased, and is now being rebuilt for the use of the Pittsburg Reduction Company. Other plants of that same general character have not paid and have been a great loss to the people who have put their money into them. The history of water power in the New England States is largely an unfortunate one. You can find records of bankruptcy in the water power interests, and very few of them have ever made a dollar.

The probability seems to be that in the future water powers may become more valuable. However, that will depend on conditions of which we know very little. In the early development of water power in this country water powers were exceedingly important. Cities were located where water powers could be developed. Communities grew up along little streams where a small power could be constructed and the mills served, and our early saw-mill interests were centered around streams where power could be obtained. Later on, as steam machinery began to be perfected, it was found that the centers of transportation were attracting manufacturing interests, that it paid better to buy fuel and to develop power locally than to utilize the water power; and there are hundreds of abandoned water power sites throughout New England and along the Atlantic coast whose values have passed, and there is a strong possibility that many of them will never be developed again.

When electrical transformation and transmission of energy became possible, it gave an additional value not to small powers, but to the large powers. The necessary investment in a transmission line is too large to run a great distance for a small power. It costs almost as much to run a transmission line 100 miles whether 1,000, 5,000 or 10,000 horsepower be transmitted over the line, for the right-of-way and cost of poles, insulation, etc., are practically the same regardless of the power transmitted, the cost of the transmission wire only varying with the amount of power. The consequence is that the small powers cannot be developed and transmitted to any great advantage. As a general proposition today I think that commercially a power of less than 1,000 horsepower is not worth developing except under most favorable conditions where it can be used locally, or with very short transmission lines. If a power is to be developed and transmitted it must be of sufficient size to afford a return on not only the cost of its development and the cost of its operation, but a return on the cost of its transmission as well.

It is true that within recent years there has been a renewed activity in the development of larger powers, but we do not know what is coming in the future. It is true our coal is being used up; it is true that many of our resources are being exhausted at a greater or less rate; and it is true that the time may come when many of these resources that we are now using cannot be used in the way that they are now being used. We do not know what else may take their place. We do not know what other sources of energy may be developed. We do know, for example, at the present day that there are some solar engines which are now largely in an experimental stage., We do know that there are hunderds of thousands of horsepower in the solar rays coming to this earth every day, and we do not know how soon the time may come when that source of energy may be made available for the use of mankind. There is also the question of the wave motor that at the present day is impracticable. How long it will remain so no one can say. We cannot look into the future even for 100 years hence and say what may be possible then.

Water powers are a valuable asset, but their value lies in their use, and it is important to utilize this valuable source ol energy. Ccal is mined and burned and it is gone forever. Wood burned for power purposes can be but slowly reproduced. Water power is practically everlasting. As long as the hills stand and the rains descend, so long will our water power exist.

Is it not therefore the part of intelligence to conserve those resources that can be exhausted and either cannot be reproduced or can be reproduced only after long lapses of time, and to encourage the substitution of those resources that are self-replenishing and hence everlasting? True conservation would encourage water power development, not hamper it, for such development would effect a saving in coal and utilize where possible the energy that is now going to waste.

Legislation should encourage such developments—not discourage them. It is more important that the state water resources be developed and utilized, that they may be made available as rapidly as possible, than that the state receive an extra tax from such properties and delay their development. The development of these properties will result in a large increase in the assessed valuation on both from the developments themselves, and the manufacturing investments, and the growth in population and property interests which they will entail. In such developments the public is more interested than in state ownership or extra taxes. Rates which will adjust themselves for water power must compete with other sources of power, and the public interest is now under the control of the Rate Commission. If the public needs require public ownership of water powers in fifty or a hundred years, they can better be acquired by condemnation by a country which has been developed through their agency than to be held available for such problematic possibilities by a "dog in the manger" policy of restriction, stagnation, and inaction.

It would seem to me therefore that the development of these water powers should be put upon a just and generous basis, a basis that in some measure is commensurate with the encouragements that surround our manufacturing establishments with just laws. Just laws are passed to encourage mining; why should not the water powers be placed on the same general basis? I believe that they should.

Forest and Stream Flow.

The relations of forests to stream flow is an important subject for your consideration on account of the bill offered at the last meeting of the legislature and which I presume is under consideration by this Committee—namely, the bill to tax the water powers of the state for the purposes of reforesting certain State lands. This bill is advocated on the theory that the development of forests on the head waters of the streams will so conserve the snows of winter and the rains of spring as to reduce floods and materially increase the low summer flow of the streams, which usually occurs in July, August, and September.

It needs no argument to prove that rainfall is the primary source of all stream flow; that other things being equal, the stream flow will increase as the rainfall increases and will diminish as the rainfall diminishes; that without rainfall there can be no stream flow. While rainfall is recognized as the most important factor in influencing the flow of streams, it is readily seen that it is not the only factor which affects stream flow. A careful consideration of the subject will show that there are a great many physical conditions on the drainage area, besides total quantity of rainfall, that are very important in their influence on the flow of streams.

Now, it is claimed by foresters and others that the influence of forests is most important in modifying stream flow, conserving and delivering the waters more slowly and regularly than would otherwise occur; that the bed of forest humus retains large quantities of the rainfall and melting snow, thus preventng floods and delivering the water slowly back to the stream when most needed, thus preventing droughts, that in this way very high water is reduced and low water increased and water powers greatly benefitted

The benefit which the bill seems to indicate may be considered as follows. I believe that the State Railway Commission has in some cases valued the water power itself, as a part of a going concern and aside from the other property and the cost of development, at $35 per horse power. On this valuation and on a 5 per cent basis, water power would be worth $1.75 per horse power per year. In many cases in localities where water power is favorably situated, with manufacturing and markets developed, and is in actual and profitable use, I believe the power itself—apart from the development—can be fairly valued at $100 per horse power (as an investment), or considered as worth $5 per horse power per annum.

This bill provides that a tax of twenty-five cents per annum shall be levied on each horsepower in use where the headwaters of the stream are reforested. Hence it is seen that the reforesting of the upper drainage area must add 14.2 per cent in the first case to 5 per cent in the second case to the power developed, in order that an actual return will be realized from the investment; and such a return is certainly the only possible excuse for such a tax levy. Even if we accept the theory of the material effect of forests on stream flow, the absurdity of such a special tax on water powers for reforesting purposes is quite apparent on careful consideration. The areas of the State which can be spared from agriculture and grazing and reforested are believed to be much less than 5 per cent and certainly in no case 14 per cent of the drainage area of any considerable stream. If we admit that the reforesting of a certain percentage of the area will increase to an equivalent percentage, the value of a stream for water power purposes—that it is the regularity and quantity of the low water flow—we must then admit that the reforesting of the entire drainage area would result in perfect regulation or in a degree of regularity that no stream from a forested area has ever possessed.

A careful consideration, however, will show that the only possible equalizing influence of forests on stream flows occurs at such a time as to render it valueless to the water power interests, that the forests exert no influence during the low water seasons

48

of winter, and the influence of the forests during the low water season of summer is wholly determinal. This will be seen by a careful study of the rainfall and factors that modify its disposal, and hence control the stream flow.

The principal conditions that modify and control the flows of streams may be briefly summarized as follows:

1. Precipitation.—Amount and character of occurrence.

(a) Whether occurring as rain or snow.

(b) Amount of each and total precipitation.

(c) Distribution and manner of occurrence.

(d) Character of storms, including their direction velocity, extent, intensity, and duration.

2. Topography of the Drainage Area.

(a) As to character of gradient, whether fairly level or highly inclined.

(b) As to character, whether smooth or rugged.

3. Geology of Drainage Area.

(A) Whether pervious or impervious.

(B) If pervious, whether such pervious deposits are (a) shallow or deep; (b) inclined or flat; whether the outcrop or discharge of the pervious deposits are (c) in the lower valley of the same river, or (d) in valleys of adjoining rivers or in the sea.

(C) As to the condition of the channel of the stream, whether (a), pervious or impervious, (b), whether or not the bed contains more or less extensive deposits of sand and gravel, permitting the development of a more or less extensive underflow.

4. The Condition of the Surface.

(a) Whether bare or covered with vegetation.

(b) Whether in natural condition or cultivated.

(c) Nature of vegetation, whether grassland, cultivated crops, or forests.

5. The Nature of Natural Storage on the Drainage Area.

(a) Nature and extent of surface storage, consisting of lakes, ponds, marshes, and swamps.

(b) Nature and extent of ground storage, consisting of gravel, sand, and other similar pervious deposits.

6. The Nature of Drainage Area Considered.

(a) As to size, whether large or small.

(b As to shape, whether long and narrow, or short and broad.

(c) The location of the area relative to prevailing winds.

(d) The direction relative to the path of storms.

7. Character of the Stream.

(a) As to slope of gradient, whether flat or inclined.

(b) As to falls and rapids on the stream.

(c) As to the arrangements of tributaries, whether joining the main stream at various points along its course or concentrated in fan-like arrangement at a more or less common point of discharge.

8. The Artificial Control of the Stream.

(a) As to dams and storage reservoirs on the drainage area.

(b) As to the restrictions of the stream's sections by dikes and levees.

(c) As to obstruction of the stream by piers, abutments, and other encroachments in or adjacent to the waterway.

9. The Artificial Use of the Stream.

(a) For irrigation.

(b) For water supply.

(c) For the supply of navigation canals.

10. As to temperature.

(a) The average and extreme temperatures on the area.

(b) The relation of extreme temperatures to the occurrence of precipitation.

(c) The accumluation of snow and ice, caused by low temperatures.

(d) The occurrence of low temperatures causing the freezing of the ground surface at times of heavy spring rains, causing excessive runoff.

11. As to the Character and Extent of the Winds on the Drainage Area.

(a) As to the intensity and direction.

(b) As to the modification of the same by mountains and forests.

12. As to the Ice Formation.

(a) As modifying the winter flows of the stream.

(b) As to the formation of ice gorges, and their accompanying floods.

I shall not attempt to discuss in detail the list of conditions named above as influencing the flow of streams; but an examination of the list will, I believe, satisfy you that each of the factors named may be of considerable importance under some particular circumstance.

I do wish, however, to call your attention to certain facts in connection with this matter in which your personal observation and experience will bear out my statements. It will be admitted by all that the primary source of stream flow is the rainfall on the drainage area. We know that in regions where there is no rain there is practically no water running in the streams, so that primarily the rainfall is the source of the flow of the stream. There can be no doubt but that temperature (as effecting freezing and evaporation), vegetation (as either a consumer or conserver of water), and the surface conditions (as promoting seepage or favoring surface flow) may have considerable effect on the amount of water reaching the streams at various times and seasons. It is within the experience of all that light rainfalls, and, under favorable conditions, rainfalls of considerable magnitude are largely or entirely taken up by vegetation and evaporation and largely or entirely lost to the streams. If, on the other hand, the rainfall is heavy during a storm, there is not the opportunity for evaporation or for vegetation to take up the water, and it will flow into the stream or seep into the ground more readily, depending on the conditions.

One of the most important factors is the geological condition,—that is, the nature and condition of the soil and rocks on which the rain falls. Sandy surfaces take in the rain rapidly as it falls, prevent evaporation, and assure the delivery of a large portion of the rain to the stream through the underflow of the ground water. The rainfall runs rapidly from mountains and slowly from the plains. It is held back by rough surfaces and its flow is hastened by smooth surfaces. So we find that conditions on the drainage area do modify and affect the disposal of the rain and the consequent stream flow.

In Wisconsin, the underlying rocks are largely covered with drifts. Sometimes under this drift, and sometimes exposed at the surface are some 14,000 square miles of Potsdam sandstone and about 2,000 sq. inches of St. Peters sandstone. Over a considerable portion of the state therefore, are these very pervious sand rock that readily take up, transmit or give out water—as the physical conditions demand. In the drift overlying these and other classes of rocks there are a great many deposits of sand, gravel, and other more or less pervious deposits; and in other geoglogical deposits of the state are strata that freely take up and transmit water.

In addition to the geological conditions which refer more particularly to the pervious or mpervious condition of the surface on which the rain falls, is the topographic condition. It makes a great deal of difference in the character of the runoff whether the slope of the country is very abrupt or quite level. In the mountains of the West the slopes are very abrupt, the mountains are rugged, and rain waters flow away quickly down the mountain sides, and the streams resulting are torrential in character. In many places the streams from this cause have high floods at certain seasons of the year, while at other seasons of the year the streams are dried up and the waters disappear entirely because there is little storage on the drainage area. Such conditions not only have the decided effect on the stream flow I have mentioned, but they also have a bearing on the relative effect of other factors in modifying flow.

There is no question but that forests do influence the disposal of the rainfall,—and hence the flow of streams—in some places and under some conditions. They always have an influence, sometimes adverse, sometimes favorable to stream flow. Some of the effects are readily recognized. A light rain falling on a forest will not reach the ground; it is simply evaporated from the leaves. As a general proposition, the water used by vegetable life is taken up by the roots and circulates through the vegetable tissues, nourishes the trees, and passes off in the outbreathing of the trees through the leaves. Therefore forests and other vegetation draw on the reservoirs of the soil and help deplete this source from which the flow of streams is replenished.

It is claimed that the soil in the woods or forests is more moist than the soil of the field and that this is caused by the protection of the forest. As a general proposition I do not believe that this is true, although there are occasions when it is so. Evaporation in the forests is less than in the open. The growth of roots in a soil prevents the free entrance of the water to a very pervious soil, while possibly in an impervious soil the reverse may be true. Under such conditions the water may be held above the surface and will not enter the soil as quickly as if no vegetation were there. The roots and humus also delay the flow of the waters over the surface and may then distribute surface runoff to a limited extent. These I believe to be the conditions under which water is sometimes found in the forests after the water of the field has seeped into the ground or flowed away on the surface. These are conditions which all have observed and are, I believe, the conditions which give rise to the claim that the forest acts as a reservoir for rain water.

There are places in which I believe even this limited action may be of value. There can be no question but that on the rugged hills of Arizona or of Utah, where the rocks are uncovered and where practically no soil exists, if forests are planted or vegetation can be grown which will interrupt the rapid runoff of rain water, the condition of stream flow will be improved for forests and vegetation would then constitute a limited form of storage which might then be of comparatively high value.

It must be admitted that forests retard the flow in the springtime by retarding the melting of snow and ice, and to this extent may influence uniformity, although it is an open question whether the delay in the gradual melting of the snows may not result in even greater flood wherever the rapid advent of warm weather affects the snows which have been sheltered from the gradual effects of the warmth of approaching spring.

The periods of lowest water in Wisconsin rivers are usually in January or February when the reservoir of the forest humus (if we admit that the forest bed ever has any particular value as a reservoir in Wisconsin) must of necessity be frozen when the spring and higher ground waters are also frozen up, and

when the precipitation is being impounded and held as ice
and snow. There is another low water period along in August
or September when the forests and other vegetation have already exhausted the immediate ground waters and the rains
that have fallen during the summer months. The action of
the forest in retarding the melting of the snow or ice may sometimes result in retarding part of the flow (that would otherwise occur in March or April) and delivering it in May or
June. The only effect that would result is that the high water
conditions would be carried to a little later period in the
season, but the runoff conditions in August and September
would not be increased thereby. Usually by April or the first
part of May, the snow even in the dense woods is very largely
gone, at least in the major portion of the state.

In the western states with streams fed from the snows of
the high mountains, the conditions are very different from
the above, for there the altitude of the snows make them available throughout the summer. But it is to be remembered
that there the snows are almost entirely above the timber line.

It should be noted that the flows which affect and control
water power developments are the low water flows of July,
August, and September; also the low flows of January and
February. On these flows the forests can have no beneficial
effect.

I think I can better illustrate the idea I wish to convey
and give you a true conception of the principles which I believe underlie this whole matter, if you will consider in the
first place a steep mountain slope surrounding a valley where
the rocks are impervious and very abrupt, such as we have
in many of the western states. A hard rainfall, upon these
steep mountains, passes quickly into the valley and serves to
form a torrential stream which passes quickly away. There
is, under such conditions, a large percentage of runoff. Evaporation takes place to a limited extent only but the rain
waters do not tarry on the surface a sufficient length of time
for evaporation to have a great effect. More or less of the
water may be absorbed by pervious rocks, but the rapid rush
of water over the rocks does not favor absorption. Some
water may reach cavities or fissures and appear at some point
down the slope as springs. Such a stream is torrential in

character for there is practically no storage on its drainage area.

Now, consider this same valley filled up 50 or 100 feet with clays, sands and gravel, consider a stream meandering down through the center, sometimes perhaps flowing over a rock bottom and sometimes flowing over sand and clay, and we will see that very different conditions have arisen and that the relation of the rainfall to the runoff will be greatly changed.

In this case, what will occur? When the rain falls on this sand bed, it sinks rapidly into the soil and forms ground water. The flow of water through the sand and gravel is usually quite slow, depending on the fineness of the grains of sand. It is sometimes in very fine soil as slow as 10 or 12 feet per year. In other cases where the gravel is coarse, the flow is quite rapid. The water that falls on this sand bed passes downward and flows slowly towards the stream. The sand, gravel, and pervious material form a reservoir which checks the flow of water and delivers it more continuously and more uniformly to the stream, and the stream is no longer torrential in character. It flows as much water as before, but the water that falls is held back by this reservoir, and instead of a torrential stream we have a perennial stream, due solely to the geological character of the drainage area.

Now, if we plant vegetation on that soil, what results will obtain? Plant a forest on that drainage area and what conditions will result—will the stream flow be conserved and increased? There is no question under such conditions but that a forest on such a drainage area would be wholly detrimental to the flow of the stream. There will be less water. Vegetation requires from 10 to 20 inches of water per year. That supply must come from some source, and as the rainfall is the only source available, it must come from the rainfall, and rain cannot run into the streams if the vegetation takes it up.

Now, let us consider the conditions in Wisconsin. We have no rugged mountain slopes, few steep declivities; the land is fairly level and regular. It is a rolling land that is geologically new. There are but few of our streams that have reached a base level; if they had, we would have no swamps and no lakes, because they would have been naturally drained out. We have no rugged valleys, but we have deep pervious deposits of glacial material and sandstone. We have the sand and gravel of the glacial epoch, and we have land comparatively level. Water in no place passes off with the rush that it does on our western slopes, or even on the slopes of the hills and mountains of Pennsylvania and therefore our conditions are quite the reverse from those in the arid West or in the mountains of the East.

Your attention is called to certain diagrams which accompany this discussion and which show the relative amount of stream flow to the amount of the rainfall upon various drainage areas of isconsin rivers. Please not that in these diagrams on the horizontal lines is a scale of rainfall, and on the vertical lines is a scale of stream flow, so that the location of any point on the diagram shows by reference to these scales the rainfall for a particular year (or for the month, as the case may be) on a given drainage area, and the relative runoff of the particular stream draining that area for the same year or month. Each of the symbols— the meaning of which is given in the legend—indicates a certain definite river of Wisconsin; and in some cases the records for a number of years are shown, so that the variations from year to year as well as from month to month may be seen.

Diagram No. 1 shows the yearly relation of the rainfall, as indicated by this horizontal sacle, to the runoff or stream flow as shown by the vertical scale. Both rainfall and stream flow are expressed in inches—that is, in inches in depth—over the entire drainage area above the point where the stream measurements were made.

The symbol O indicates the Wisconsin river. The location of each symbol of this kind on the diagram indicates that in a certain year the rainfall on the watershed equaled the corresponding amount indicated on the horizontal scale at the bottom of the diagram, and the runoff or stream flow was as indicated on the left hand vertical scale. The other diagrams indicate the same conditions for each particular month. The diagonal lines show the percentage relations of runoff to rainfall. These data are from the records of runoff as measured by the United States Geological Survey on various rivers and by the Army Engineer on the Fox river, together with similar information from other sources compared with the rainfall records as determined by the United States Weather Bureau.

Now, if we consider the actual conditions as found in Wisconsin rivers, we find that the annual flow of these streams varies from as low as 16 per cent to as high as 70 per cent of the rainfall, and that the average flow will be about 33 per cent of the rainfall. The Menominee, the Chippewa, the Wisconsin, and the Peshtigo rivers are rivers of high flow, averaging about 55 per cent of the rainfall. These rivers all rise in the high Archean region of the state where many lakes and swamp areas and extensive glacial deposits tend to conserve and regulate the streams, where no deep preglacial valleys are believed to exist, and where—in consequence—no extensive underflow is possible and the measured flow of the streams is high. The Fox, the Rock, and the St. Croix rivers rise and flow over the later and softer geological deposits which are often deeply cut by valleys formed in pre-glacial times and whihc have since been filled by pervious deposits of sands and gravels. These conditions probably give rise to large overflow, and these rivers—in consequence—are rivers of low flow, averaging only about 25 per cent of the rainfall.

Comparing the Rock and the Wisconsin rivers it will be noted that the flow of the Rock is only about one-half of the flow of the Wisconsin, while the rainfalls on their two drainage areas are not greatly different. What is the reason of the difference in flow? One reason is that the Rick river is flowing down through Wisconsin and Illinois as far as Rockford over its old pre-glacial valley. I do not know how many thousand years ago—some geoolgists say 30,000 years and some say 100,000 years—this country was entirely different, and the old Rock river flowed at an elevation 300 feet or more lower than it does now in an old valley that was filled up during the glacial epoch. In 1897 I dug down 100 feet into this valley at Rockford and found great deposits of water bearing sand and gravel and old cedar logs that had been there at least 30,000 years. The volumes of water was so great that pumping was impossible and we were obliged to hold back the waters by pnuematic pressure in order to do our work. Through this sand and gravel deposit, which largely fills the old valley, a great amount of water is flowing away, and that is, I believe, one of the reasons why the Rock river flows so much less in proportion than the Wisconsin river which in most cases flows in a modern bed with no chance for a great underflow.

The various other diagrams show the conditions of rainfall and stream flow for individual months. You will note by reference to the diagrams for January that in this month the percentage of runoff is high but the actual rainfall is low, not averaging more than an inch and a half for the month; and the runoff as a rule is equal to or greater than the rainfall being often over 100 per cent. Such a condition simply means that the stored ground water has helped the flow, or perhaps that the snow from the previous month has melted and run off, so that the monthly runoff was greater than the monthly rainfall and consequently the rainfall for the month is here not the principal factor of flow. The same condition is shown in the diagram for February, March and April. As we examine the latter months we note the rainfall and runoff have increased somewhat. The April runoff is often much greater than the rainfall because during March and April the snows which fell through the winter months are melted and run away, and the actual runoff of the stream may be much above the rainfall, especially where the rainfall for the month is low, and in some cases the actual runoff is three times the rainfall for particular years and particular drainage areas.

On account of the temperature conditions in January and February, due to the freezing up of the springs and the shallow ground waters, we very frequently get the lowest stream flow of the year. In March and April, and sometimes in May, we get very high stream flows because of the stored waters in the form of ice and snow of the preceding winter.

As we examine the diagrams of the later months we see that the runoff begins to grow less. In the June diagram you will note a decided reduction. The flow would perhaps average over 50 per cent in May; it is less than 50 per cent, probably not more than 40 per cent in June; and in July the percentage of flow is still less. You will note that many of the observations fall below the 25 per cent line in July; in August the percentage of flow drops still further, and in some cases, the runoff is not more than 5 per cent of the rainfall. In September it is still low but is beginning to raise again.

Now, why does this percentage fall off during May, June, July, and August, and sometimes in September? The reason is not very far to seek. The rainfall is very much heavier in these months than it is earlier in the season, yet the stream flow is much less than earlier in the season. Why is this? It is so most largely because the vegetation on the drainage area is absorbing the rainfall for its growth and development, and because evaporation is also greatly increased. Evaporation takes up a considerable share, but the loss of evaporation does not approach the amount that is used by plant life. Plant life frequently consumes during the summer months practically all the water that falls, and the flow of the stream is kept up simply from the waters that are stored in the lakes and ground, which waters gradually flow out and make a perennial stream possible. Very heavy rainfall may occur and sometimes does occur during the summer months. A rainfall of six or seven inches during the month of March, or earlier in the season would cause a great flood; but in the later summer time, with vegetation at its best, such a rainfall will often cause no rise whatever. It is all taken up by vegetation, or evaporated and is lost—so far as stream flow is concerned. Where such previous strata or extensive underground storage exist on a waterhead, vegetation of any kind is an absolute detriment to stream flow:

On the Western mountains I do not question the value of forests as a betterment to stream flow conditions. There is no doubt but that in France the steep slopes were saved from denudation by the planting of forests on the hills and mountains of the Pyrenees and the Alps, and that extensive improvement resulted; but we have no Pyrenees or Alps in Wisconsin, and conditions are entirely different.

So we can trace the stream flow by these diagrams through the later season and see that the flow begins to increase as vegetation decreases. In November the flow is increased materially, and in December it is still higher—although in these months other conditions besides the dearth of vegetation may control. There is no question as to the clear meaning indicated by these diagrams or as to the reason for the results shown by them.

I believe that forests have an influence on the flow of streams

and that in Wisconsin that influence is usually detrimental. I
do not believe however, that we can ever re-forest this State to
an extent that will have any serious effect on stream flow one
way or the other. The amount of land that can be devoted to
re-forestation is so small as to be insignificant, and other forms
of vegetation will in any event demand their tribute from the
water supply. I know from a personal examination on some
streams that the re-foresting of the stream would be an absolute detriment. I am satisfied that is true of the Peshtigo river.
On the Peshtigo drainage area, on the White river in Michigan,
and on many other rivers through the drift covered region, the
soil is sandy and the water which falls on it sinks immediately
into the sandy soil. In many places you can go out within fifteen
minutes after a heavy rainfall and not wet your feet because the
water has gone down into this great sandy reservoir from which
the stream is fed. The country on the Peshtigo drainage area
has very little vegetation, and is not well suited for farming.
Much of it is the kind of country that should be re-forested and
you will please understand that I am not arguing against forests
but stating what I believe to be a fact—that the planting of
forests in the northern part of Wisconsin and in northern Michigan would not decrease the flood height one inch, or increase the
rivers of Wisconsin in their low stages an additional horse power.
I believe the effect would be practically nothing so far as that is
concerned, for I would practically place forests and vegetation
in the same class as to the consumption of water.

Considering for a moment the question of storage. If you go
into the country along the streams in Wisconsin and dig down
into the sands and gravels, you will be convinced that there is no
question about the storage of water in these deposits. The sand
and gravel furnish immense quantities of water that we use for
extensive public and private water supplies. It is readily found
moving slowly through these deposits towards the respective
streams on the drainage areas of which the sand and gravel exist.
If you go to the lakes and swamps, you find the water is there—
not in theory but in fact. But if you go into the forests to find
this mythical storage which is heralded as of such great value
to water power, your disappointment is quite complete. In a dry
season the swamp is low, but water is still in evidence, while in
the forest is quite dry underneath the soil. The soil has been

drained to the depth of the taproot to supply the plant with the water needed to maintain its life.

Lakes and ground waters are well known sources from which water supplies are secured for many purposes. but the history of engineering enterprises fails to show one instance where a water supply for any purpose was secured from a forest as a source.

We cannot conserve the water of our streams by planting forests. Now, what we can and should have in this state and other states is the building of reservoir systems that will unquestionably store water and permit it to be delivered as needed for water powers, navigation. or other uses. Even this method is expensive, and unless conditions are favorable, the large expense involved may not be warranted by the benefits resulting under present conditions.

I do not wish to give the impression that there are not many places where foresting certain areas may not add materially to the regularity of streams; but I do not believe that the conditions in Wisconsin are conditions where such results can possibly obtain. I do not believe the reforesting of any lands that the state can re-forest, will add or detract particularly from the stream flow. We cannot re-forest our farms. We must drain the swamps. We cannot leave the state in a state of nature: and even if we could there were floods in this country before Columbus came to America, and the records along the Mississippi and the Ohio rivers show that the floods are no higher and the low water is no lower than they were 60 or 80 years ago. And I believe the same thing is true of the conditions in Wisconsin.

I am ready to admit that there are places where it is quite possible that local springs have dried up, due to conditions peculiar to that locality. If there is a spring that occurs surrounded by trees, perhaps, and the trees are cut away, and the light and air get access to the spring, it is quite possible that the amount of water there may be reduced. We are taught in our elementary course that the spring is the source of the creek and of the river—but that is not so. The stream is fed by the ground water, and if we dig along a stream and trace the ground water course through any pervious strata along the stream's side we will find the ground water plain, which begins at the level water and may be of the depth the soil reaches below the bed of the stream, will gradually rise back from the stream in the country from which it is bringing down the rain waters through their underground channel in which they are free from evaporation effects.

These conditions all have far greater influence than the forests can possibly have. In some cases the influence of the forests may be large ,but certainly not in Wisconsin.

Before closing in regard to this matter, I want to say that I do not wish you to conclude from what I have said that I am an opponent to re-foresting. I believe it is the duty of the legislature to provide means for the re-foresting of the waste lands of the northern part of the state. I believe that it is a duty that this state owes to posterity, and I believe that the importance of reforesting is sufficient in itself without dragging into consideration a theoretical influence and mythical benefit that I do not believe have any existence in fact.

The Water Power Trust.

In the discussion of the control of water powers, certain popular writers have raised a warning cry against a so-called water power trust which they seem to think is to be the controlling factor in the future in almost all affairs, state and national, if not held in check. I believe that the term "water power trust" is an exceedingly misleading one, and I believe that in some cases popular writers have used it with an intent to mislead. Popular attention, with the multitude of interests which occupy it, is attracted only by something startling, and the pictures painted of this mythical trust are sufficiently startling to attract at least passing attention from all readers.

My practice as an engineer has led me pretty well over the United States, and I have a considerable knowledge of water powers outside of the state of Wisconsin, and I do not believe that it is possible to create a "water power trust"—using the ordinary significance of the word "trust." There can be no possible competition between a water power plant in Washington, and a water power plant in Wisconsin; and so far as the people of Wisconsin or the people of Washington are concerned, it makes n difference whether a single company owns one plant or both plants, provided, of course, the individual may not be interested in investment in water power securities or water power installations.

It is undoubtedly true that those who are interested in water powers are the people who are carrying out water power developments.

In regard to the so-called monopoly that is said to exist in the state of Michigan, I think reference is intended to what is, I believe, called the Commonwelth Company of Michigan. This company has developed a number of small water powers on various rivers in Southern Michigan, and its works have been, I think, the outgrowth from a single development. That company has, I believe, been the result of gradual development in the power business. When this company has reached the capacity of the power it already owned, it added additional powers. I know of no objectionable results of the increase in capacity or capital of this company; and the organization of large companies for business purposes and the combination of small companies in larger single companies for economical reasons is both authorized by law and seems to be economic necessity for modern business success. I believe that the General Electric Company is interested in water power in the same way—not as a company, but through other companies associated with it, principally, I believe, through the Electric Bond and Share Company of New York. I think this company found it sometimes necessary, in order to sell their goods, to take in some measure an interest in certain water power projects. This may have been particularly true in some of our Western projects, and they have possibly had to take some of these powers in self-protection. In other cases those who have owned powers, or had certain rights, and desired to develop water powers, naturally looked for capital to assist them and would go prehaps, to this subsidiary company whose business it was to invest in lines that were associated with the business of the General Electric. So the General Electric, I presume, has, indirectly, a considerable investment in water powers, scattered over considerable territory, largely in the western and southern part of the country. Are such investments a menace or a benefit to the country? Are such investments to be encouraged or discouraged?

This segregation of water power interests in a few companies is not in the nature of a trust. This matter should be discussed and

considered in its true light. The organization of large companies
and the uniting of many small concerns into a single large one
may be objectionable. If so, our corporation laws should be
changed. But let us face the question as it is—honestly and
fairly, and not with any misconception of the facts.

If a company has certain water power rights that it thinks
can be developed to financial advantage, it is quite apparent and
quite natural that it should seek the people who know something
about water powers for assistance in financing the same. If such
a project is taken to those who are interested in other lines—say
timber lands—the project would get no attention. Such investors
would say: "We know nothing about water powers. If you have
a timber proposition to present to us, we shall be glad to consider it." But the men who have already investigated and invested profitably in water powers are the men who will invest
in new water powers, and the result is to be anticipated that
there will be to a considerable extent a development of water
by the present water power interests, both in Wisconsin and
elsewhere. Other investors will not go into such projects. You
might bring into Milwaukee any water power project in Wis-
cousin and offer stock or bonds on the market, and I will venture
to say you will not get a purchaser, because they know—or think
they know—that there is a great opportunity for them to lose
by such investment. They have no means of or experience in
judging the safety of the project, and they prefer eo invest only
in those projects in which they have successfully invested before. The consequence is that such investments naturally go to
the people who know something of the subject and who are interested in such investments and hence they are naturally carried to the bond houses who have investigated and successfully
financed water powers—and there is a general tendency, in consequence. for a company that has successfully developed one
project to develop still other projects of the same character.

I believe that this is the extent of the water power trust. I
do not believe there is any tendency to combine these plants except in a legitimate business way. There is a tendency toward
combinations in a great many projects of all kinds, in ordeh to
reduce the operating and general expenses, and this tendency may
have and probably will have more or less of a bearing on water
power developments; but that there ever can be a water power

49

trust that will seriously affect the cost of delivered power is
exceedingly doubtful. Any company that owns a water power is
to an extent a trust in itself, but a trust that will and can be
regulated in its public dealings by the state. The great grasp-
ing water power trust that we read of in the popular prints is,
I think, entirely fallacious—I think it is a phantom.

The Legal Phase.

It has been called to your attention that in certain Western
States certain constitutional provisions have been adopted providing for the state ownership of waters, with the inference at
least that Wisconsin should follow so admirable an example. I
think it is desirable to call your attention in a very general way,
to the general lines of development of the legal aspect of waters
in the United States.

West of the line of the Missouri river the conditions of development have been considerably different from those in the
eastern part of the country. In the East there is ample rainfall for agriculture. In the West, the states are arid or semi-
arid in character, and in some states even dry farming is impossible. The rainfall is sometimes only two or three inches per
year, and in some cases for a whole year no rain will fall at all;
and yet it is found that when many of these lands are irrigated,
they are among the most productive lands in the United States.

Now, in the development of mining in California the miners
who went there, not for agriculture but for gold, took the water
from the streams and used it for panning the gravel for which
water was a necessity. The waters of the streams were often diverted and carried into other valleys and were often not returned to the streams, and in that way a great many appropriations of water were made in a way not permissible under the common law. Such uses of water were permitted by the United
States Government, the owner of both the land and the water
rights. Mining was an important industry in California, and
from California as a center there evolved what is termed the
California system of land tenures. If I may read a statement
contained in Mill's Irrigation Manual, the situation will be explained more briefly and more correctly than if I try to discuss

it myself. This statement is based on a California decision and is as follows:

> "In the states adopting the California system the courts have taken the position that as the common law has been adopted by legislative enactment as the rule of decision, except where changed by statutes, the rights of a riparian owner (in the waters) when they have once been attained cannot be diverted except by grant or condemnation for public use; the United States being the owner of the fee of all public lands is also the riparian proprietor. and so long as the government is the sole riparian proprietor it can grant the right to appropriate and divert the waters of the streams and apply then to beneficial uses; but the moment its title to the land passes to an individual the riparian rights of the individual immediatelyvest, and no subsequent appropriations or diversions can be made unless by grant or condemnation. In these states the courts have sustained the statutes relating to the appropriation and diversion of water for use upon non-riparian lands and have protected all appropriations made prior to the vesting of riparian rights in any individual, also those appropriations made thereafter where the right to divert the waters had been acquired by adverse use, condemnation or grant." .

A number of states have adopted this California system—I think some 8 or 10—and carry both the idea of the prior appropriation of waters from streams bordering on lands the ownership of which has not yet passed from the United States, together with the common law doctrine or riparian ownership in the waters when the lands have so passed.

In regard to what is termed the Colorado system, which has been adopted by the states of Colorado, Wyoming, and a number of others, a different doctrine has been held. Extracts from various decisions of United States courts are found on page 41 of the same manual, and I quote the following:

> "It would reasonably appear, not speaking now with reference to interstate waters, that the conflict between the doctrine of appropriation and riparian rights would in evevry case be decided according to the rules, customs, laws and decisions of the state or territory where the controversy arises. In a case that arose in the Dakotas, the United

States court expressly said: 'The local custom is set forth
in the findings to have consisted in the recognition and ac-
knowledgement of the rights to local water rights and to
divert, appropriate and use the waters of the flowing
streams for purposes of irrigation where such location, diversion and use do not conflict with rights vested and acquired prior thereto.' Thus under the laws of congress in
the territories and under the applicable custom, priority of
use gives priority of rights.''

Now, in a number of western states that have been more recently organized. and where the appropriation of waters has
been made necessary by the arid conditions, it has been held that
the law of riparian ownership—the common law—was inapplicable, and it has been discarded entirely, based on the grounds
of the necessity of those particular states, and in some of those
states there have been constitutional declarations that, on account of the conditions that there obtain, the ownership of the
waters shall be vested in the state, and that the waters can be
appropriated only under legislative regulation, which always
entails priority of appropriation and continuous use.

In the states east of the Missouri other conditions have obtained, and the common law has been adopted with minor
changes.

I do not desire to discuss these legal questions only to this
extent—to show that in these western states where a different
constitutional law is in force and where different customs obtain
at the present time, that these customs and laws have grown
out of the necessary conditions that have arisen there, as developed before the land passed from the government to the
present owners. Such laws cannot apply or be applied to Wisconsin conditions where the common law has been adopted and
in force for many years.

State Regulation and Control.

I understand that one of the questions you have under consideration is the question of state regulation and control of
water powers.

It has been suggested that dams have not always been located
in such places that the river, when fully developed, will generate
the maximum possible amount of power. It has been suggested

that the state through some board or official might be able to decide these matters more intelligently than they can be or are decided by the private interests involved.

If the state, or if a private corporation owned a particular river system and had immediate or early use for all of the power· the first thing that would be desirable would be a survey similar to those that Professor Smith has carried out on a number of the rivers of Wisconsin. Such a survey would give in general a knowledge as to what developments were possible and would necessarily be followed by an approximate location of different installations along the course of the stream and a detailed survey of the various sites at which power plants might be constructed. If there was an immediate or early demand or market for all of the power of such streams at a profitable price, it would under such circumstances be possible to develop these powers fully or with due reference to one another, and perhaps to get the maximum possible development from the stream. Such conditions are only ideal and not practical. The conditions that actually obtain in the state on any stream are quite different from these.

The question of the development of a power is purely a commercial one at the present time. Will it pay to develop a power, and to what extent will it pay to develop? The restriction of the height of the dam, whether to make it a maximum or minimum height, must be largely a commercial one. It may be limited, possibly, by state authority, so that the dam cannot be built above a certain height; but there is a limit to the maximum height of that dam that the legislature cannot govern, and that is the commercial limit as to how far it will pay to raise the dam. No water power company can afford to submerge an exceedingly large amount of valuable land, or to lay themselves open to claims for extensive damages from back water, and if required by the legislature to do so, the plant could not be financed and built. The extent of development must be determined from both the physical and the commercial conditions that surround the plant, and it will frequently be found that such commercial conditions will necessitate a development that is less extensive and less expensive than might be possible if the maximum development only was considered. It is therefore impossible to separate, even partially, the question of location from the practical design and the commercial relation of the development of a water power.

The limitations or restrictions that have been placed by the state in the past on these water powers have sometimes been unfortunate. One limitation is usually made, that the dam shall not exceed a certain height. If the state desires to develop its hydraulic resources to the greatest practical extent, it is apparent that the requirements should be that the dam should not be *less* than a certain height, and that the commercial requirements must then settle the ultimate height to which such a dam can be constructed. Some of the legislative limitations that have been placed on the height of dams are indefinite and meaningless. Take, for example, the limiting height of the Kilbourn dam. The state permit provided that a dam might be constructed 17 feet in height. No explanation of this limitation was made. The water at the site of the dam was at one point 30 feet deep. Now, the limit fixed could not mean that the dam was to have a height only 17 feet above the bed of the river, because if so constructed it would have been 13 feet below the surface of the water. The limit could not mean that it should be 17 above the extreme low water, for no one oculd settle just where extreme low water was; and if it was built only to that height it would mean that for the major portion of the time the water power company would not secure the head to which it seemed plainly entitled by the act. It could not mean 17 feet above high water, because high water rose 18 feet, and that would have required a dam 35 feet above mean low water and would have flooded much valuable property. The conclusion was finally reached that 17 feet above the ordinary low water would be a fair and equitable interpretation of the permit, and the dam was built on that basis, 17 feet being, you understand, the height of the top of the flash-boards. The act also specified that adjustable flash-boards two feet in height should be constructed on the dam. It was found that on account of occasional high floods such flash-boards were not a proper protection, and the flash boards (the adjustable portions of the dam) were made 6 feet in height; so that instead of having a dam 15 feet above ordinary water, as the water company is apparently entitled to by the permit, it has a dam that in 12 feet above ordinary water—a precaution that as engineer of the company I felt was necessary for both the interests of the company and the interests of the riparian owners along the stream. These matters were very carefully considered in the design of the Kilbourn plant, and there were many facts determined and considered in the design that could not have been taken up in the cursory way that these things must be taken up and de- termined by state authority.

It has been assumed that dams will not wash out, that construction will not be imperiled, and that lives and property will be safe if the state had the supervision of the design and construction of dams. Such conclusions are not warranted or borne out by experience. One serious feature in regard to state control of water power matters is the political influence that is very apt to creep into state offices. As a general prop- osition, in such professional lines as offer fair returns to pro- fessional men, it is frequently difficult, if not impossible, to secure the best and most experienced services in state offices having such work in charge. By this I do not mean that the state does not, in many cases, secure good expert advice, and that the state is not able to secure in many technical places as good men as there are in those particular lines; but when poli- tics and salary are both considered, it is exceedingly difficult to get high technical skill and broad experience into the service of the state when general practice offers a broader and more remunerative field. The result is that men of average ability are often secured for such offices and the result of their work is anything but that which safety and efficiency require. For example, I had occasion recently to examine an irrigation pro- ject in one of our arid states. In that state the welfare of the farmer and of the investor were safeguarded and protected by state supervision. It was the duty of the official in charge to look over the question of water supply and approve or condemn it in order to prevent the construction of expensive but useless works, and to prevent the selling of land to farmers under conditions that would lead to their failure or loss. In due course of their official work, the expert of the state examined this property and issued a report. In this report an estimate was made of the quantity of water that could be obtained from the proposed source of supply, and the amount estimated was nearly three times the amount that could possibly be obtained, even with a very extensive reservoir system which was not a part of the plans for development. In the interest of the parties who had proposed to develop this tract, I was obliged to examine this matter and to reject the proposition, and the state authorities afterward acknowledged that their estimate was in error as stated above. It is well to note also that the official mentioned above was a man of more than average ability, and, I think, was well qualified for his work; but the amount of such work that he was called upon to do rendered uniformly accurate work difficult—if not impossible.

This is only one of a hundred instances of a similar kind in which state supervision has not only been useless but seriously misleading inasmuch as the approval of the state is assumed to be conclusive and to give a project an assurance of safety to which it is frequently not entitled.

I believe that when an application for a water power permit is made, the state legislature should adopt some method that would enable it to act with at least better results than it can under present conditions, and in what I have said I do not wish to be understood as speaking against that general proposition. I believe, however, that the control should be limited to the examination and the approval of such plans as may affect the public interest or the public safety. Such a supervision is a function that could be exercised to advantage by the state. I think that the legislature is in duty bound, when granting permits for the construction of dams, to know just what they are granting and to what extent the proposed development is to be made. Both the public and private interests might be subserved by requiring the filing, examination, and approval of such plans as affect either the navigability of the stream, including logways and fishways, and also the safety of the people living along the stream below the structure. In the construction of dams that may affect the lives and property of riparian owners farther down the stream, and of those who live on the shore or on low lands that may be affected by imperfect construction, the question of safety of the dam is of great importance. I do not believe, however, that state supervision should be carried to the extent that will relieve the parties undertaking the construction from the responsibilities that should be entailed by such construction. There is always a tendency, if state regulation is carried too far, to relieve from responsibility the parties on whom such responsibility should rest.

The requirement to submit complete plans of such parts of the construction as may involve hazard to life or property will result in more mature and careful design; and state inspection and approval, if carefully carried out, offer an additional safeguard to which the people of the state are entitled.

It is probably true that a judicious state supervision or regulation would not have a tendency to hamper investments if it *is a judicious* supervision.   I believe that if there is to be a supervision of any kind, or if the state is to grant permits with certain restrictions, that those permits should be made on intelligent lines.

The examination of the plans for the dam by a state officer, without the assumption of the authority to design and locate the dam would be an additional safeguard, and, while it would not prevent the occurrence of accidents, it would be an additional safeguard against such accidents, and at the same time it would not inflict any large additional expense upon the water power owners; in fact, those who owned the water power would have the advantage of such advice and such inspection. In some cases such advice might be quite valuable because water powers are sometimes built without careful consideration of expert advice, and dams are constructed on improper lines and sometimes fail,—and the more plans of that kind are examined, the more chances there are that defects will be noted, that errors will be caught, and not only public, but private interests as well, will be protected.   There is no man or no company who care to build a dam that will be destroyed by the first freshet; yet we find dams of this kind have been built and have been destroyed in this and in other states.   In some states in the case of any dam over 5 ft. high, duplicate plans must be furnished, and one set of the approved plans is retained by the state authorities.

This same power is exercised by the United States War Department in passing permits for building structures, or in carrying wires across navigable streams.   In this case plans must be submitted to the United States engineer, and these are returned with corrections if not satisfactory.   The plans, when satisfactory, are finally approved, and the structure must be constructed on those approved lines.

Stream Flow Measurements.

I believe that the state should undertake the measurement of stream flow as already advocated by Prof. L. S. Smith. In answer to the question raised as to why this should be done by the state, I would say that private interests cannot undertake the extended and general investigation of these matters that is desirable. The matter of stream flow is of very great importance not only to water power interests, but to all water interests. In the question of water supply for our cities, in drainage and in navigation, this information is important and the state should do this work for the same reasons that the state has established and maintains a state university; that it maintains an agricultural experiment station; that it has undertaken the investigation of the geological resources or the supervision of its forests.

It is true that in a narrow sense these matters are of no immediate interest to each individual in the state; but in a broad sense, such matters are of the greatest importance to the state, and to all of its citizens, for they affect the public welfare.

It is a fact that in some of the localities where water powers have been developed, stream flow records have been kept for a number of years, and we have—in a limited way—some knowledge of the flow of the streams of the state. In Wisconsin I think perhaps the longest records have been kept by the United States engineer on the Upper Fox, Wisconsin, and Mississippi rivers. Work of this character has also been carried on by the United States Geological Survey, beginning about 1903. Congress, however, has not realized the great importance of this work, and about 1908 the amount of money that was appropriated for this service was reduced and has since been inadequate for the work. The consequence was that about that date the gauging stations throughout the state were abandoned, and the only observations that have been carried on since have been at private expense. The observations thus being made are very limited. The Wisconsin Valley Improvement Association is making some observations, and I have been having observations taken on a number of streams on which I am carrying on investigations. All these observations are being

furnished gratuitously to the Geological Survey.   This work
can be done without large expense and many who are interested
in the subject will gladly co-operate with the state and thus
reduce the expense.   The matter can be carried on by the Geological and Natural History Survey, and it is quite likely that
the United States Geological Survey would co-operate and so
reduce the expense.

A knowledge of the flow of our streams under all of the conditions of wet and dry seasons that obtain from year to year
through a long series of years is of very great importance and
I believe that the state should provide for this work.